풀 Grass by Keum Suk Gendry-Kim
First published in 2017 by Bori Publishing Co., Korea.
© Keum Suk Gendry-Kim c/o HAN Agency Co., Korea.

drawnandquarterly.com

978-1-77046-362-2
First edition: June 2019
Printed in Canada
10 9 8 7 6 5 4 3 2 1

Cataloguing data available from Library and Archives Canada

Published in the USA by Drawn & Quarterly,
a client publisher of Farrar, Straus and Giroux

Published in Canada by Drawn & Quarterly,
a client publisher of Raincoast Books

Published in the United Kingdom by Drawn & Quarterly,
a client publisher of Publishers Group UK

This book is published with the support of the Literature Translation Institute of Korea (LTI Korea)

# GRASS

## KEUM SUK GENDRY-KIM

Translated by Janet Hong

Drawn & Quarterly

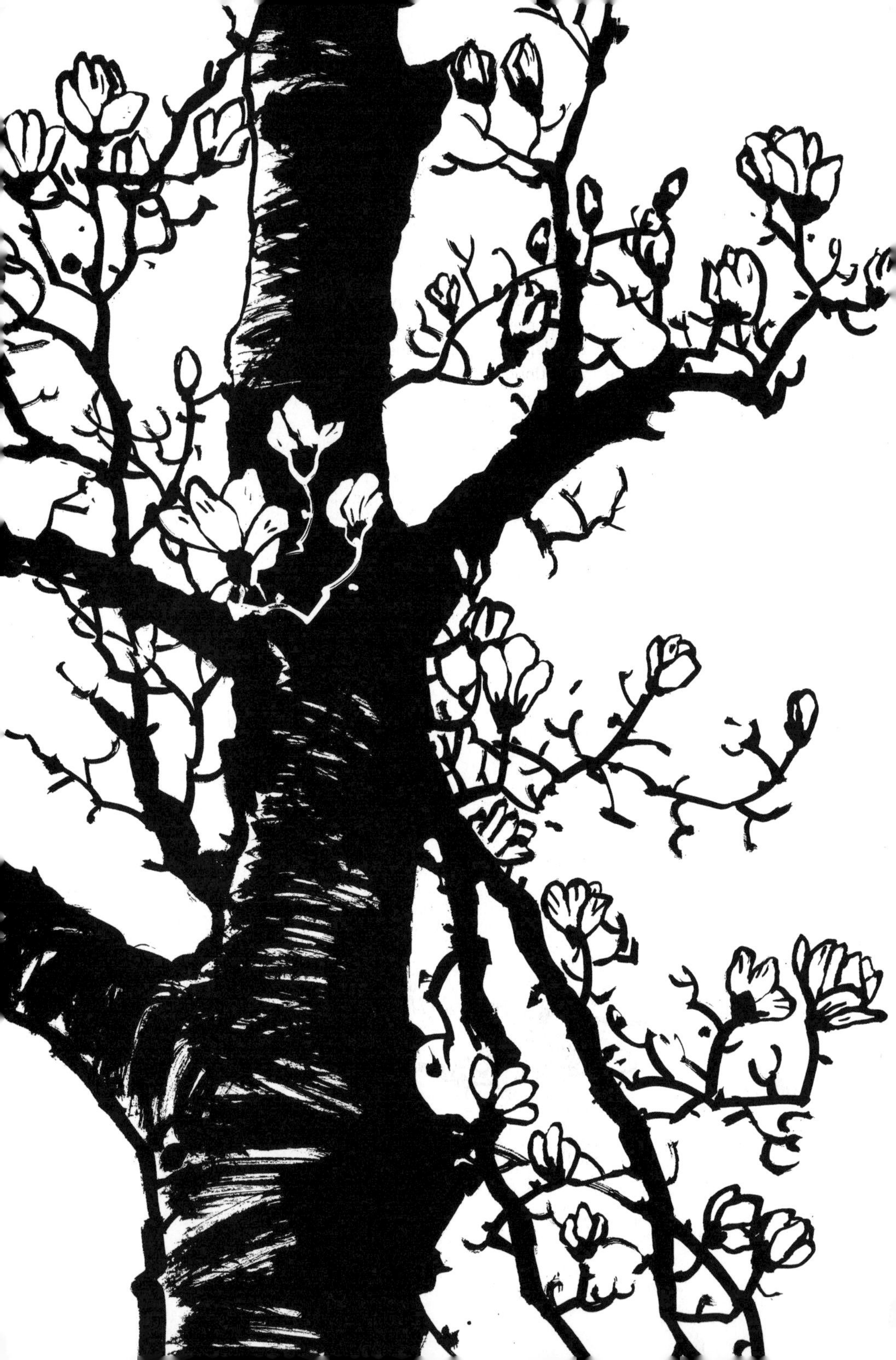

The term "comfort women" is widely used to refer to the victims of Japanese military sexual slavery. A direct translation of the Japanese euphemism for "prostitute," *ianfu*, the term continues to be controversial, especially among survivors and the countries from which they were taken, since it reflects only the perspective of the Japanese military and distorts the victims' experiences. For the purposes of this book, despite its very clear failings, we've opted to use the literal translation, given its common usage within Korea, to refer to this specific form of forced sexual slavery.

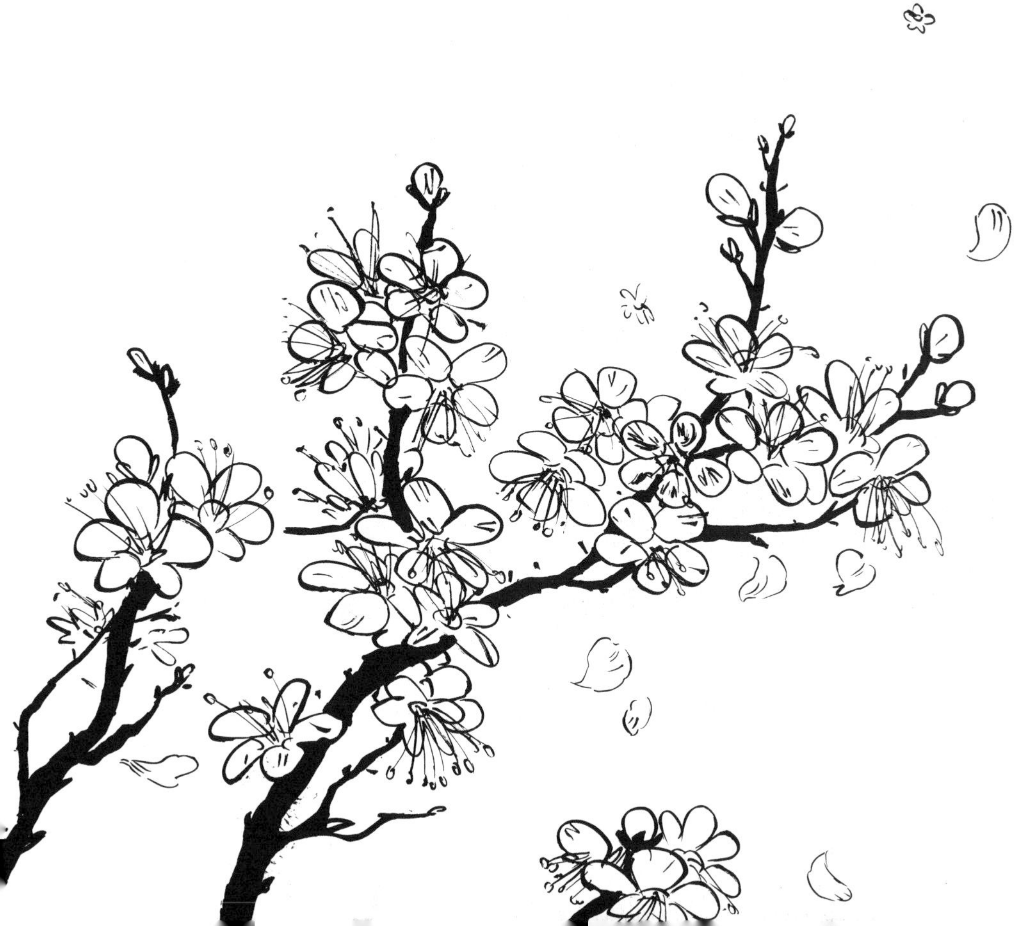

# THE WAY HOME

LONGJING, CHINA, 1996

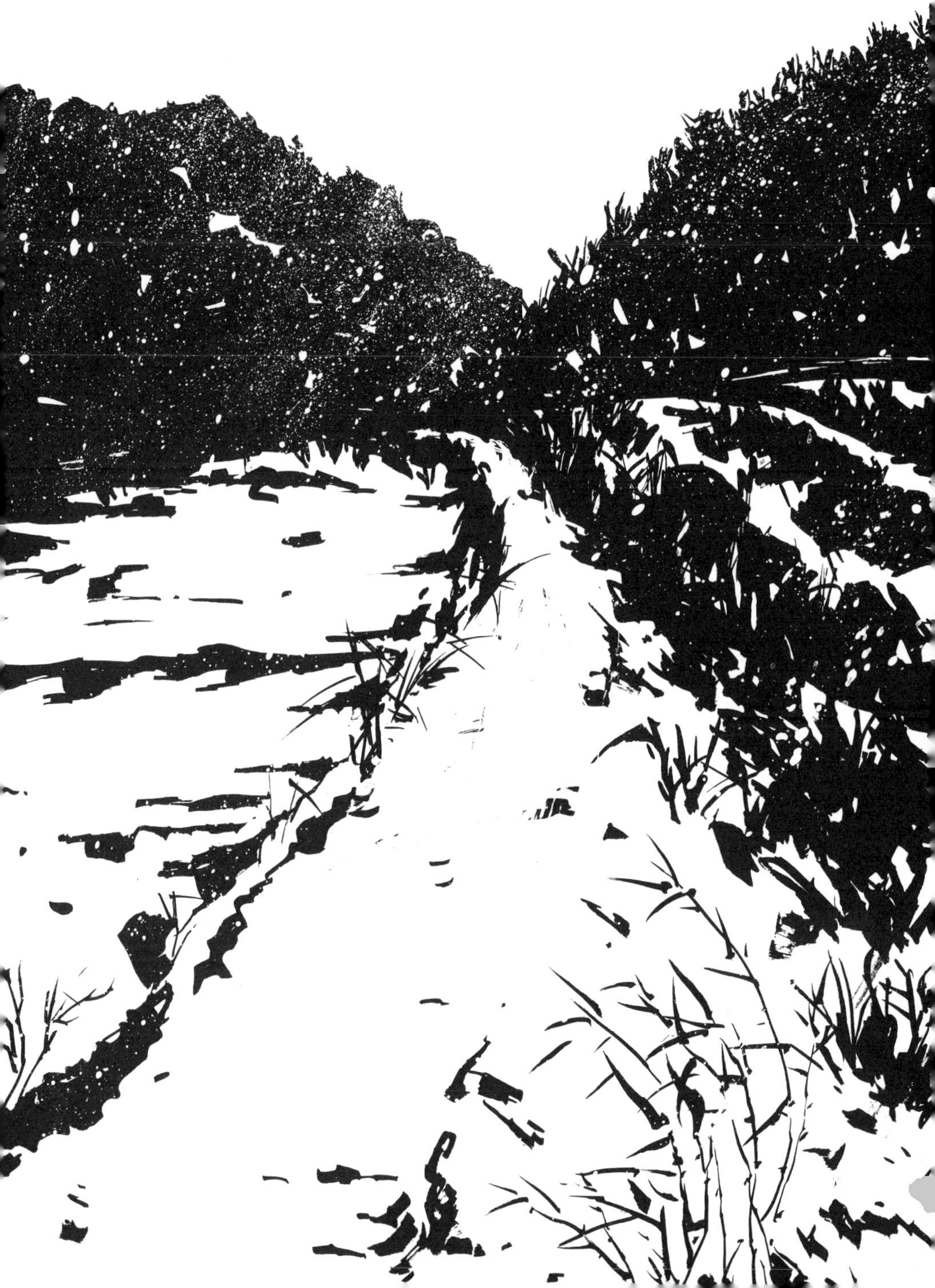

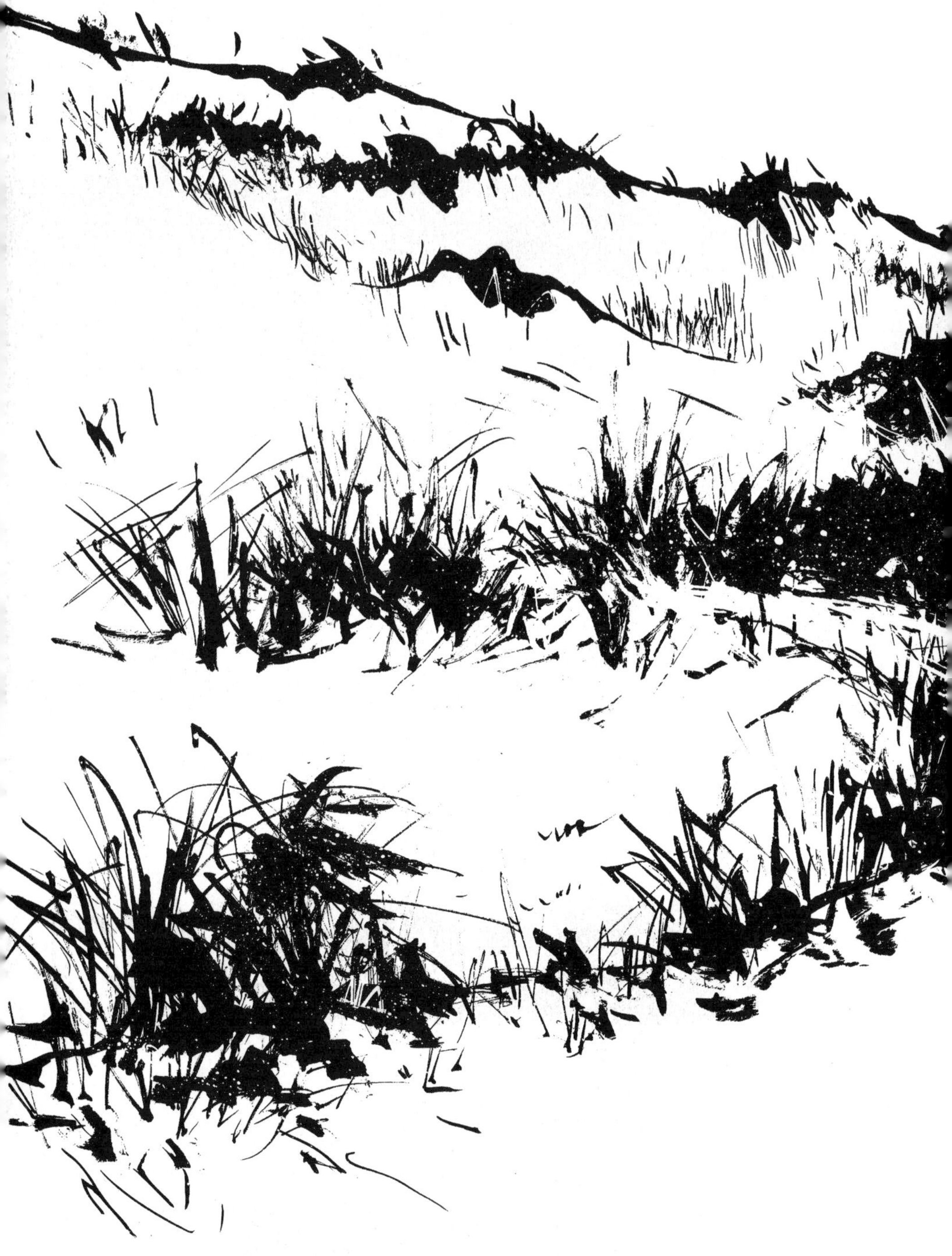

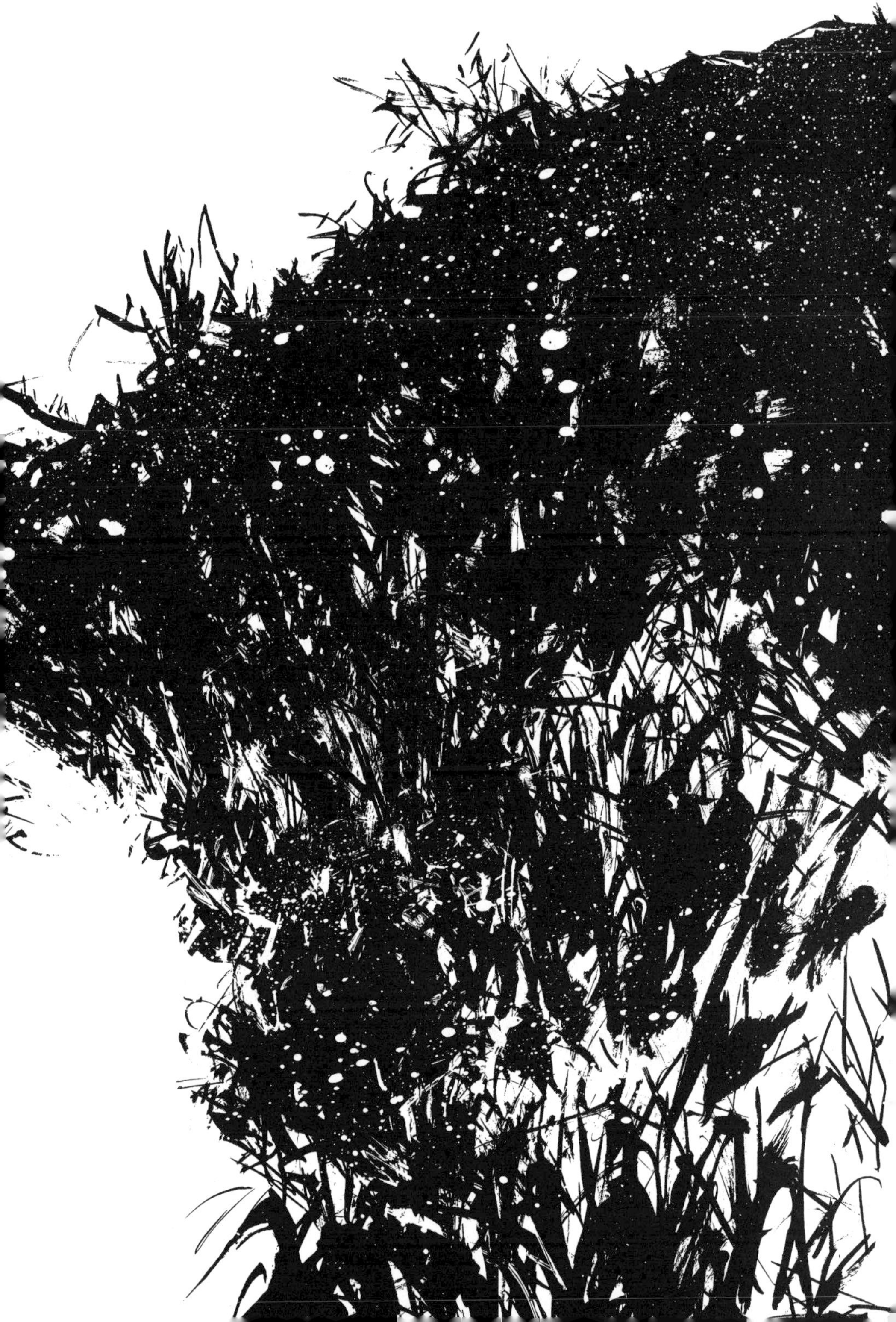

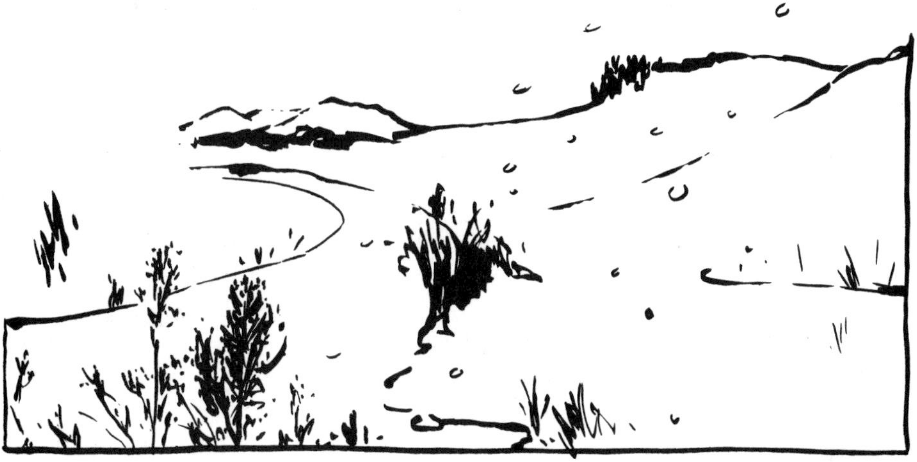

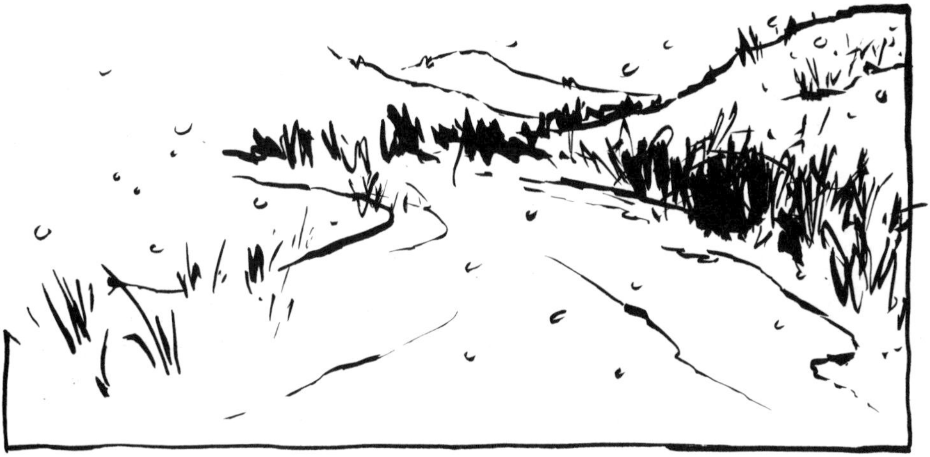

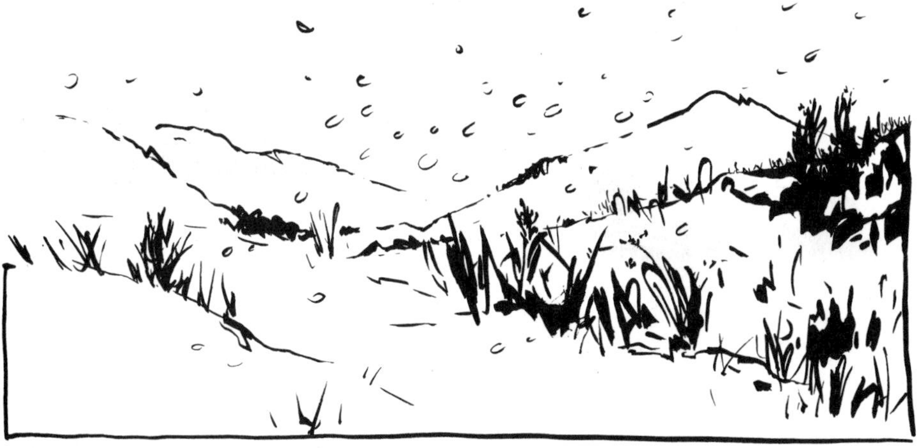

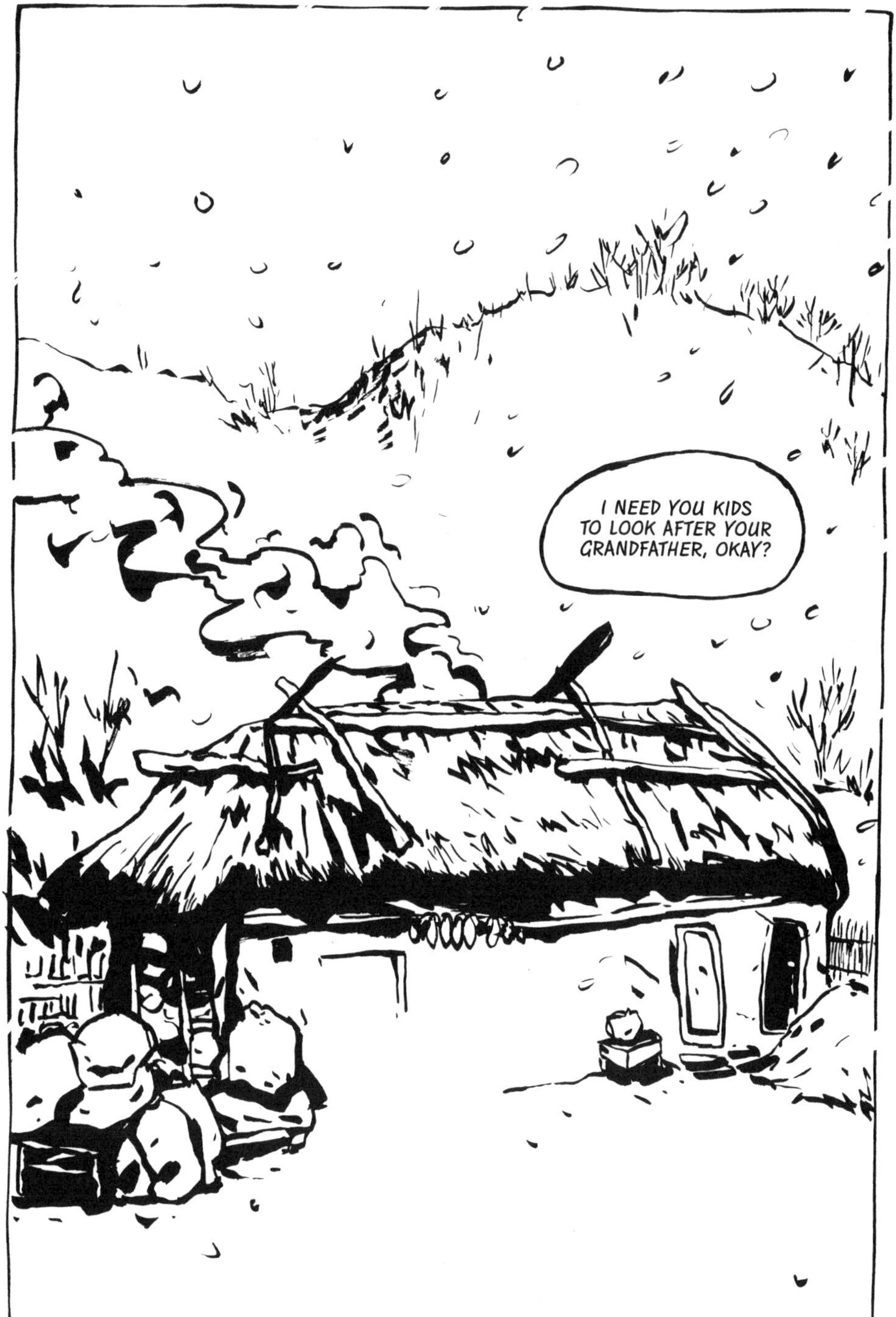
I NEED YOU KIDS TO LOOK AFTER YOUR GRANDFATHER, OKAY?

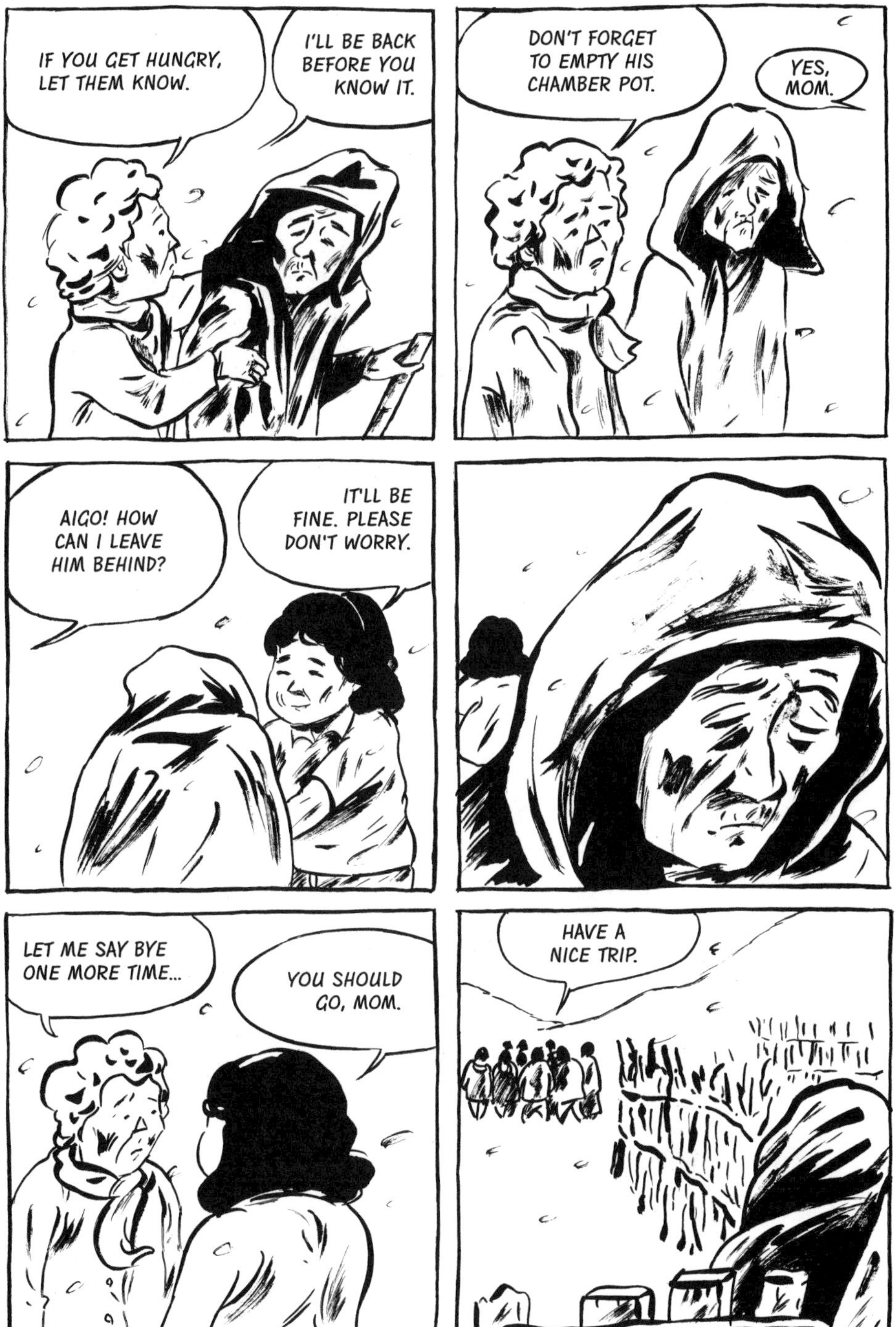
IF YOU GET HUNGRY, LET THEM KNOW.
I'LL BE BACK BEFORE YOU KNOW IT.
DON'T FORGET TO EMPTY HIS CHAMBER POT.
YES, MOM.
AIGO! HOW CAN I LEAVE HIM BEHIND?
IT'LL BE FINE. PLEASE DON'T WORRY.
LET ME SAY BYE ONE MORE TIME...
YOU SHOULD GO, MOM.
HAVE A NICE TRIP.

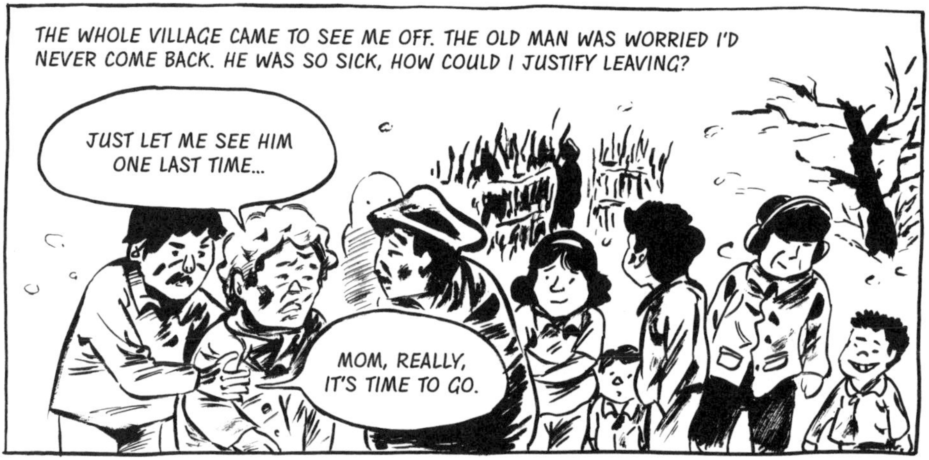
THE WHOLE VILLAGE CAME TO SEE ME OFF. THE OLD MAN WAS WORRIED I'D NEVER COME BACK. HE WAS SO SICK, HOW COULD I JUSTIFY LEAVING?
JUST LET ME SEE HIM ONE LAST TIME...
MOM, REALLY, IT'S TIME TO GO.

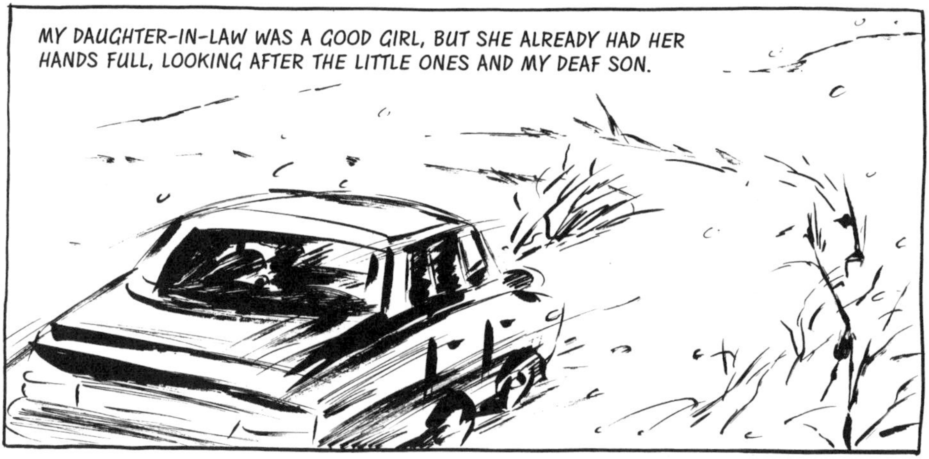
MY DAUGHTER-IN-LAW WAS A GOOD GIRL, BUT SHE ALREADY HAD HER HANDS FULL, LOOKING AFTER THE LITTLE ONES AND MY DEAF SON.

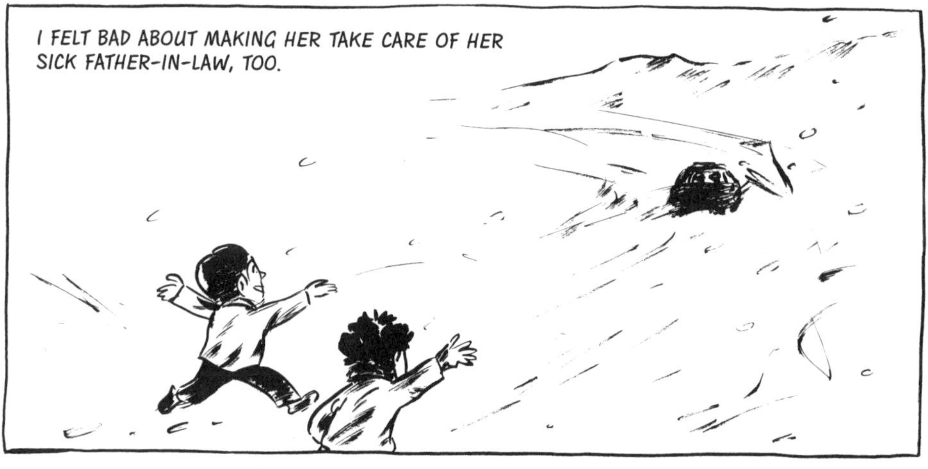
I FELT BAD ABOUT MAKING HER TAKE CARE OF HER SICK FATHER-IN-LAW, TOO.

I NEEDED MY VISA FROM THE KOREAN EMBASSY IN BEIJING

BECAUSE I WAS REPORTED DEAD IN KOREA.

NO MATTER HOW LONG IT'S BEEN, I CAN FIND MY WAY BACK HOME WITH MY EYES CLOSED. BOSU, BUSAN...

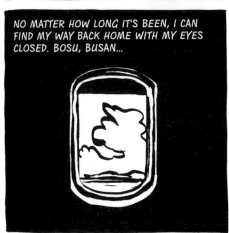

IT TOOK ME FIFTY-FIVE YEARS TO RETURN, AND YET THE FLIGHT WAS ONLY TWO HOURS.

FIFTY-FIVE YEARS.

THAT'S HOW LONG IT TOOK TO GO HOME.

*IN THE WINTER OF 1996, THE SBS DOCUDRAMA *TRACKING EVENTS AND PEOPLE* HELPED GRANNY LEE OK-SUN GO BACK TO KOREA FOR THE FIRST TIME IN FIFTY-FIVE YEARS. THE EPISODE "COMFORT WOMEN LEFT IN CHINA RETURN HOME" AIRED JANUARY 4, 1997.

# THE GIRL WHO DREAMED OF GOING TO SCHOOL

BUSAN, 1934

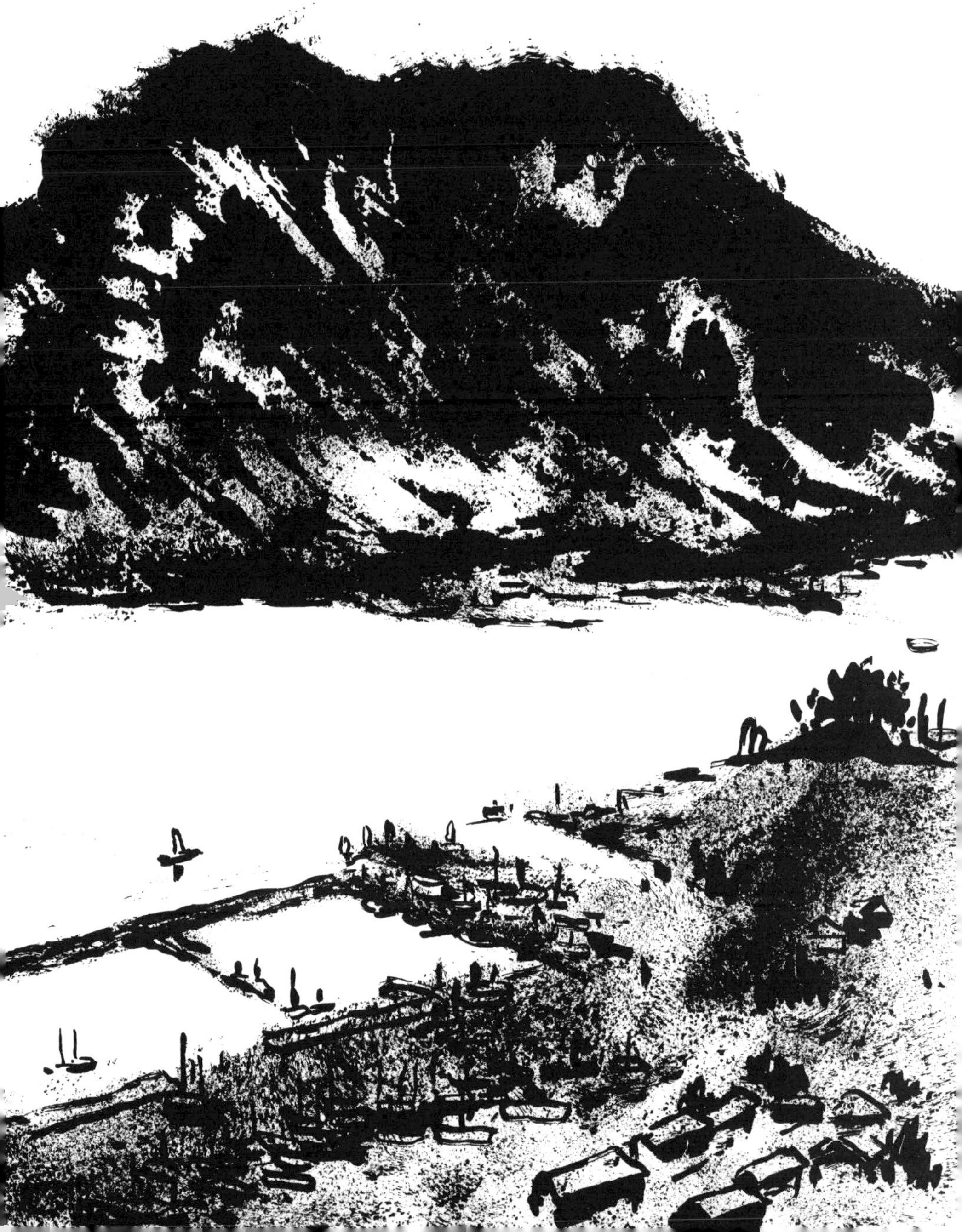

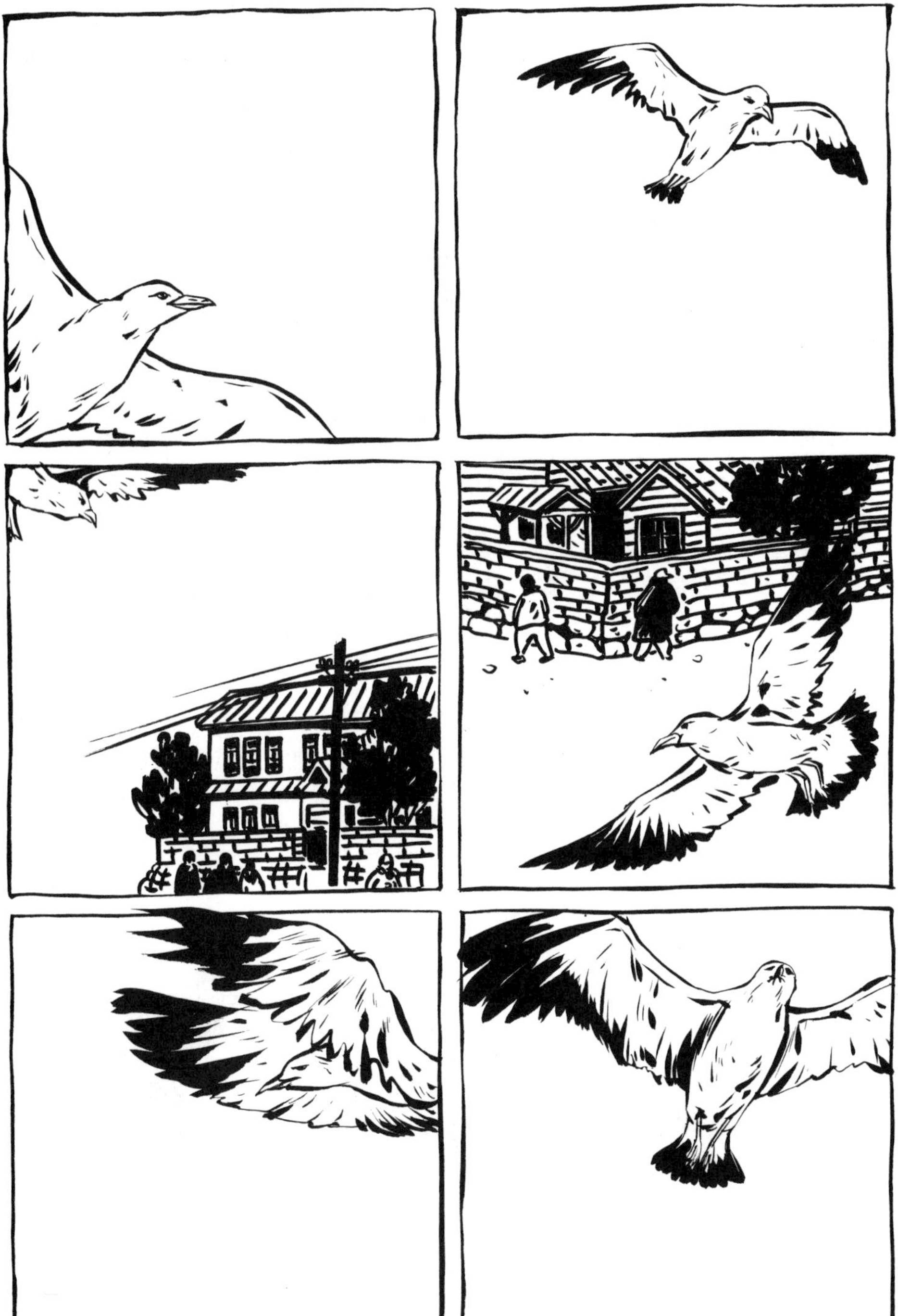

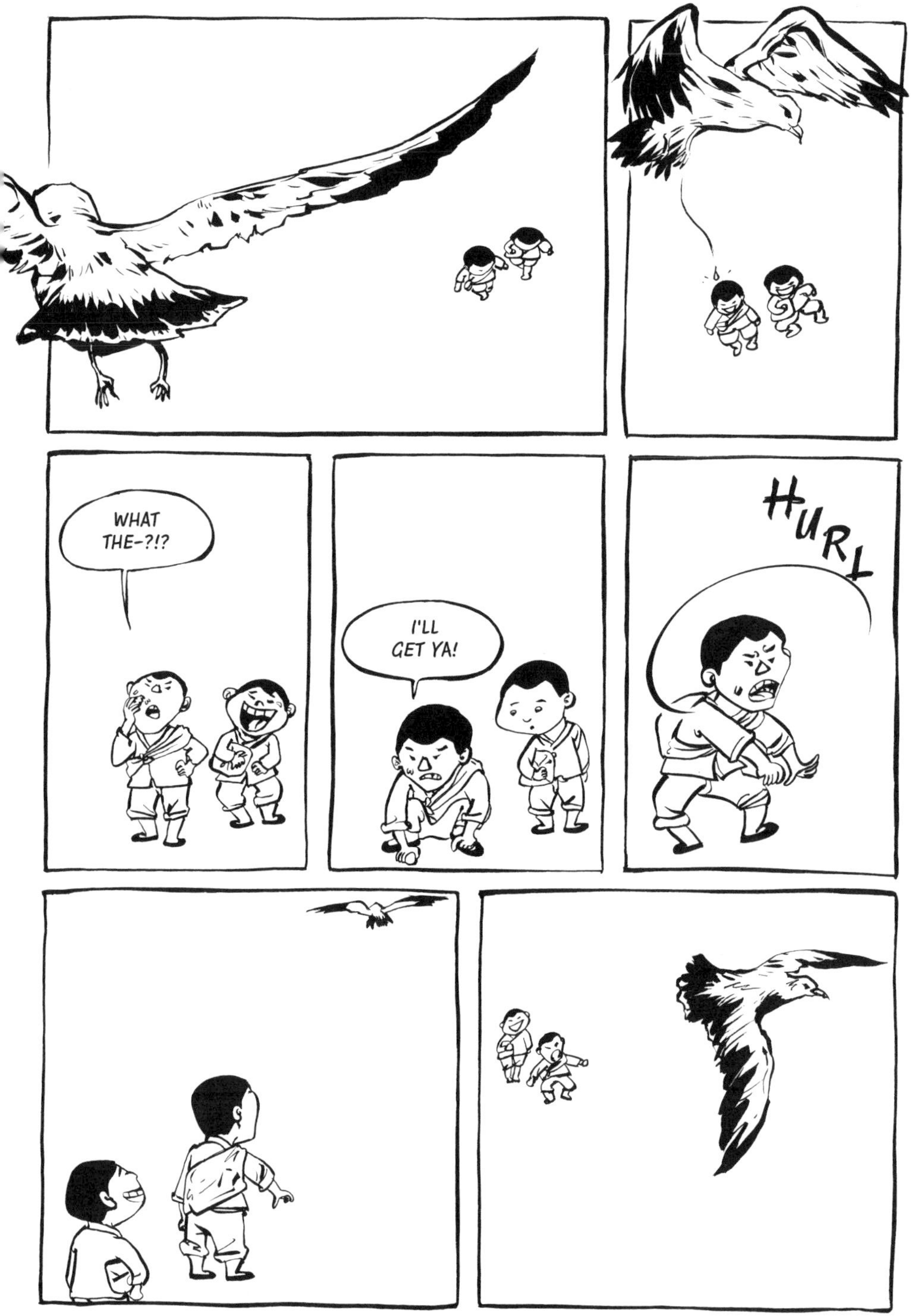
WHAT THE-?!?
I'LL GET YA!
HURL

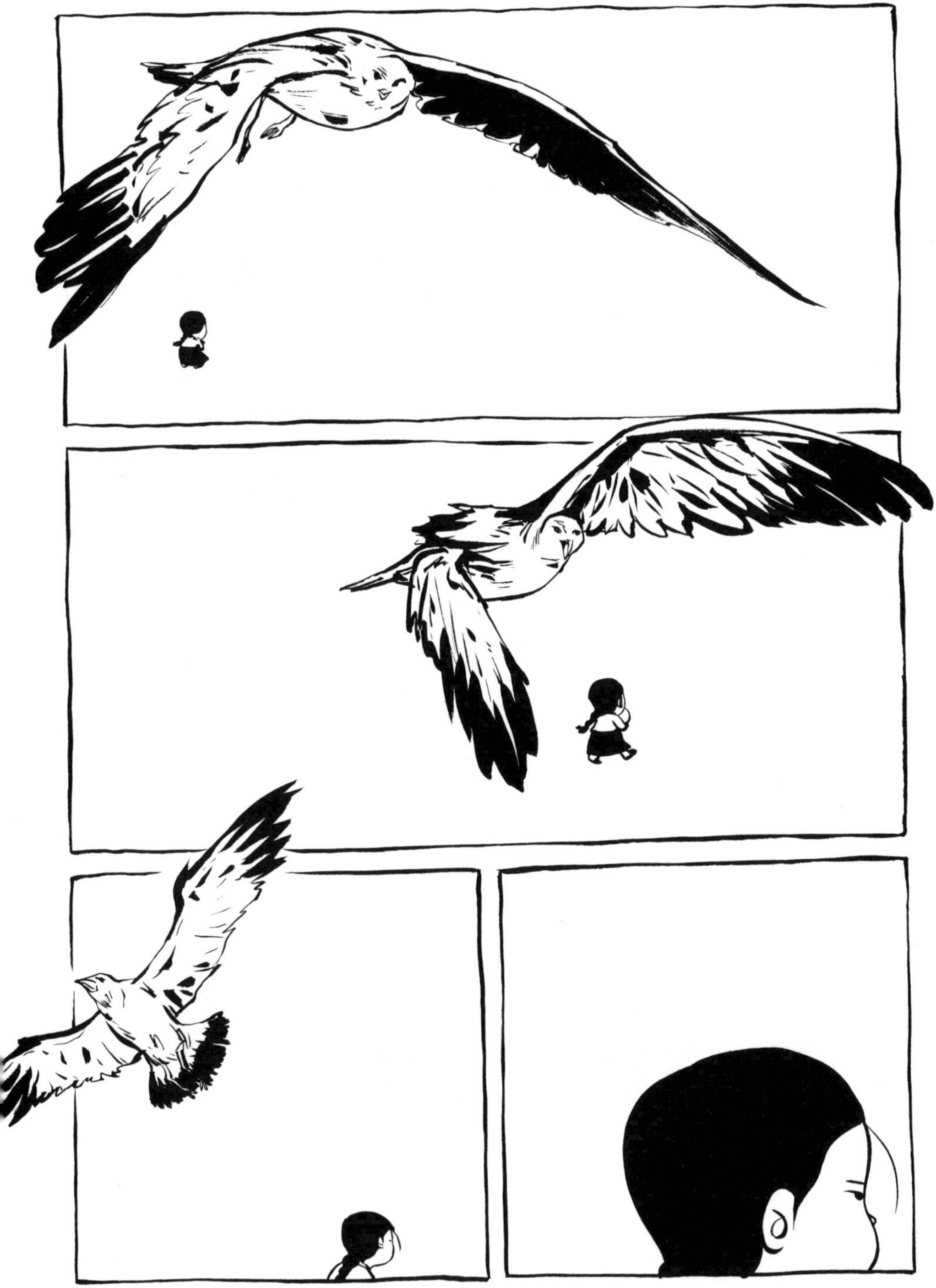

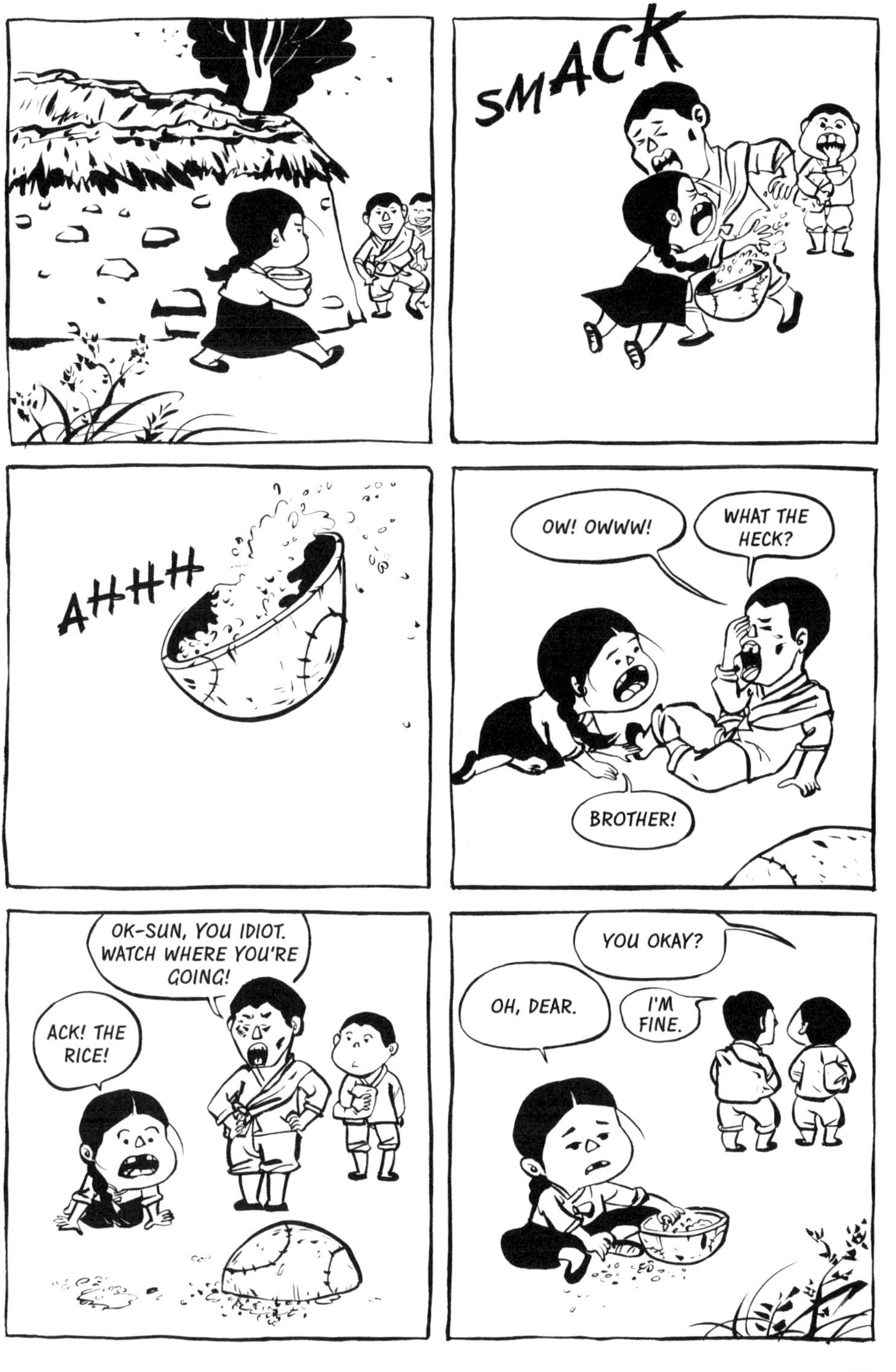
SMACK
AHHH
OW! OWWW!
WHAT THE HECK?
BROTHER!
OK-SUN, YOU IDIOT. WATCH WHERE YOU'RE GOING!
ACK! THE RICE!
YOU OKAY?
OH, DEAR.
I'M FINE.

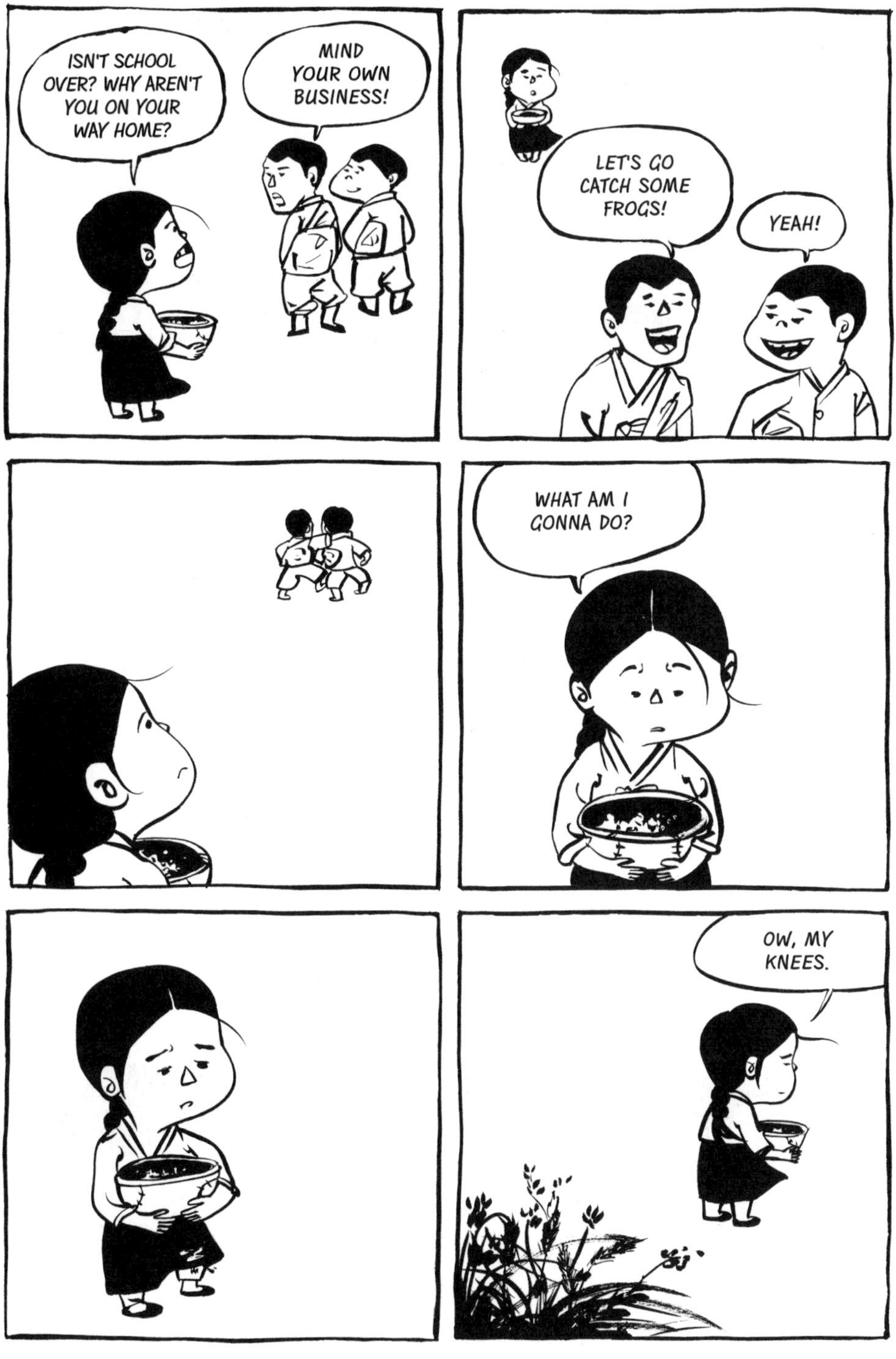
ISN'T SCHOOL OVER? WHY AREN'T YOU ON YOUR WAY HOME?
MIND YOUR OWN BUSINESS!
LET'S GO CATCH SOME FROGS!
YEAH!
WHAT AM I GONNA DO?
OW, MY KNEES.

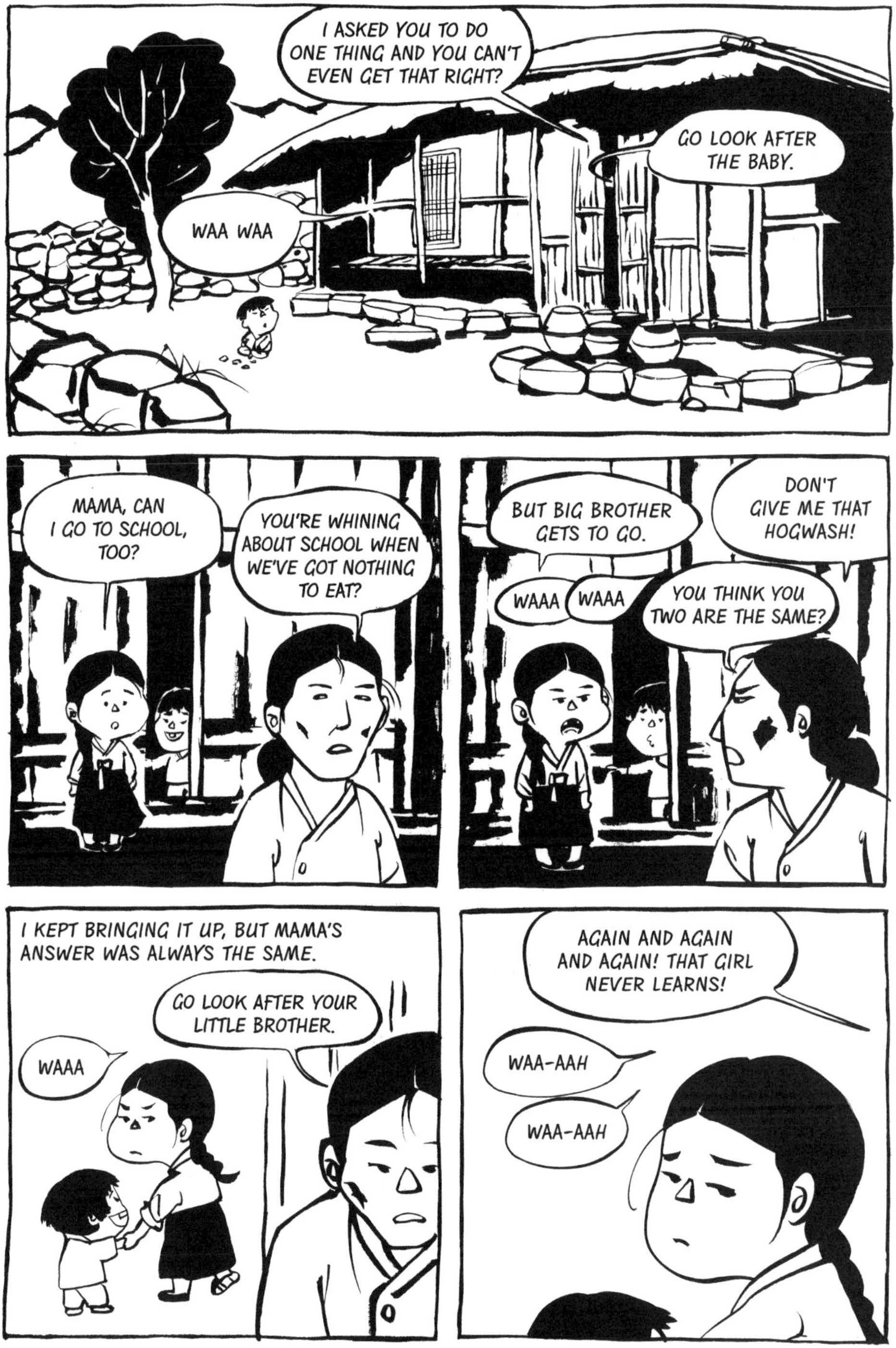
I ASKED YOU TO DO ONE THING AND YOU CAN'T EVEN GET THAT RIGHT?
GO LOOK AFTER THE BABY.
WAA WAA
MAMA, CAN I GO TO SCHOOL, TOO?
YOU'RE WHINING ABOUT SCHOOL WHEN WE'VE GOT NOTHING TO EAT?
BUT BIG BROTHER GETS TO GO.
WAAA
WAAA
DON'T GIVE ME THAT HOGWASH!
YOU THINK YOU TWO ARE THE SAME?
I KEPT BRINGING IT UP, BUT MAMA'S ANSWER WAS ALWAYS THE SAME.
GO LOOK AFTER YOUR LITTLE BROTHER.
WAAA
AGAIN AND AGAIN AND AGAIN! THAT GIRL NEVER LEARNS!
WAA-AAH
WAA-AAH

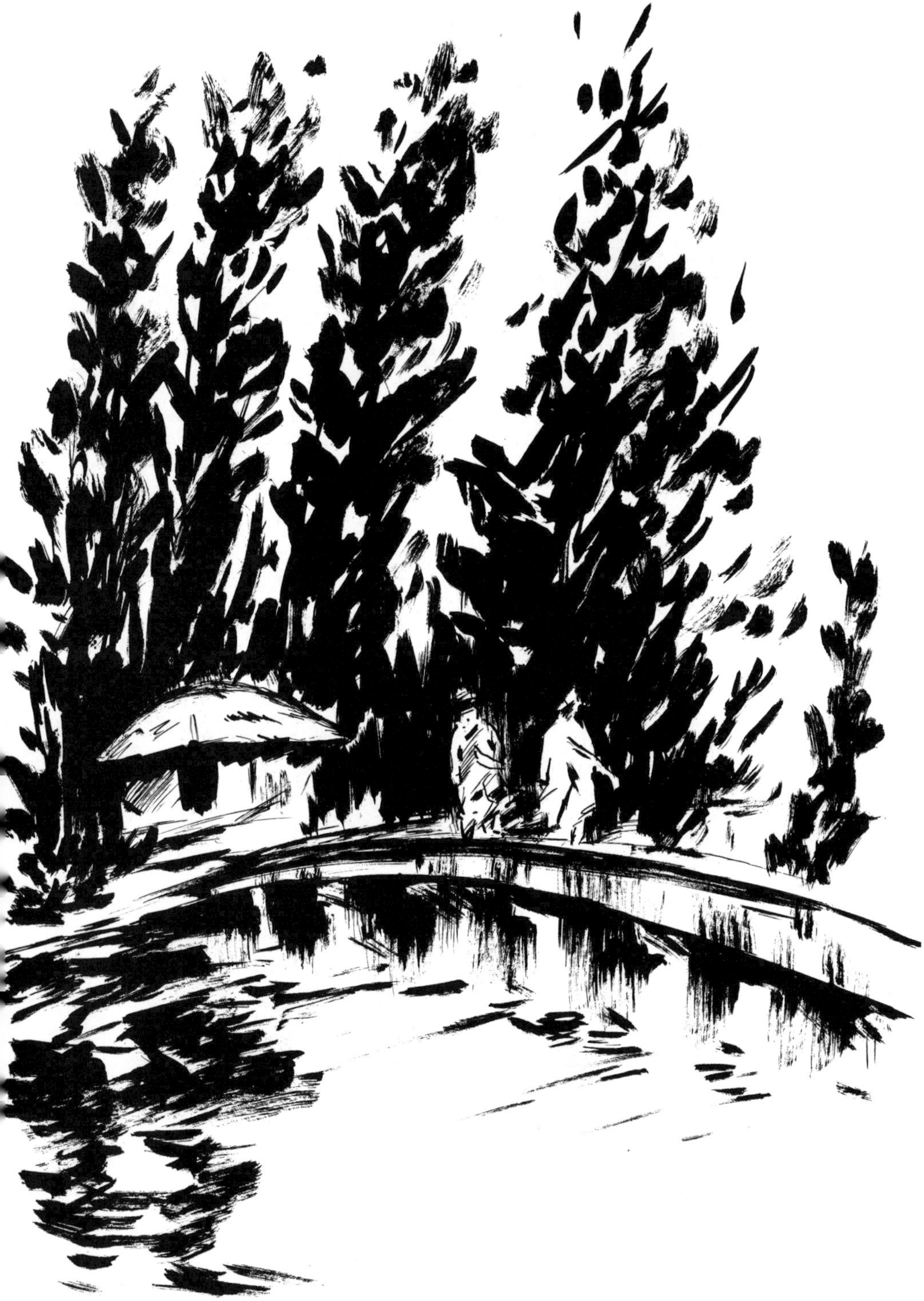

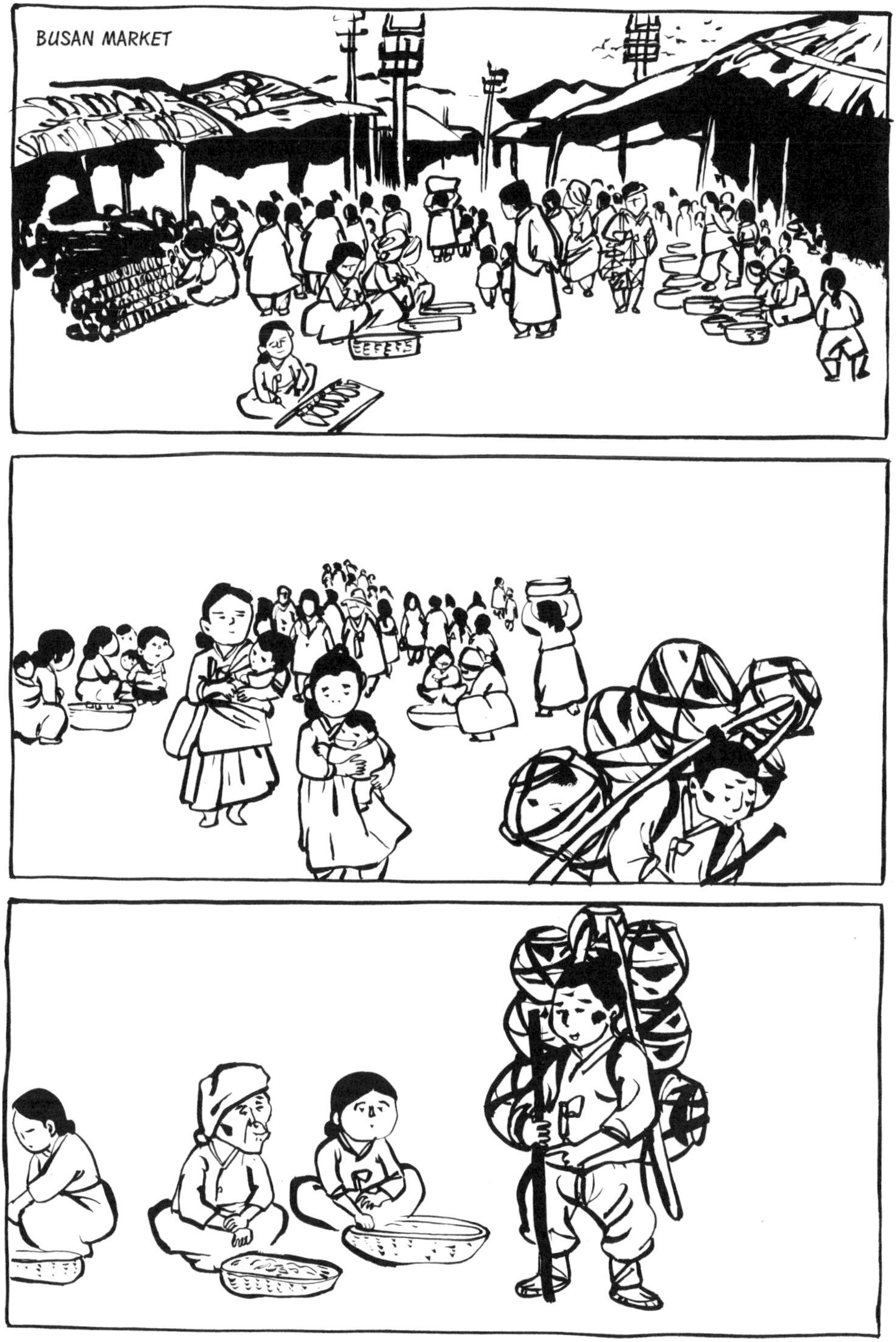
BUSAN MARKET

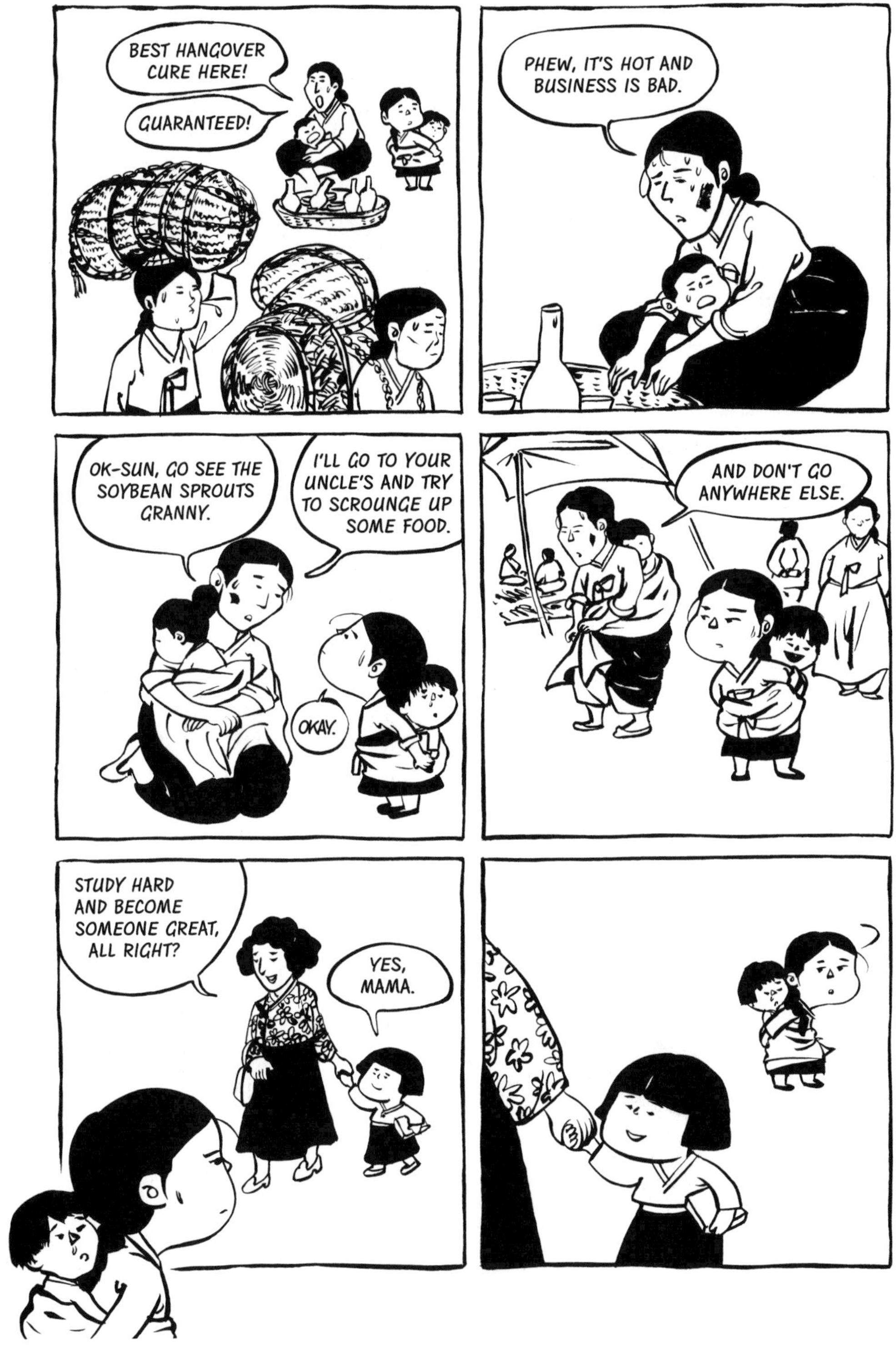
BEST HANGOVER CURE HERE!
GUARANTEED!
PHEW, IT'S HOT AND BUSINESS IS BAD.
OK-SUN, GO SEE THE SOYBEAN SPROUTS GRANNY.
I'LL GO TO YOUR UNCLE'S AND TRY TO SCROUNGE UP SOME FOOD.
OKAY.
AND DON'T GO ANYWHERE ELSE.
STUDY HARD AND BECOME SOMEONE GREAT, ALL RIGHT?
YES, MAMA.

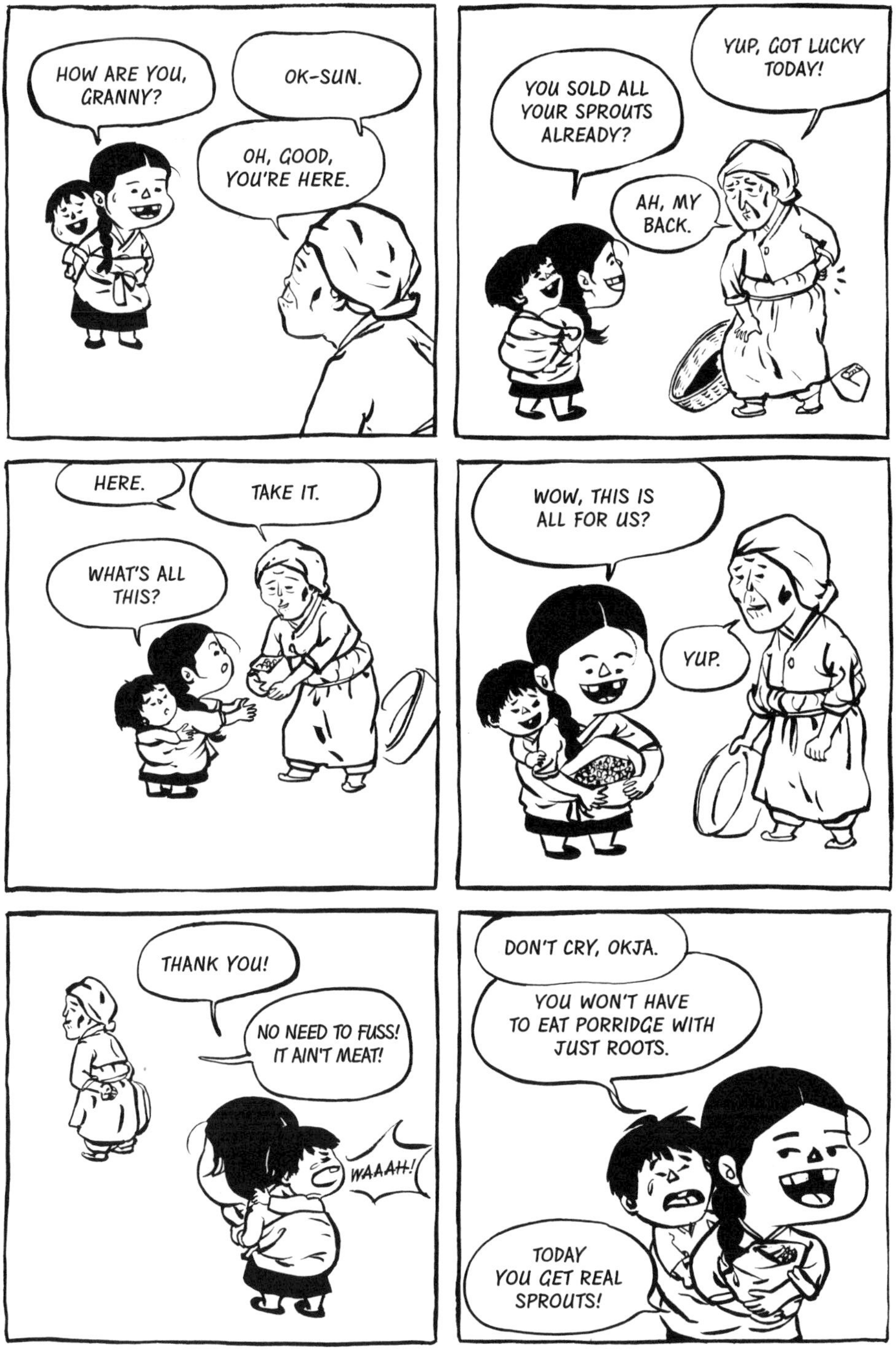
HOW ARE YOU, GRANNY?
OK-SUN.
OH, GOOD, YOU'RE HERE.
YOU SOLD ALL YOUR SPROUTS ALREADY?
YUP, GOT LUCKY TODAY!
AH, MY BACK.
HERE.
TAKE IT.
WHAT'S ALL THIS?
WOW, THIS IS ALL FOR US?
YUP.
THANK YOU!
NO NEED TO FUSS! IT AIN'T MEAT!
WAAAH!
DON'T CRY, OKJA.
YOU WON'T HAVE TO EAT PORRIDGE WITH JUST ROOTS.
TODAY YOU GET REAL SPROUTS!

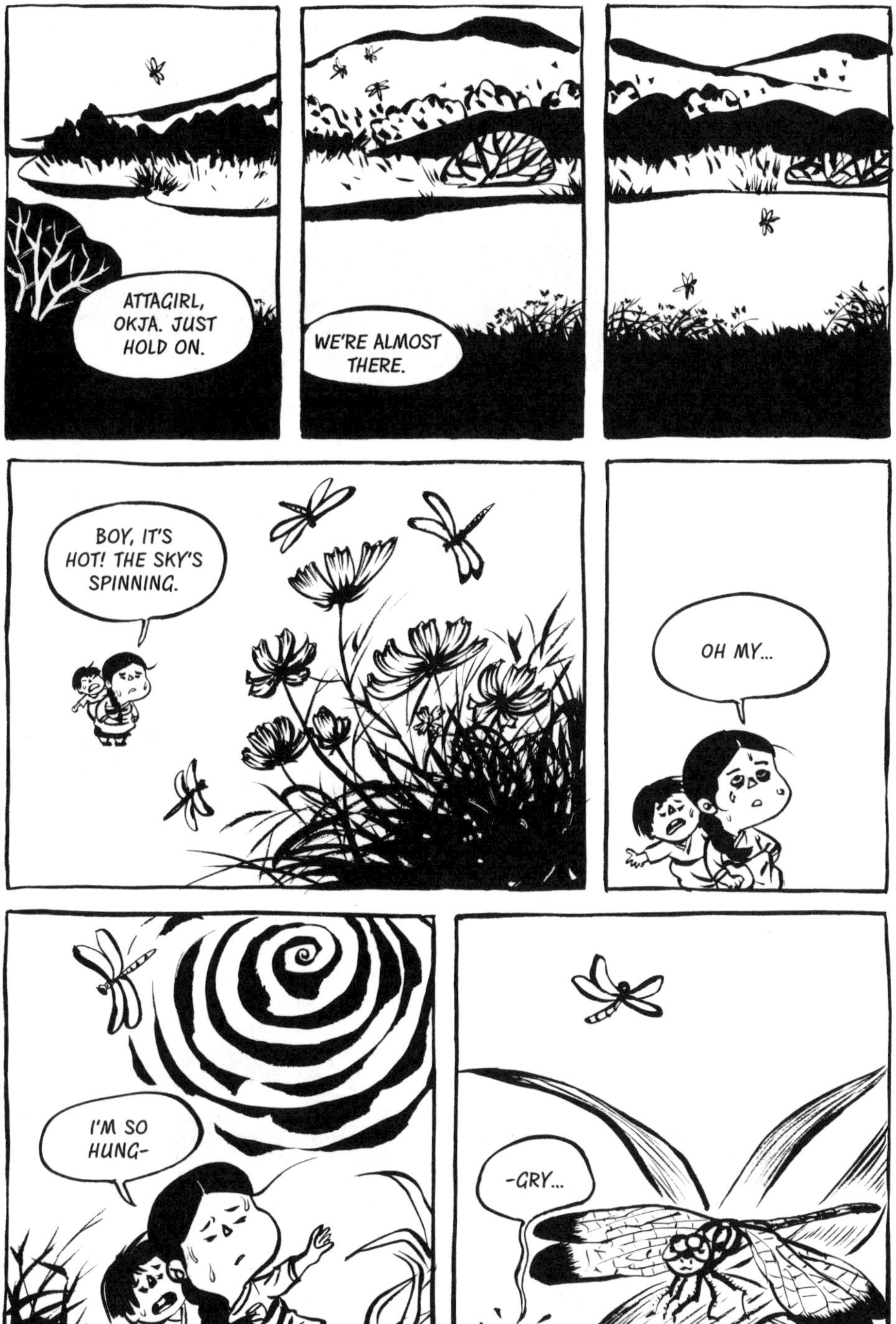
ATTAGIRL, OKJA. JUST HOLD ON.
WE'RE ALMOST THERE.
BOY, IT'S HOT! THE SKY'S SPINNING.
OH MY...
I'M SO HUNG-
-GRY...

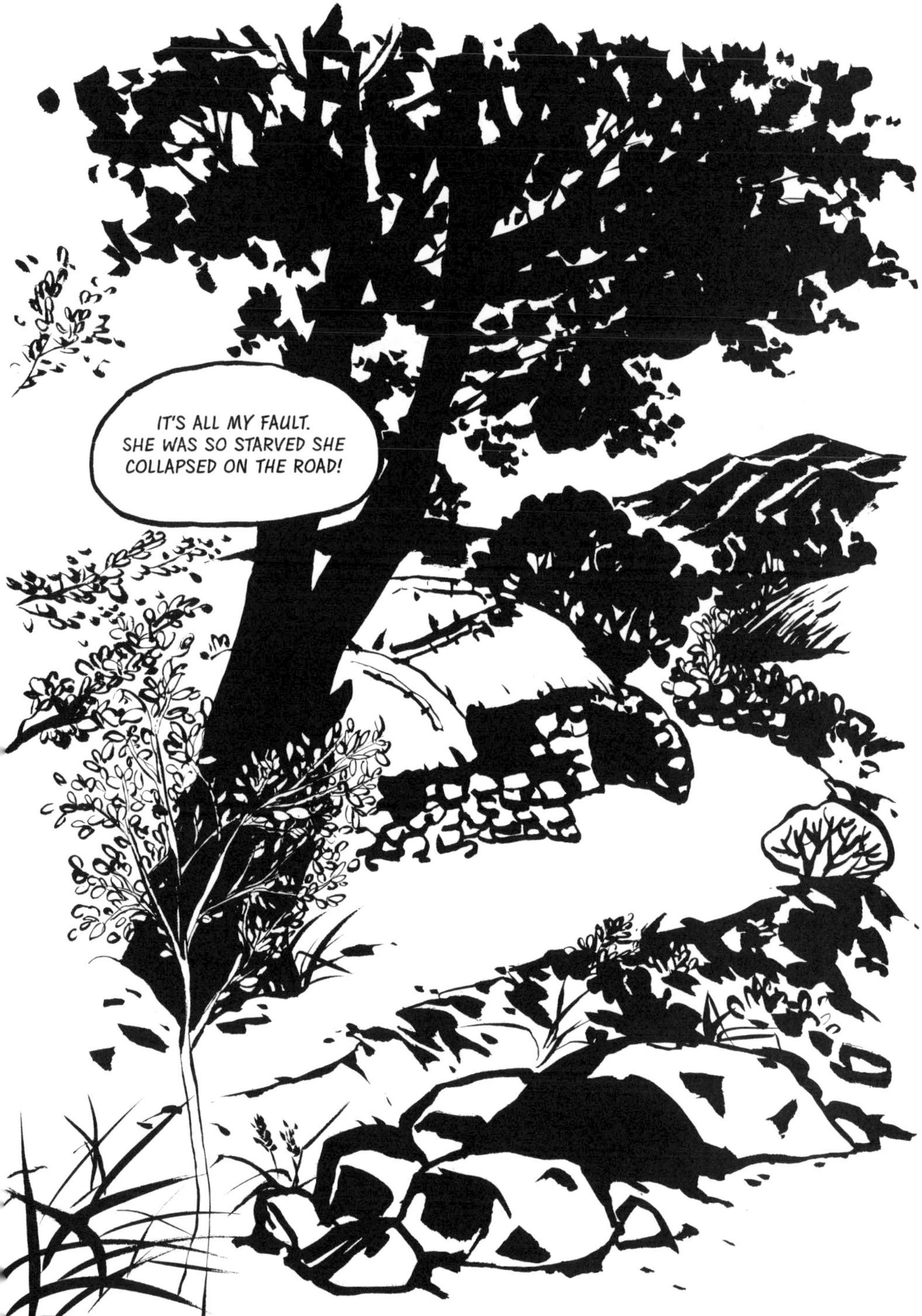
IT'S ALL MY FAULT. SHE WAS SO STARVED SHE COLLAPSED ON THE ROAD!

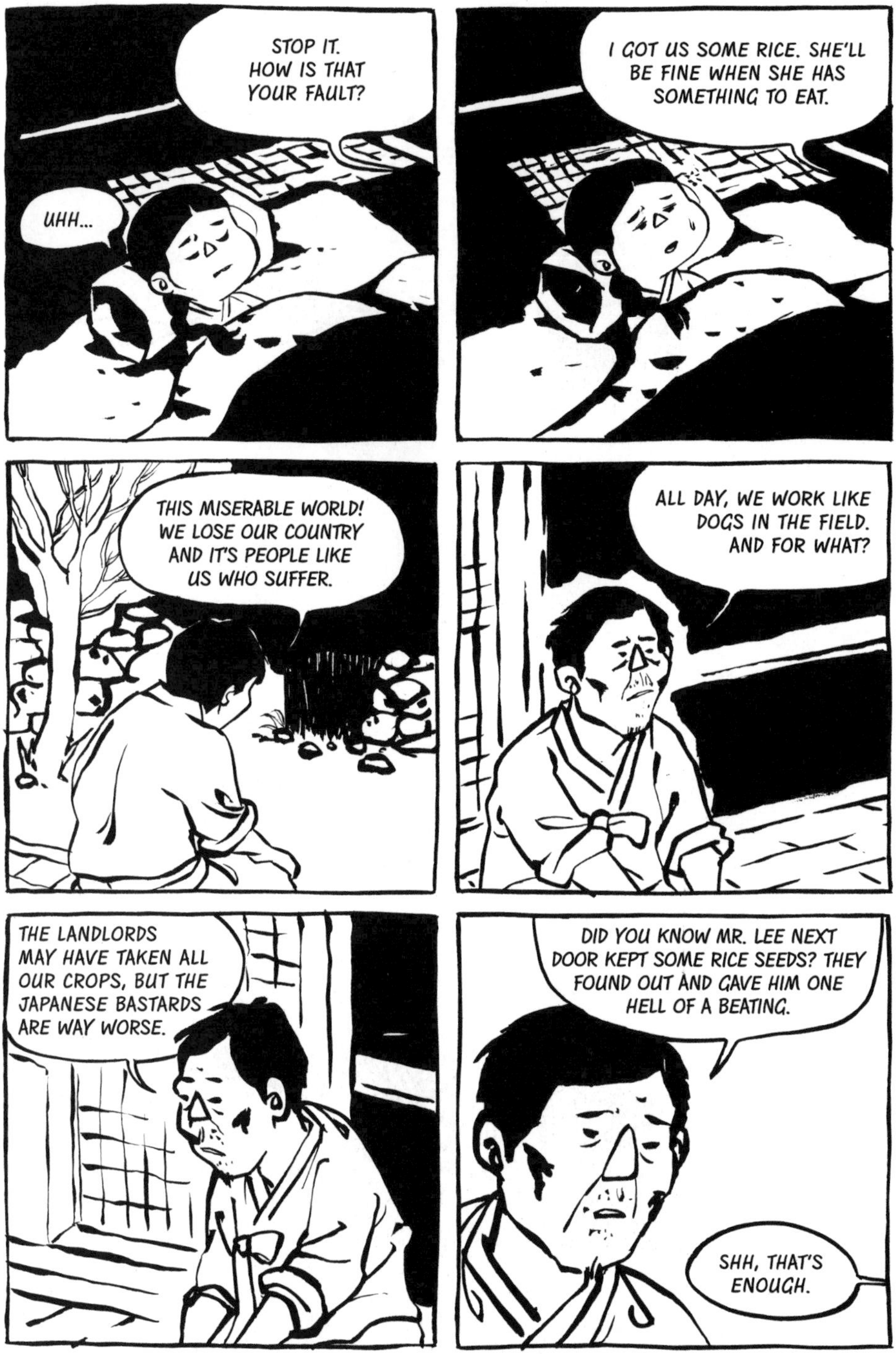
STOP IT. HOW IS THAT YOUR FAULT?
UHH...
I GOT US SOME RICE. SHE'LL BE FINE WHEN SHE HAS SOMETHING TO EAT.
THIS MISERABLE WORLD! WE LOSE OUR COUNTRY AND IT'S PEOPLE LIKE US WHO SUFFER.
ALL DAY, WE WORK LIKE DOGS IN THE FIELD. AND FOR WHAT?
THE LANDLORDS MAY HAVE TAKEN ALL OUR CROPS, BUT THE JAPANESE BASTARDS ARE WAY WORSE.
DID YOU KNOW MR. LEE NEXT DOOR KEPT SOME RICE SEEDS? THEY FOUND OUT AND GAVE HIM ONE HELL OF A BEATING.
SHH, THAT'S ENOUGH.

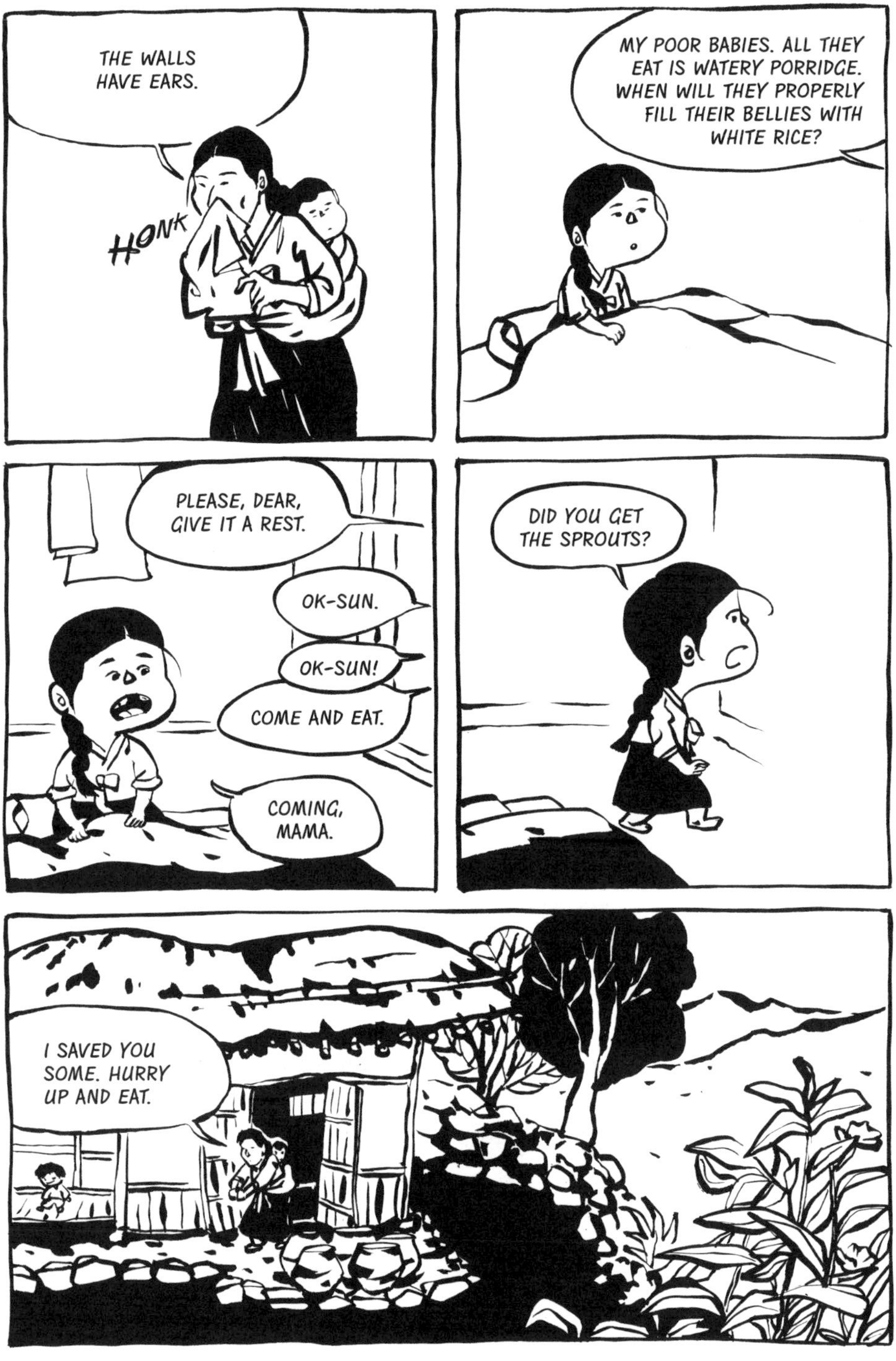
THE WALLS HAVE EARS.
HONK
MY POOR BABIES. ALL THEY EAT IS WATERY PORRIDGE. WHEN WILL THEY PROPERLY FILL THEIR BELLIES WITH WHITE RICE?
PLEASE, DEAR, GIVE IT A REST.
OK-SUN.
OK-SUN!
COME AND EAT.
COMING, MAMA.
DID YOU GET THE SPROUTS?
I SAVED YOU SOME. HURRY UP AND EAT.

# PERSIMMONS AND CANDY

THE HOUSE OF SHARING,*
GYEONGGI PROVINCE,
SOUTH KOREA

SEE THIS SCAR ON MY HAND?

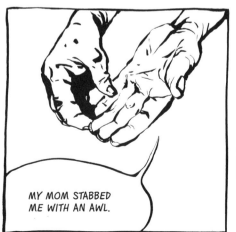

MY MOM STABBED ME WITH AN AWL.

SHE CALLED ME A DISGRACE AND SAID SHE'D TEACH ME TO NEVER STEAL AGAIN.

*THE HOUSE OF SHARING IN GWANGJU, GYEONGGI PROVINCE, IS A NURSING HOME FOR SURVIVING COMFORT WOMEN. LOCATED ON THE GROUNDS IS A MEMORIAL HALL AND MUSEUM.

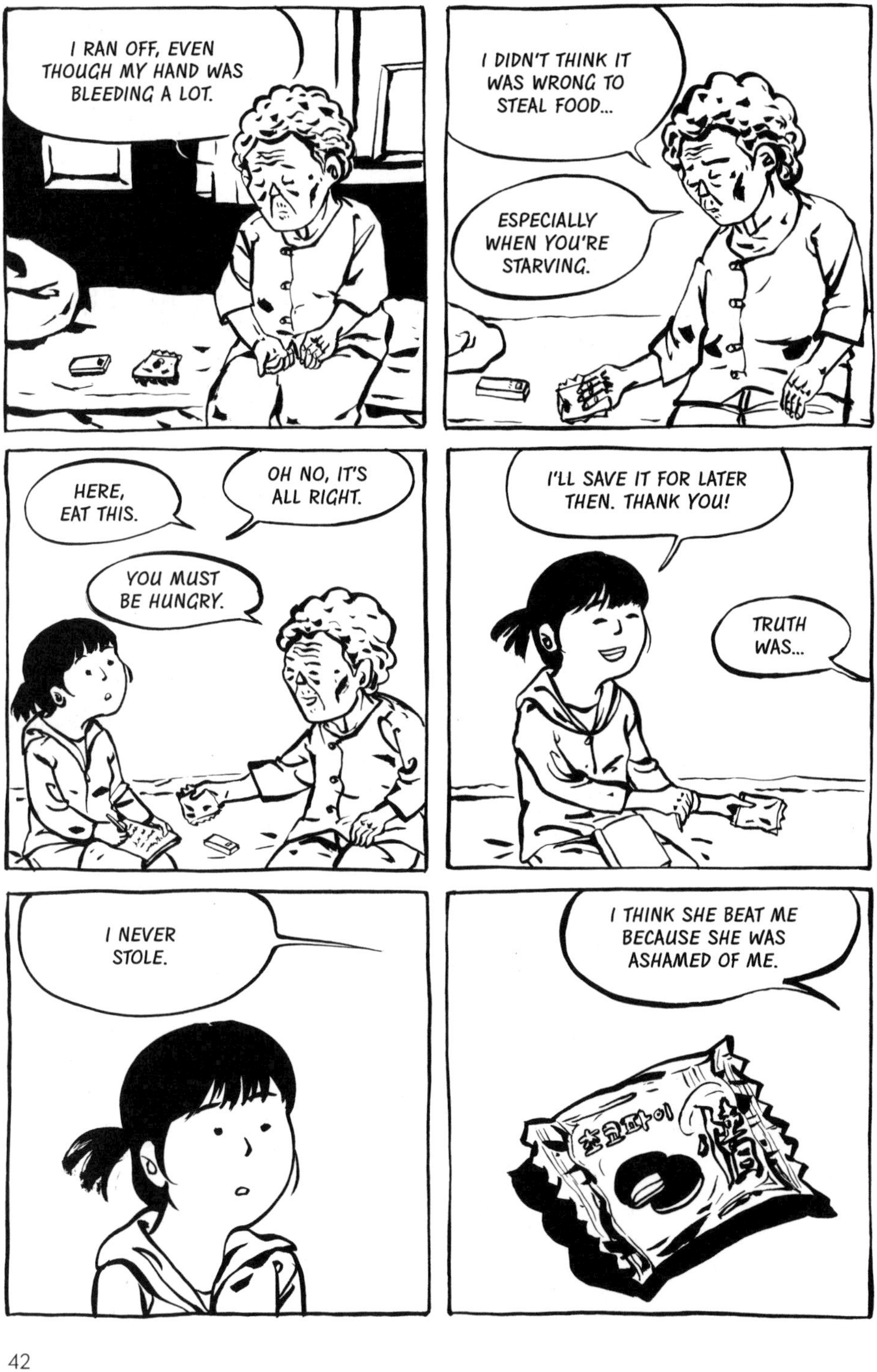
I RAN OFF, EVEN THOUGH MY HAND WAS BLEEDING A LOT.
I DIDN'T THINK IT WAS WRONG TO STEAL FOOD...
ESPECIALLY WHEN YOU'RE STARVING.
HERE, EAT THIS.
OH NO, IT'S ALL RIGHT.
YOU MUST BE HUNGRY.
I'LL SAVE IT FOR LATER THEN. THANK YOU!
TRUTH WAS...
I NEVER STOLE.
I THINK SHE BEAT ME BECAUSE SHE WAS ASHAMED OF ME.

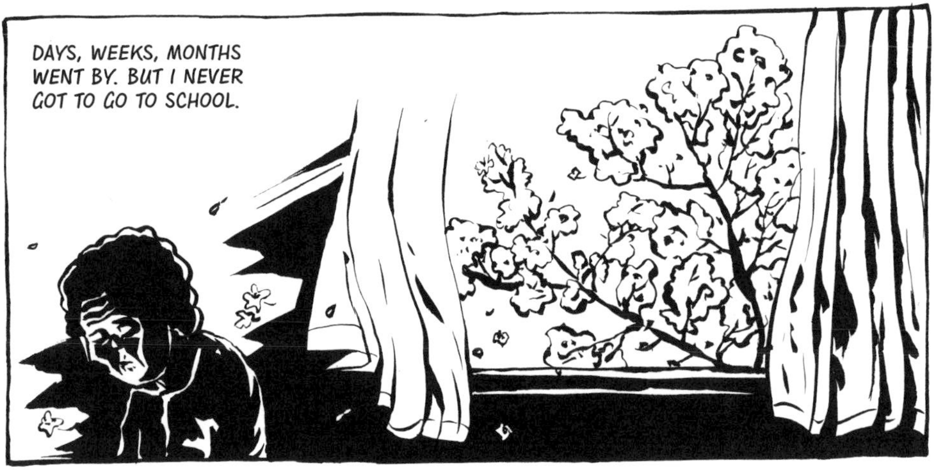
DAYS, WEEKS, MONTHS WENT BY. BUT I NEVER GOT TO GO TO SCHOOL.

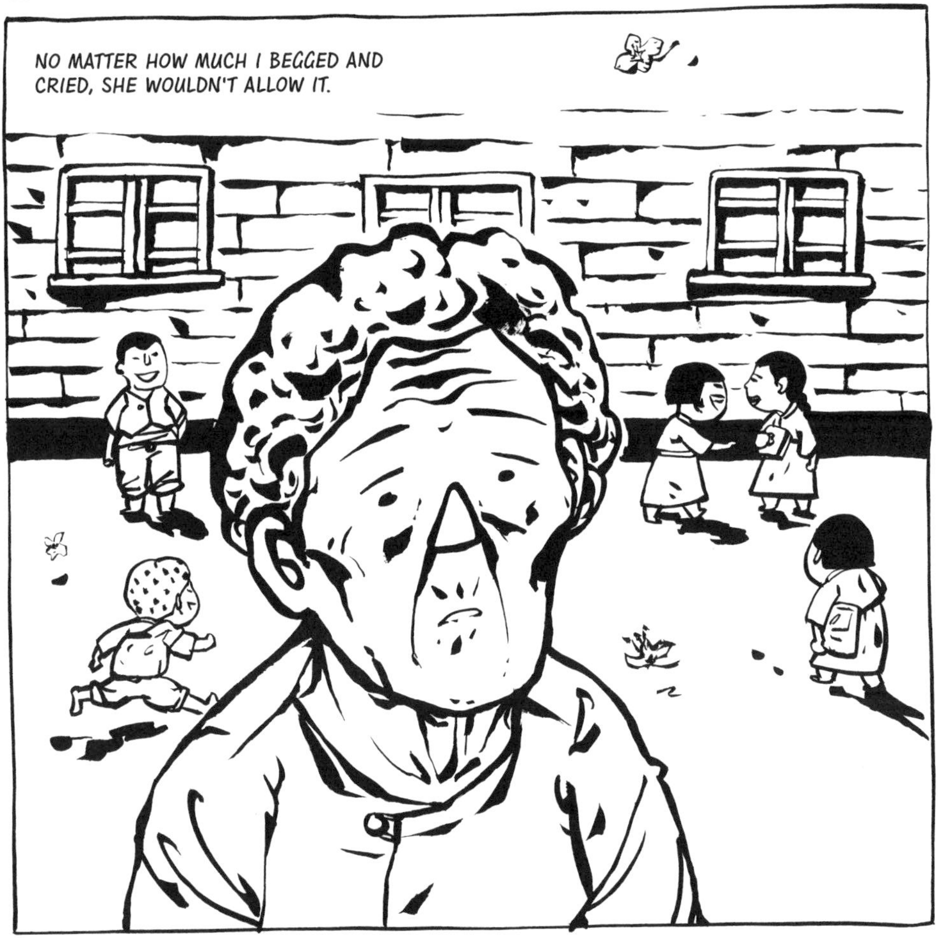
NO MATTER HOW MUCH I BEGGED AND CRIED, SHE WOULDN'T ALLOW IT.

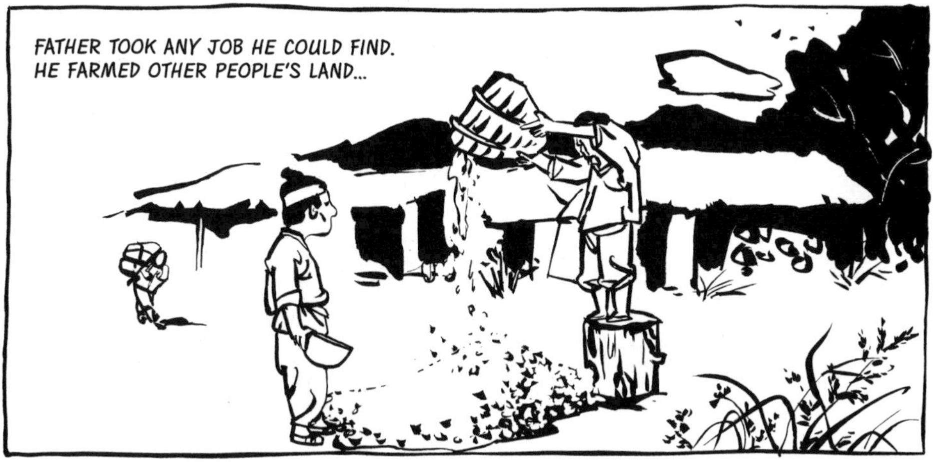
FATHER TOOK ANY JOB HE COULD FIND.
HE FARMED OTHER PEOPLE'S LAND...

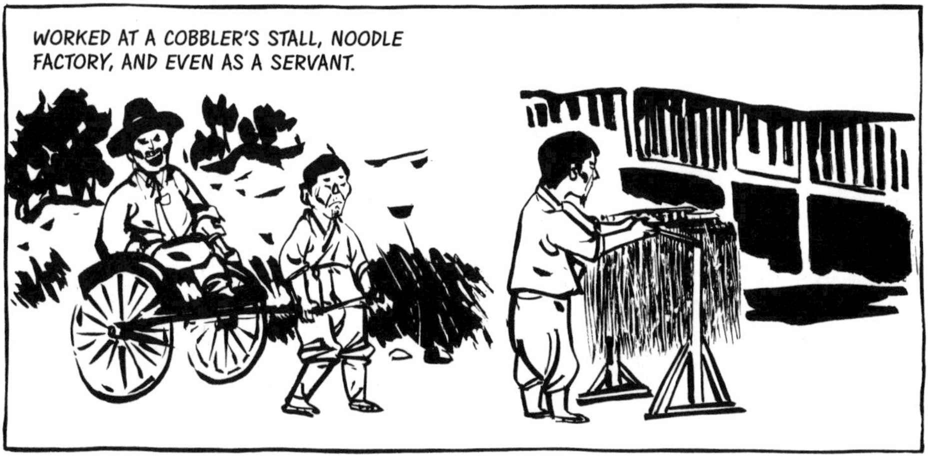
WORKED AT A COBBLER'S STALL, NOODLE FACTORY, AND EVEN AS A SERVANT.

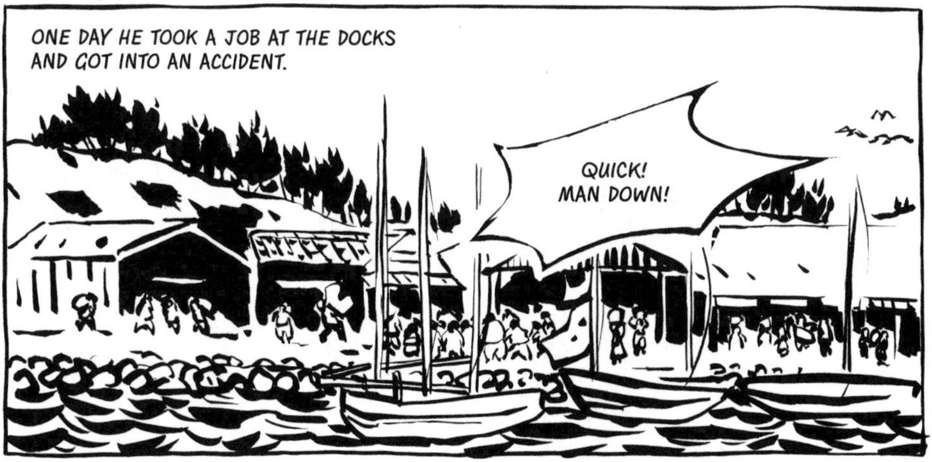
ONE DAY HE TOOK A JOB AT THE DOCKS AND GOT INTO AN ACCIDENT.
QUICK! MAN DOWN!

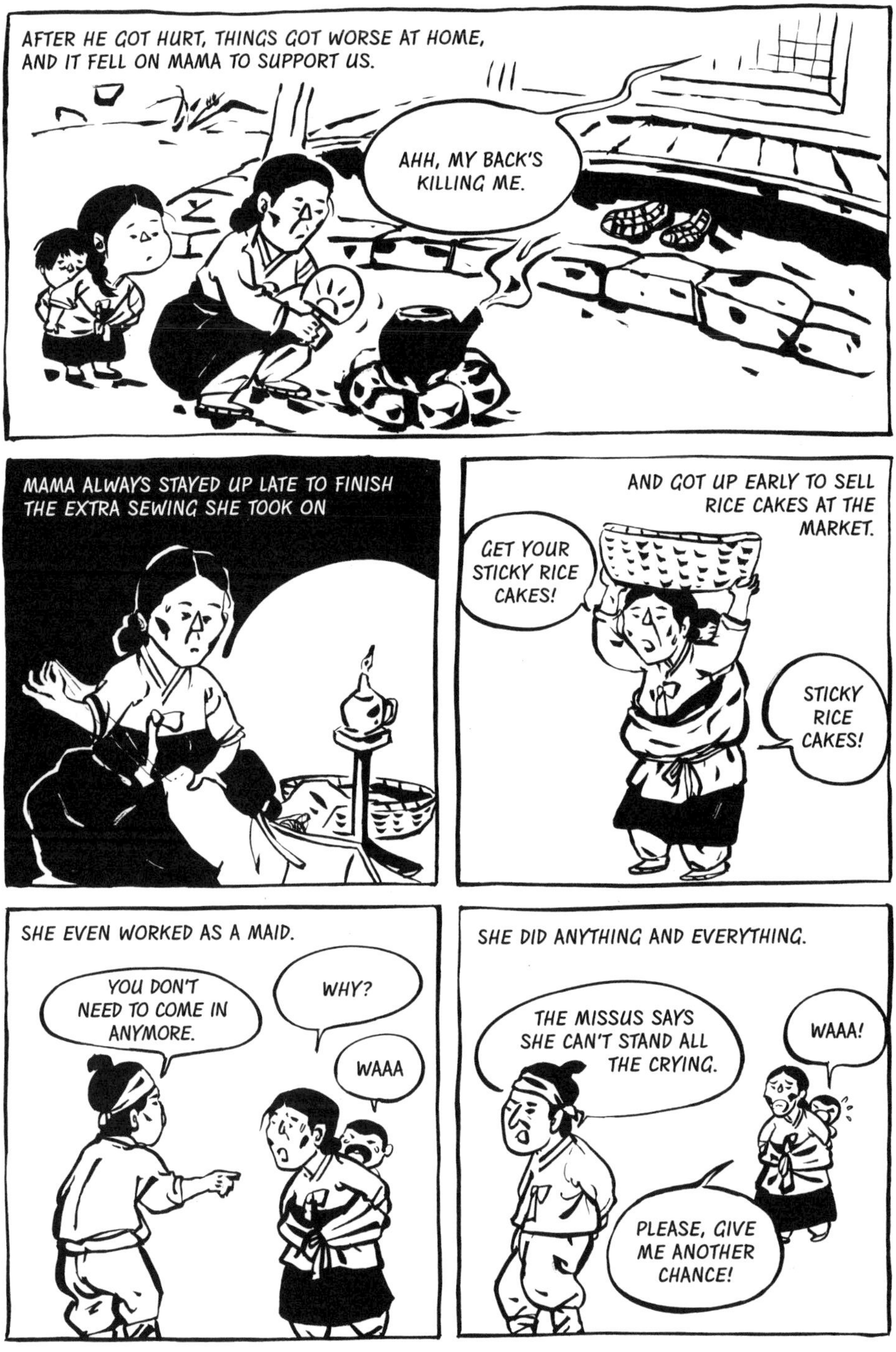

AFTER HE GOT HURT, THINGS GOT WORSE AT HOME, AND IT FELL ON MAMA TO SUPPORT US.
AHH, MY BACK'S KILLING ME.
MAMA ALWAYS STAYED UP LATE TO FINISH THE EXTRA SEWING SHE TOOK ON
AND GOT UP EARLY TO SELL RICE CAKES AT THE MARKET.
GET YOUR STICKY RICE CAKES!
STICKY RICE CAKES!
SHE EVEN WORKED AS A MAID.
YOU DON'T NEED TO COME IN ANYMORE.
WHY?
WAAA
SHE DID ANYTHING AND EVERYTHING.
THE MISSUS SAYS SHE CAN'T STAND ALL THE CRYING.
WAAA!
PLEASE, GIVE ME ANOTHER CHANCE!

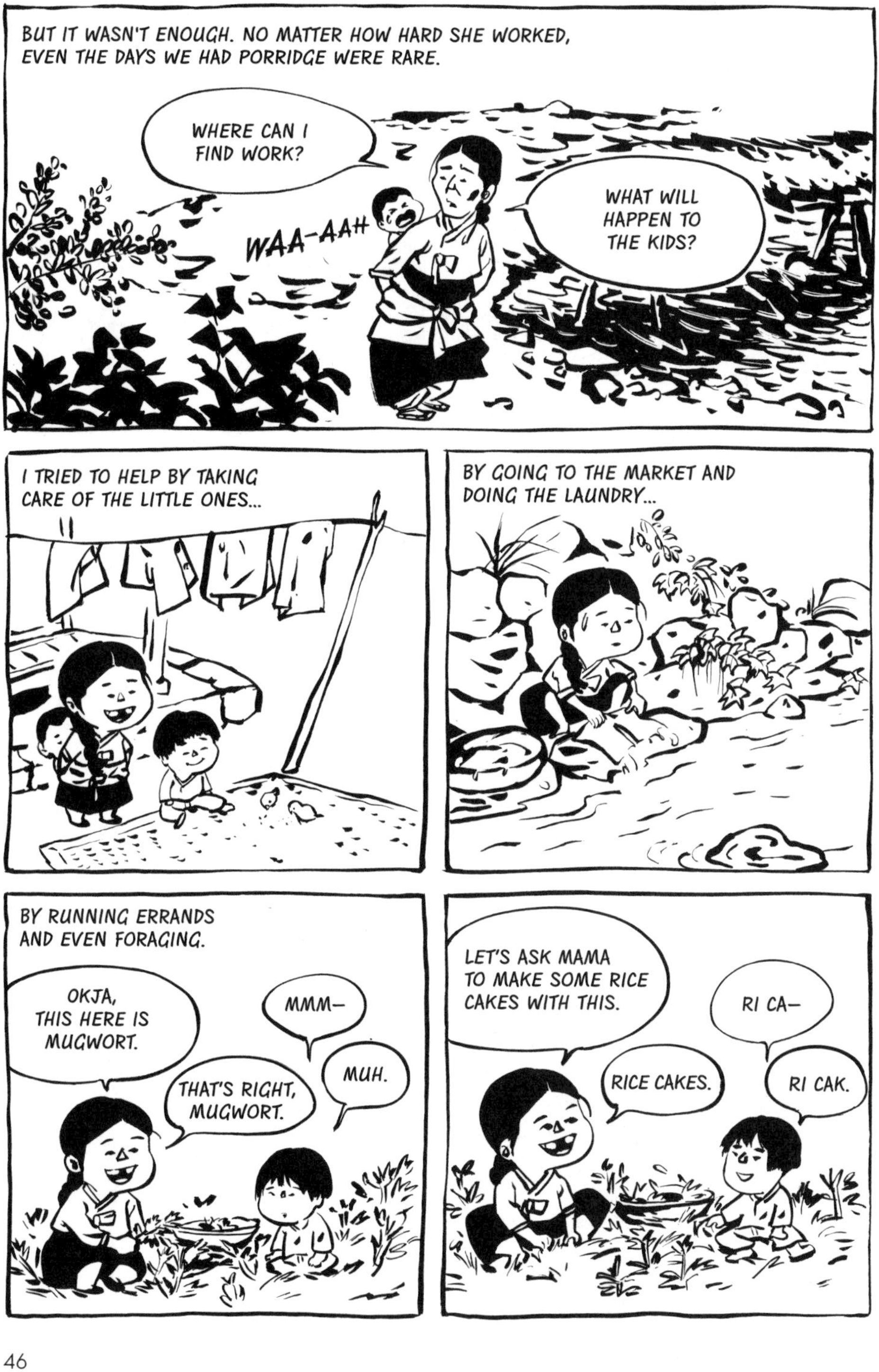
BUT IT WASN'T ENOUGH. NO MATTER HOW HARD SHE WORKED, EVEN THE DAYS WE HAD PORRIDGE WERE RARE.
WHERE CAN I FIND WORK?
WAA-AAH
WHAT WILL HAPPEN TO THE KIDS?
I TRIED TO HELP BY TAKING CARE OF THE LITTLE ONES...
BY GOING TO THE MARKET AND DOING THE LAUNDRY...
BY RUNNING ERRANDS AND EVEN FORAGING.
OKJA, THIS HERE IS MUGWORT.
MMM-
MUH.
THAT'S RIGHT, MUGWORT.
LET'S ASK MAMA TO MAKE SOME RICE CAKES WITH THIS.
RI CA-
RICE CAKES.
RI CAK.

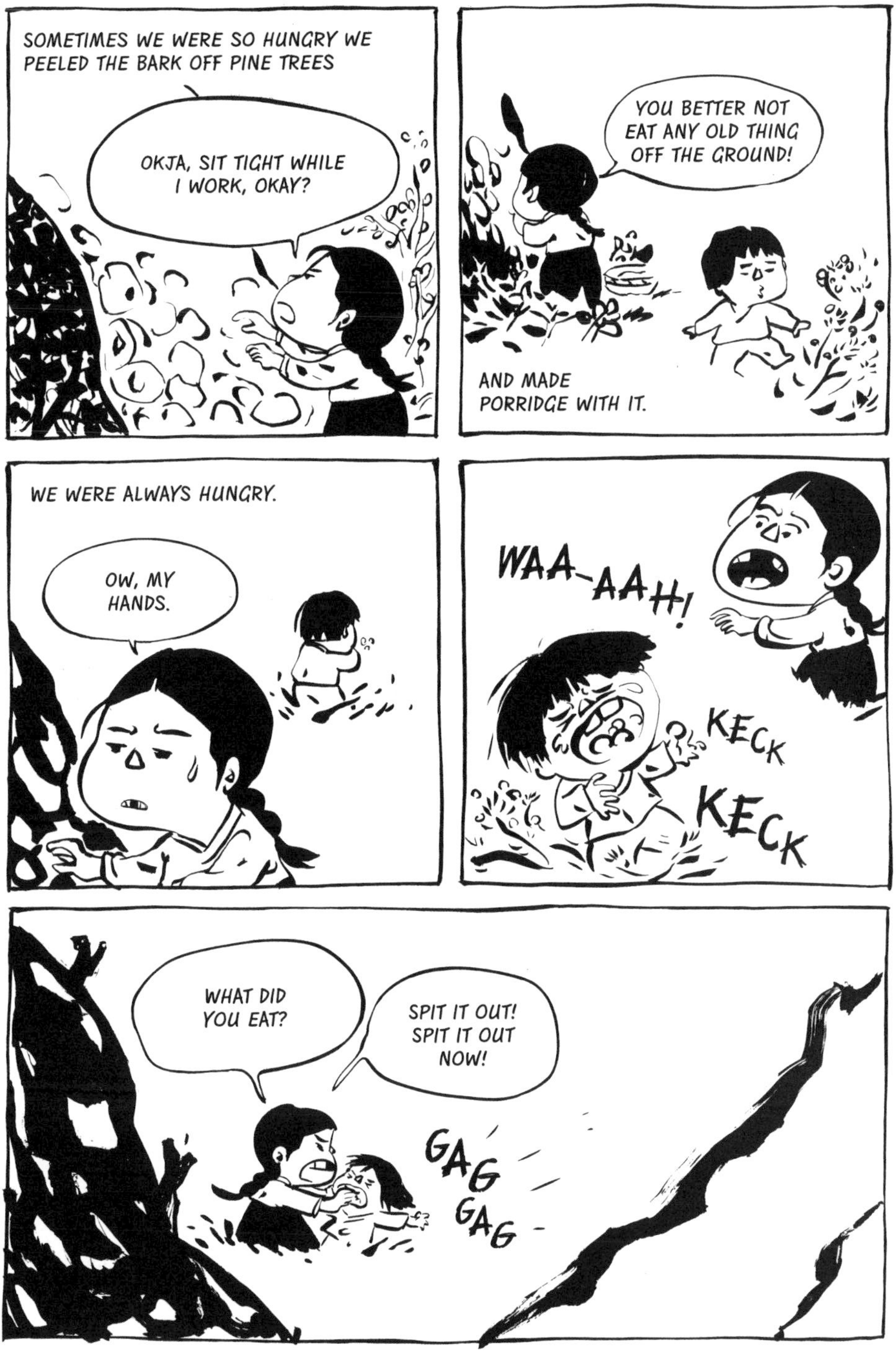

SOMETIMES WE WERE SO HUNGRY WE PEELED THE BARK OFF PINE TREES
OKJA, SIT TIGHT WHILE I WORK, OKAY?
YOU BETTER NOT EAT ANY OLD THING OFF THE GROUND!
AND MADE PORRIDGE WITH IT.
WE WERE ALWAYS HUNGRY.
OW, MY HANDS.
WAA-AAH!
KECK
KECK
WHAT DID YOU EAT?
SPIT IT OUT! SPIT IT OUT NOW!
GAG
GAG

ONE DAY WHEN OUR SITUATION COULDN'T GET ANY WORSE, MAMA SENT ME TO THE NEXT VILLAGE WHERE MY GRANDMOTHER LIVED. SHE TOLD ME TO COME BACK WITH SOME FOOD NO MATTER WHAT.

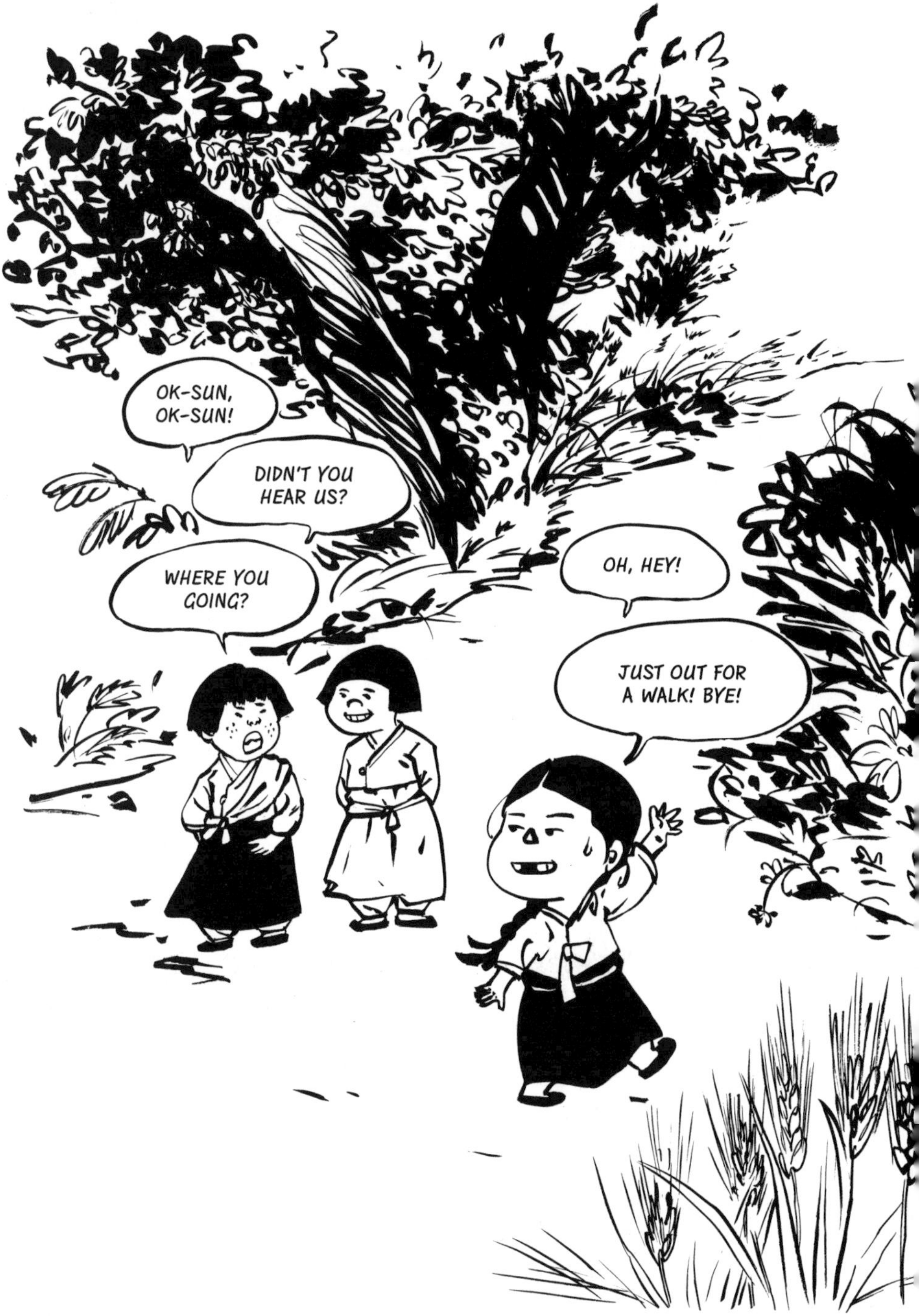
OK-SUN, OK-SUN!
DIDN'T YOU HEAR US?
WHERE YOU GOING?
OH, HEY!
JUST OUT FOR A WALK! BYE!

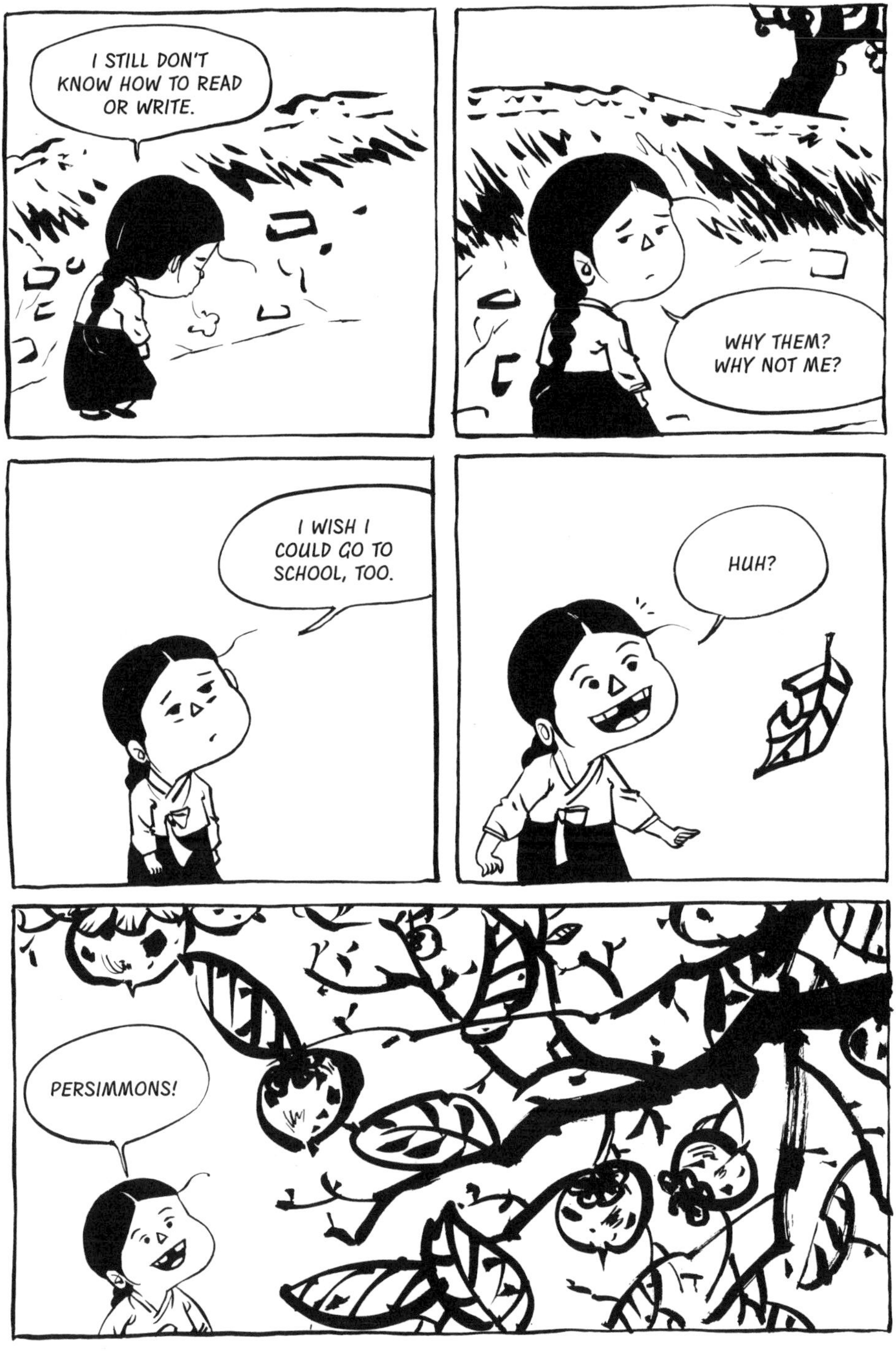
I STILL DON'T KNOW HOW TO READ OR WRITE.
WHY THEM? WHY NOT ME?
I WISH I COULD GO TO SCHOOL, TOO.
HUH?
PERSIMMONS!

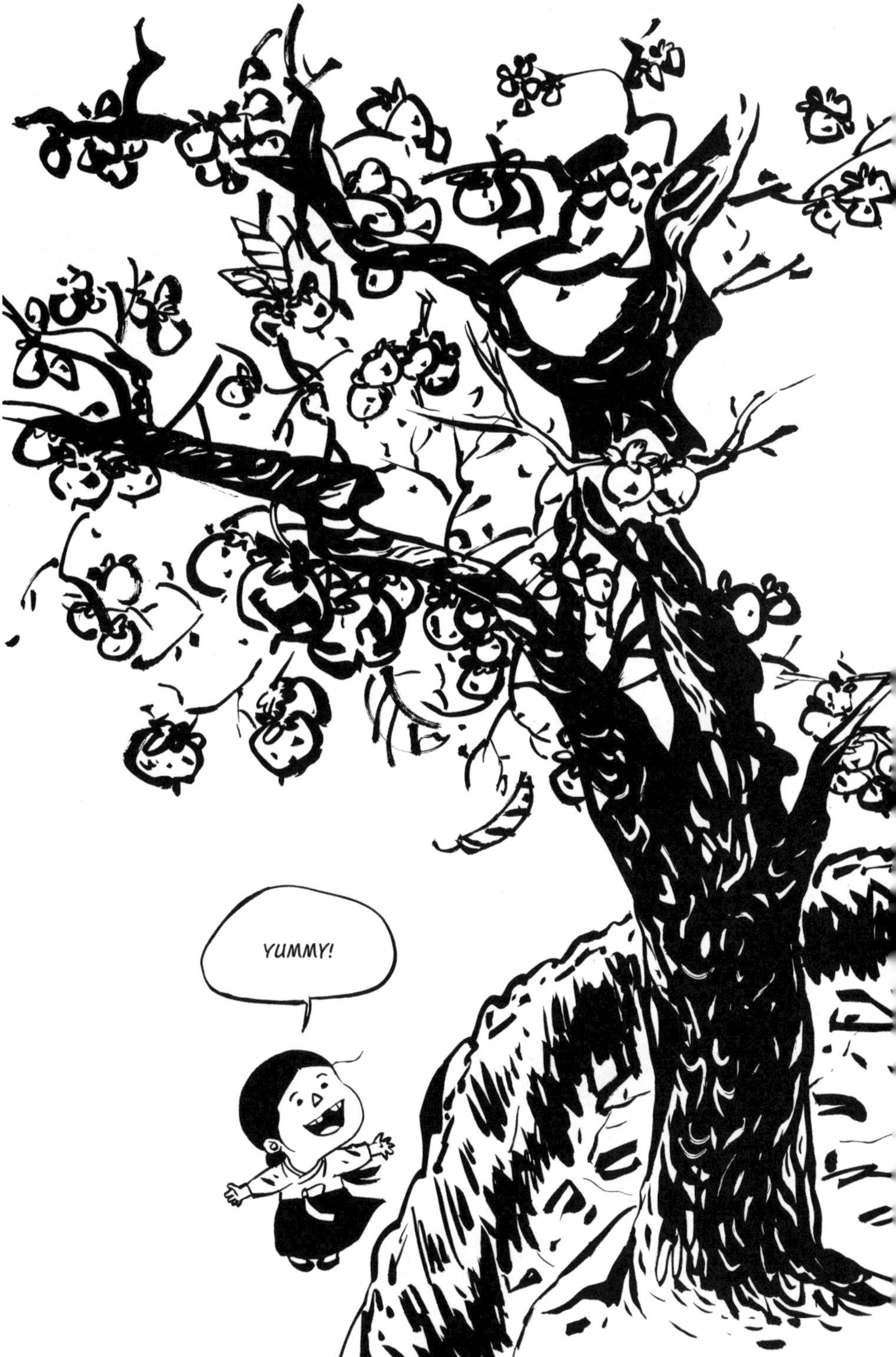
YUMMY!

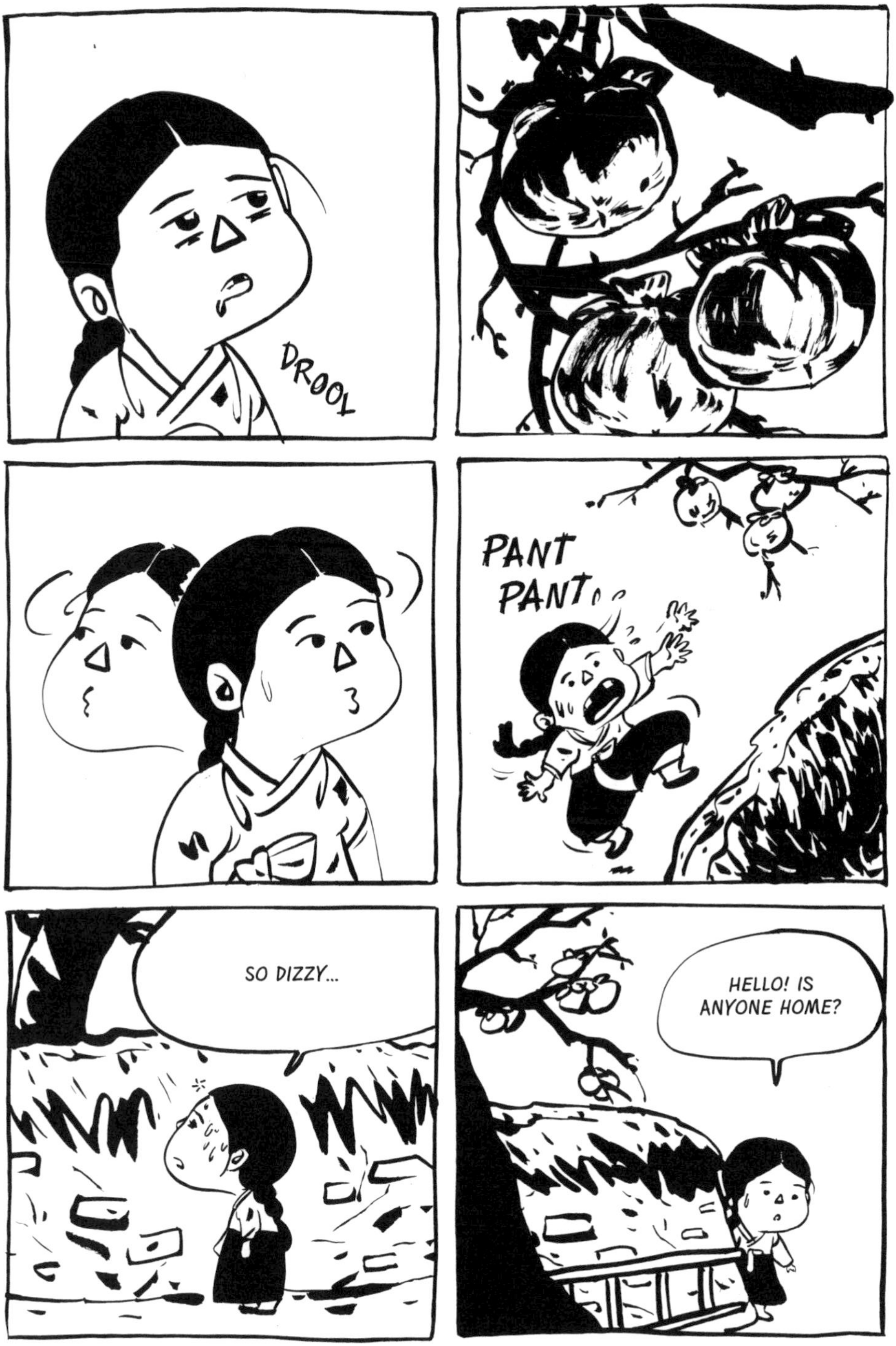
DROOL
PANT
PANT
SO DIZZY...
HELLO! IS
ANYONE HOME?

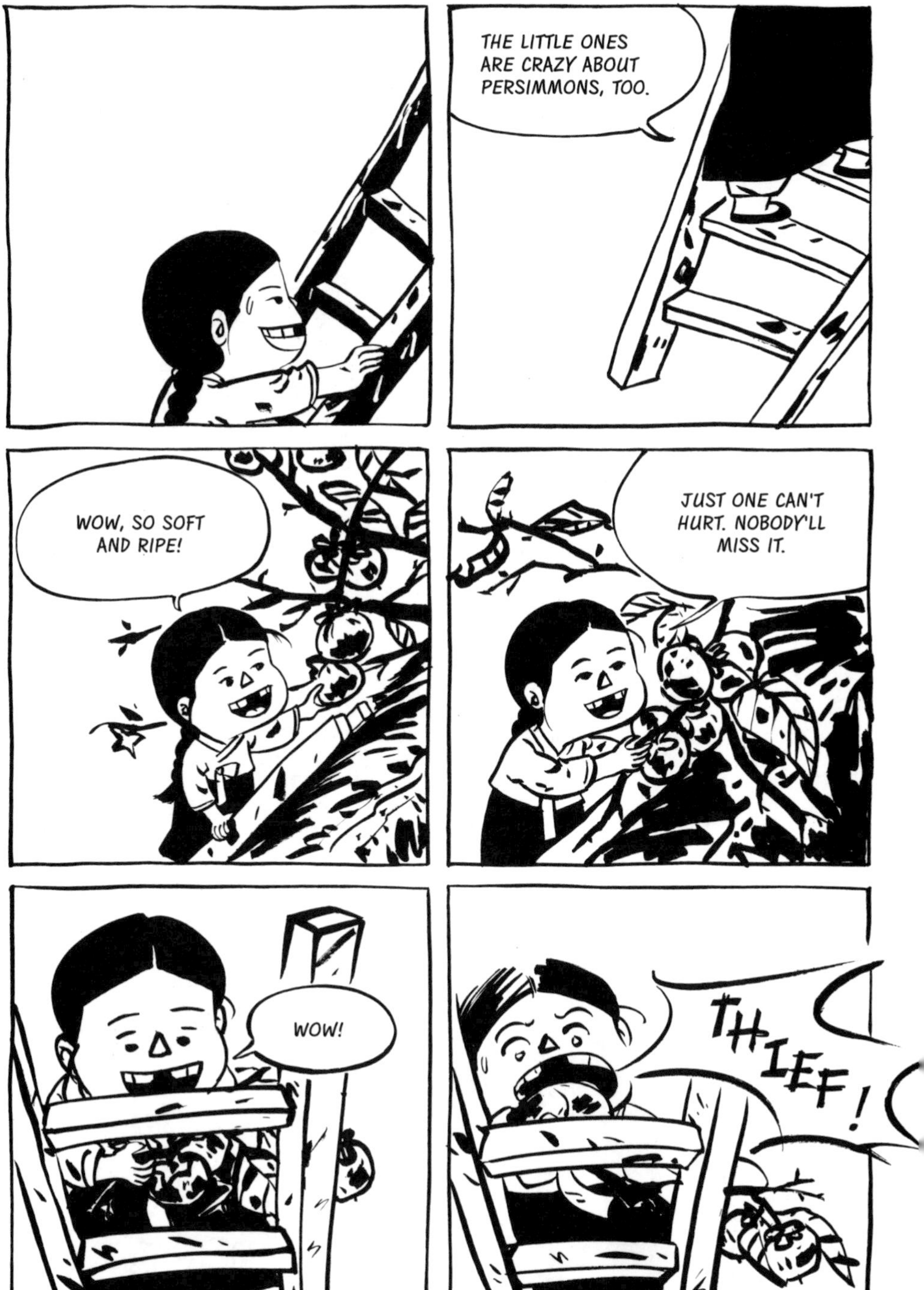
THE LITTLE ONES ARE CRAZY ABOUT PERSIMMONS, TOO.
WOW, SO SOFT AND RIPE!
JUST ONE CAN'T HURT. NOBODY'LL MISS IT.
WOW!
THIEF!

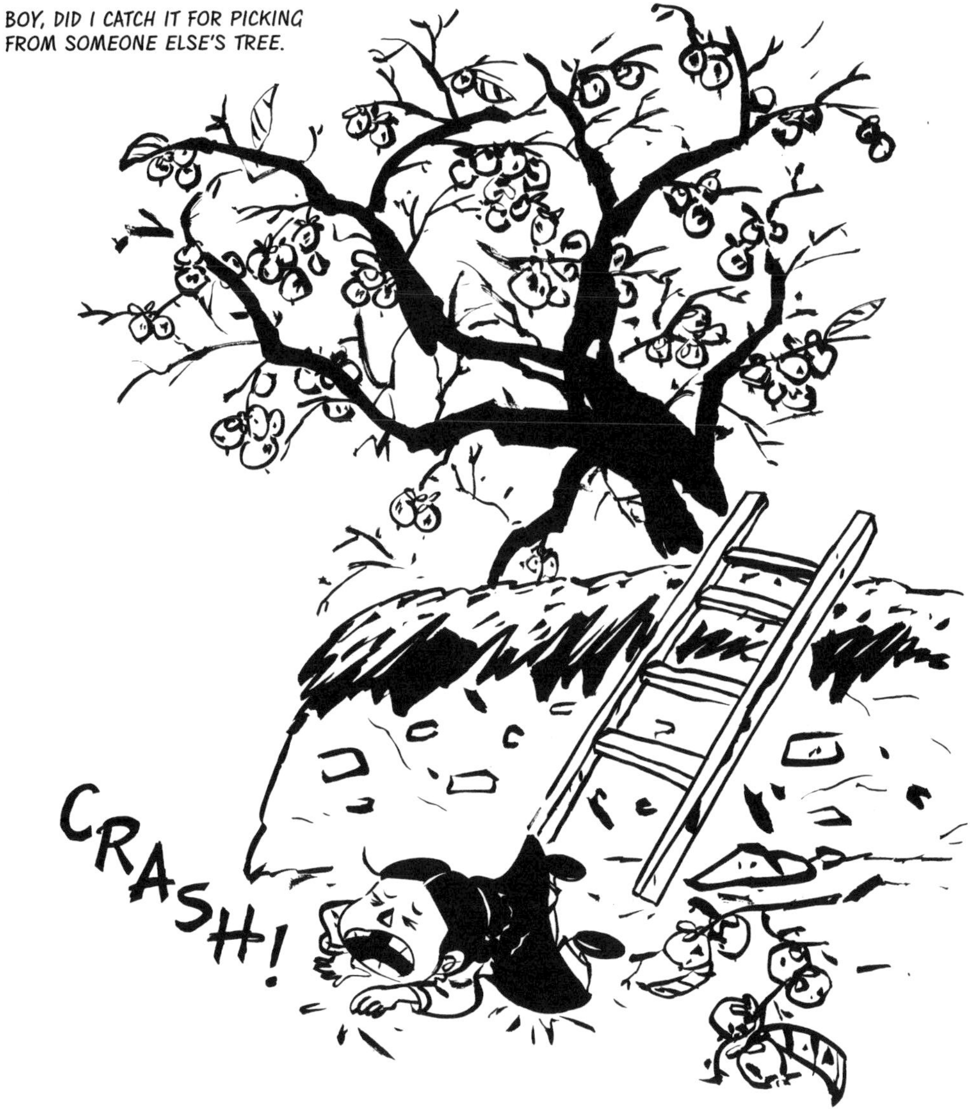
BOY, DID I CATCH IT FOR PICKING FROM SOMEONE ELSE'S TREE.
CRASH!

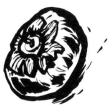

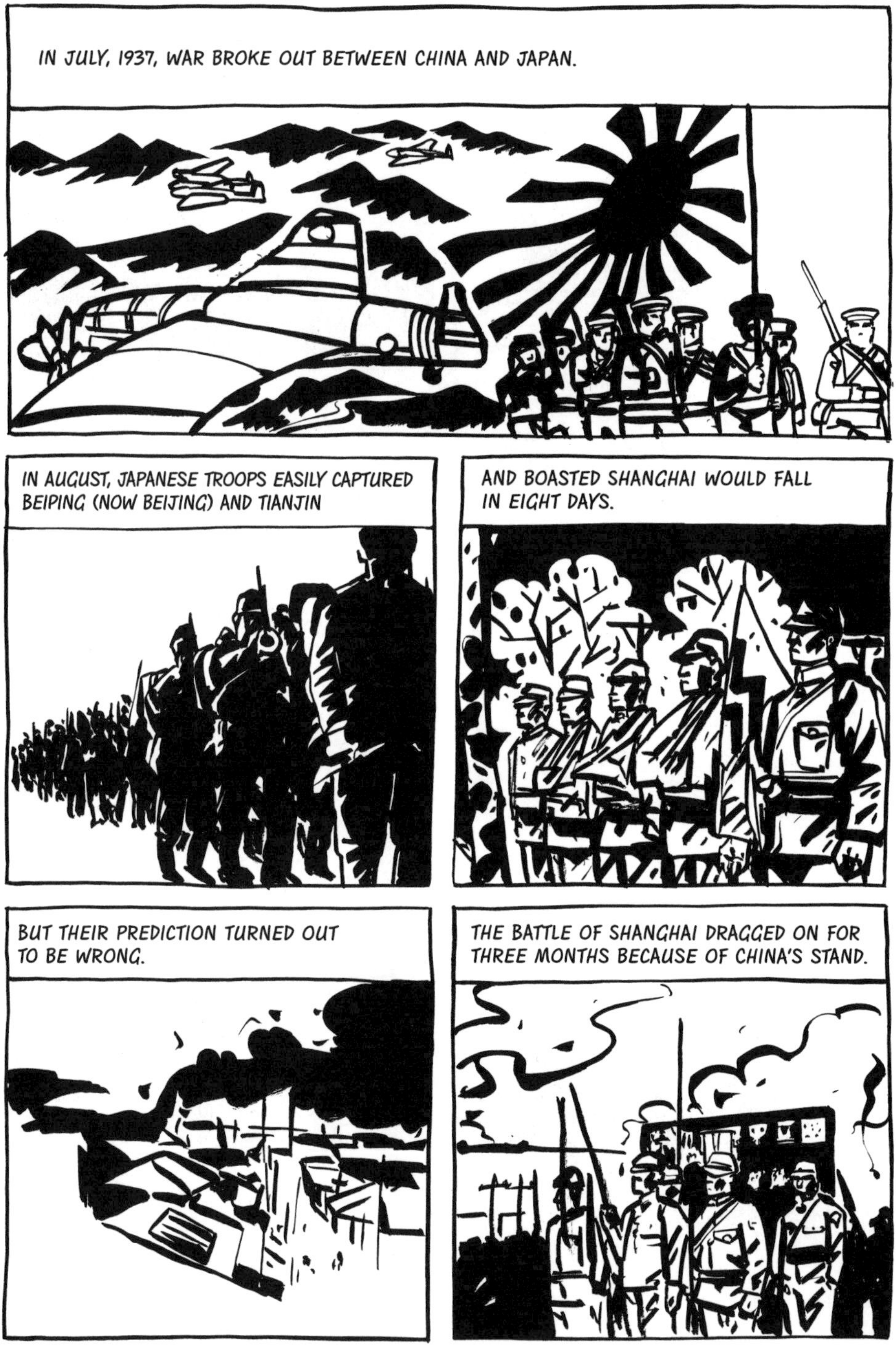
IN JULY, 1937, WAR BROKE OUT BETWEEN CHINA AND JAPAN.
IN AUGUST, JAPANESE TROOPS EASILY CAPTURED BEIPING (NOW BEIJING) AND TIANJIN
AND BOASTED SHANGHAI WOULD FALL IN EIGHT DAYS.
BUT THEIR PREDICTION TURNED OUT TO BE WRONG.
THE BATTLE OF SHANGHAI DRAGGED ON FOR THREE MONTHS BECAUSE OF CHINA'S STAND.

IN NOVEMBER, AFTER A HARD-WON VICTORY IN SHANGHAI

THE JAPANESE TROOPS

MARCHED 300 KILOMETERS WESTWARD AT A BREAKNECK SPEED

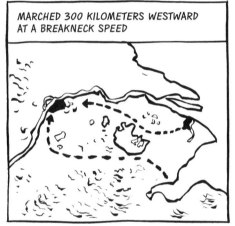

TO THE "SOUTHERN CAPITAL": NANJING.

ALONG THE WAY

THEY SET FIRE TO ALL THE VILLAGES THEY PASSED

AND RAPED AND MURDERED COUNTLESS CIVILIANS.

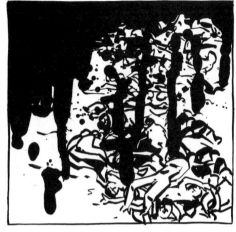

ON DECEMBER 13, 1937

THE SAME YEAR GRANNY LEE OK-SUN WAS PUNISHED FOR STEALING A PERSIMMON...

THE JAPANESE ARMY INVADED NANJING

AND STORMED THE CITY'S FORTIFIED WALLS.

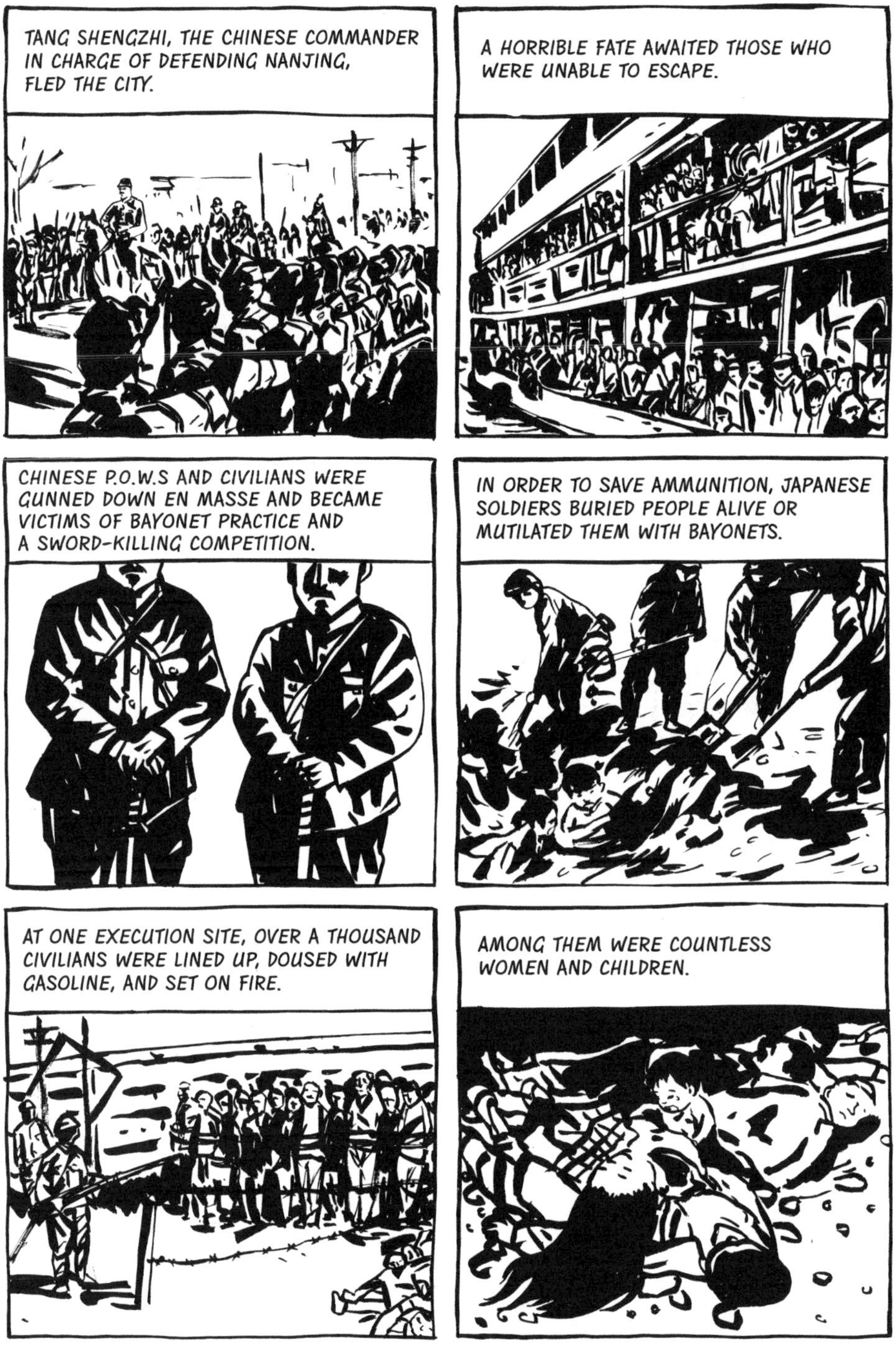
TANG SHENGZHI, THE CHINESE COMMANDER IN CHARGE OF DEFENDING NANJING, FLED THE CITY.
A HORRIBLE FATE AWAITED THOSE WHO WERE UNABLE TO ESCAPE.
CHINESE P.O.W.S AND CIVILIANS WERE GUNNED DOWN EN MASSE AND BECAME VICTIMS OF BAYONET PRACTICE AND A SWORD-KILLING COMPETITION.
IN ORDER TO SAVE AMMUNITION, JAPANESE SOLDIERS BURIED PEOPLE ALIVE OR MUTILATED THEM WITH BAYONETS.
AT ONE EXECUTION SITE, OVER A THOUSAND CIVILIANS WERE LINED UP, DOUSED WITH GASOLINE, AND SET ON FIRE.
AMONG THEM WERE COUNTLESS WOMEN AND CHILDREN.

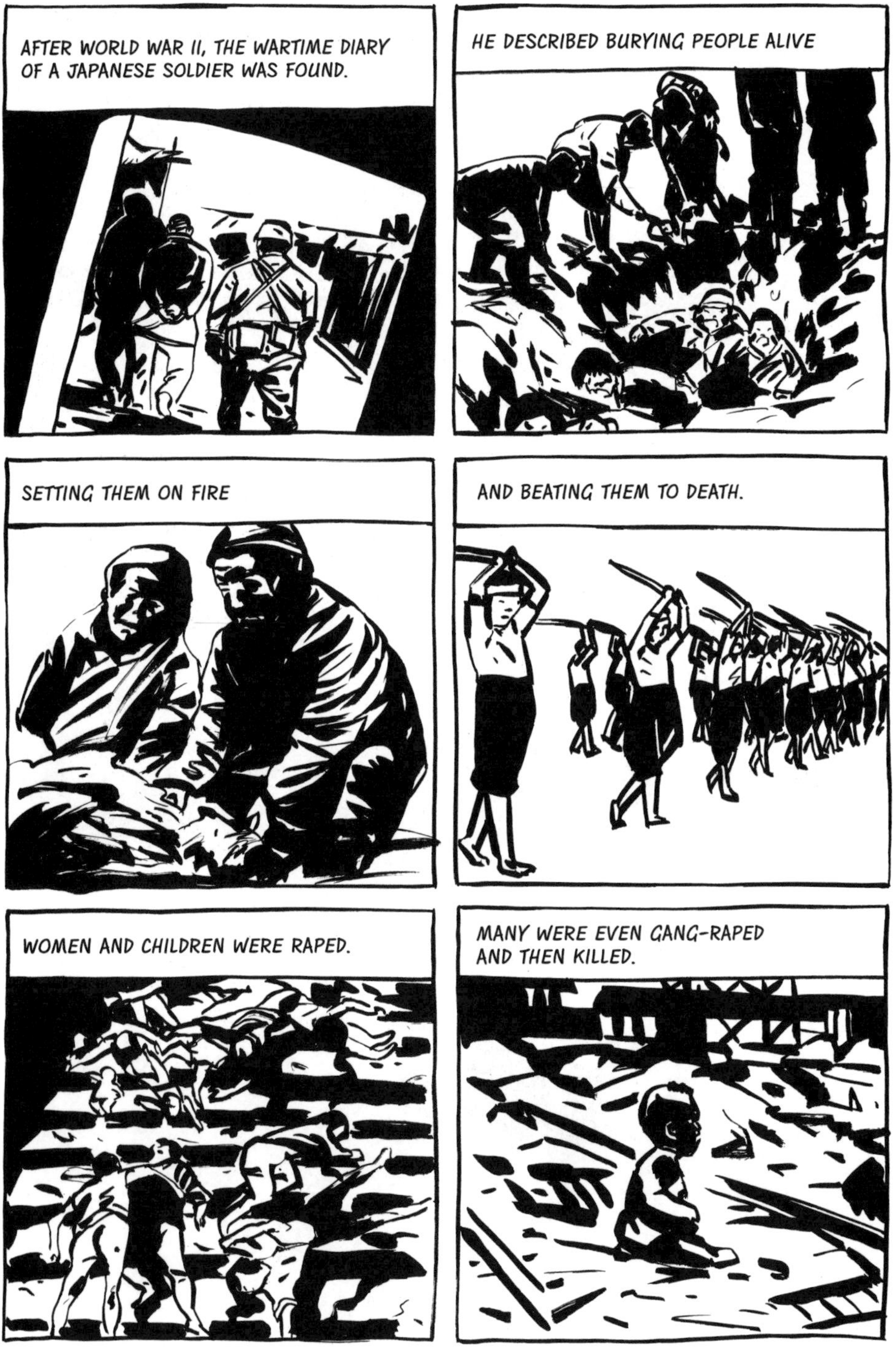
AFTER WORLD WAR II, THE WARTIME DIARY OF A JAPANESE SOLDIER WAS FOUND.
HE DESCRIBED BURYING PEOPLE ALIVE
SETTING THEM ON FIRE
AND BEATING THEM TO DEATH.
WOMEN AND CHILDREN WERE RAPED.
MANY WERE EVEN GANG-RAPED AND THEN KILLED.

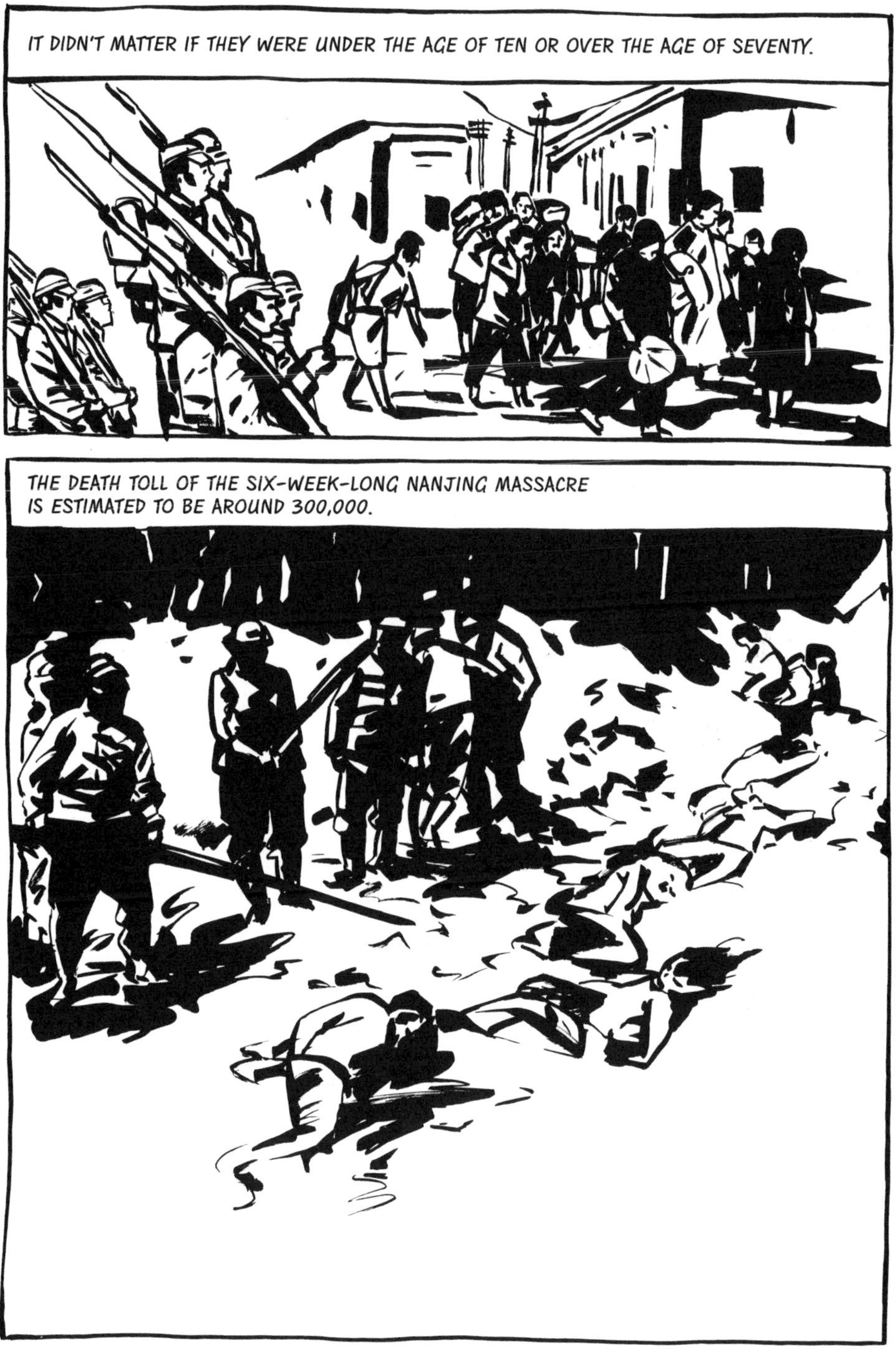
IT DIDN'T MATTER IF THEY WERE UNDER THE AGE OF TEN OR OVER THE AGE OF SEVENTY.
THE DEATH TOLL OF THE SIX-WEEK-LONG NANJING MASSACRE IS ESTIMATED TO BE AROUND 300,000.

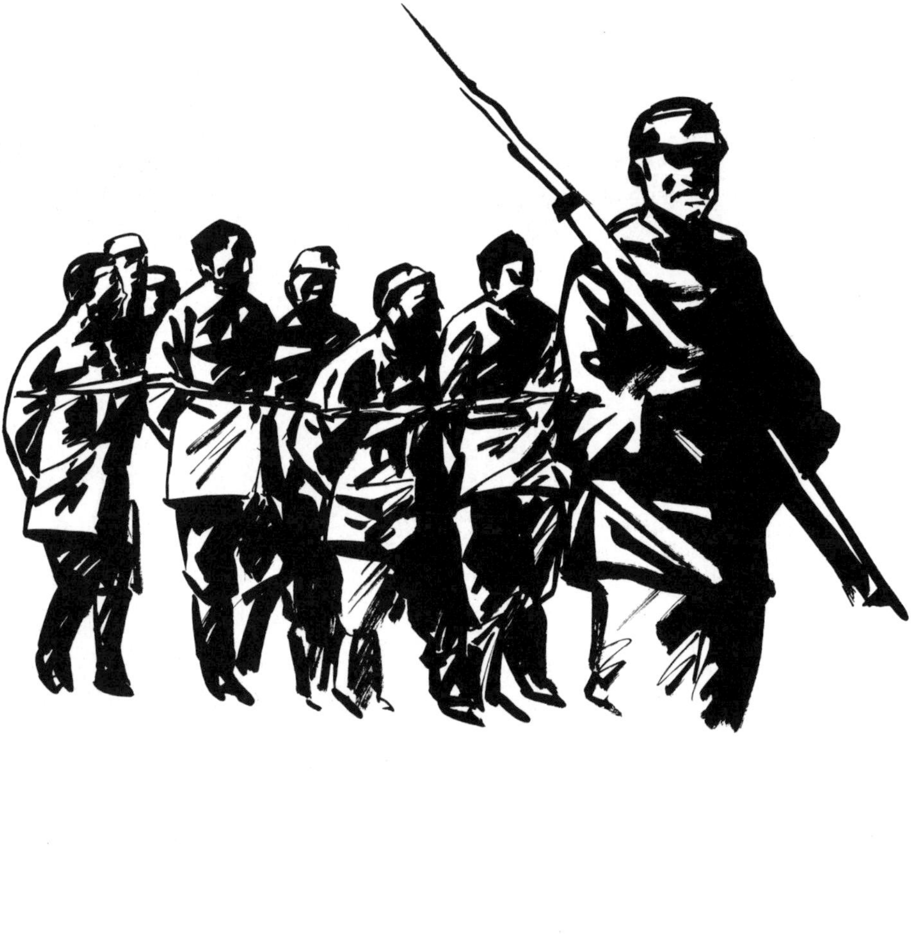

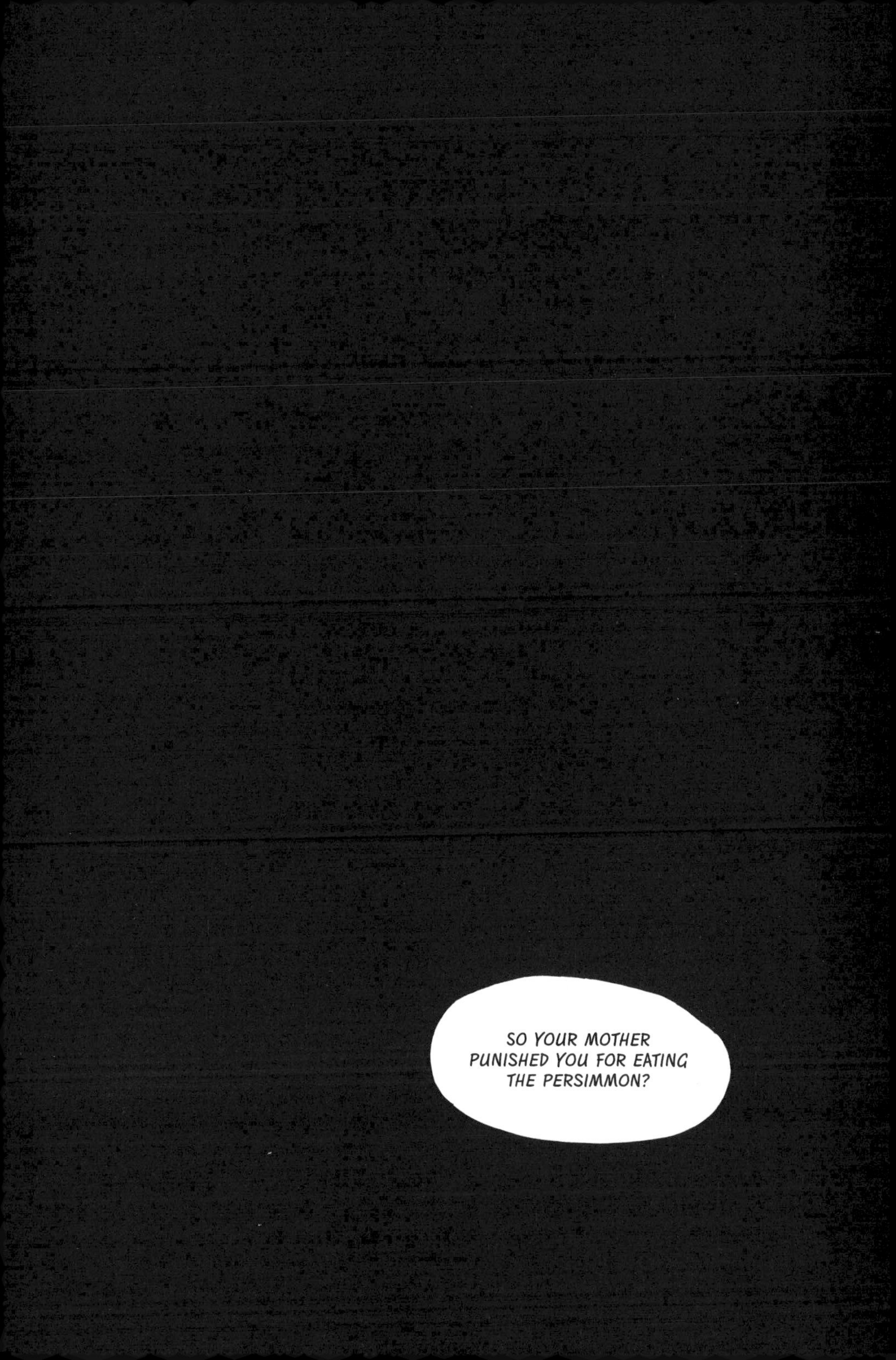
SO YOUR MOTHER PUNISHED YOU FOR EATING THE PERSIMMON?

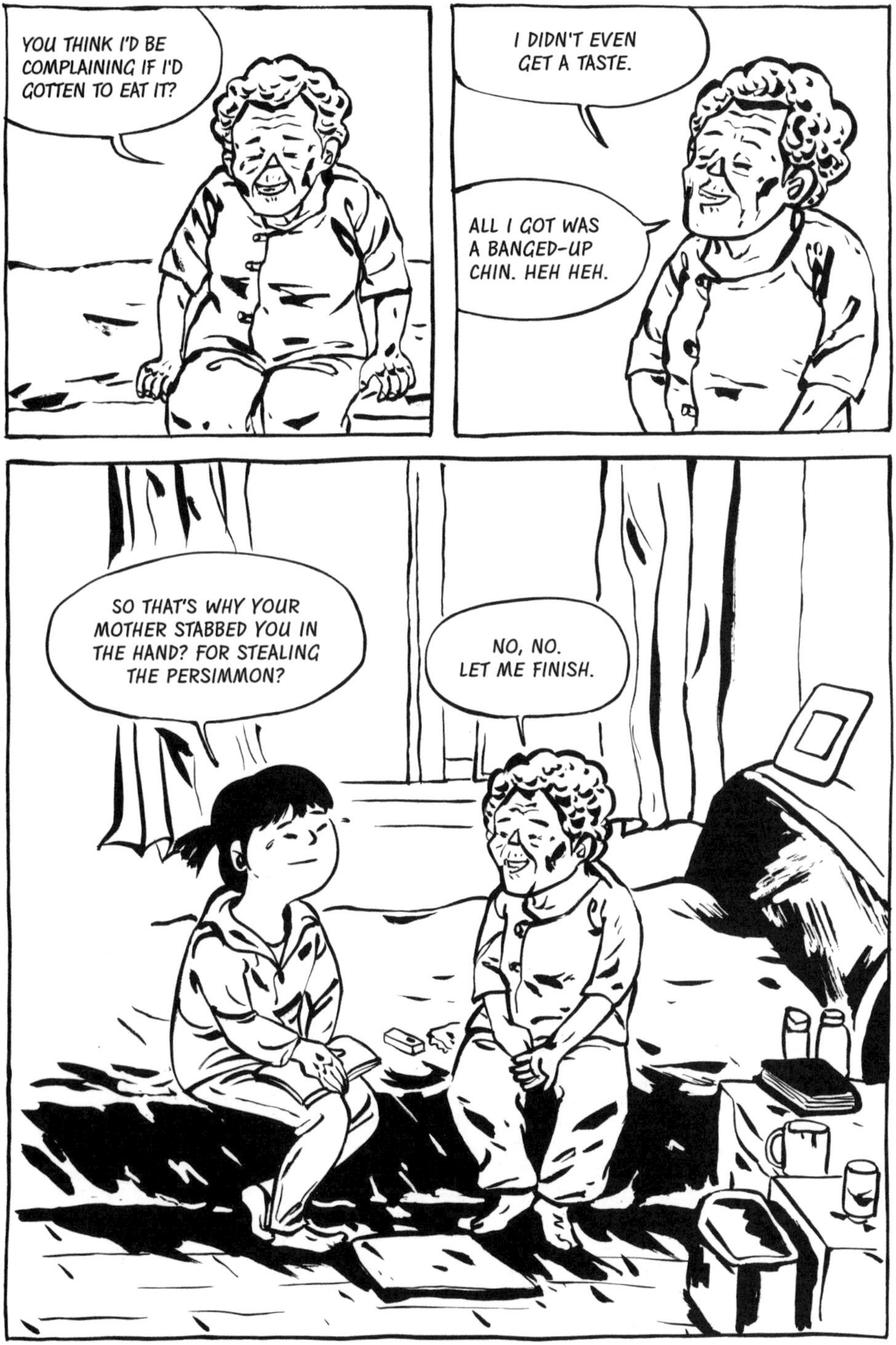
YOU THINK I'D BE COMPLAINING IF I'D GOTTEN TO EAT IT?
I DIDN'T EVEN GET A TASTE.
ALL I GOT WAS A BANGED-UP CHIN. HEH HEH.
SO THAT'S WHY YOUR MOTHER STABBED YOU IN THE HAND? FOR STEALING THE PERSIMMON?
NO, NO. LET ME FINISH.

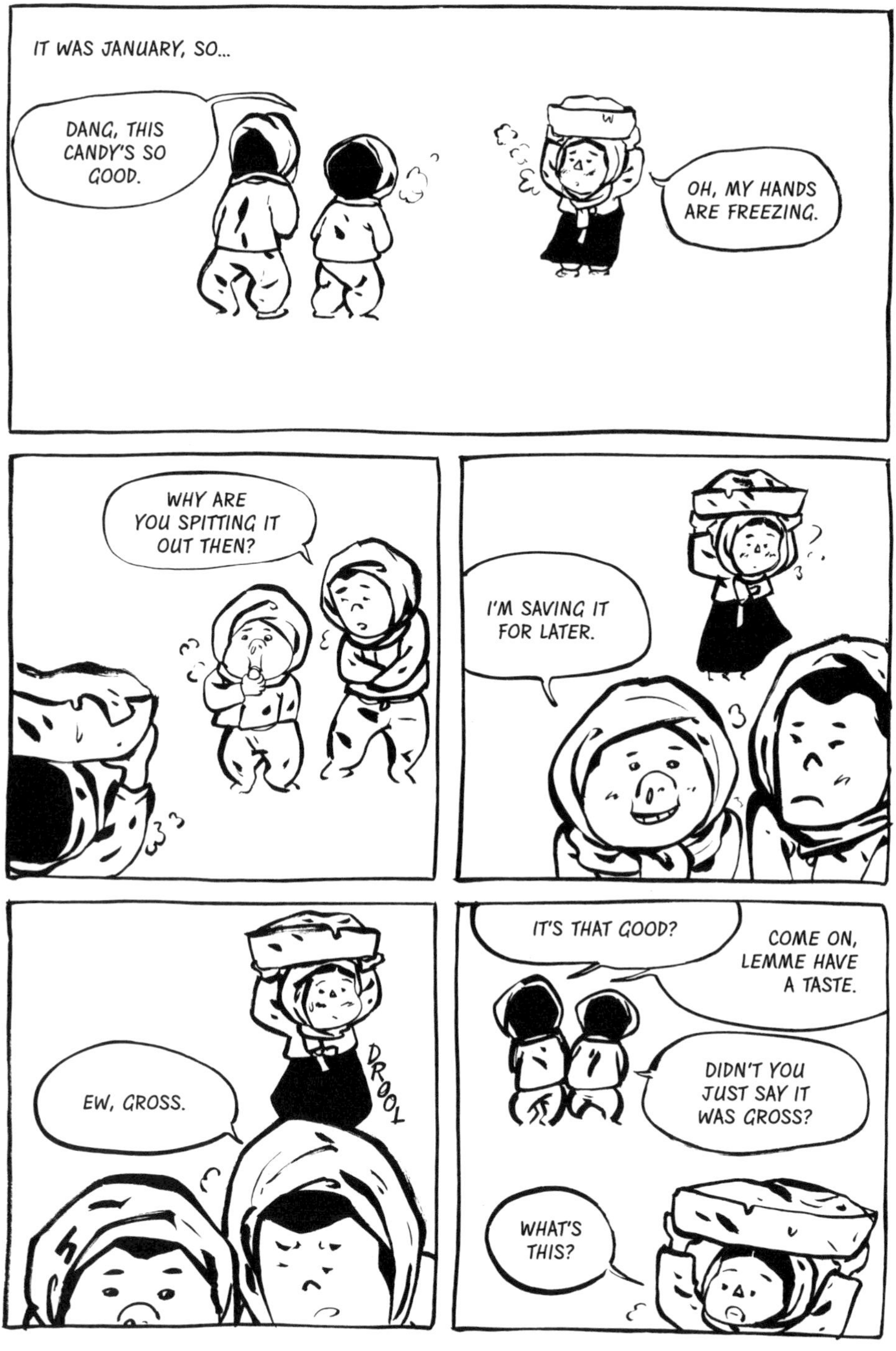

IT WAS JANUARY, SO...
DANG, THIS CANDY'S SO GOOD.
OH, MY HANDS ARE FREEZING.
WHY ARE YOU SPITTING IT OUT THEN?
I'M SAVING IT FOR LATER.
EW, GROSS.
DROOL
IT'S THAT GOOD?
COME ON, LEMME HAVE A TASTE.
DIDN'T YOU JUST SAY IT WAS GROSS?
WHAT'S THIS?

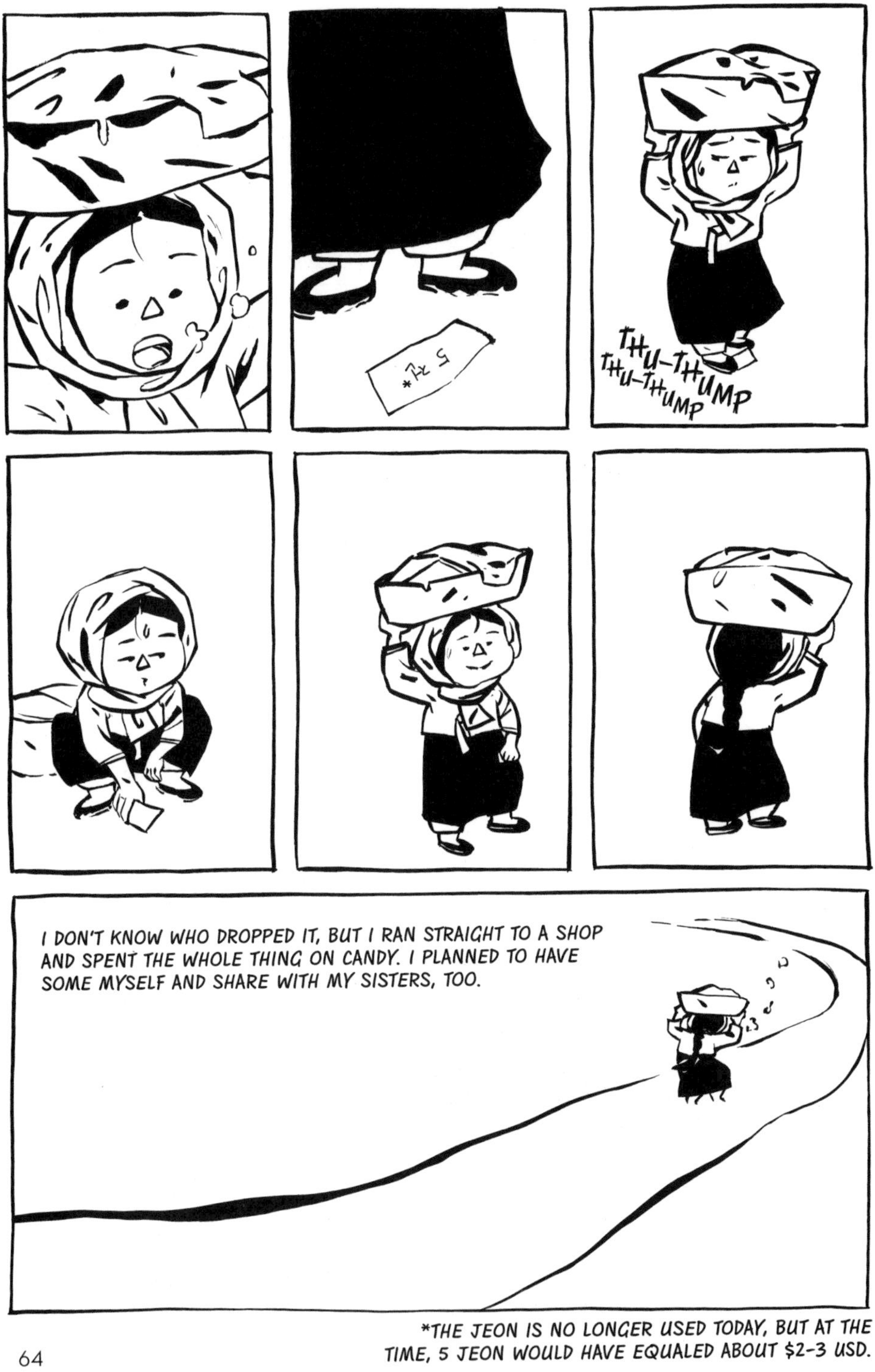
THU-THUMP
THU-THUMP
I DON'T KNOW WHO DROPPED IT, BUT I RAN STRAIGHT TO A SHOP AND SPENT THE WHOLE THING ON CANDY. I PLANNED TO HAVE SOME MYSELF AND SHARE WITH MY SISTERS, TOO.

*THE JEON IS NO LONGER USED TODAY, BUT AT THE TIME, 5 JEON WOULD HAVE EQUALED ABOUT $2–3 USD.

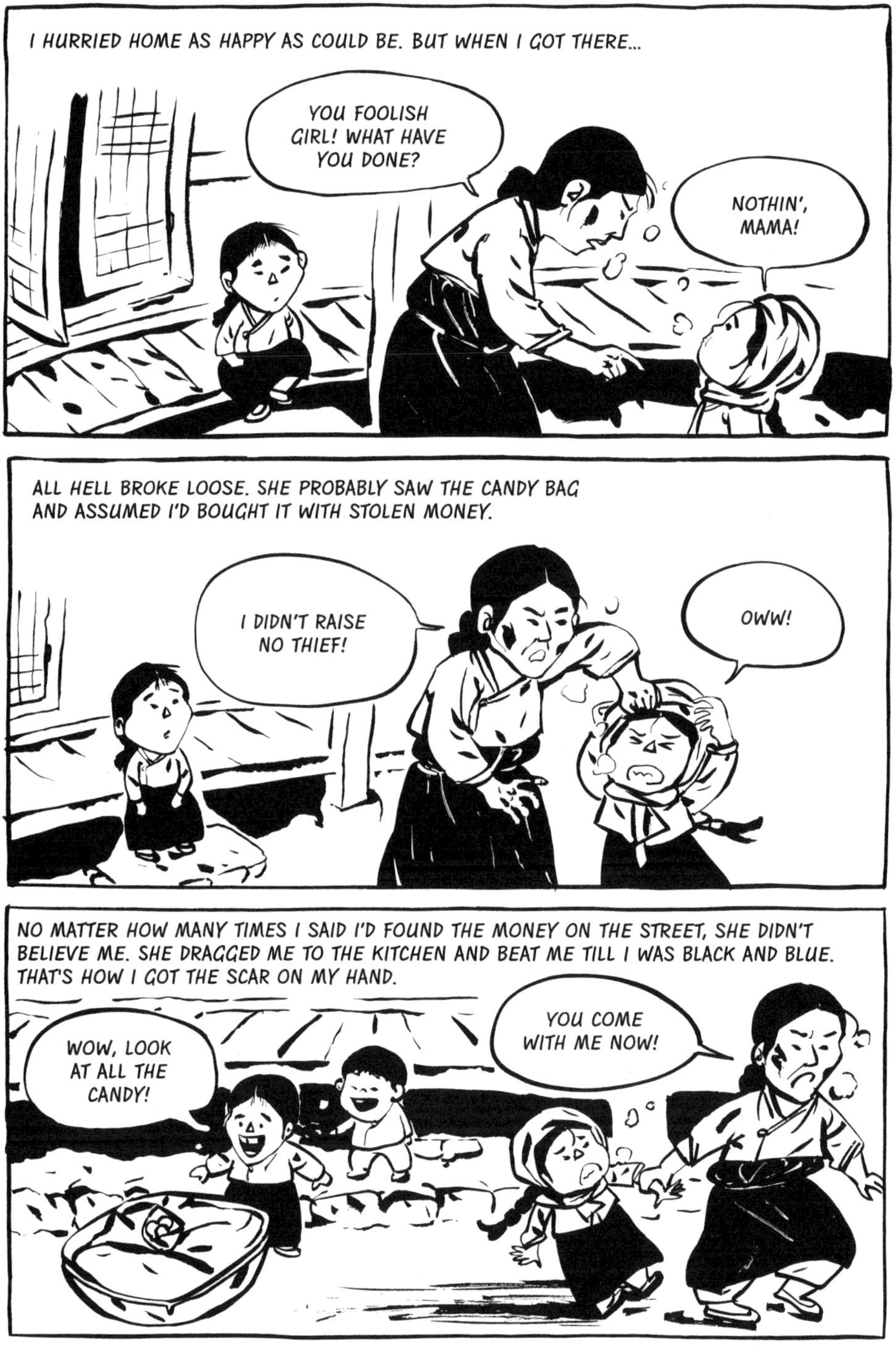
I HURRIED HOME AS HAPPY AS COULD BE. BUT WHEN I GOT THERE...
YOU FOOLISH GIRL! WHAT HAVE YOU DONE?
NOTHIN', MAMA!
ALL HELL BROKE LOOSE. SHE PROBABLY SAW THE CANDY BAG AND ASSUMED I'D BOUGHT IT WITH STOLEN MONEY.
I DIDN'T RAISE NO THIEF!
OWW!
NO MATTER HOW MANY TIMES I SAID I'D FOUND THE MONEY ON THE STREET, SHE DIDN'T BELIEVE ME. SHE DRAGGED ME TO THE KITCHEN AND BEAT ME TILL I WAS BLACK AND BLUE. THAT'S HOW I GOT THE SCAR ON MY HAND.
WOW, LOOK AT ALL THE CANDY!
YOU COME WITH ME NOW!

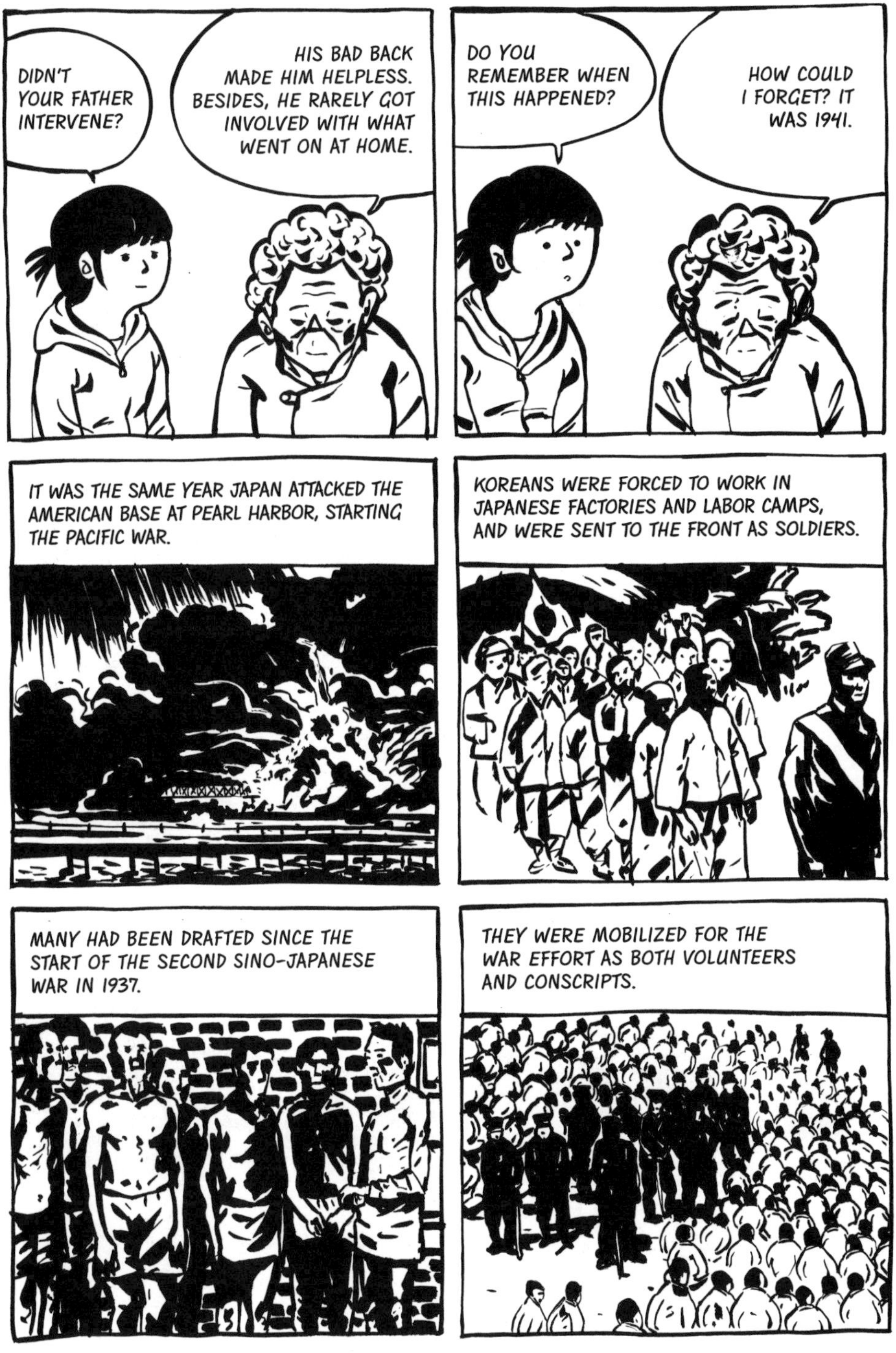
DIDN'T YOUR FATHER INTERVENE?
HIS BAD BACK MADE HIM HELPLESS. BESIDES, HE RARELY GOT INVOLVED WITH WHAT WENT ON AT HOME.
DO YOU REMEMBER WHEN THIS HAPPENED?
HOW COULD I FORGET? IT WAS 1941.
IT WAS THE SAME YEAR JAPAN ATTACKED THE AMERICAN BASE AT PEARL HARBOR, STARTING THE PACIFIC WAR.
KOREANS WERE FORCED TO WORK IN JAPANESE FACTORIES AND LABOR CAMPS, AND WERE SENT TO THE FRONT AS SOLDIERS.
MANY HAD BEEN DRAFTED SINCE THE START OF THE SECOND SINO-JAPANESE WAR IN 1937.
THEY WERE MOBILIZED FOR THE WAR EFFORT AS BOTH VOLUNTEERS AND CONSCRIPTS.

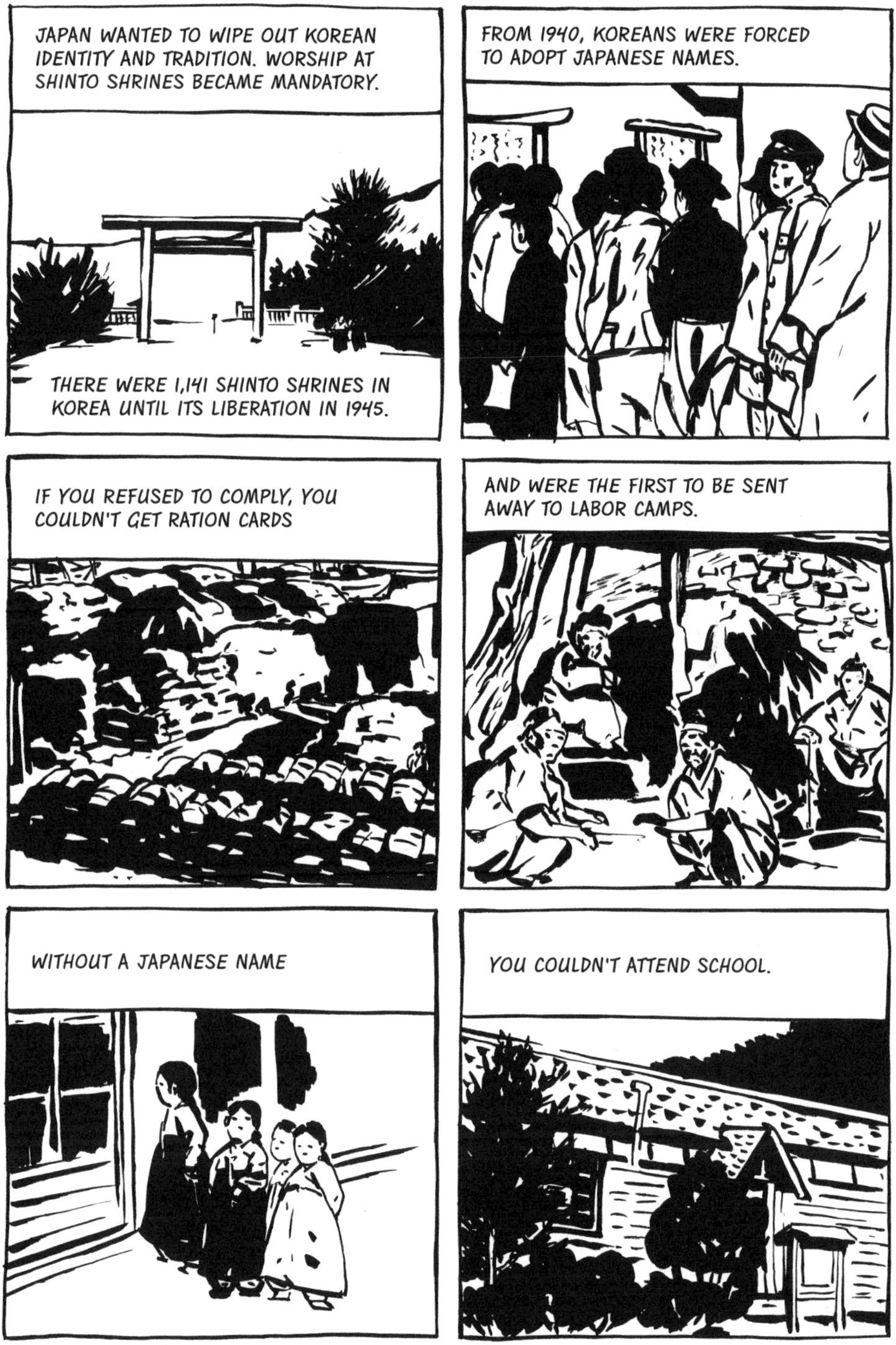
JAPAN WANTED TO WIPE OUT KOREAN IDENTITY AND TRADITION. WORSHIP AT SHINTO SHRINES BECAME MANDATORY.
THERE WERE 1,141 SHINTO SHRINES IN KOREA UNTIL ITS LIBERATION IN 1945.
FROM 1940, KOREANS WERE FORCED TO ADOPT JAPANESE NAMES.
IF YOU REFUSED TO COMPLY, YOU COULDN'T GET RATION CARDS
AND WERE THE FIRST TO BE SENT AWAY TO LABOR CAMPS.
WITHOUT A JAPANESE NAME
YOU COULDN'T ATTEND SCHOOL.

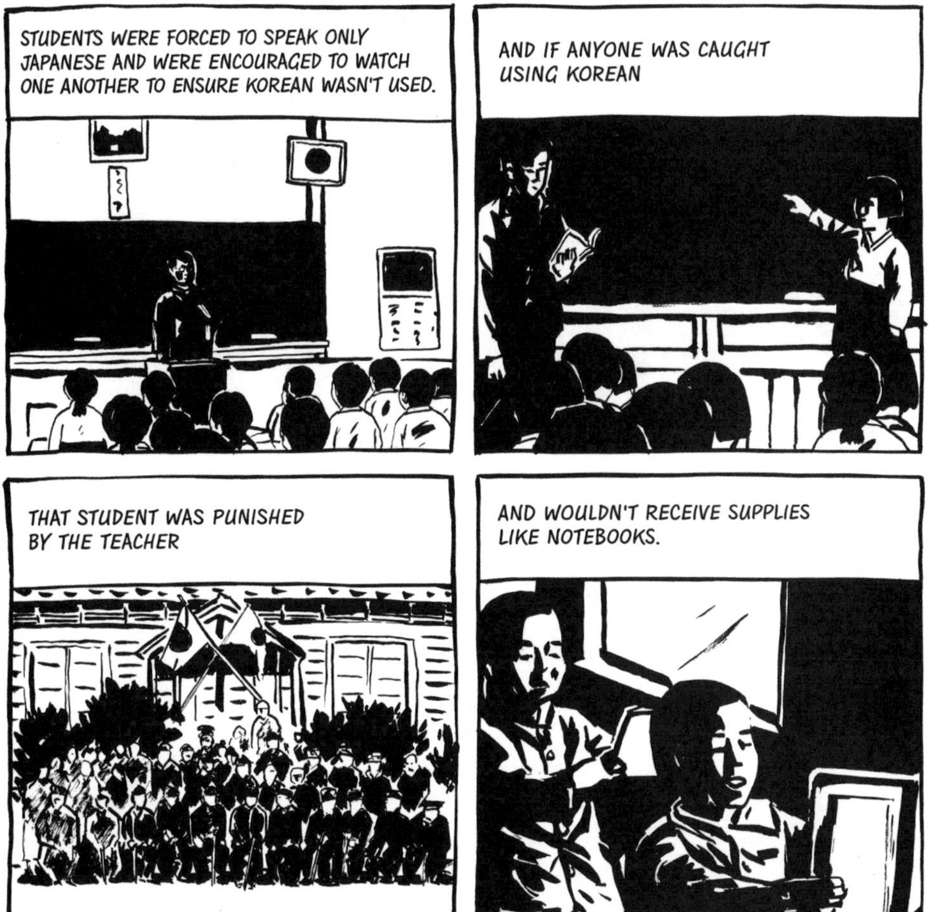
STUDENTS WERE FORCED TO SPEAK ONLY JAPANESE AND WERE ENCOURAGED TO WATCH ONE ANOTHER TO ENSURE KOREAN WASN'T USED.
AND IF ANYONE WAS CAUGHT USING KOREAN
THAT STUDENT WAS PUNISHED BY THE TEACHER
AND WOULDN'T RECEIVE SUPPLIES LIKE NOTEBOOKS.
CHALKBOARDS WERE FILLED WITH QUESTIONS LIKE "WHY IS JAPAN AT WAR?" AND "WHEN YOU'RE PERFORMING THE EMPEROR BOW,* WHAT POSTURE SHOULD YOUR HEART ASSUME?"
THE KOREAN LEAGUE FOR NATIONAL MOBILIZATION WAS ESTABLISHED AND JAPANESE PROPAGANDA COVERED EVERY STREET.

*PEOPLE WERE INSTRUCTED TO BOW IN THE DIRECTION OF JAPAN'S IMPERIAL PALACE WHERE THE EMPEROR RESIDED.

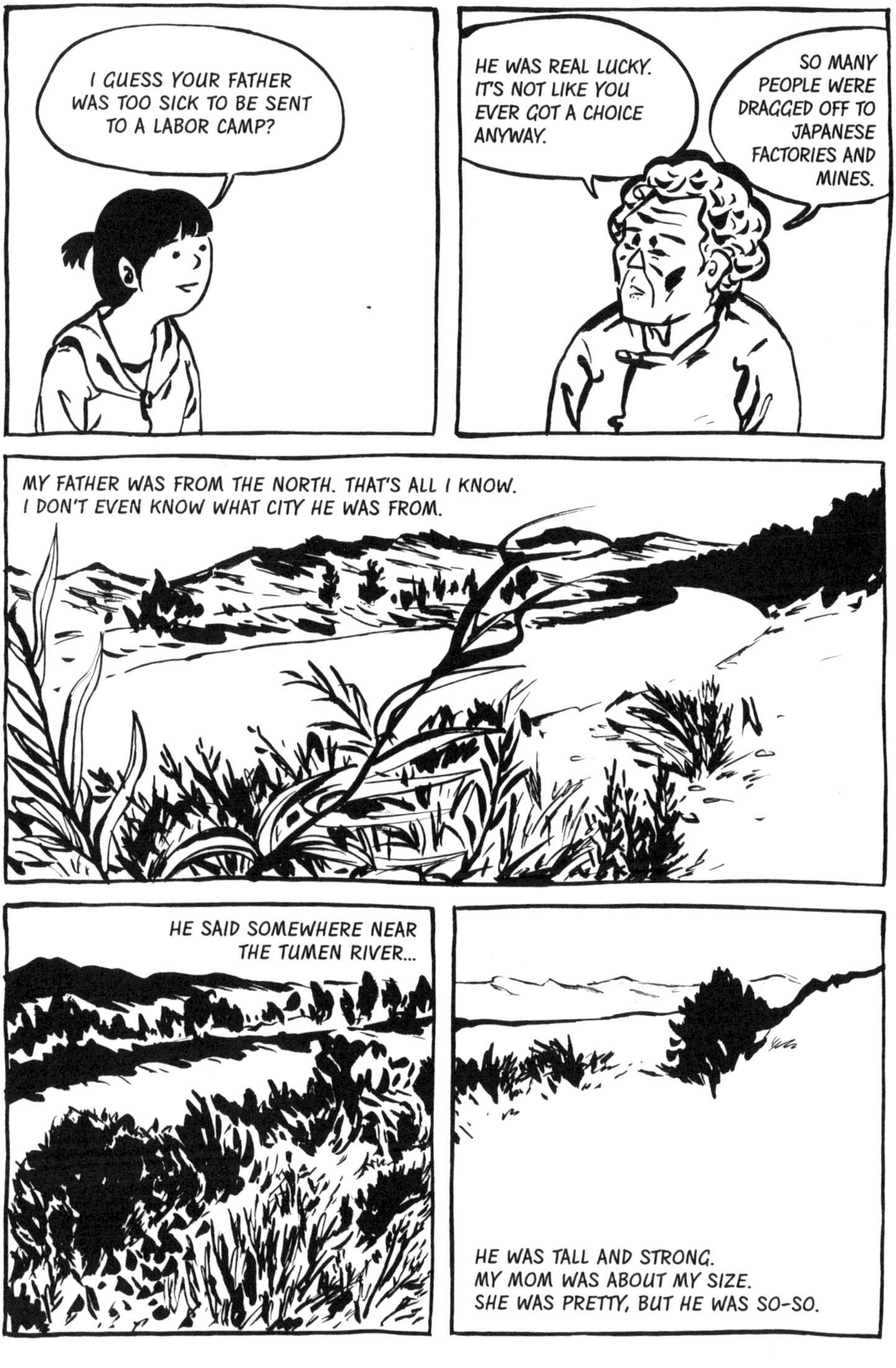
I GUESS YOUR FATHER WAS TOO SICK TO BE SENT TO A LABOR CAMP?
HE WAS REAL LUCKY. IT'S NOT LIKE YOU EVER GOT A CHOICE ANYWAY.
SO MANY PEOPLE WERE DRAGGED OFF TO JAPANESE FACTORIES AND MINES.
MY FATHER WAS FROM THE NORTH. THAT'S ALL I KNOW. I DON'T EVEN KNOW WHAT CITY HE WAS FROM.
HE SAID SOMEWHERE NEAR THE TUMEN RIVER...
HE WAS TALL AND STRONG. MY MOM WAS ABOUT MY SIZE. SHE WAS PRETTY, BUT HE WAS SO-SO.

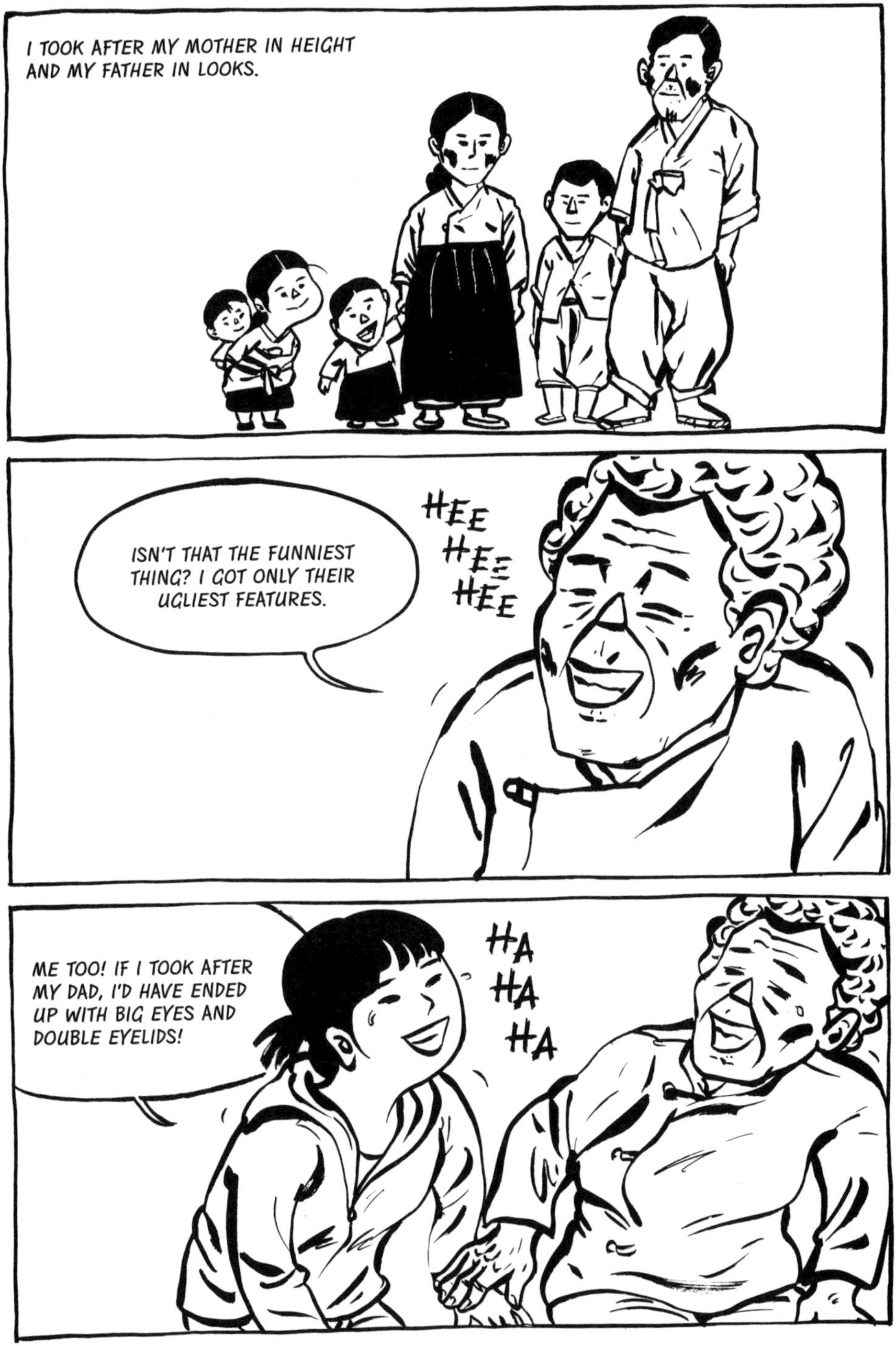
I TOOK AFTER MY MOTHER IN HEIGHT AND MY FATHER IN LOOKS.
ISN'T THAT THE FUNNIEST THING? I GOT ONLY THEIR UGLIEST FEATURES.
HEE HEE HEE
ME TOO! IF I TOOK AFTER MY DAD, I'D HAVE ENDED UP WITH BIG EYES AND DOUBLE EYELIDS!
HA HA HA

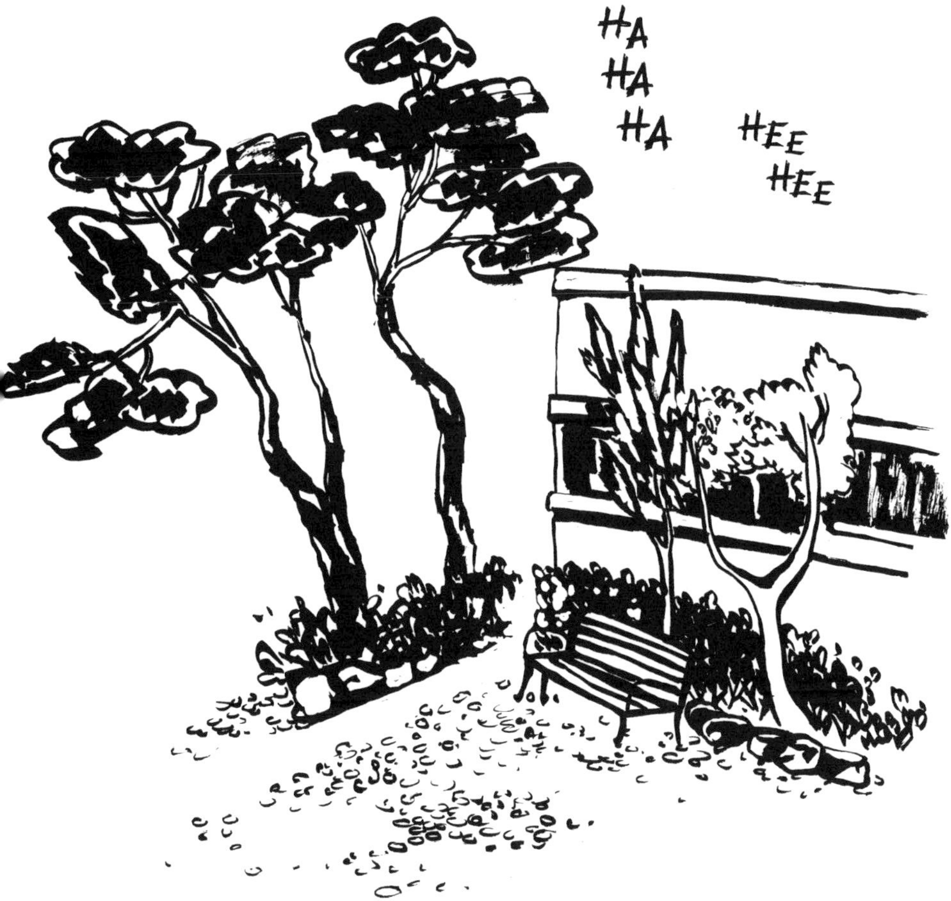
HA
HA
HA
HEE
HEE

# ADOPTION

ONE DAY A STRANGER CAME
TO OUR HOUSE.

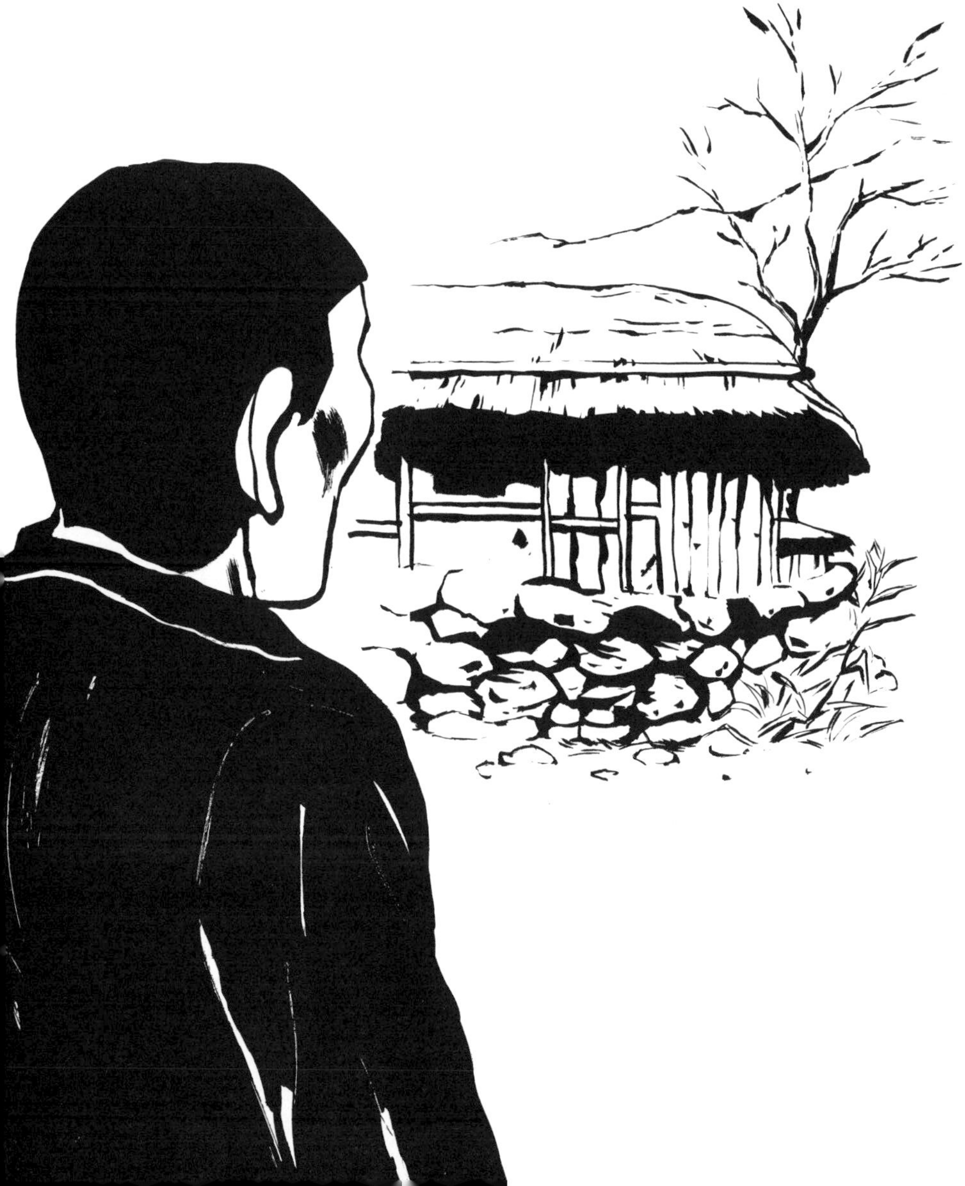

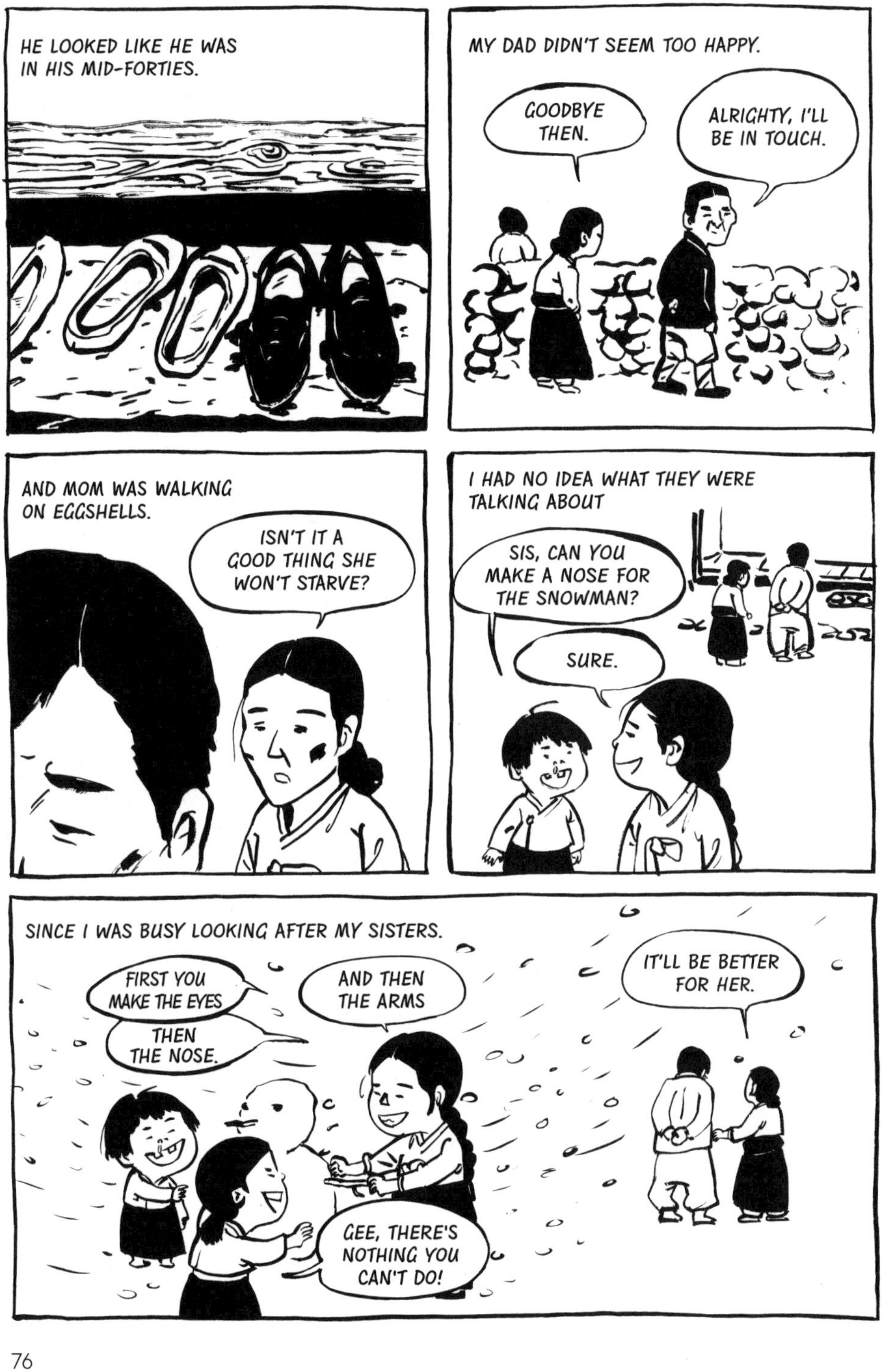
HE LOOKED LIKE HE WAS IN HIS MID-FORTIES.
MY DAD DIDN'T SEEM TOO HAPPY.
GOODBYE THEN.
ALRIGHTY, I'LL BE IN TOUCH.
AND MOM WAS WALKING ON EGGSHELLS.
ISN'T IT A GOOD THING SHE WON'T STARVE?
I HAD NO IDEA WHAT THEY WERE TALKING ABOUT
SIS, CAN YOU MAKE A NOSE FOR THE SNOWMAN?
SURE.
SINCE I WAS BUSY LOOKING AFTER MY SISTERS.
FIRST YOU MAKE THE EYES
THEN THE NOSE.
AND THEN THE ARMS
IT'LL BE BETTER FOR HER.
GEE, THERE'S NOTHING YOU CAN'T DO!

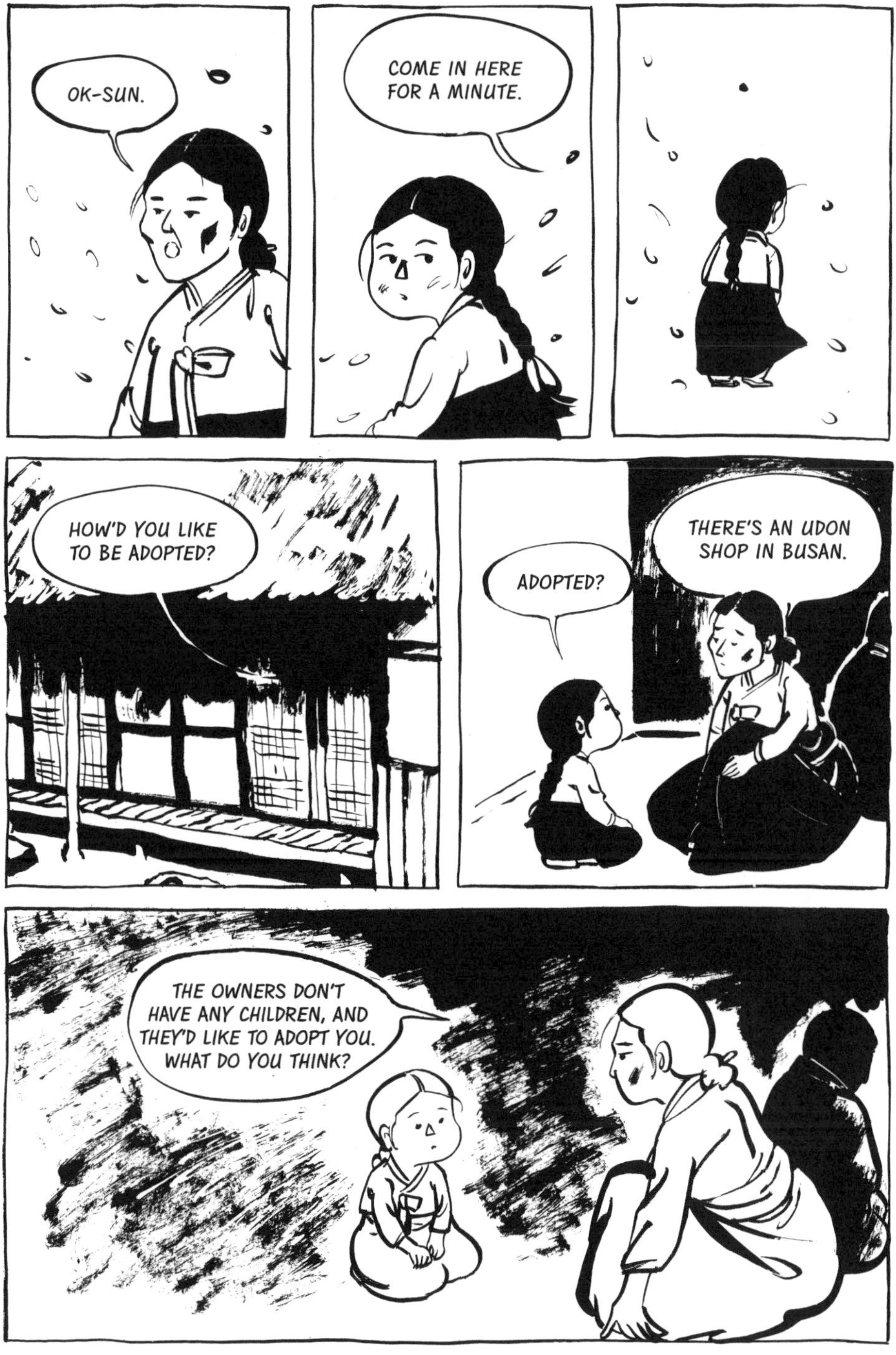
OK-SUN.
COME IN HERE FOR A MINUTE.
HOW'D YOU LIKE TO BE ADOPTED?
ADOPTED?
THERE'S AN UDON SHOP IN BUSAN.
THE OWNERS DON'T HAVE ANY CHILDREN, AND THEY'D LIKE TO ADOPT YOU. WHAT DO YOU THINK?

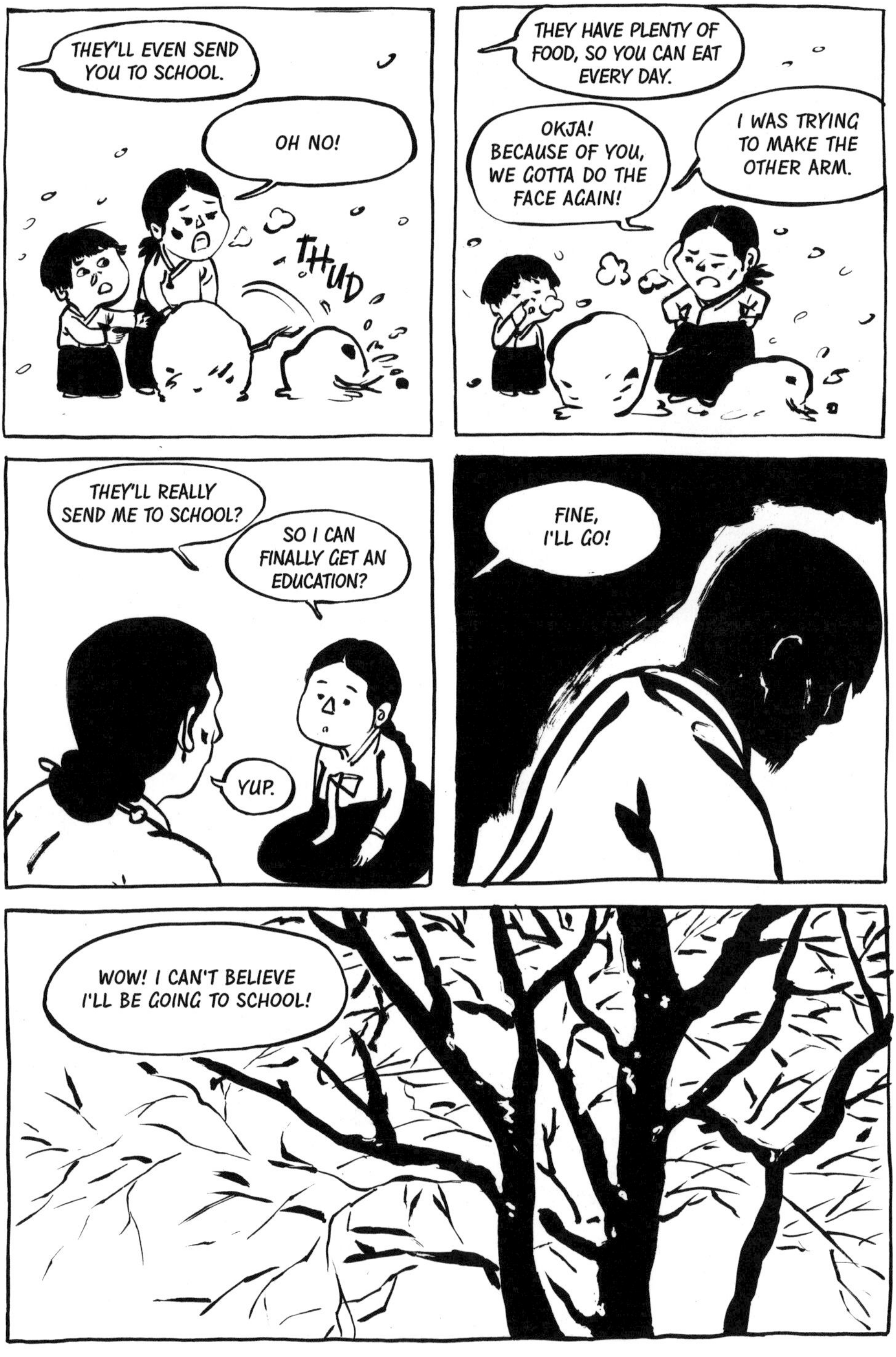
THEY'LL EVEN SEND YOU TO SCHOOL.
OH NO!
THUD
THEY HAVE PLENTY OF FOOD, SO YOU CAN EAT EVERY DAY.
OKJA! BECAUSE OF YOU, WE GOTTA DO THE FACE AGAIN!
I WAS TRYING TO MAKE THE OTHER ARM.
THEY'LL REALLY SEND ME TO SCHOOL?
SO I CAN FINALLY GET AN EDUCATION?
YUP.
FINE, I'LL GO!
WOW! I CAN'T BELIEVE I'LL BE GOING TO SCHOOL!

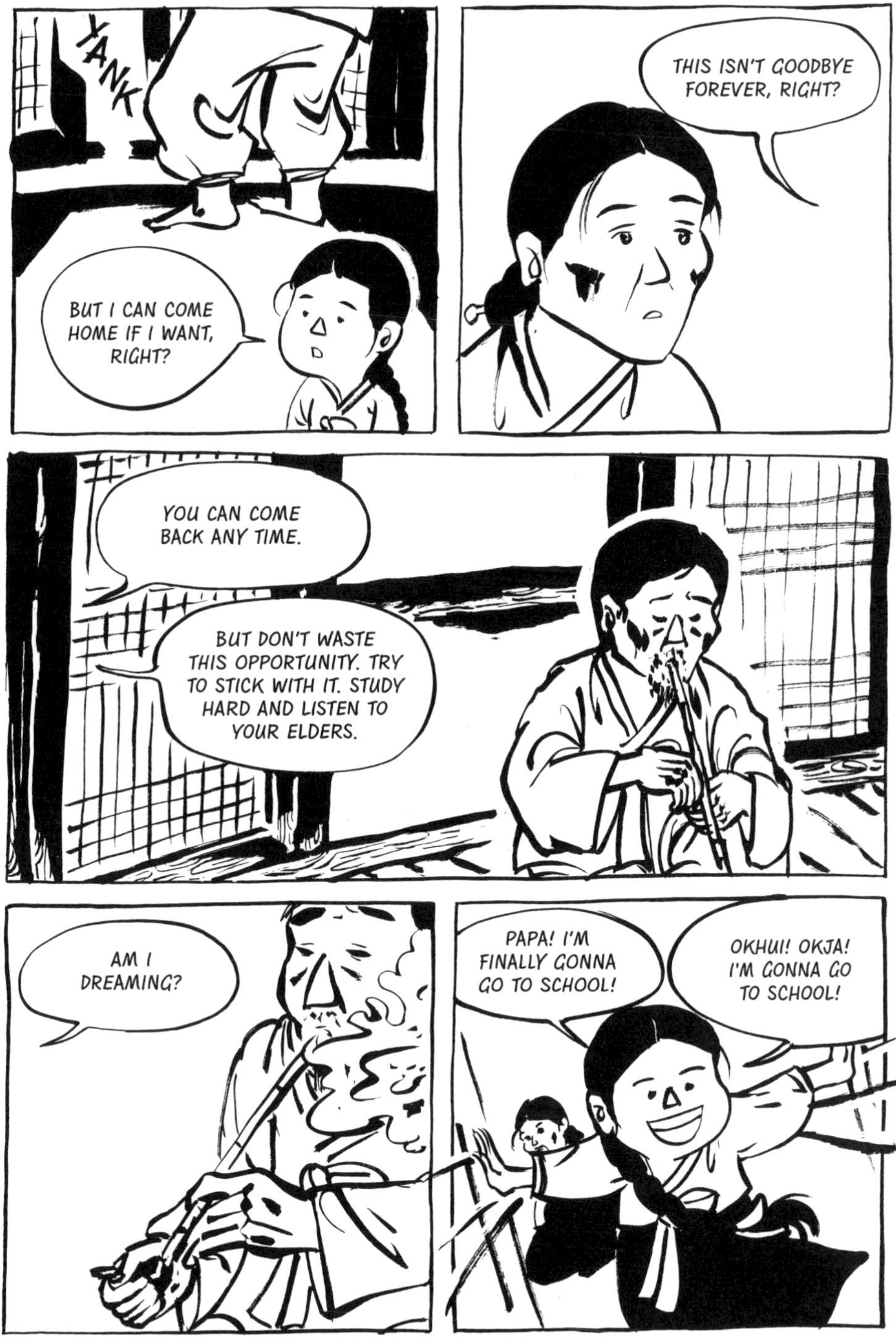
YANK
BUT I CAN COME HOME IF I WANT, RIGHT?
THIS ISN'T GOODBYE FOREVER, RIGHT?
YOU CAN COME BACK ANY TIME.
BUT DON'T WASTE THIS OPPORTUNITY. TRY TO STICK WITH IT. STUDY HARD AND LISTEN TO YOUR ELDERS.
AM I DREAMING?
PAPA! I'M FINALLY GONNA GO TO SCHOOL!
OKHUI! OKJA! I'M GONNA GO TO SCHOOL!

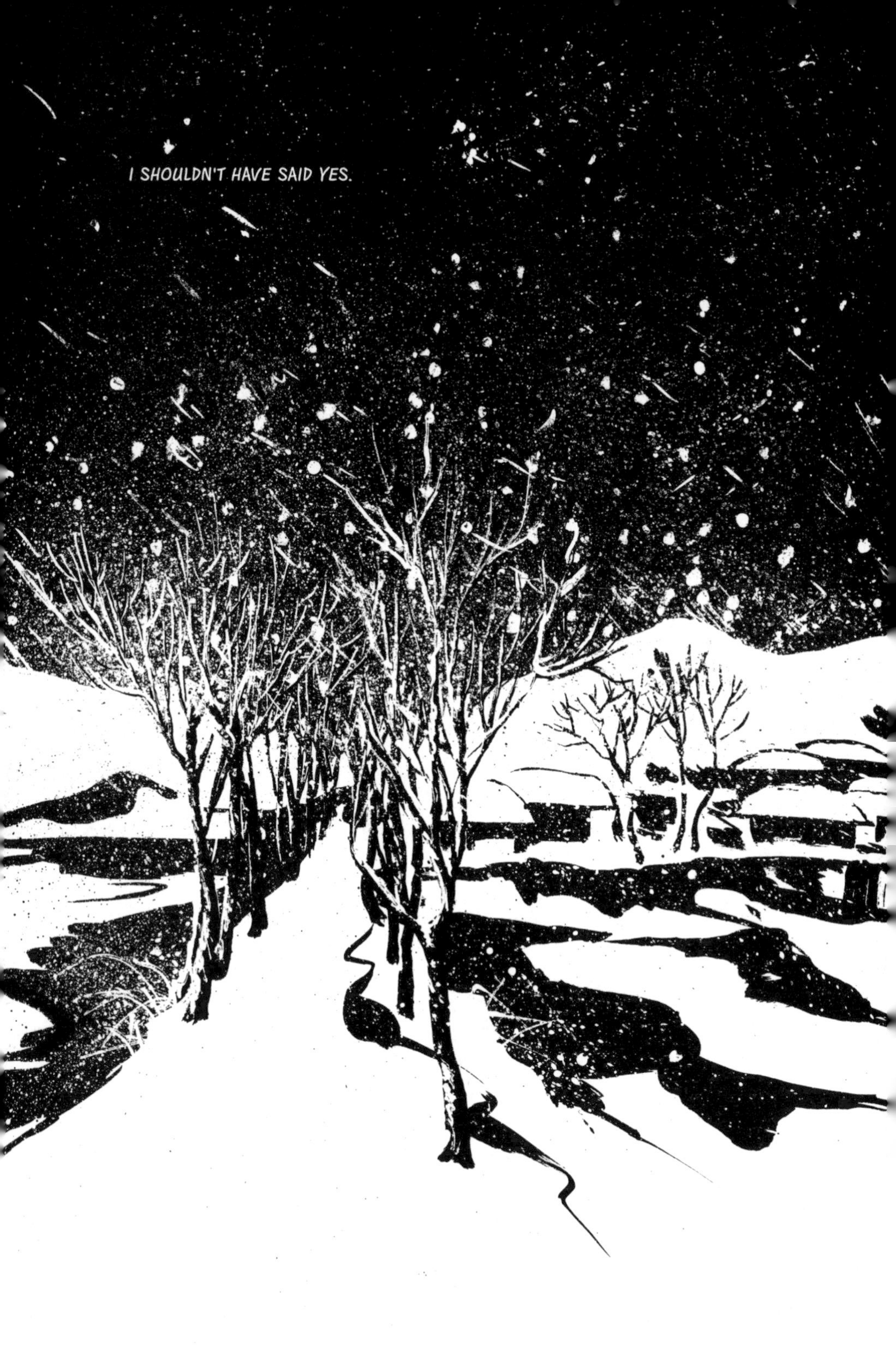
I SHOULDN'T HAVE SAID YES.

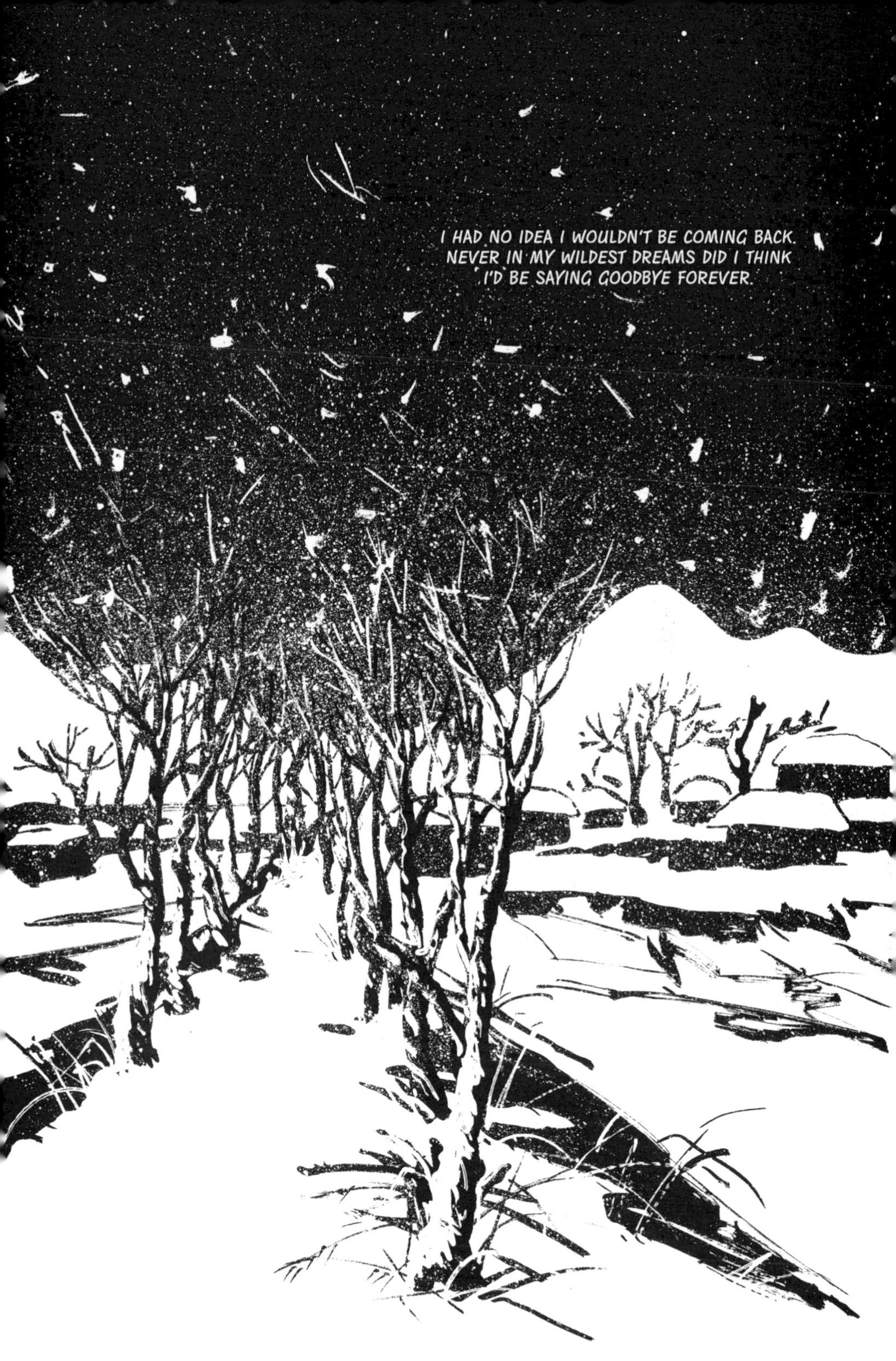
I HAD NO IDEA I WOULDN'T BE COMING BACK. NEVER IN MY WILDEST DREAMS DID I THINK I'D BE SAYING GOODBYE FOREVER.

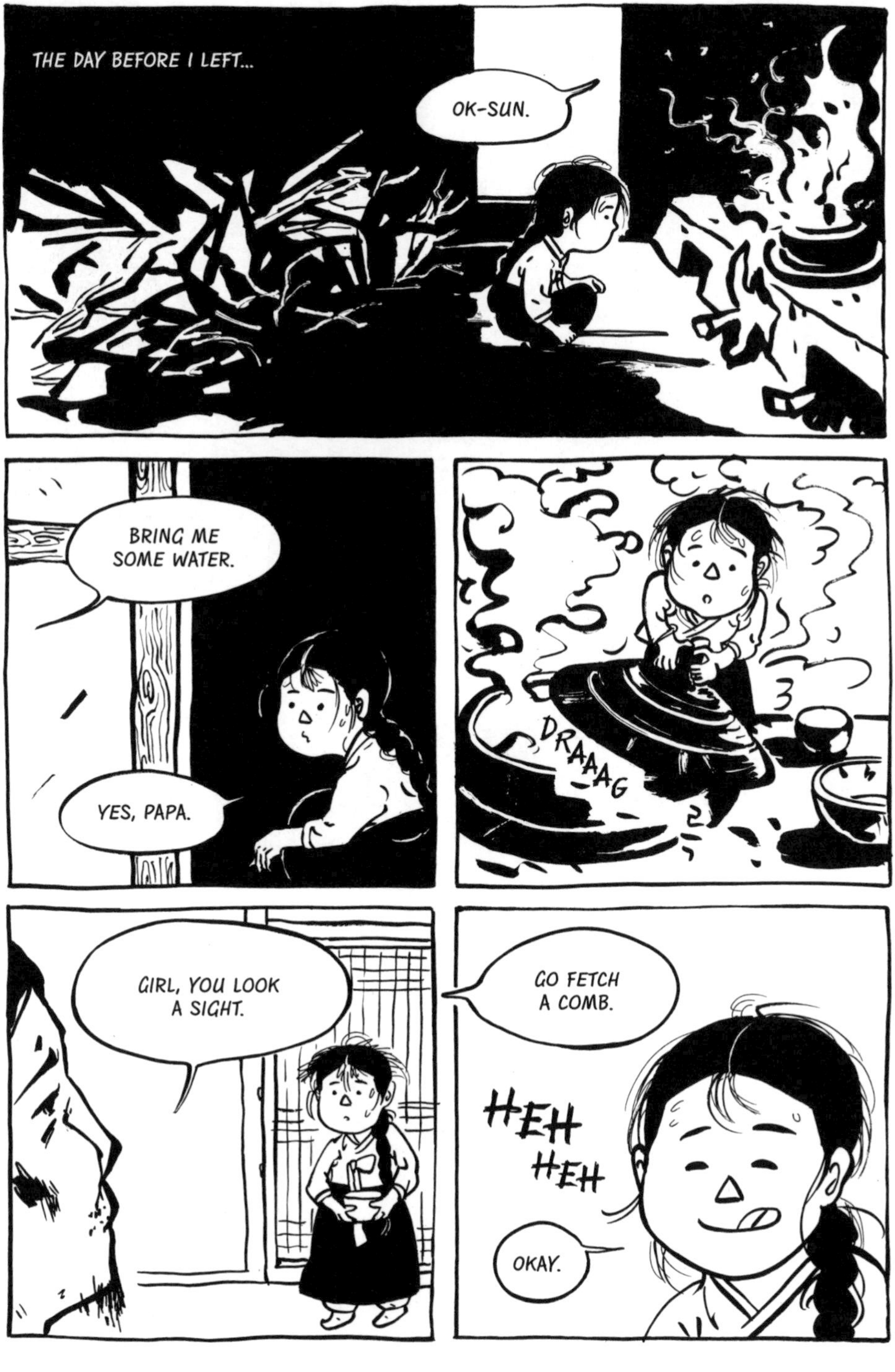
THE DAY BEFORE I LEFT...
OK-SUN.
BRING ME SOME WATER.
YES, PAPA.
DRAAAG
GIRL, YOU LOOK A SIGHT.
GO FETCH A COMB.
HEH HEH
OKAY.

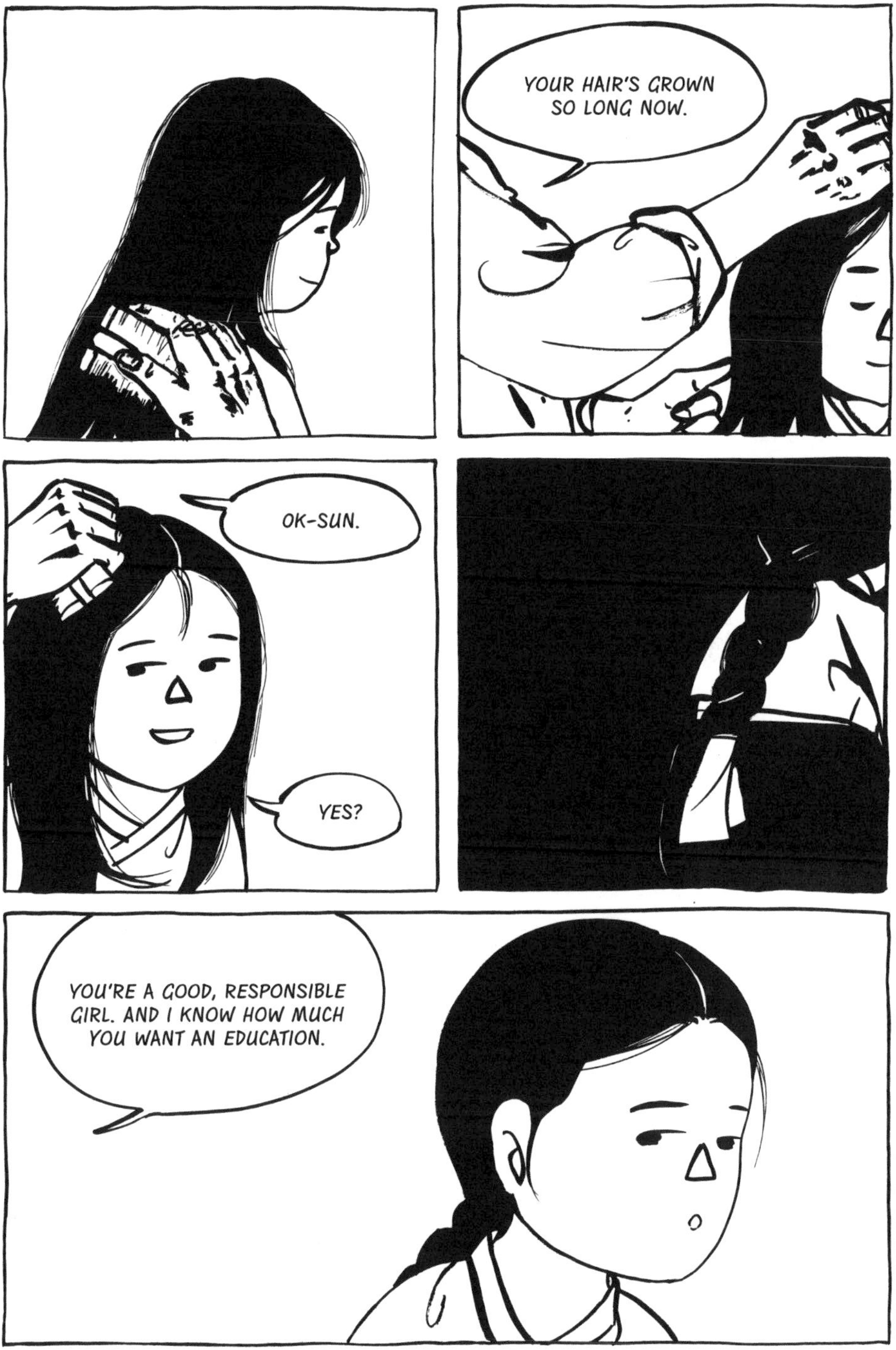
YOUR HAIR'S GROWN SO LONG NOW.
OK-SUN.
YES?
YOU'RE A GOOD, RESPONSIBLE GIRL. AND I KNOW HOW MUCH YOU WANT AN EDUCATION.

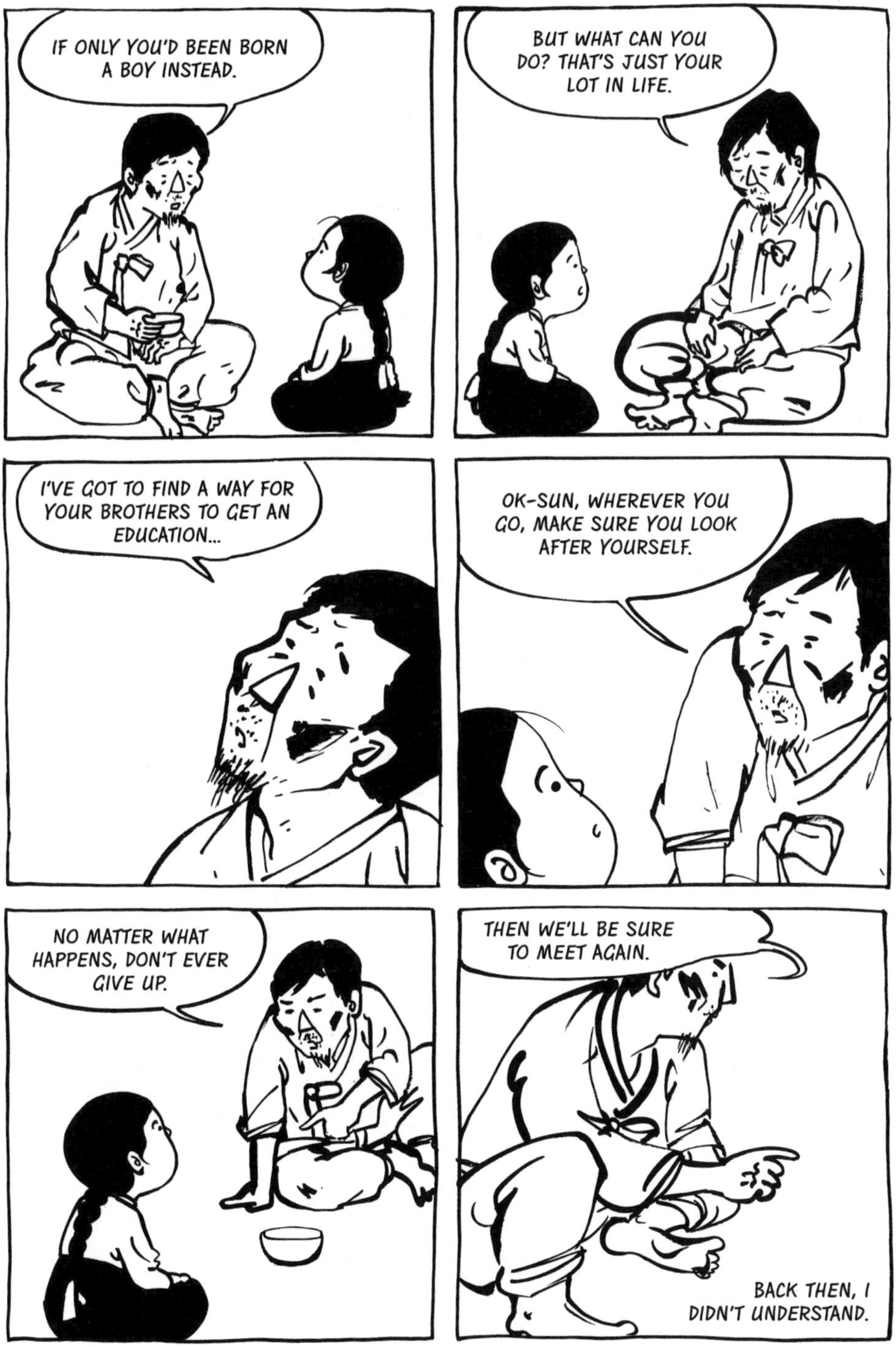
IF ONLY YOU'D BEEN BORN A BOY INSTEAD.
BUT WHAT CAN YOU DO? THAT'S JUST YOUR LOT IN LIFE.
I'VE GOT TO FIND A WAY FOR YOUR BROTHERS TO GET AN EDUCATION...
OK-SUN, WHEREVER YOU GO, MAKE SURE YOU LOOK AFTER YOURSELF.
NO MATTER WHAT HAPPENS, DON'T EVER GIVE UP.
THEN WE'LL BE SURE TO MEET AGAIN.
BACK THEN, I DIDN'T UNDERSTAND.

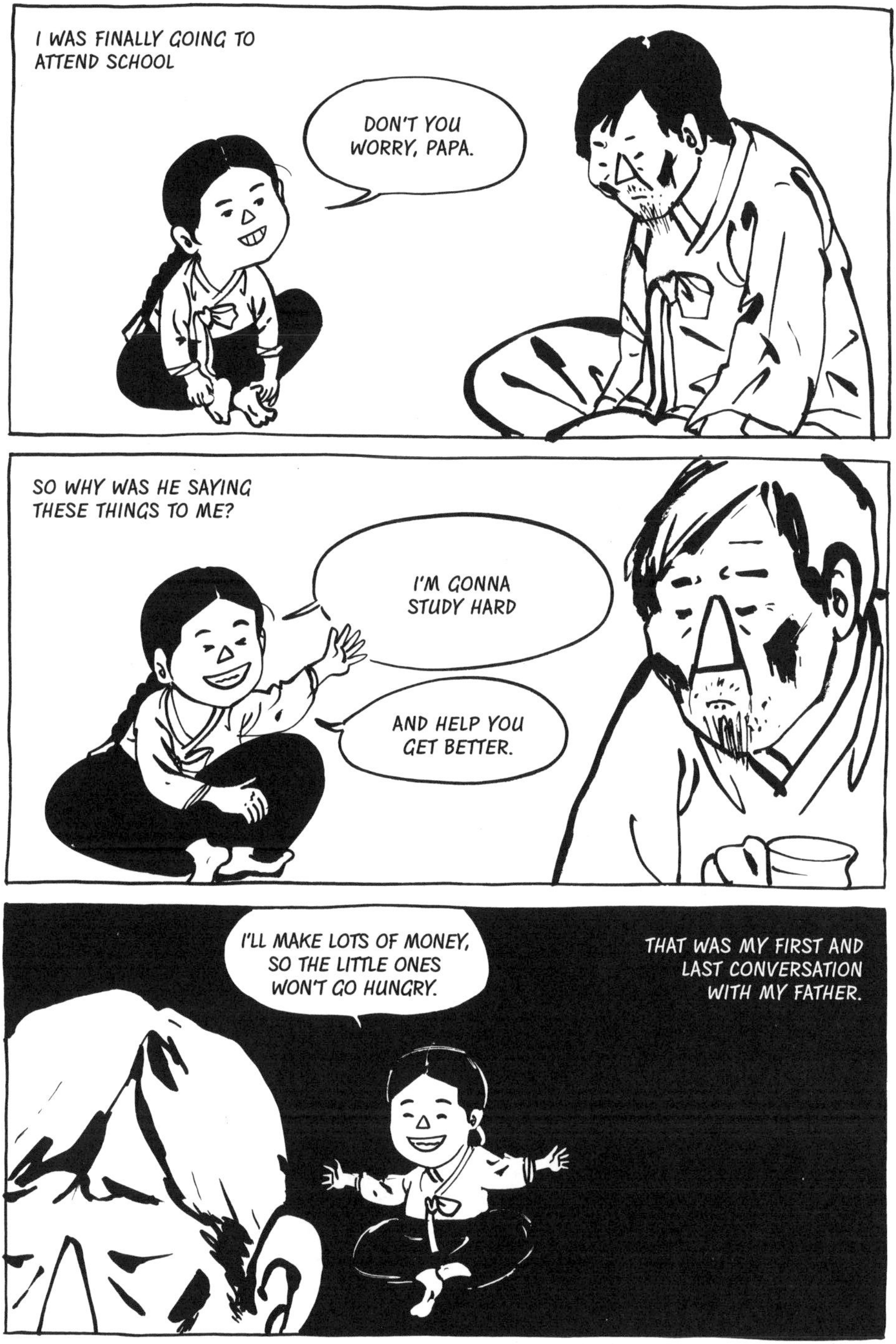
I WAS FINALLY GOING TO ATTEND SCHOOL
DON'T YOU WORRY, PAPA.
SO WHY WAS HE SAYING THESE THINGS TO ME?
I'M GONNA STUDY HARD
AND HELP YOU GET BETTER.
I'LL MAKE LOTS OF MONEY, SO THE LITTLE ONES WON'T GO HUNGRY.
THAT WAS MY FIRST AND LAST CONVERSATION WITH MY FATHER.

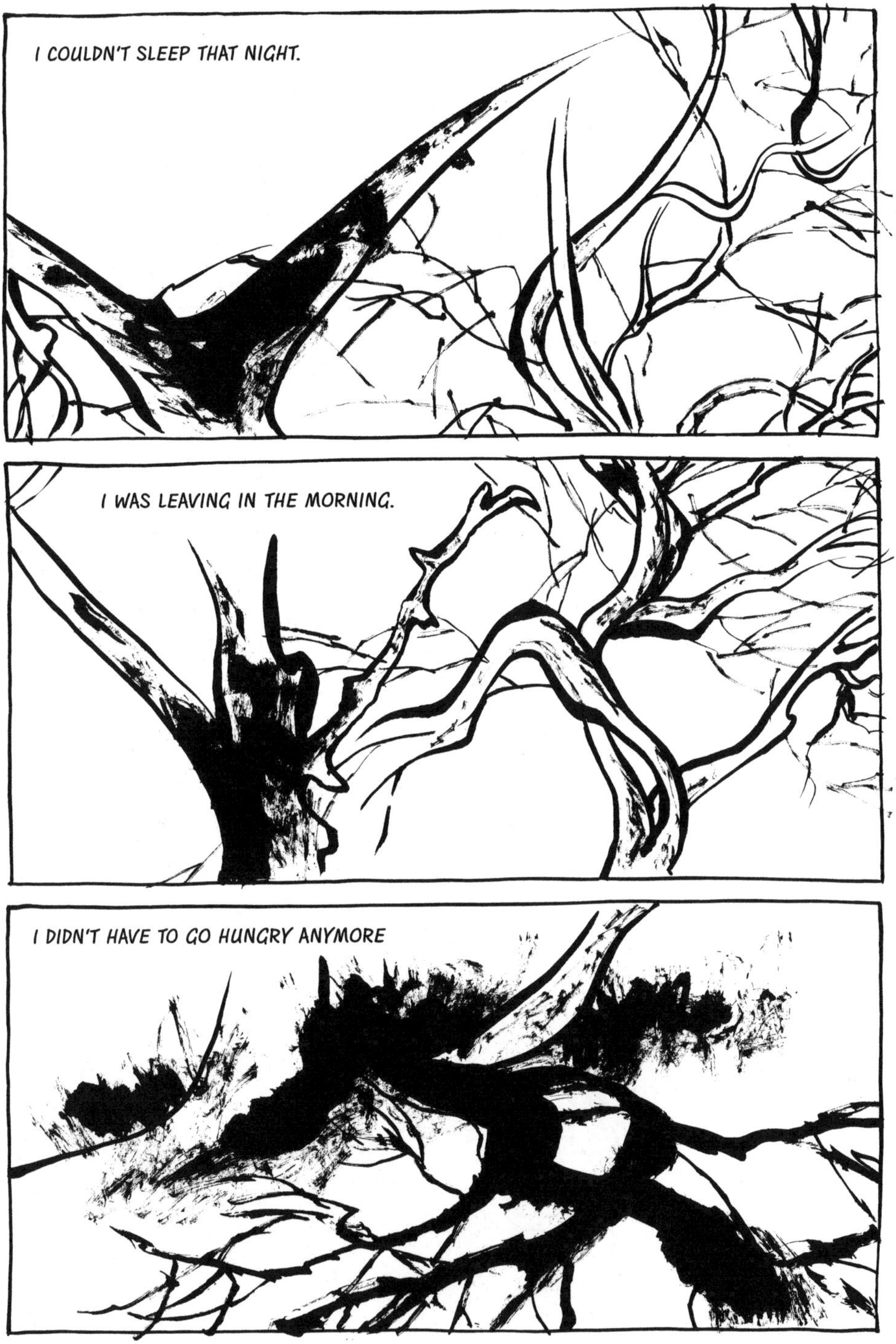
I COULDN'T SLEEP THAT NIGHT.
I WAS LEAVING IN THE MORNING.
I DIDN'T HAVE TO GO HUNGRY ANYMORE

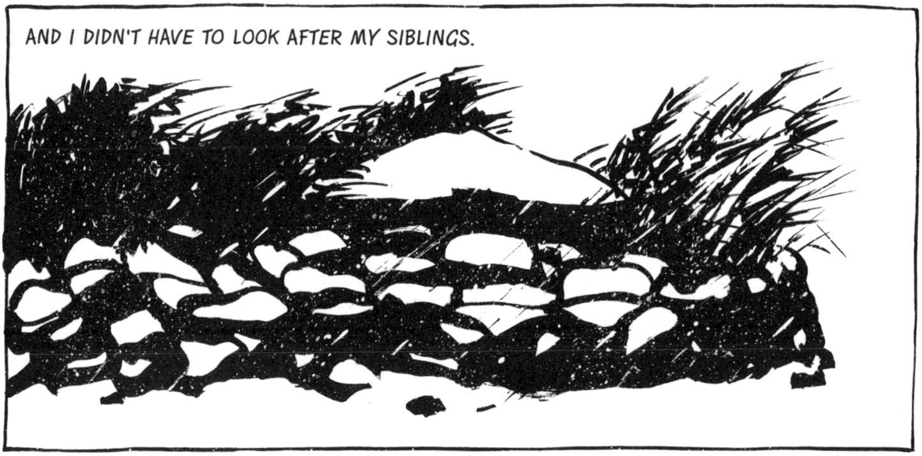
AND I DIDN'T HAVE TO LOOK AFTER MY SIBLINGS.

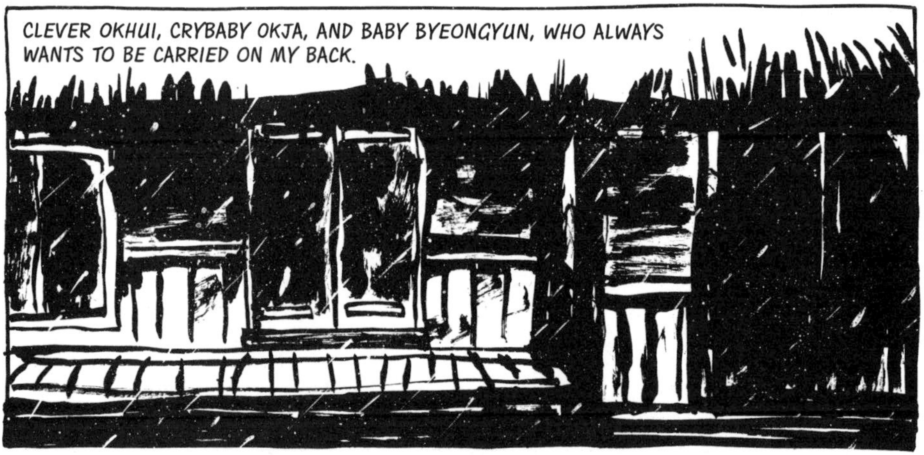
CLEVER OKHUI, CRYBABY OKJA, AND BABY BYEONGYUN, WHO ALWAYS WANTS TO BE CARRIED ON MY BACK.

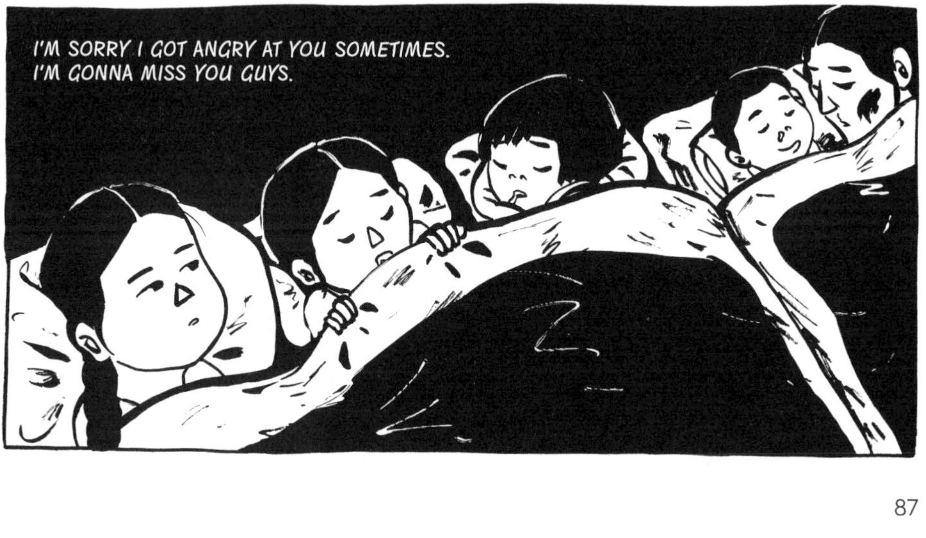
I'M SORRY I GOT ANGRY AT YOU SOMETIMES.
I'M GONNA MISS YOU GUYS.

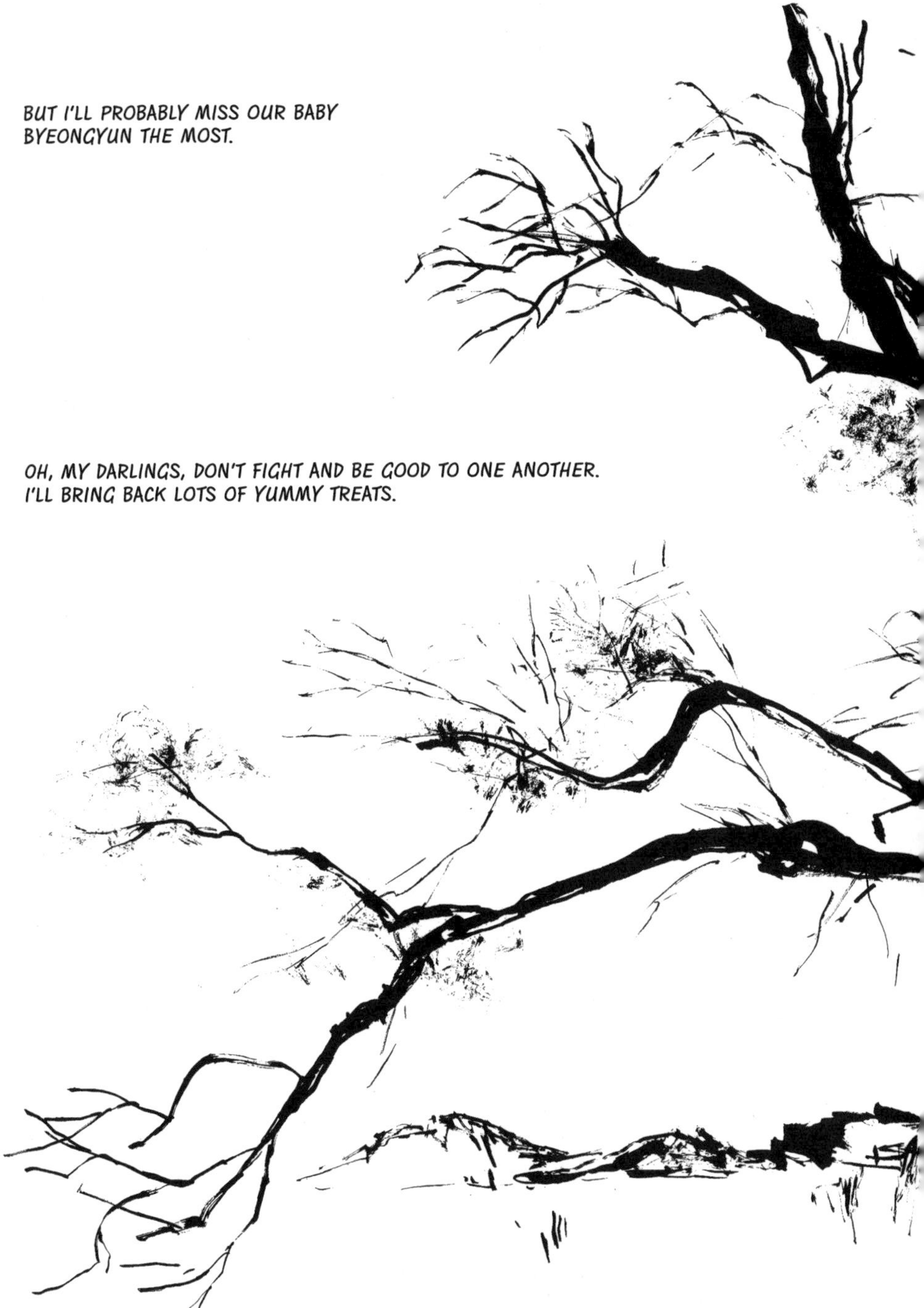
BUT I'LL PROBABLY MISS OUR BABY BYEONGYUN THE MOST.
OH, MY DARLINGS, DON'T FIGHT AND BE GOOD TO ONE ANOTHER. I'LL BRING BACK LOTS OF YUMMY TREATS.

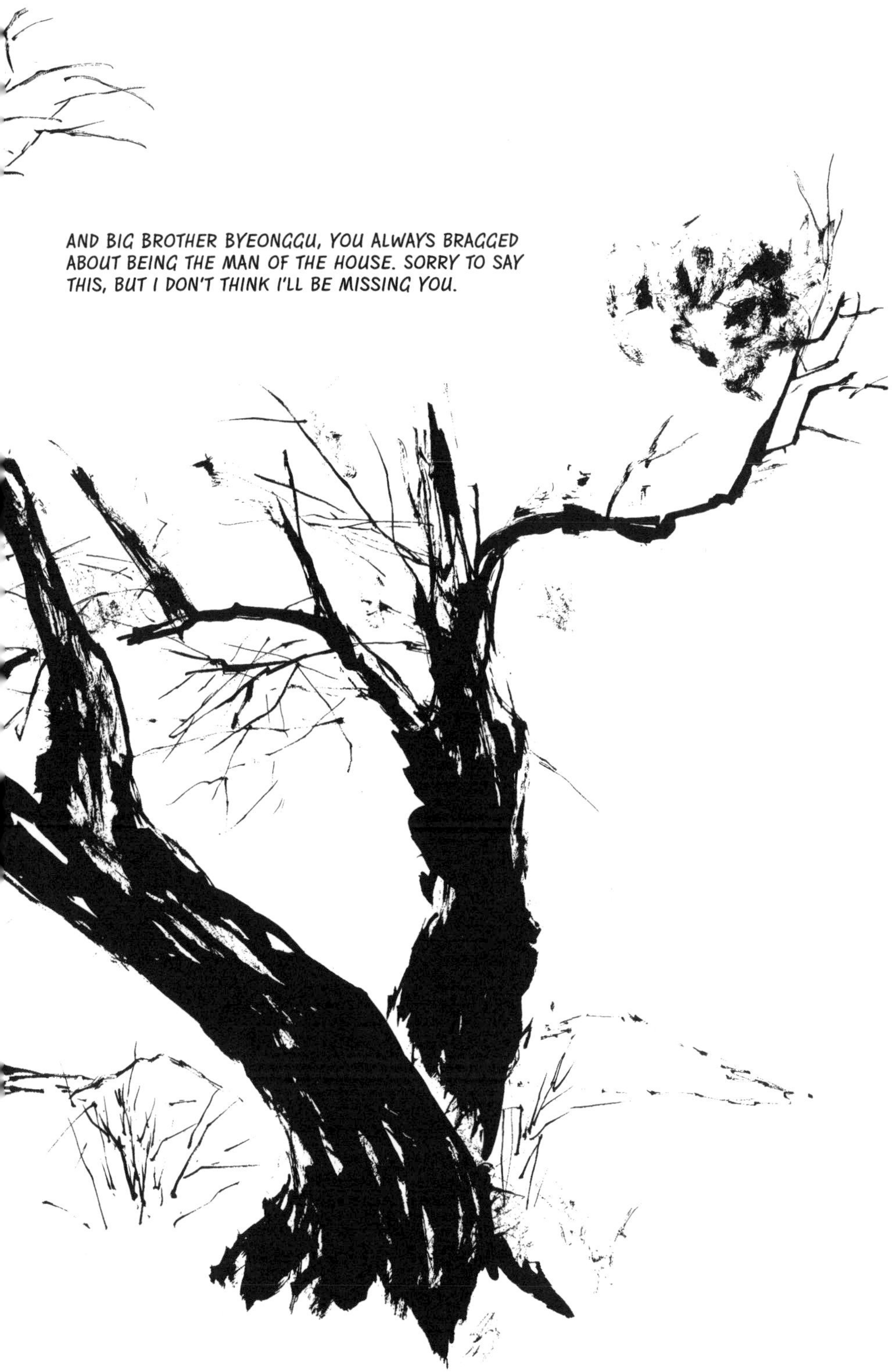
AND BIG BROTHER BYEONGGU, YOU ALWAYS BRAGGED ABOUT BEING THE MAN OF THE HOUSE. SORRY TO SAY THIS, BUT I DON'T THINK I'LL BE MISSING YOU.

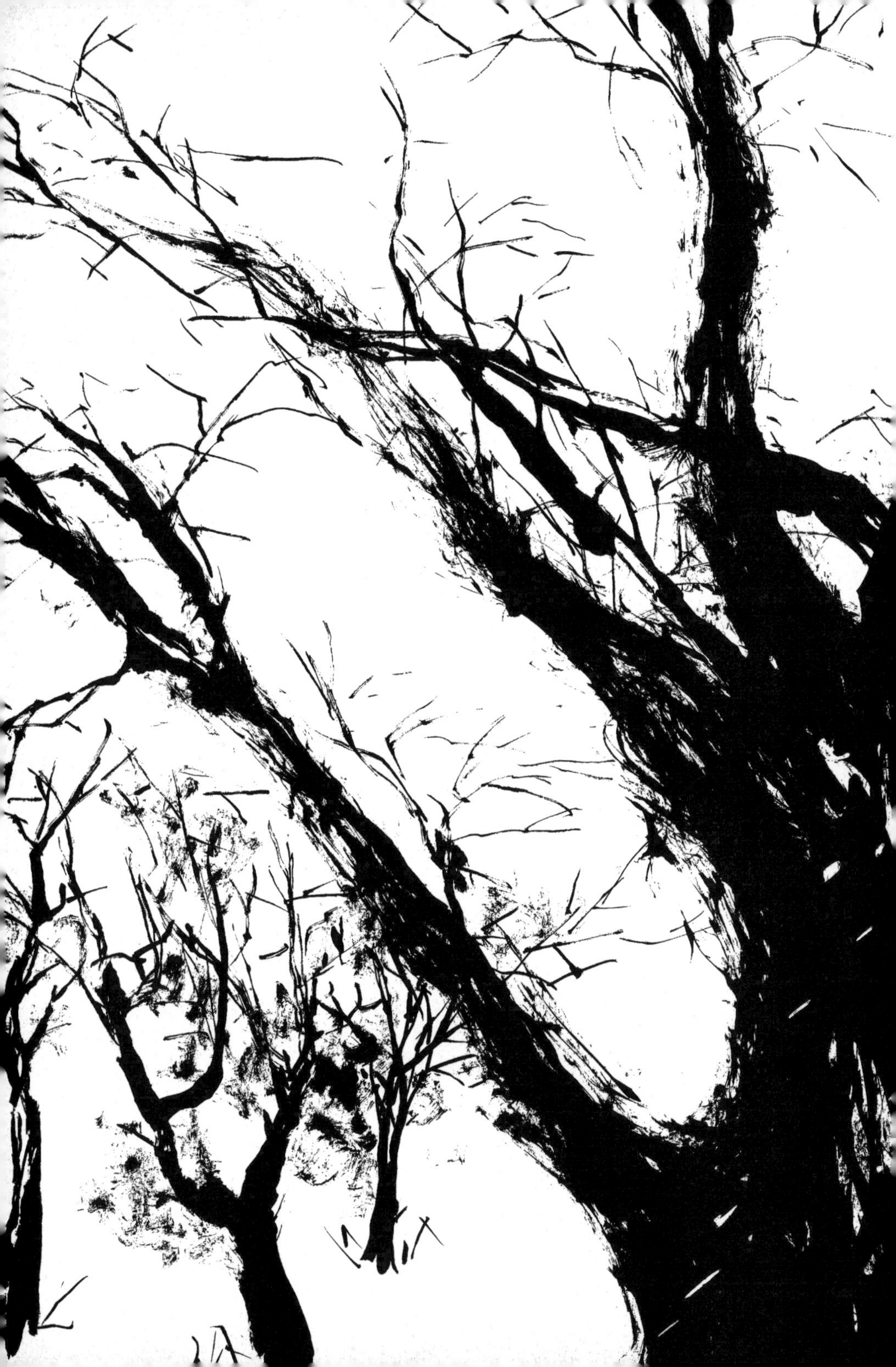

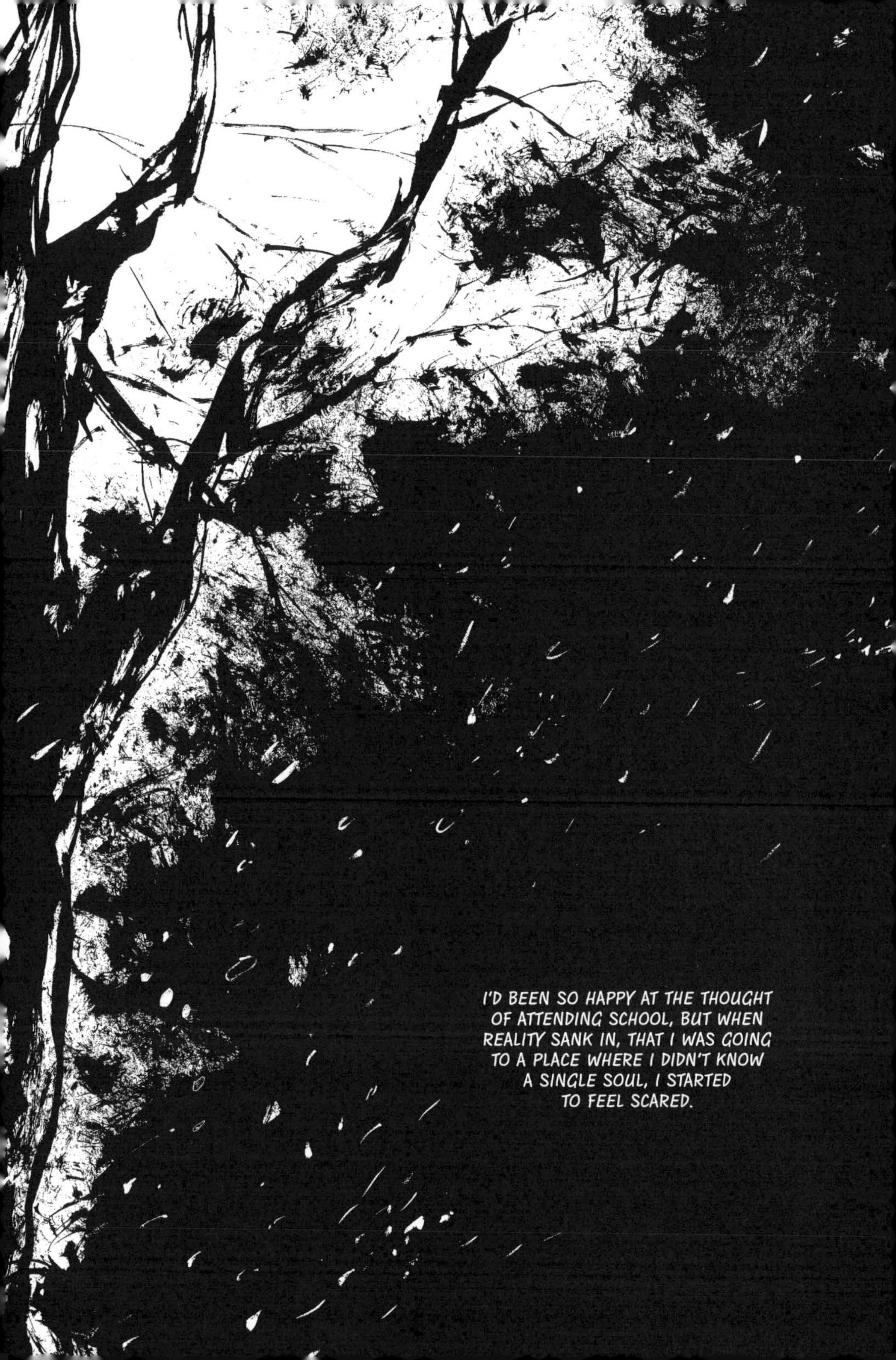
I'D BEEN SO HAPPY AT THE THOUGHT OF ATTENDING SCHOOL, BUT WHEN REALITY SANK IN, THAT I WAS GOING TO A PLACE WHERE I DIDN'T KNOW A SINGLE SOUL, I STARTED TO FEEL SCARED.

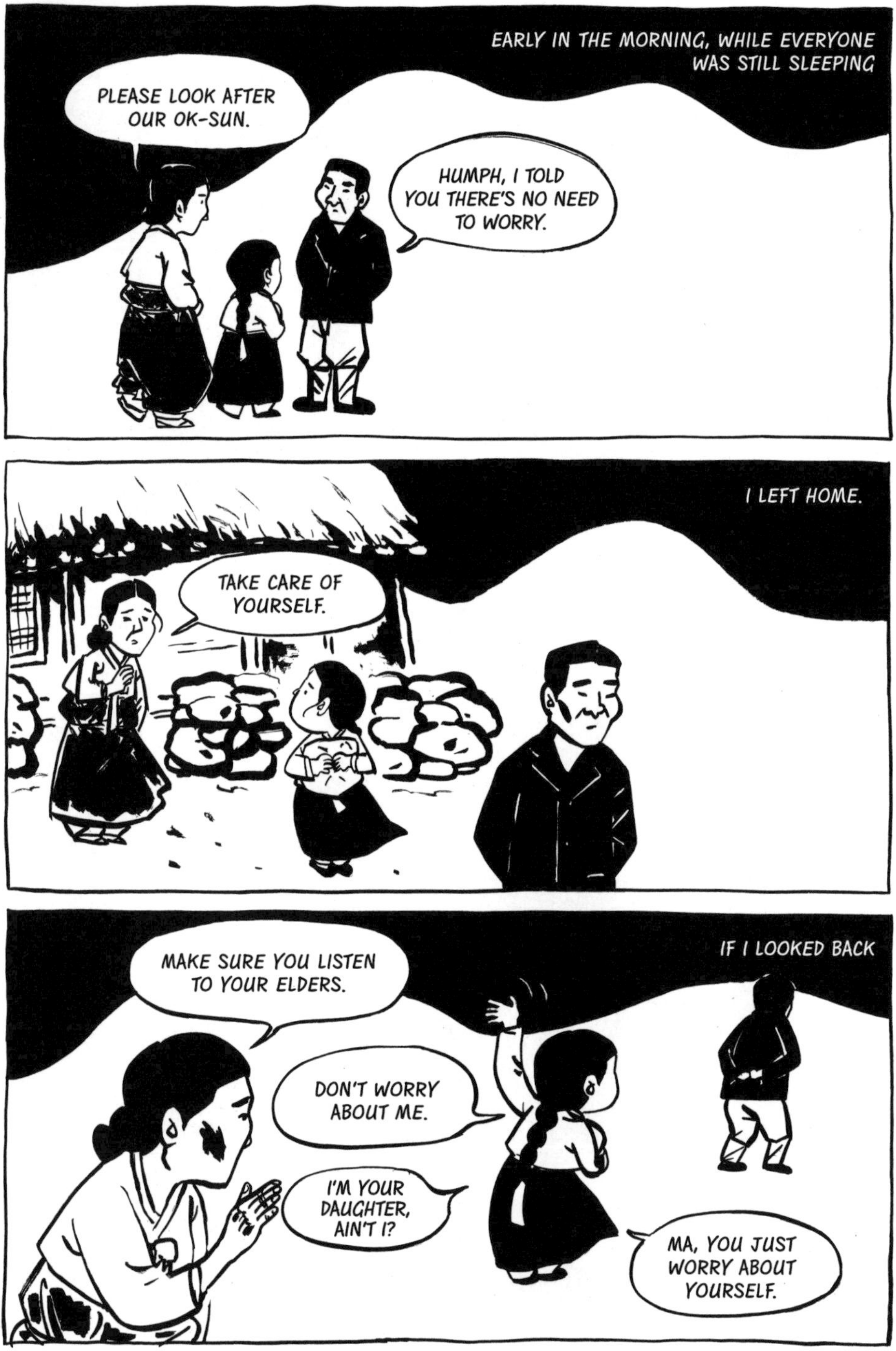
EARLY IN THE MORNING, WHILE EVERYONE WAS STILL SLEEPING
PLEASE LOOK AFTER OUR OK-SUN.
HUMPH, I TOLD YOU THERE'S NO NEED TO WORRY.
I LEFT HOME.
TAKE CARE OF YOURSELF.
IF I LOOKED BACK
MAKE SURE YOU LISTEN TO YOUR ELDERS.
DON'T WORRY ABOUT ME.
I'M YOUR DAUGHTER, AIN'T I?
MA, YOU JUST WORRY ABOUT YOURSELF.

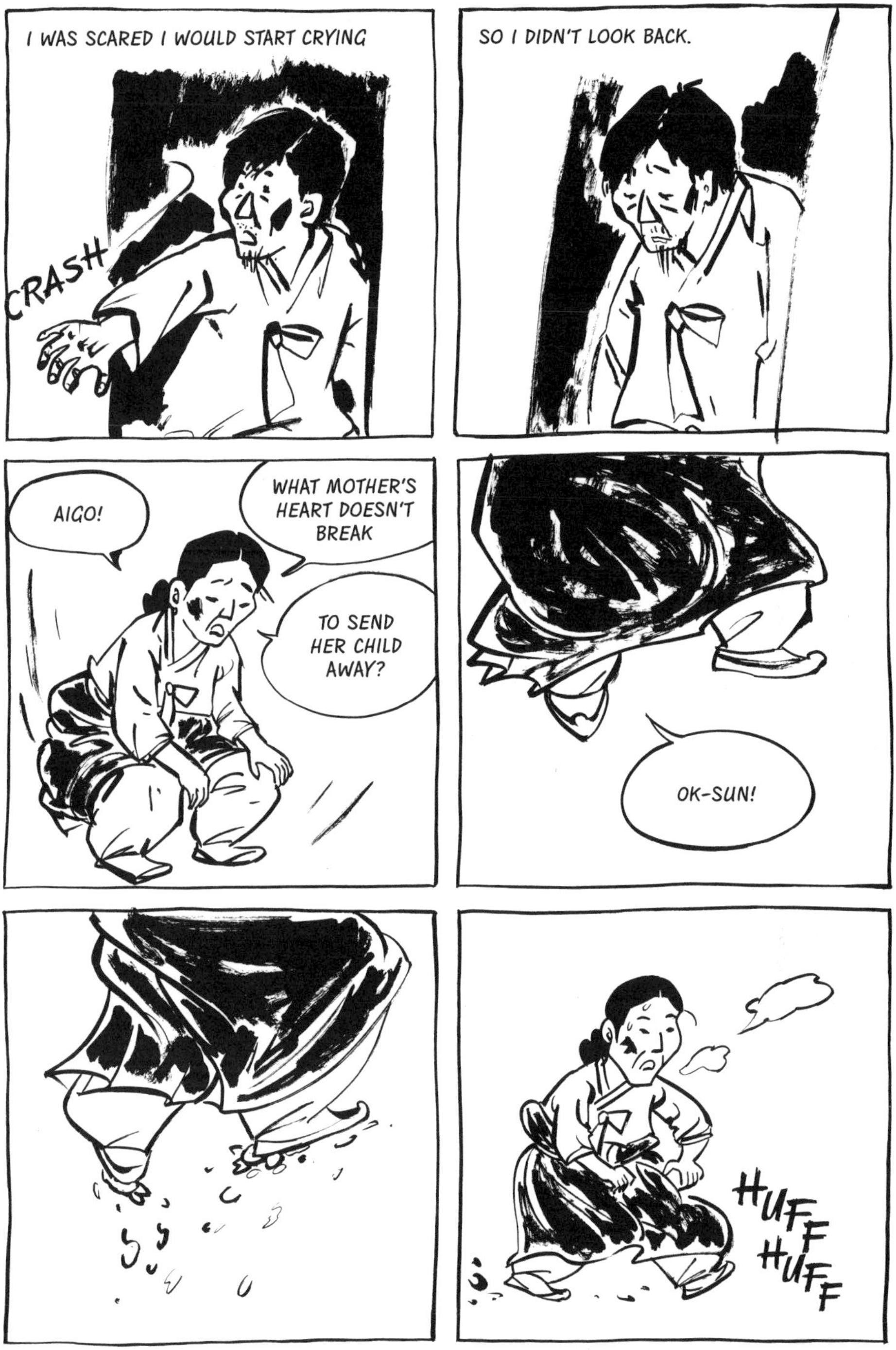
I WAS SCARED I WOULD START CRYING
CRASH
SO I DIDN'T LOOK BACK.
AIGO!
WHAT MOTHER'S HEART DOESN'T BREAK
TO SEND HER CHILD AWAY?
OK-SUN!
HUFF
HUFF

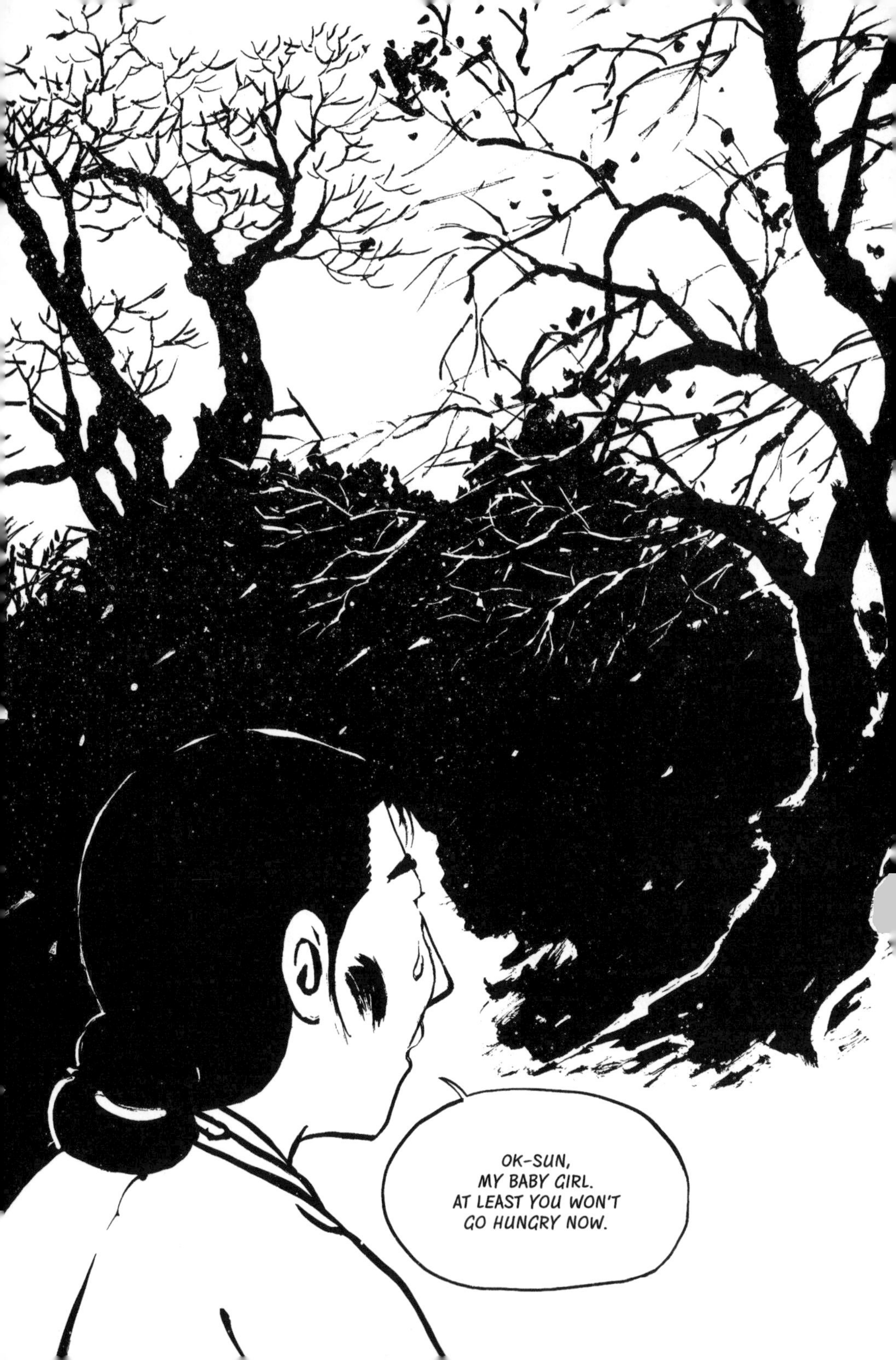
OK-SUN, MY BABY GIRL. AT LEAST YOU WON'T GO HUNGRY NOW.

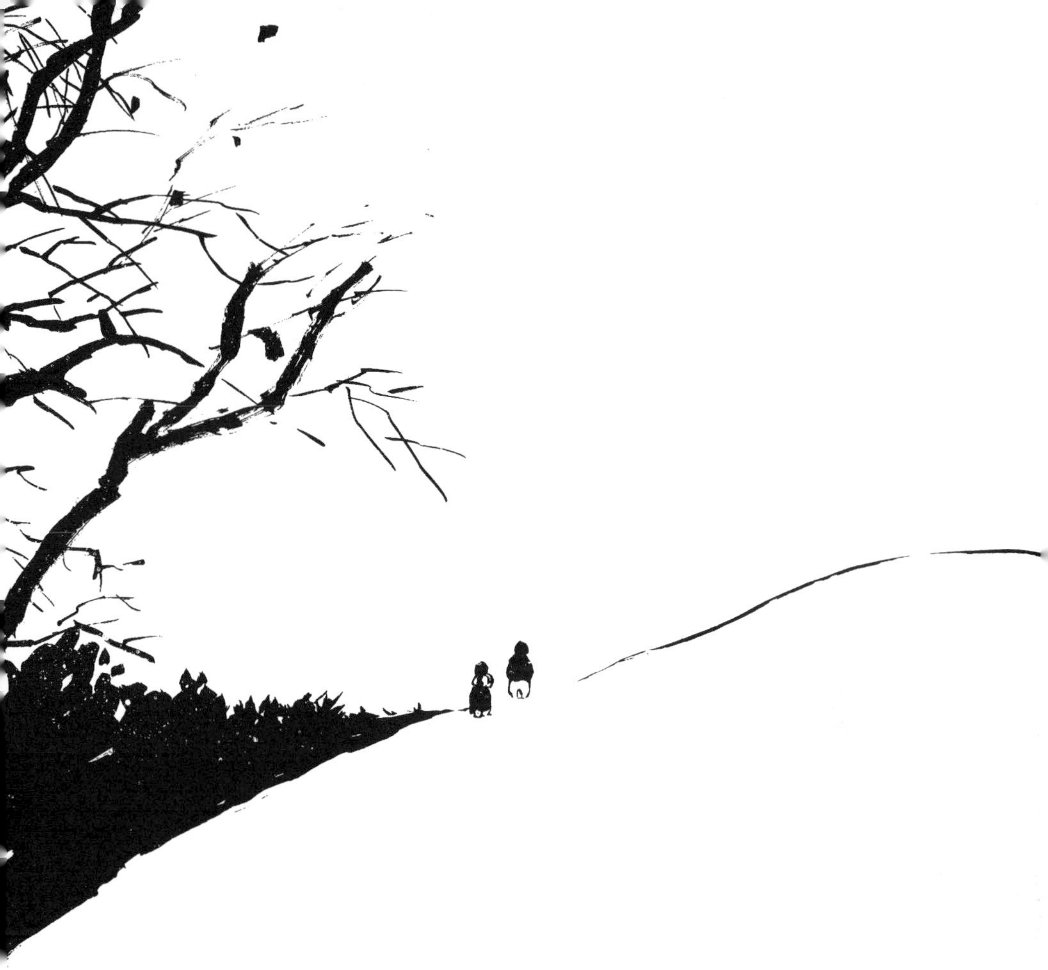

# BUSAN UDON SHOP

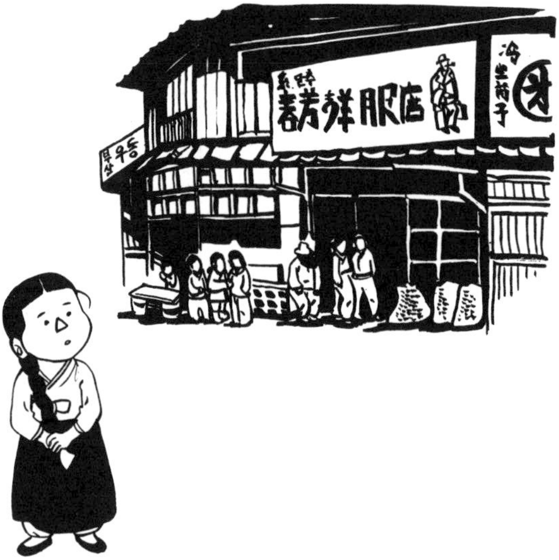
春芳洋服店

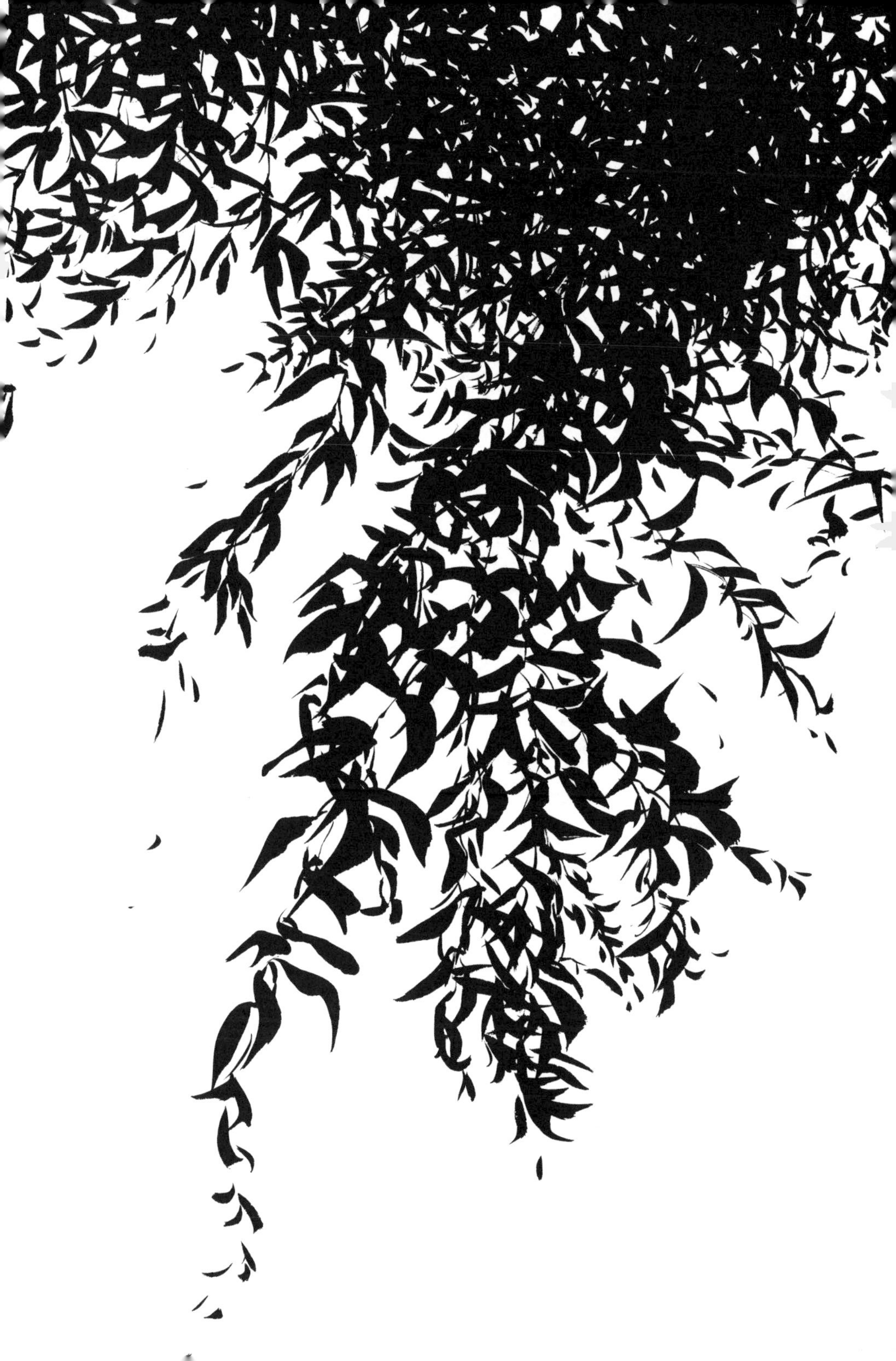

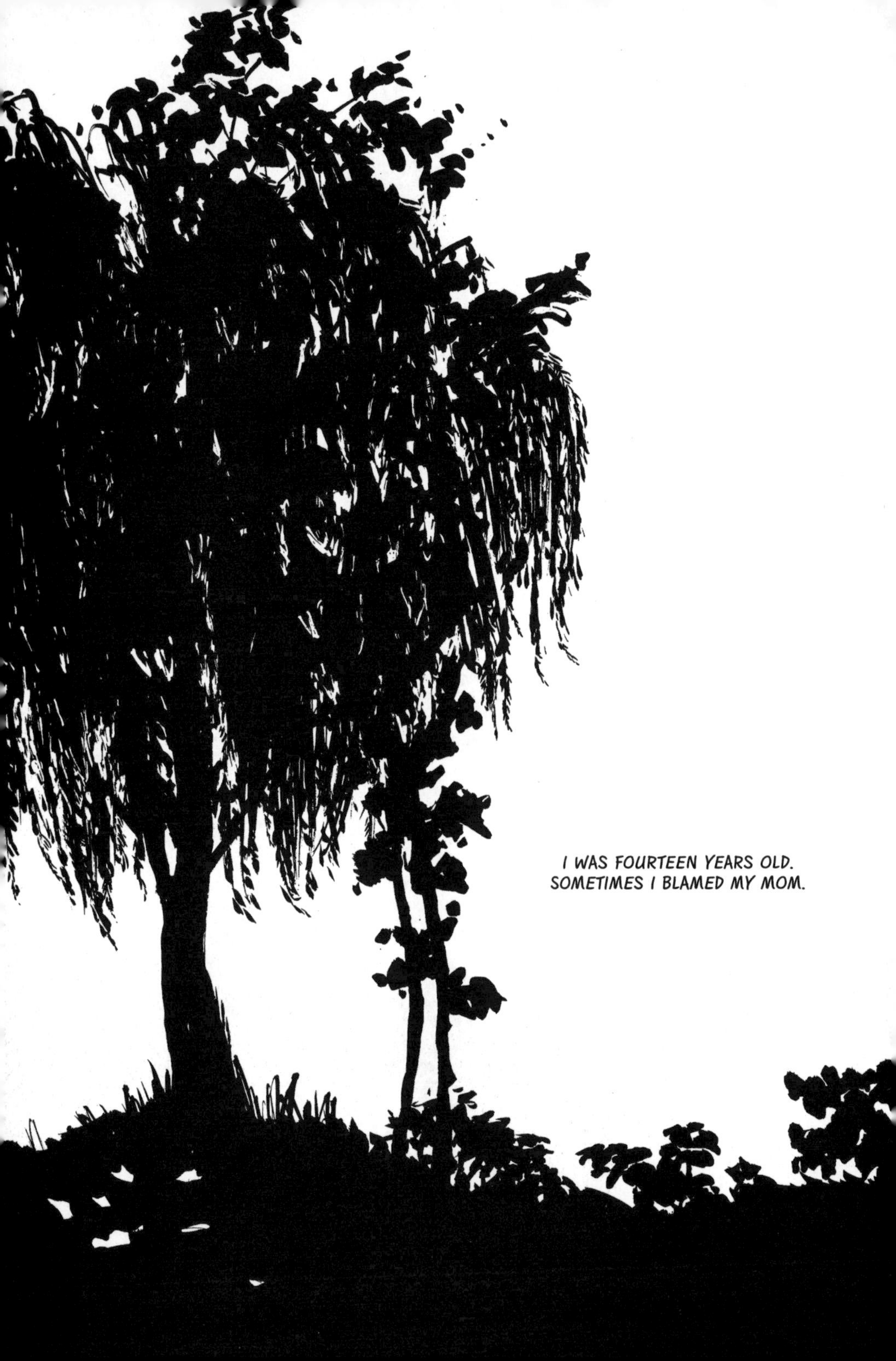
I WAS FOURTEEN YEARS OLD.
SOMETIMES I BLAMED MY MOM.

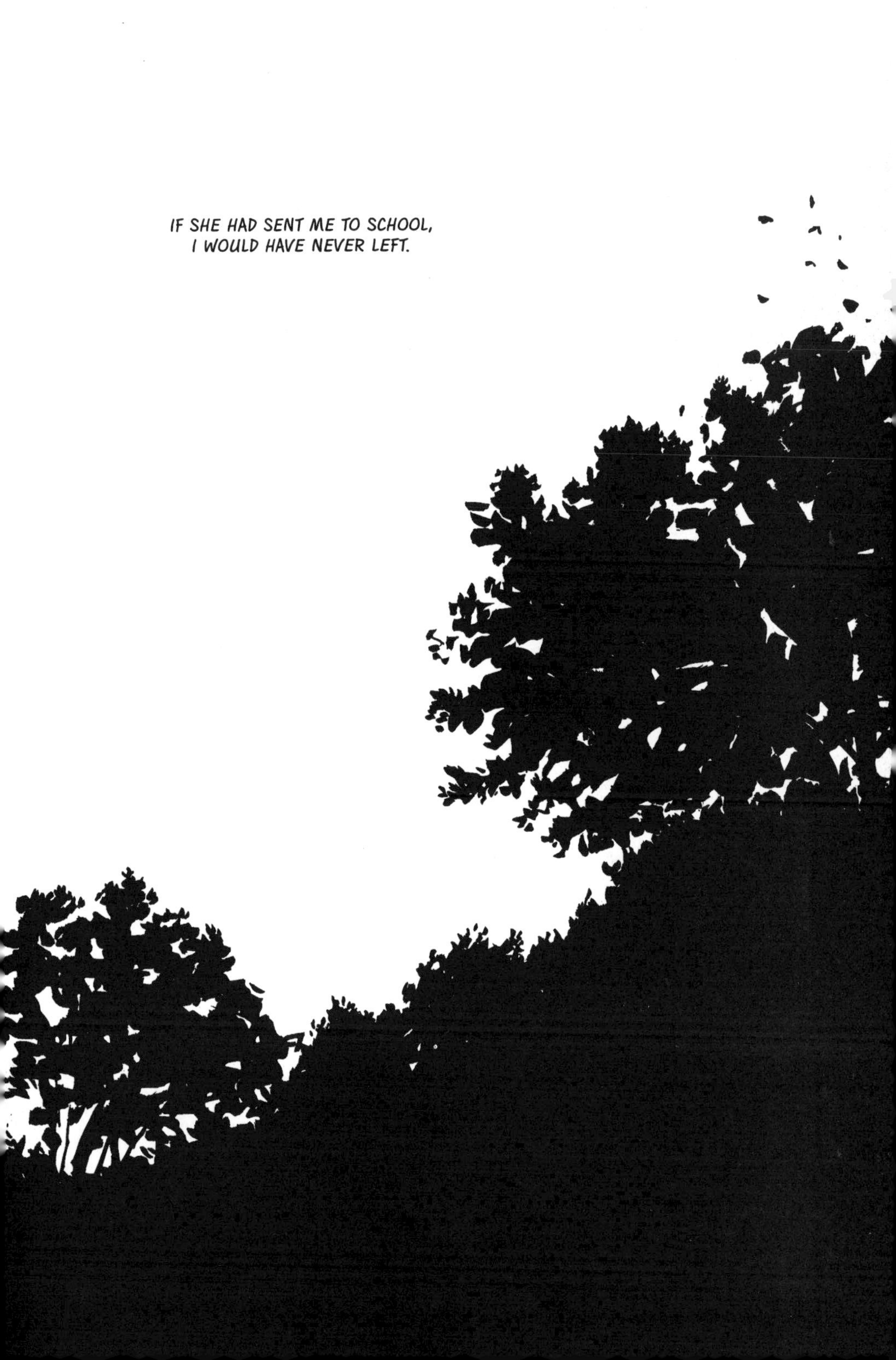
IF SHE HAD SENT ME TO SCHOOL,
I WOULD HAVE NEVER LEFT.

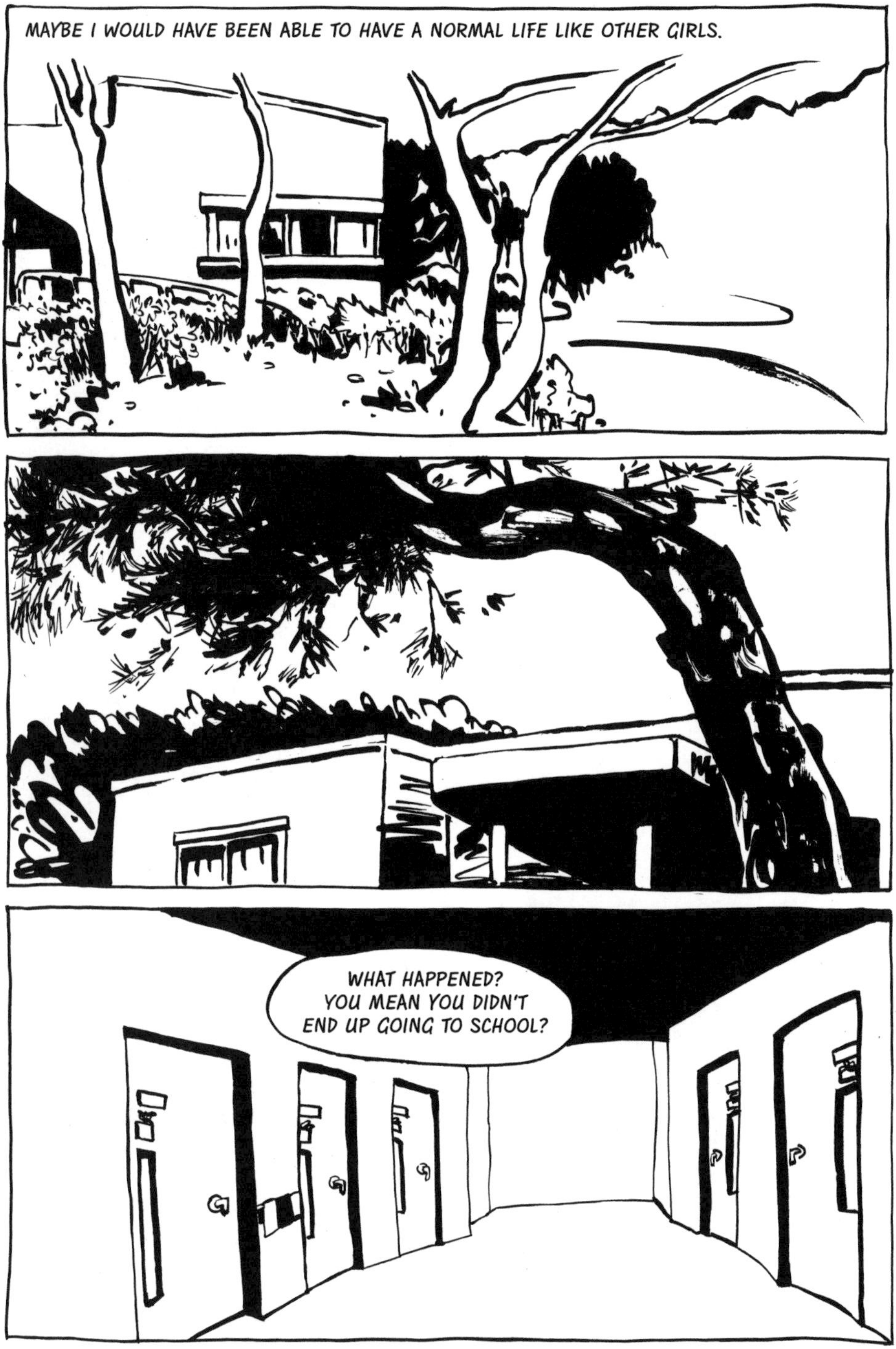
MAYBE I WOULD HAVE BEEN ABLE TO HAVE A NORMAL LIFE LIKE OTHER GIRLS.
WHAT HAPPENED? YOU MEAN YOU DIDN'T END UP GOING TO SCHOOL?

GRANNY LEE OK-SUN
OF COURSE I WENT.
I MAY NOT LOOK IT, BUT I GRADUATED FROM HOMI UNIVERSITY.
REALLY?
HOMI UNIVERSITY?
I'VE NEVER HEARD OF IT.
IS IT IN CHINA?
우리 시간표
http://twitter.com
homestory
YOU'LL NEVER FIND IT EVEN IF YOU LOOKED FOR A HUNDRED DAYS.
HEH HEH
?
I WORKED EVERY DAY IN THE FIELD WITH A HOMI,* SO I WENT TO HOMI UNIVERSITY.

*THE HOMI IS A VERSATILE HAND HOE USED EXTENSIVELY IN KOREA FOR PLOWING, PLANTING, AND DIGGING.

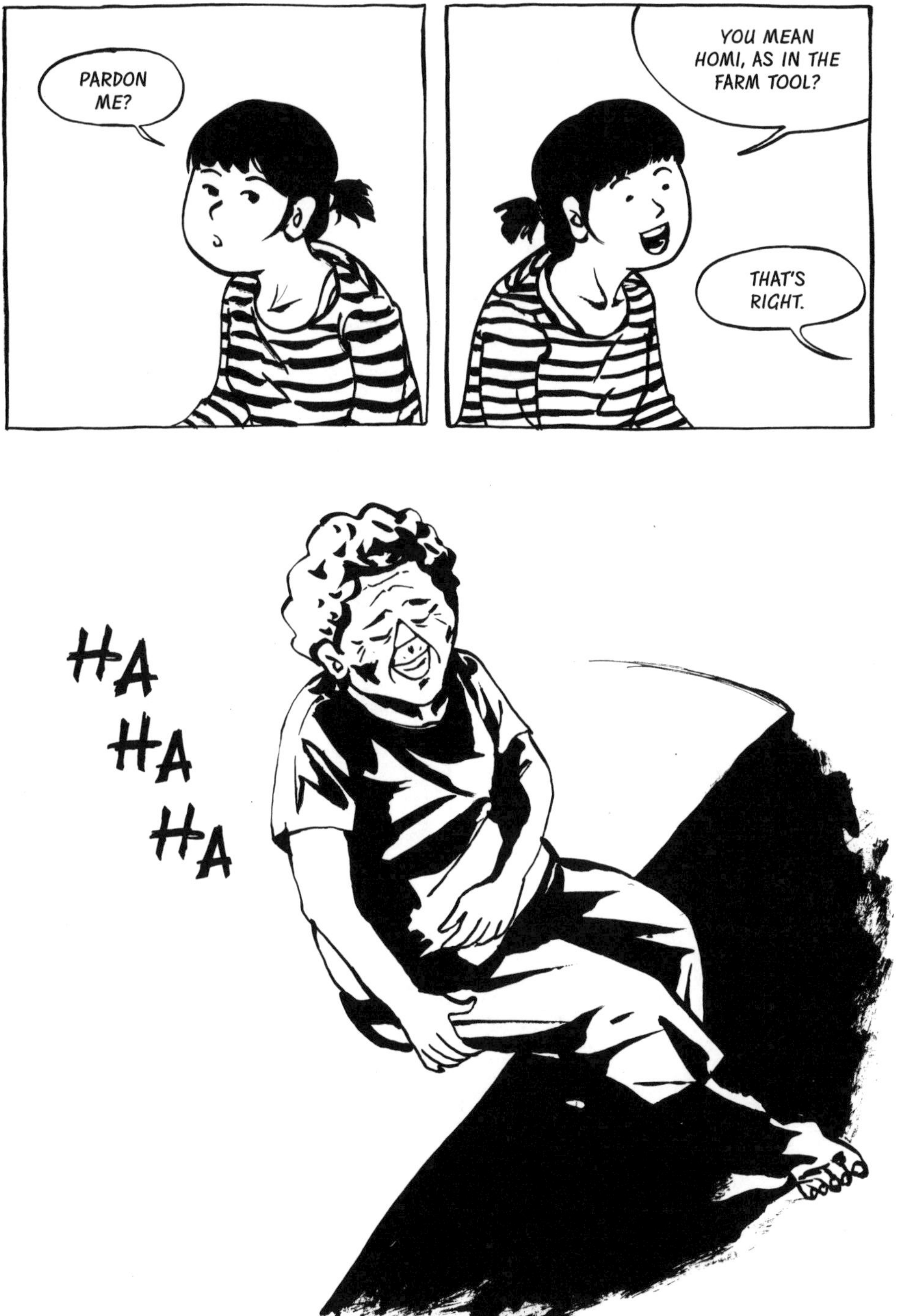
PARDON ME?
YOU MEAN HOMI, AS IN THE FARM TOOL?
THAT'S RIGHT.
HA HA HA

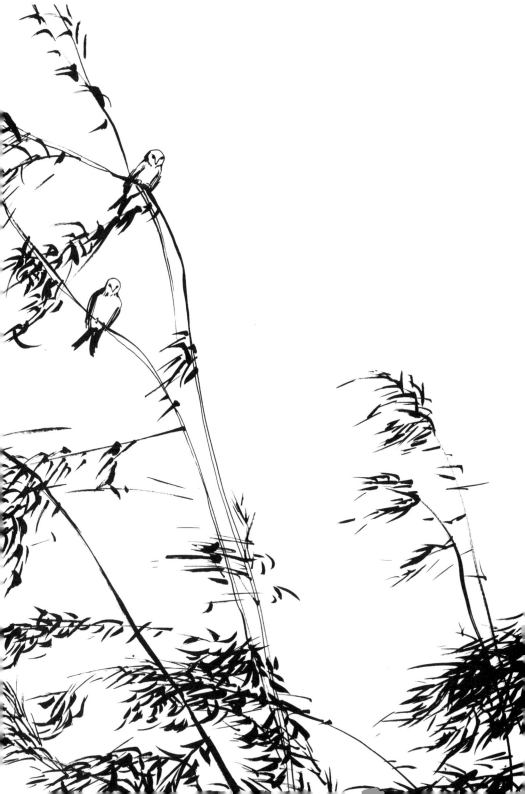

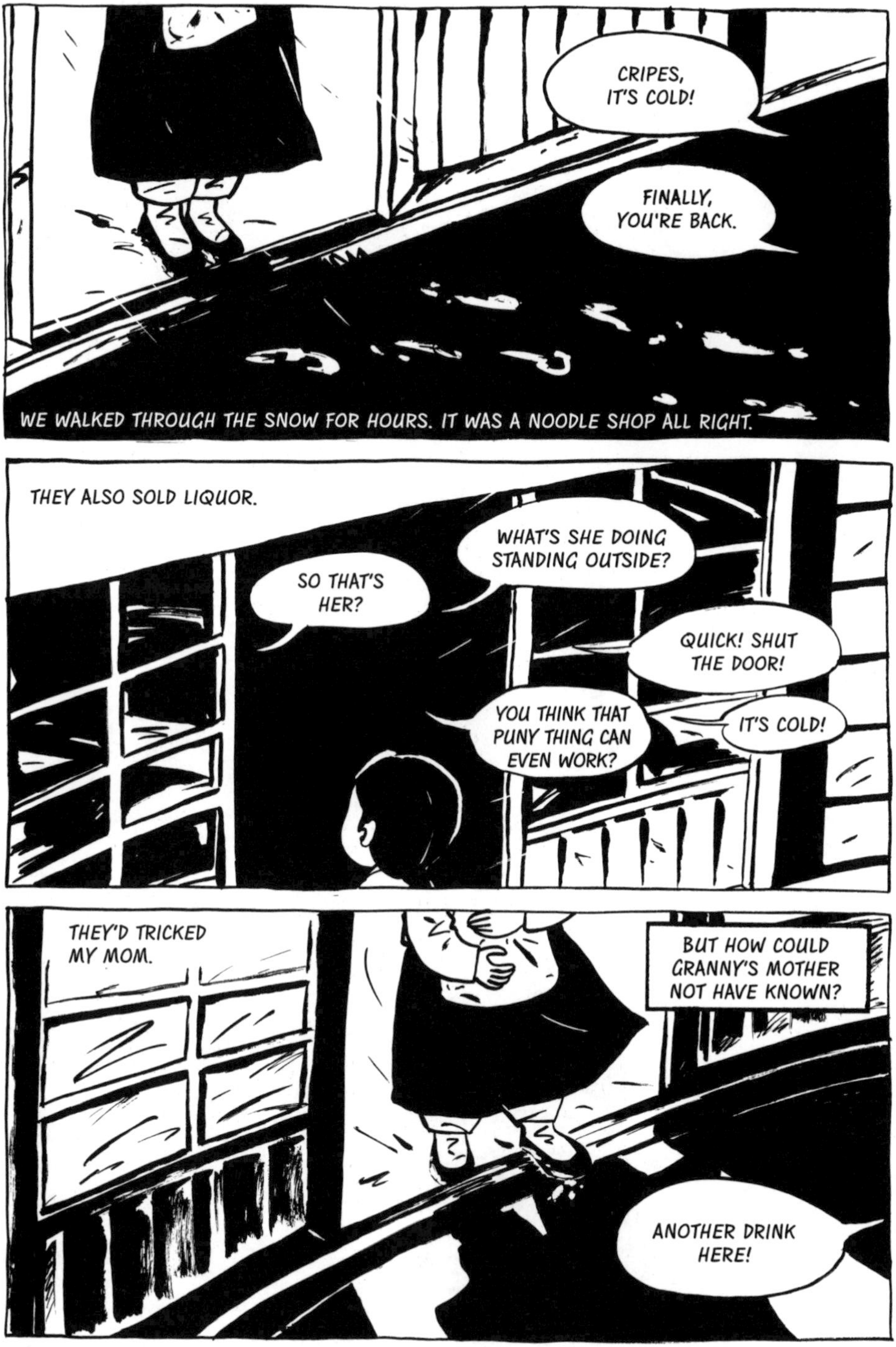
CRIPES, IT'S COLD!
FINALLY, YOU'RE BACK.
WE WALKED THROUGH THE SNOW FOR HOURS. IT WAS A NOODLE SHOP ALL RIGHT.
THEY ALSO SOLD LIQUOR.
SO THAT'S HER?
WHAT'S SHE DOING STANDING OUTSIDE?
QUICK! SHUT THE DOOR!
YOU THINK THAT PUNY THING CAN EVEN WORK?
IT'S COLD!
THEY'D TRICKED MY MOM.
BUT HOW COULD GRANNY'S MOTHER NOT HAVE KNOWN?
ANOTHER DRINK HERE!

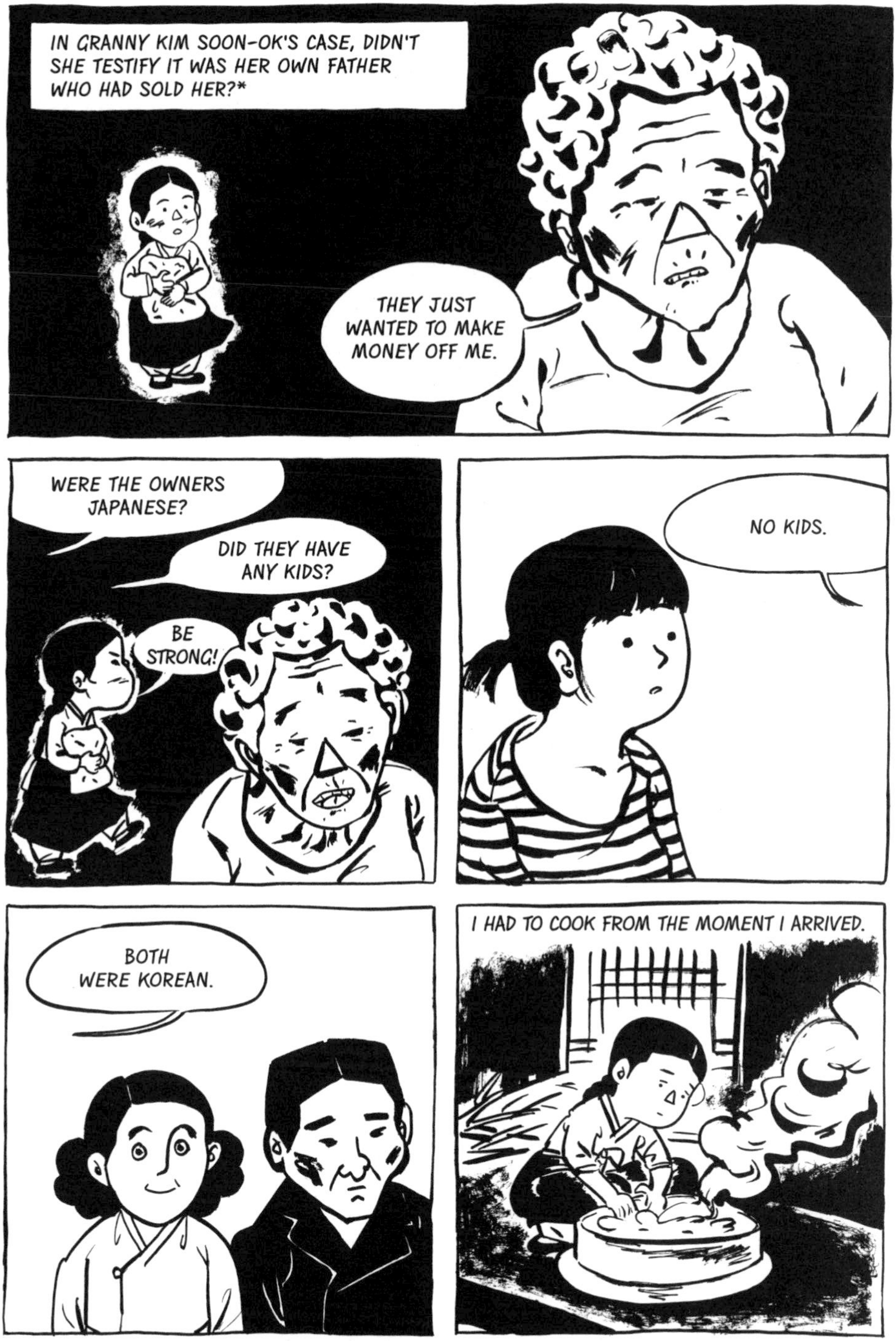
IN GRANNY KIM SOON-OK'S CASE, DIDN'T SHE TESTIFY IT WAS HER OWN FATHER WHO HAD SOLD HER?*
THEY JUST WANTED TO MAKE MONEY OFF ME.
WERE THE OWNERS JAPANESE?
DID THEY HAVE ANY KIDS?
BE STRONG!
NO KIDS.
BOTH WERE KOREAN.
I HAD TO COOK FROM THE MOMENT I ARRIVED.

*KIM SOON-OK WAS BORN IN PYEONGYANG IN 1922. IN 1940, SHE WAS TAKEN TO HEILONGJIANG PROVINCE, CHINA, WHERE SHE WAS FORCED TO SERVE AS A COMFORT WOMAN.

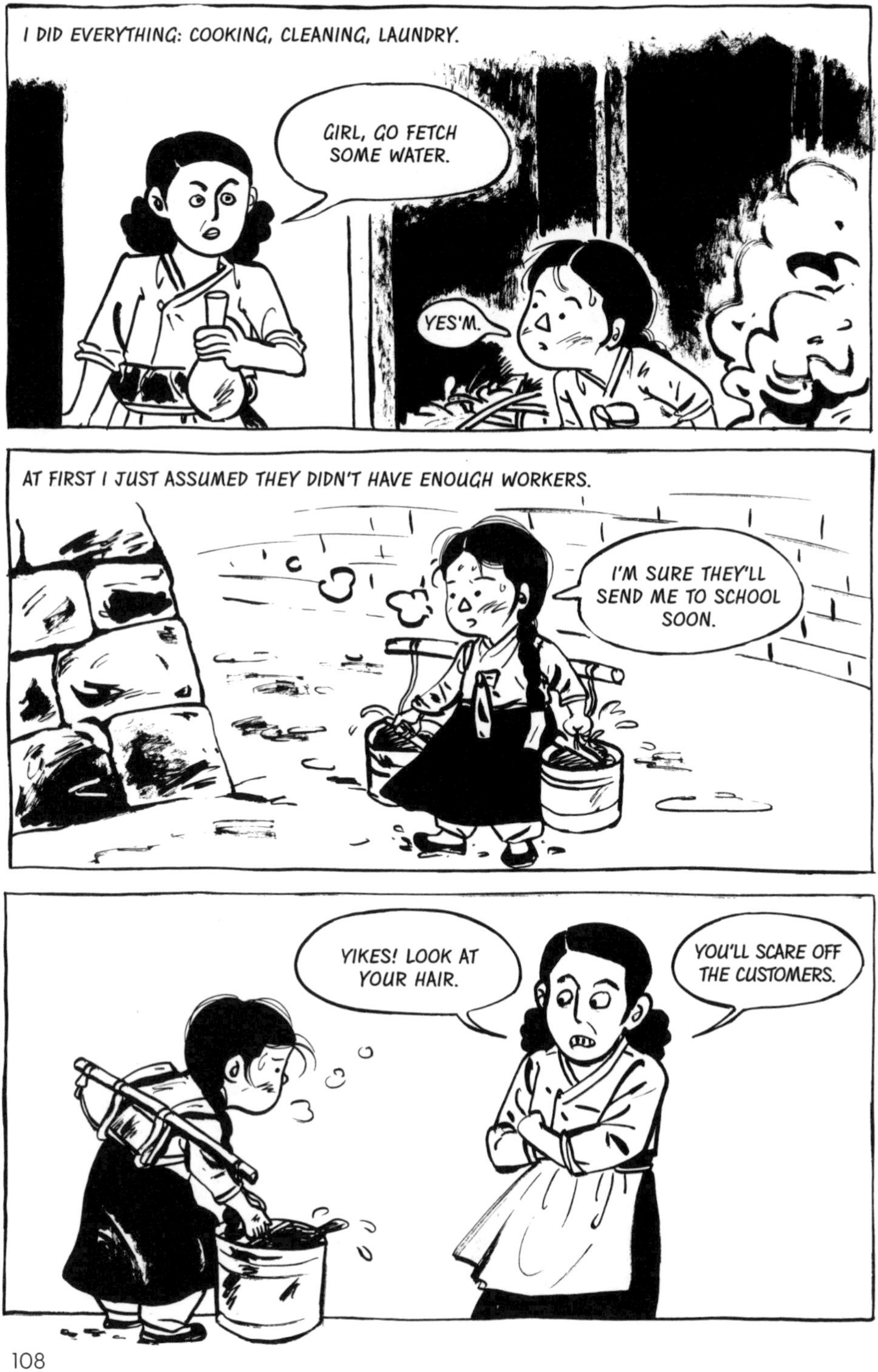
I DID EVERYTHING: COOKING, CLEANING, LAUNDRY.
GIRL, GO FETCH SOME WATER.
YES'M.
AT FIRST I JUST ASSUMED THEY DIDN'T HAVE ENOUGH WORKERS.
I'M SURE THEY'LL SEND ME TO SCHOOL SOON.
YIKES! LOOK AT YOUR HAIR.
YOU'LL SCARE OFF THE CUSTOMERS.

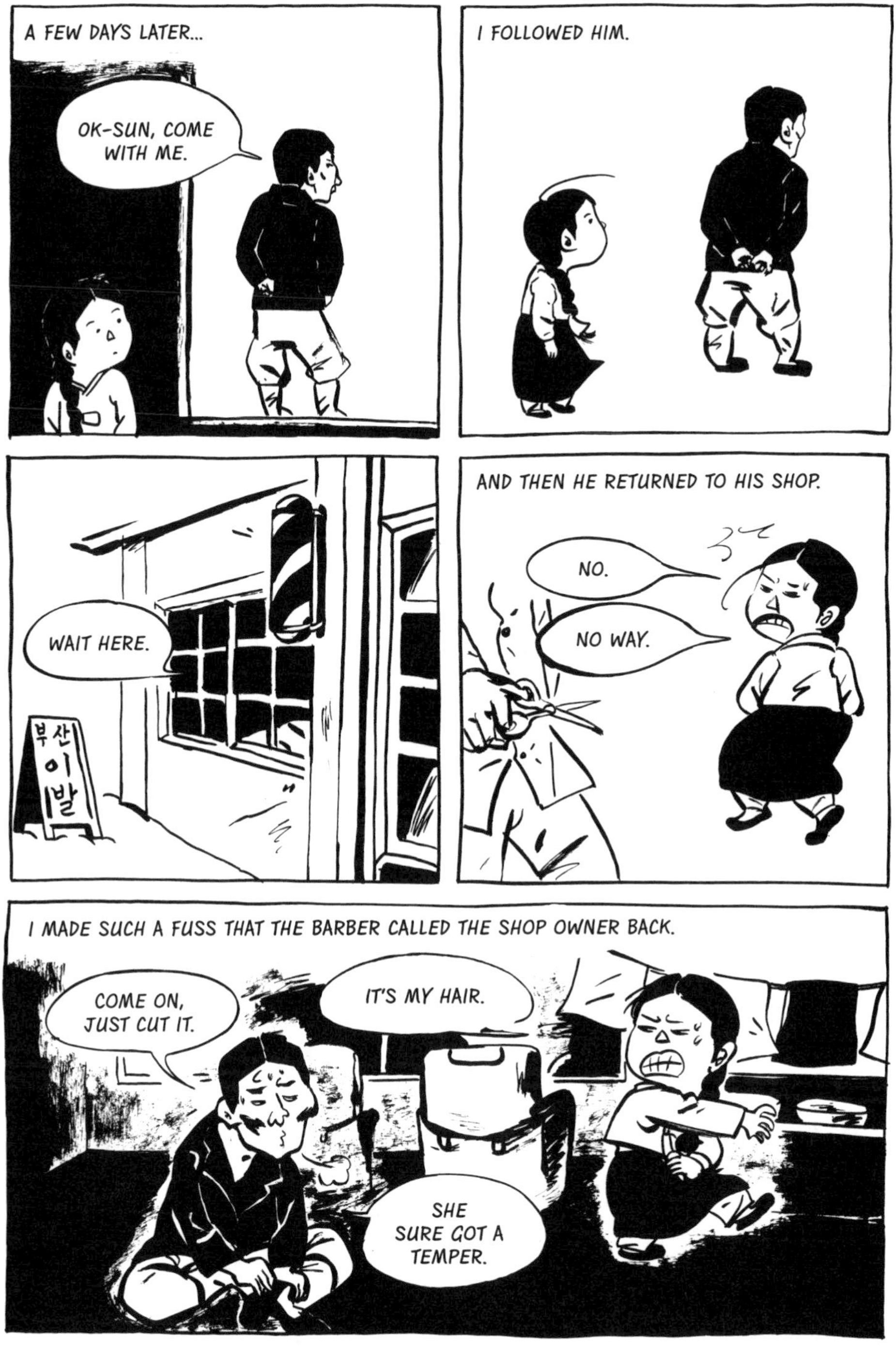
A FEW DAYS LATER...
OK-SUN, COME WITH ME.
I FOLLOWED HIM.
WAIT HERE.
부산 이발
AND THEN HE RETURNED TO HIS SHOP.
NO.
NO WAY.
I MADE SUCH A FUSS THAT THE BARBER CALLED THE SHOP OWNER BACK.
COME ON, JUST CUT IT.
IT'S MY HAIR.
SHE SURE GOT A TEMPER.

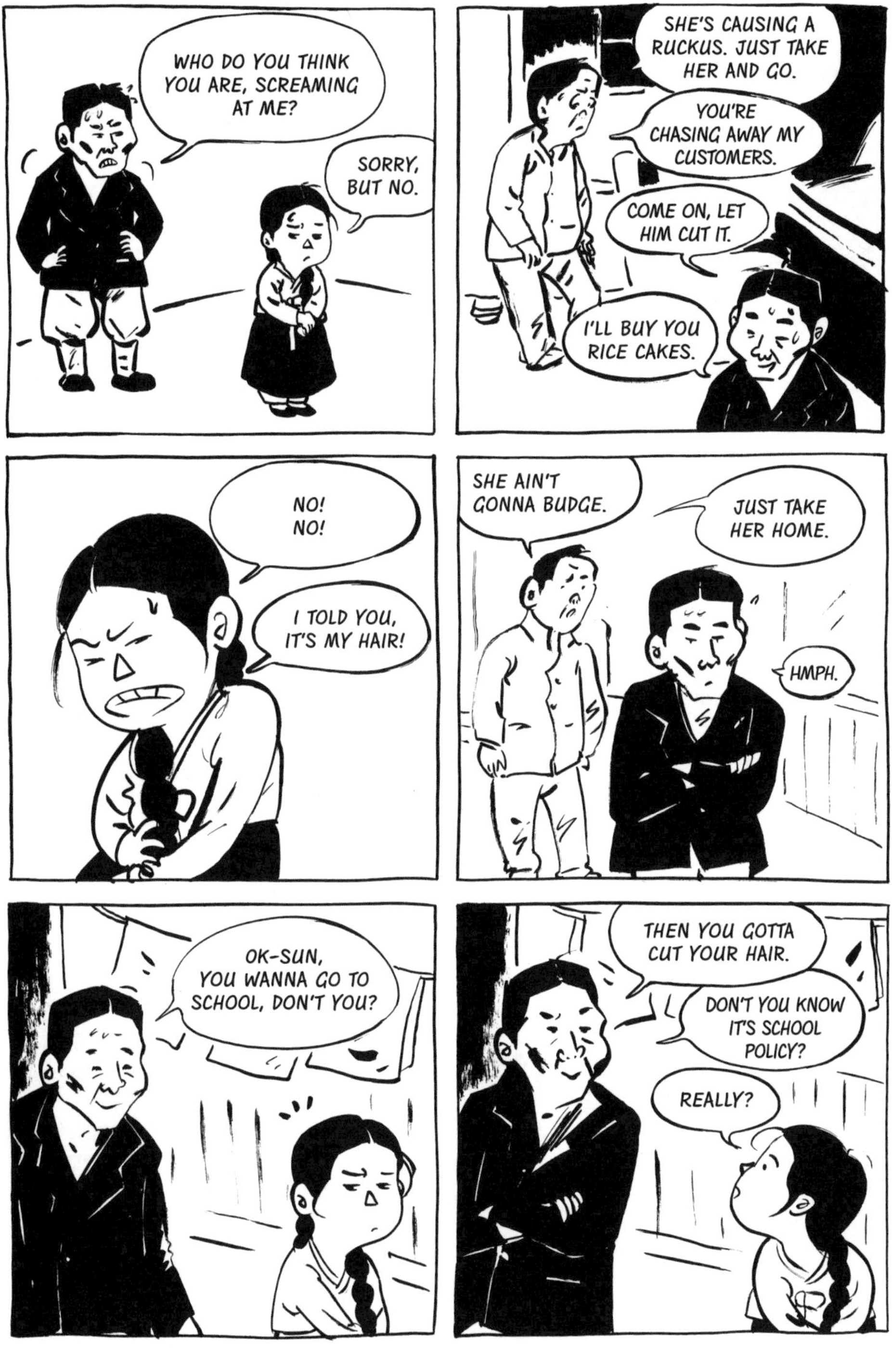
WHO DO YOU THINK YOU ARE, SCREAMING AT ME?
SORRY, BUT NO.
SHE'S CAUSING A RUCKUS. JUST TAKE HER AND GO.
YOU'RE CHASING AWAY MY CUSTOMERS.
COME ON, LET HIM CUT IT.
I'LL BUY YOU RICE CAKES.
NO! NO!
I TOLD YOU, IT'S MY HAIR!
SHE AIN'T GONNA BUDGE.
JUST TAKE HER HOME.
HMPH.
OK-SUN, YOU WANNA GO TO SCHOOL, DON'T YOU?
THEN YOU GOTTA CUT YOUR HAIR.
DON'T YOU KNOW IT'S SCHOOL POLICY?
REALLY?

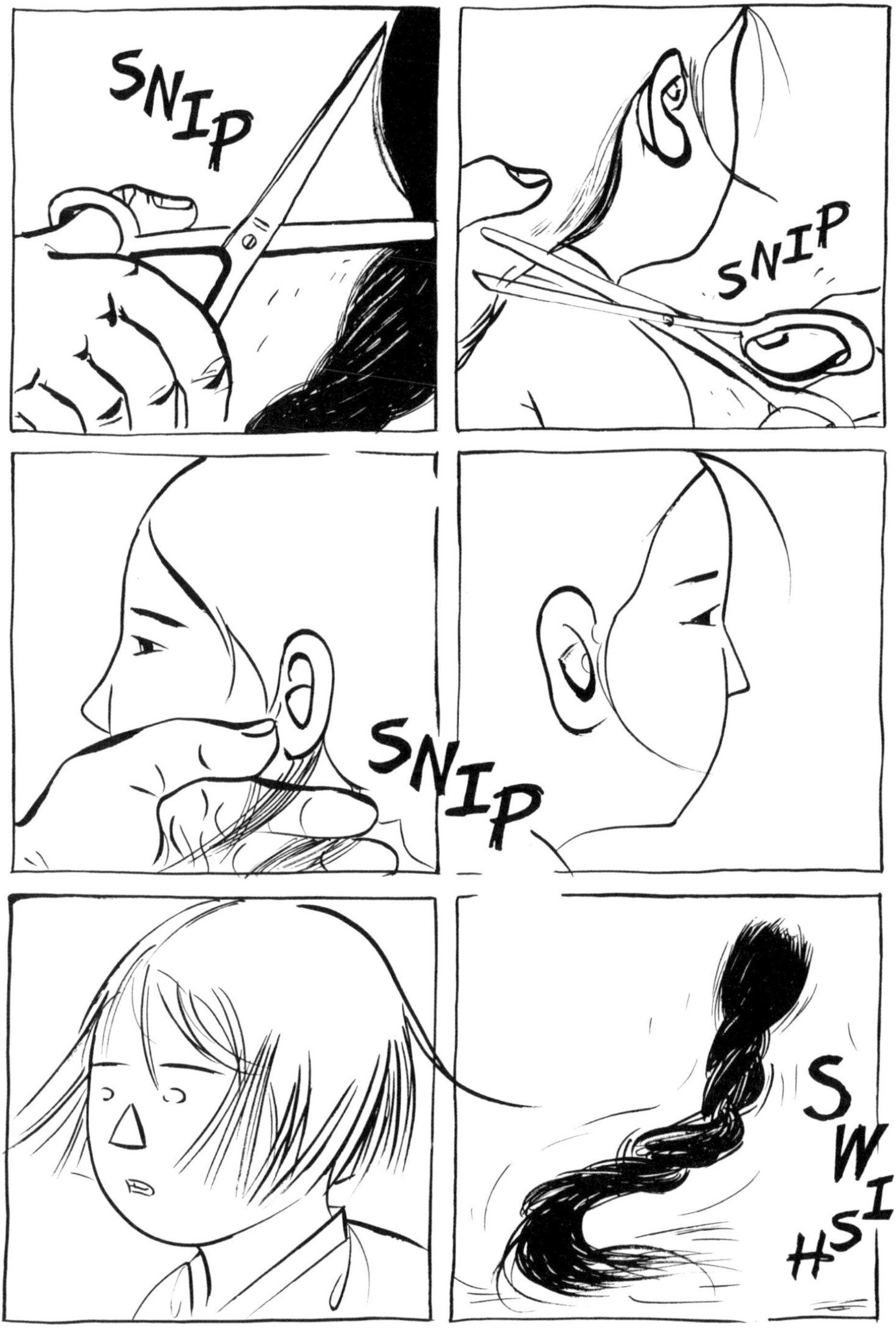
SNIP
SNIP
SNIP
SWISH

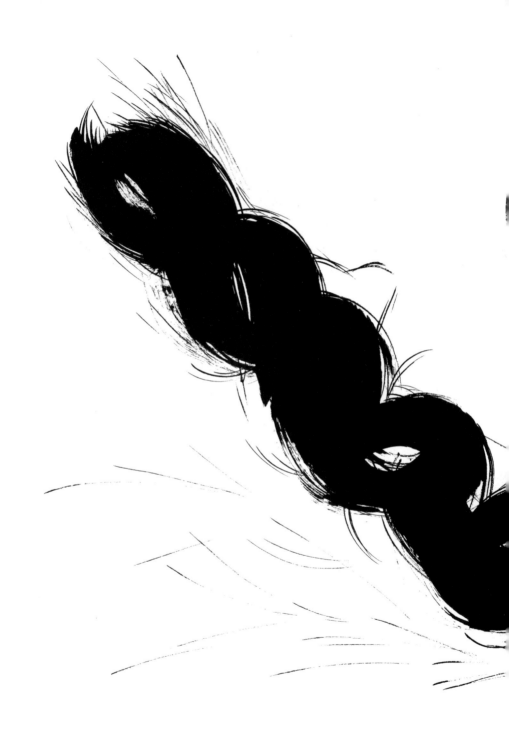

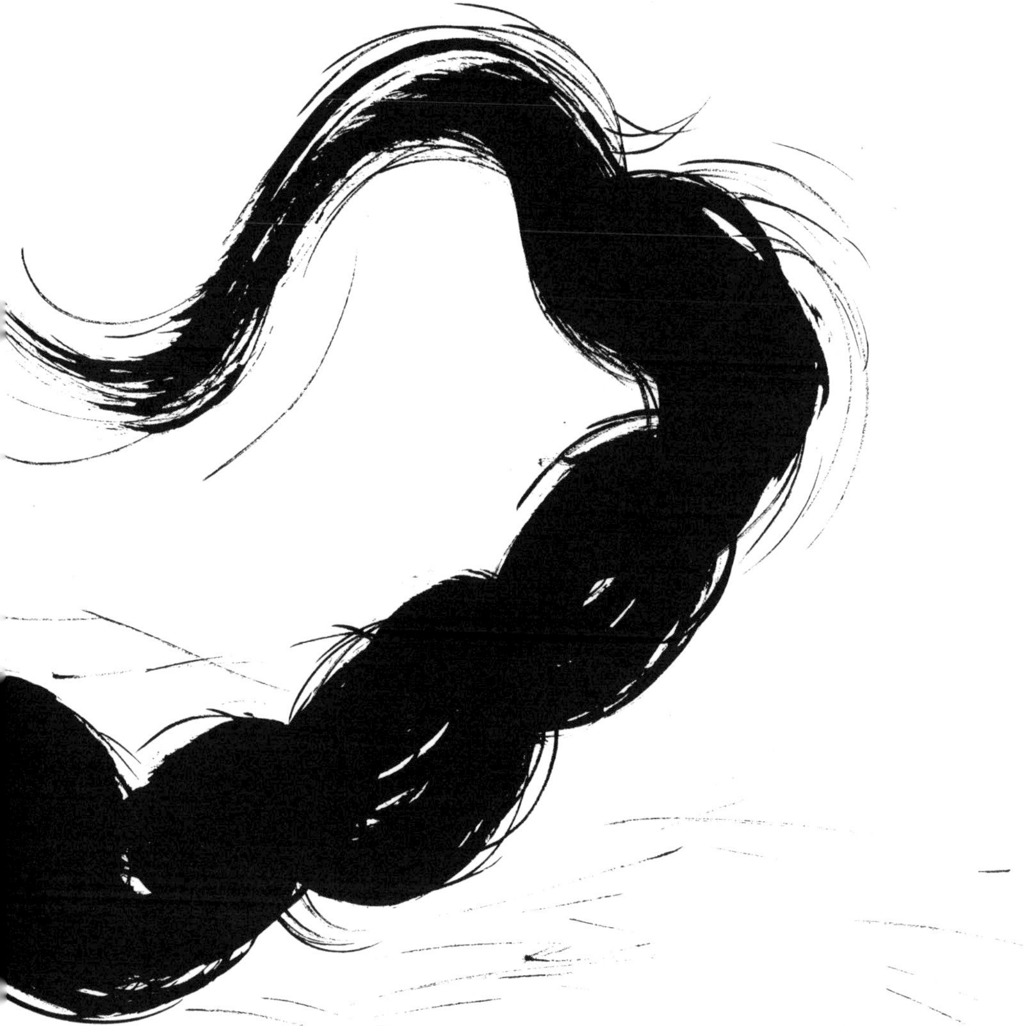

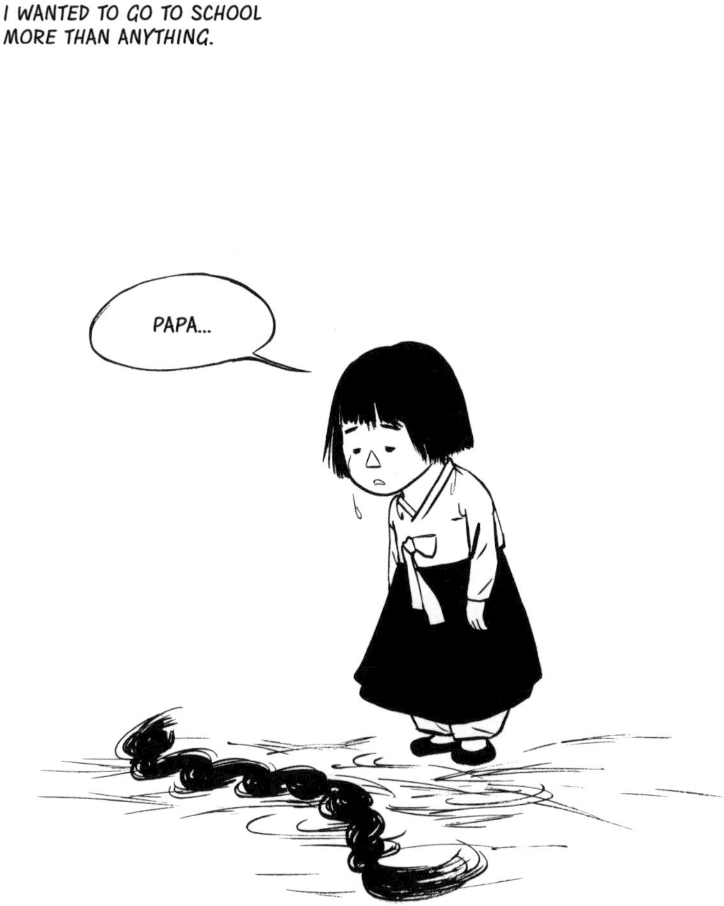
I WANTED TO GO TO SCHOOL MORE THAN ANYTHING.
PAPA...

IT WAS ALL A TRICK. A MONTH PASSED AND NOTHING CHANGED.
THEY WERE NEVER GOING TO SEND ME TO SCHOOL.

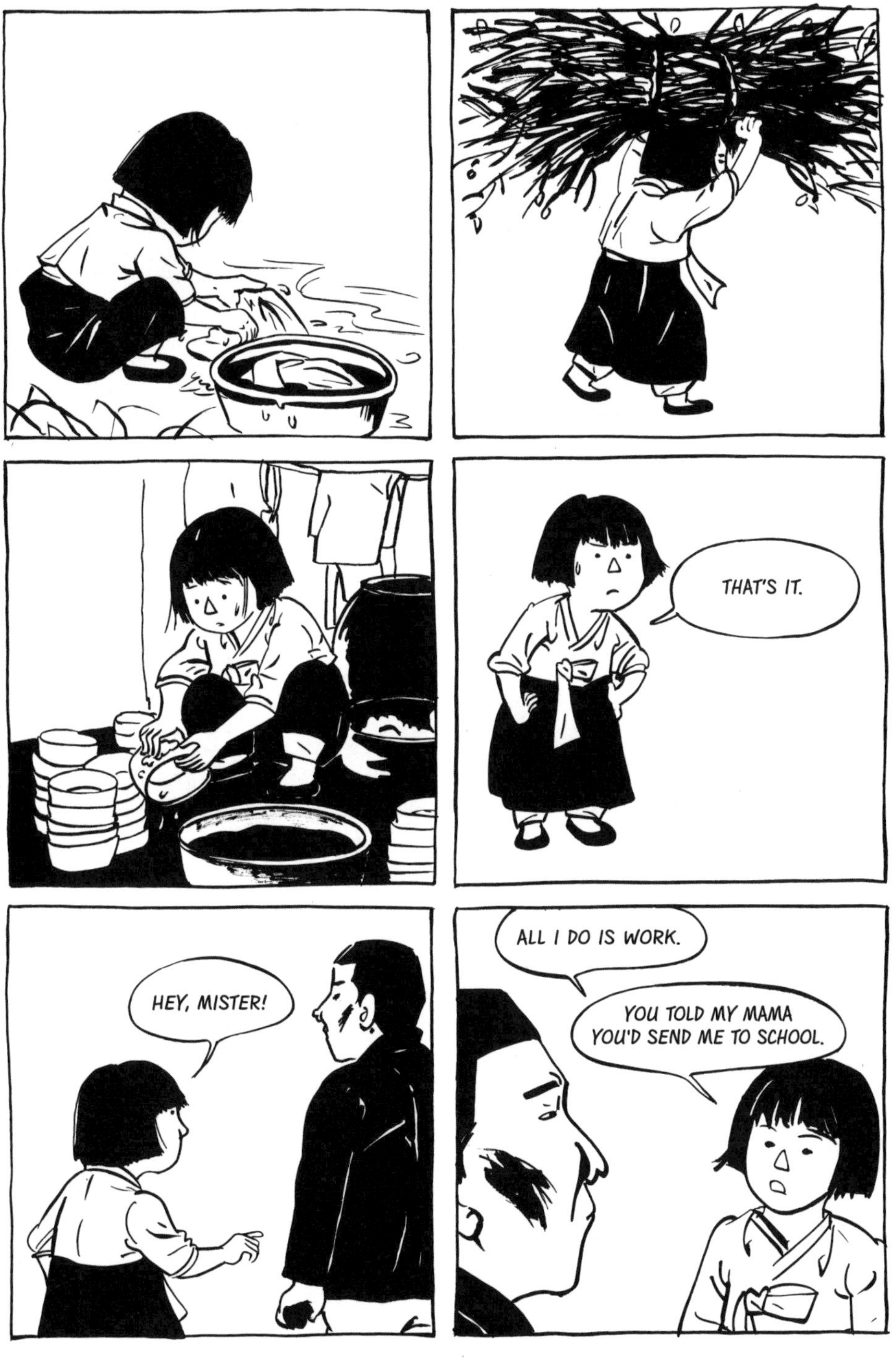
THAT'S IT.
HEY, MISTER!
ALL I DO IS WORK.
YOU TOLD MY MAMA YOU'D SEND ME TO SCHOOL.

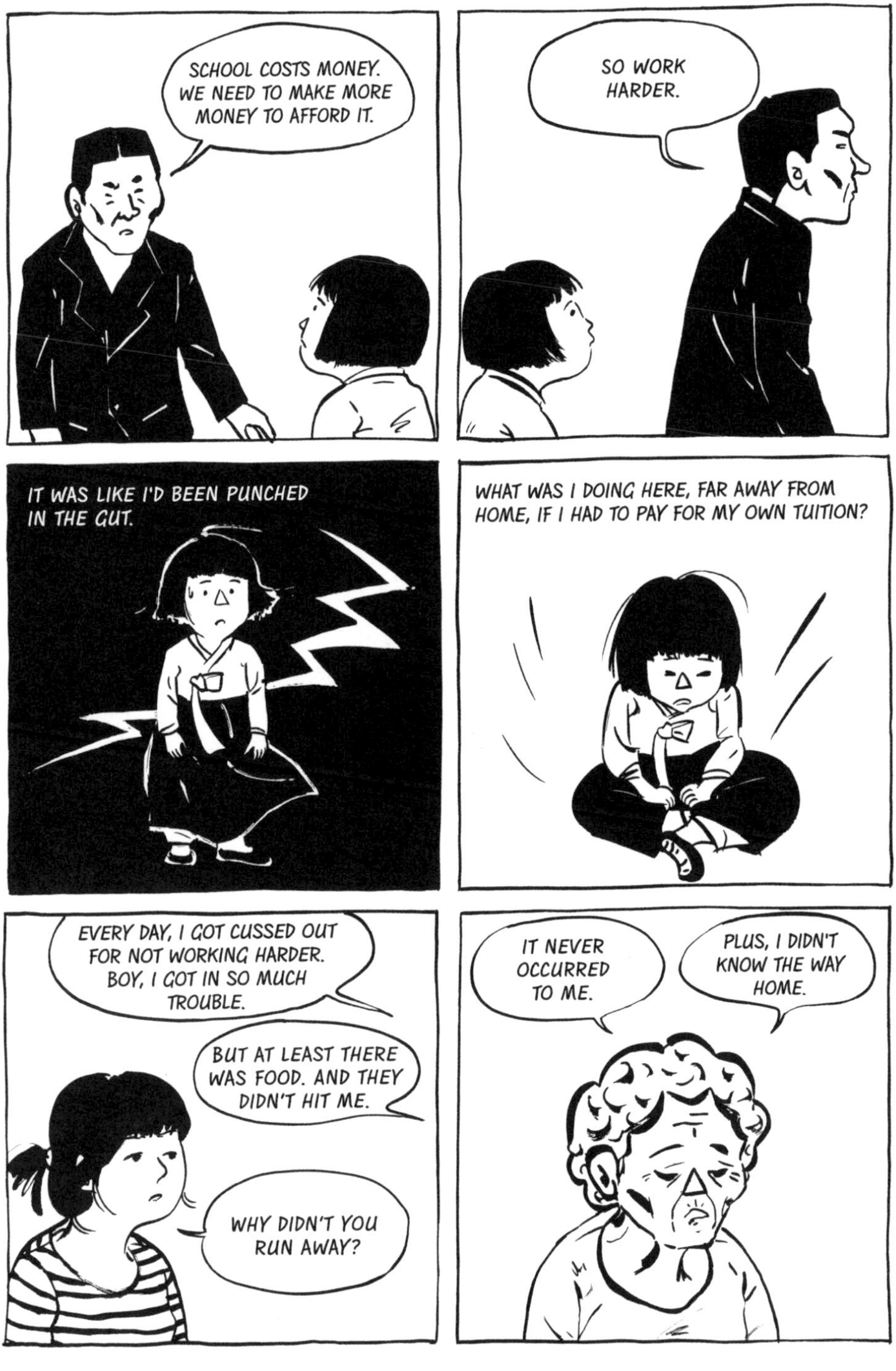
SCHOOL COSTS MONEY. WE NEED TO MAKE MORE MONEY TO AFFORD IT.
SO WORK HARDER.
IT WAS LIKE I'D BEEN PUNCHED IN THE GUT.
WHAT WAS I DOING HERE, FAR AWAY FROM HOME, IF I HAD TO PAY FOR MY OWN TUITION?
EVERY DAY, I GOT CUSSED OUT FOR NOT WORKING HARDER. BOY, I GOT IN SO MUCH TROUBLE.
BUT AT LEAST THERE WAS FOOD. AND THEY DIDN'T HIT ME.
WHY DIDN'T YOU RUN AWAY?
IT NEVER OCCURRED TO ME.
PLUS, I DIDN'T KNOW THE WAY HOME.

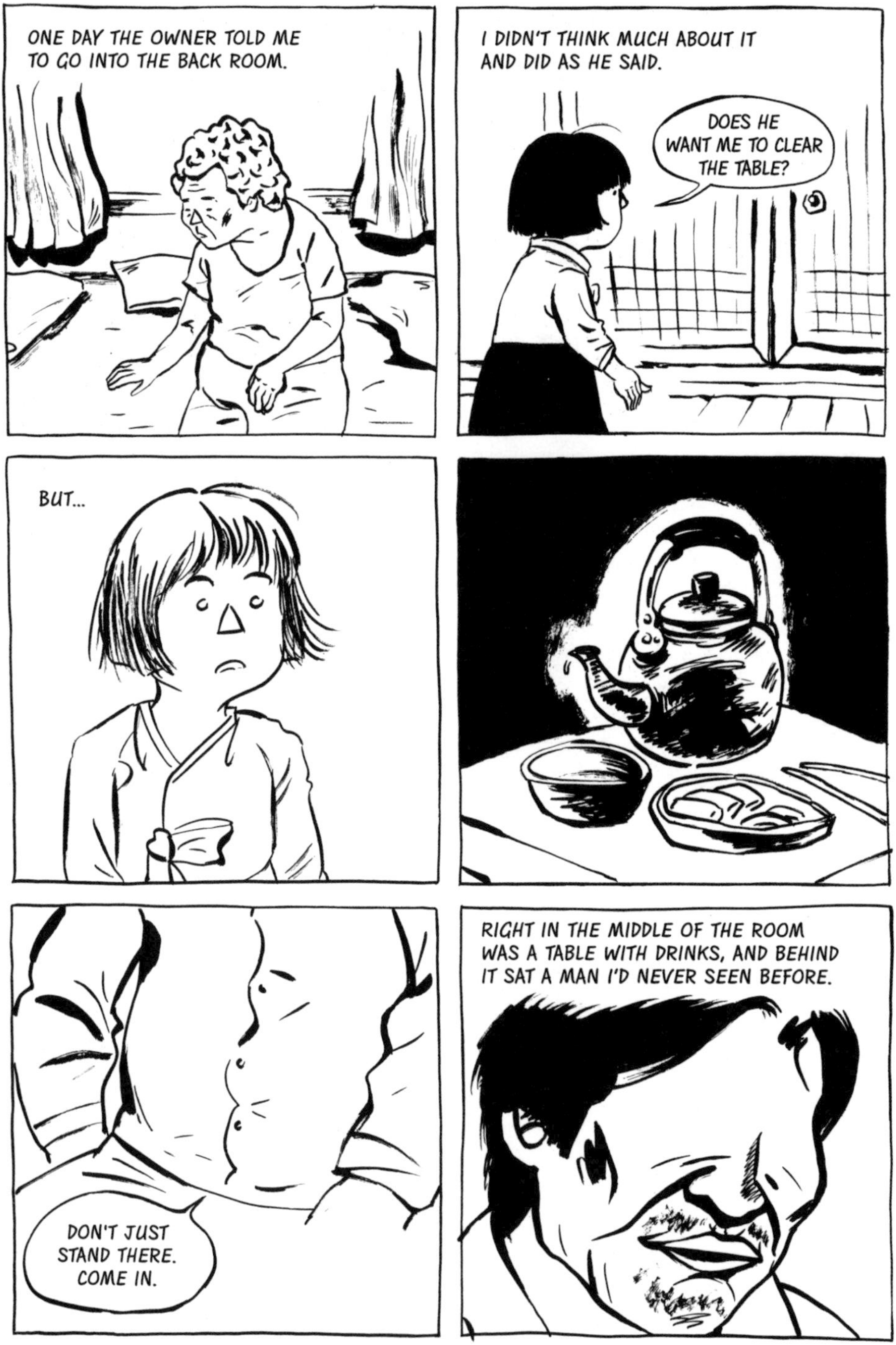
ONE DAY THE OWNER TOLD ME TO GO INTO THE BACK ROOM.
I DIDN'T THINK MUCH ABOUT IT AND DID AS HE SAID.
DOES HE WANT ME TO CLEAR THE TABLE?
BUT...
DON'T JUST STAND THERE. COME IN.
RIGHT IN THE MIDDLE OF THE ROOM WAS A TABLE WITH DRINKS, AND BEHIND IT SAT A MAN I'D NEVER SEEN BEFORE.

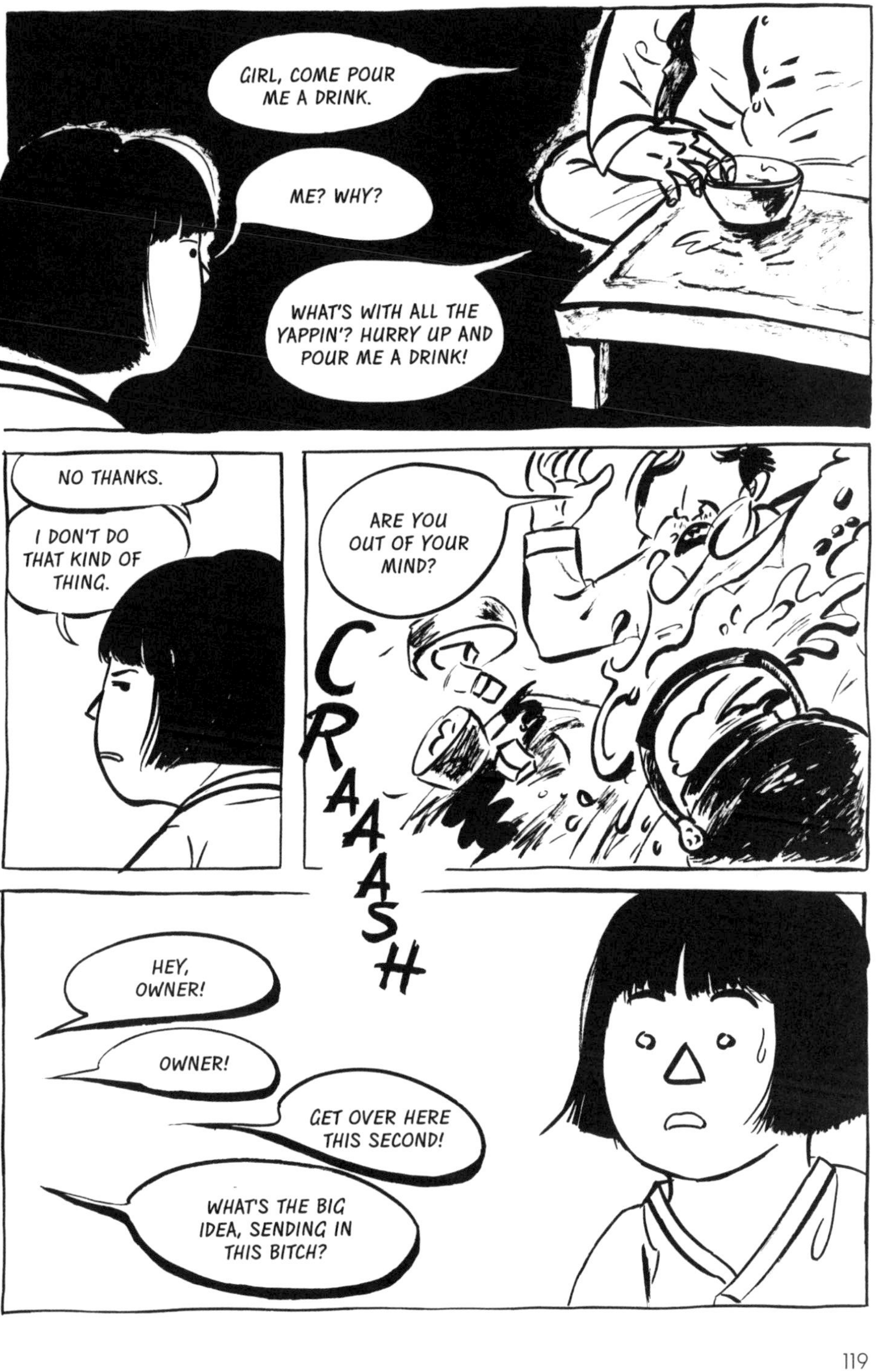
GIRL, COME POUR ME A DRINK.
ME? WHY?
WHAT'S WITH ALL THE YAPPIN'? HURRY UP AND POUR ME A DRINK!
NO THANKS.
I DON'T DO THAT KIND OF THING.
ARE YOU OUT OF YOUR MIND?
CRAAASH
HEY, OWNER!
OWNER!
GET OVER HERE THIS SECOND!
WHAT'S THE BIG IDEA, SENDING IN THIS BITCH?

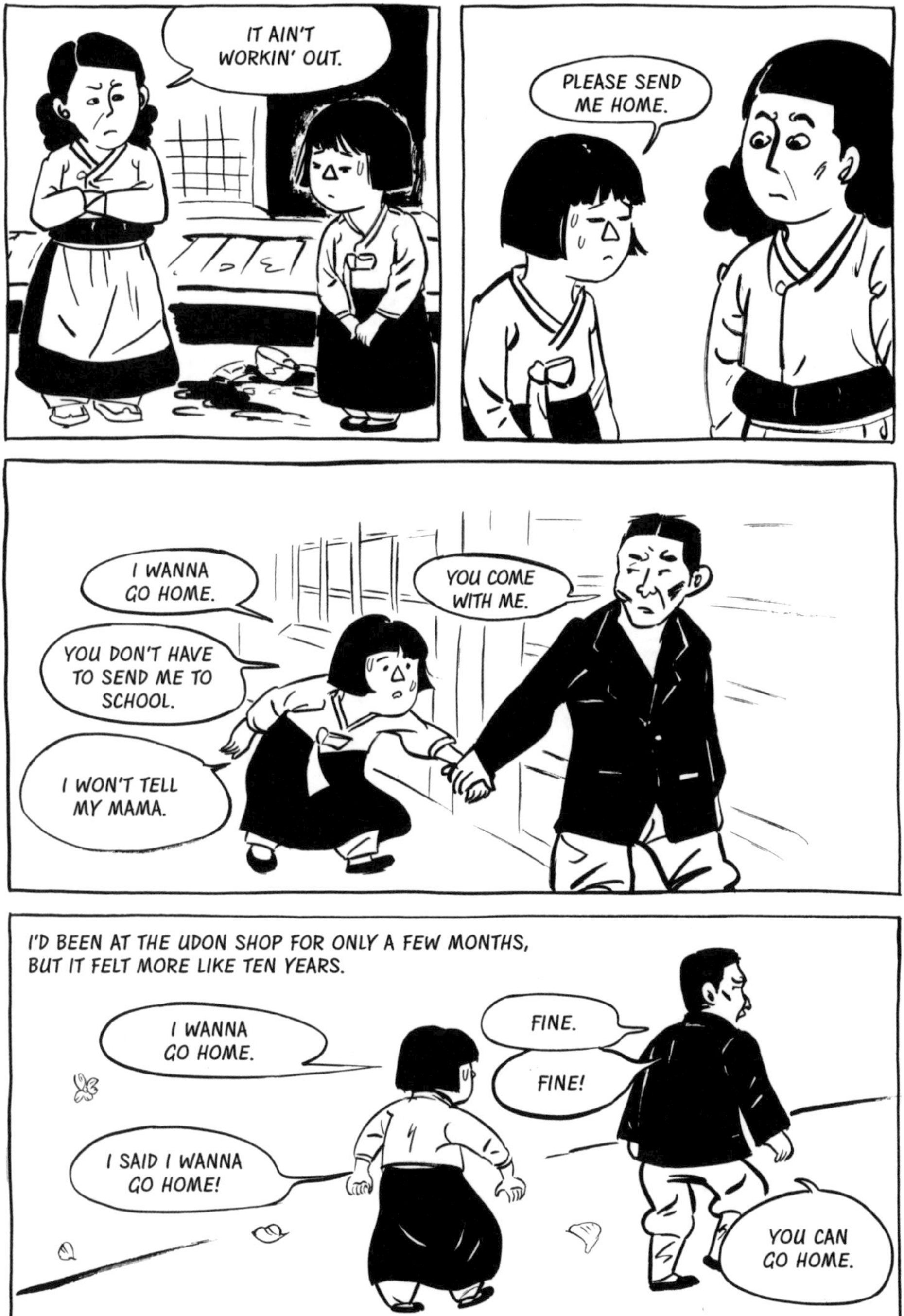
IT AIN'T WORKIN' OUT.
PLEASE SEND ME HOME.
I WANNA GO HOME.
YOU COME WITH ME.
YOU DON'T HAVE TO SEND ME TO SCHOOL.
I WON'T TELL MY MAMA.
I'D BEEN AT THE UDON SHOP FOR ONLY A FEW MONTHS, BUT IT FELT MORE LIKE TEN YEARS.
I WANNA GO HOME.
FINE.
FINE!
I SAID I WANNA GO HOME!
YOU CAN GO HOME.

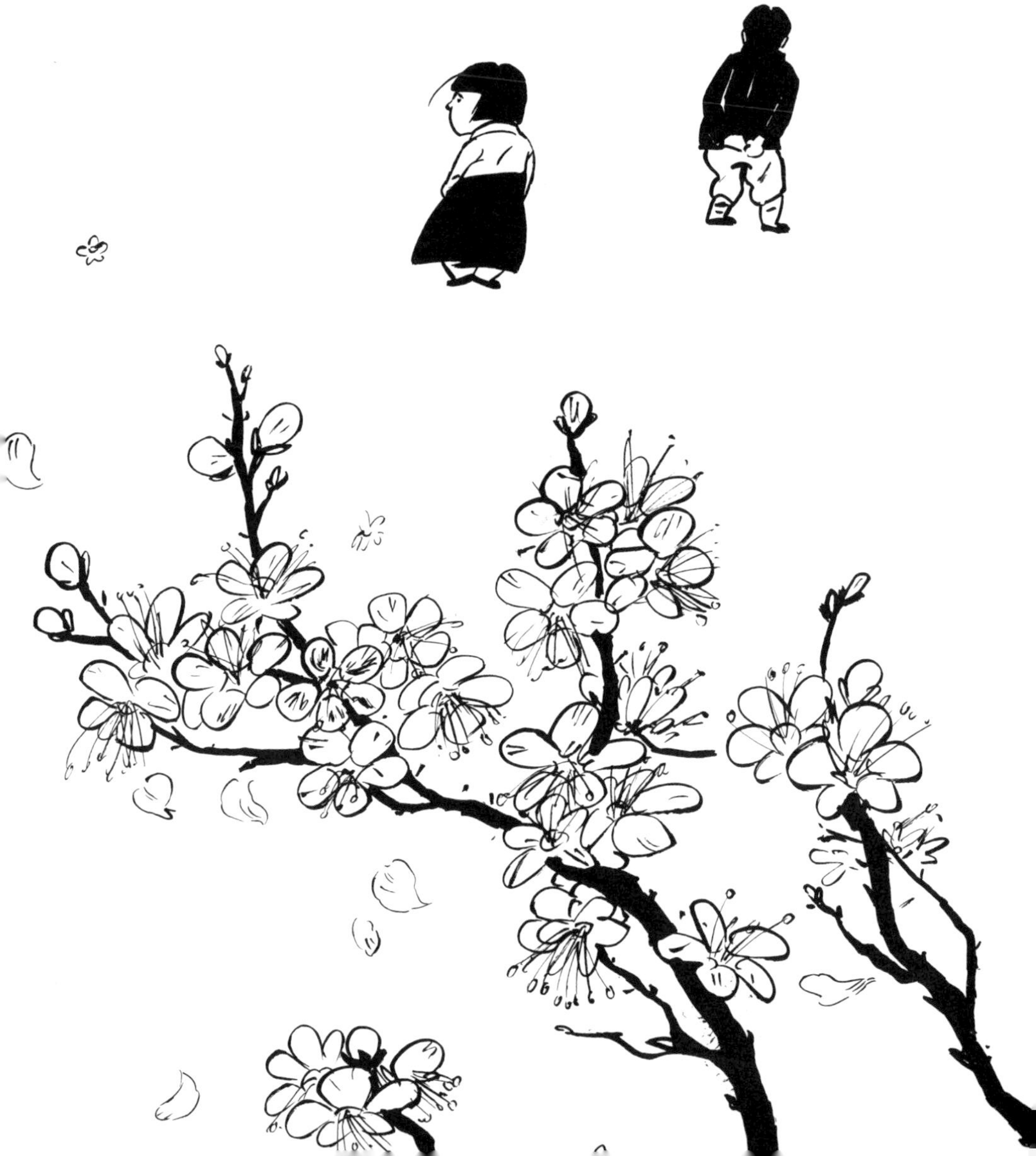

# ULSAN TAVERN

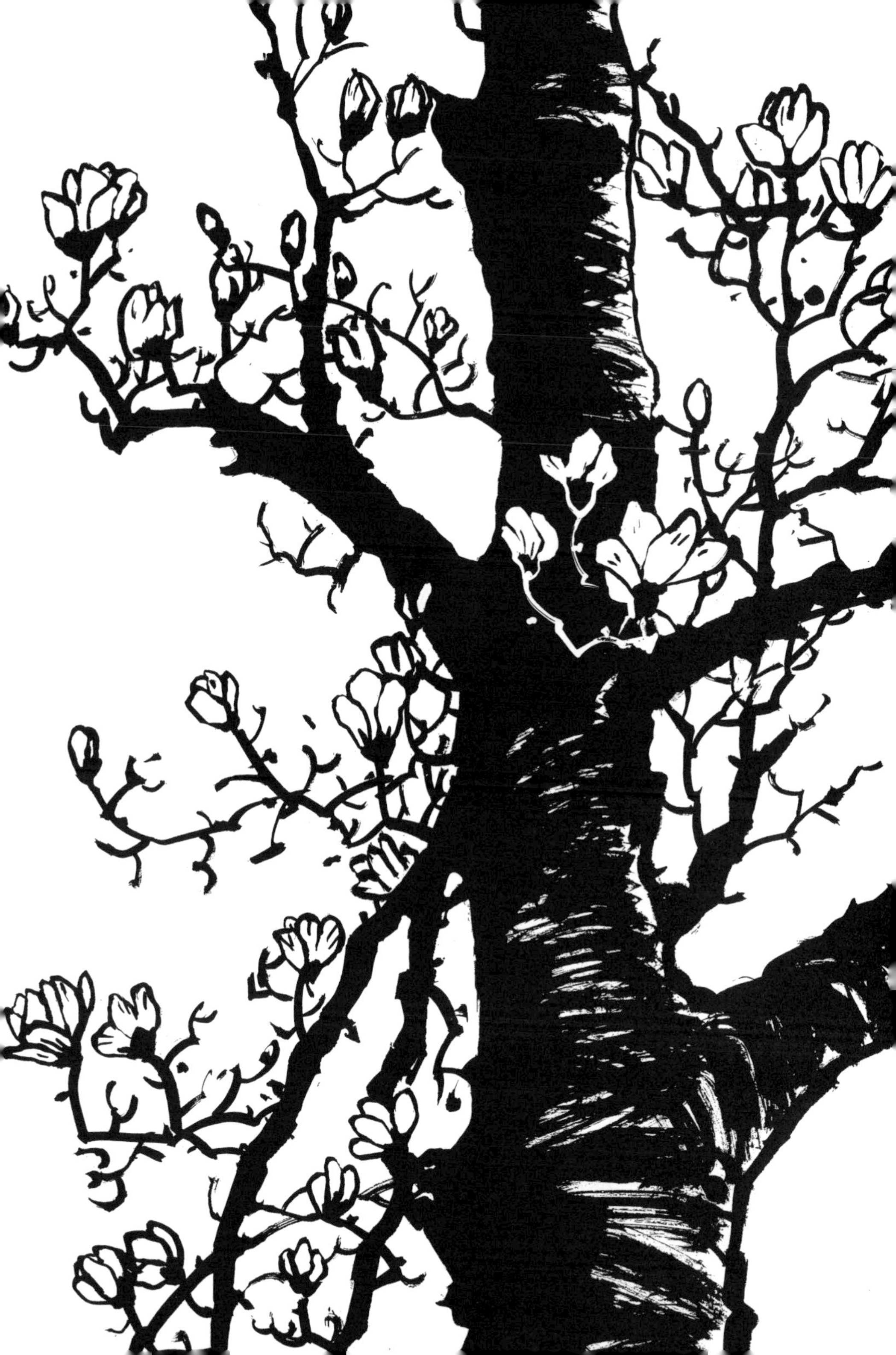

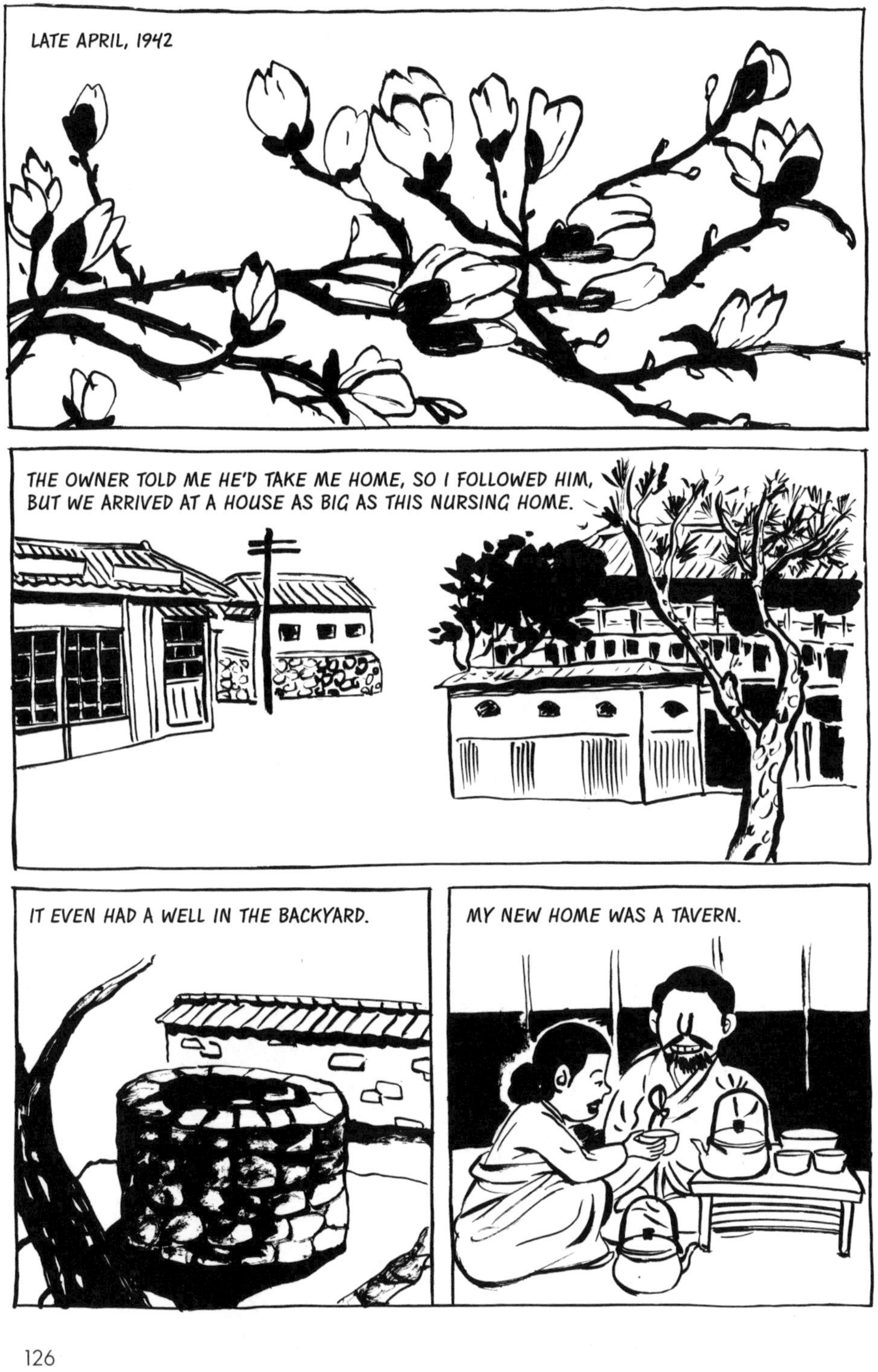
LATE APRIL, 1942
THE OWNER TOLD ME HE'D TAKE ME HOME, SO I FOLLOWED HIM, BUT WE ARRIVED AT A HOUSE AS BIG AS THIS NURSING HOME.
IT EVEN HAD A WELL IN THE BACKYARD.
MY NEW HOME WAS A TAVERN.

HERE, WOMEN DANCED, SANG, AND PLAYED THE JANGGU DRUMS. THEY WERE CALLED THE GISAENG.*

AND I BECAME A MAID ONCE MORE.

THERE WAS A GIRL MY AGE WHO DID ALL THE COOKING AND CLEANING. SHE'D ARRIVED A YEAR BEFORE.

BUT THERE WAS TOO MUCH WORK FOR JUST ONE PERSON

SO I'D BEEN PURCHASED TO HELP HER.

DID THE GISAENG LIVE THERE, TOO?

*THE GISAENG WERE HIGHLY SKILLED FEMALE PERFORMERS, WHO ENTERTAINED MEN OF WEALTH OR NOBLE BIRTH WITH MUSIC, DANCE, AND LITERATURE, OFTEN PROVIDING SEXUAL SERVICES.

127

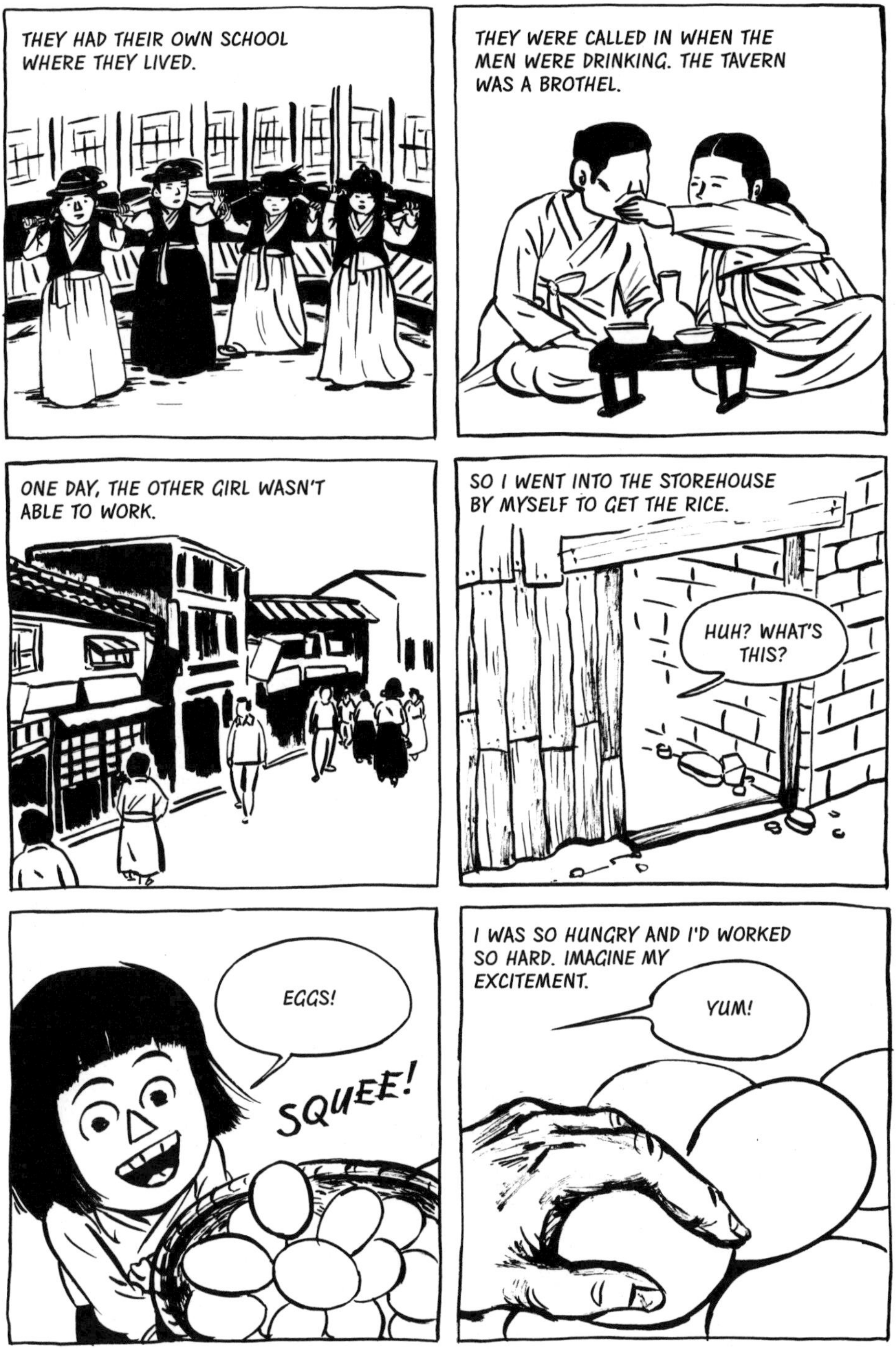
THEY HAD THEIR OWN SCHOOL WHERE THEY LIVED.
THEY WERE CALLED IN WHEN THE MEN WERE DRINKING. THE TAVERN WAS A BROTHEL.
ONE DAY, THE OTHER GIRL WASN'T ABLE TO WORK.
SO I WENT INTO THE STOREHOUSE BY MYSELF TO GET THE RICE.
HUH? WHAT'S THIS?
EGGS!
SQUEE!
I WAS SO HUNGRY AND I'D WORKED SO HARD. IMAGINE MY EXCITEMENT.
YUM!

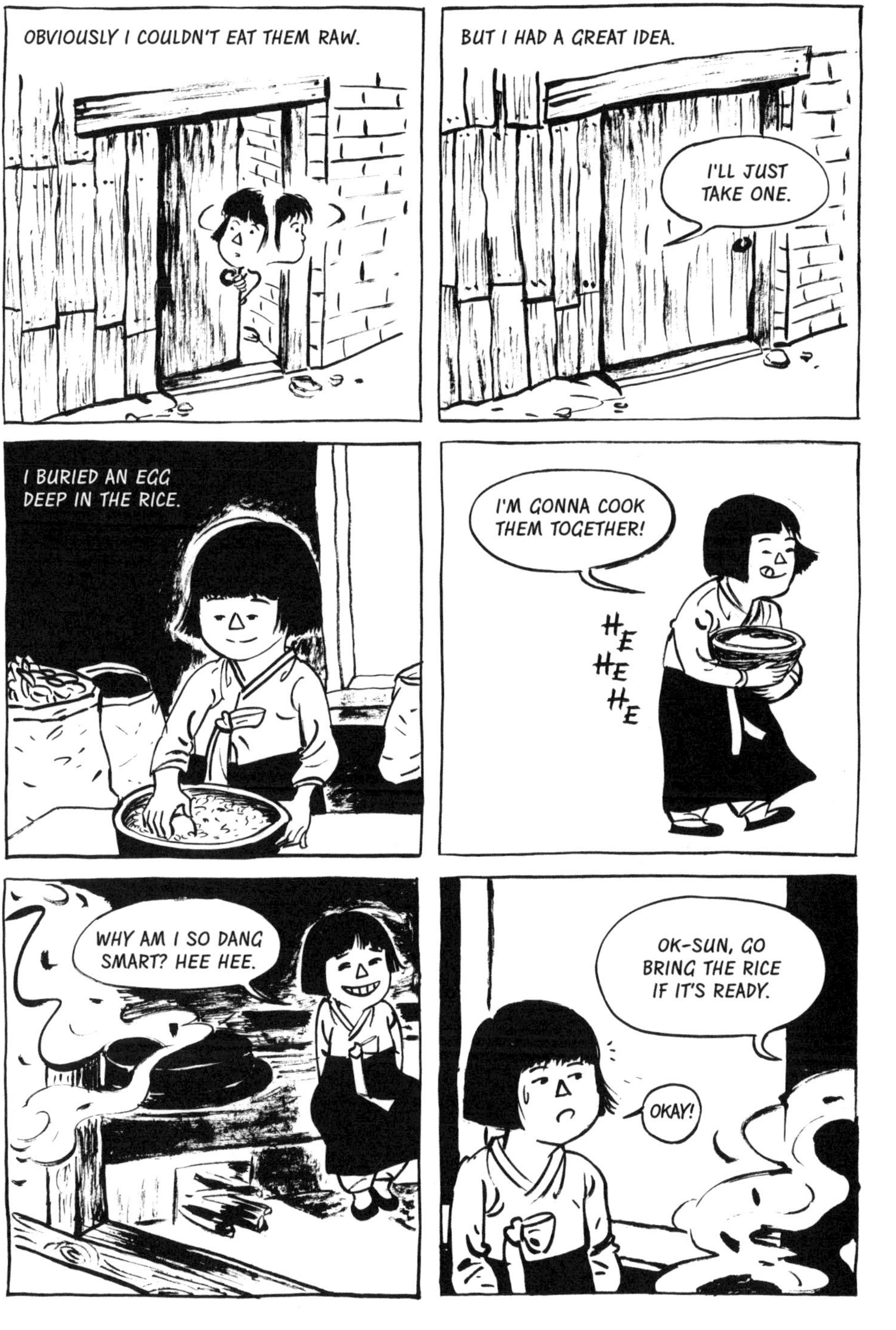
OBVIOUSLY I COULDN'T EAT THEM RAW.
BUT I HAD A GREAT IDEA.
I'LL JUST TAKE ONE.
I BURIED AN EGG DEEP IN THE RICE.
I'M GONNA COOK THEM TOGETHER!
HE HE HE
WHY AM I SO DANG SMART? HEE HEE.
OK-SUN, GO BRING THE RICE IF IT'S READY.
OKAY!

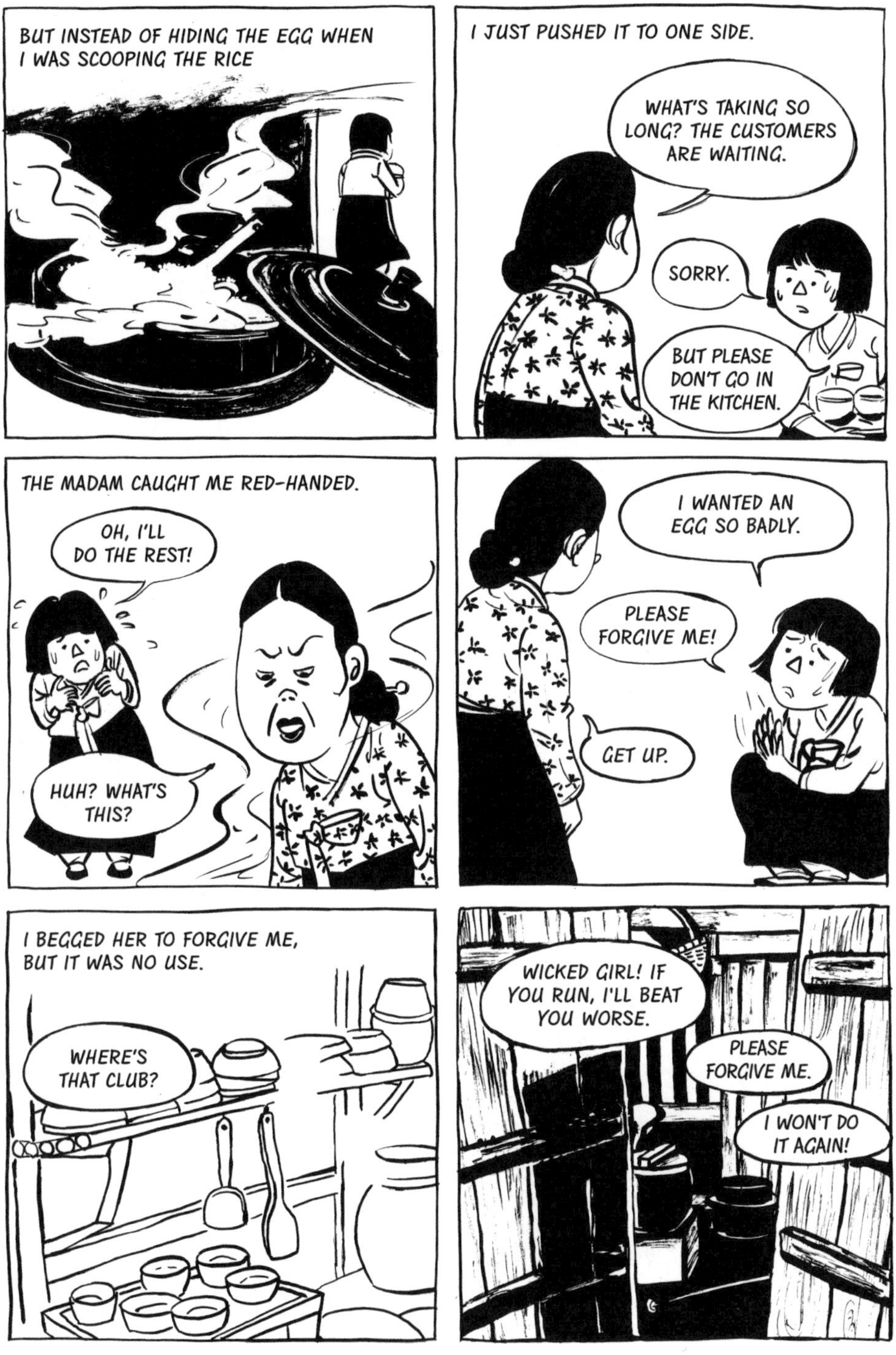
BUT INSTEAD OF HIDING THE EGG WHEN I WAS SCOOPING THE RICE
I JUST PUSHED IT TO ONE SIDE.
WHAT'S TAKING SO LONG? THE CUSTOMERS ARE WAITING.
SORRY.
BUT PLEASE DON'T GO IN THE KITCHEN.
THE MADAM CAUGHT ME RED-HANDED.
OH, I'LL DO THE REST!
HUH? WHAT'S THIS?
I WANTED AN EGG SO BADLY.
PLEASE FORGIVE ME!
GET UP.
I BEGGED HER TO FORGIVE ME, BUT IT WAS NO USE.
WHERE'S THAT CLUB?
WICKED GIRL! IF YOU RUN, I'LL BEAT YOU WORSE.
PLEASE FORGIVE ME.
I WON'T DO IT AGAIN!

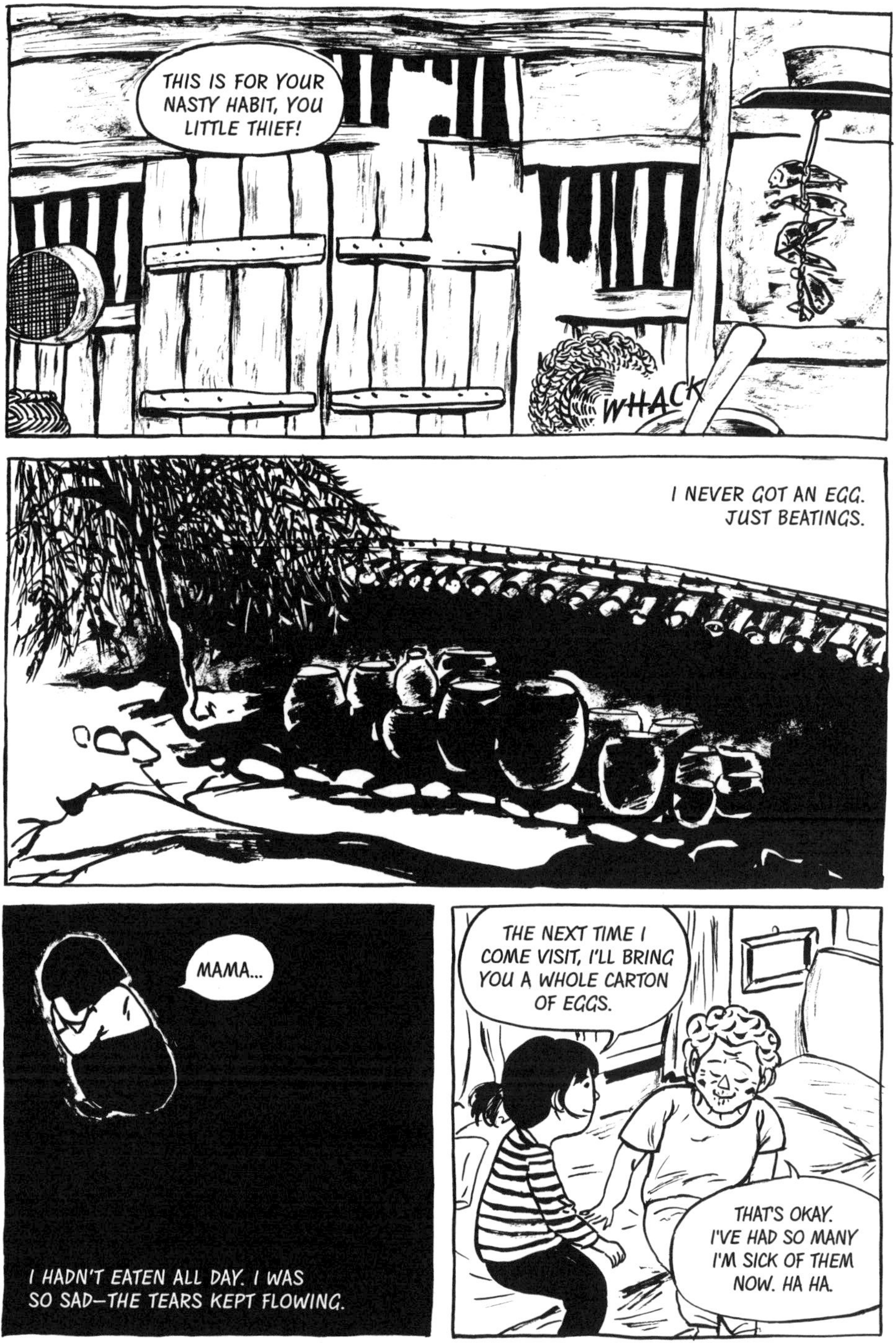
THIS IS FOR YOUR NASTY HABIT, YOU LITTLE THIEF!
WHACK
I NEVER GOT AN EGG. JUST BEATINGS.
MAMA...
I HADN'T EATEN ALL DAY. I WAS SO SAD—THE TEARS KEPT FLOWING.
THE NEXT TIME I COME VISIT, I'LL BRING YOU A WHOLE CARTON OF EGGS.
THAT'S OKAY. I'VE HAD SO MANY I'M SICK OF THEM NOW. HA HA.

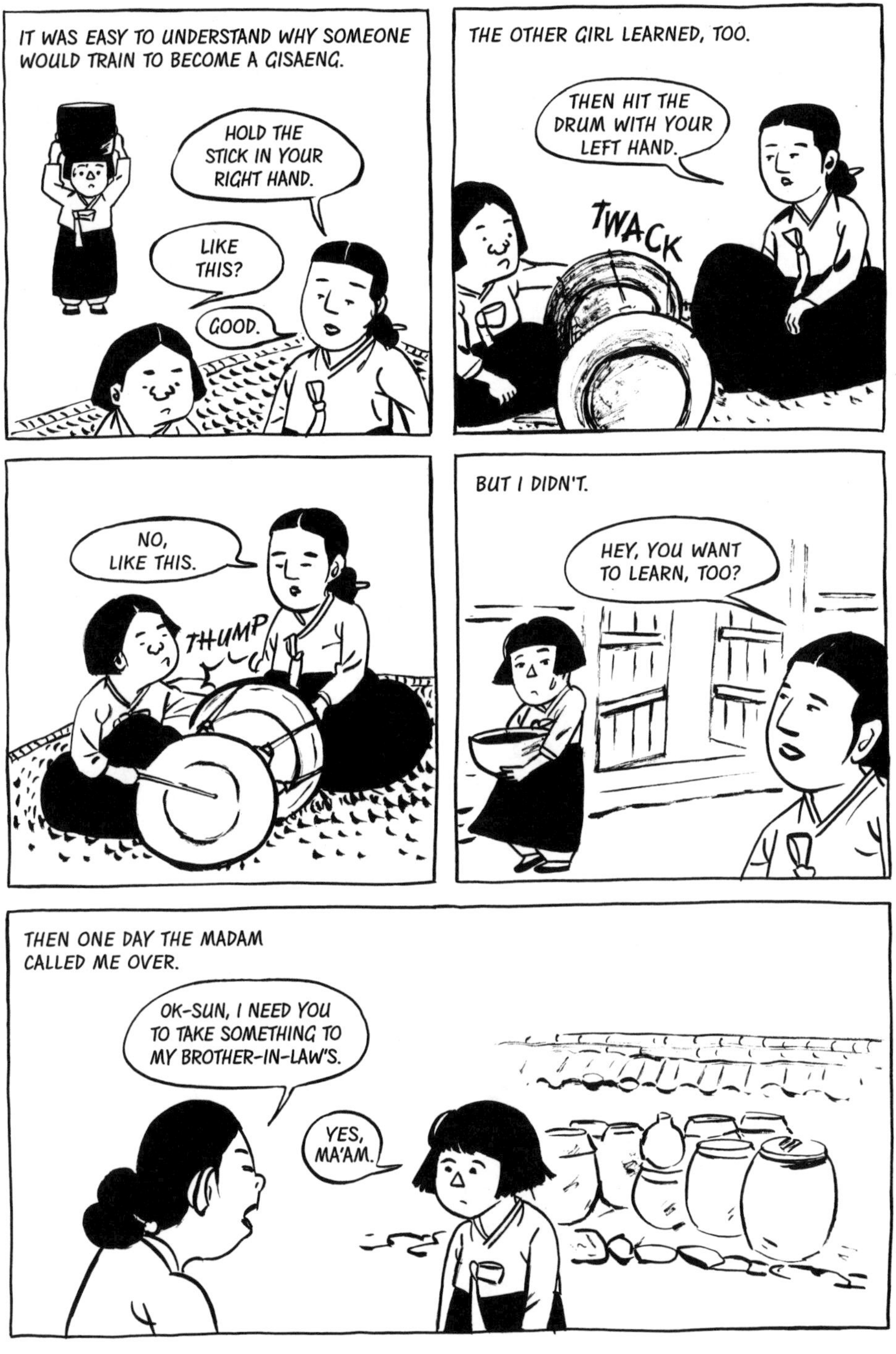

IT WAS EASY TO UNDERSTAND WHY SOMEONE WOULD TRAIN TO BECOME A GISAENG.
HOLD THE STICK IN YOUR RIGHT HAND.
LIKE THIS?
GOOD.
THE OTHER GIRL LEARNED, TOO.
THEN HIT THE DRUM WITH YOUR LEFT HAND.
TWACK
NO, LIKE THIS.
THUMP
BUT I DIDN'T.
HEY, YOU WANT TO LEARN, TOO?
THEN ONE DAY THE MADAM CALLED ME OVER.
OK-SUN, I NEED YOU TO TAKE SOMETHING TO MY BROTHER-IN-LAW'S.
YES, MA'AM.

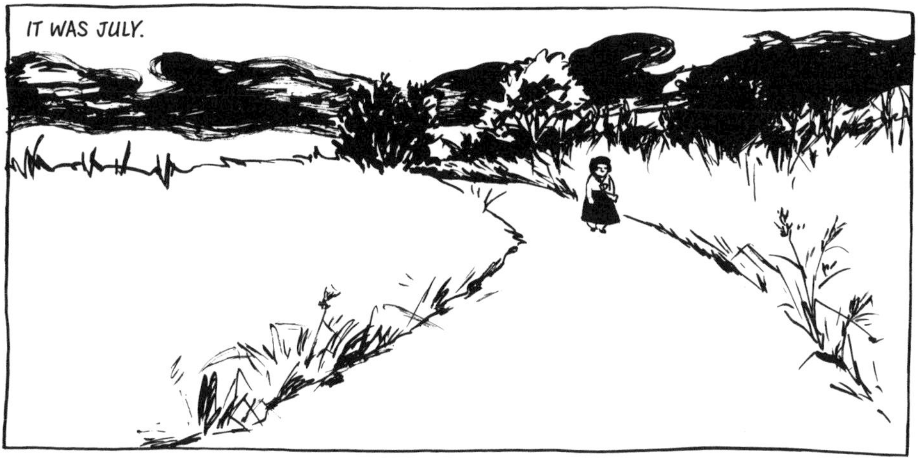
IT WAS JULY.

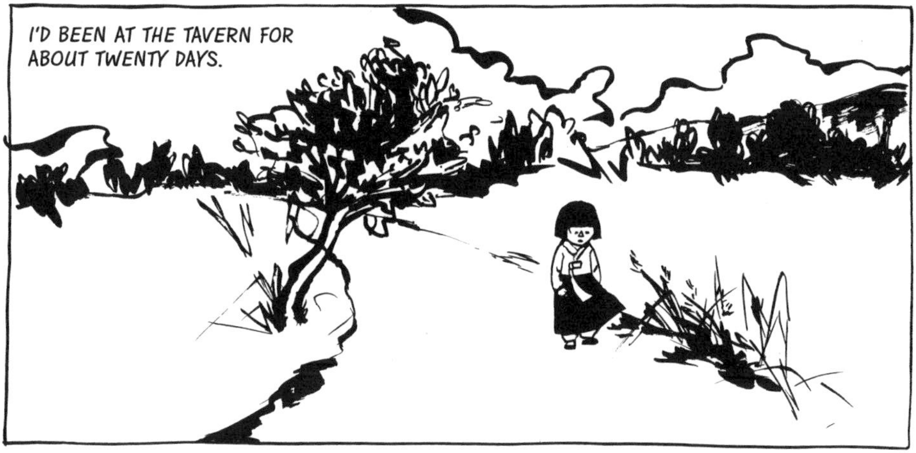
I'D BEEN AT THE TAVERN FOR
ABOUT TWENTY DAYS.

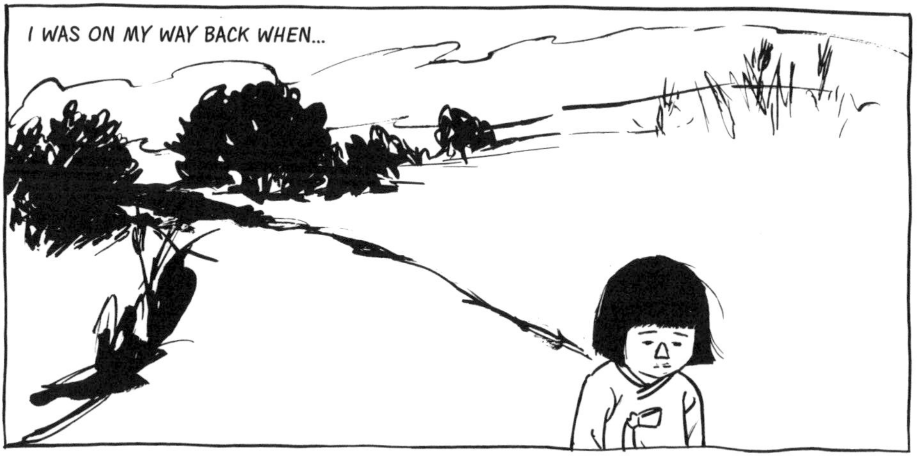
I WAS ON MY WAY BACK WHEN...

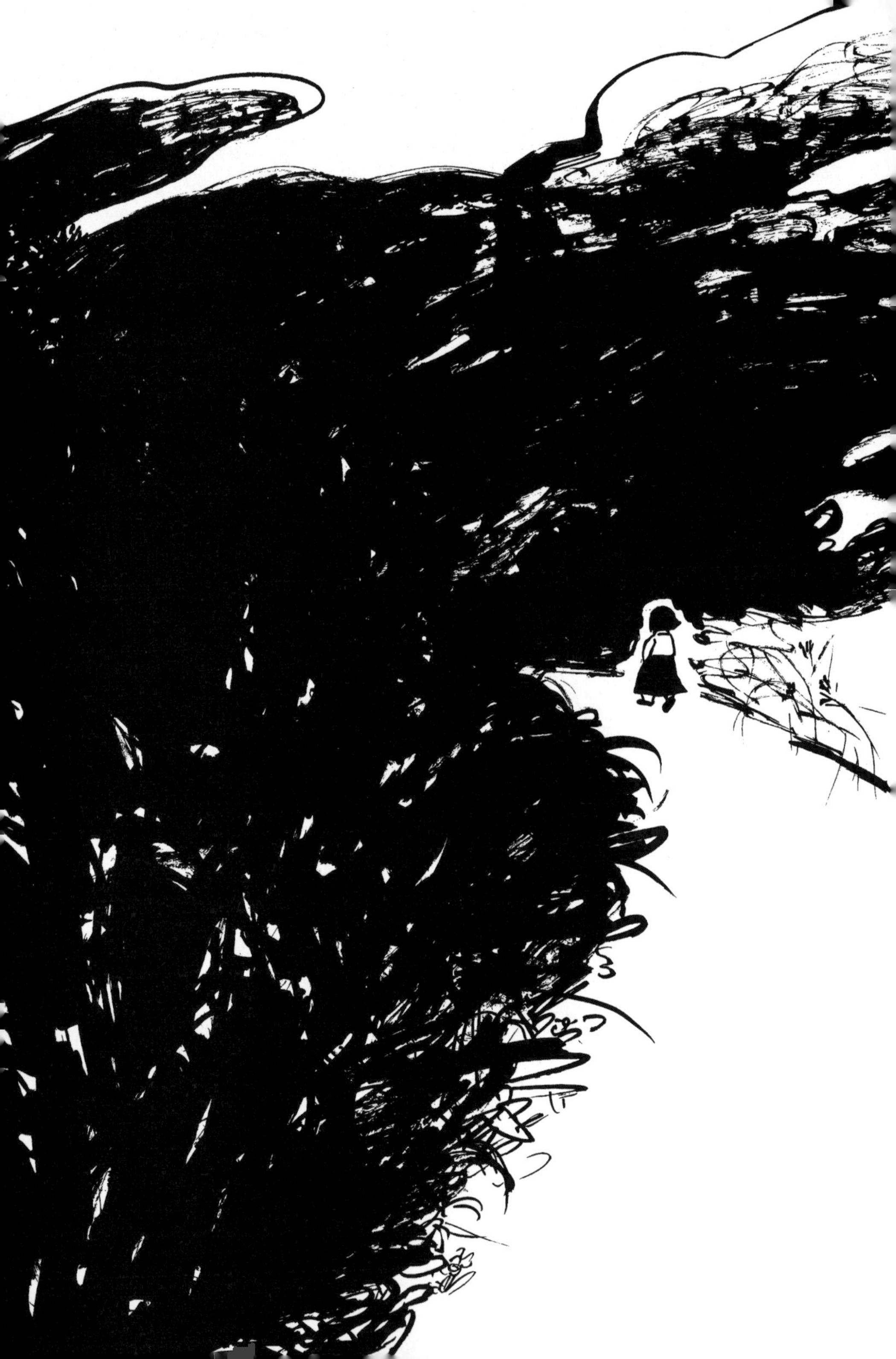

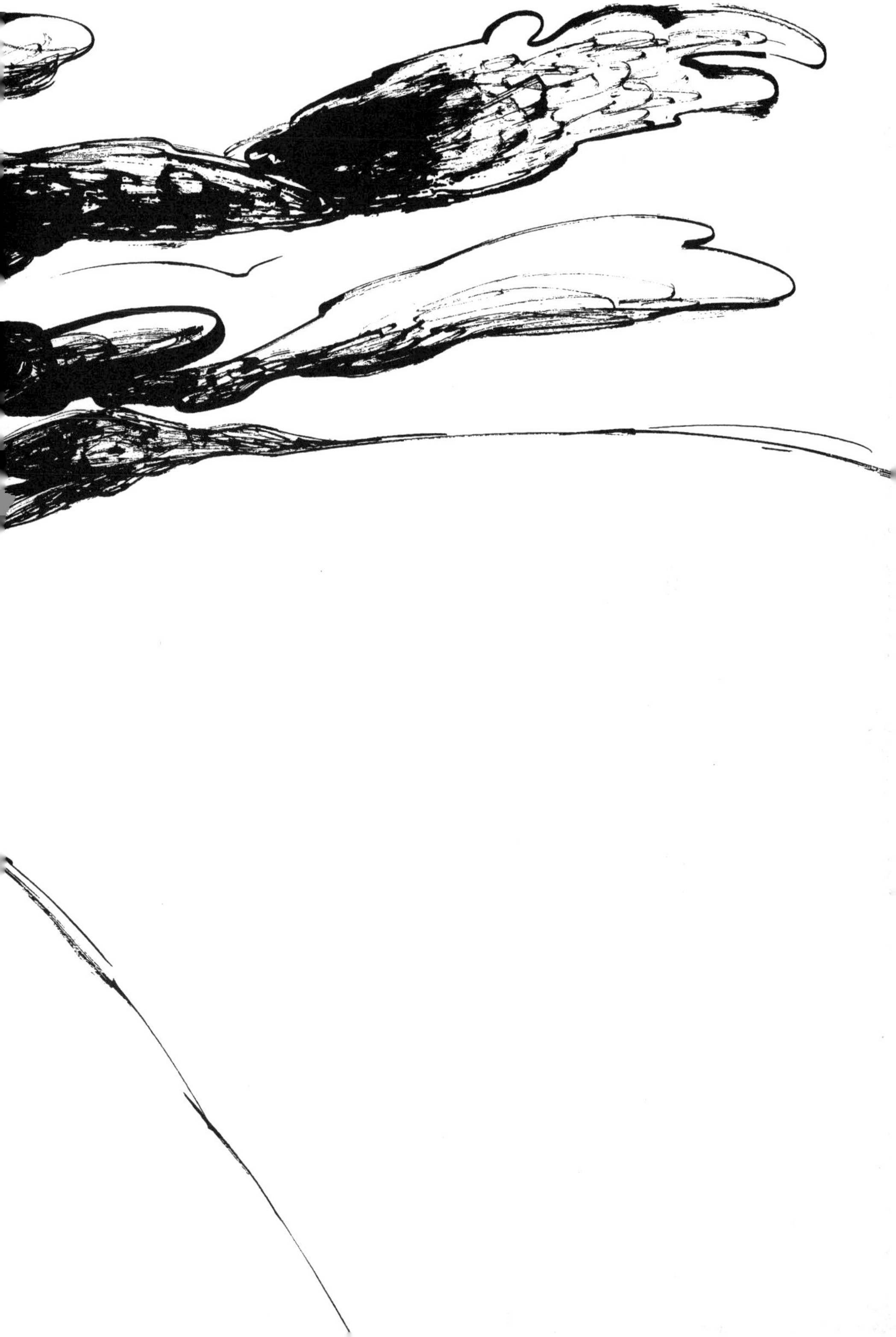

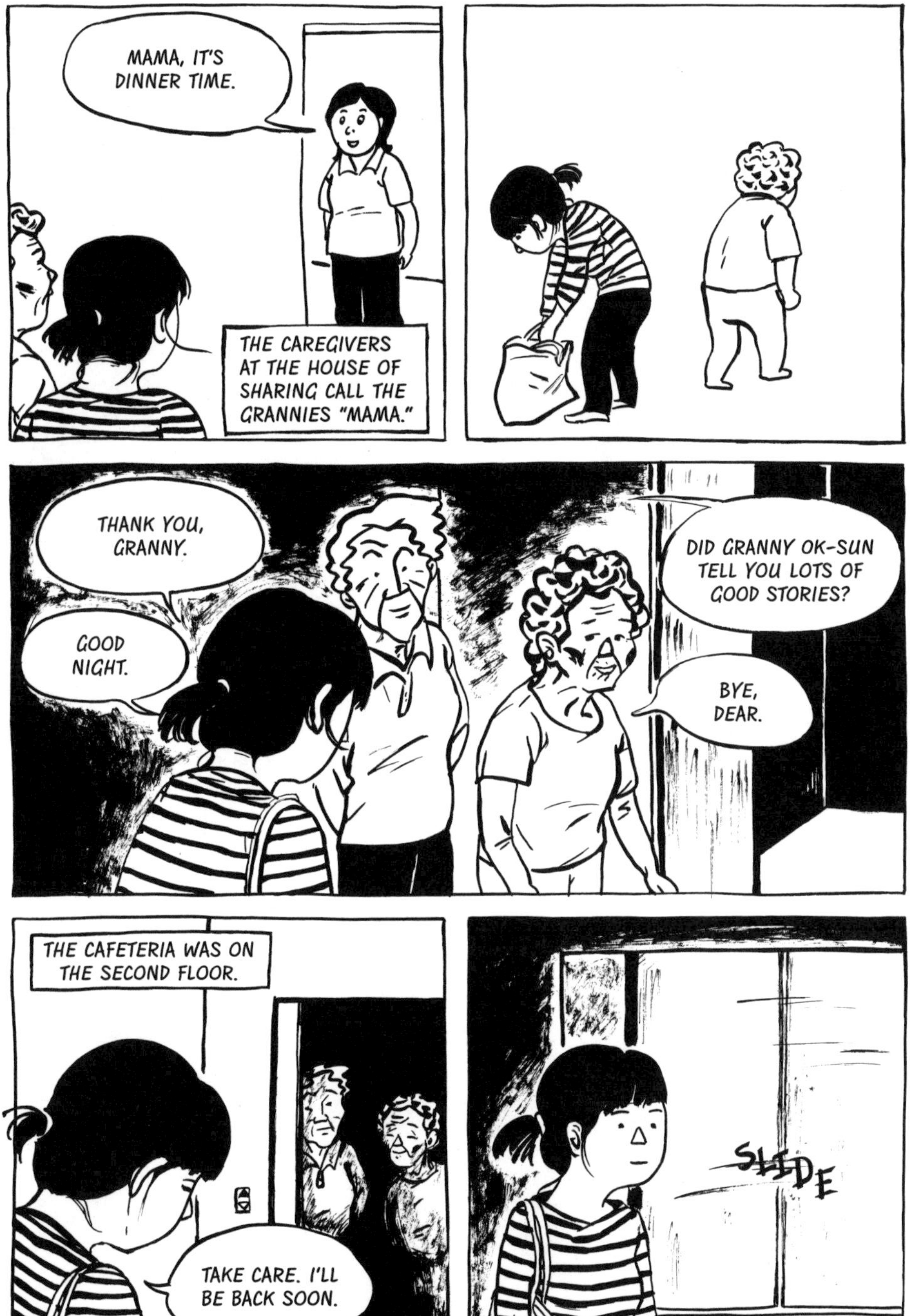
MAMA, IT'S DINNER TIME.
THE CAREGIVERS AT THE HOUSE OF SHARING CALL THE GRANNIES "MAMA."
THANK YOU, GRANNY.
GOOD NIGHT.
DID GRANNY OK-SUN TELL YOU LOTS OF GOOD STORIES?
BYE, DEAR.
THE CAFETERIA WAS ON THE SECOND FLOOR.
TAKE CARE. I'LL BE BACK SOON.
SLIDE

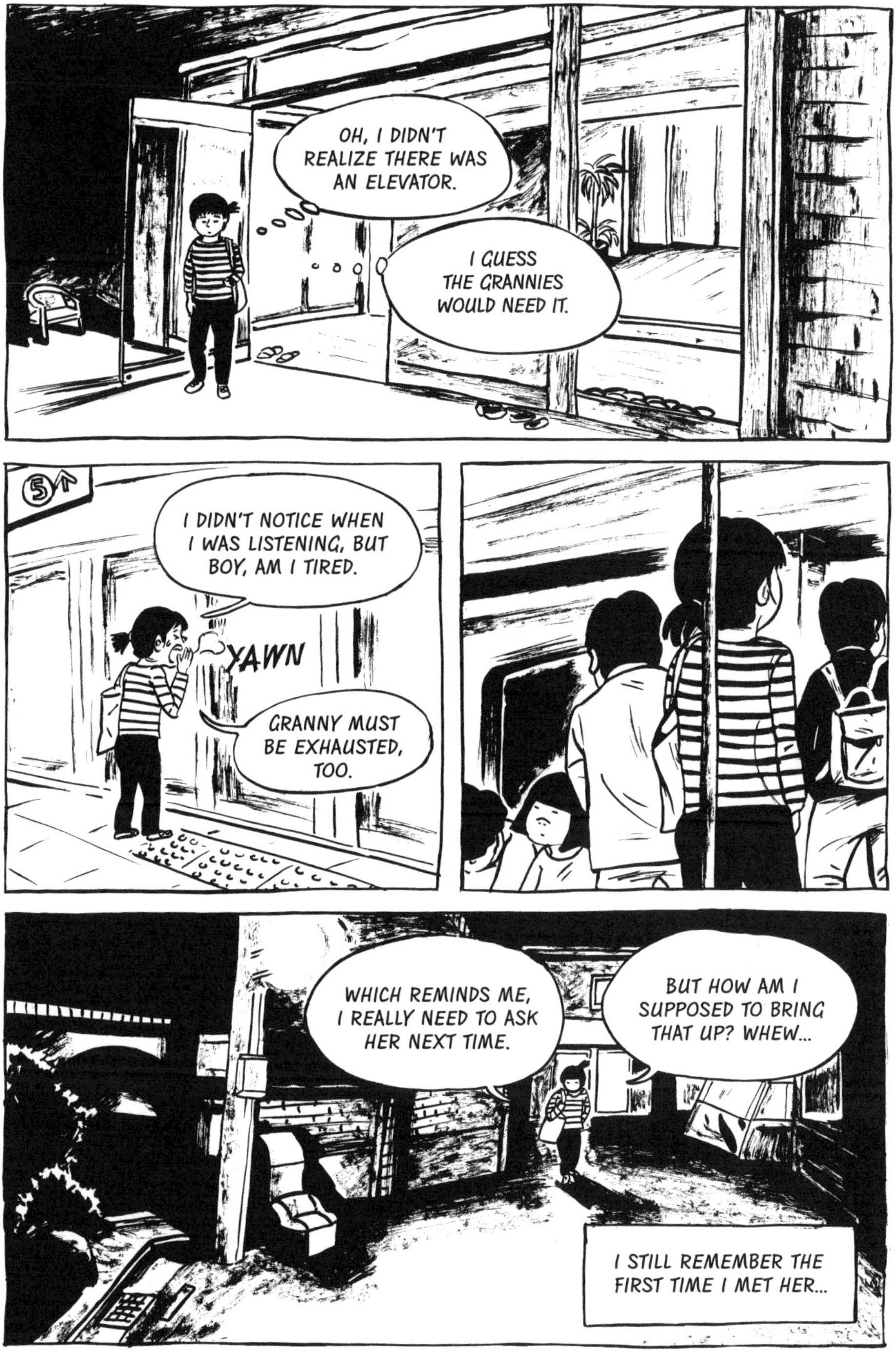
OH, I DIDN'T REALIZE THERE WAS AN ELEVATOR.
I GUESS THE GRANNIES WOULD NEED IT.
I DIDN'T NOTICE WHEN I WAS LISTENING, BUT BOY, AM I TIRED.
YAWN
GRANNY MUST BE EXHAUSTED, TOO.
WHICH REMINDS ME, I REALLY NEED TO ASK HER NEXT TIME.
BUT HOW AM I SUPPOSED TO BRING THAT UP? WHEW...
I STILL REMEMBER THE FIRST TIME I MET HER...

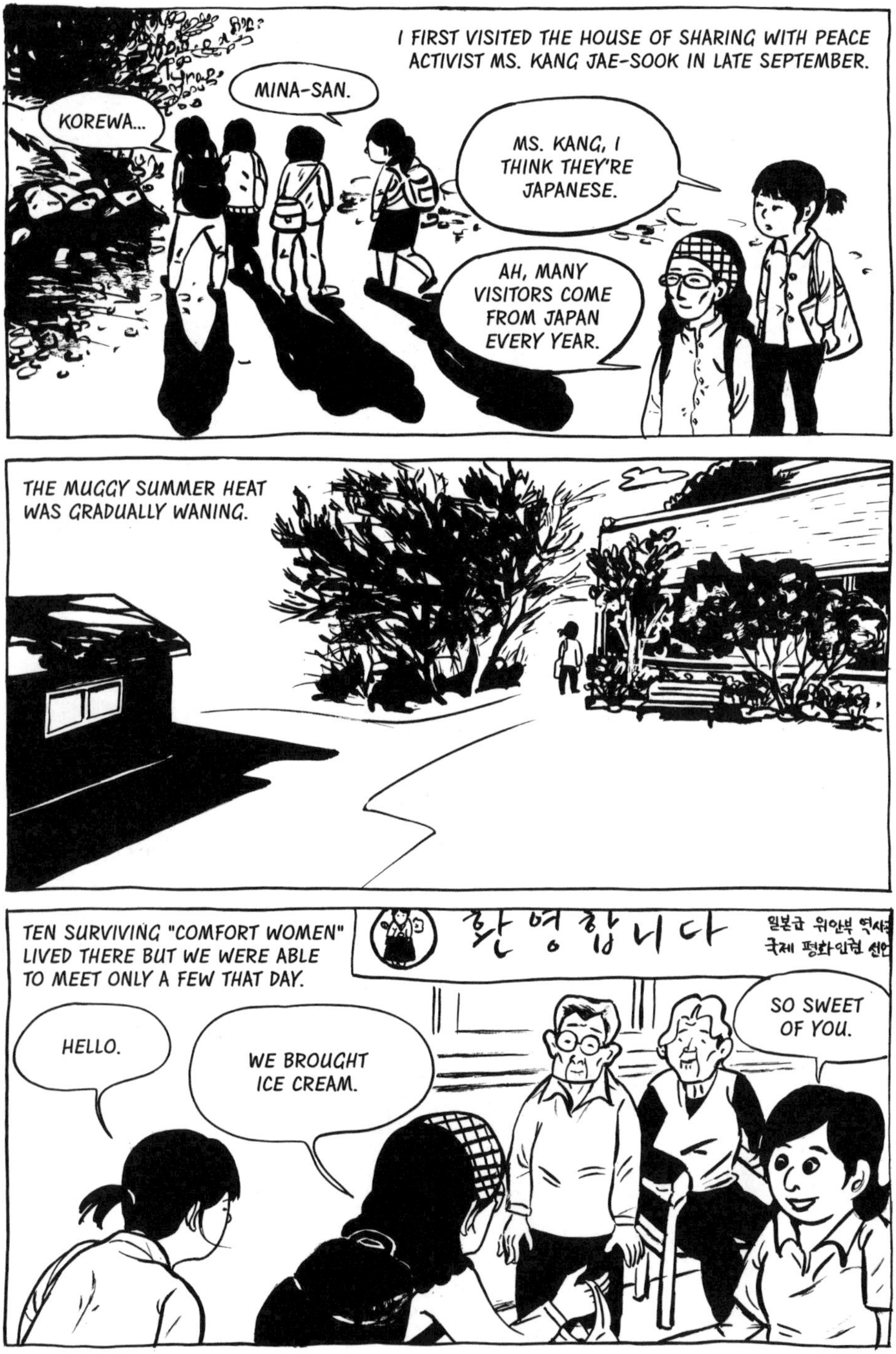
I FIRST VISITED THE HOUSE OF SHARING WITH PEACE ACTIVIST MS. KANG JAE-SOOK IN LATE SEPTEMBER.
KOREWA...
MINA-SAN.
MS. KANG, I THINK THEY'RE JAPANESE.
AH, MANY VISITORS COME FROM JAPAN EVERY YEAR.
THE MUGGY SUMMER HEAT WAS GRADUALLY WANING.
TEN SURVIVING "COMFORT WOMEN" LIVED THERE BUT WE WERE ABLE TO MEET ONLY A FEW THAT DAY.
환영합니다
HELLO.
WE BROUGHT ICE CREAM.
SO SWEET OF YOU.

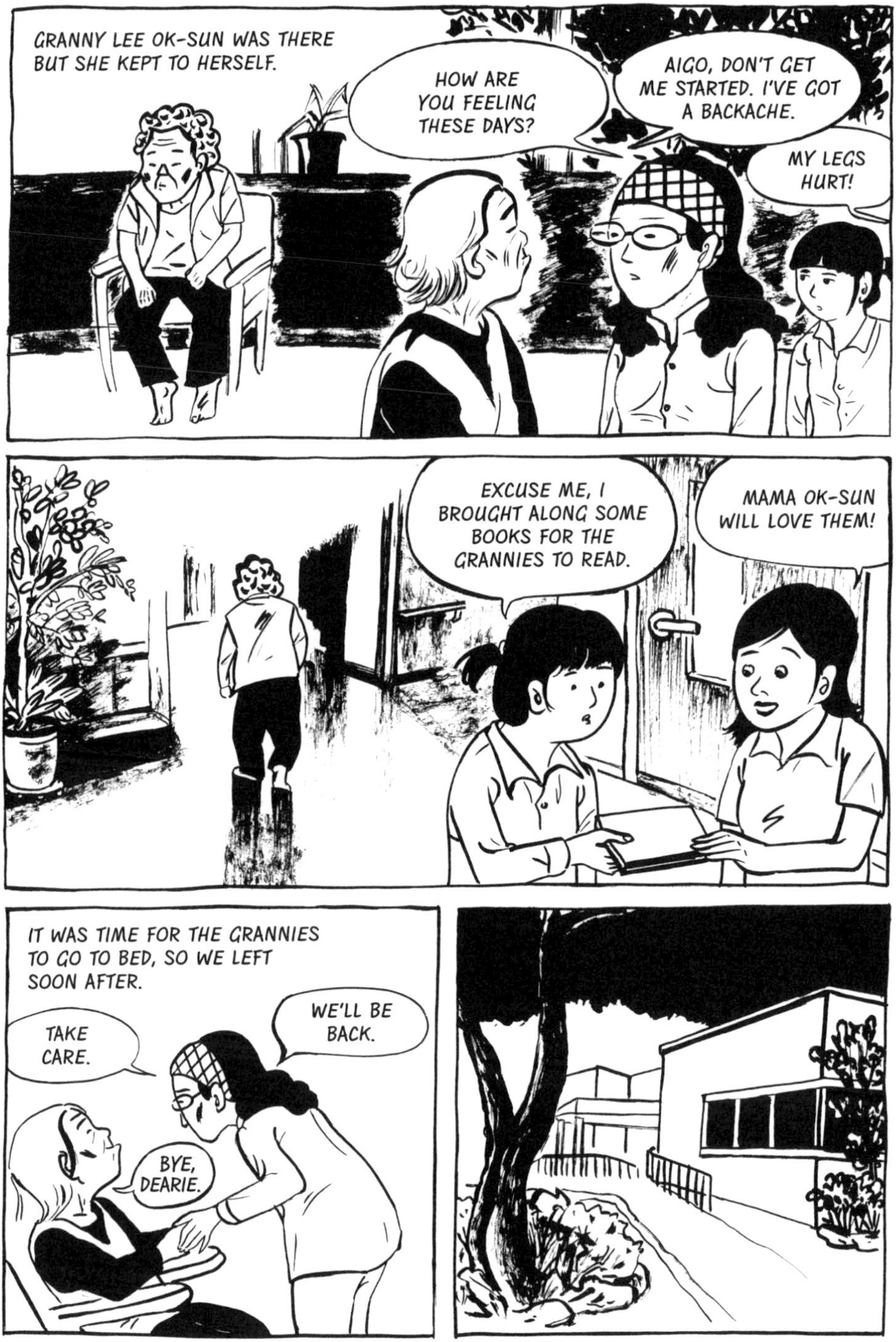
GRANNY LEE OK-SUN WAS THERE BUT SHE KEPT TO HERSELF.
HOW ARE YOU FEELING THESE DAYS?
AIGO, DON'T GET ME STARTED. I'VE GOT A BACKACHE.
MY LEGS HURT!
EXCUSE ME, I BROUGHT ALONG SOME BOOKS FOR THE GRANNIES TO READ.
MAMA OK-SUN WILL LOVE THEM!
IT WAS TIME FOR THE GRANNIES TO GO TO BED, SO WE LEFT SOON AFTER.
TAKE CARE.
WE'LL BE BACK.
BYE, DEARIE.

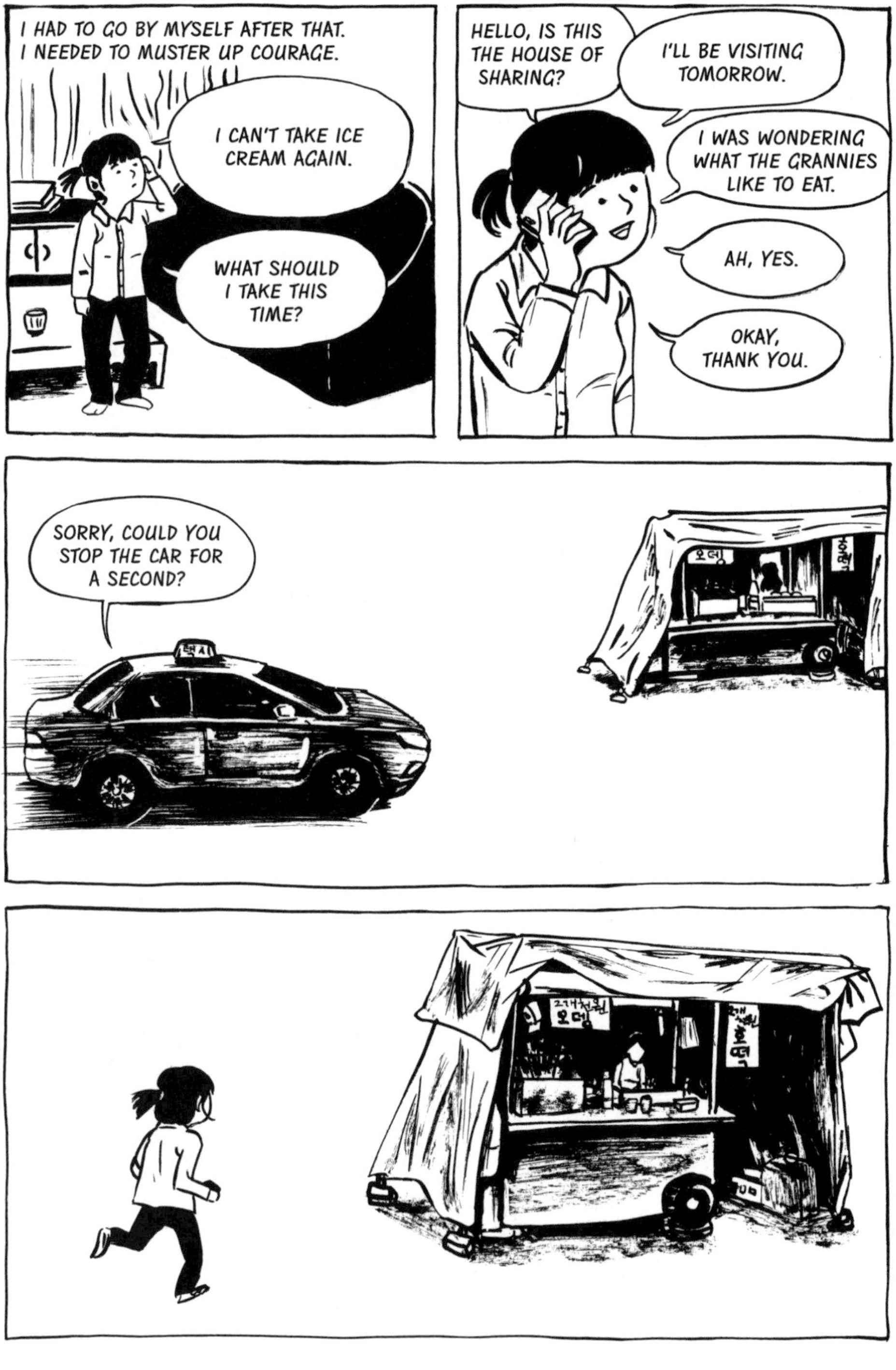
I HAD TO GO BY MYSELF AFTER THAT.
I NEEDED TO MUSTER UP COURAGE.
I CAN'T TAKE ICE CREAM AGAIN.
WHAT SHOULD I TAKE THIS TIME?
HELLO, IS THIS THE HOUSE OF SHARING?
I'LL BE VISITING TOMORROW.
I WAS WONDERING WHAT THE GRANNIES LIKE TO EAT.
AH, YES.
OKAY, THANK YOU.
SORRY, COULD YOU STOP THE CAR FOR A SECOND?

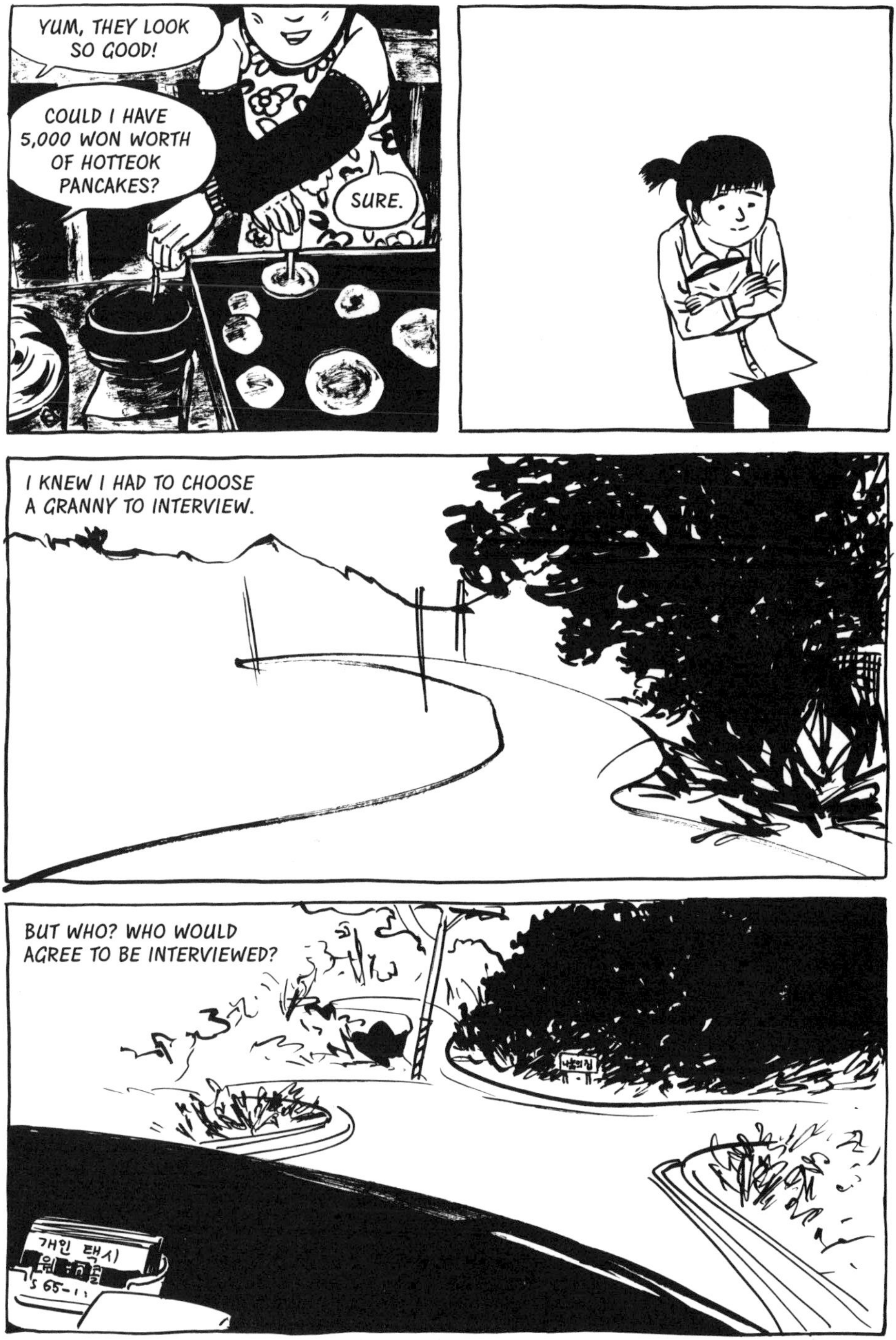
YUM, THEY LOOK SO GOOD!
COULD I HAVE 5,000 WON WORTH OF HOTTEOK PANCAKES?
SURE.
I KNEW I HAD TO CHOOSE A GRANNY TO INTERVIEW.
BUT WHO? WHO WOULD AGREE TO BE INTERVIEWED?
개인 택시

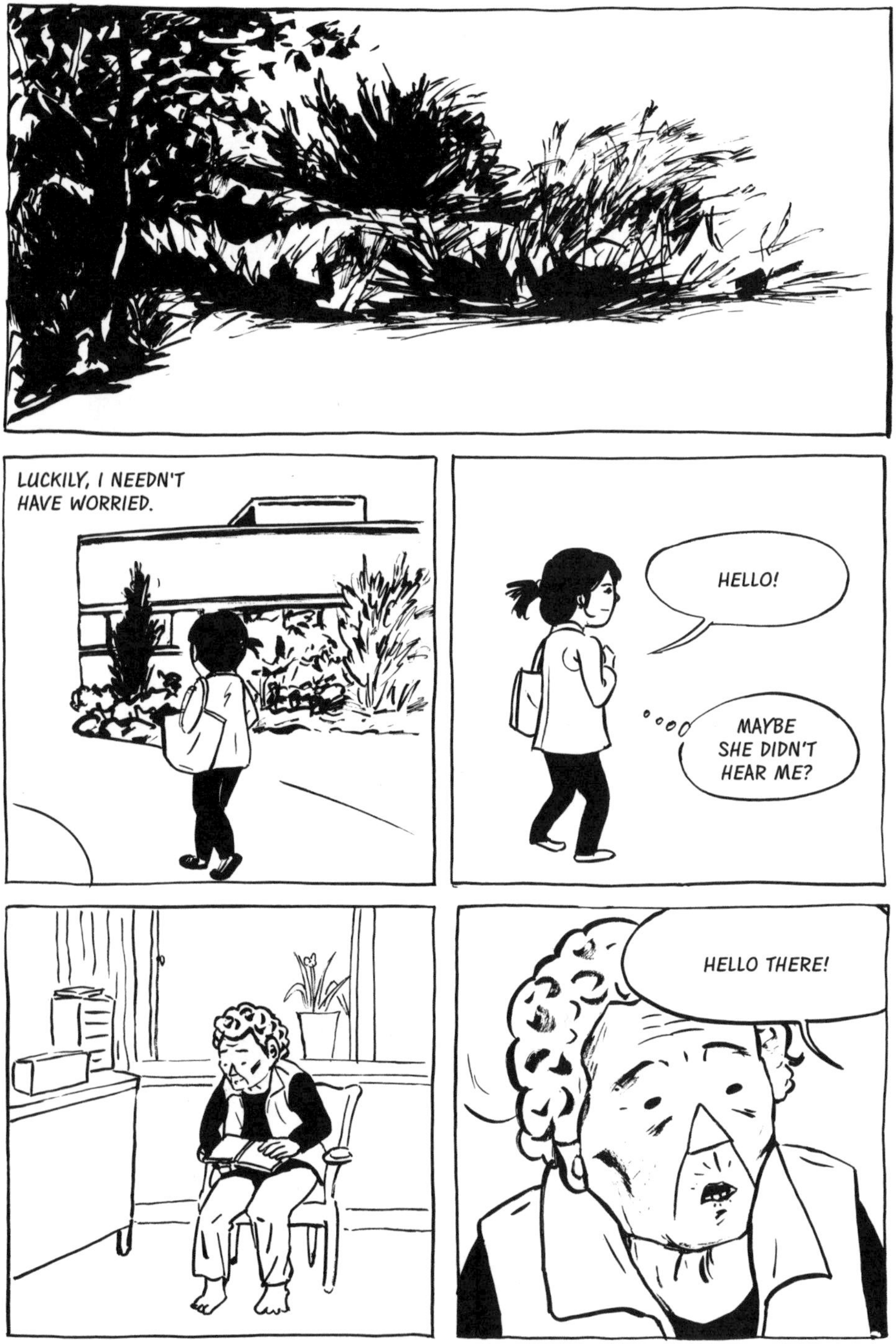
LUCKILY, I NEEDN'T HAVE WORRIED.
HELLO!
MAYBE SHE DIDN'T HEAR ME?
HELLO THERE!

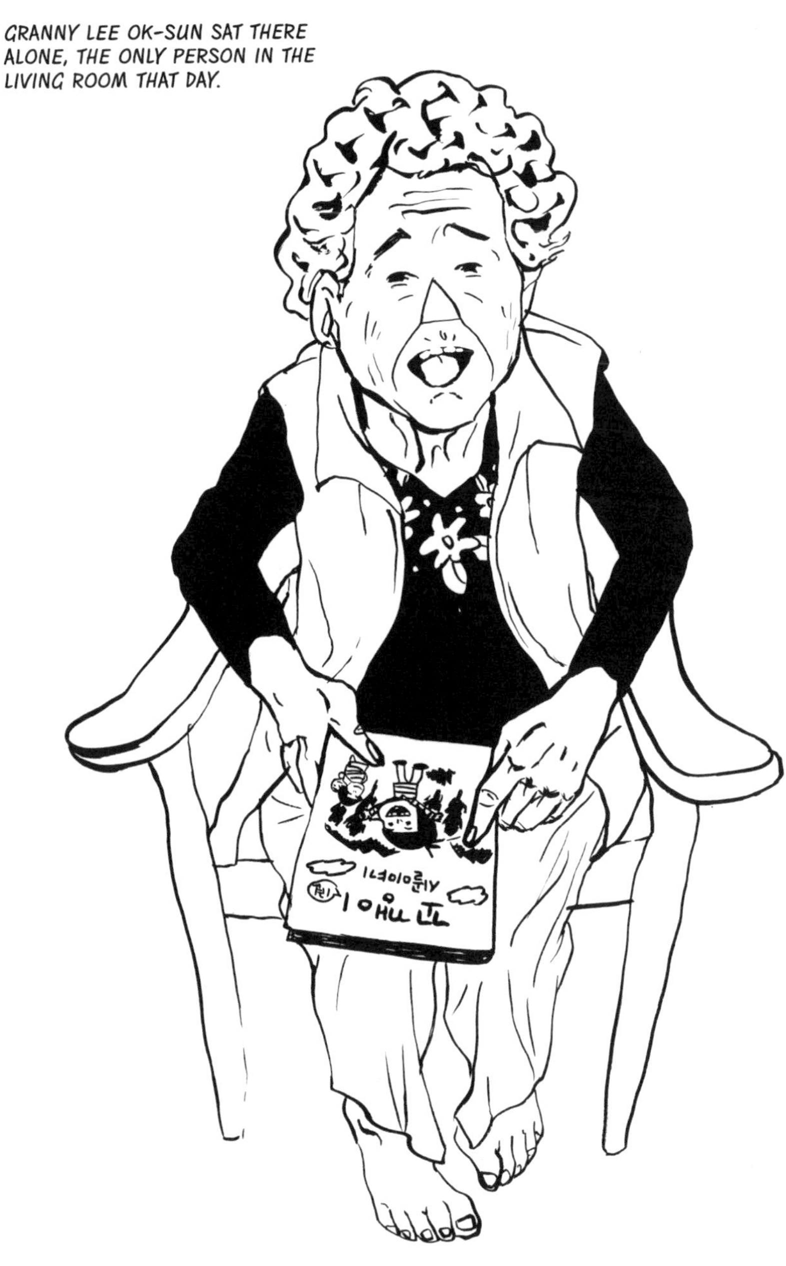
GRANNY LEE OK-SUN SAT THERE ALONE, THE ONLY PERSON IN THE LIVING ROOM THAT DAY.

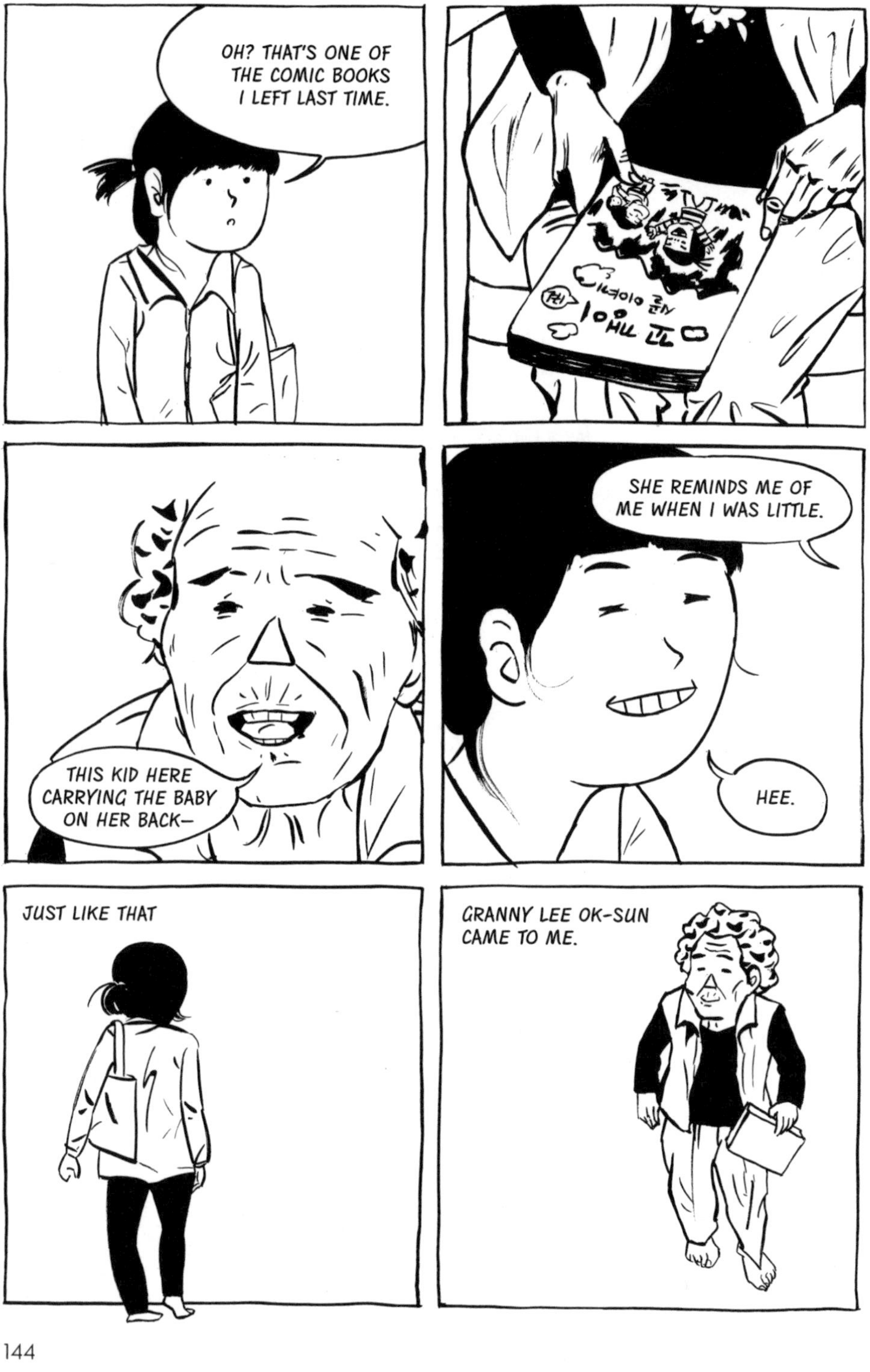
OH? THAT'S ONE OF THE COMIC BOOKS I LEFT LAST TIME.
THIS KID HERE CARRYING THE BABY ON HER BACK—
SHE REMINDS ME OF ME WHEN I WAS LITTLE.
HEE.
JUST LIKE THAT
GRANNY LEE OK-SUN CAME TO ME.

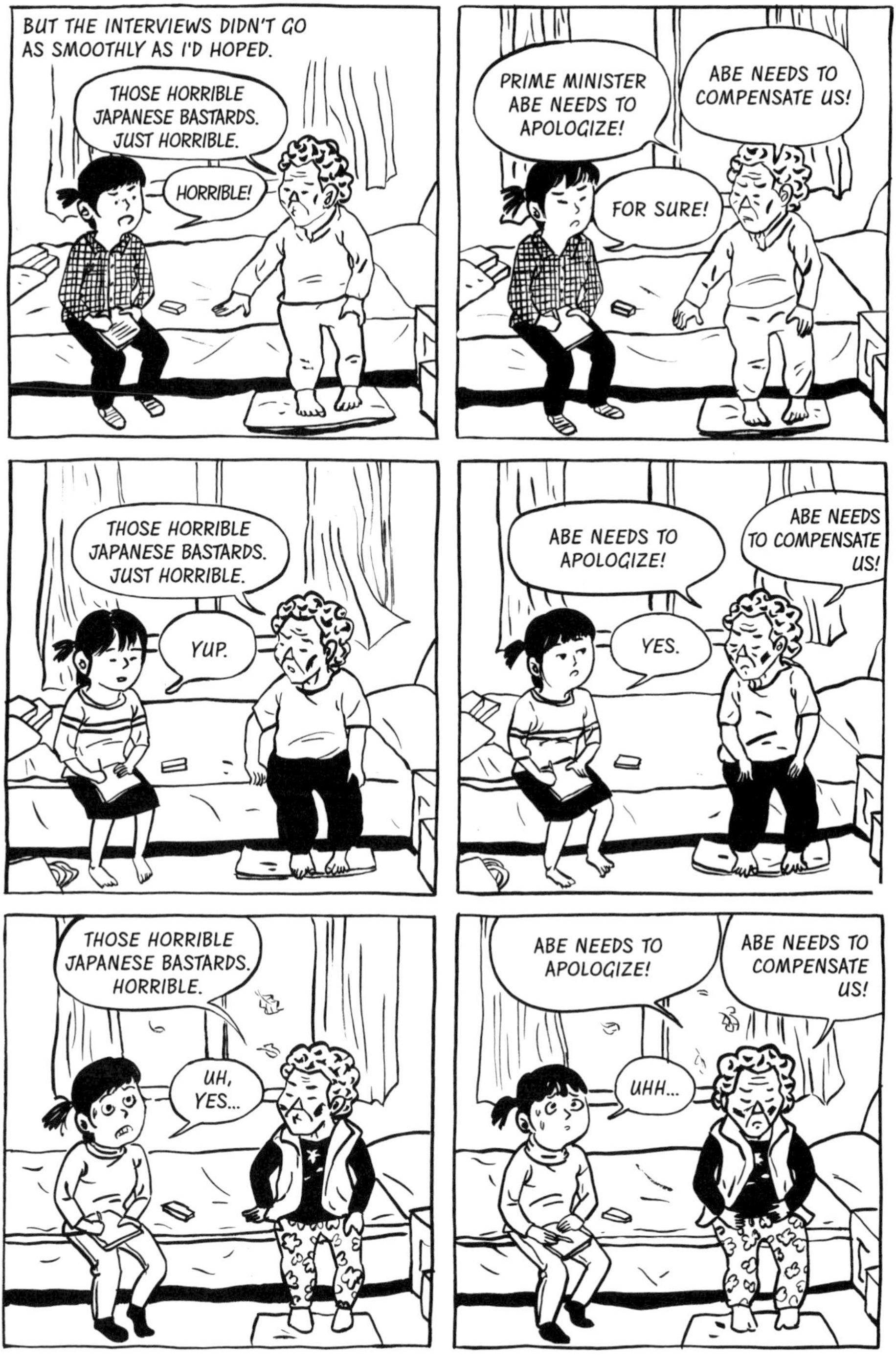
BUT THE INTERVIEWS DIDN'T GO AS SMOOTHLY AS I'D HOPED.
THOSE HORRIBLE JAPANESE BASTARDS. JUST HORRIBLE.
HORRIBLE!
PRIME MINISTER ABE NEEDS TO APOLOGIZE!
ABE NEEDS TO COMPENSATE US!
FOR SURE!
THOSE HORRIBLE JAPANESE BASTARDS. JUST HORRIBLE.
YUP.
ABE NEEDS TO APOLOGIZE!
ABE NEEDS TO COMPENSATE US!
YES.
THOSE HORRIBLE JAPANESE BASTARDS. HORRIBLE.
UH, YES...
ABE NEEDS TO APOLOGIZE!
ABE NEEDS TO COMPENSATE US!
UHH...

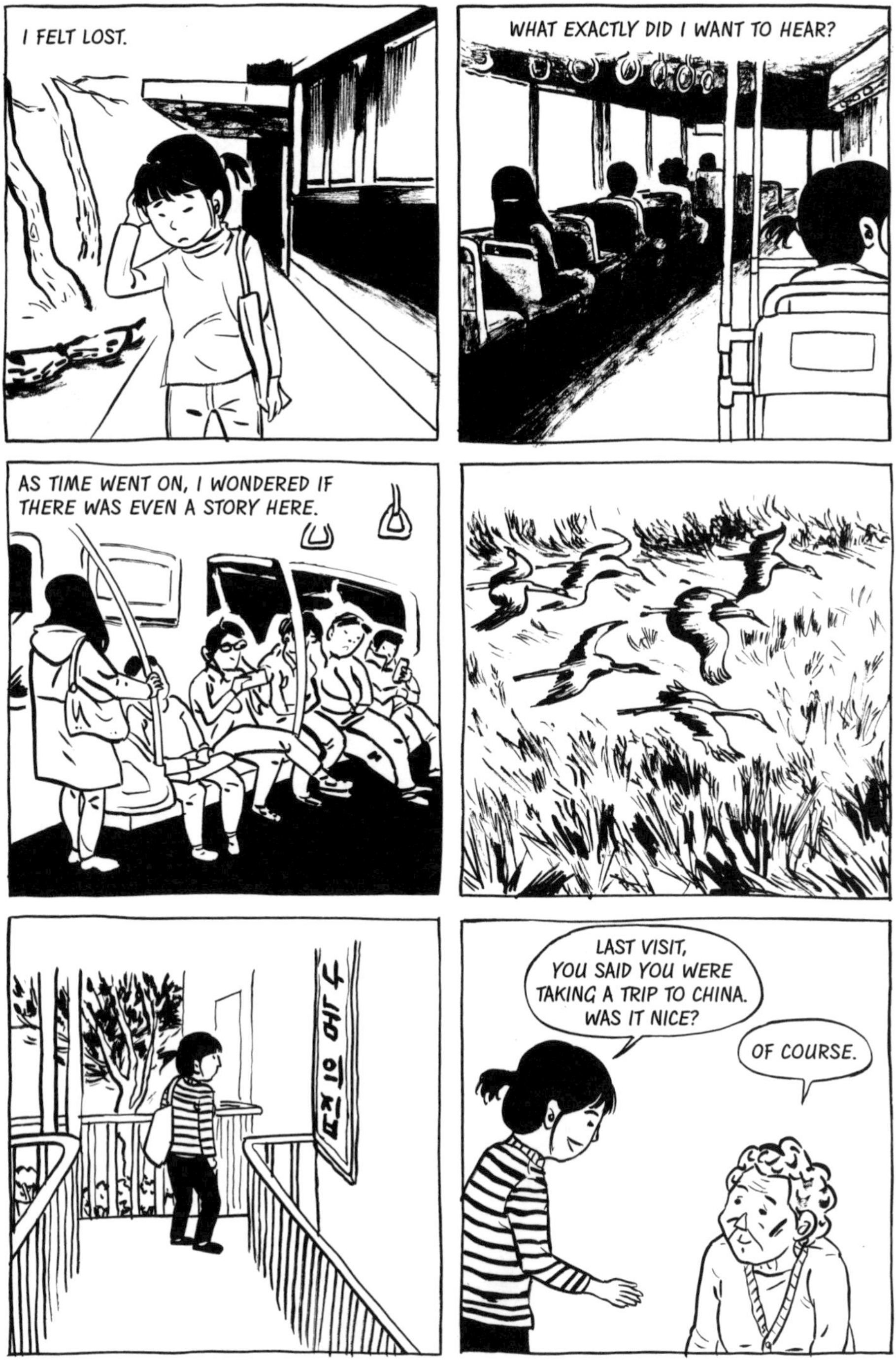
I FELT LOST.
WHAT EXACTLY DID I WANT TO HEAR?
AS TIME WENT ON, I WONDERED IF THERE WAS EVEN A STORY HERE.
나눔의 집
LAST VISIT, YOU SAID YOU WERE TAKING A TRIP TO CHINA. WAS IT NICE?
OF COURSE.

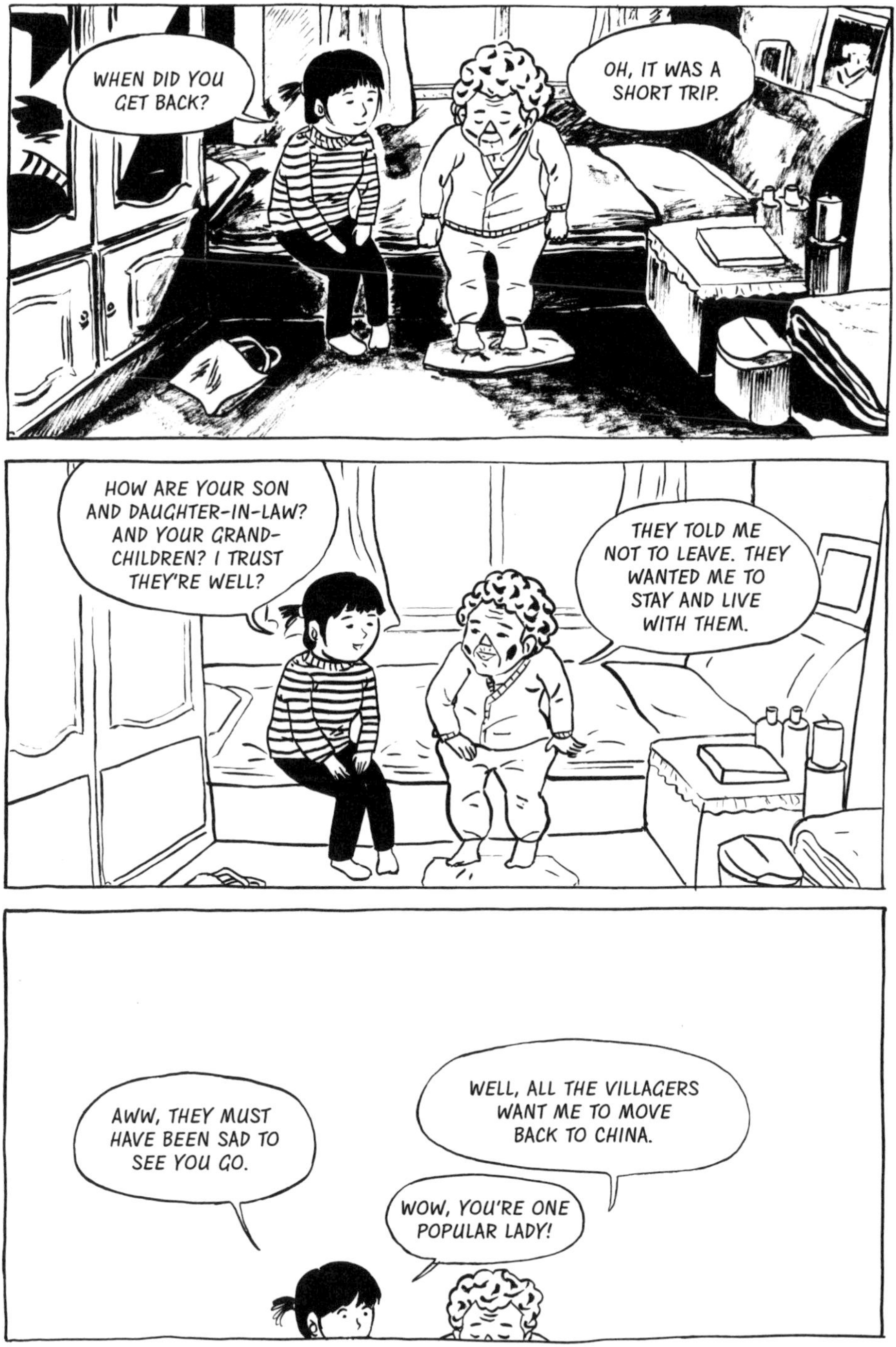
WHEN DID YOU GET BACK?
OH, IT WAS A SHORT TRIP.
HOW ARE YOUR SON AND DAUGHTER-IN-LAW? AND YOUR GRAND-CHILDREN? I TRUST THEY'RE WELL?
THEY TOLD ME NOT TO LEAVE. THEY WANTED ME TO STAY AND LIVE WITH THEM.
AWW, THEY MUST HAVE BEEN SAD TO SEE YOU GO.
WELL, ALL THE VILLAGERS WANT ME TO MOVE BACK TO CHINA.
WOW, YOU'RE ONE POPULAR LADY!

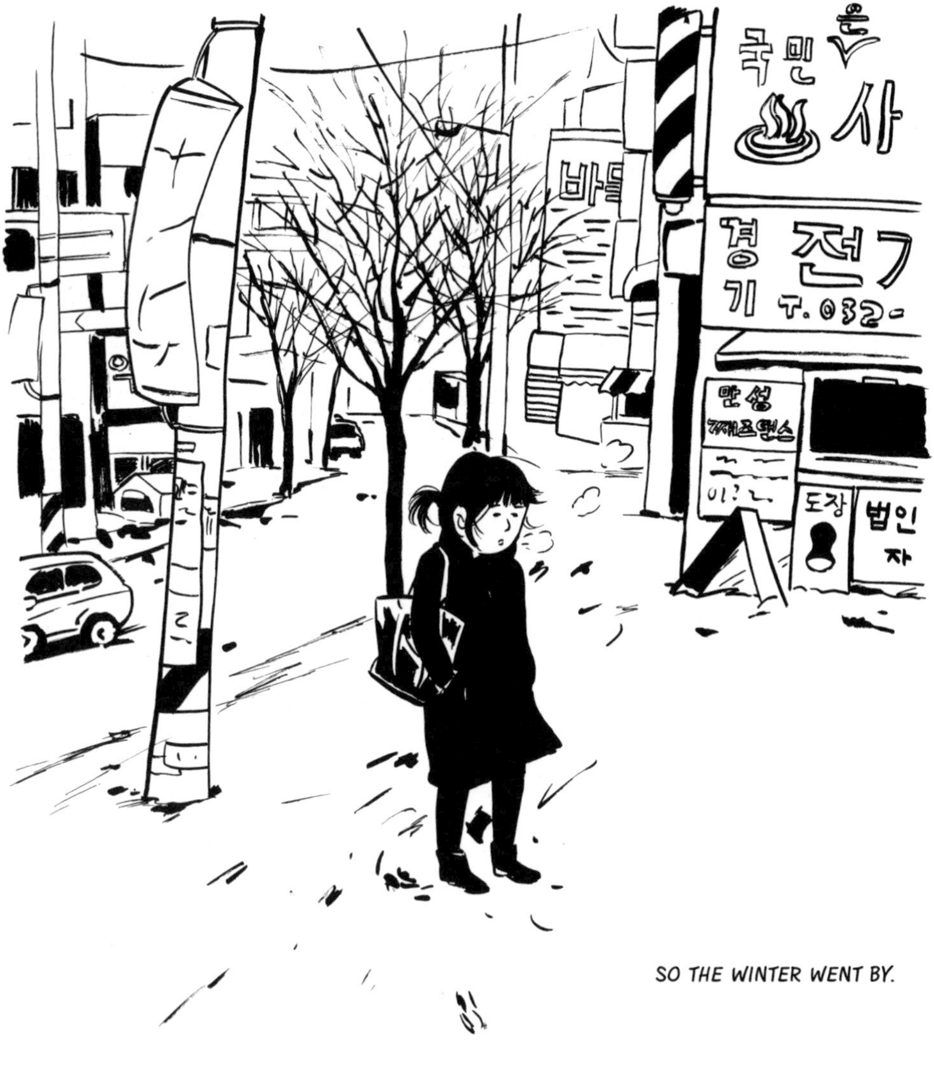
국민
사
경기 전기
T.032-
도장
법인
자

SO THE WINTER WENT BY.

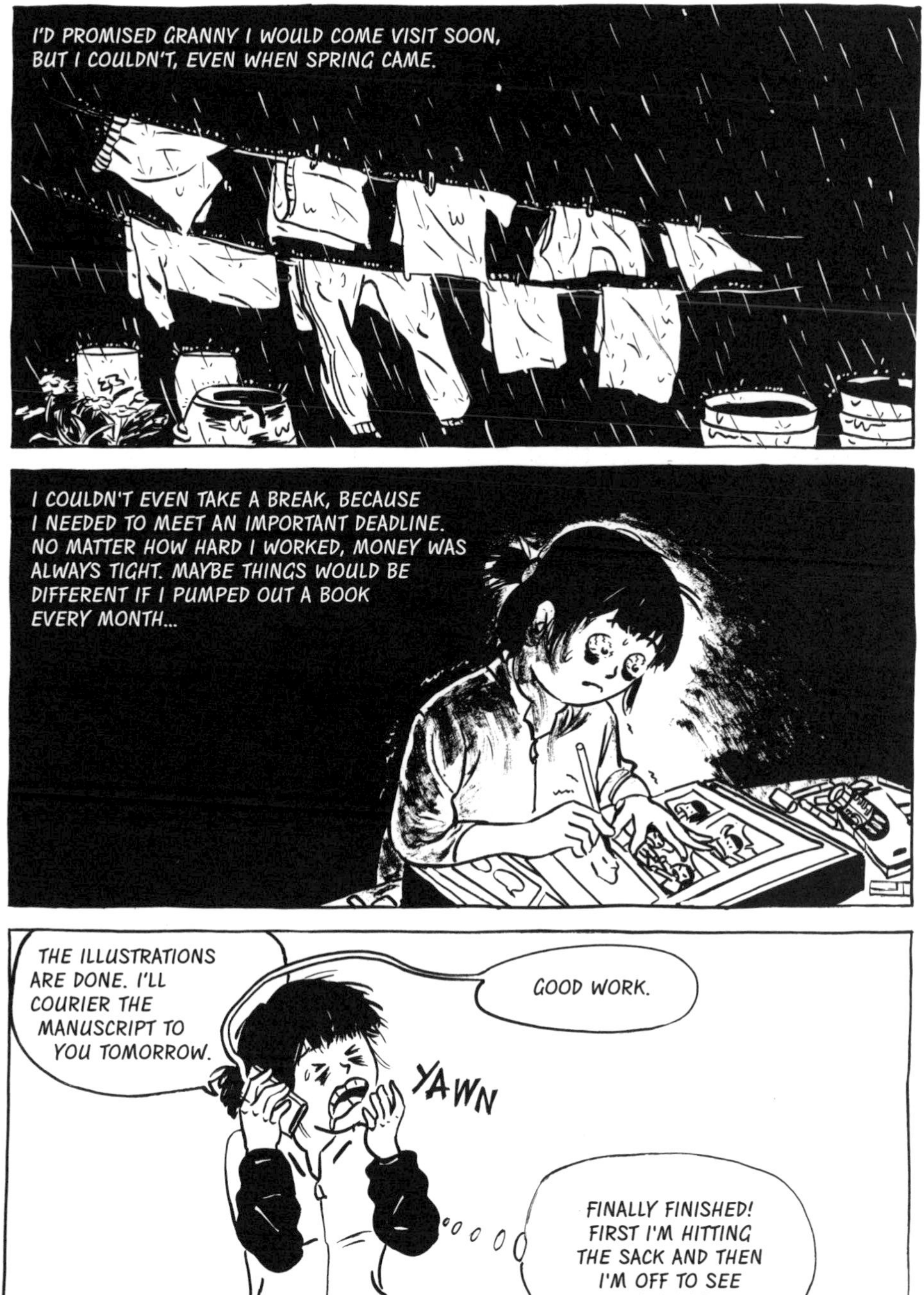
I'D PROMISED GRANNY I WOULD COME VISIT SOON, BUT I COULDN'T, EVEN WHEN SPRING CAME.
I COULDN'T EVEN TAKE A BREAK, BECAUSE I NEEDED TO MEET AN IMPORTANT DEADLINE. NO MATTER HOW HARD I WORKED, MONEY WAS ALWAYS TIGHT. MAYBE THINGS WOULD BE DIFFERENT IF I PUMPED OUT A BOOK EVERY MONTH...
THE ILLUSTRATIONS ARE DONE. I'LL COURIER THE MANUSCRIPT TO YOU TOMORROW.
GOOD WORK.
YAWN
FINALLY FINISHED! FIRST I'M HITTING THE SACK AND THEN I'M OFF TO SEE GRANNY.

# EAST YANJI AIRPORT

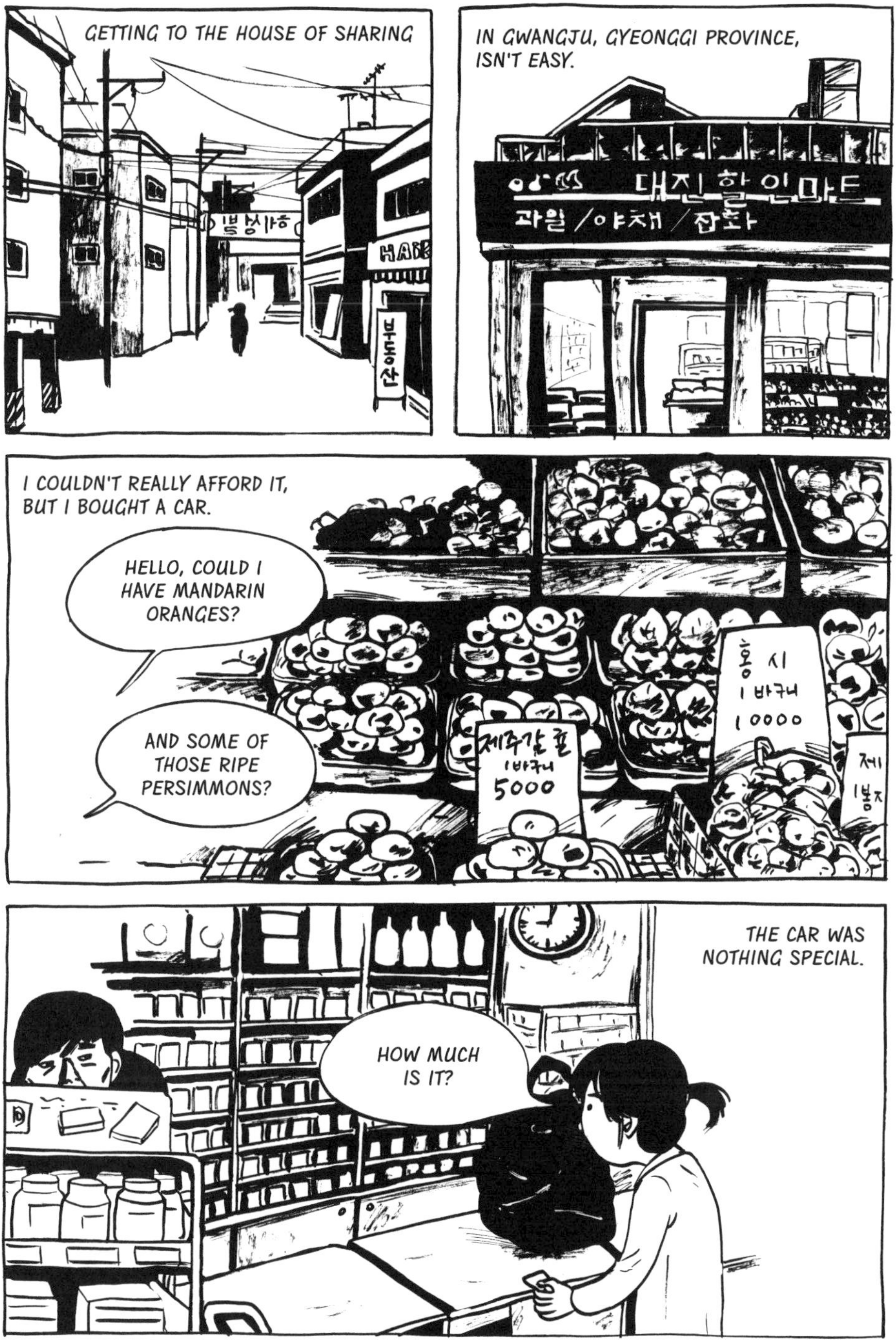
GETTING TO THE HOUSE OF SHARING
부동산
IN GWANGJU, GYEONGGI PROVINCE, ISN'T EASY.
대진할인마트
과일/야채/잡화
I COULDN'T REALLY AFFORD IT, BUT I BOUGHT A CAR.
HELLO, COULD I HAVE MANDARIN ORANGES?
AND SOME OF THOSE RIPE PERSIMMONS?
홍시
1바구니
10000
제주감귤
1바구니
5000
THE CAR WAS NOTHING SPECIAL.
HOW MUCH IS IT?

IT WAS A THIRTEEN-YEAR-OLD COMPACT
WITH NO AIRBAGS. MY FRIENDS TEASED
ME ABOUT IT. THEY CALLED IT A WRECK.

BUT A TRIP REQUIRING SUBWAY, BUS,
AND TAXI

OVER THE COURSE OF
NEARLY FOUR HOURS

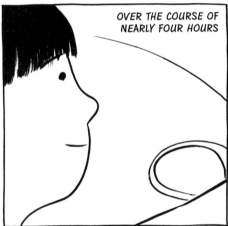

NOW TOOK ONLY TWO.

SIGN: "THE HOUSE OF SHARING"

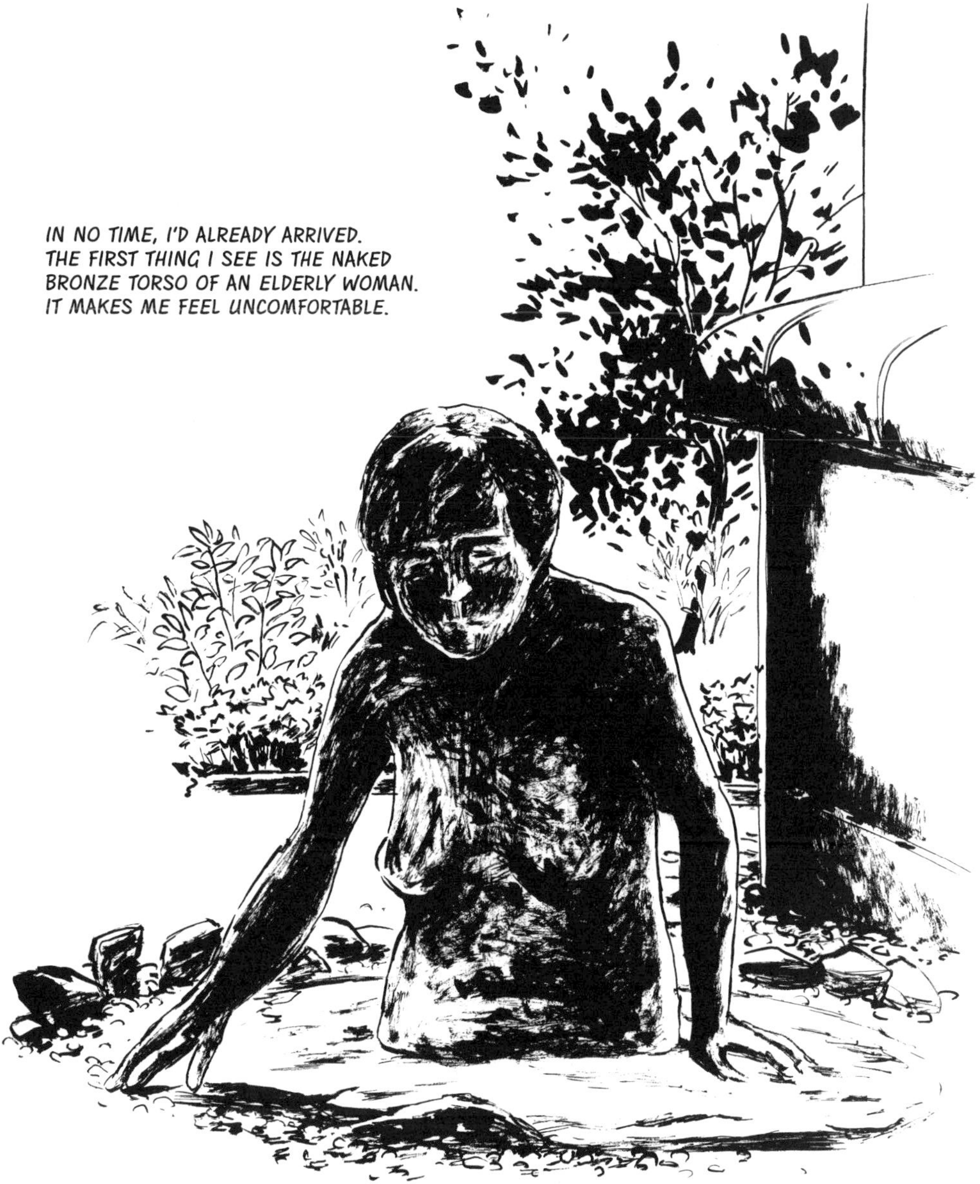
IN NO TIME, I'D ALREADY ARRIVED. THE FIRST THING I SEE IS THE NAKED BRONZE TORSO OF AN ELDERLY WOMAN. IT MAKES ME FEEL UNCOMFORTABLE.
WAS I JUST STIRRING UP PAINFUL MEMORIES FOR GRANNY LEE BY TRYING TO TELL HER STORY AS A COMIC WHEN ALL SHE WANTED WAS TO PUT THE PAST BEHIND HER? I KNOW MANY PEOPLE HAVE COME TO HER WITH SIMILAR AGENDAS...

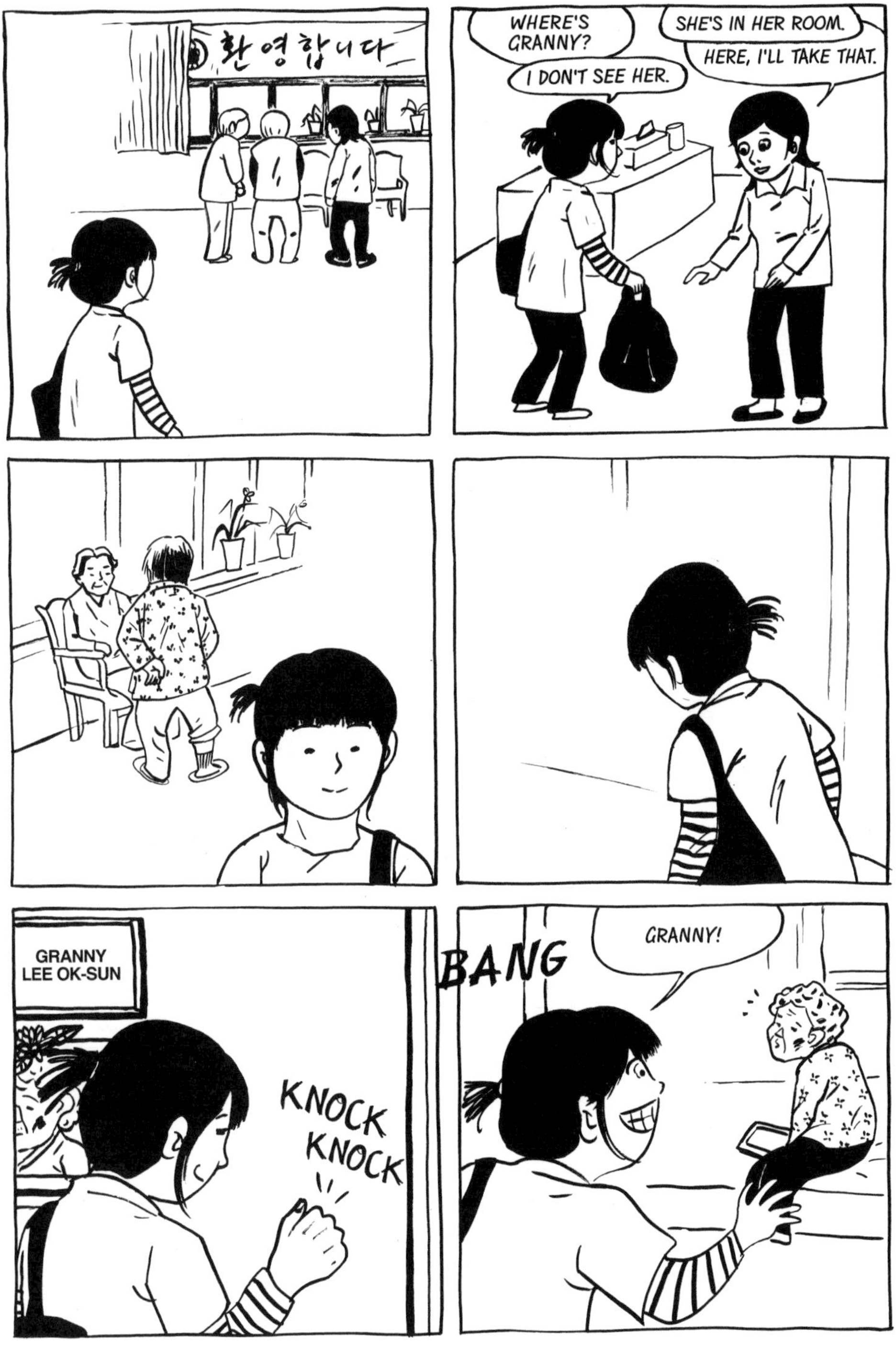
환영합니다
WHERE'S GRANNY?
I DON'T SEE HER.
SHE'S IN HER ROOM.
HERE, I'LL TAKE THAT.
GRANNY LEE OK-SUN
KNOCK KNOCK
BANG
GRANNY!

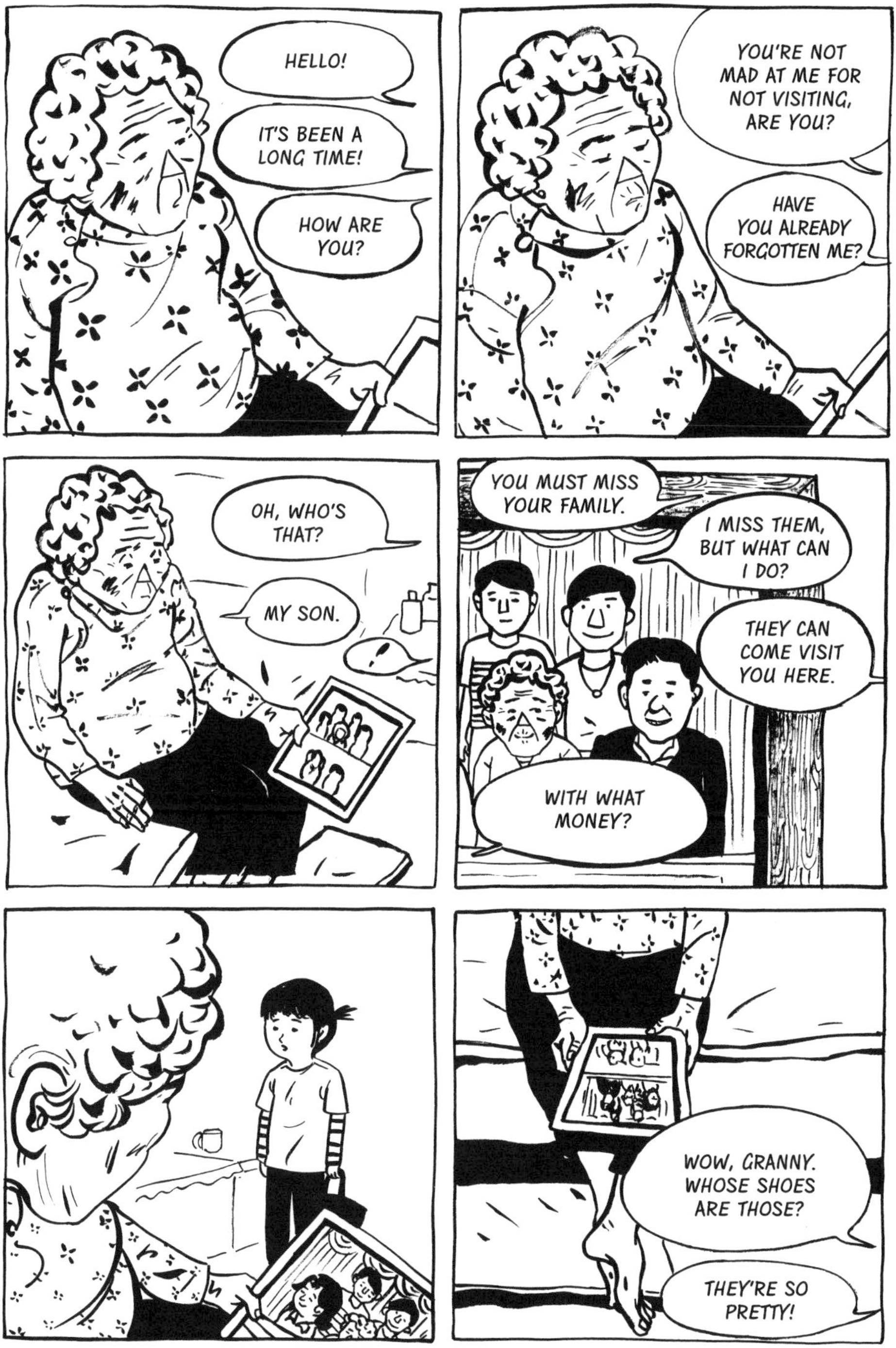
HELLO!
IT'S BEEN A LONG TIME!
HOW ARE YOU?
YOU'RE NOT MAD AT ME FOR NOT VISITING, ARE YOU?
HAVE YOU ALREADY FORGOTTEN ME?
OH, WHO'S THAT?
MY SON.
!
YOU MUST MISS YOUR FAMILY.
I MISS THEM, BUT WHAT CAN I DO?
THEY CAN COME VISIT YOU HERE.
WITH WHAT MONEY?
WOW, GRANNY. WHOSE SHOES ARE THOSE?
THEY'RE SO PRETTY!

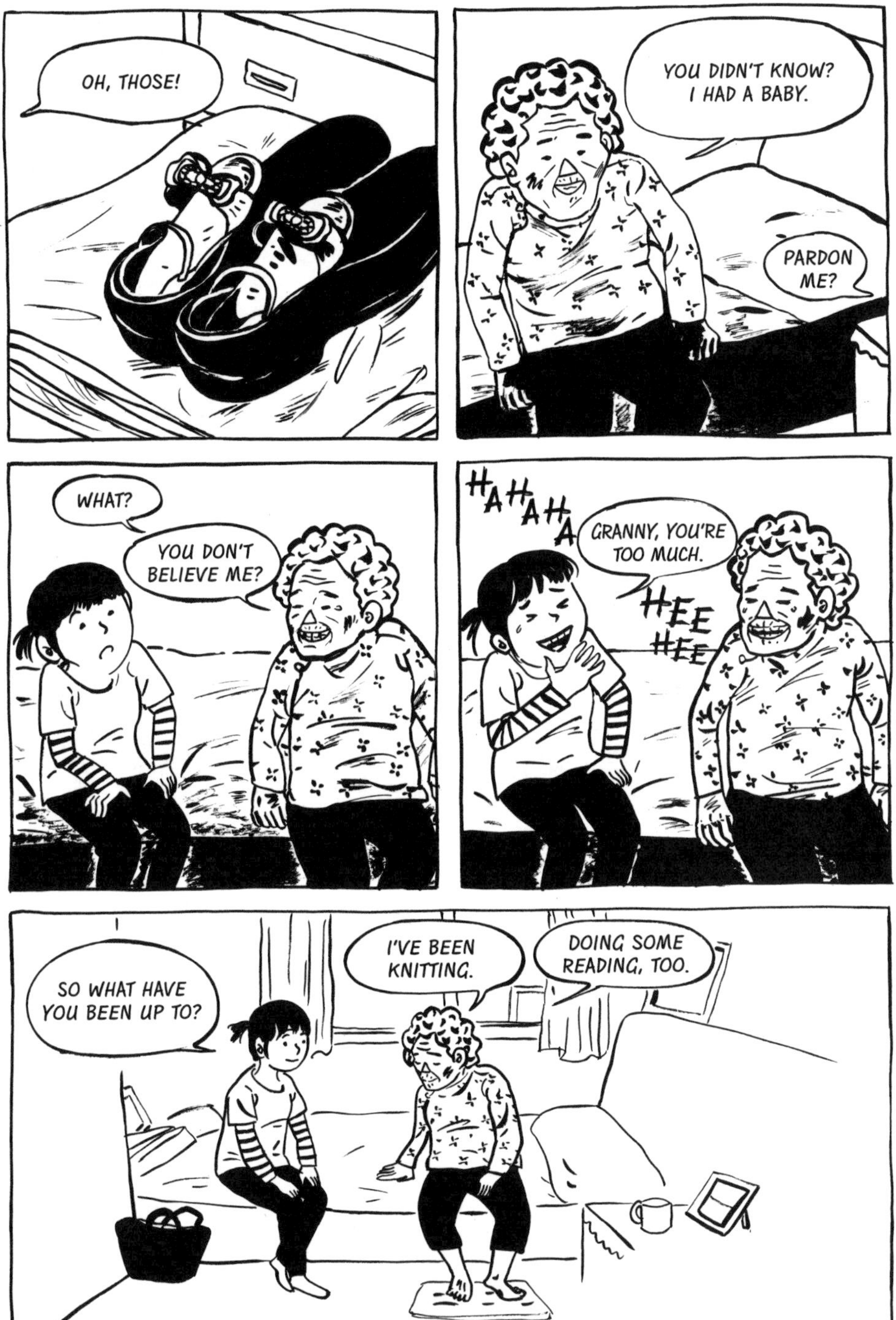
OH, THOSE!
YOU DIDN'T KNOW? I HAD A BABY.
PARDON ME?
WHAT?
YOU DON'T BELIEVE ME?
HAHAHA
GRANNY, YOU'RE TOO MUCH.
HEE HEE
SO WHAT HAVE YOU BEEN UP TO?
I'VE BEEN KNITTING.
DOING SOME READING, TOO.

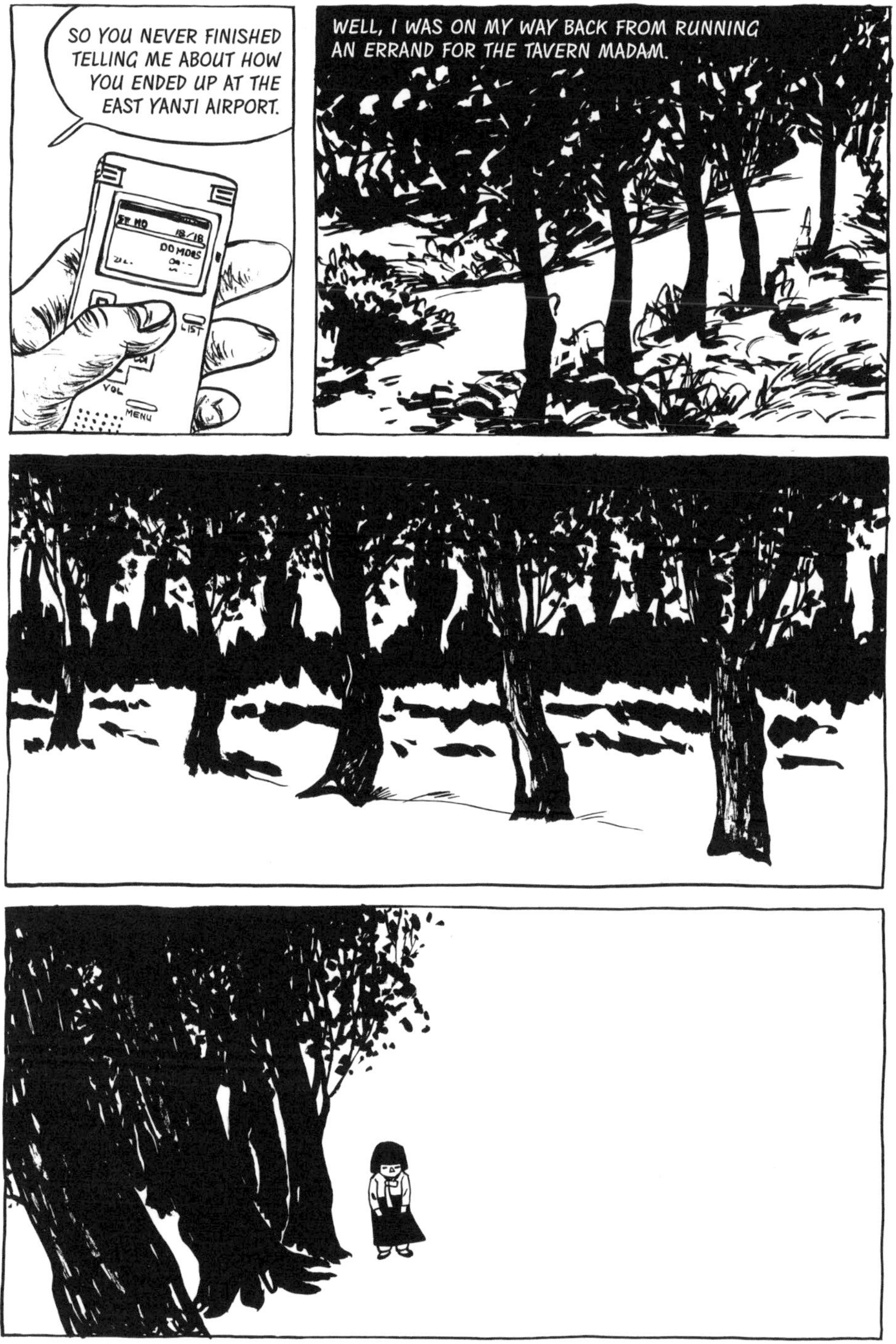
SO YOU NEVER FINISHED TELLING ME ABOUT HOW YOU ENDED UP AT THE EAST YANJI AIRPORT.
LIST
VOL
MENU
WELL, I WAS ON MY WAY BACK FROM RUNNING AN ERRAND FOR THE TAVERN MADAM.

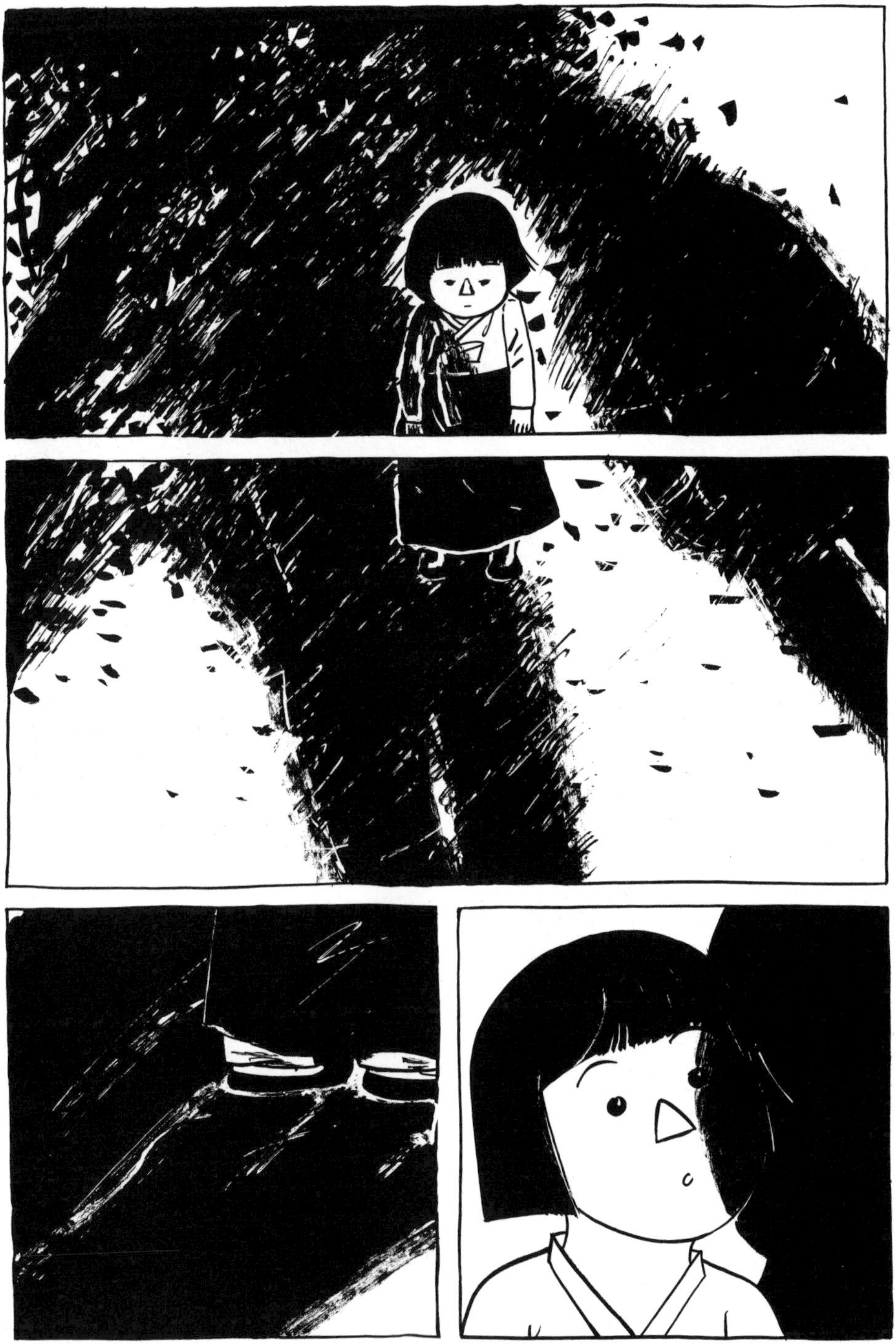

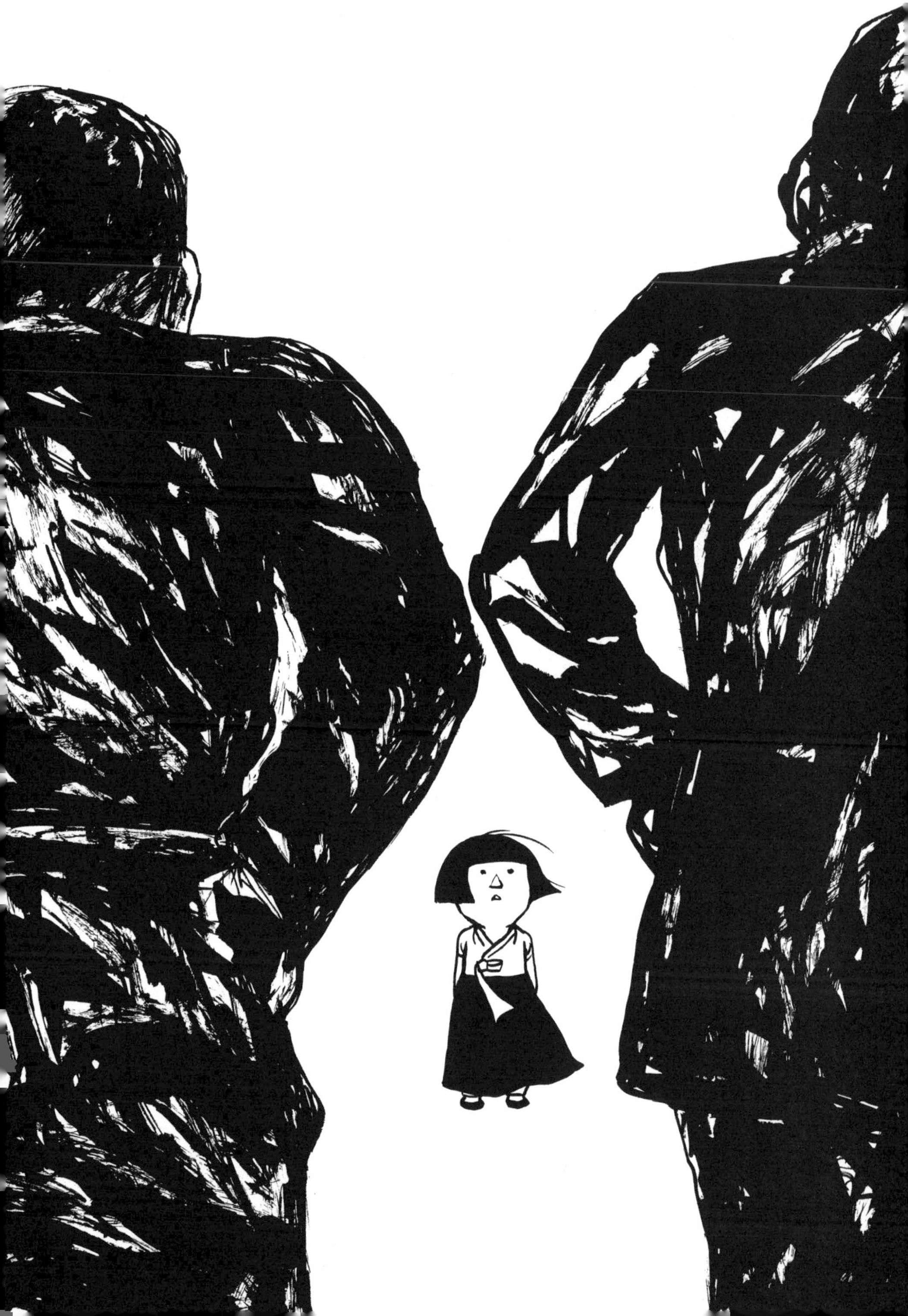

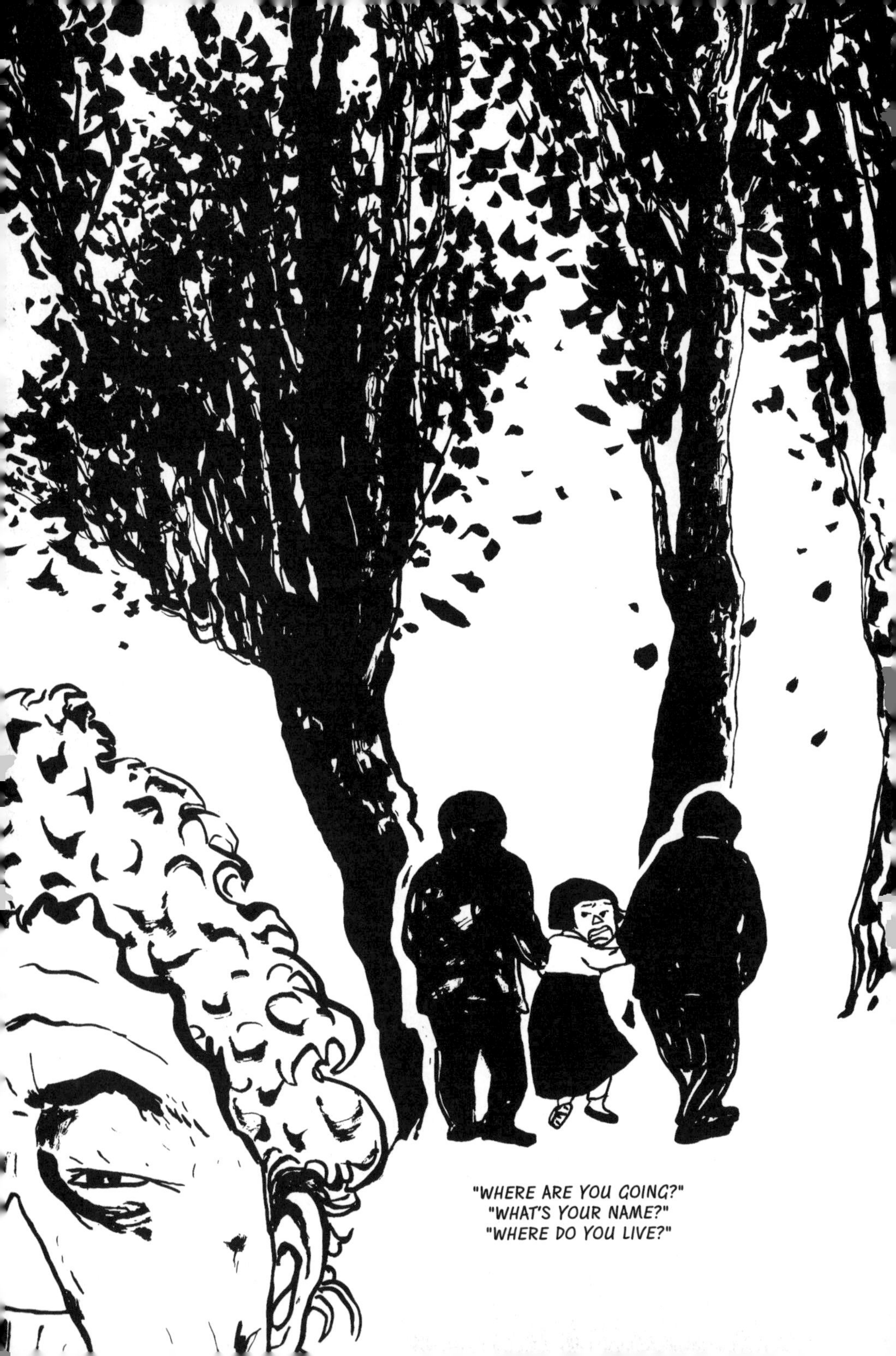
"WHERE ARE YOU GOING?"
"WHAT'S YOUR NAME?"
"WHERE DO YOU LIVE?"

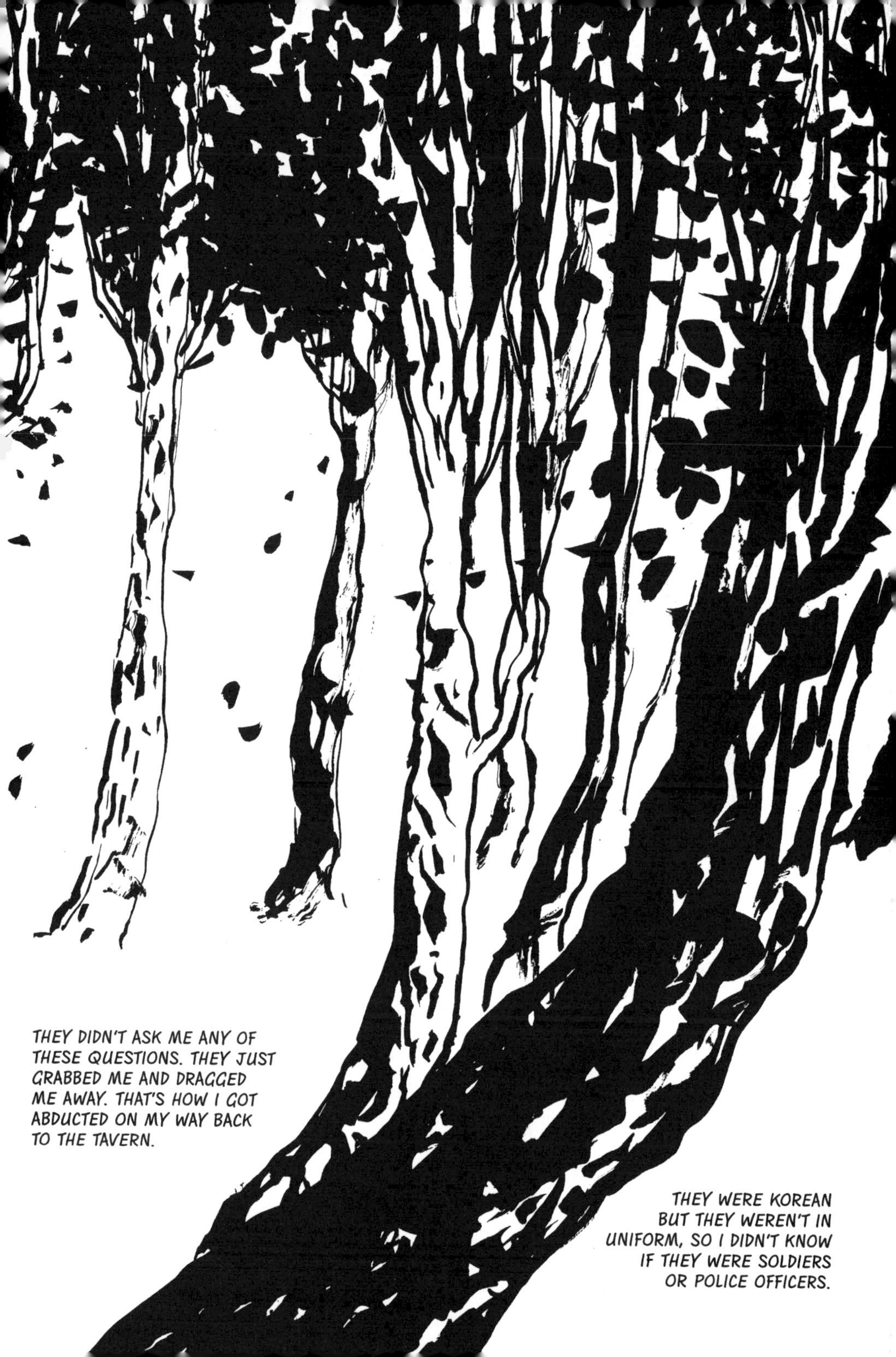
THEY DIDN'T ASK ME ANY OF THESE QUESTIONS. THEY JUST GRABBED ME AND DRAGGED ME AWAY. THAT'S HOW I GOT ABDUCTED ON MY WAY BACK TO THE TAVERN.
THEY WERE KOREAN BUT THEY WEREN'T IN UNIFORM, SO I DIDN'T KNOW IF THEY WERE SOLDIERS OR POLICE OFFICERS.

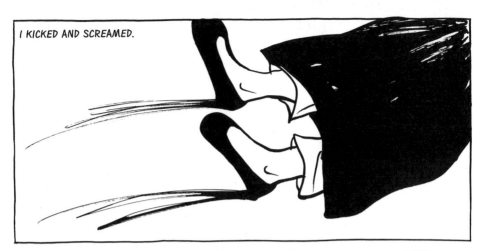

I KICKED AND SCREAMED.

I ASKED THEM WHY THEY WERE TAKING ME.

I SAID MY PARENTS WERE WAITING FOR ME AT HOME.

MAMA!

PAPA!

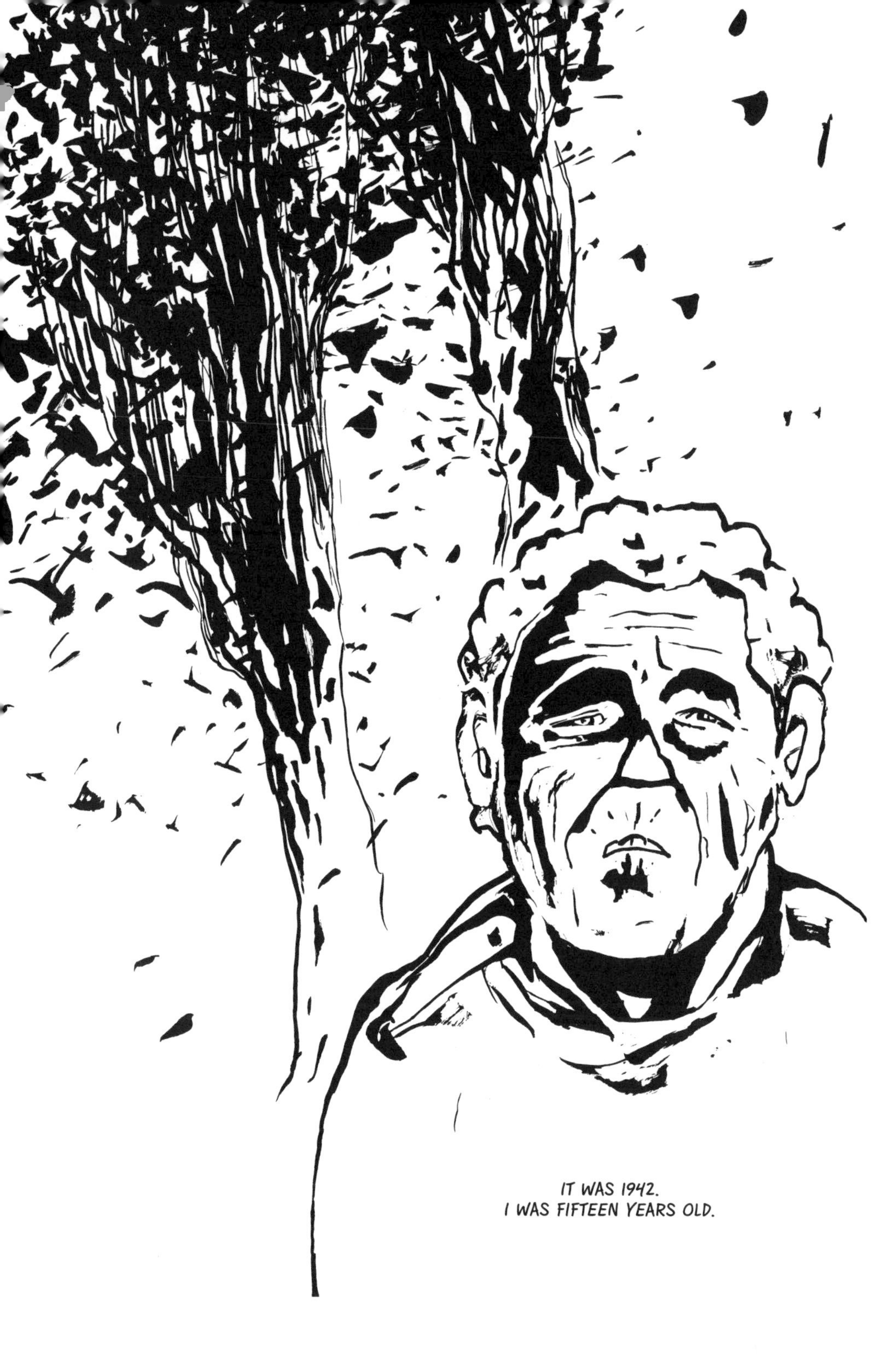
IT WAS 1942.
I WAS FIFTEEN YEARS OLD.

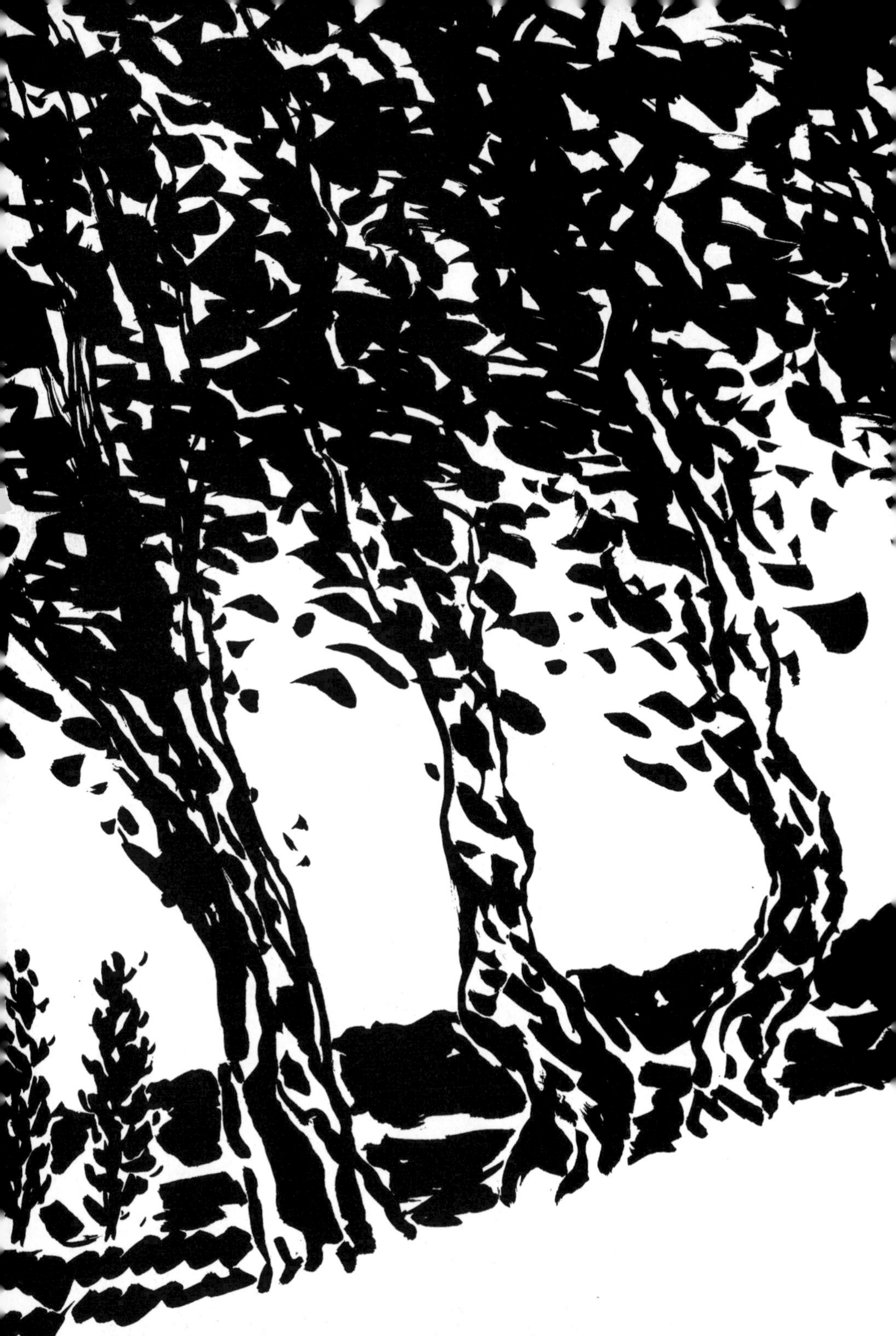

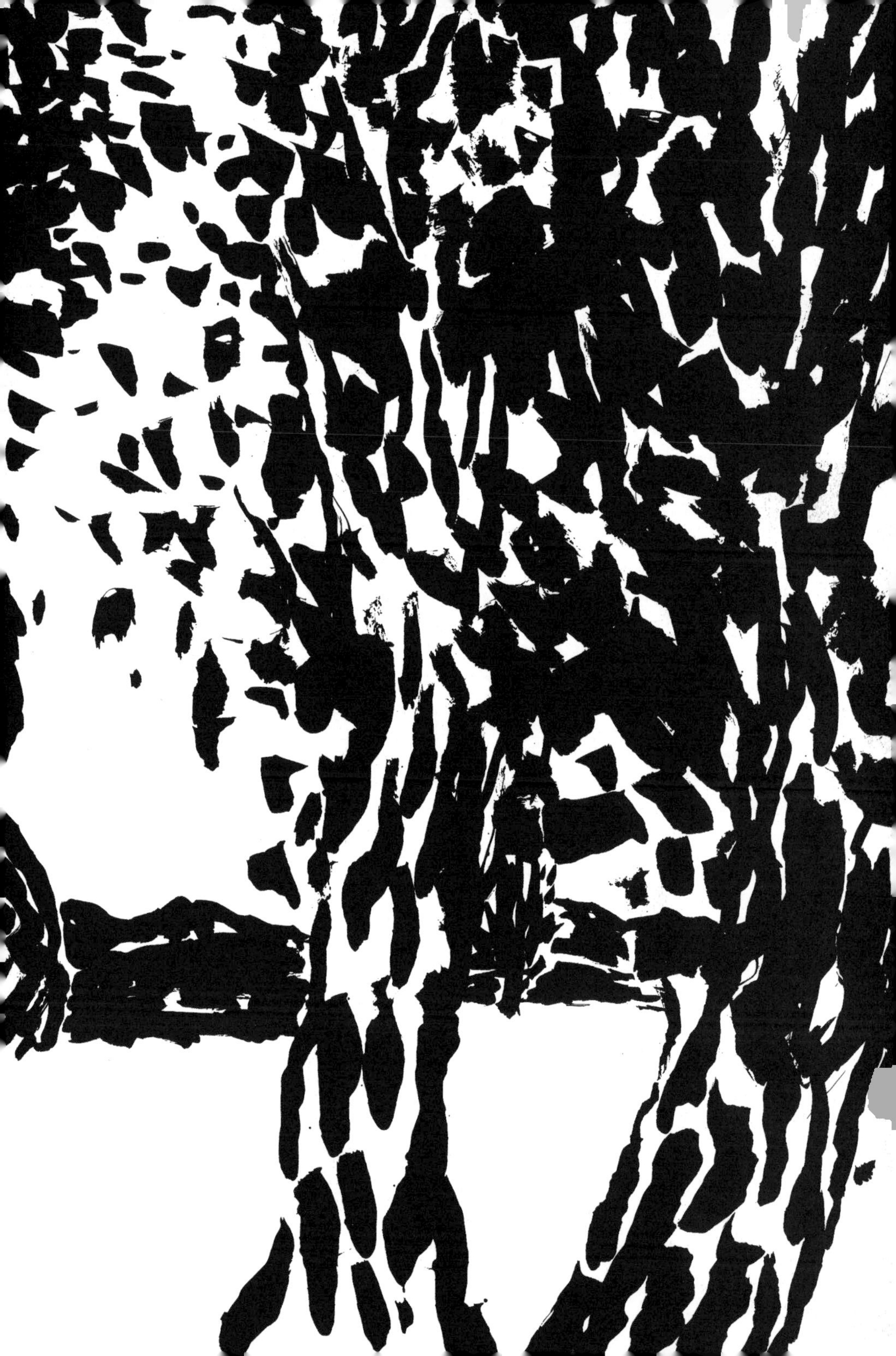

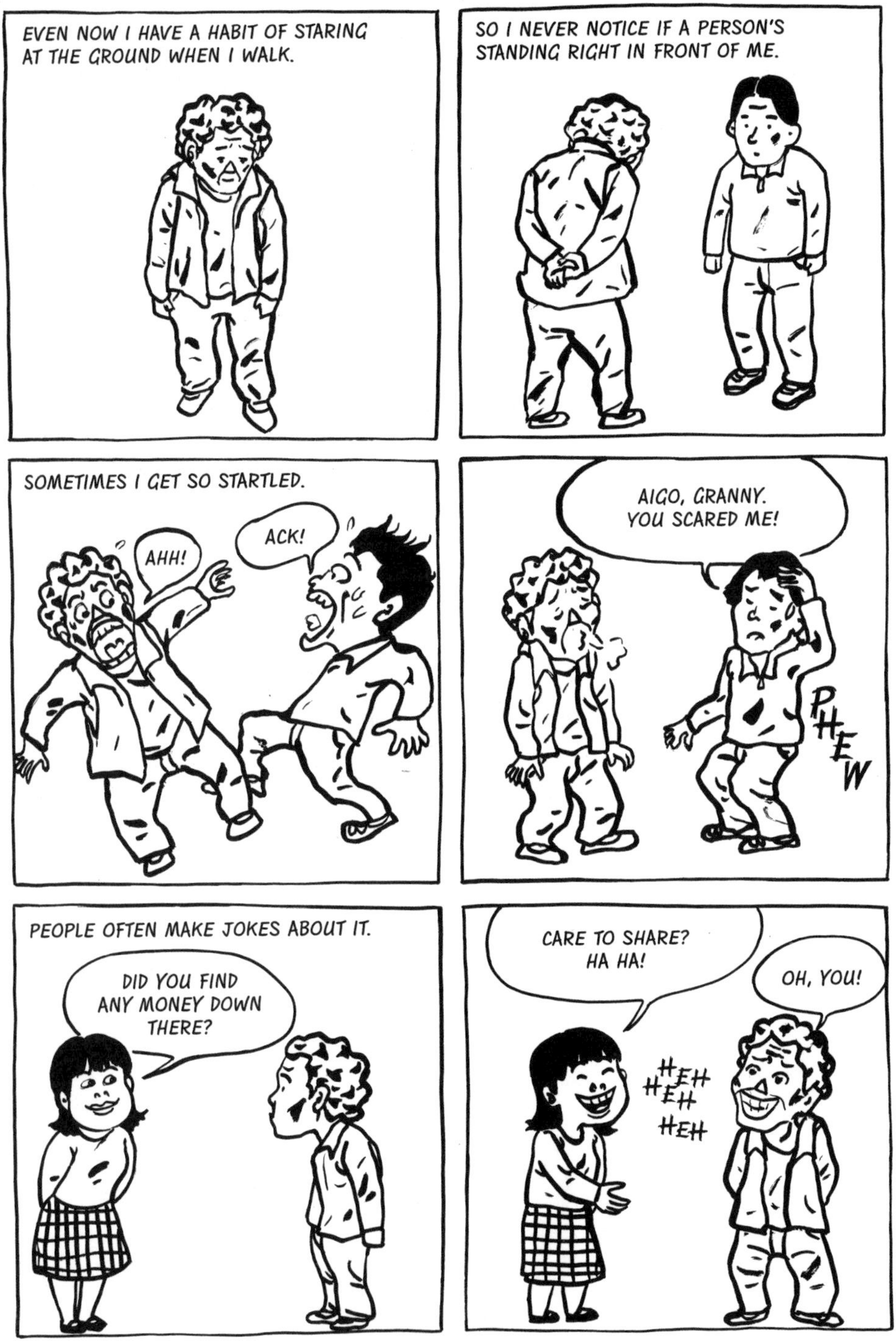
EVEN NOW I HAVE A HABIT OF STARING AT THE GROUND WHEN I WALK.
SO I NEVER NOTICE IF A PERSON'S STANDING RIGHT IN FRONT OF ME.
SOMETIMES I GET SO STARTLED.
AHH!
ACK!
AIGO, GRANNY. YOU SCARED ME!
PHEW
PEOPLE OFTEN MAKE JOKES ABOUT IT.
DID YOU FIND ANY MONEY DOWN THERE?
CARE TO SHARE? HA HA!
OH, YOU!
HEH HEH HEH

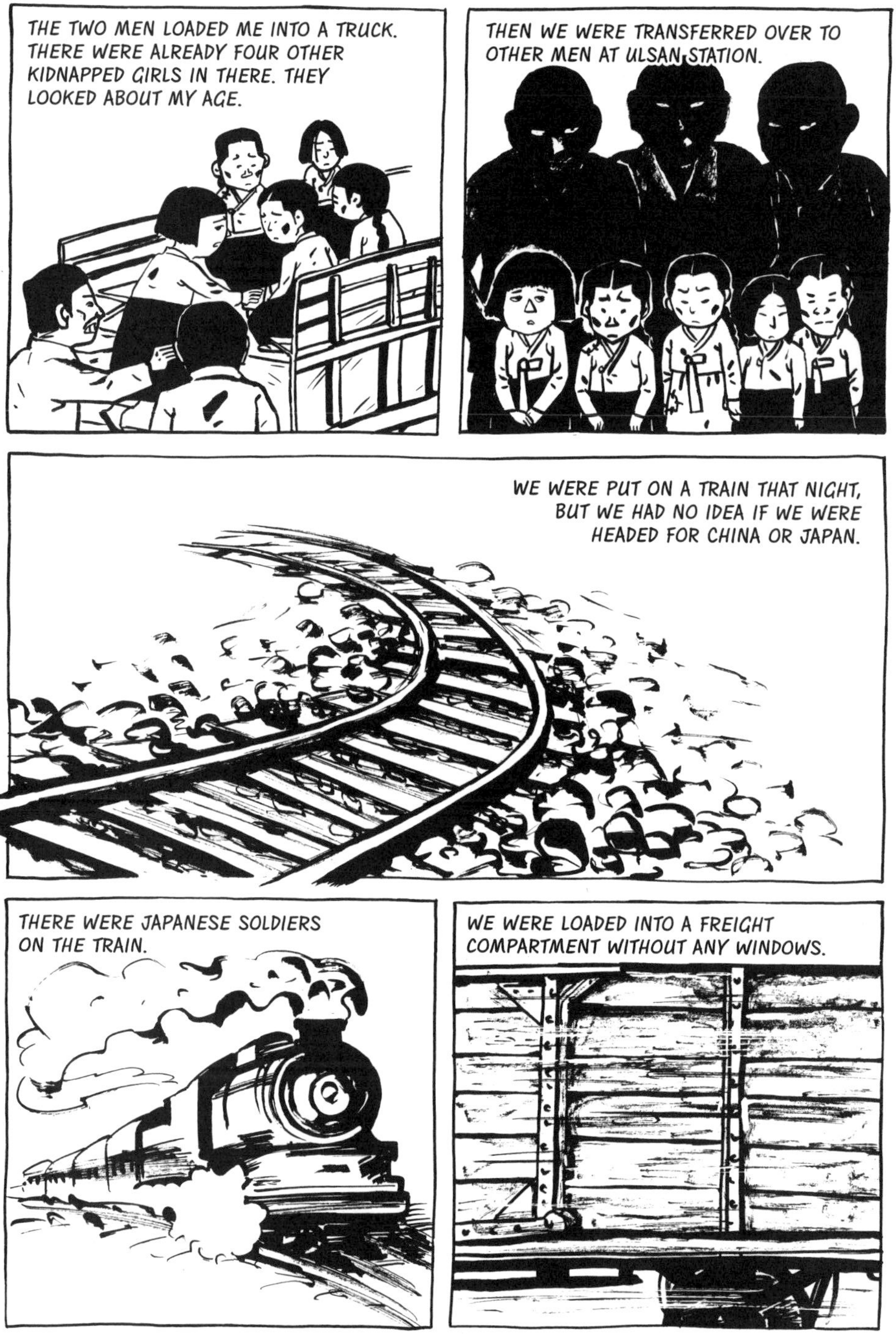
THE TWO MEN LOADED ME INTO A TRUCK. THERE WERE ALREADY FOUR OTHER KIDNAPPED GIRLS IN THERE. THEY LOOKED ABOUT MY AGE.
THEN WE WERE TRANSFERRED OVER TO OTHER MEN AT ULSAN STATION.
WE WERE PUT ON A TRAIN THAT NIGHT, BUT WE HAD NO IDEA IF WE WERE HEADED FOR CHINA OR JAPAN.
THERE WERE JAPANESE SOLDIERS ON THE TRAIN.
WE WERE LOADED INTO A FREIGHT COMPARTMENT WITHOUT ANY WINDOWS.

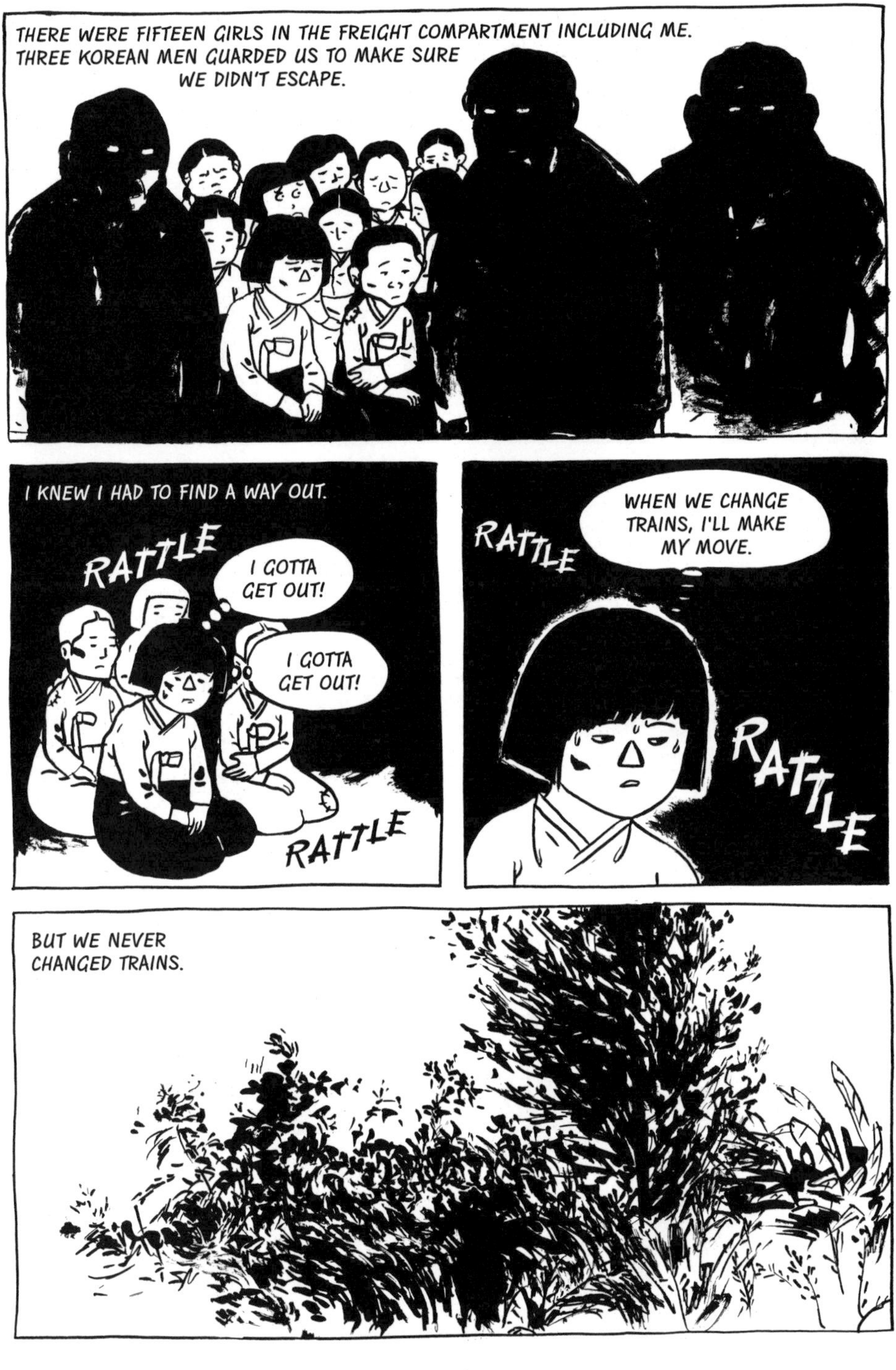

THERE WERE FIFTEEN GIRLS IN THE FREIGHT COMPARTMENT INCLUDING ME. THREE KOREAN MEN GUARDED US TO MAKE SURE WE DIDN'T ESCAPE.
I KNEW I HAD TO FIND A WAY OUT.
RATTLE
I GOTTA GET OUT!
I GOTTA GET OUT!
RATTLE
RATTLE
WHEN WE CHANGE TRAINS, I'LL MAKE MY MOVE.
RATTLE
BUT WE NEVER CHANGED TRAINS.

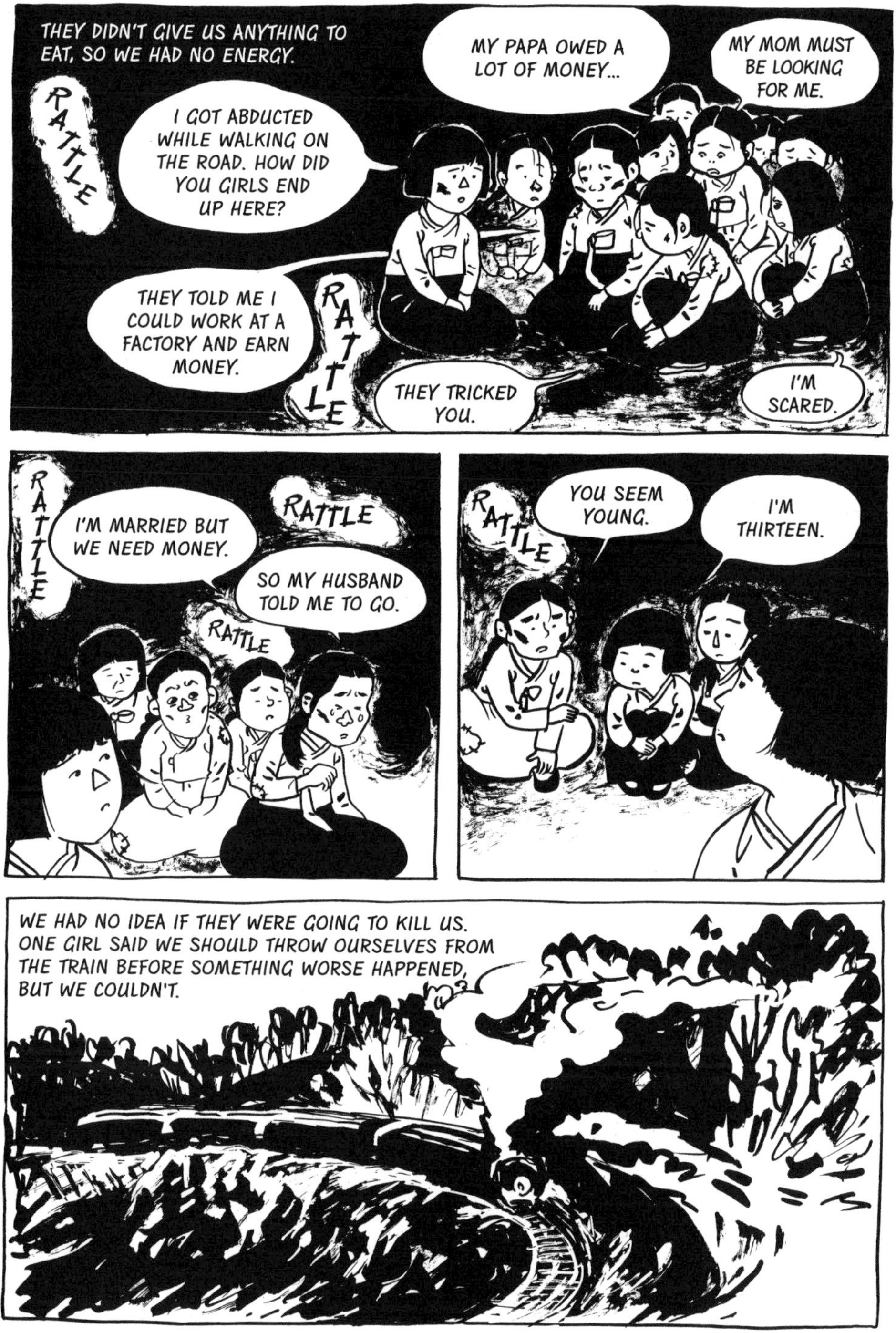
THEY DIDN'T GIVE US ANYTHING TO EAT, SO WE HAD NO ENERGY.
RATTLE
MY PAPA OWED A LOT OF MONEY...
MY MOM MUST BE LOOKING FOR ME.
I GOT ABDUCTED WHILE WALKING ON THE ROAD. HOW DID YOU GIRLS END UP HERE?
THEY TOLD ME I COULD WORK AT A FACTORY AND EARN MONEY.
RATTLE
THEY TRICKED YOU.
I'M SCARED.
RATTLE
RATTLE
I'M MARRIED BUT WE NEED MONEY.
SO MY HUSBAND TOLD ME TO GO.
RATTLE
RATTLE
YOU SEEM YOUNG.
I'M THIRTEEN.
WE HAD NO IDEA IF THEY WERE GOING TO KILL US. ONE GIRL SAID WE SHOULD THROW OURSELVES FROM THE TRAIN BEFORE SOMETHING WORSE HAPPENED, BUT WE COULDN'T.

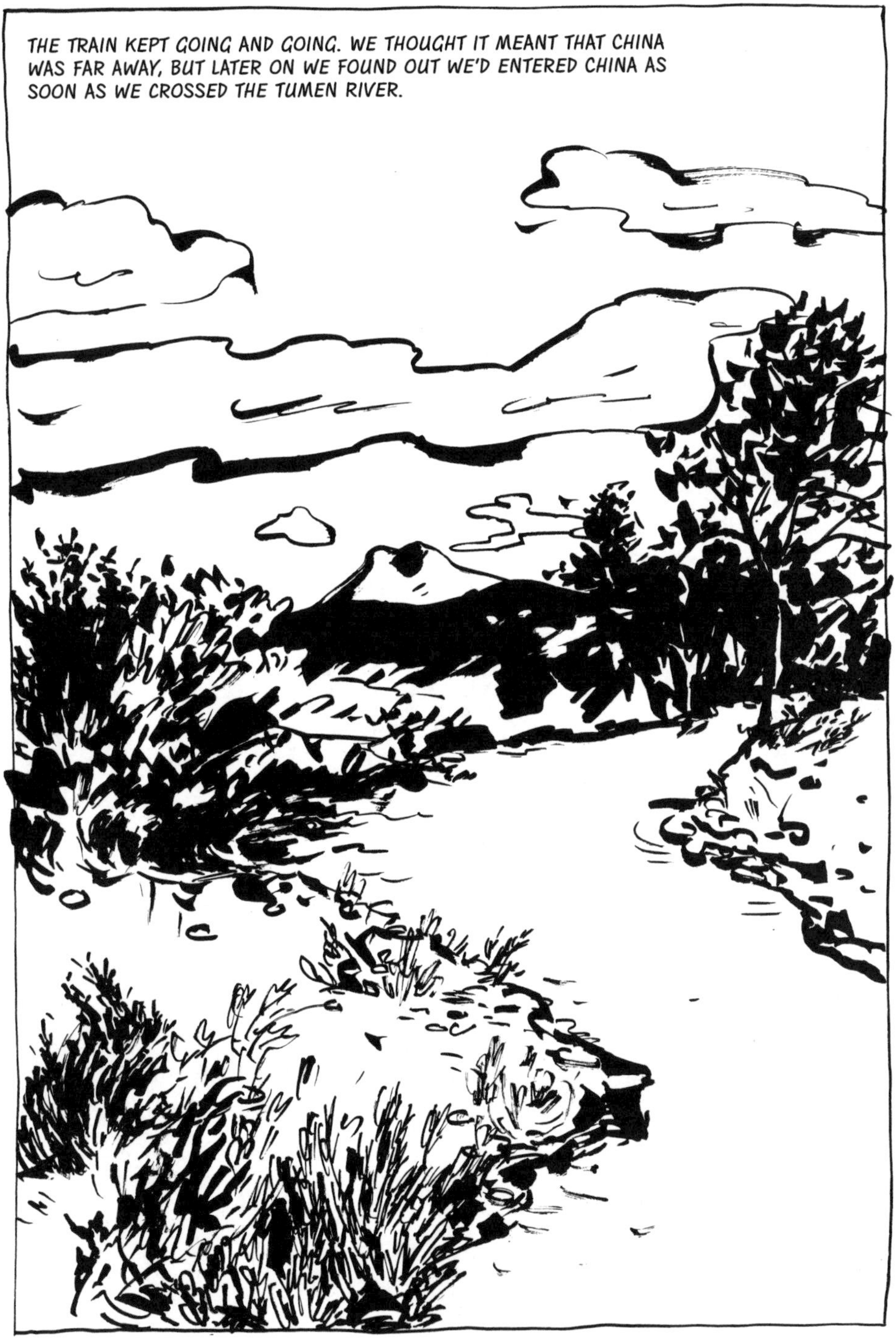
THE TRAIN KEPT GOING AND GOING. WE THOUGHT IT MEANT THAT CHINA WAS FAR AWAY, BUT LATER ON WE FOUND OUT WE'D ENTERED CHINA AS SOON AS WE CROSSED THE TUMEN RIVER.

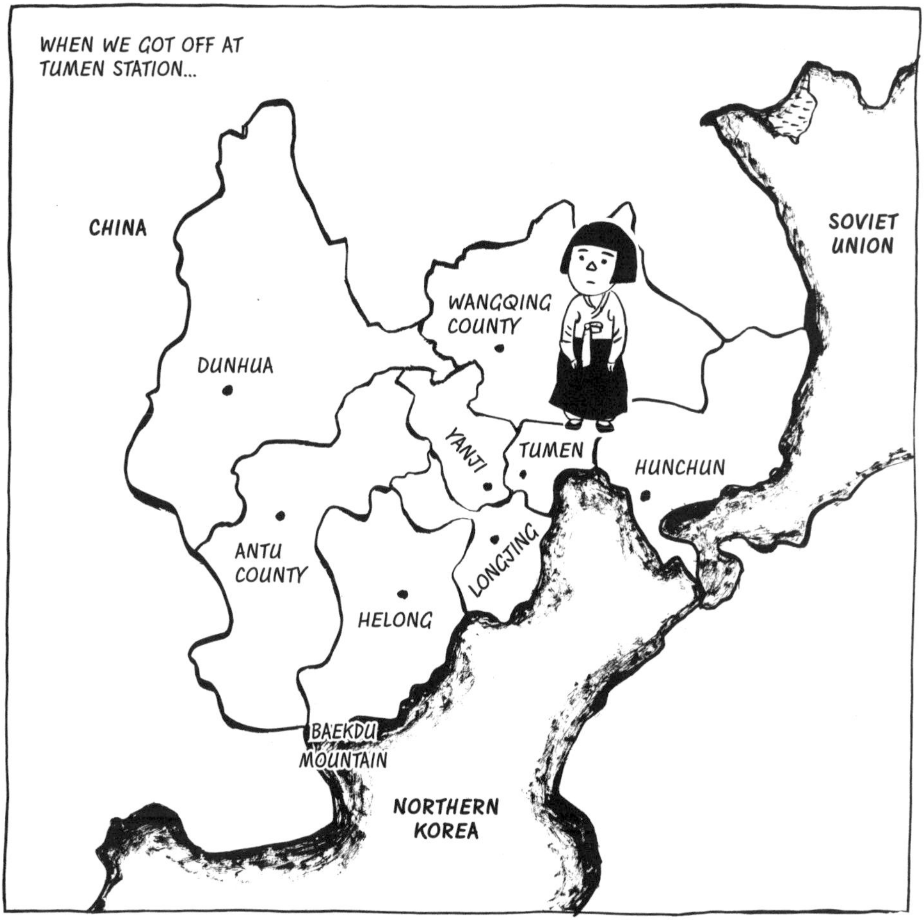
WHEN WE GOT OFF AT
TUMEN STATION...
CHINA
SOVIET
UNION
WANGQING
COUNTY
DUNHUA
YANJI
TUMEN
HUNCHUN
ANTU
COUNTY
LONGJING
HELONG
BAEKDU
MOUNTAIN
NORTHERN
KOREA

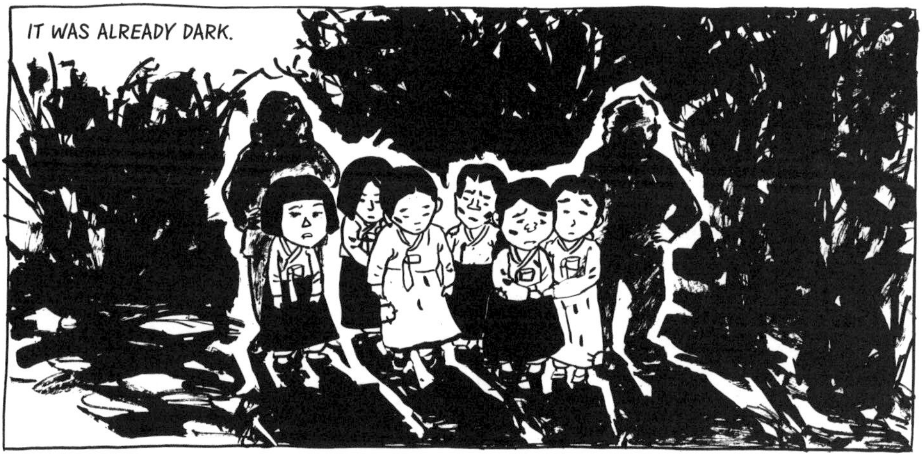
IT WAS ALREADY DARK.

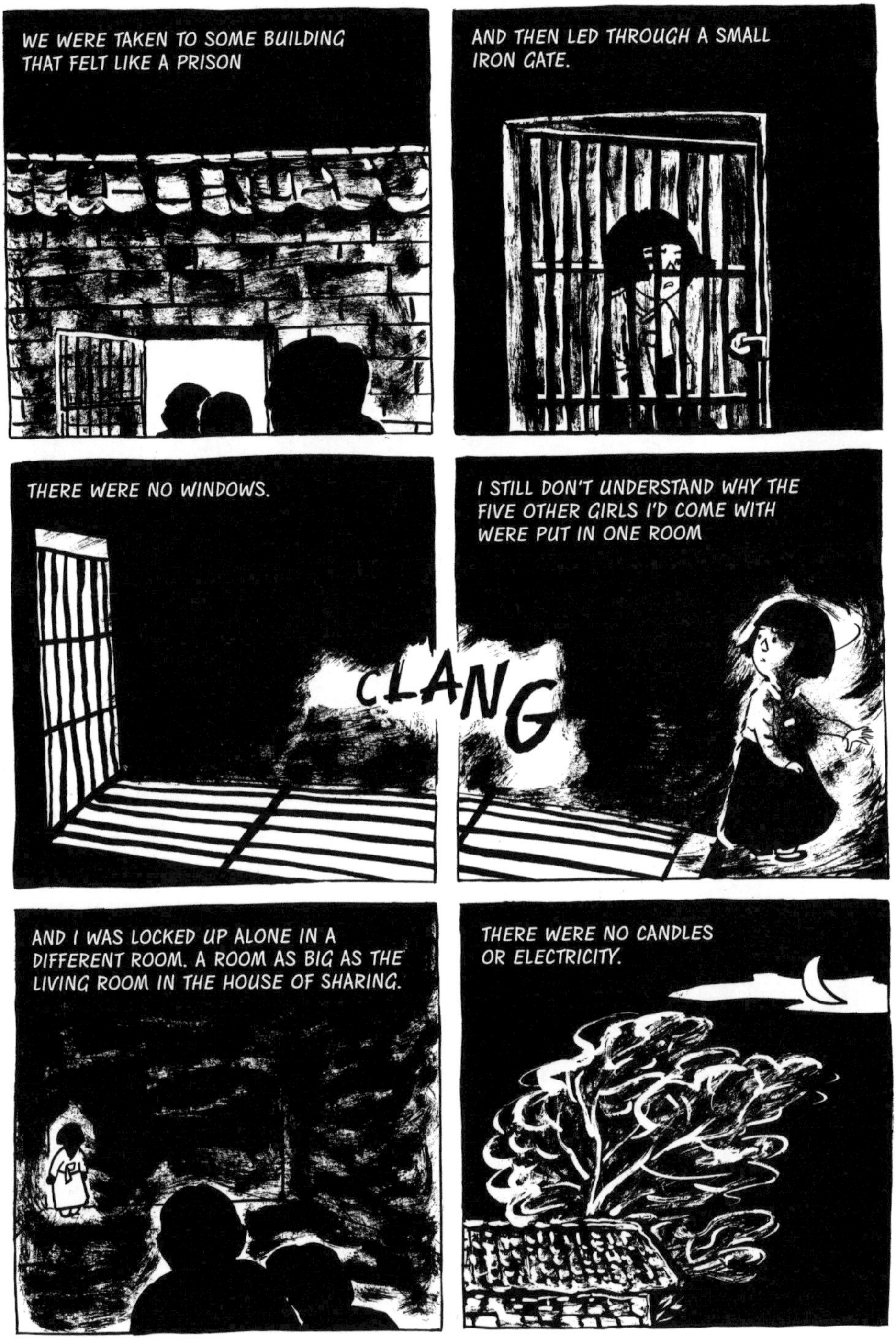
WE WERE TAKEN TO SOME BUILDING THAT FELT LIKE A PRISON
AND THEN LED THROUGH A SMALL IRON GATE.
THERE WERE NO WINDOWS.
I STILL DON'T UNDERSTAND WHY THE FIVE OTHER GIRLS I'D COME WITH WERE PUT IN ONE ROOM
CLANG
AND I WAS LOCKED UP ALONE IN A DIFFERENT ROOM. A ROOM AS BIG AS THE LIVING ROOM IN THE HOUSE OF SHARING.
THERE WERE NO CANDLES OR ELECTRICITY.

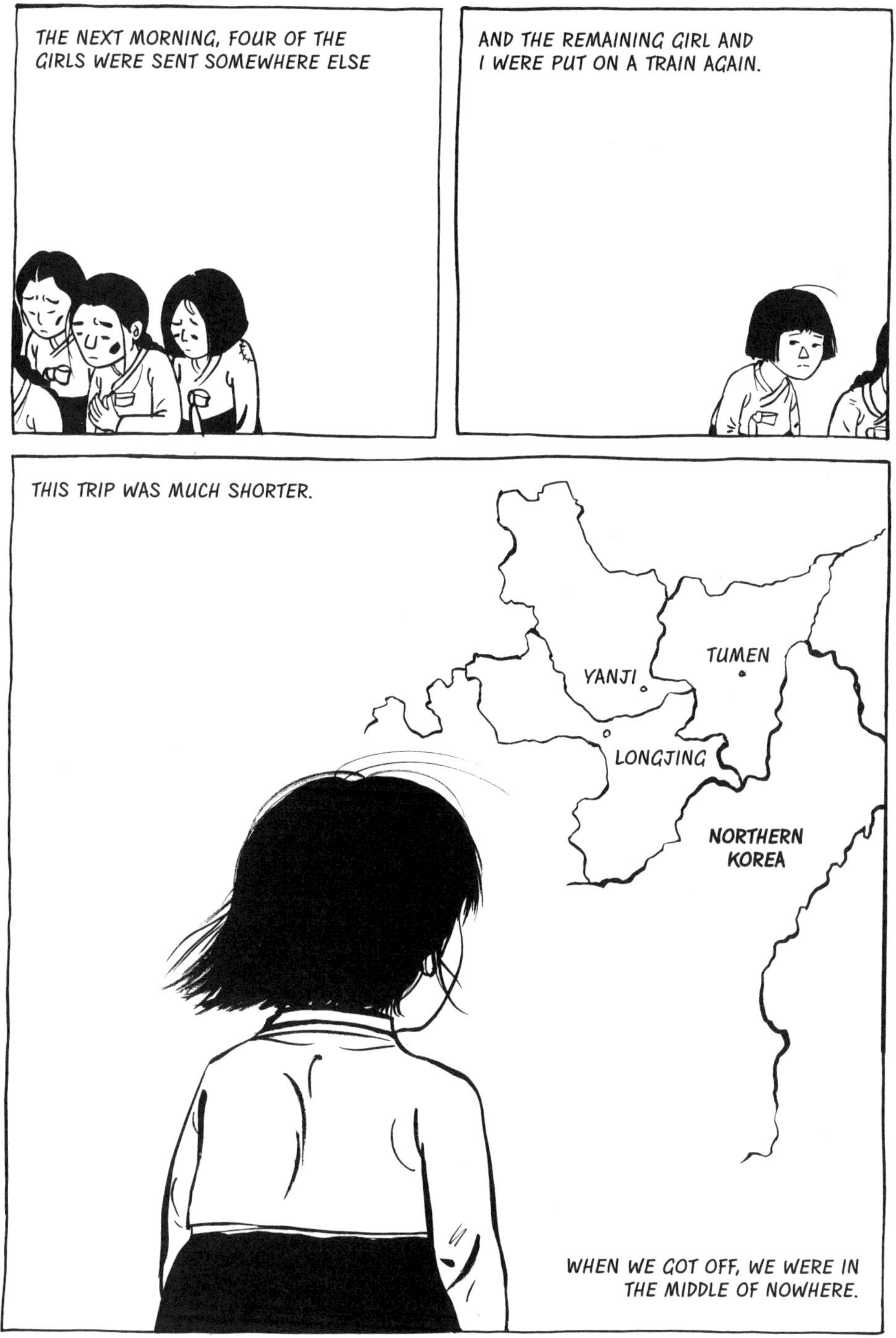
THE NEXT MORNING, FOUR OF THE GIRLS WERE SENT SOMEWHERE ELSE
AND THE REMAINING GIRL AND I WERE PUT ON A TRAIN AGAIN.
THIS TRIP WAS MUCH SHORTER.
YANJI
TUMEN
LONGJING
NORTHERN KOREA
WHEN WE GOT OFF, WE WERE IN THE MIDDLE OF NOWHERE.

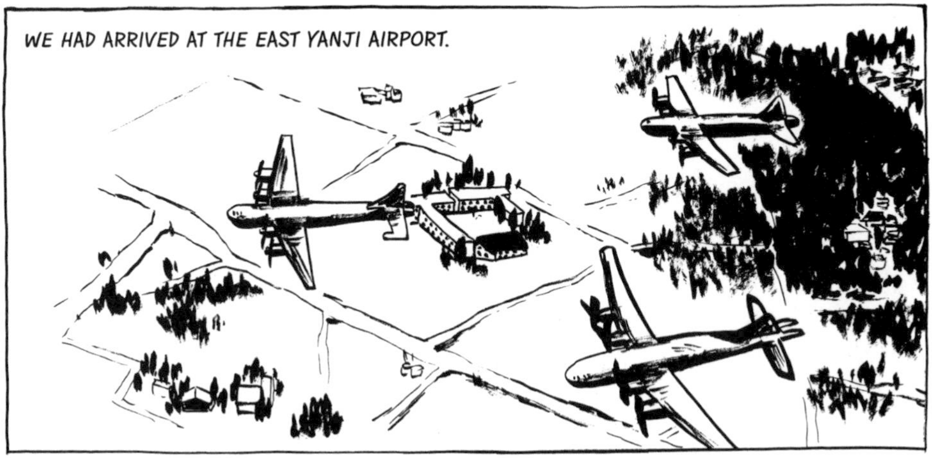
WE HAD ARRIVED AT THE EAST YANJI AIRPORT.

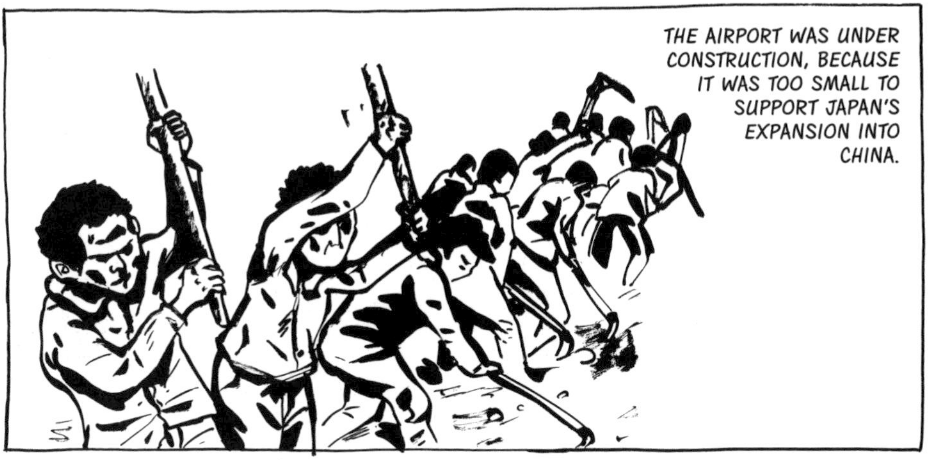
THE AIRPORT WAS UNDER CONSTRUCTION, BECAUSE IT WAS TOO SMALL TO SUPPORT JAPAN'S EXPANSION INTO CHINA.

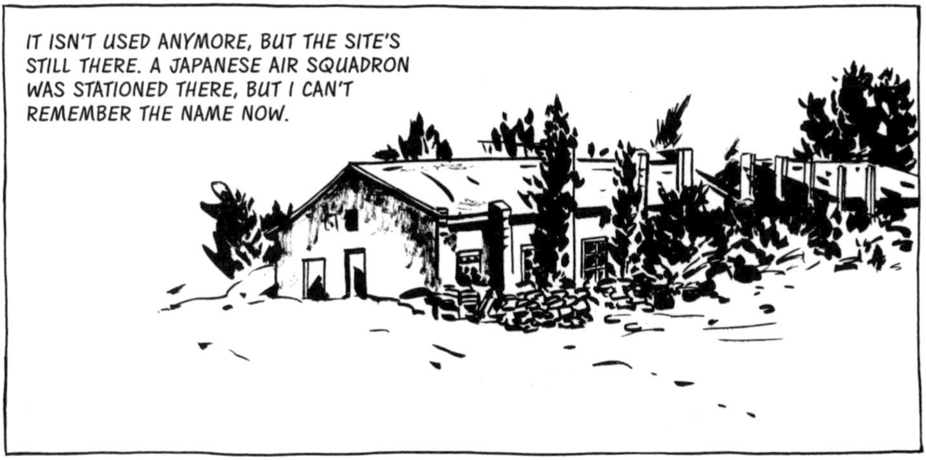
IT ISN'T USED ANYMORE, BUT THE SITE'S STILL THERE. A JAPANESE AIR SQUADRON WAS STATIONED THERE, BUT I CAN'T REMEMBER THE NAME NOW.

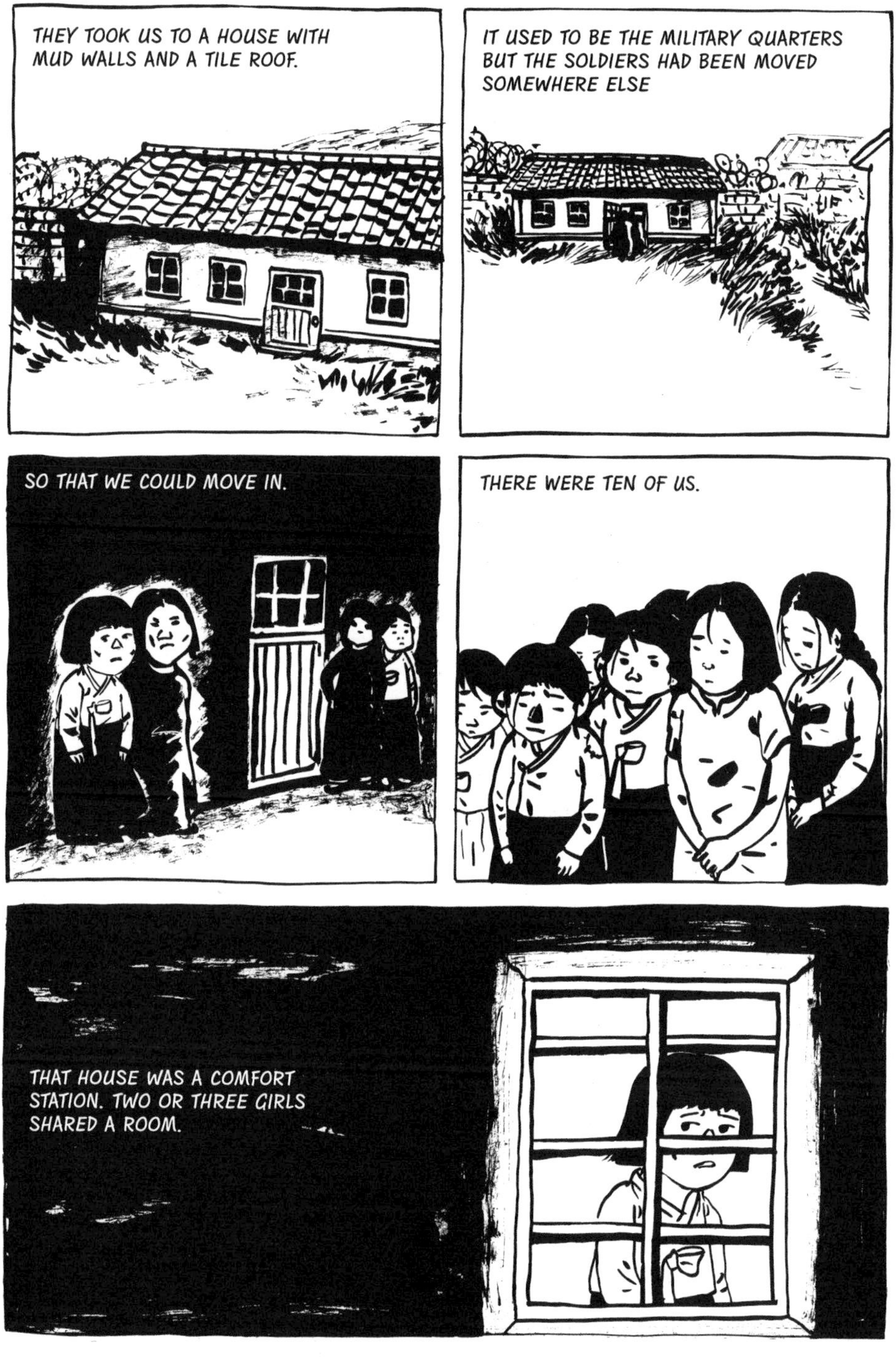
THEY TOOK US TO A HOUSE WITH MUD WALLS AND A TILE ROOF.
IT USED TO BE THE MILITARY QUARTERS BUT THE SOLDIERS HAD BEEN MOVED SOMEWHERE ELSE
SO THAT WE COULD MOVE IN.
THERE WERE TEN OF US.
THAT HOUSE WAS A COMFORT STATION. TWO OR THREE GIRLS SHARED A ROOM.

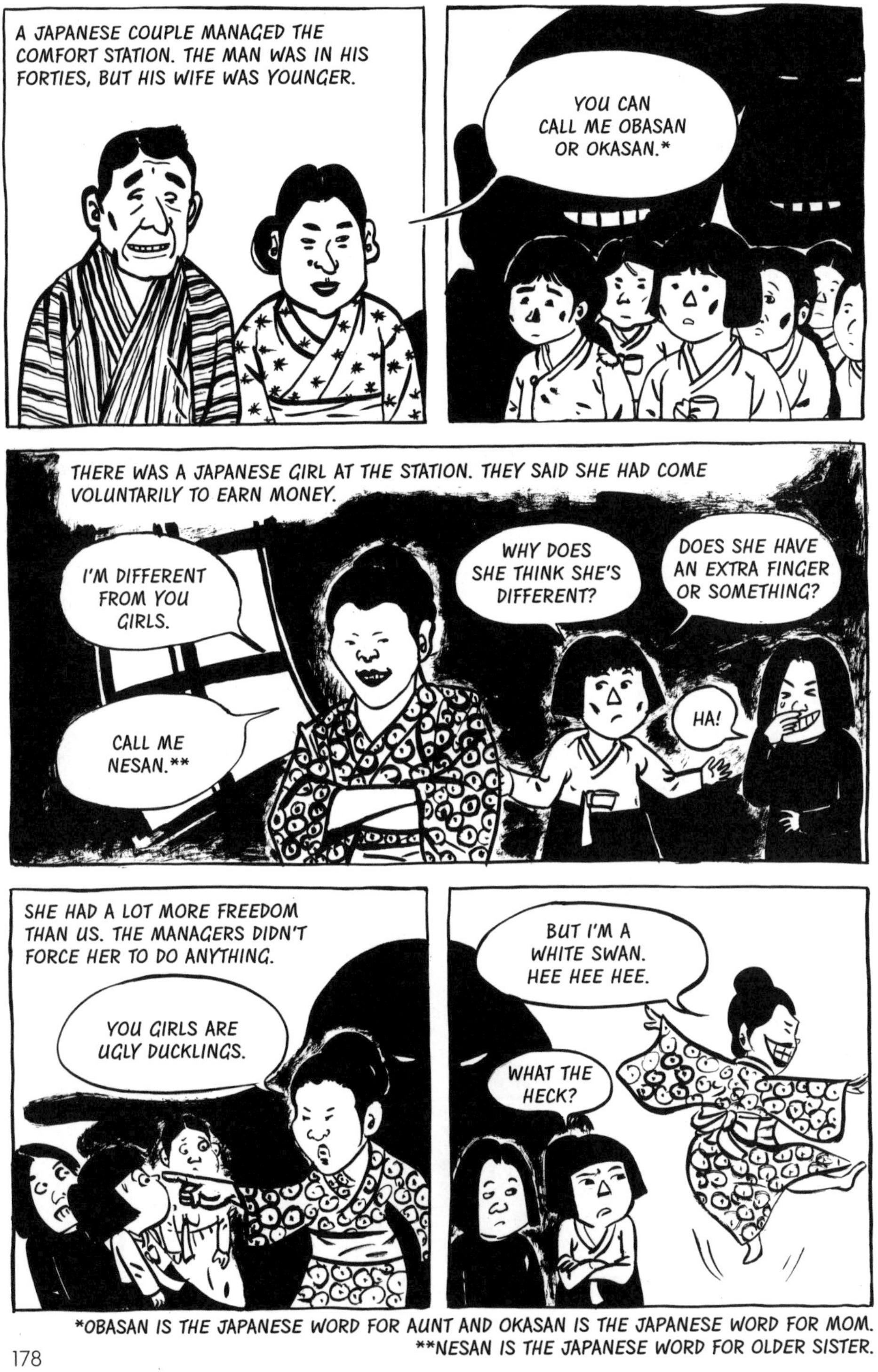
A JAPANESE COUPLE MANAGED THE COMFORT STATION. THE MAN WAS IN HIS FORTIES, BUT HIS WIFE WAS YOUNGER.
YOU CAN CALL ME OBASAN OR OKASAN.*
THERE WAS A JAPANESE GIRL AT THE STATION. THEY SAID SHE HAD COME VOLUNTARILY TO EARN MONEY.
I'M DIFFERENT FROM YOU GIRLS.
CALL ME NESAN.**
WHY DOES SHE THINK SHE'S DIFFERENT?
DOES SHE HAVE AN EXTRA FINGER OR SOMETHING?
HA!
SHE HAD A LOT MORE FREEDOM THAN US. THE MANAGERS DIDN'T FORCE HER TO DO ANYTHING.
YOU GIRLS ARE UGLY DUCKLINGS.
BUT I'M A WHITE SWAN. HEE HEE HEE.
WHAT THE HECK?

*OBASAN IS THE JAPANESE WORD FOR AUNT AND OKASAN IS THE JAPANESE WORD FOR MOM.

**NESAN IS THE JAPANESE WORD FOR OLDER SISTER.

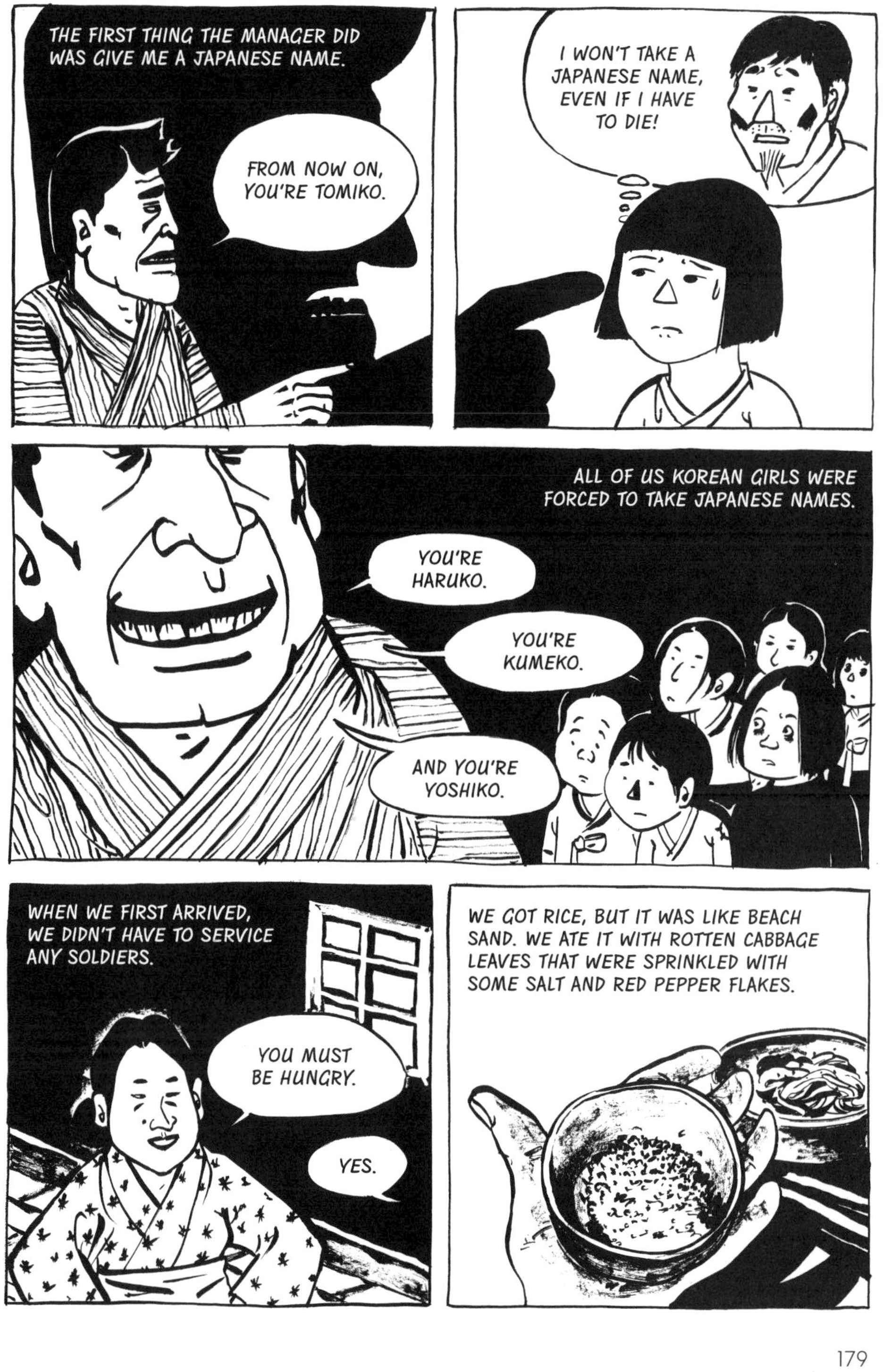
THE FIRST THING THE MANAGER DID WAS GIVE ME A JAPANESE NAME.
FROM NOW ON, YOU'RE TOMIKO.
I WON'T TAKE A JAPANESE NAME, EVEN IF I HAVE TO DIE!
ALL OF US KOREAN GIRLS WERE FORCED TO TAKE JAPANESE NAMES.
YOU'RE HARUKO.
YOU'RE KUMEKO.
AND YOU'RE YOSHIKO.
WHEN WE FIRST ARRIVED, WE DIDN'T HAVE TO SERVICE ANY SOLDIERS.
YOU MUST BE HUNGRY.
YES.
WE GOT RICE, BUT IT WAS LIKE BEACH SAND. WE ATE IT WITH ROTTEN CABBAGE LEAVES THAT WERE SPRINKLED WITH SOME SALT AND RED PEPPER FLAKES.

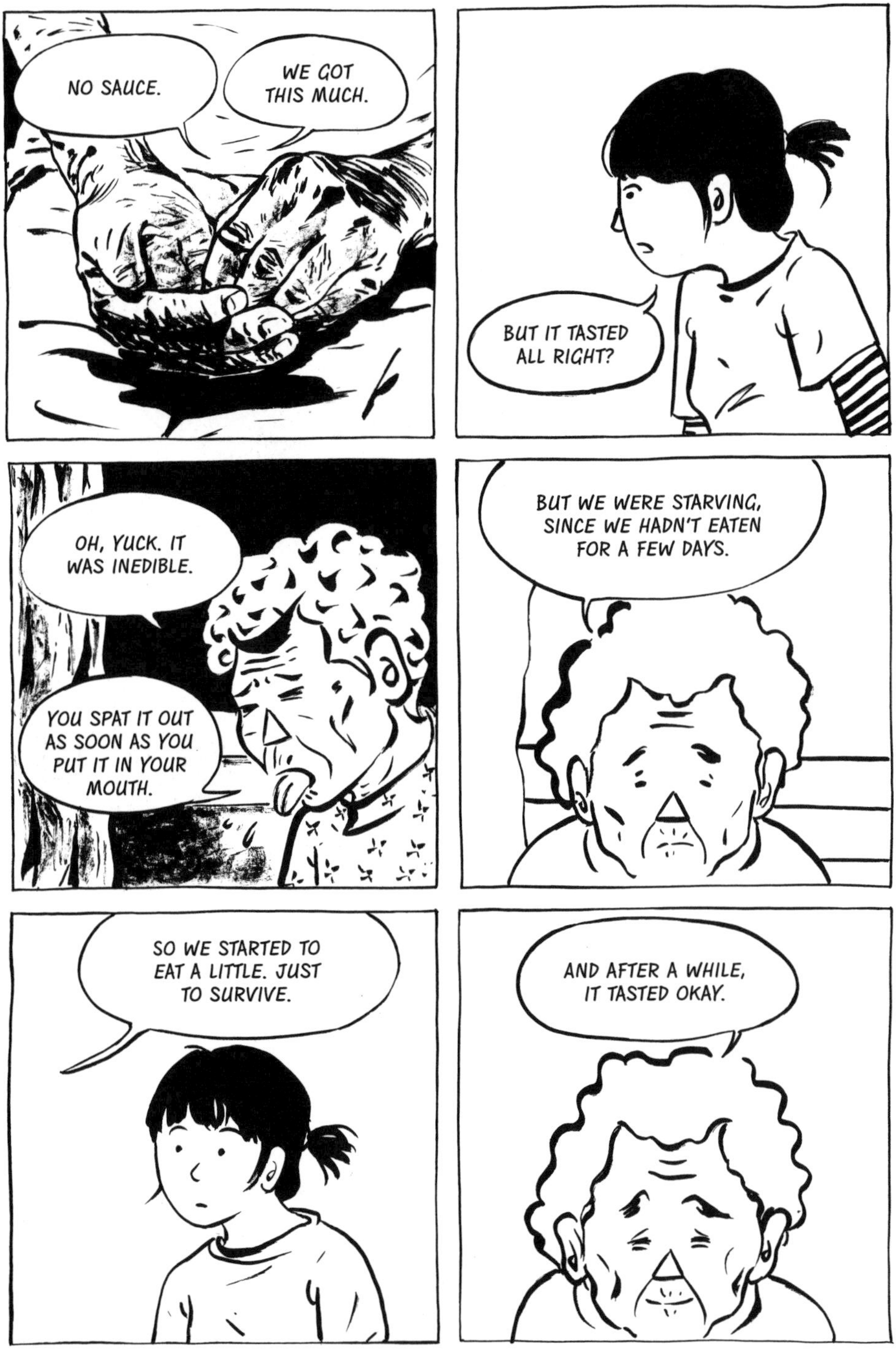
NO SAUCE.
WE GOT THIS MUCH.
BUT IT TASTED ALL RIGHT?
OH, YUCK. IT WAS INEDIBLE.
YOU SPAT IT OUT AS SOON AS YOU PUT IT IN YOUR MOUTH.
BUT WE WERE STARVING, SINCE WE HADN'T EATEN FOR A FEW DAYS.
SO WE STARTED TO EAT A LITTLE. JUST TO SURVIVE.
AND AFTER A WHILE, IT TASTED OKAY.

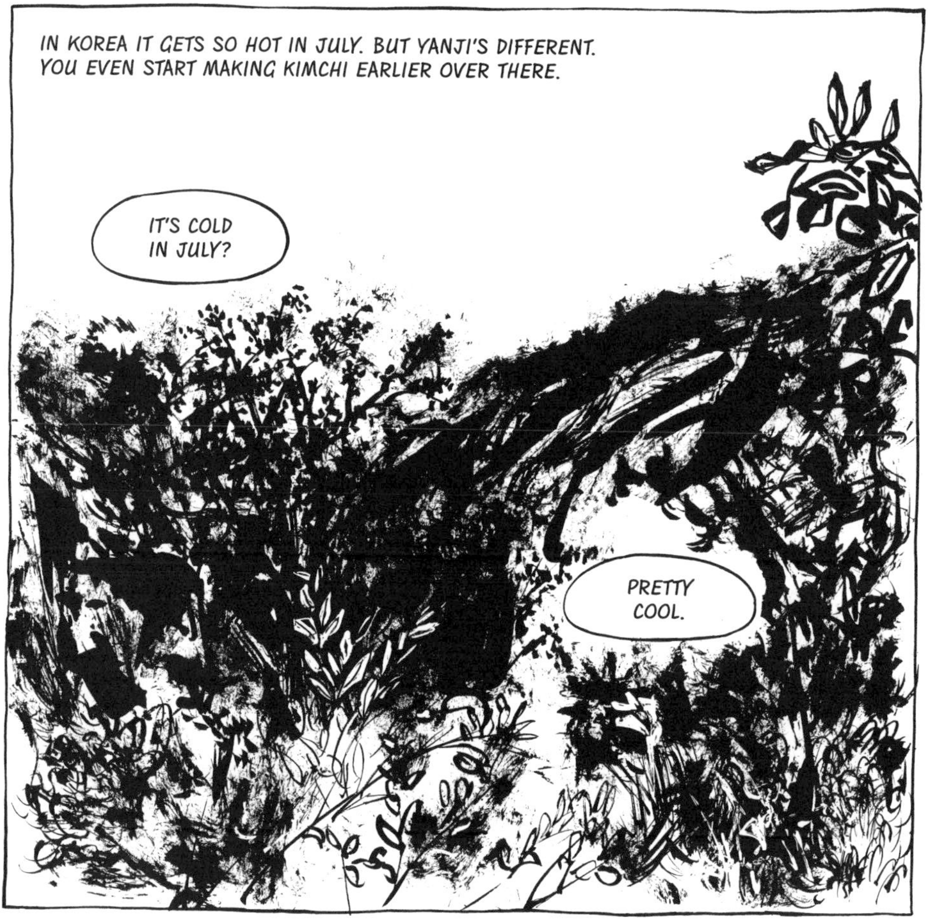
IN KOREA IT GETS SO HOT IN JULY. BUT YANJI'S DIFFERENT. YOU EVEN START MAKING KIMCHI EARLIER OVER THERE.
IT'S COLD IN JULY?
PRETTY COOL.

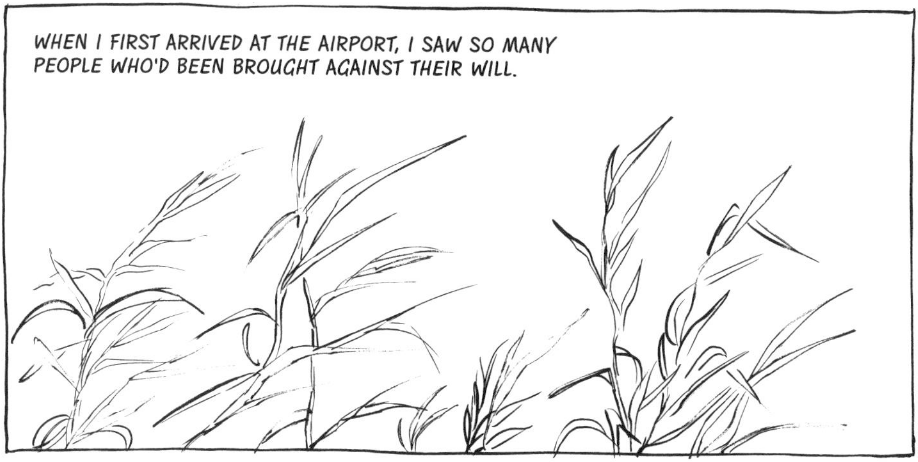
WHEN I FIRST ARRIVED AT THE AIRPORT, I SAW SO MANY PEOPLE WHO'D BEEN BROUGHT AGAINST THEIR WILL.

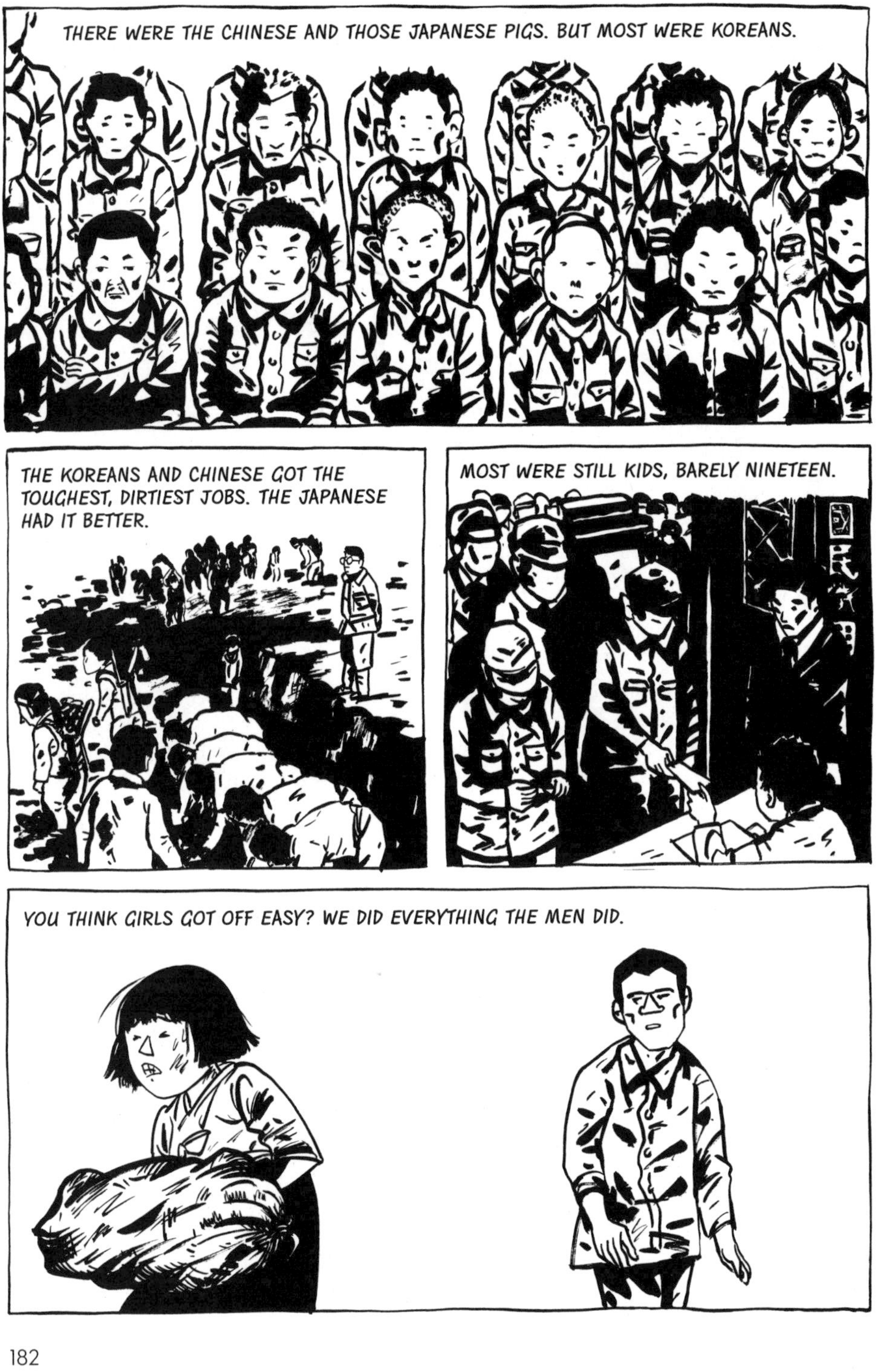
THERE WERE THE CHINESE AND THOSE JAPANESE PIGS. BUT MOST WERE KOREANS.
THE KOREANS AND CHINESE GOT THE TOUGHEST, DIRTIEST JOBS. THE JAPANESE HAD IT BETTER.
MOST WERE STILL KIDS, BARELY NINETEEN.
YOU THINK GIRLS GOT OFF EASY? WE DID EVERYTHING THE MEN DID.

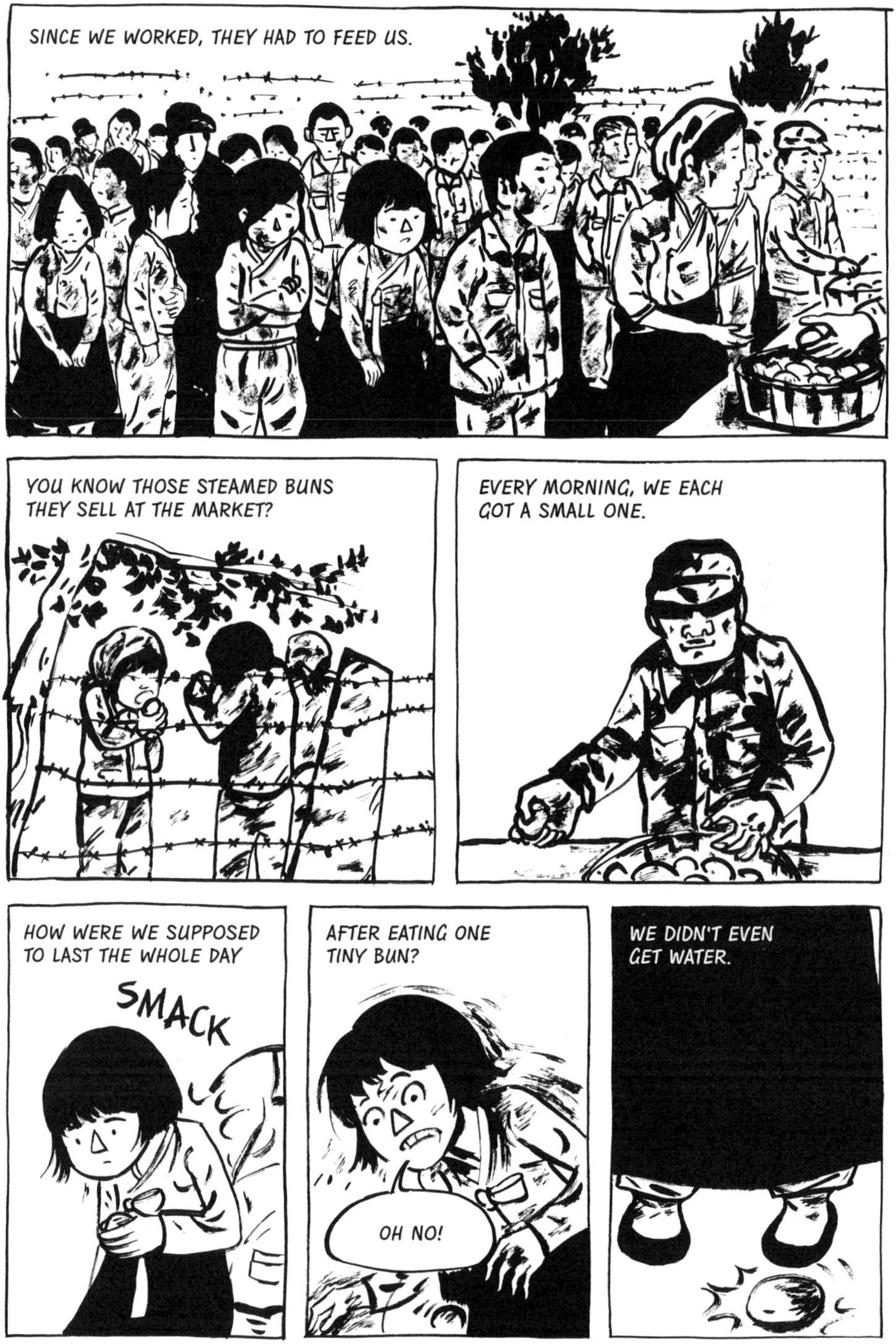
SINCE WE WORKED, THEY HAD TO FEED US.
YOU KNOW THOSE STEAMED BUNS THEY SELL AT THE MARKET?
EVERY MORNING, WE EACH GOT A SMALL ONE.
HOW WERE WE SUPPOSED TO LAST THE WHOLE DAY
SMACK
AFTER EATING ONE TINY BUN?
OH NO!
WE DIDN'T EVEN GET WATER.

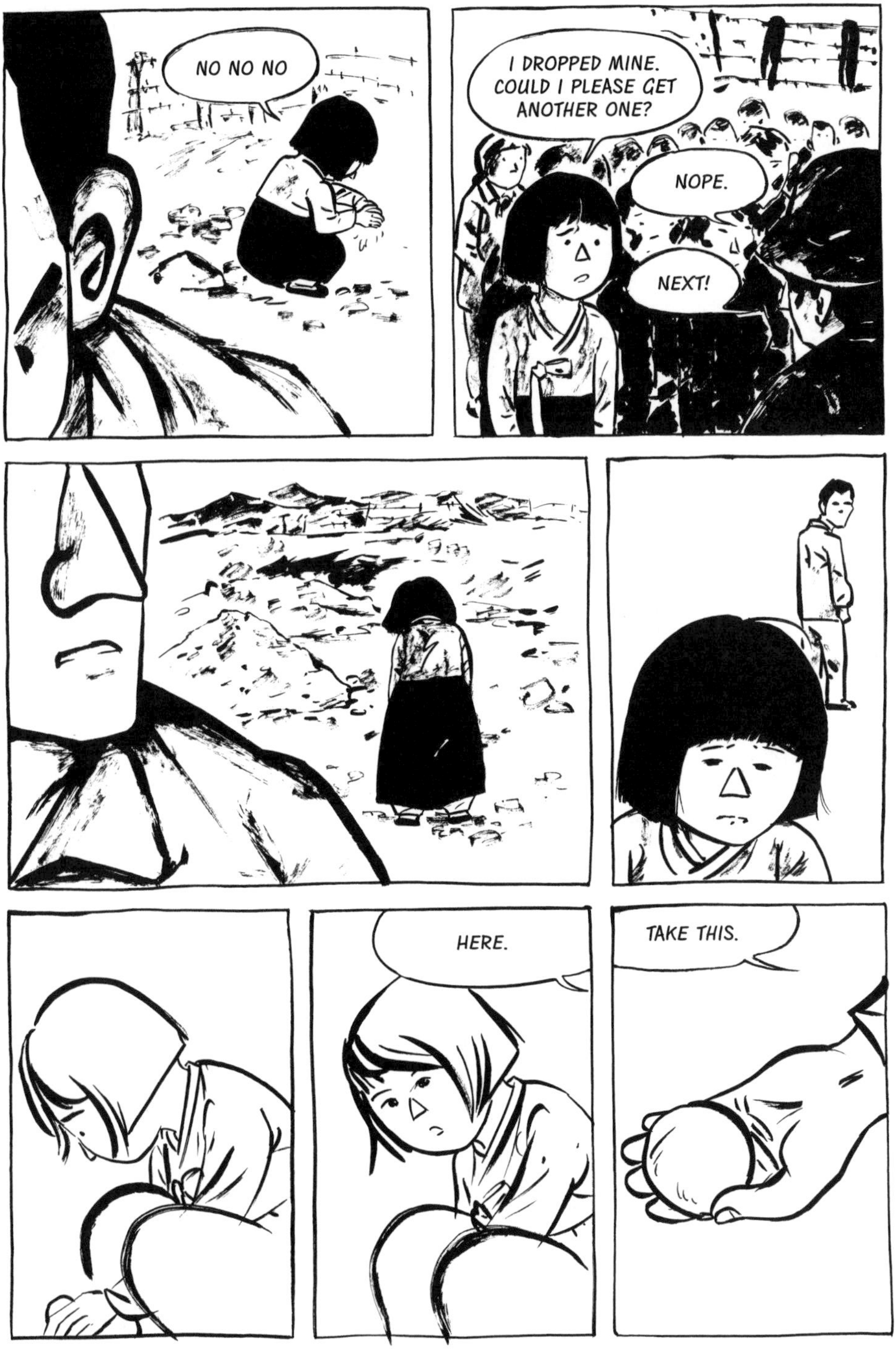
NO NO NO
I DROPPED MINE. COULD I PLEASE GET ANOTHER ONE?
NOPE.
NEXT!
HERE.
TAKE THIS.

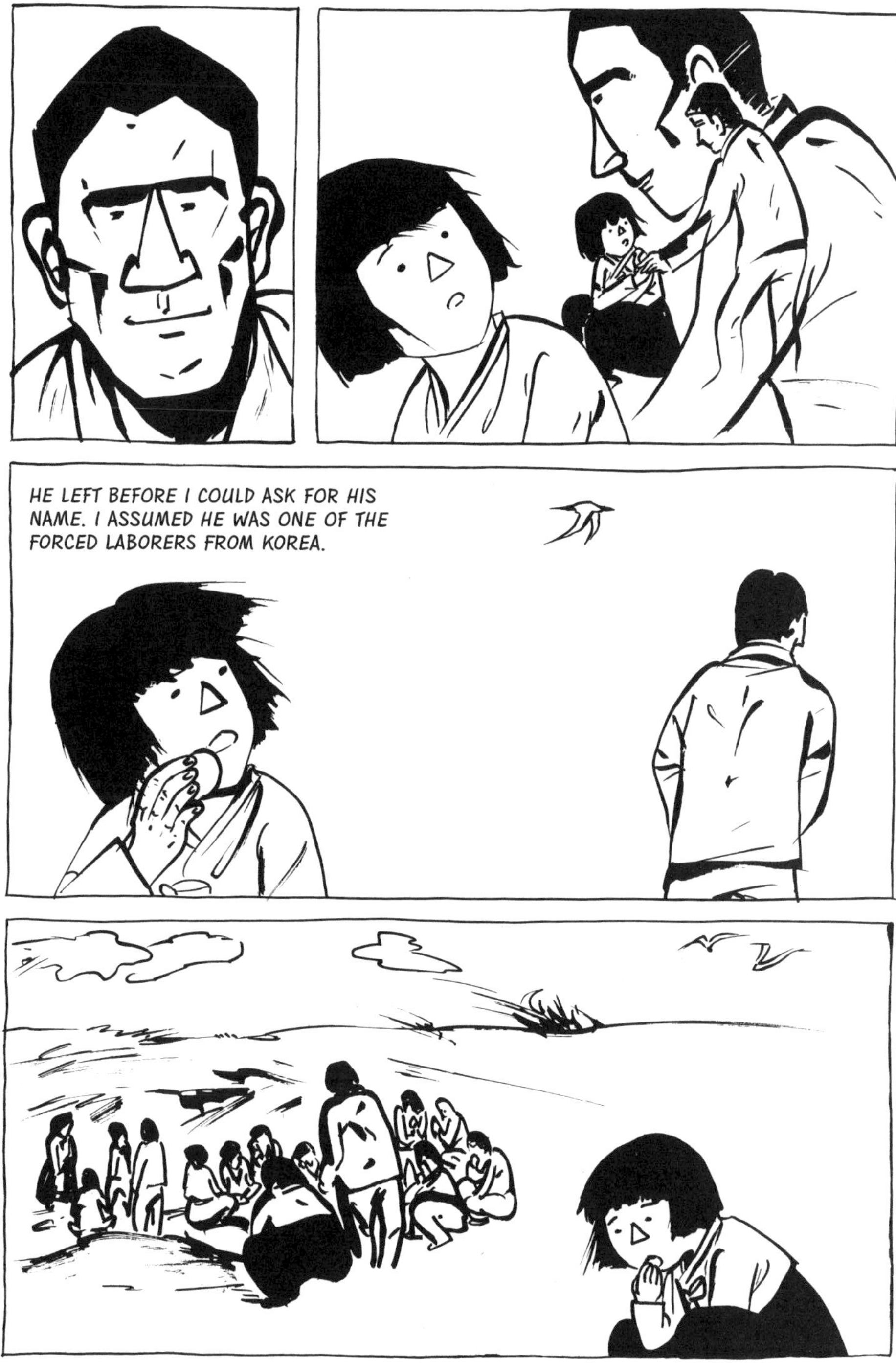
HE LEFT BEFORE I COULD ASK FOR HIS NAME. I ASSUMED HE WAS ONE OF THE FORCED LABORERS FROM KOREA.

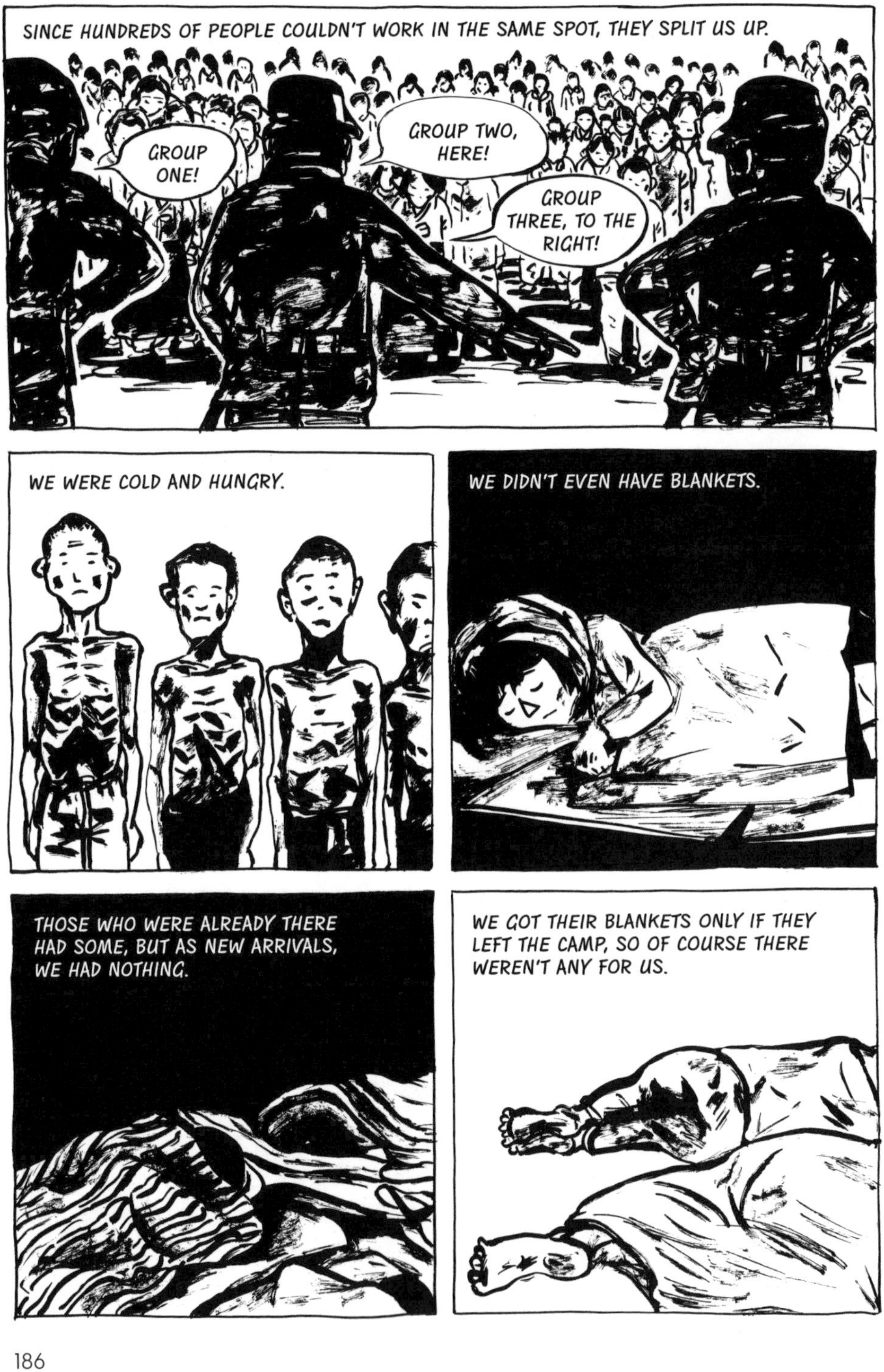

SINCE HUNDREDS OF PEOPLE COULDN'T WORK IN THE SAME SPOT, THEY SPLIT US UP.
GROUP ONE!
GROUP TWO, HERE!
GROUP THREE, TO THE RIGHT!
WE WERE COLD AND HUNGRY.
WE DIDN'T EVEN HAVE BLANKETS.
THOSE WHO WERE ALREADY THERE HAD SOME, BUT AS NEW ARRIVALS, WE HAD NOTHING.
WE GOT THEIR BLANKETS ONLY IF THEY LEFT THE CAMP, SO OF COURSE THERE WEREN'T ANY FOR US.

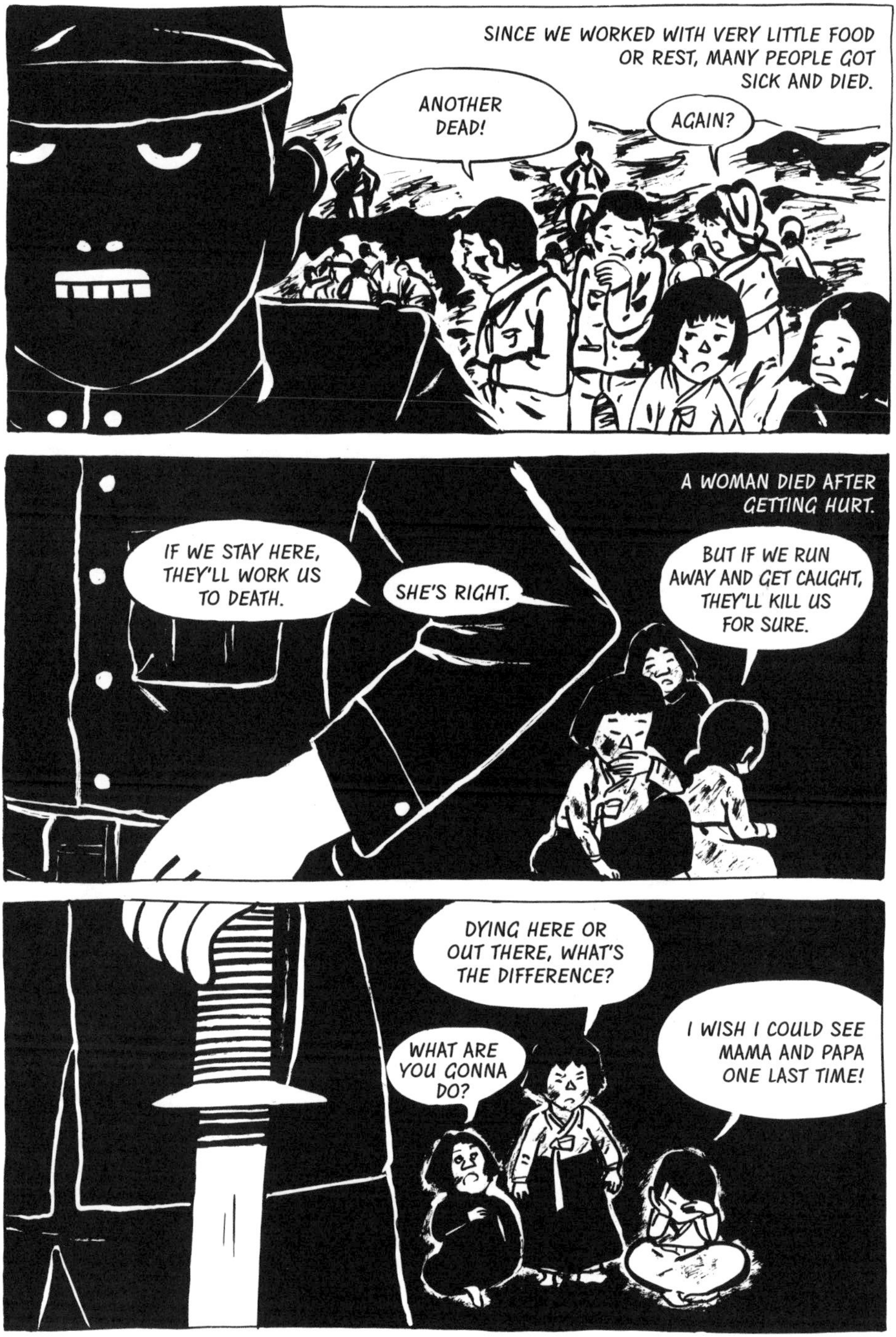
SINCE WE WORKED WITH VERY LITTLE FOOD OR REST, MANY PEOPLE GOT SICK AND DIED.
ANOTHER DEAD!
AGAIN?
A WOMAN DIED AFTER GETTING HURT.
IF WE STAY HERE, THEY'LL WORK US TO DEATH.
SHE'S RIGHT.
BUT IF WE RUN AWAY AND GET CAUGHT, THEY'LL KILL US FOR SURE.
DYING HERE OR OUT THERE, WHAT'S THE DIFFERENCE?
WHAT ARE YOU GONNA DO?
I WISH I COULD SEE MAMA AND PAPA ONE LAST TIME!

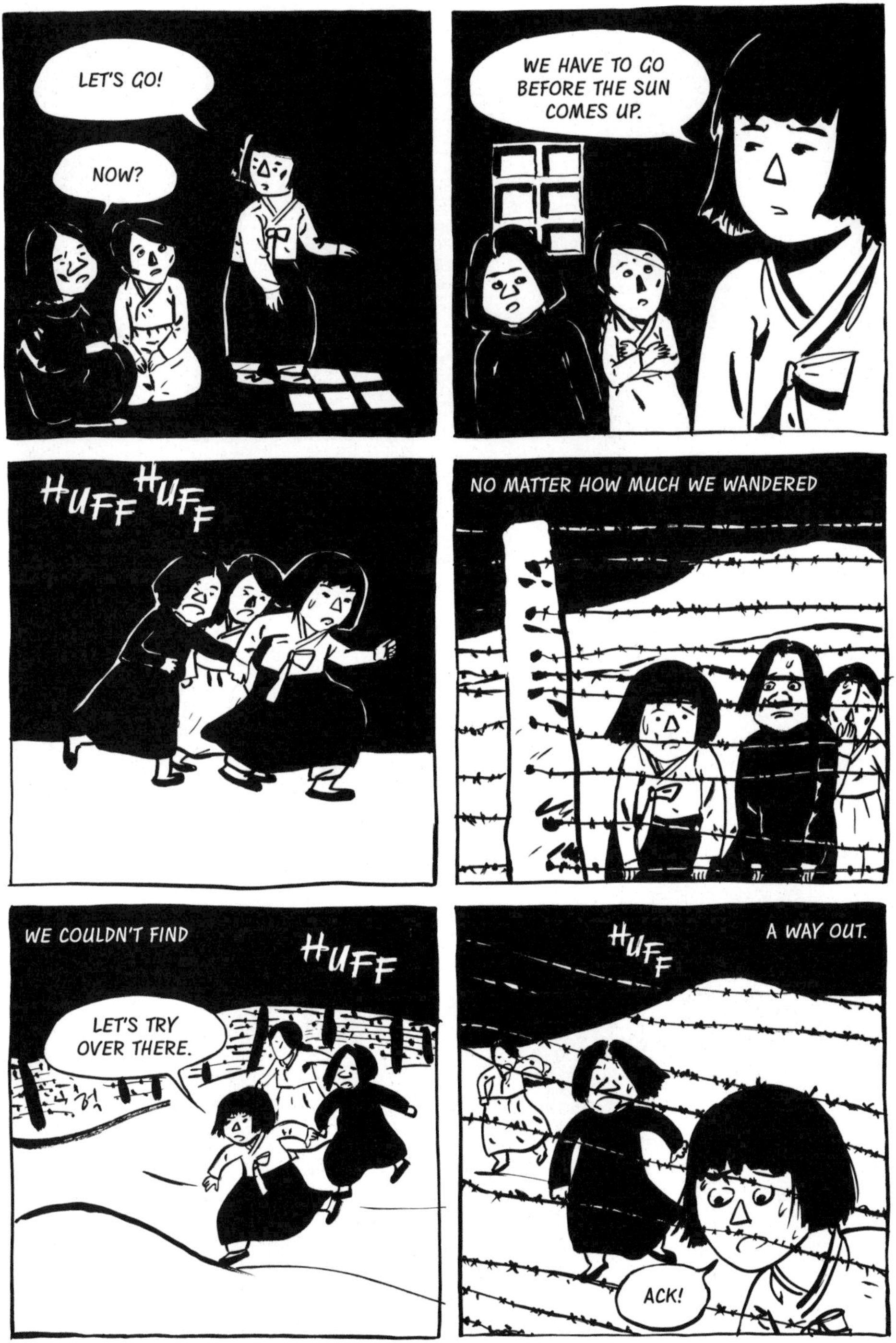
LET'S GO!
NOW?
WE HAVE TO GO BEFORE THE SUN COMES UP.
HUFF HUFF
NO MATTER HOW MUCH WE WANDERED
WE COULDN'T FIND
HUFF
LET'S TRY OVER THERE.
HUFF
A WAY OUT.
ACK!

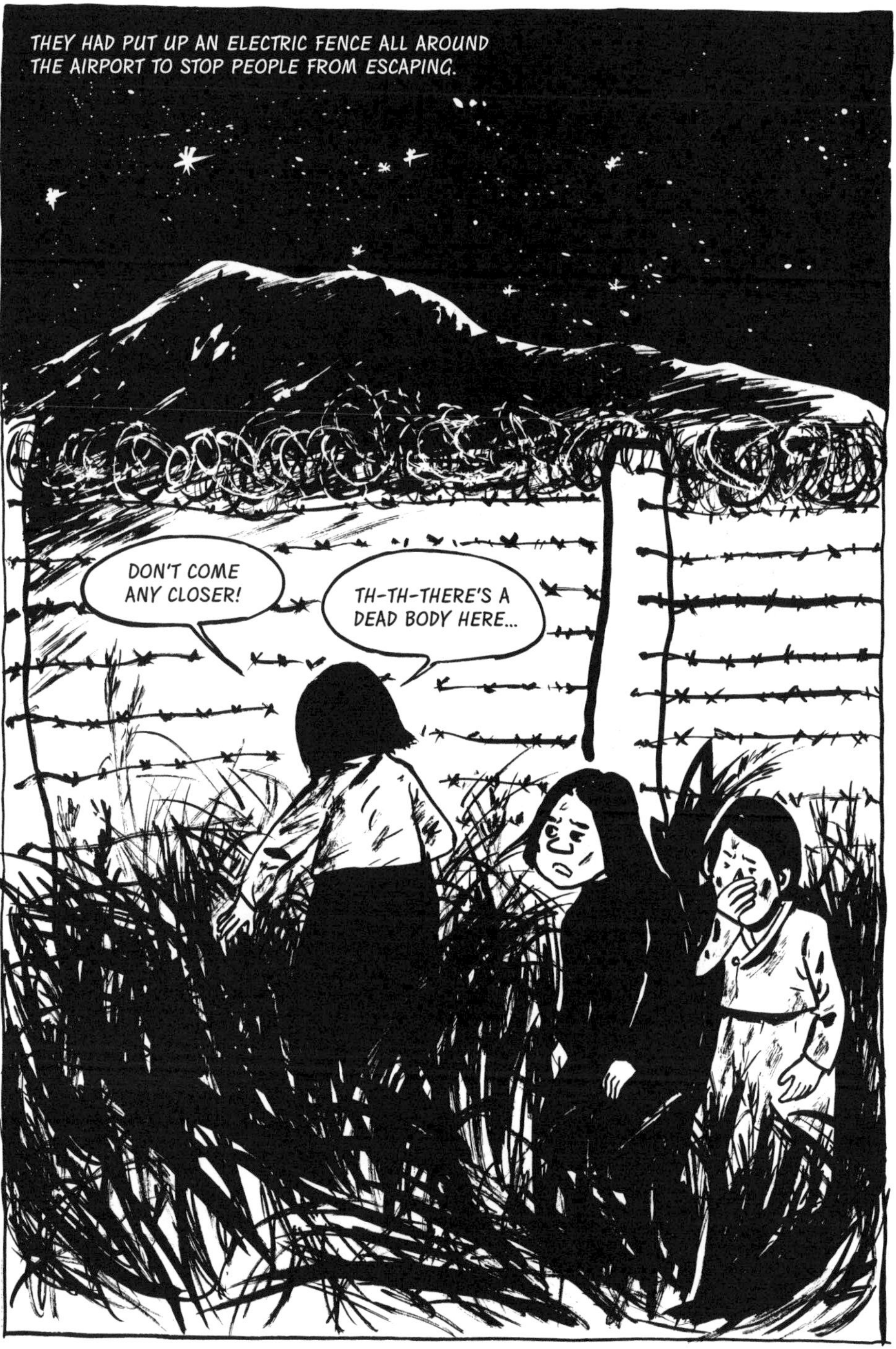
THEY HAD PUT UP AN ELECTRIC FENCE ALL AROUND THE AIRPORT TO STOP PEOPLE FROM ESCAPING.
DON'T COME ANY CLOSER!
TH-TH-THERE'S A DEAD BODY HERE...

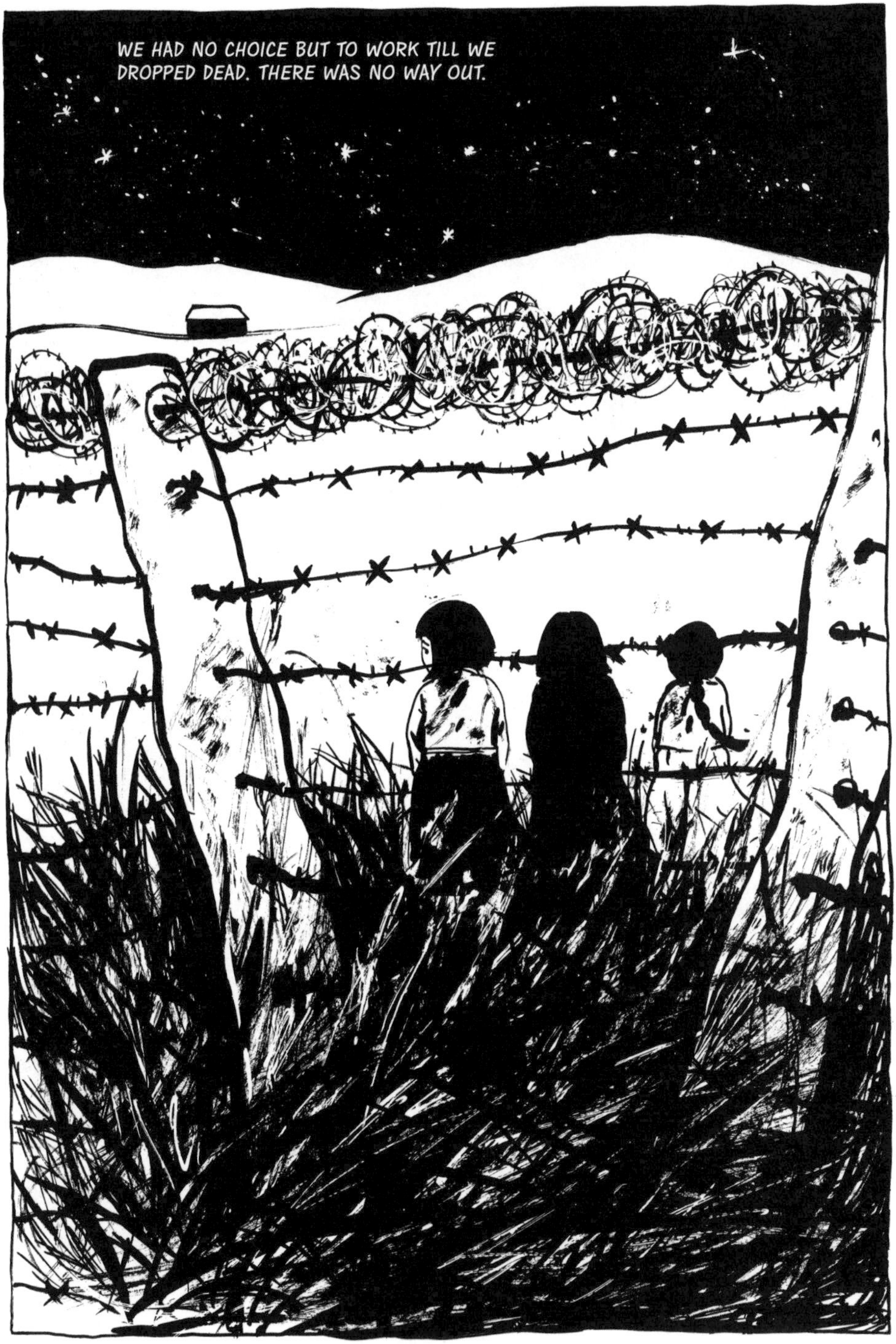
WE HAD NO CHOICE BUT TO WORK TILL WE DROPPED DEAD. THERE WAS NO WAY OUT.

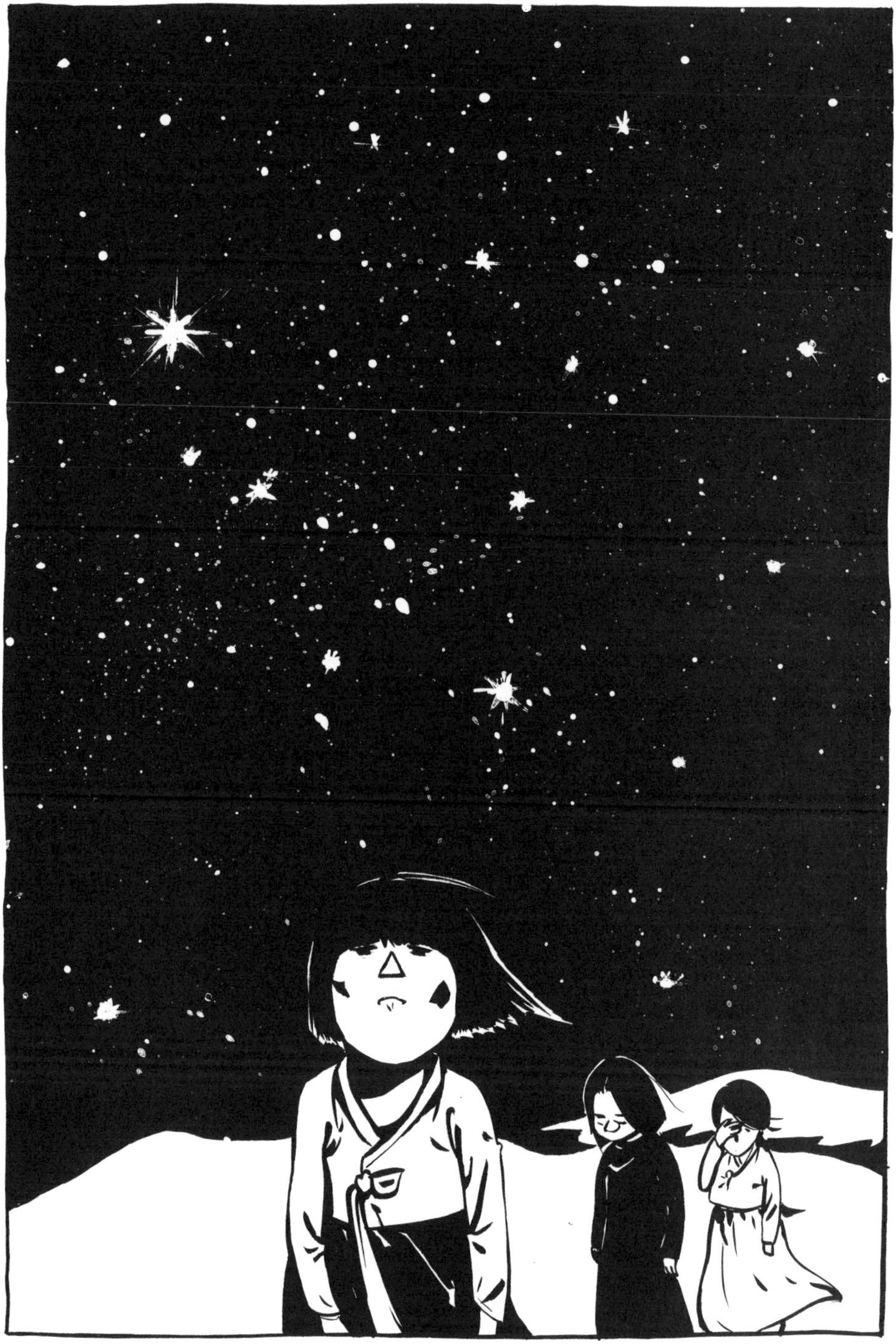

# CHASTITY

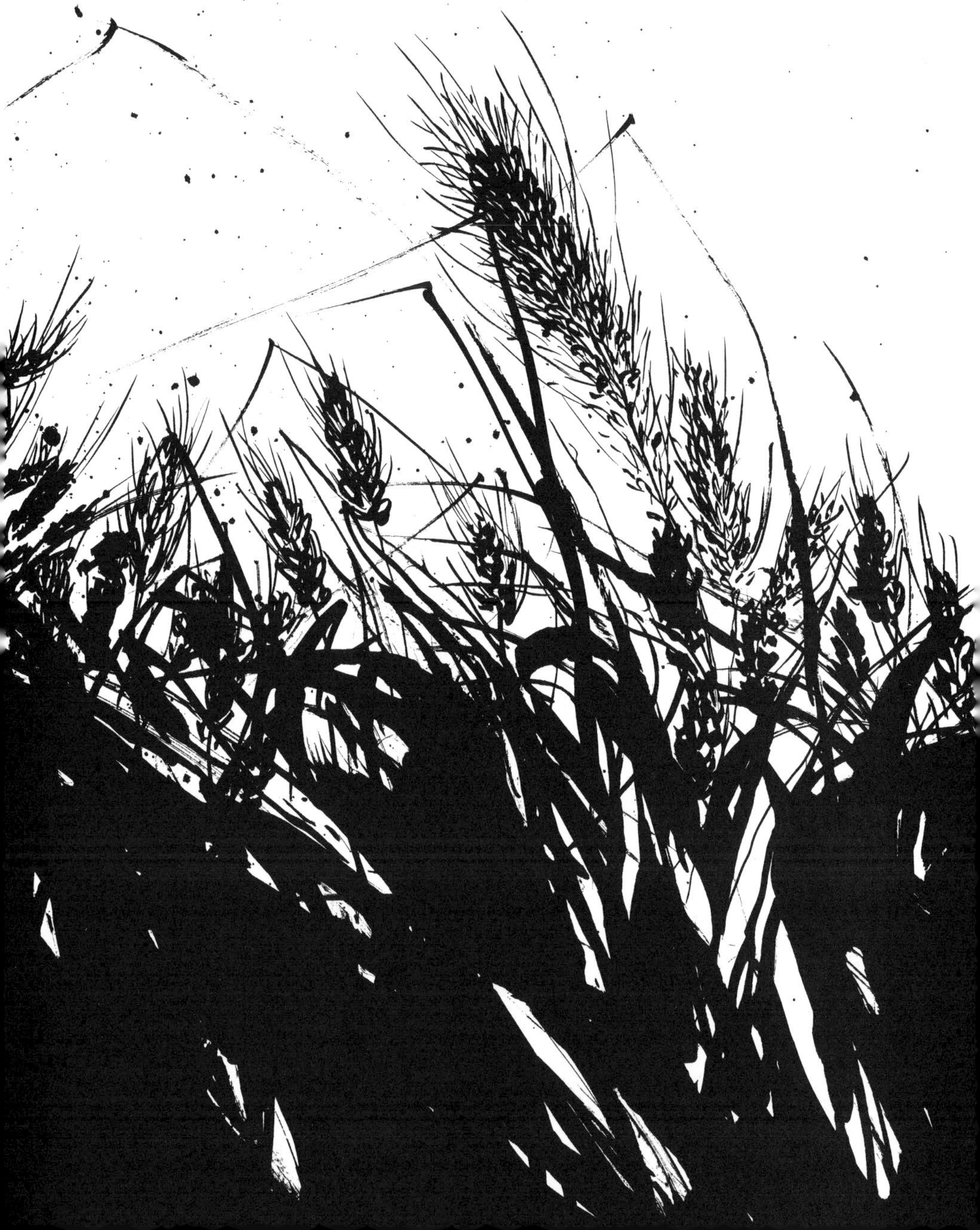

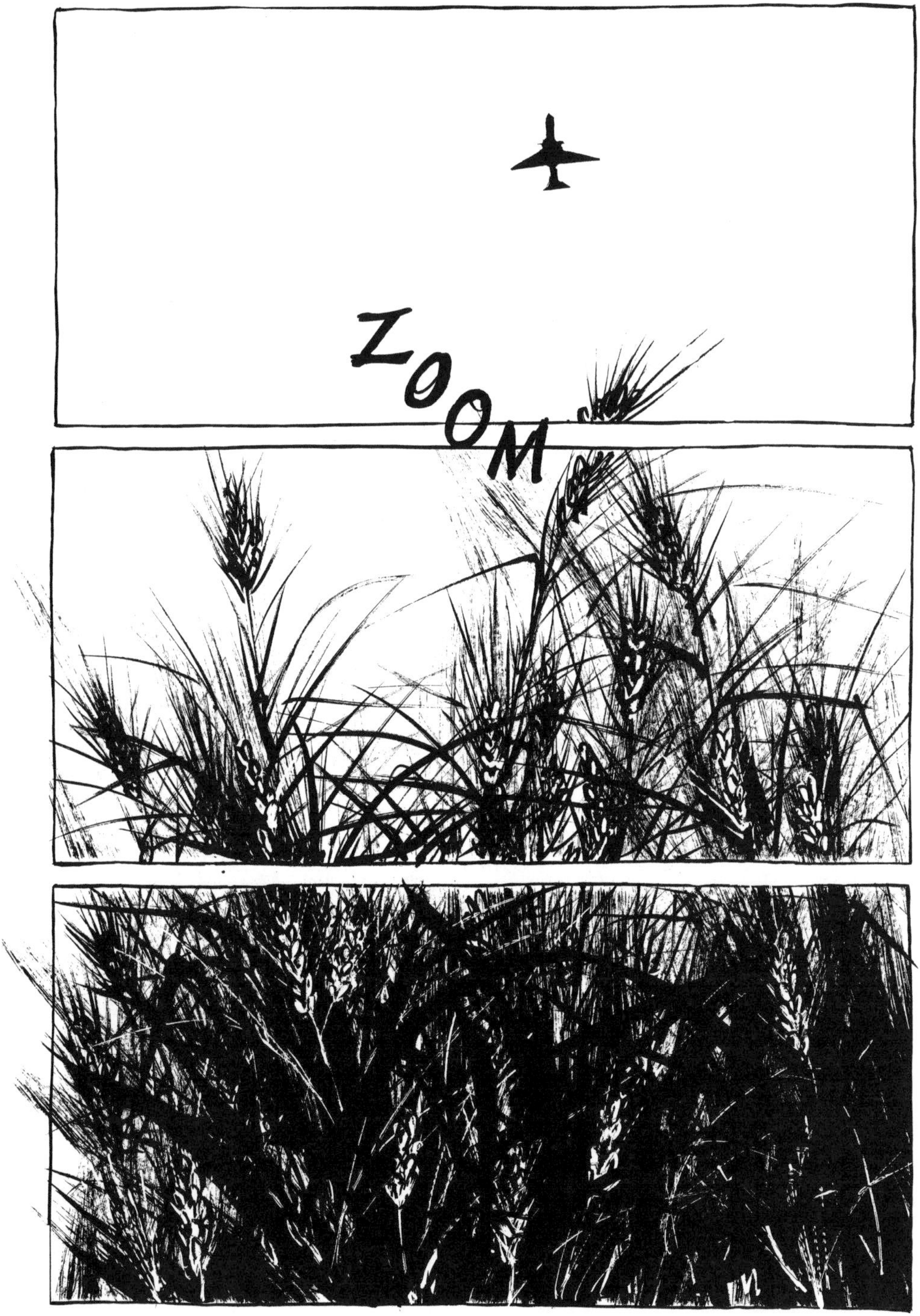
ZOOM

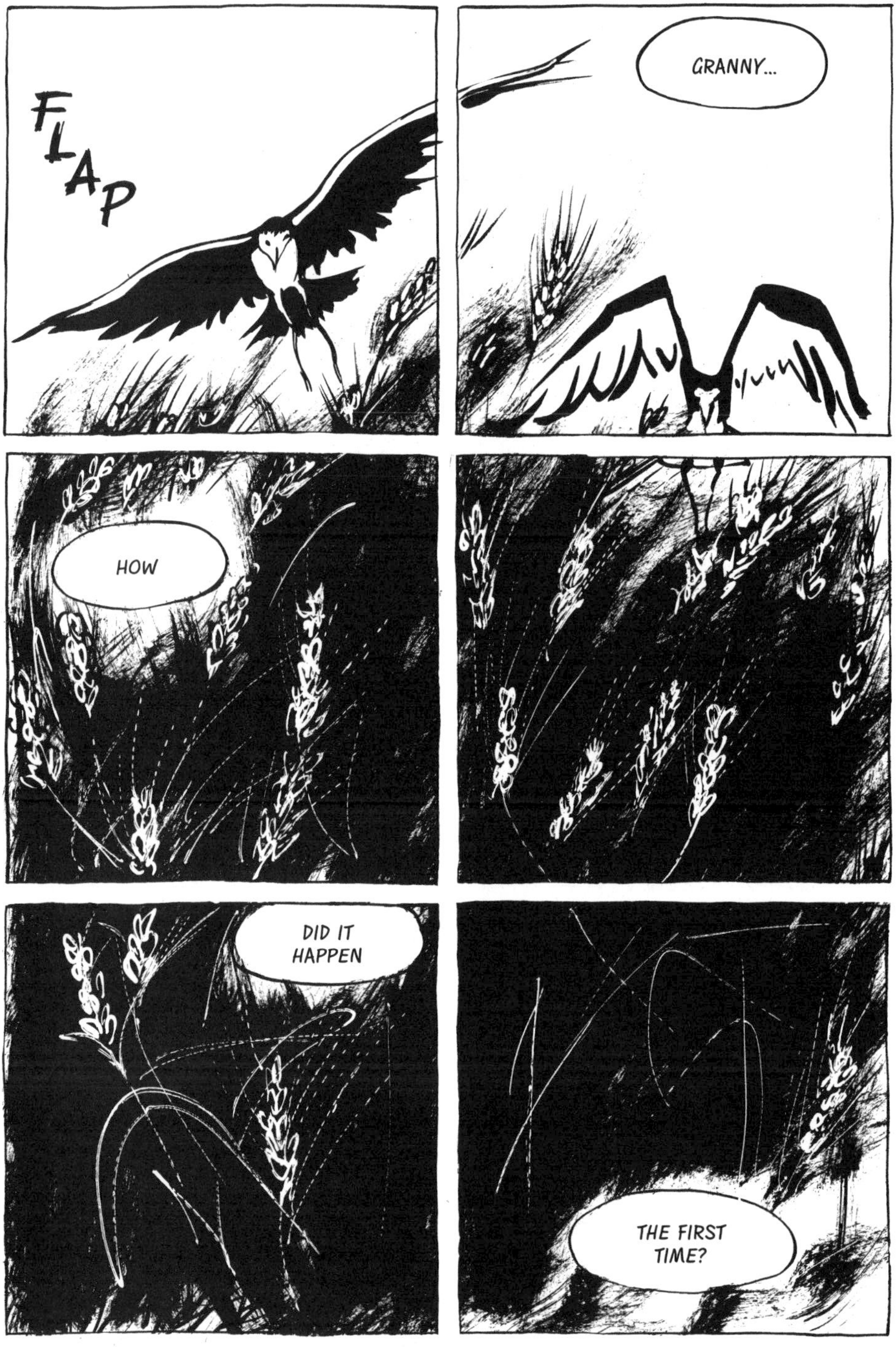
FLAP
GRANNY...
HOW
DID IT HAPPEN
THE FIRST TIME?

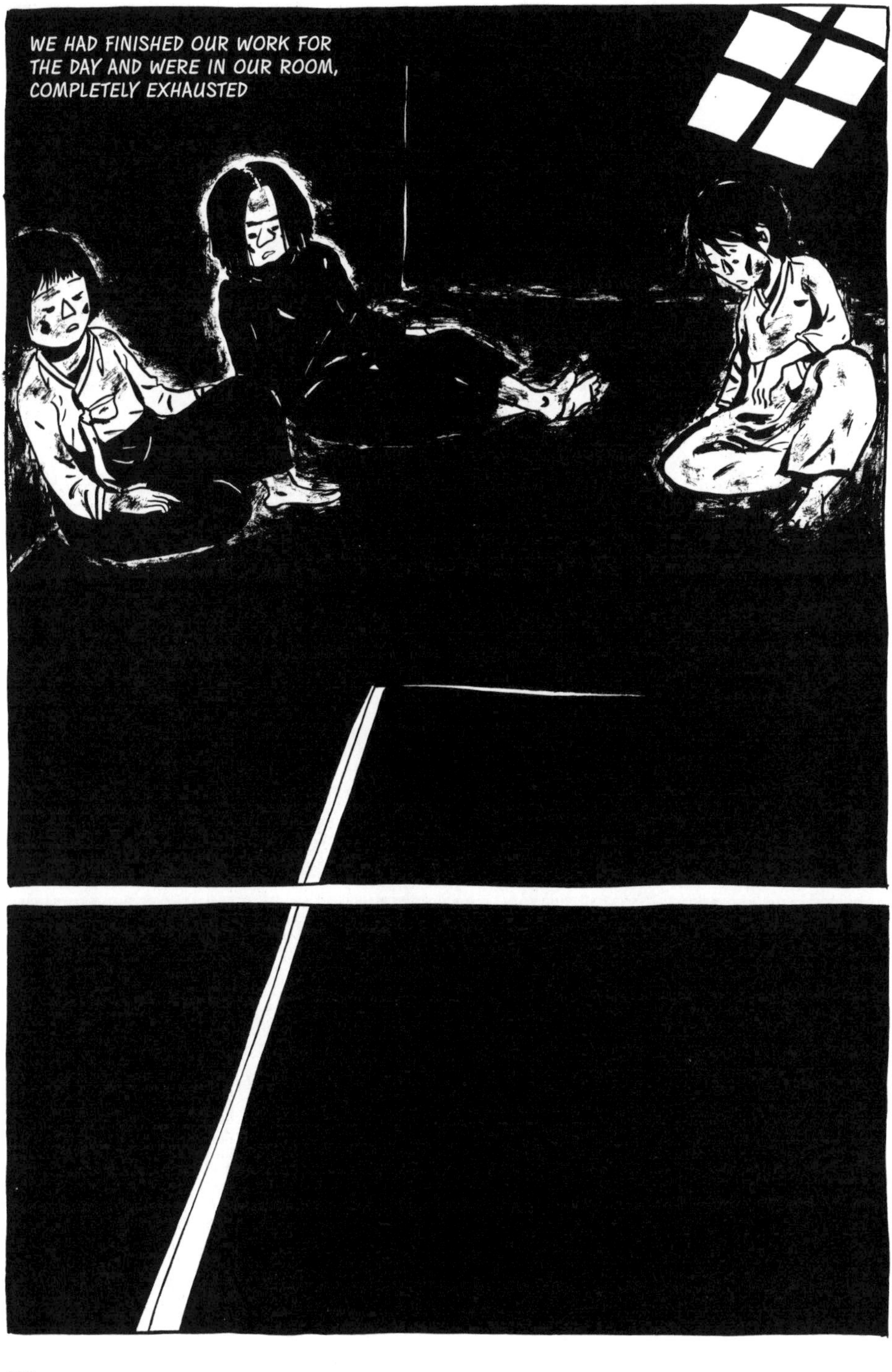
WE HAD FINISHED OUR WORK FOR THE DAY AND WERE IN OUR ROOM, COMPLETELY EXHAUSTED

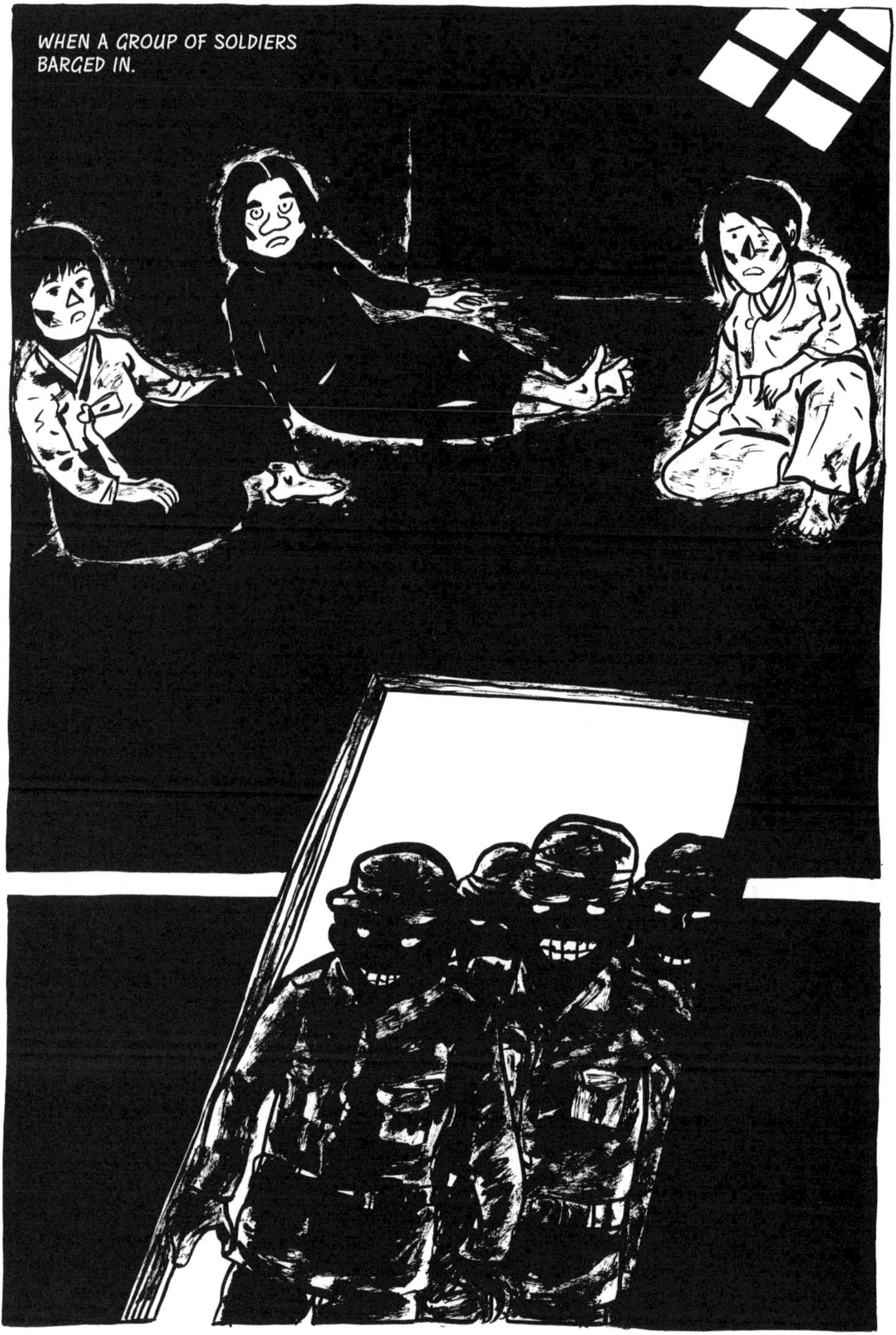
WHEN A GROUP OF SOLDIERS
BARGED IN.

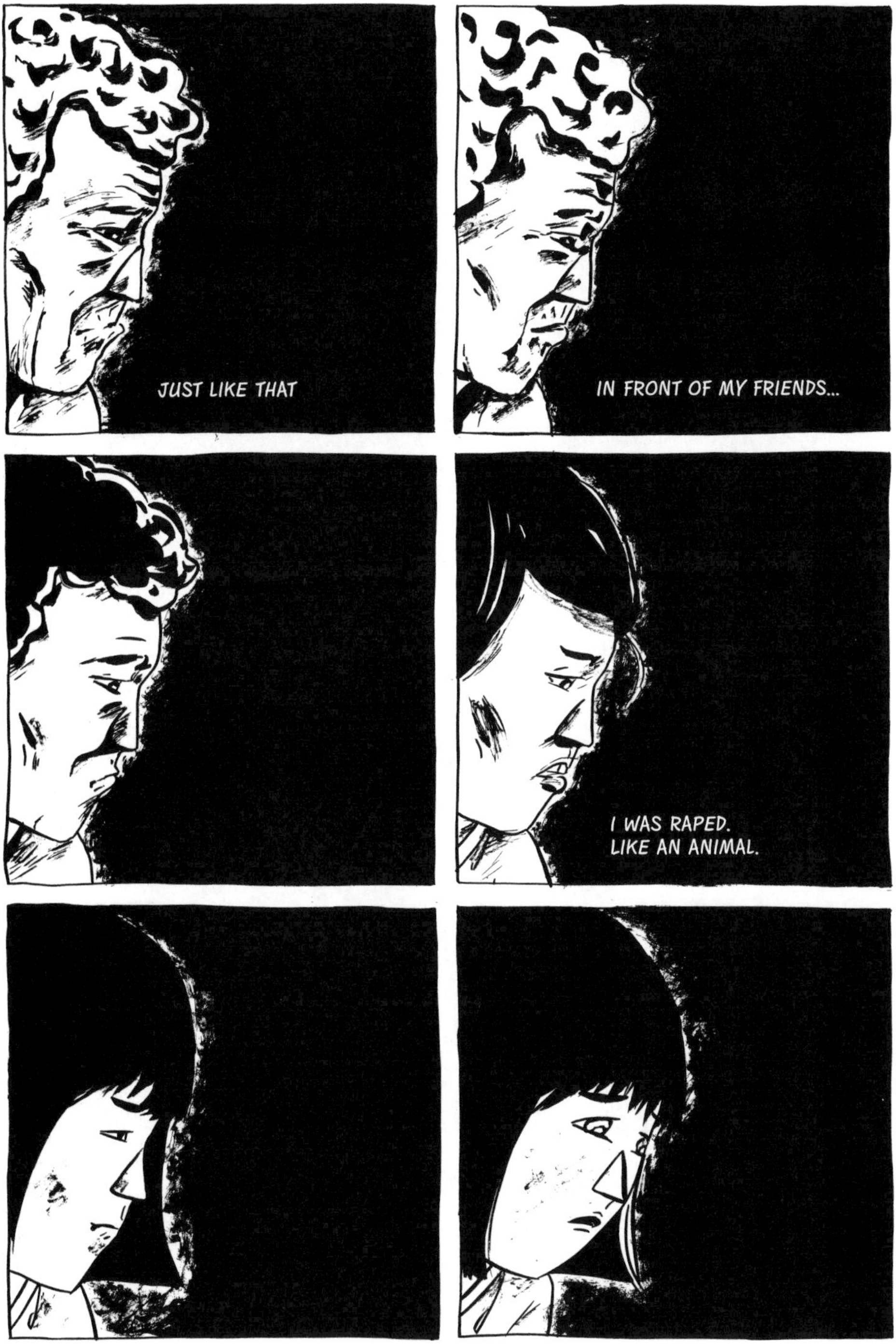
JUST LIKE THAT
IN FRONT OF MY FRIENDS...
I WAS RAPED.
LIKE AN ANIMAL.

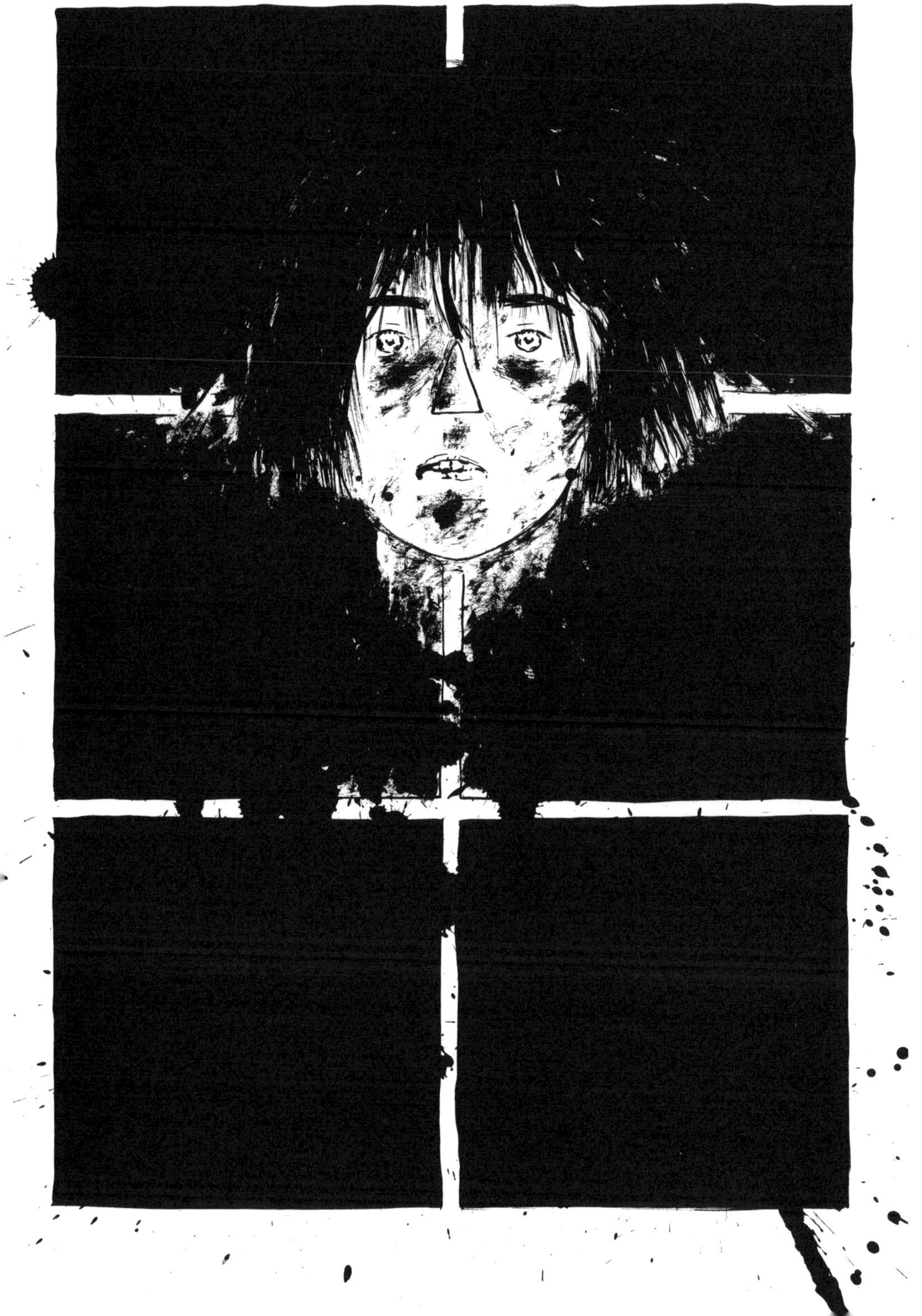

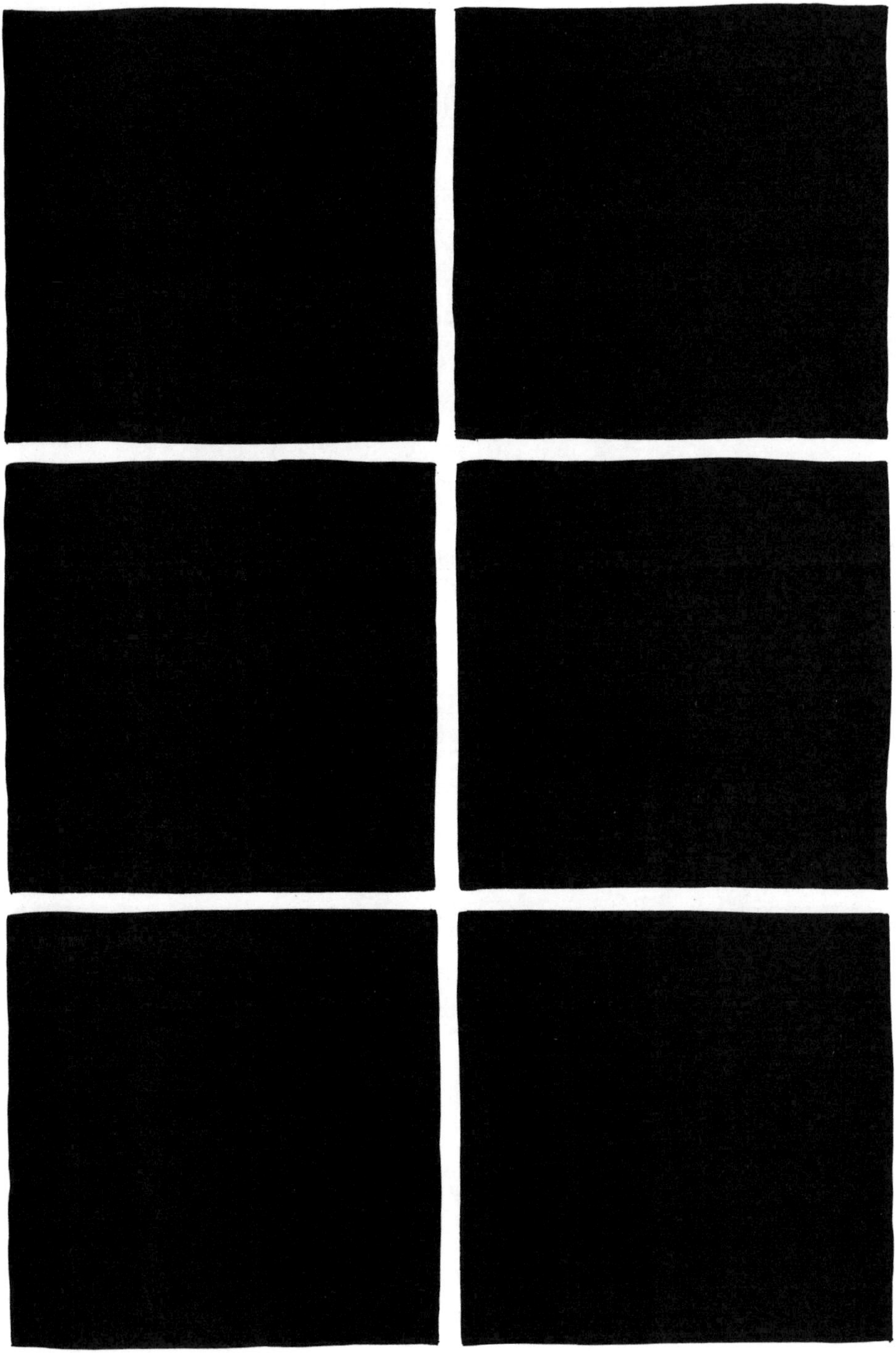

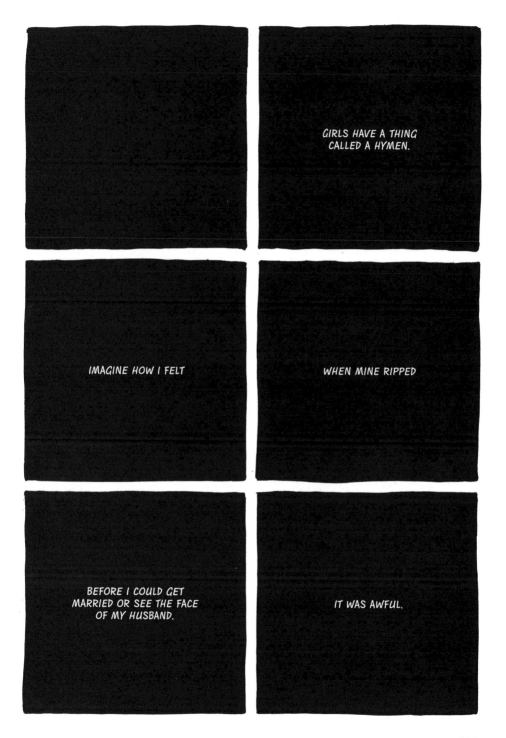

GIRLS HAVE A THING CALLED A HYMEN.

IMAGINE HOW I FELT

WHEN MINE RIPPED

BEFORE I COULD GET MARRIED OR SEE THE FACE OF MY HUSBAND.

IT WAS AWFUL.

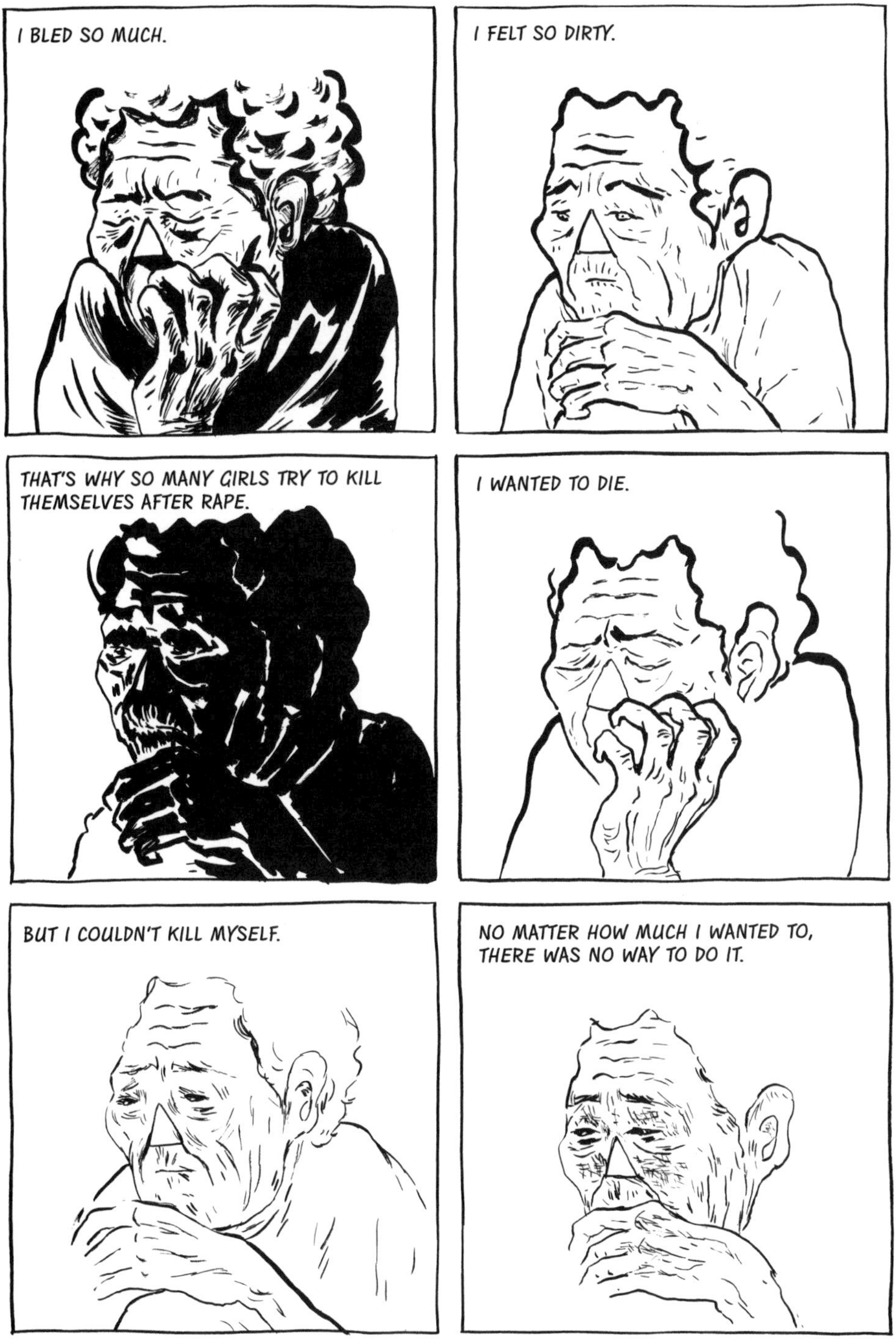
I BLED SO MUCH.
I FELT SO DIRTY.
THAT'S WHY SO MANY GIRLS TRY TO KILL THEMSELVES AFTER RAPE.
I WANTED TO DIE.
BUT I COULDN'T KILL MYSELF.
NO MATTER HOW MUCH I WANTED TO, THERE WAS NO WAY TO DO IT.

I WAS ALIVE,
BUT I WASN'T LIVING.

MY MOTHER, MY FATHER,
MY BROTHERS, MY SISTERS,
MY HOME.

I COULDN'T GO BACK
TO THEM NOW.

NOT EVER.

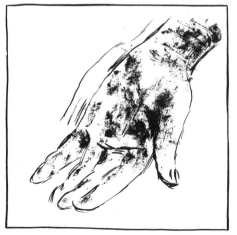

MORE SOLDIERS CAME. THEY NEVER WORE CONDOMS.

SOON MEDICS CAME FROM THE MILITARY HOSPITAL TO CHECK US FOR VENEREAL DISEASES.

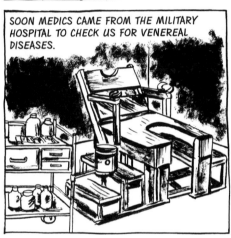

CONDUCT THOROUGH EXAMS SO OUR IMPERIAL FORCES DON'T CONTRACT DISEASES.

THESE ARE THE ORDERS.

HAI.

EVERY WEEK AT THE COMFORT STATION

WE HAD TO UNDERGO MEDICAL EXAMS.

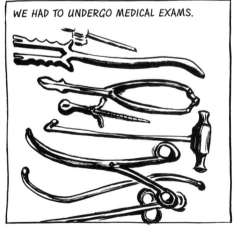

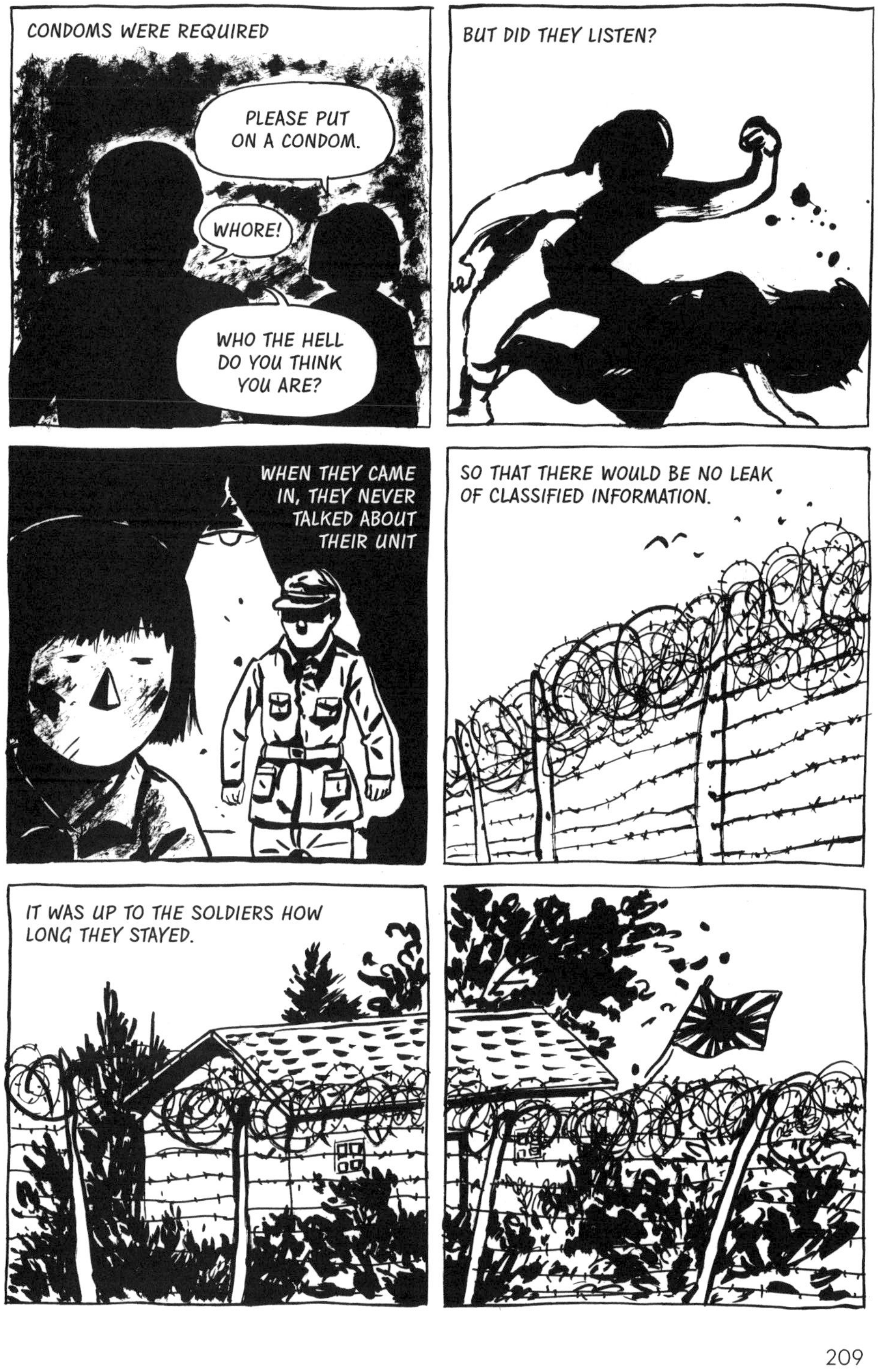
CONDOMS WERE REQUIRED
PLEASE PUT ON A CONDOM.
WHORE!
WHO THE HELL DO YOU THINK YOU ARE?
BUT DID THEY LISTEN?
WHEN THEY CAME IN, THEY NEVER TALKED ABOUT THEIR UNIT
SO THAT THERE WOULD BE NO LEAK OF CLASSIFIED INFORMATION.
IT WAS UP TO THE SOLDIERS HOW LONG THEY STAYED.

THEY CLIMBED ABOARD PLANES TO CARRY OUT SORTIES.

SINCE WE WEREN'T ALLOWED NEAR THE PLANES, WE DIDN'T KNOW HOW MANY THERE WERE OR WHERE THEY WERE HEADED.

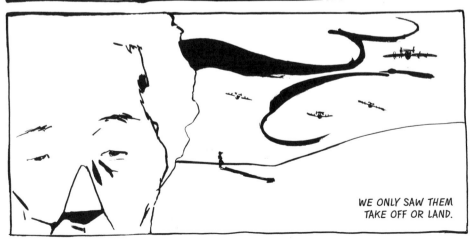

WE ONLY SAW THEM TAKE OFF OR LAND.

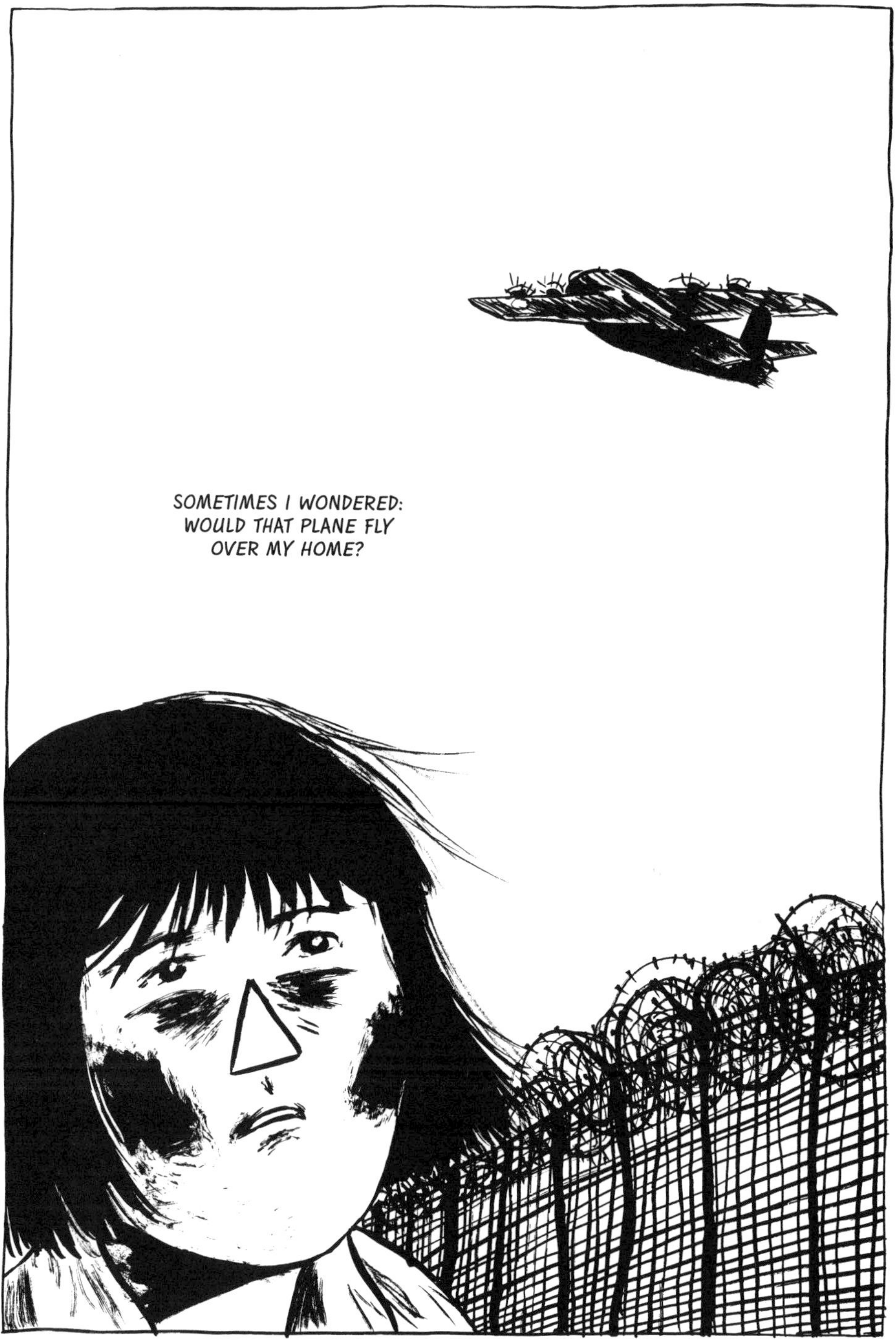
SOMETIMES I WONDERED: WOULD THAT PLANE FLY OVER MY HOME?

HIM

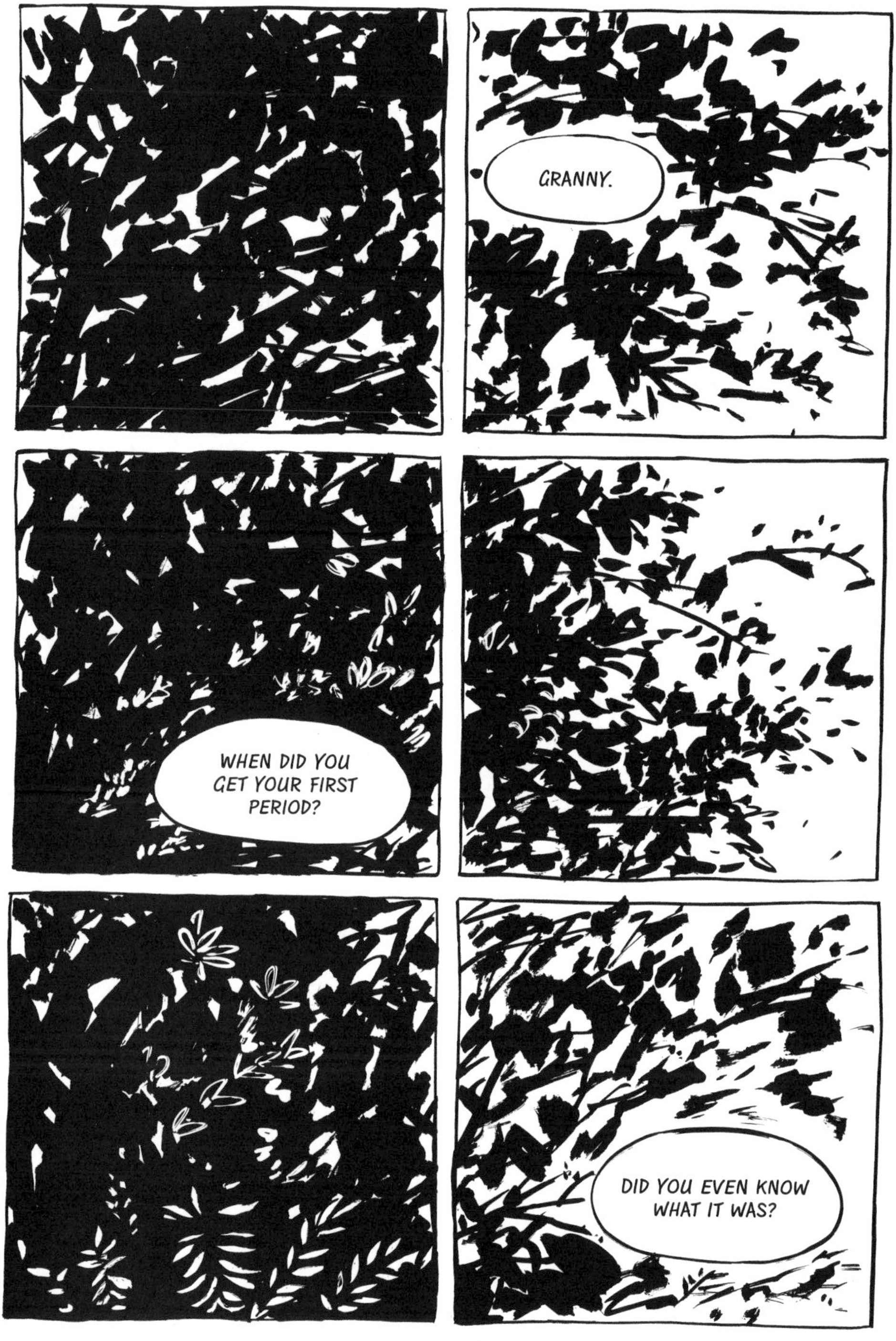
GRANNY.
WHEN DID YOU GET YOUR FIRST PERIOD?
DID YOU EVEN KNOW WHAT IT WAS?

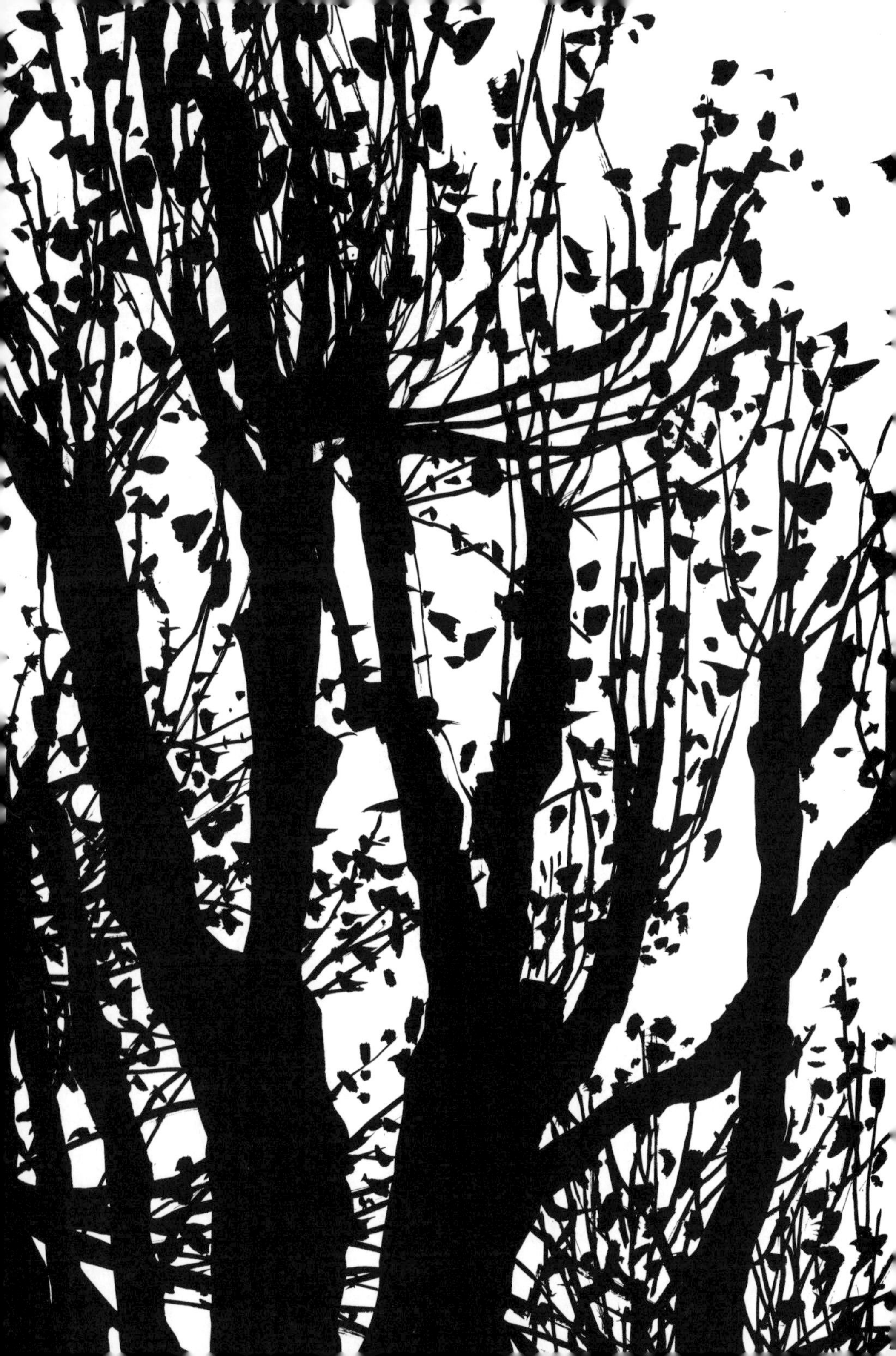

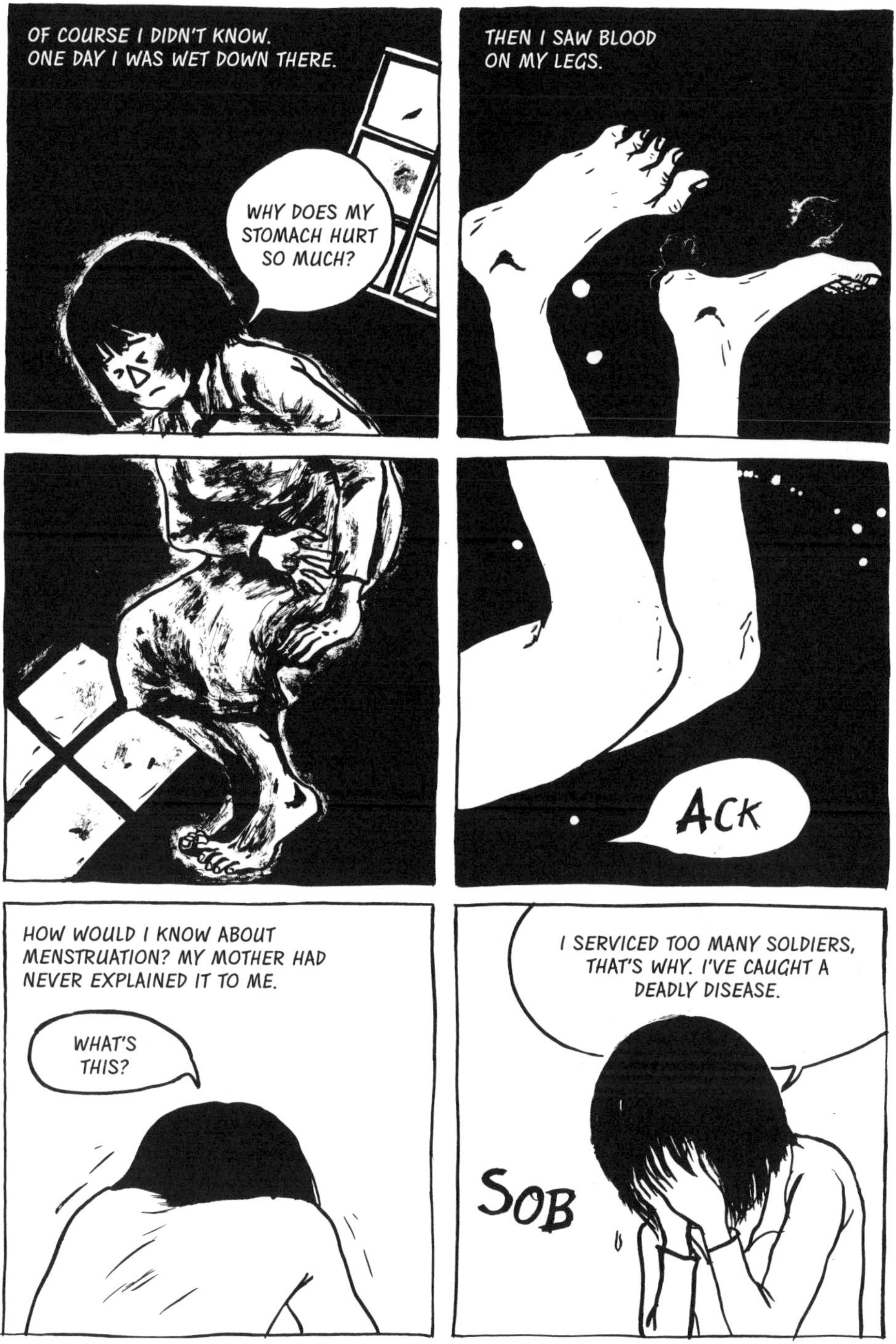
OF COURSE I DIDN'T KNOW.
ONE DAY I WAS WET DOWN THERE.
WHY DOES MY STOMACH HURT SO MUCH?
THEN I SAW BLOOD ON MY LEGS.
ACK
HOW WOULD I KNOW ABOUT MENSTRUATION? MY MOTHER HAD NEVER EXPLAINED IT TO ME.
WHAT'S THIS?
I SERVICED TOO MANY SOLDIERS, THAT'S WHY. I'VE CAUGHT A DEADLY DISEASE.
SOB

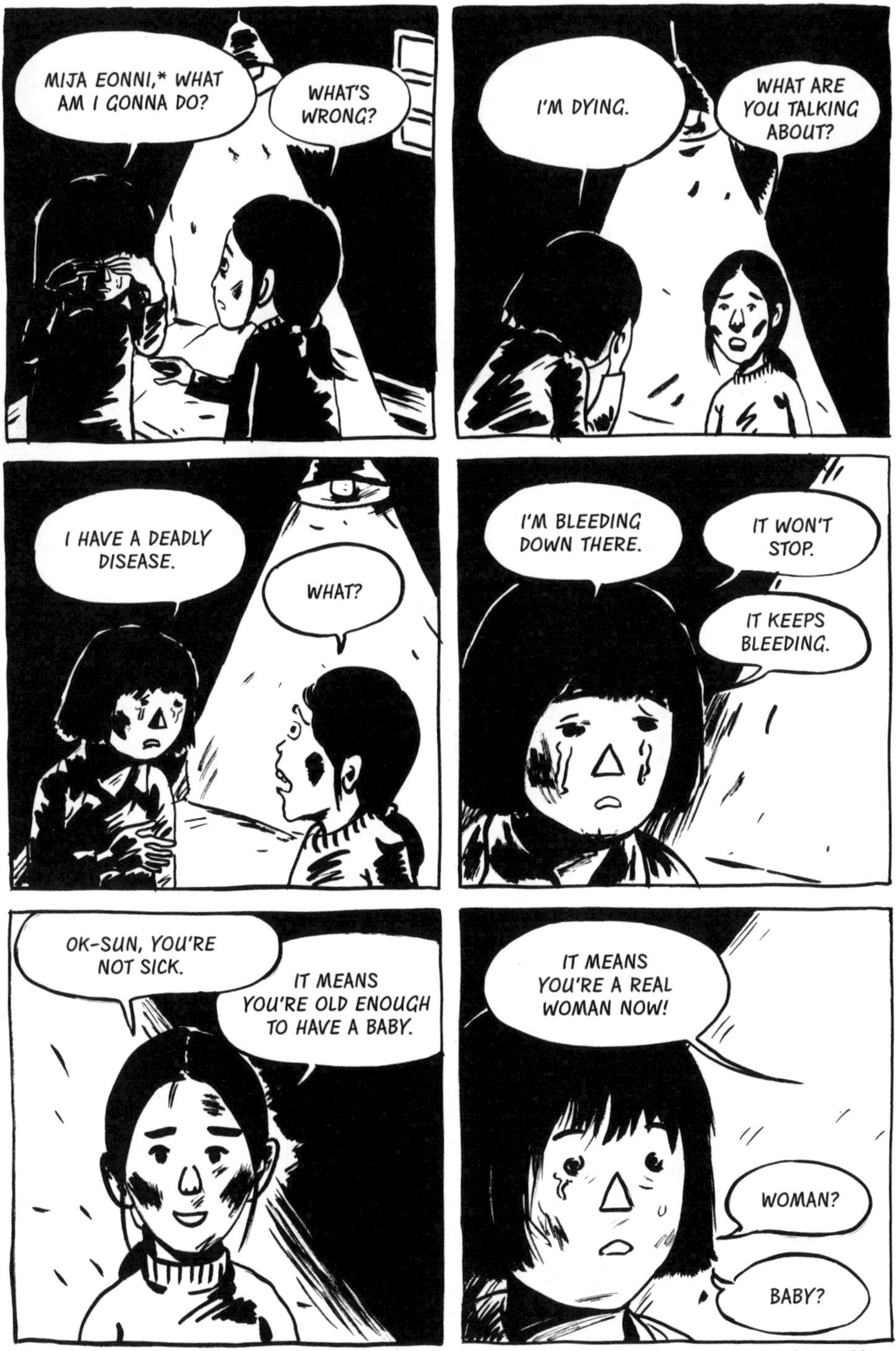
MIJA EONNI,* WHAT AM I GONNA DO?
WHAT'S WRONG?
I'M DYING.
WHAT ARE YOU TALKING ABOUT?
I HAVE A DEADLY DISEASE.
WHAT?
I'M BLEEDING DOWN THERE.
IT WON'T STOP.
IT KEEPS BLEEDING.
OK-SUN, YOU'RE NOT SICK.
IT MEANS YOU'RE OLD ENOUGH TO HAVE A BABY.
IT MEANS YOU'RE A REAL WOMAN NOW!
WOMAN?
BABY?

*EONNI IS THE KOREAN WORD FOR OLDER SISTER USED BY A FEMALE.

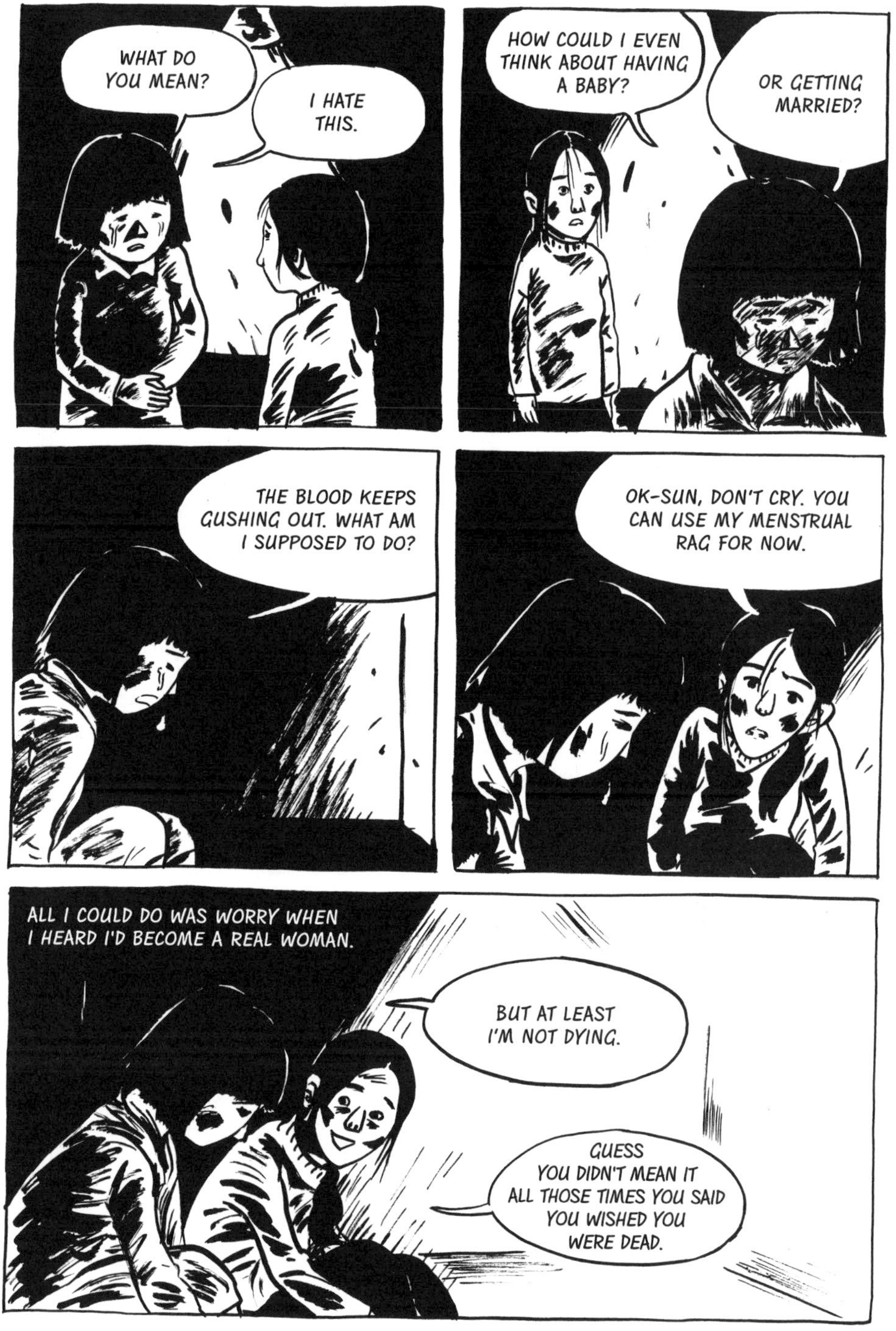
WHAT DO YOU MEAN?
I HATE THIS.
HOW COULD I EVEN THINK ABOUT HAVING A BABY?
OR GETTING MARRIED?
THE BLOOD KEEPS GUSHING OUT. WHAT AM I SUPPOSED TO DO?
OK-SUN, DON'T CRY. YOU CAN USE MY MENSTRUAL RAG FOR NOW.
ALL I COULD DO WAS WORRY WHEN I HEARD I'D BECOME A REAL WOMAN.
BUT AT LEAST I'M NOT DYING.
GUESS YOU DIDN'T MEAN IT ALL THOSE TIMES YOU SAID YOU WISHED YOU WERE DEAD.

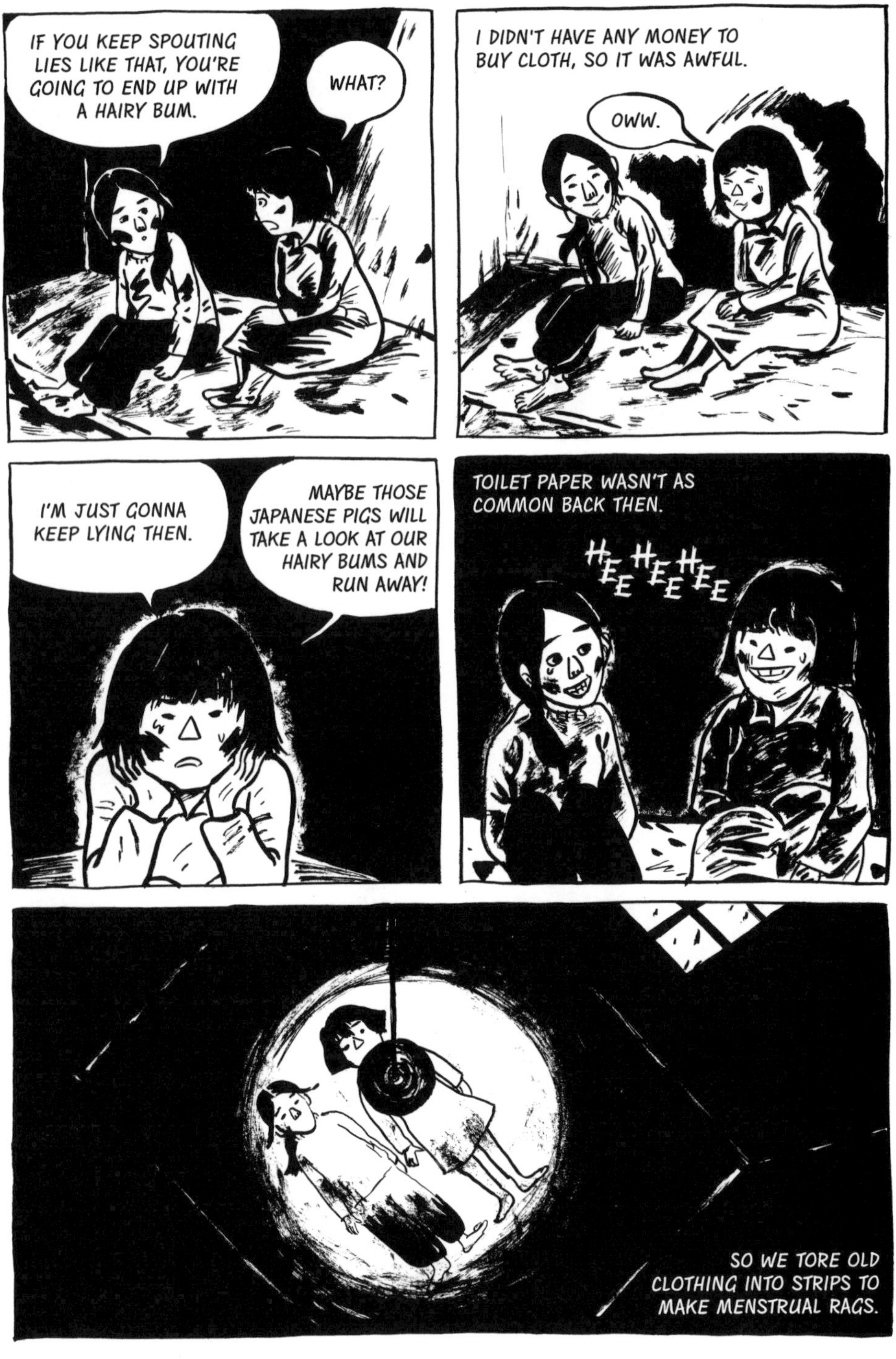
IF YOU KEEP SPOUTING LIES LIKE THAT, YOU'RE GOING TO END UP WITH A HAIRY BUM.
WHAT?
I DIDN'T HAVE ANY MONEY TO BUY CLOTH, SO IT WAS AWFUL.
OWW.
I'M JUST GONNA KEEP LYING THEN.
MAYBE THOSE JAPANESE PIGS WILL TAKE A LOOK AT OUR HAIRY BUMS AND RUN AWAY!
TOILET PAPER WASN'T AS COMMON BACK THEN.
HEE HEE HEE
SO WE TORE OLD CLOTHING INTO STRIPS TO MAKE MENSTRUAL RAGS.

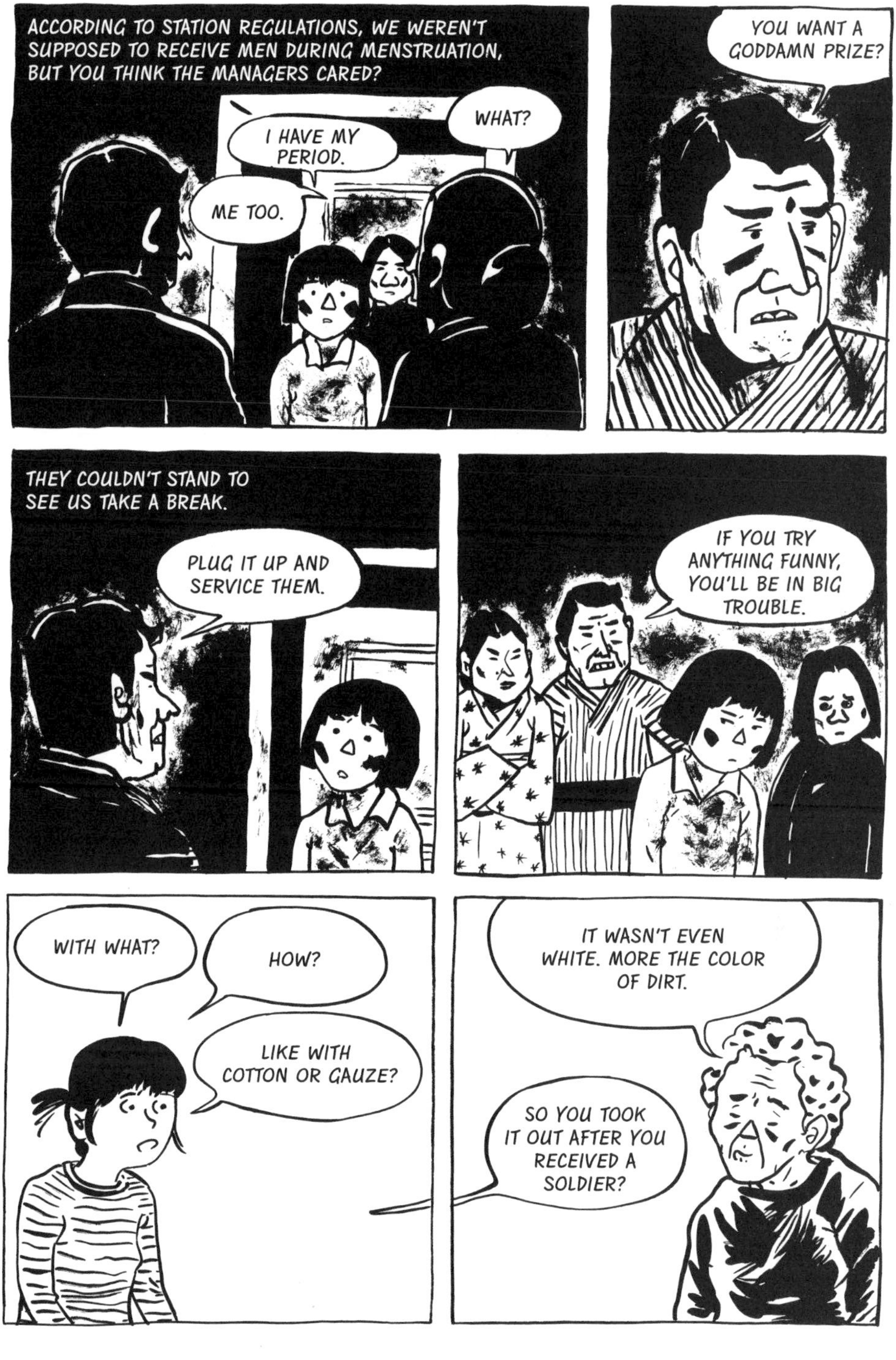
ACCORDING TO STATION REGULATIONS, WE WEREN'T SUPPOSED TO RECEIVE MEN DURING MENSTRUATION, BUT YOU THINK THE MANAGERS CARED?
I HAVE MY PERIOD.
WHAT?
ME TOO.
YOU WANT A GODDAMN PRIZE?
THEY COULDN'T STAND TO SEE US TAKE A BREAK.
PLUG IT UP AND SERVICE THEM.
IF YOU TRY ANYTHING FUNNY, YOU'LL BE IN BIG TROUBLE.
WITH WHAT?
HOW?
LIKE WITH COTTON OR GAUZE?
IT WASN'T EVEN WHITE. MORE THE COLOR OF DIRT.
SO YOU TOOK IT OUT AFTER YOU RECEIVED A SOLDIER?

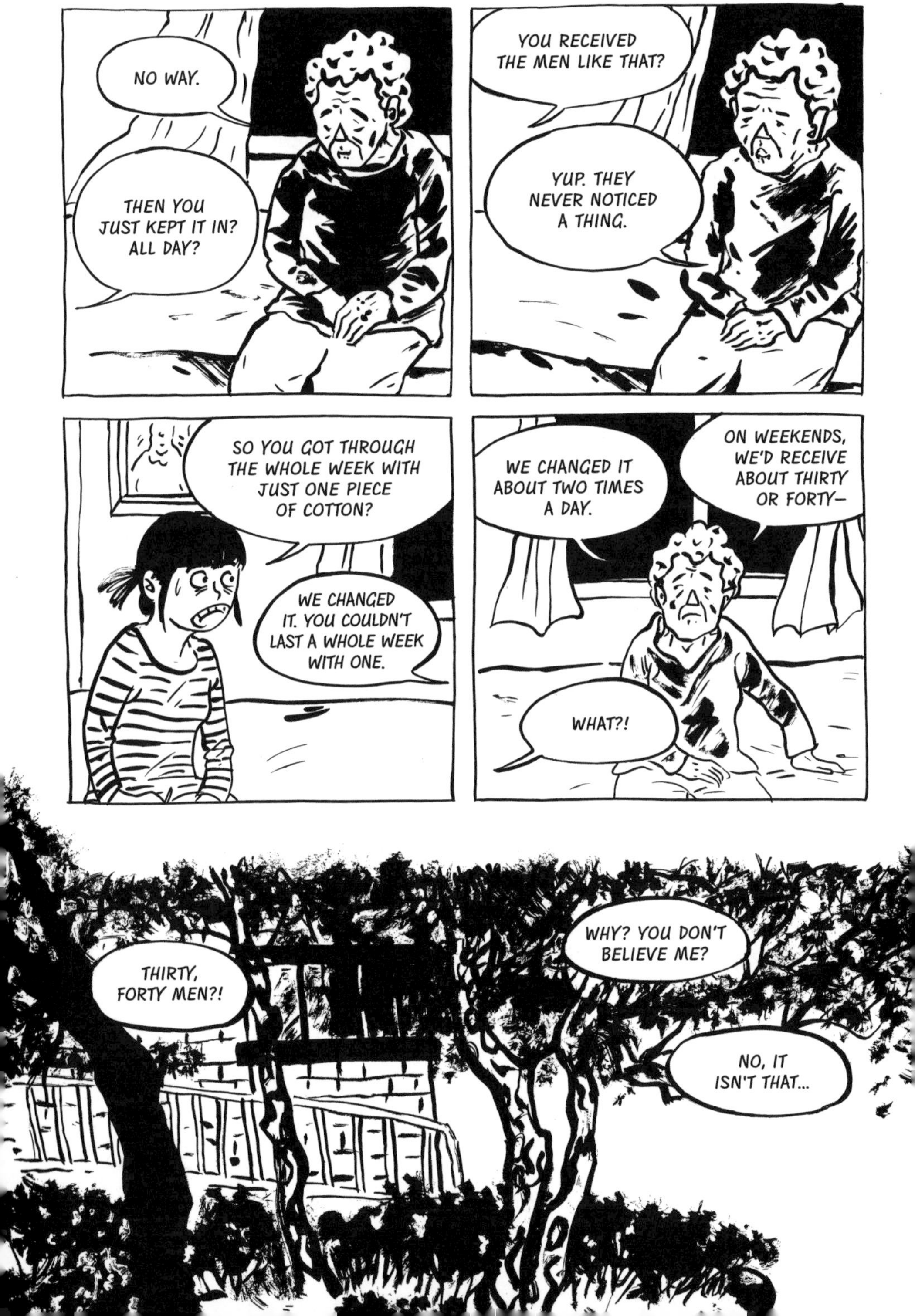
NO WAY.
THEN YOU JUST KEPT IT IN? ALL DAY?
YOU RECEIVED THE MEN LIKE THAT?
YUP. THEY NEVER NOTICED A THING.
SO YOU GOT THROUGH THE WHOLE WEEK WITH JUST ONE PIECE OF COTTON?
WE CHANGED IT. YOU COULDN'T LAST A WHOLE WEEK WITH ONE.
WE CHANGED IT ABOUT TWO TIMES A DAY.
ON WEEKENDS, WE'D RECEIVE ABOUT THIRTY OR FORTY—
WHAT?!
THIRTY, FORTY MEN?!
WHY? YOU DON'T BELIEVE ME?
NO, IT ISN'T THAT...

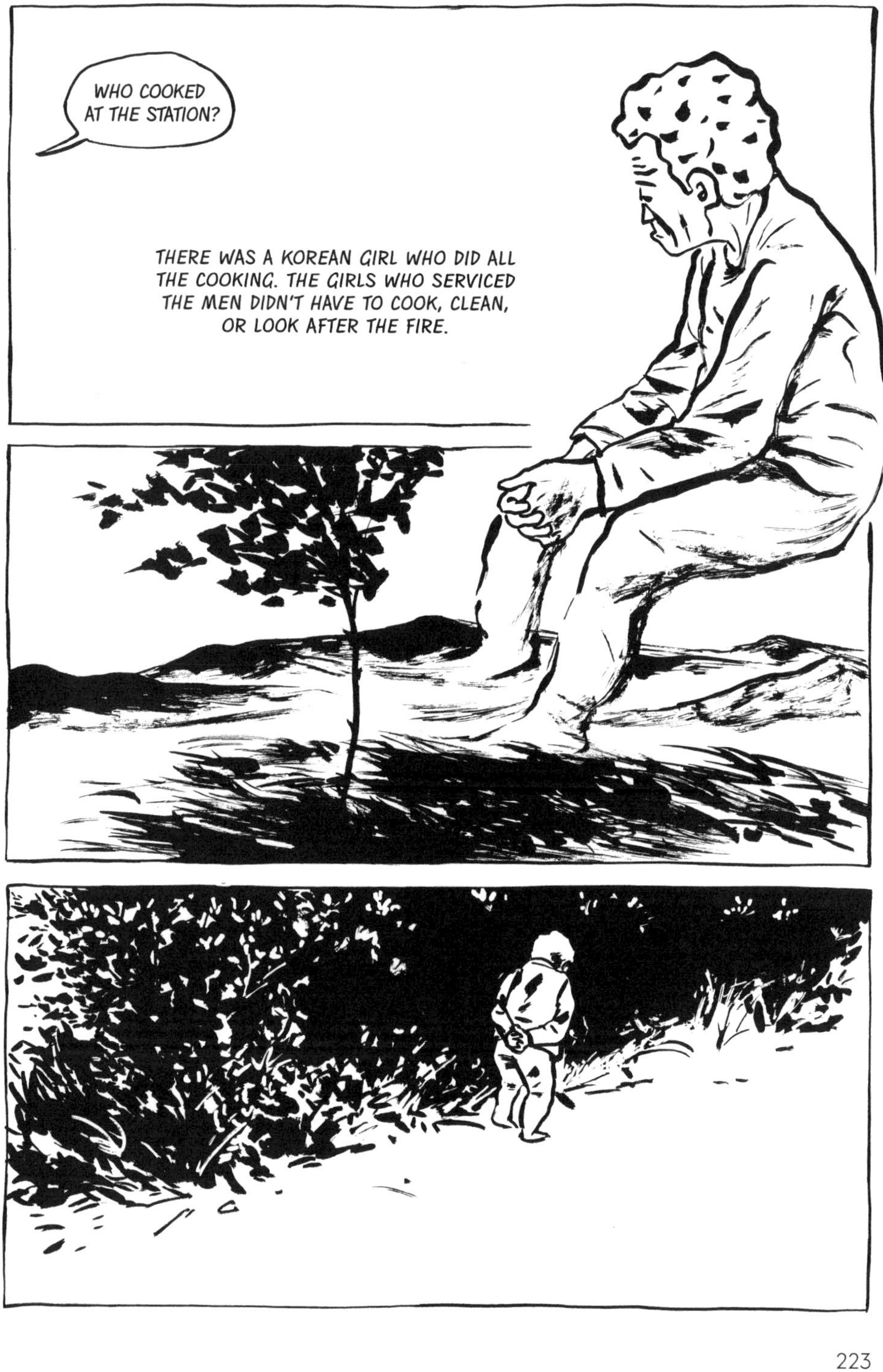
WHO COOKED AT THE STATION?
THERE WAS A KOREAN GIRL WHO DID ALL THE COOKING. THE GIRLS WHO SERVICED THE MEN DIDN'T HAVE TO COOK, CLEAN, OR LOOK AFTER THE FIRE.

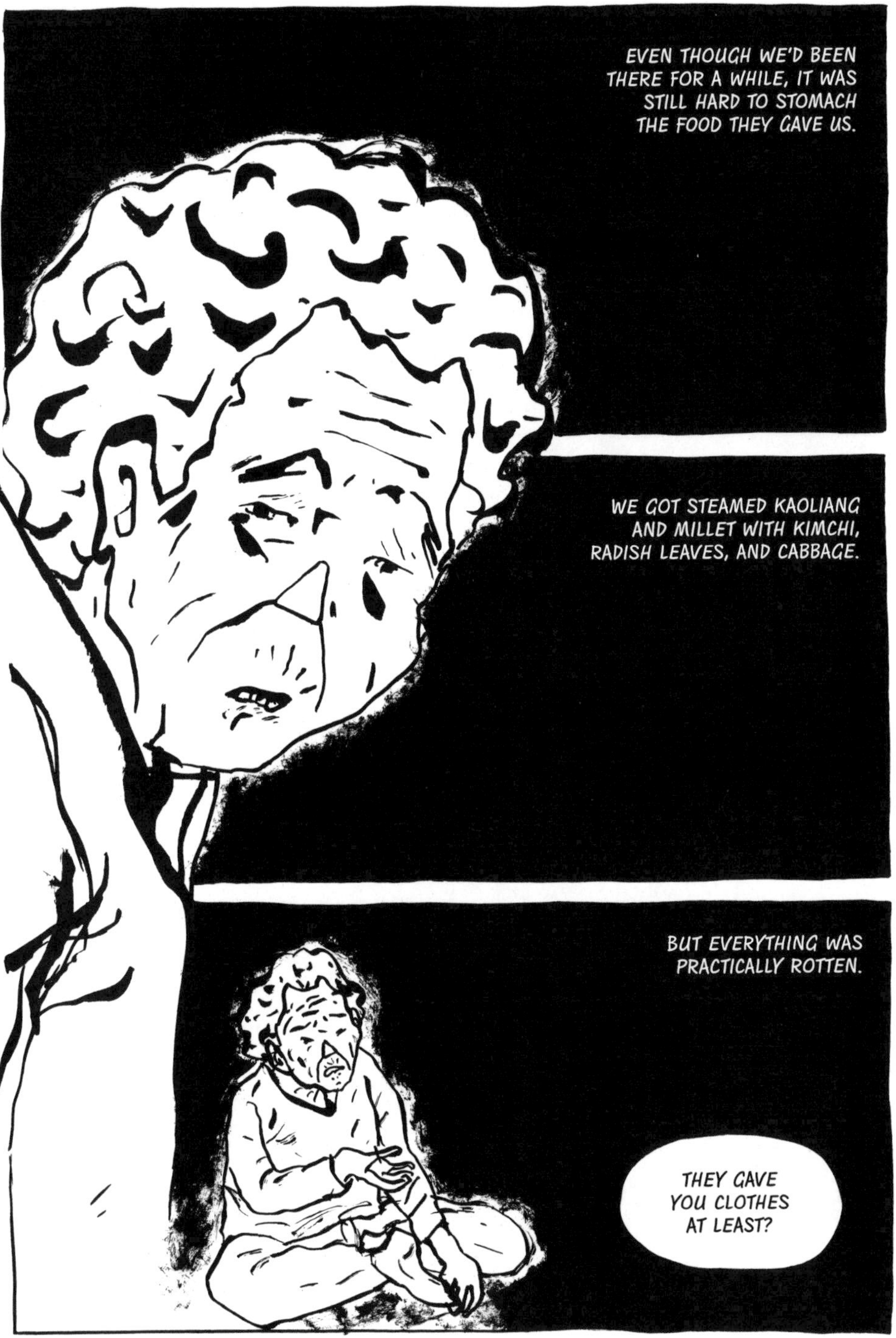
EVEN THOUGH WE'D BEEN THERE FOR A WHILE, IT WAS STILL HARD TO STOMACH THE FOOD THEY GAVE US.
WE GOT STEAMED KAOLIANG AND MILLET WITH KIMCHI, RADISH LEAVES, AND CABBAGE.
BUT EVERYTHING WAS PRACTICALLY ROTTEN.
THEY GAVE YOU CLOTHES AT LEAST?

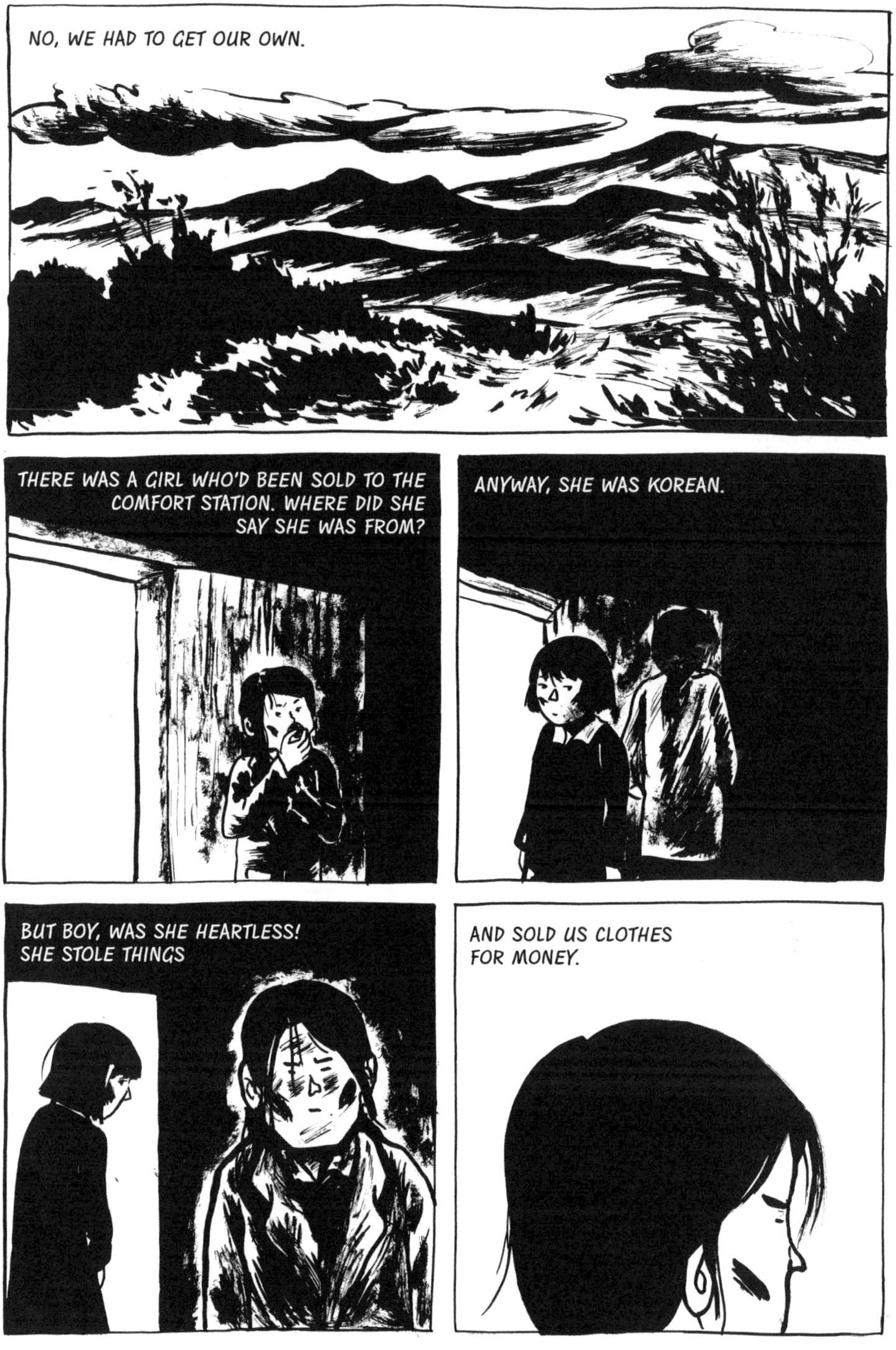
NO, WE HAD TO GET OUR OWN.
THERE WAS A GIRL WHO'D BEEN SOLD TO THE COMFORT STATION. WHERE DID SHE SAY SHE WAS FROM?
ANYWAY, SHE WAS KOREAN.
BUT BOY, WAS SHE HEARTLESS! SHE STOLE THINGS
AND SOLD US CLOTHES FOR MONEY.

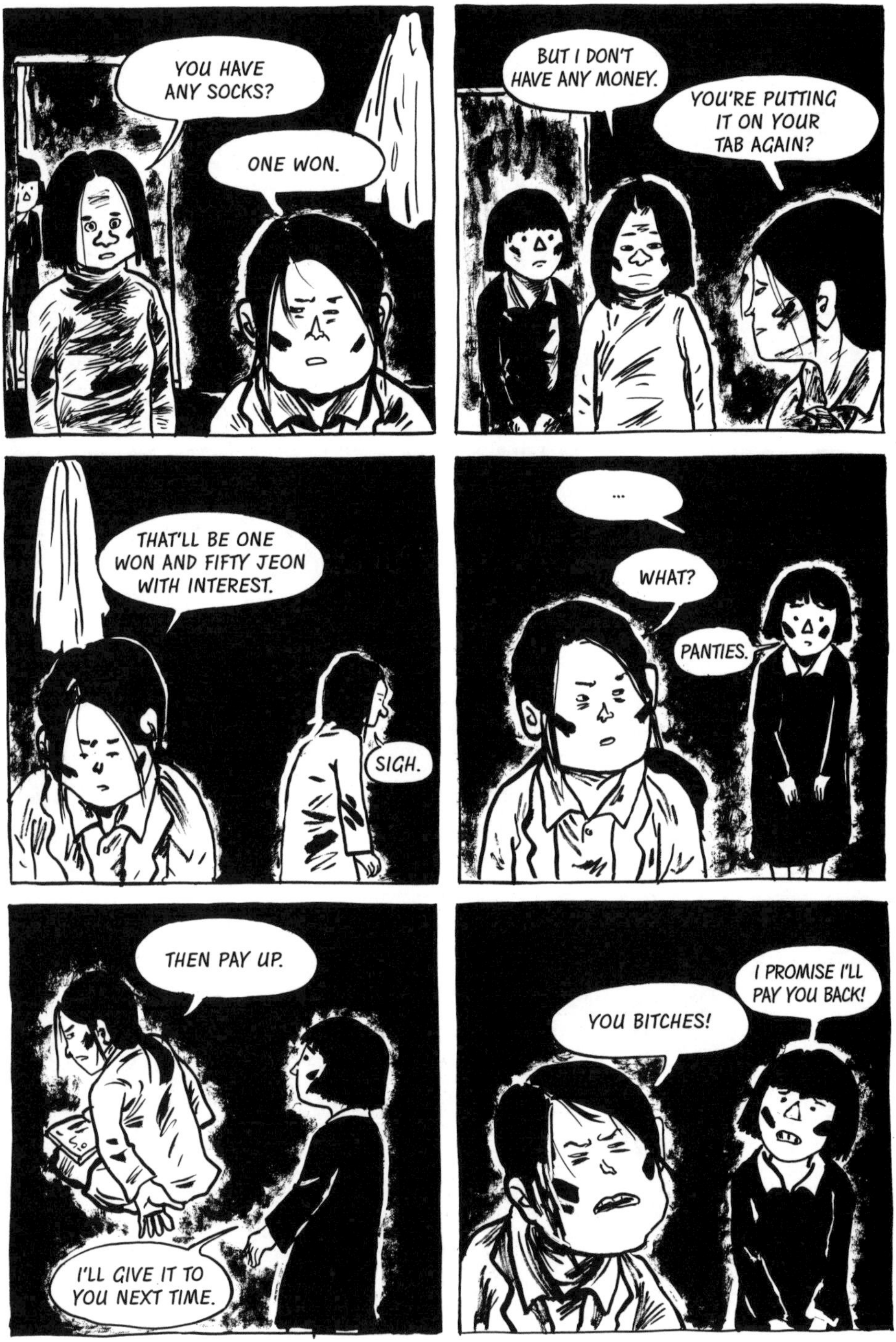
YOU HAVE ANY SOCKS?
ONE WON.
BUT I DON'T HAVE ANY MONEY.
YOU'RE PUTTING IT ON YOUR TAB AGAIN?
THAT'LL BE ONE WON AND FIFTY JEON WITH INTEREST.
SIGH.
...
WHAT?
PANTIES.
THEN PAY UP.
I'LL GIVE IT TO YOU NEXT TIME.
YOU BITCHES!
I PROMISE I'LL PAY YOU BACK!

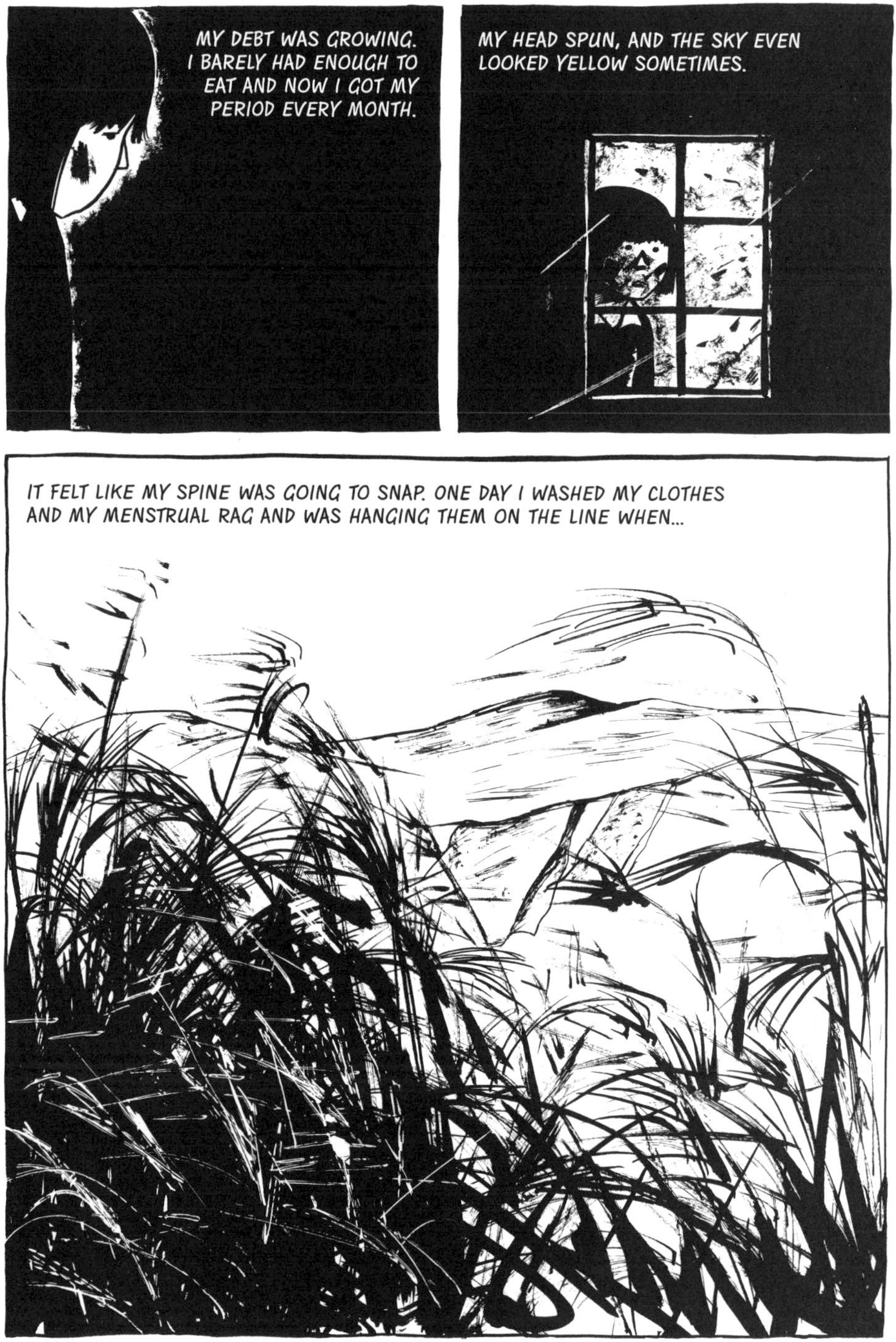
MY DEBT WAS GROWING. I BARELY HAD ENOUGH TO EAT AND NOW I GOT MY PERIOD EVERY MONTH.
MY HEAD SPUN, AND THE SKY EVEN LOOKED YELLOW SOMETIMES.
IT FELT LIKE MY SPINE WAS GOING TO SNAP. ONE DAY I WASHED MY CLOTHES AND MY MENSTRUAL RAG AND WAS HANGING THEM ON THE LINE WHEN...

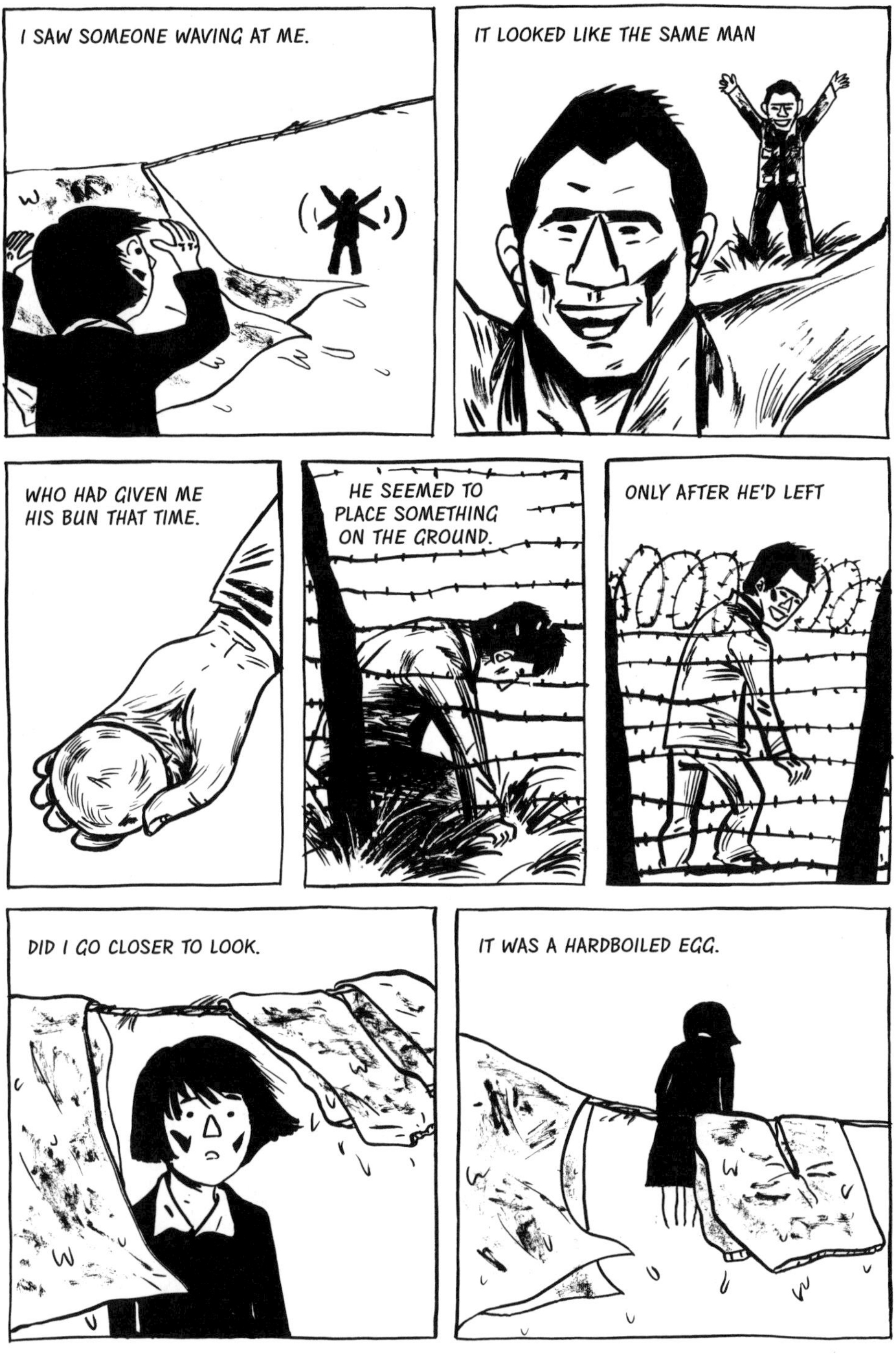
I SAW SOMEONE WAVING AT ME.
IT LOOKED LIKE THE SAME MAN
WHO HAD GIVEN ME HIS BUN THAT TIME.
HE SEEMED TO PLACE SOMETHING ON THE GROUND.
ONLY AFTER HE'D LEFT
DID I GO CLOSER TO LOOK.
IT WAS A HARDBOILED EGG.

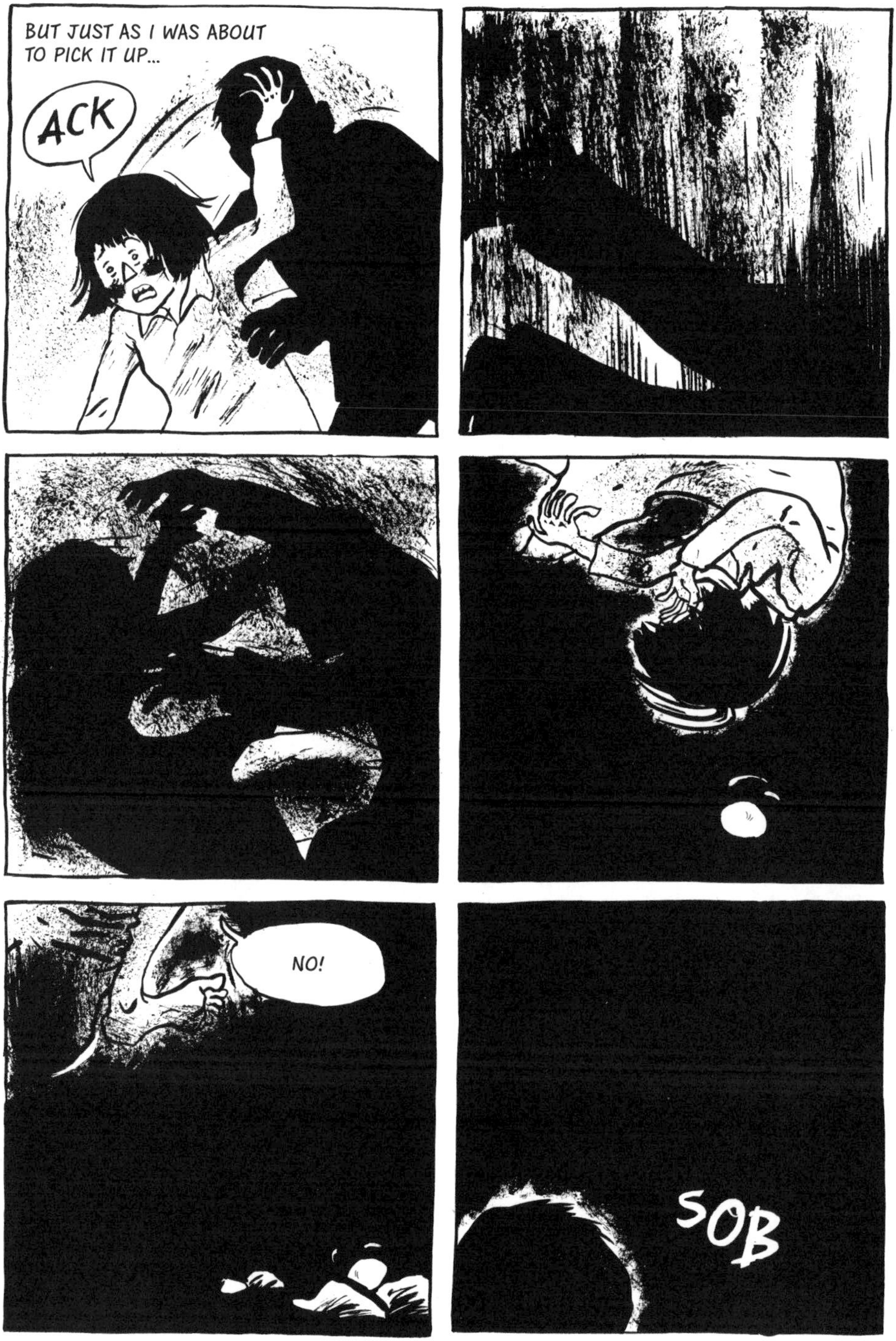
BUT JUST AS I WAS ABOUT TO PICK IT UP...
ACK
NO!
SOB

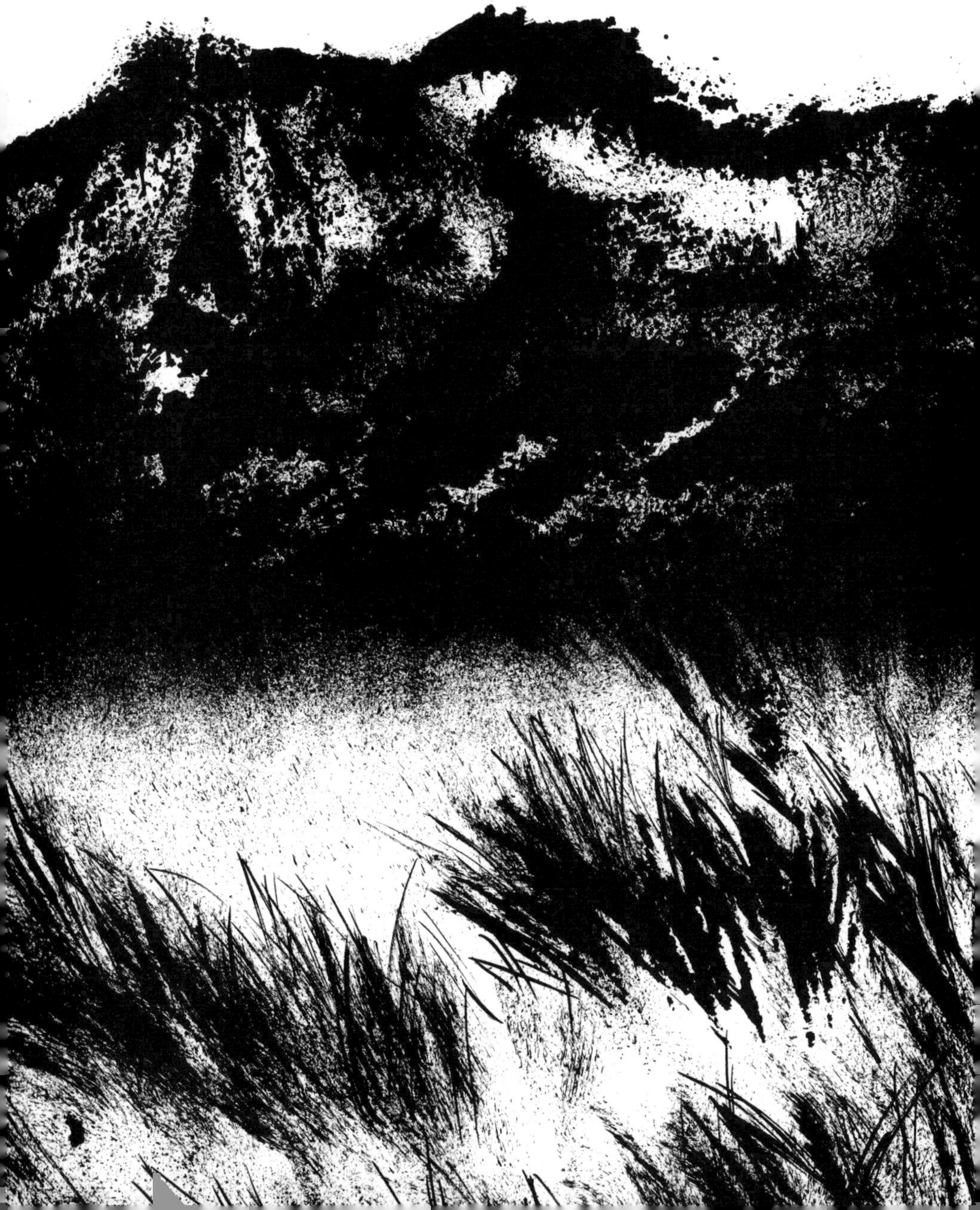

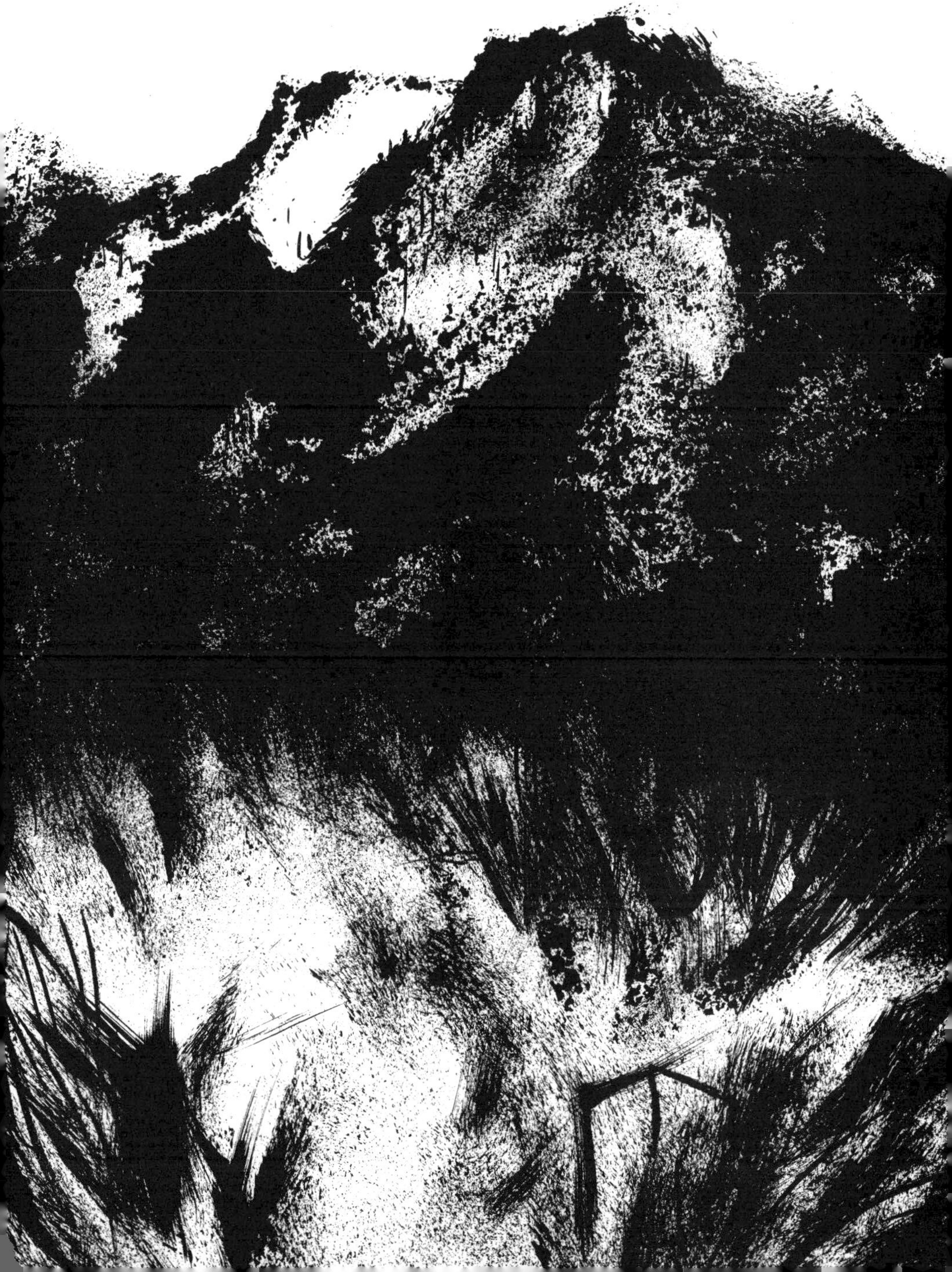

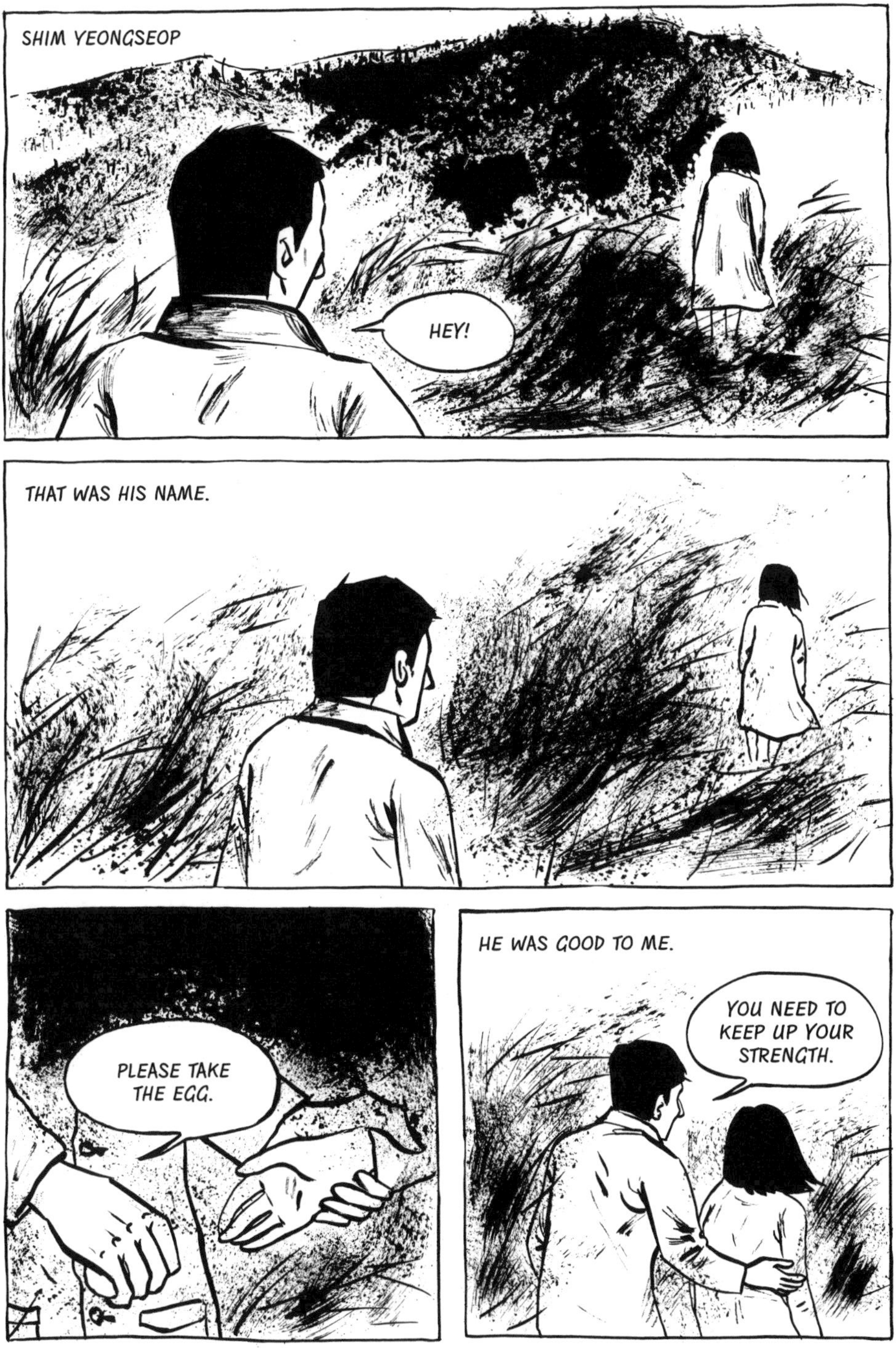
SHIM YEONGSEOP
HEY!
THAT WAS HIS NAME.
PLEASE TAKE THE EGG.
HE WAS GOOD TO ME.
YOU NEED TO KEEP UP YOUR STRENGTH.

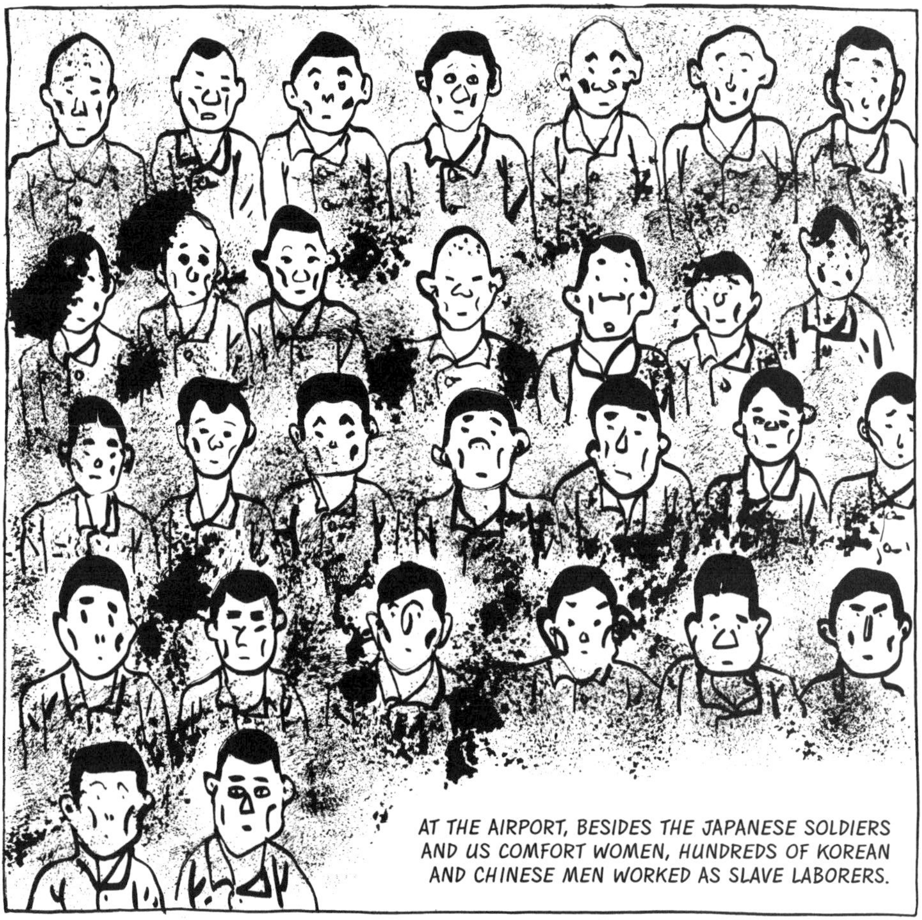
AT THE AIRPORT, BESIDES THE JAPANESE SOLDIERS AND US COMFORT WOMEN, HUNDREDS OF KOREAN AND CHINESE MEN WORKED AS SLAVE LABORERS.

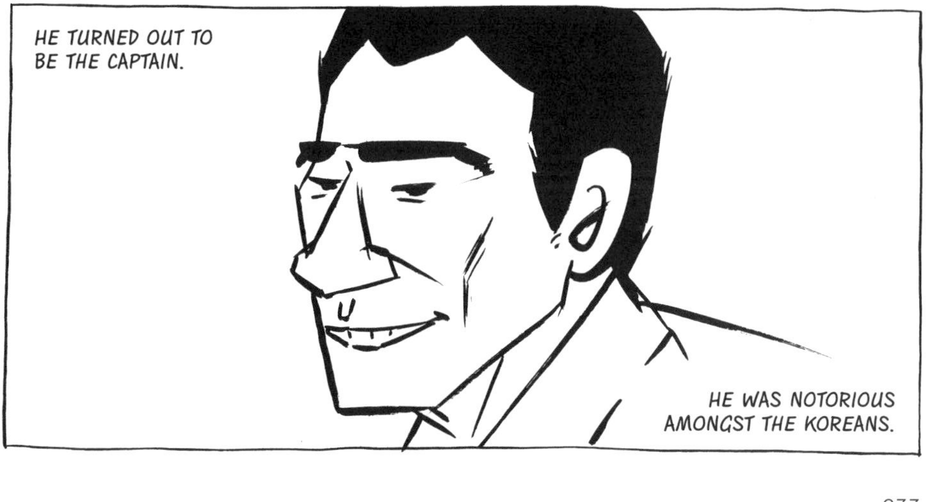
HE TURNED OUT TO BE THE CAPTAIN.
HE WAS NOTORIOUS AMONGST THE KOREANS.

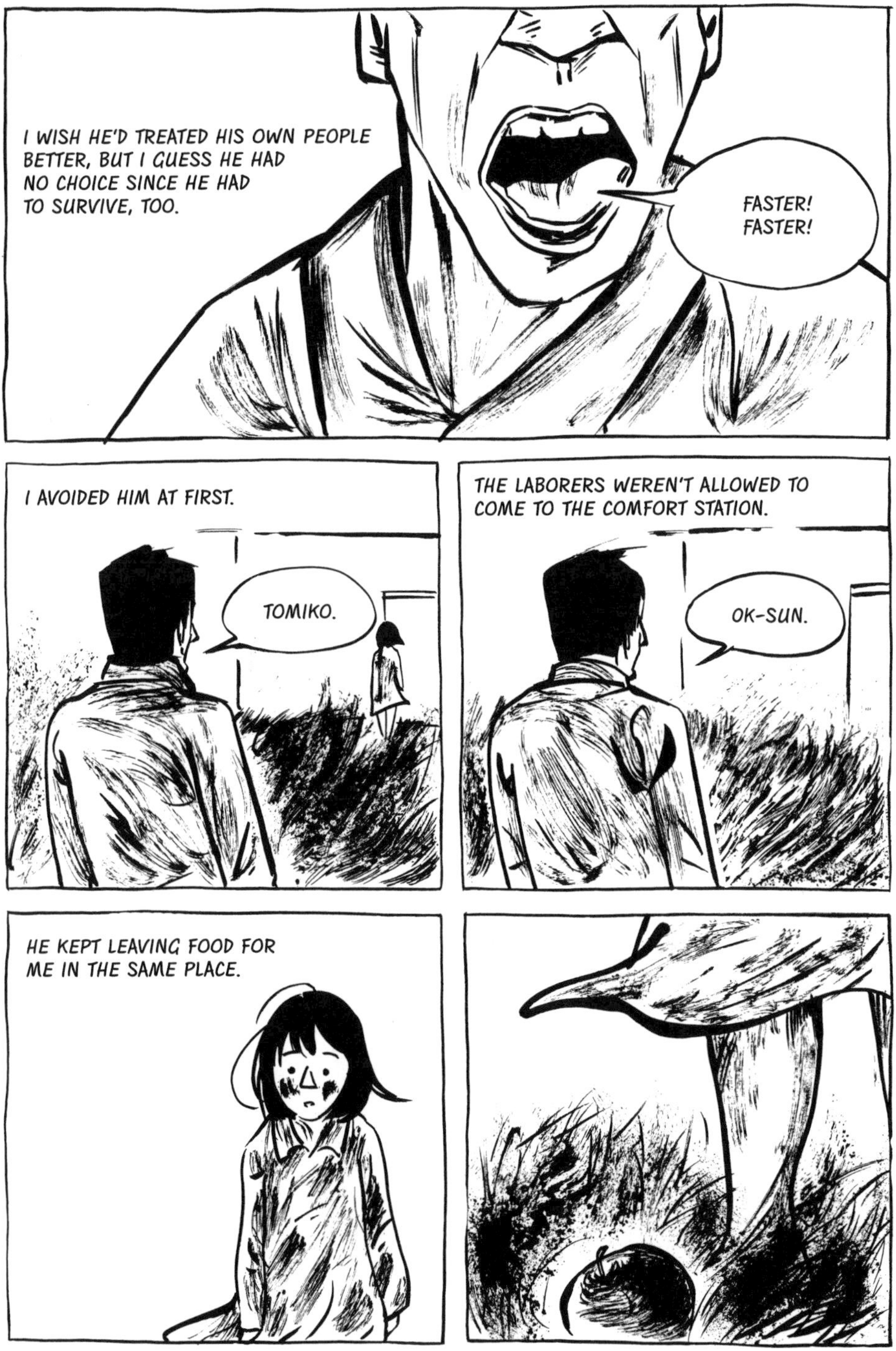
I WISH HE'D TREATED HIS OWN PEOPLE BETTER, BUT I GUESS HE HAD NO CHOICE SINCE HE HAD TO SURVIVE, TOO.
FASTER! FASTER!
I AVOIDED HIM AT FIRST.
TOMIKO.
THE LABORERS WEREN'T ALLOWED TO COME TO THE COMFORT STATION.
OK-SUN.
HE KEPT LEAVING FOOD FOR ME IN THE SAME PLACE.

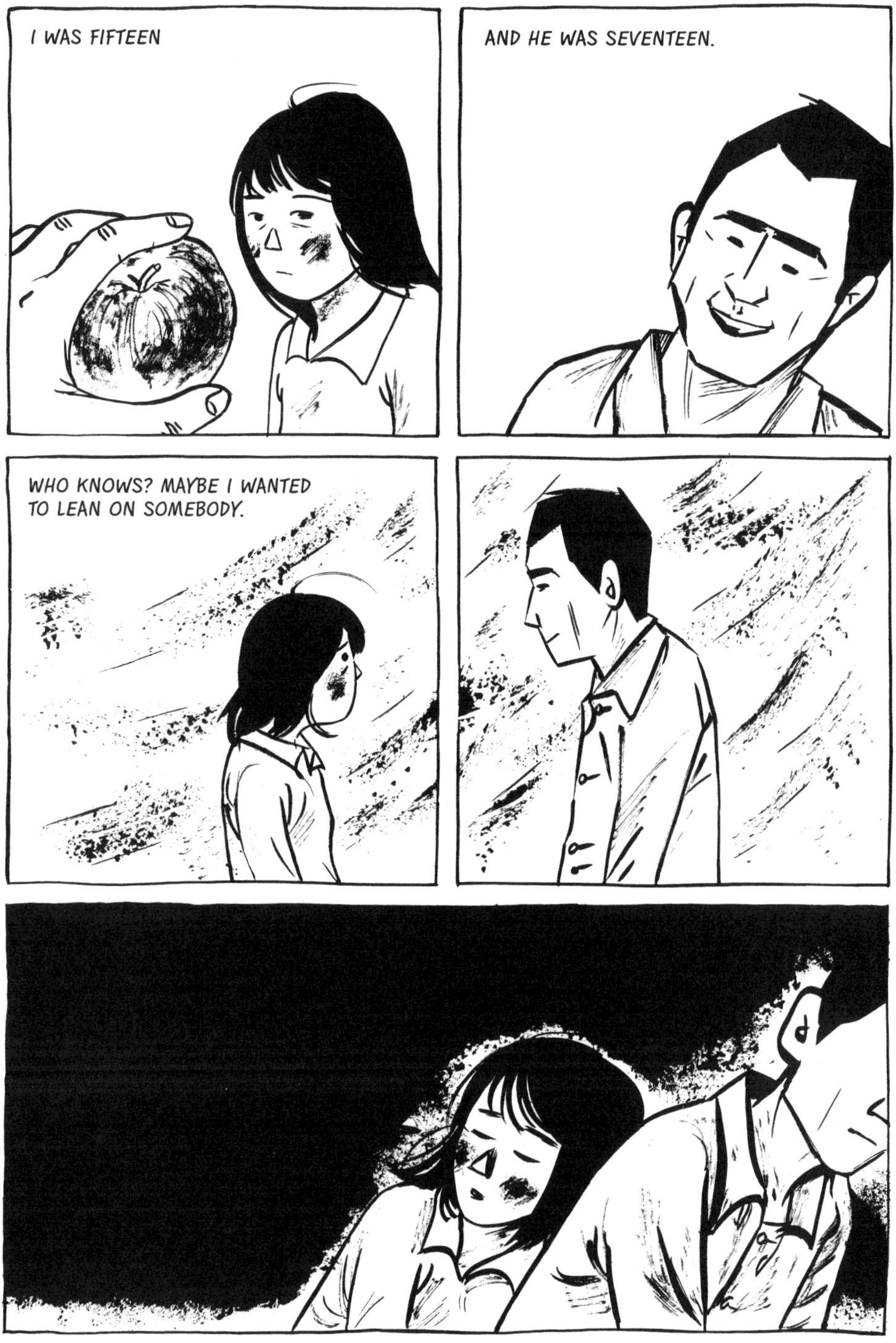
I WAS FIFTEEN
AND HE WAS SEVENTEEN.
WHO KNOWS? MAYBE I WANTED TO LEAN ON SOMEBODY.

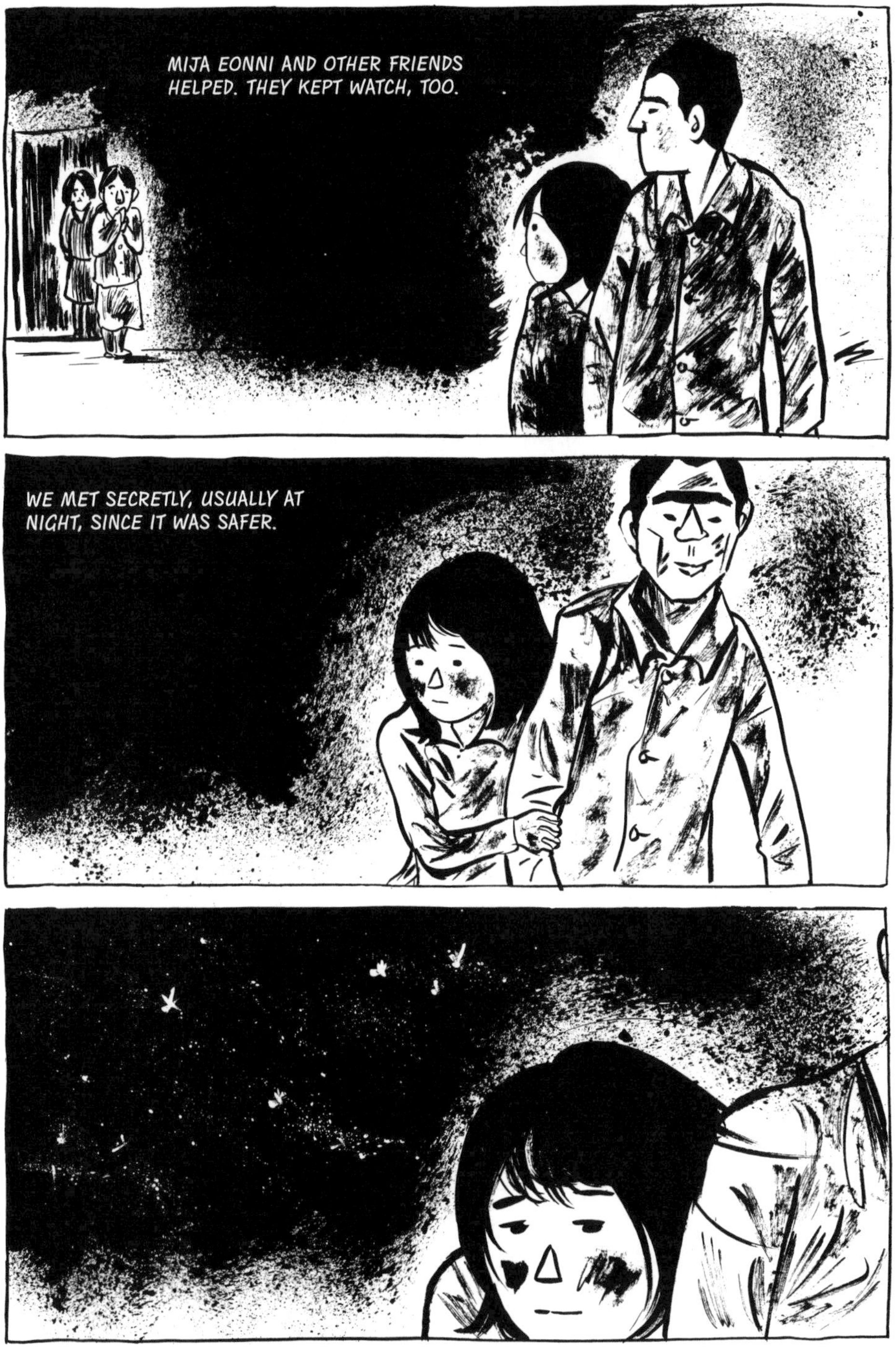
MIJA EONNI AND OTHER FRIENDS HELPED. THEY KEPT WATCH, TOO.
WE MET SECRETLY, USUALLY AT NIGHT, SINCE IT WAS SAFER.

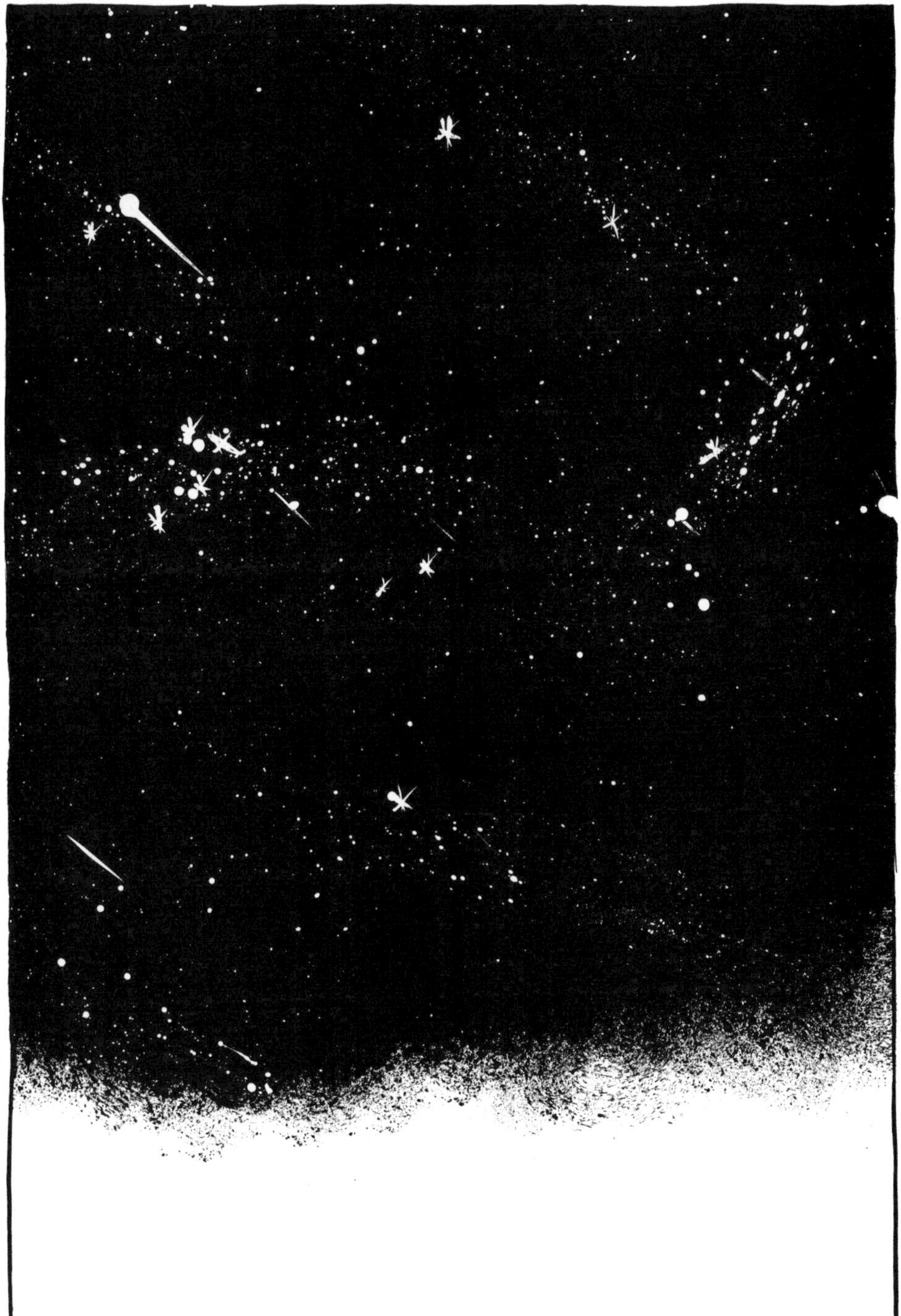

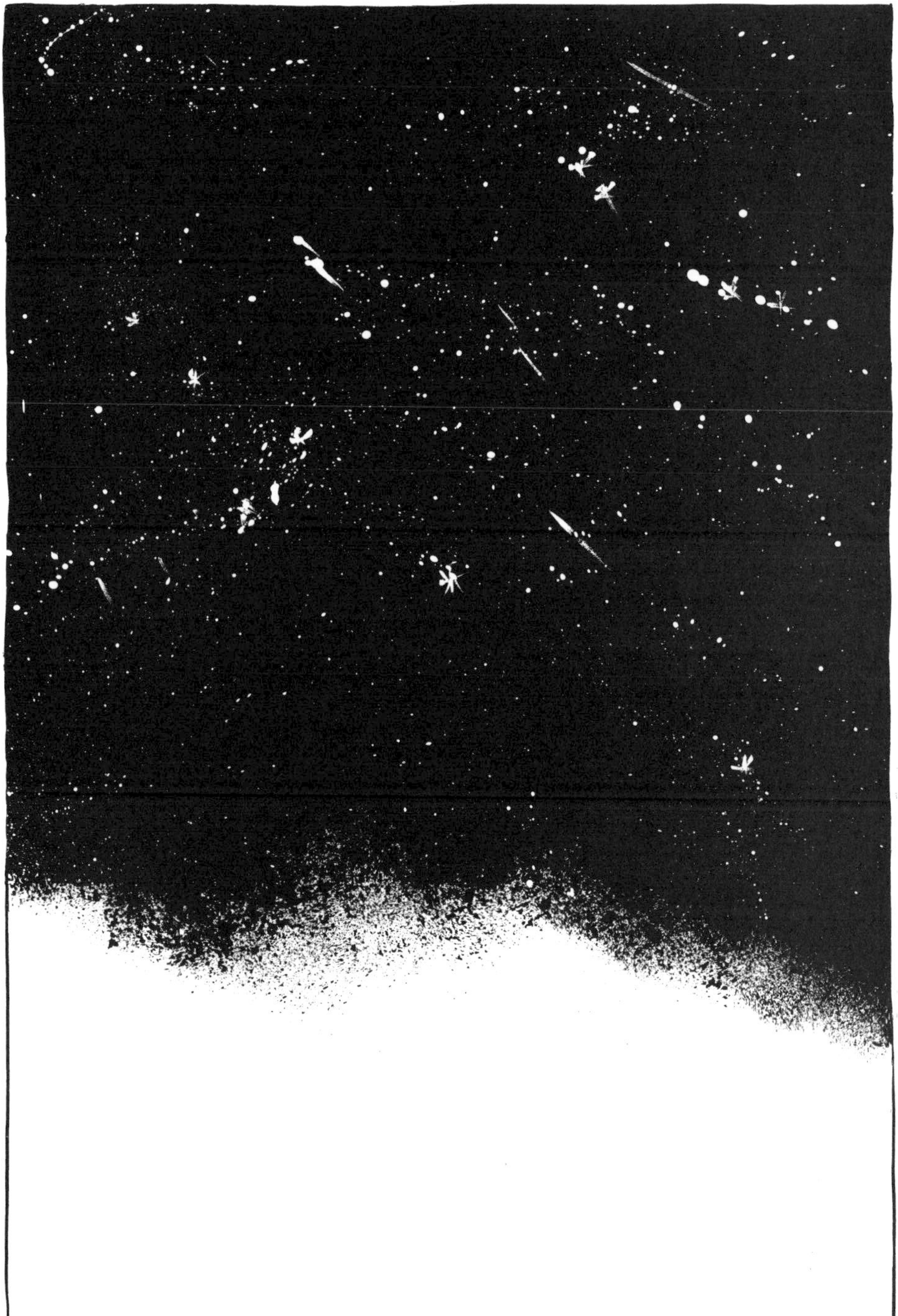

# TO DOWNTOWN YANJI

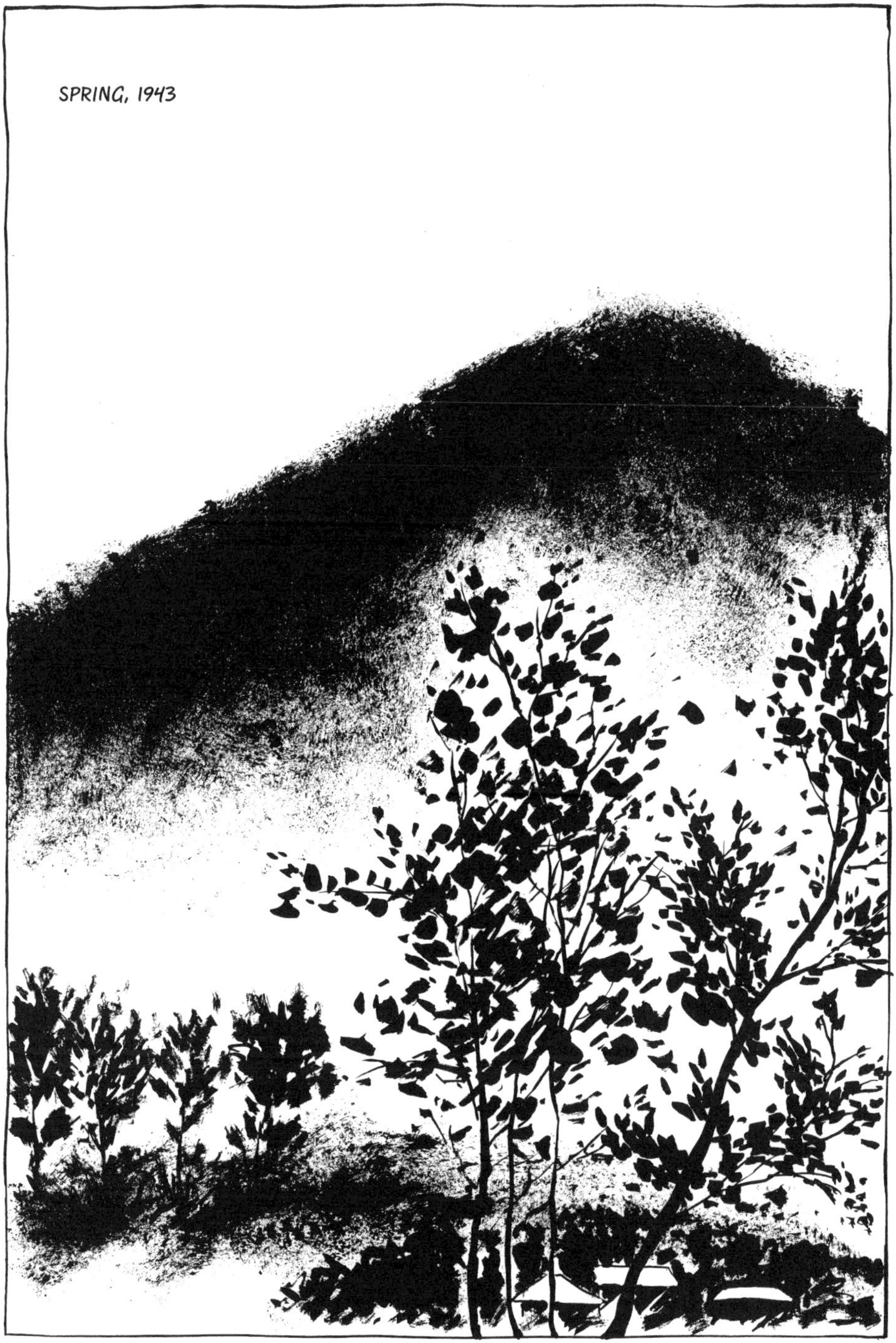
SPRING, 1943

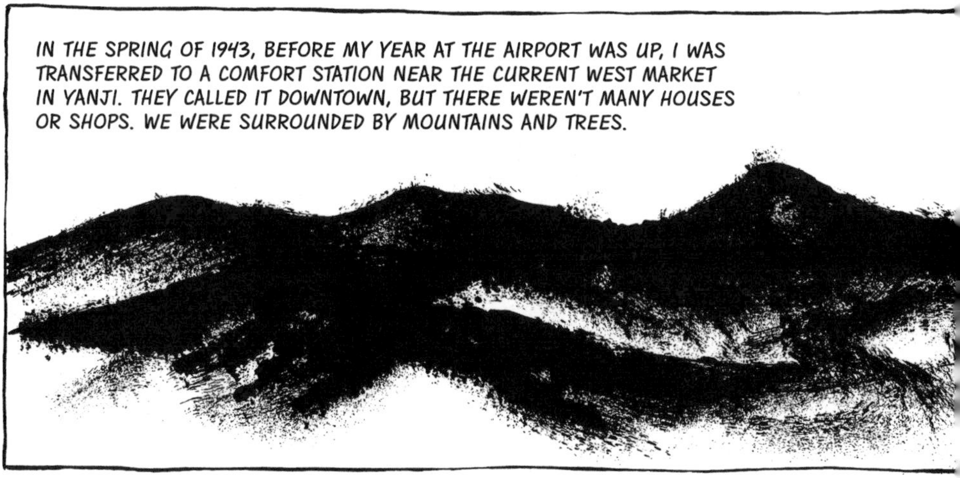
IN THE SPRING OF 1943, BEFORE MY YEAR AT THE AIRPORT WAS UP, I WAS TRANSFERRED TO A COMFORT STATION NEAR THE CURRENT WEST MARKET IN YANJI. THEY CALLED IT DOWNTOWN, BUT THERE WEREN'T MANY HOUSES OR SHOPS. WE WERE SURROUNDED BY MOUNTAINS AND TREES.

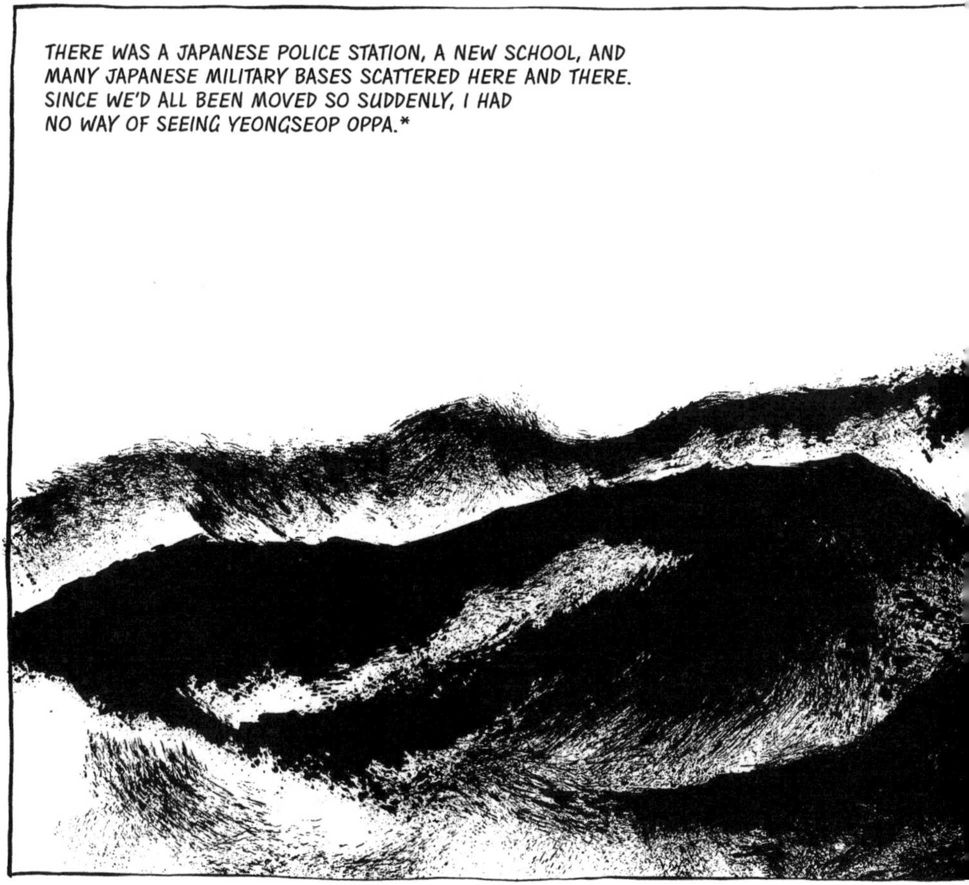
THERE WAS A JAPANESE POLICE STATION, A NEW SCHOOL, AND MANY JAPANESE MILITARY BASES SCATTERED HERE AND THERE. SINCE WE'D ALL BEEN MOVED SO SUDDENLY, I HAD NO WAY OF SEEING YEONGSEOP OPPA.*

*OPPA IS THE KOREAN WORD FOR OLDER BROTHER USED BY A FEMALE.

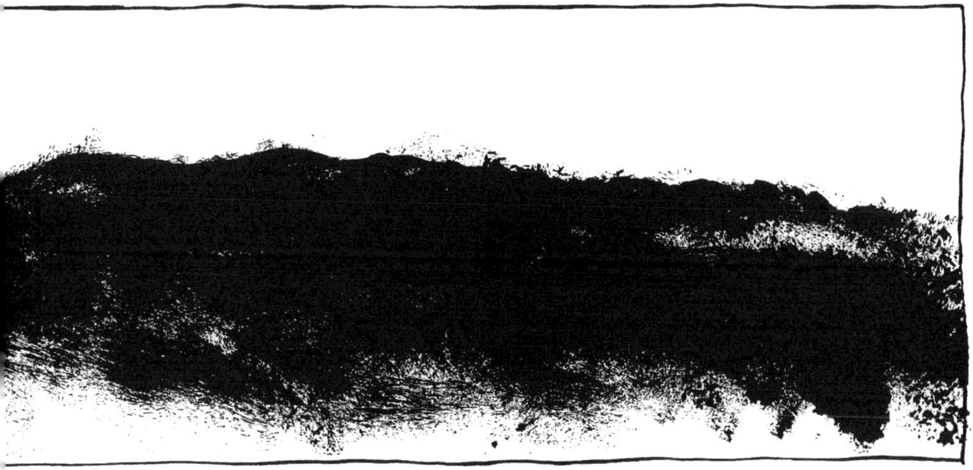

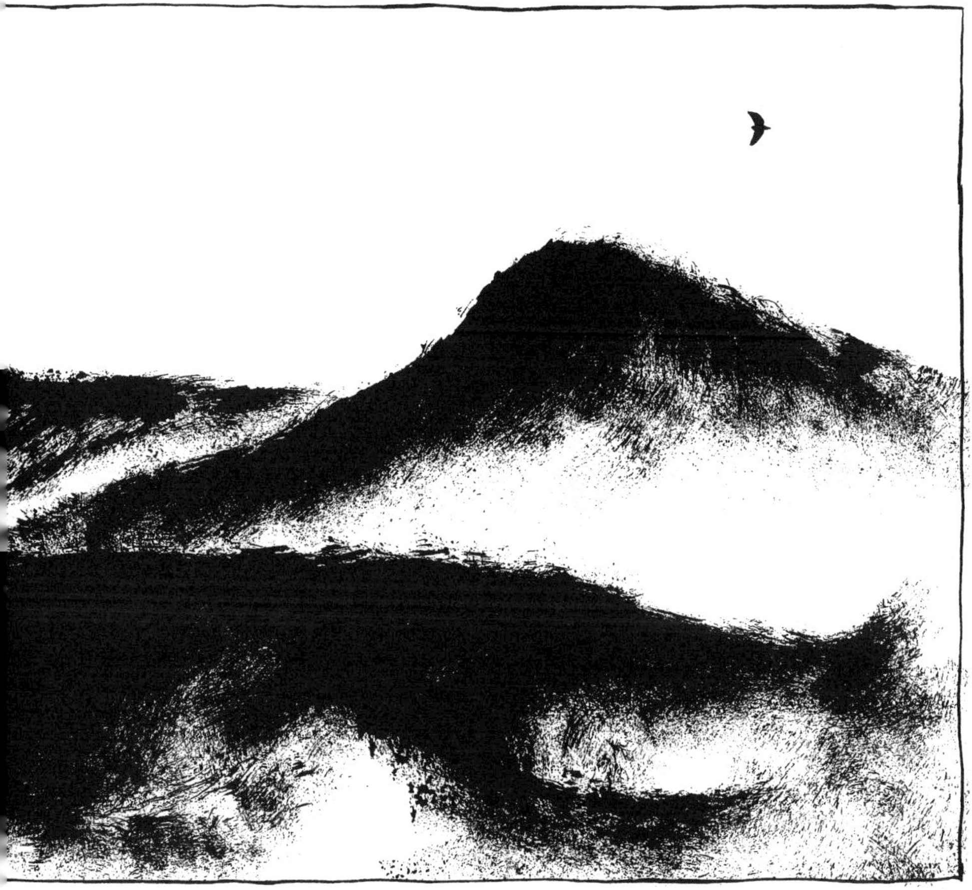

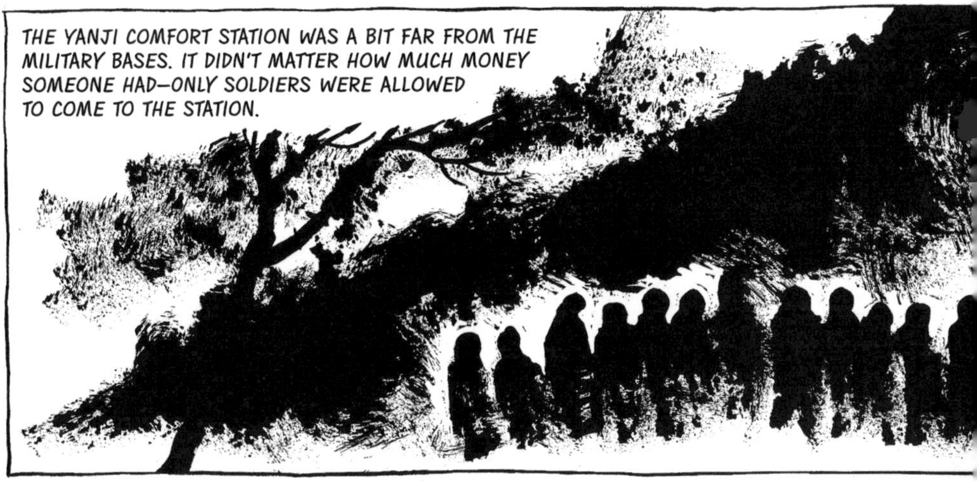
THE YANJI COMFORT STATION WAS A BIT FAR FROM THE MILITARY BASES. IT DIDN'T MATTER HOW MUCH MONEY SOMEONE HAD—ONLY SOLDIERS WERE ALLOWED TO COME TO THE STATION.

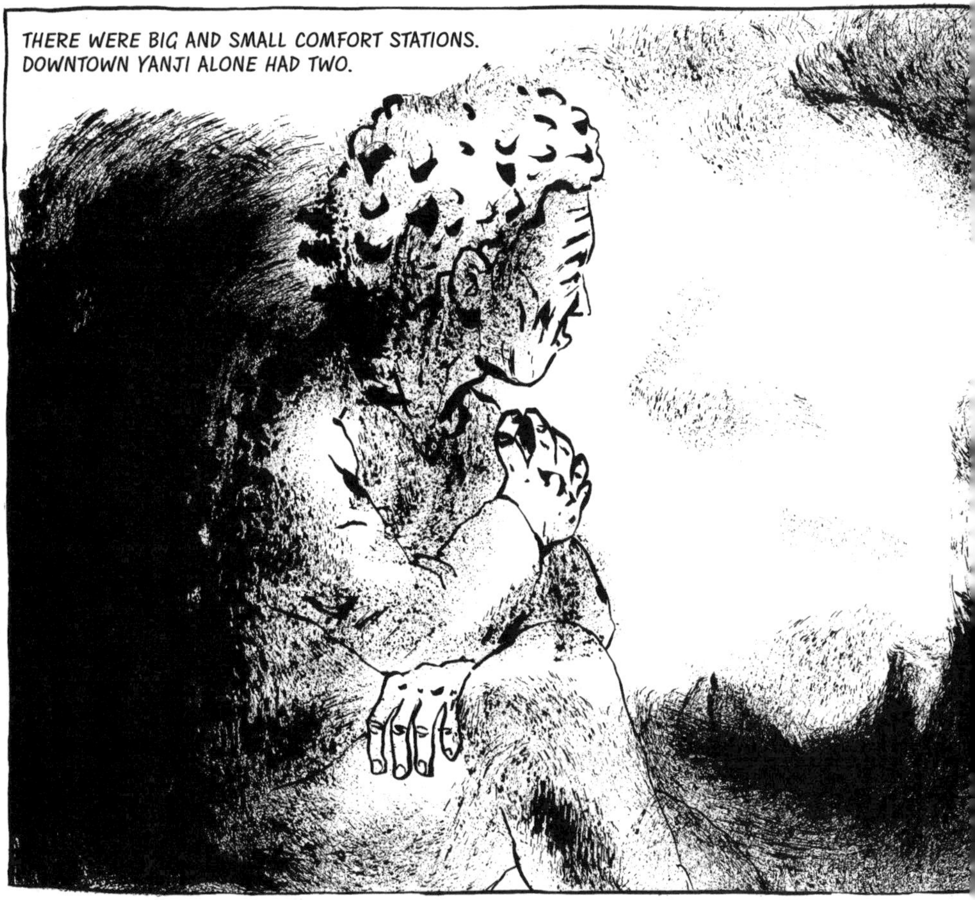
THERE WERE BIG AND SMALL COMFORT STATIONS. DOWNTOWN YANJI ALONE HAD TWO.

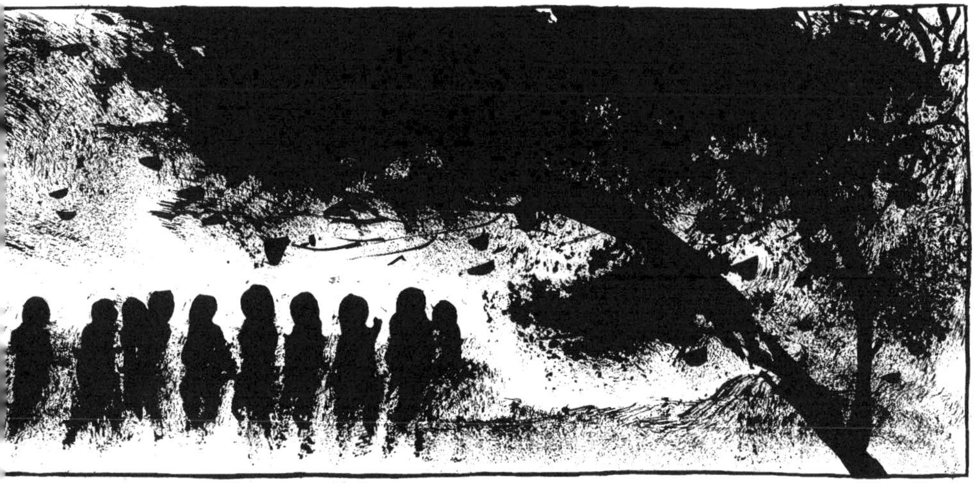

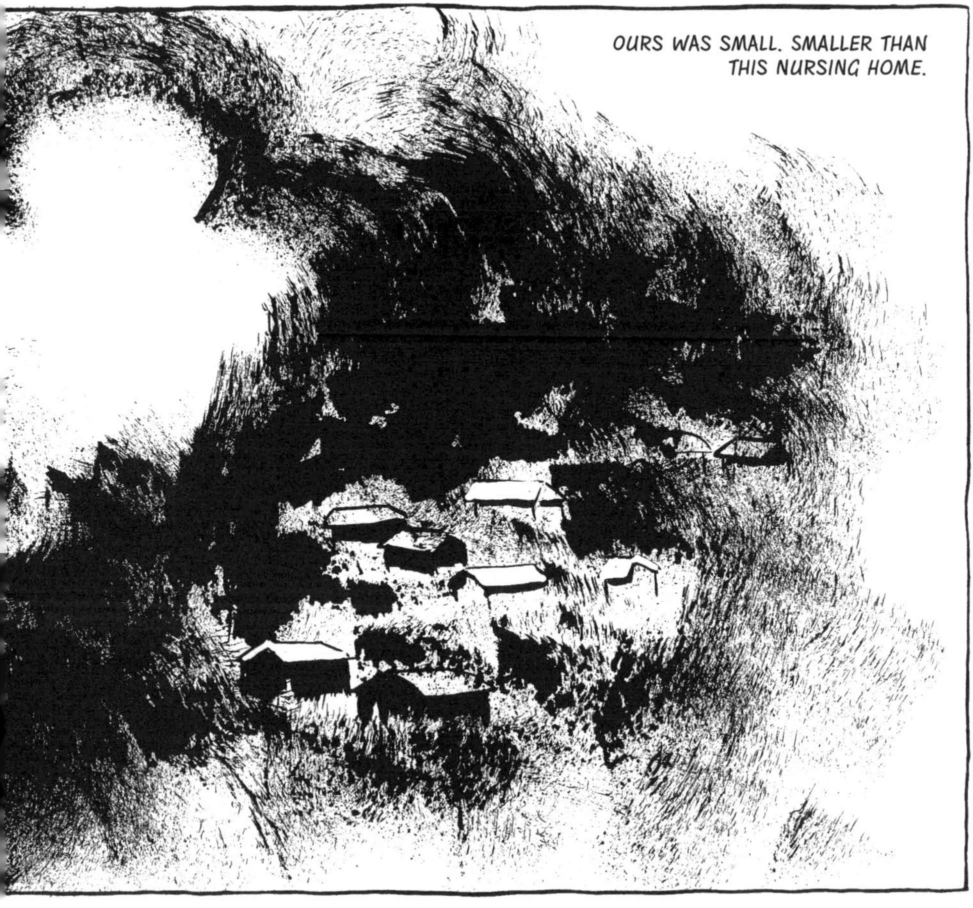
OURS WAS SMALL. SMALLER THAN THIS NURSING HOME.

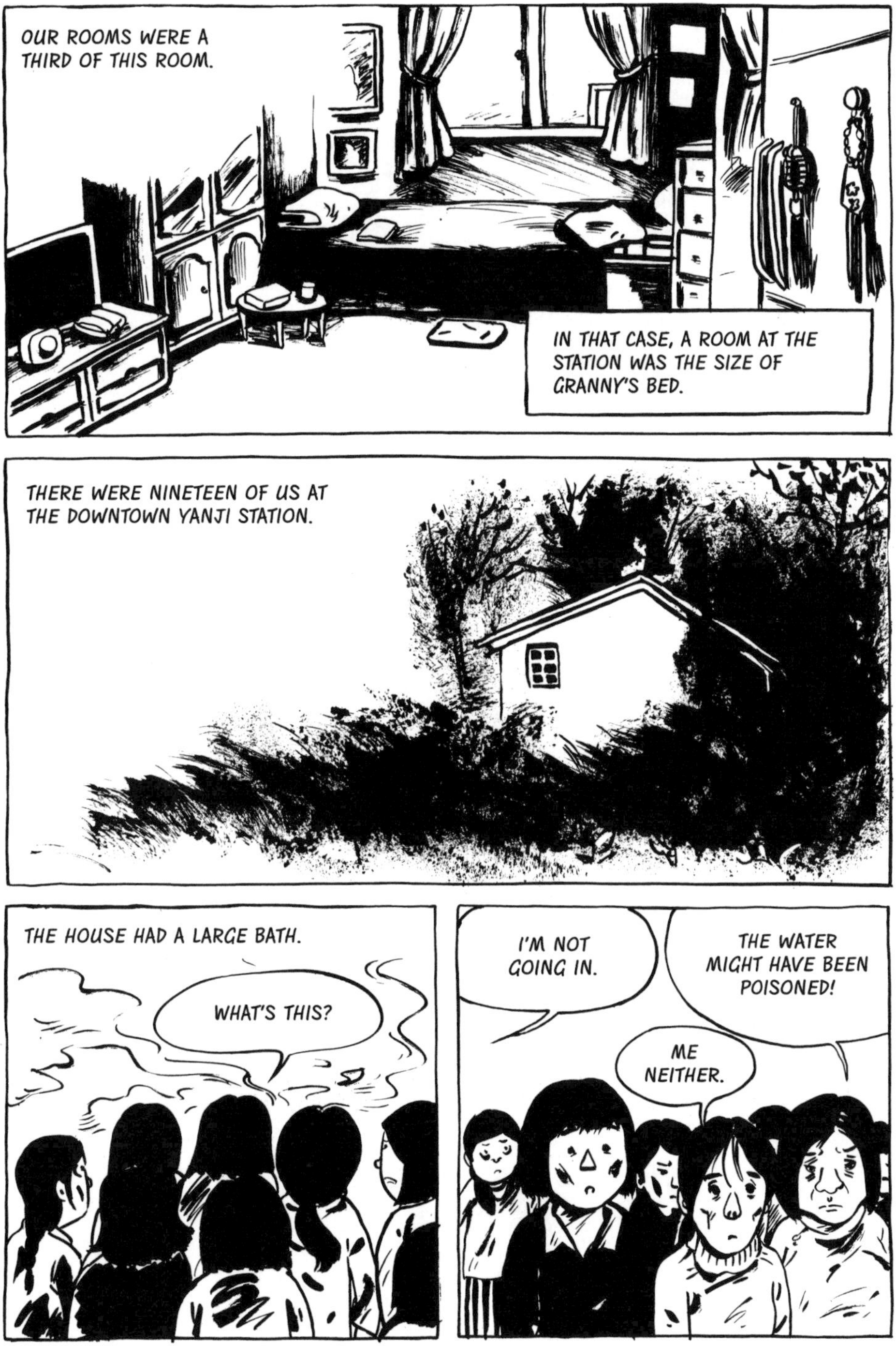
OUR ROOMS WERE A THIRD OF THIS ROOM.
IN THAT CASE, A ROOM AT THE STATION WAS THE SIZE OF GRANNY'S BED.
THERE WERE NINETEEN OF US AT THE DOWNTOWN YANJI STATION.
THE HOUSE HAD A LARGE BATH.
WHAT'S THIS?
I'M NOT GOING IN.
THE WATER MIGHT HAVE BEEN POISONED!
ME NEITHER.

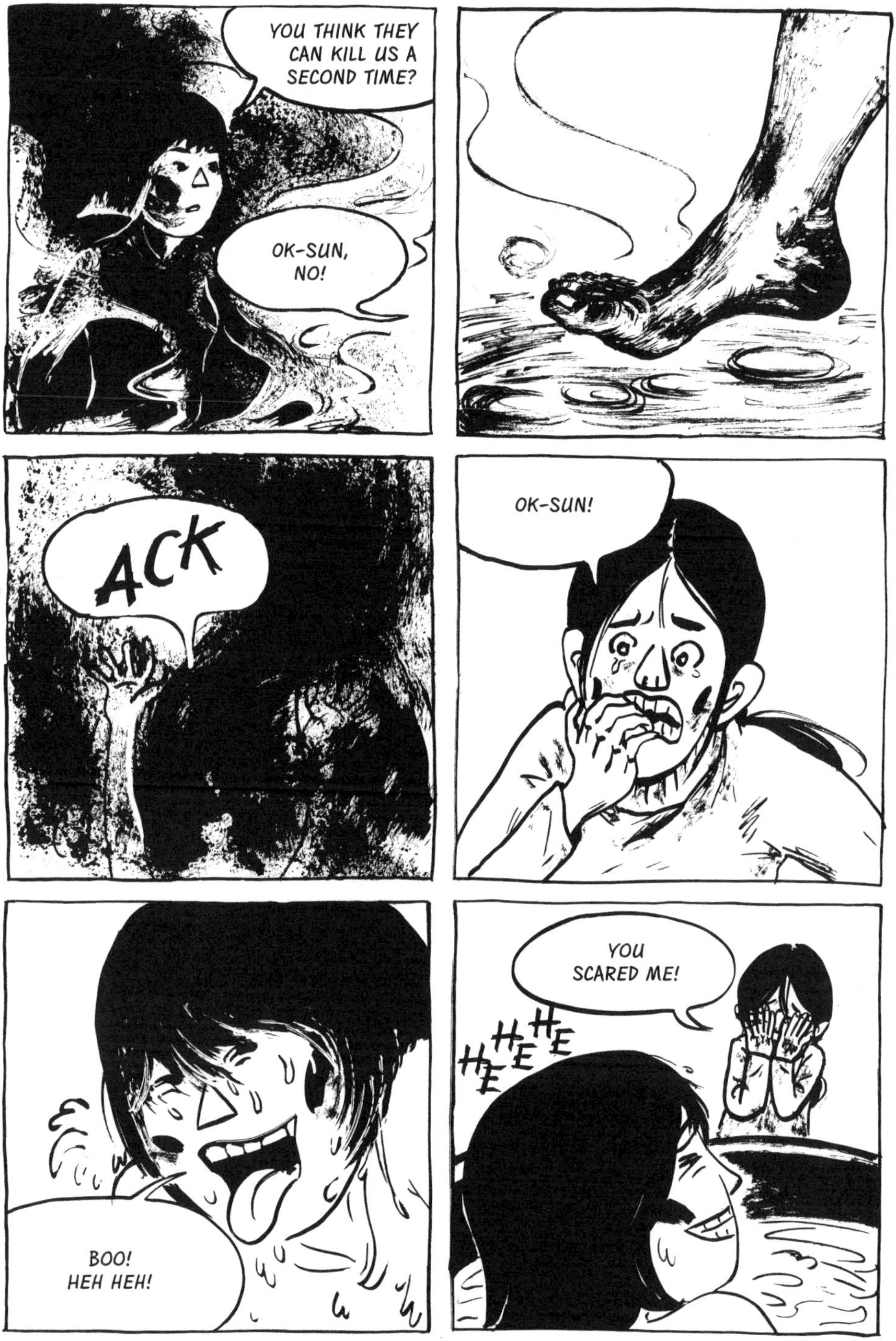
YOU THINK THEY CAN KILL US A SECOND TIME?
OK-SUN, NO!
ACK
OK-SUN!
BOO! HEH HEH!
YOU SCARED ME!
HEHEHEHE

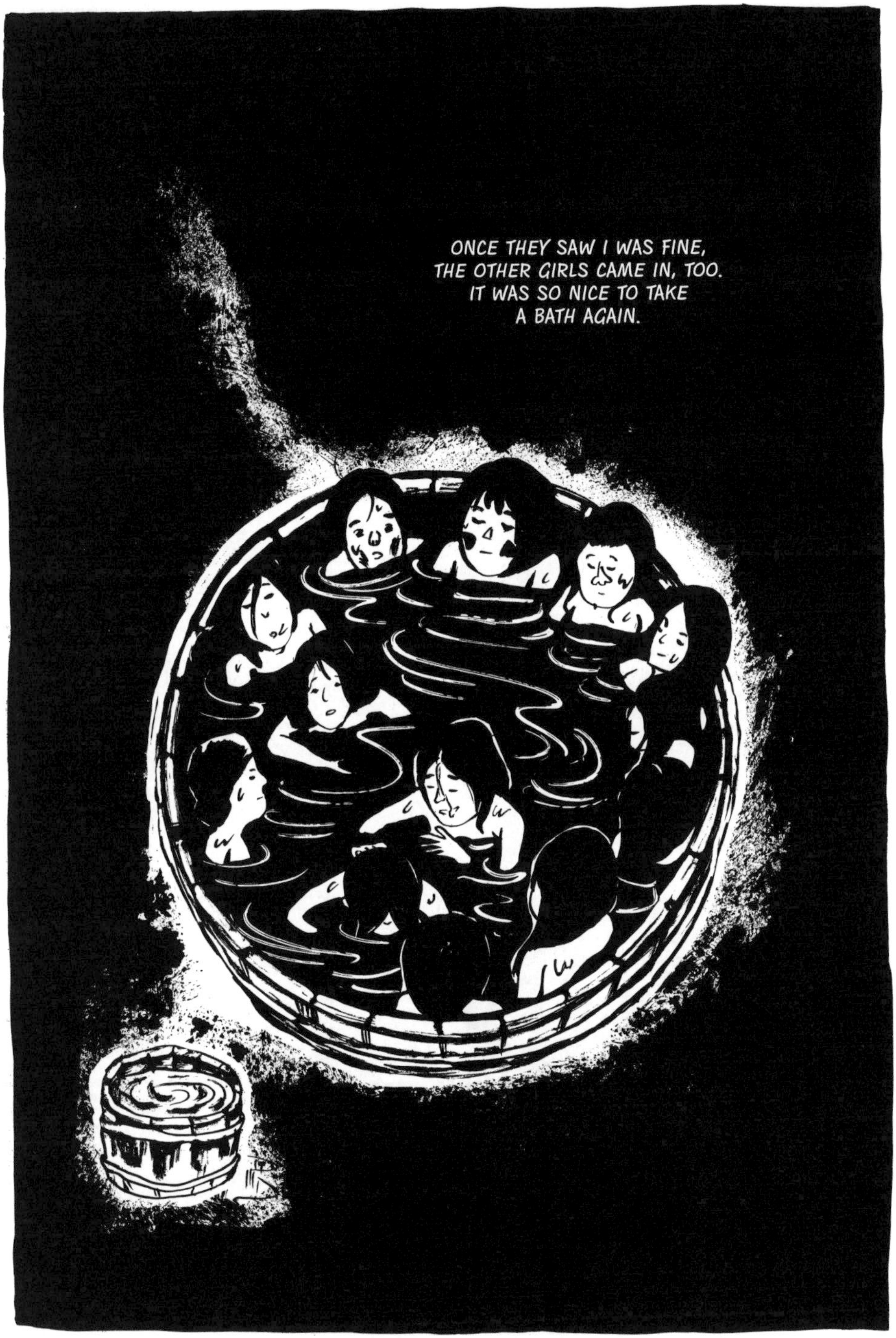
ONCE THEY SAW I WAS FINE, THE OTHER GIRLS CAME IN, TOO. IT WAS SO NICE TO TAKE A BATH AGAIN.

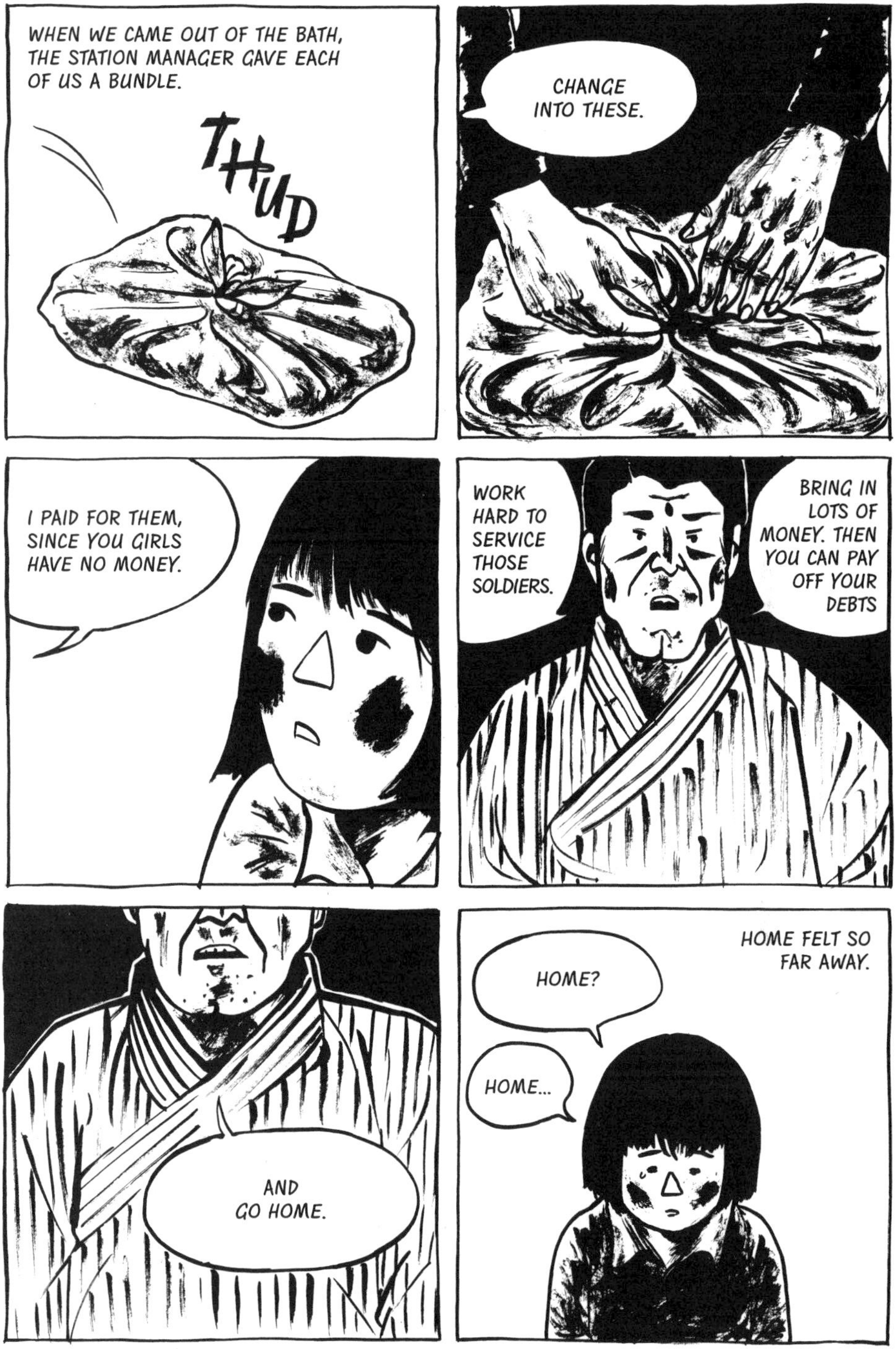
WHEN WE CAME OUT OF THE BATH, THE STATION MANAGER GAVE EACH OF US A BUNDLE.
THUD
CHANGE INTO THESE.
I PAID FOR THEM, SINCE YOU GIRLS HAVE NO MONEY.
WORK HARD TO SERVICE THOSE SOLDIERS.
BRING IN LOTS OF MONEY. THEN YOU CAN PAY OFF YOUR DEBTS
AND GO HOME.
HOME FELT SO FAR AWAY.
HOME?
HOME...

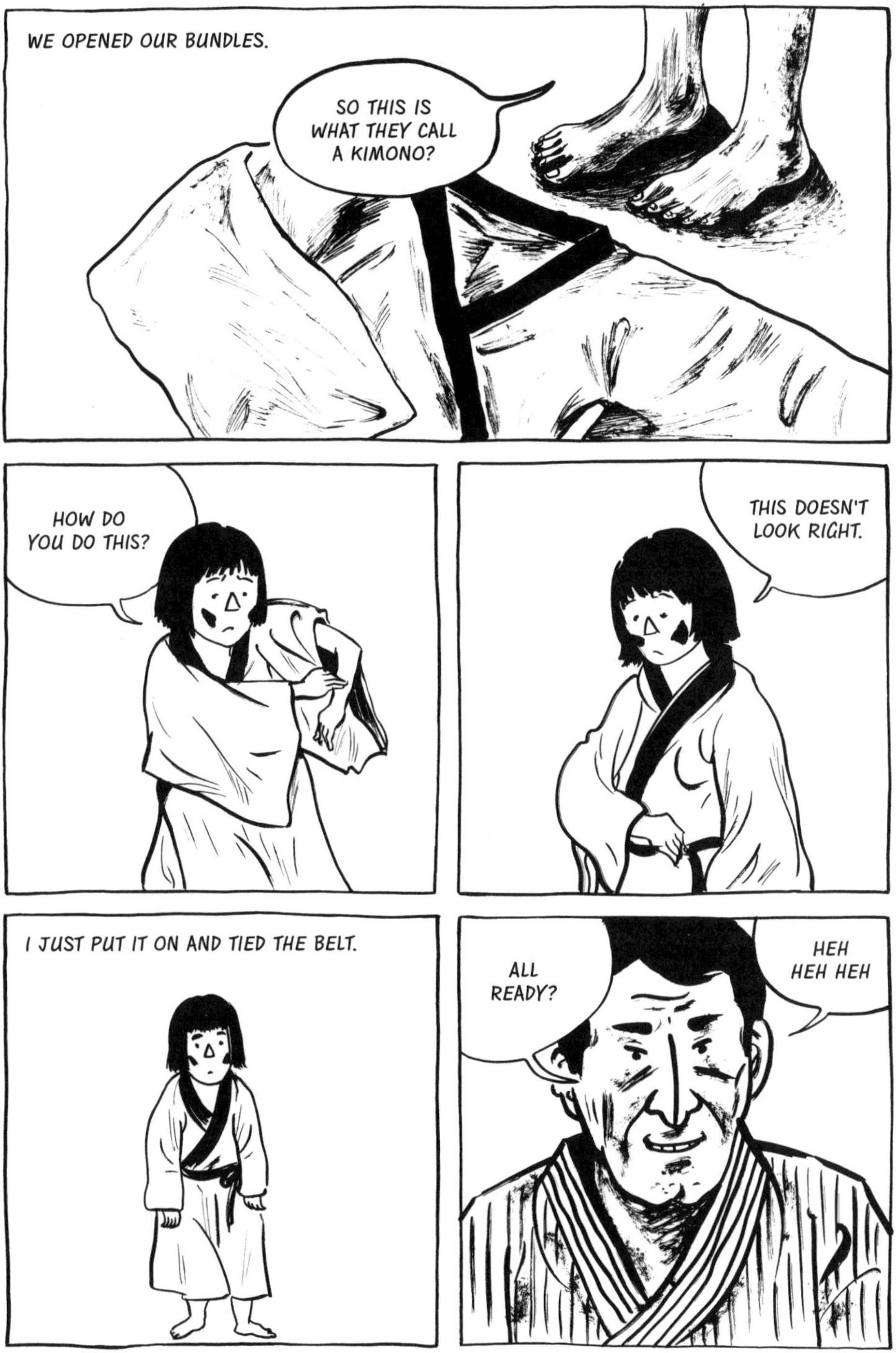
WE OPENED OUR BUNDLES.
SO THIS IS WHAT THEY CALL A KIMONO?
HOW DO YOU DO THIS?
THIS DOESN'T LOOK RIGHT.
I JUST PUT IT ON AND TIED THE BELT.
ALL READY?
HEH HEH HEH

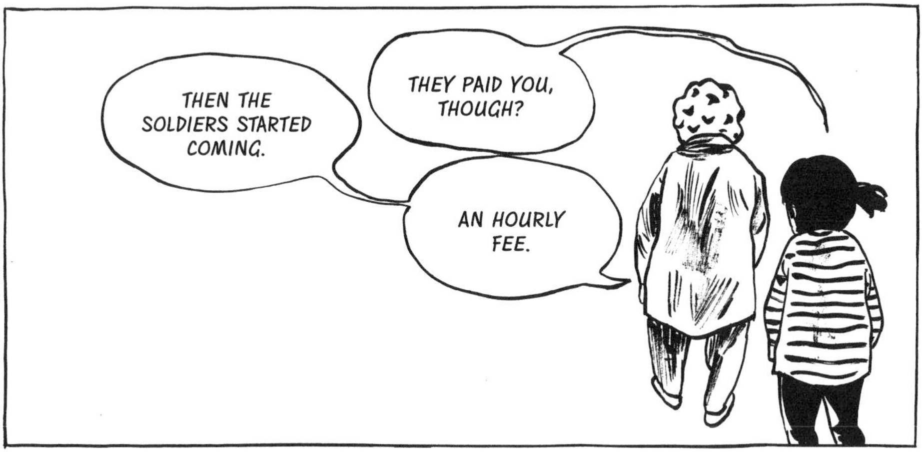
THEN THE SOLDIERS STARTED COMING.
THEY PAID YOU, THOUGH?
AN HOURLY FEE.
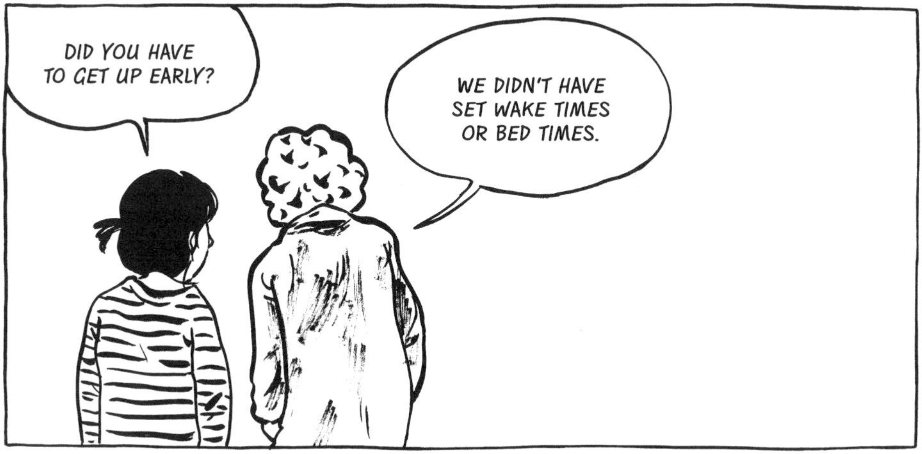
DID YOU HAVE TO GET UP EARLY?
WE DIDN'T HAVE SET WAKE TIMES OR BED TIMES.
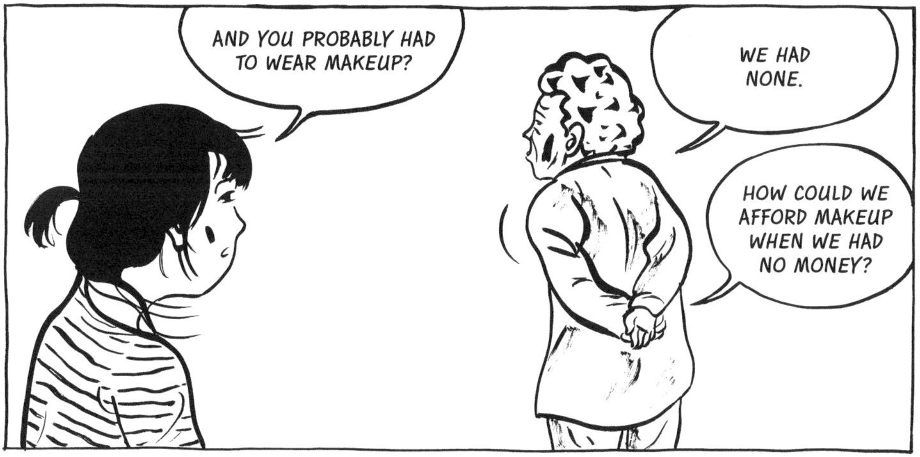
AND YOU PROBABLY HAD TO WEAR MAKEUP?
WE HAD NONE.
HOW COULD WE AFFORD MAKEUP WHEN WE HAD NO MONEY?

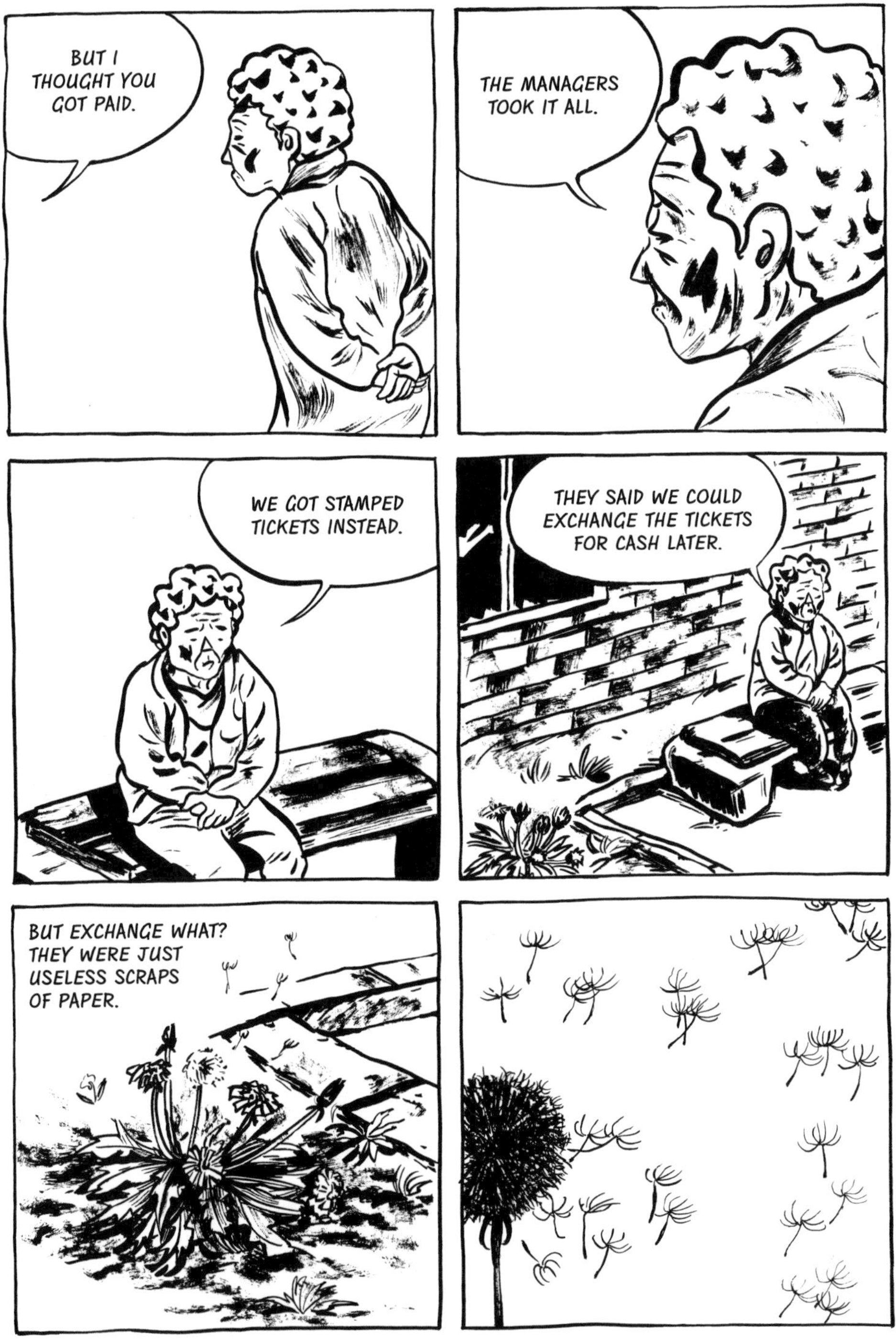
BUT I THOUGHT YOU GOT PAID.
THE MANAGERS TOOK IT ALL.
WE GOT STAMPED TICKETS INSTEAD.
THEY SAID WE COULD EXCHANGE THE TICKETS FOR CASH LATER.
BUT EXCHANGE WHAT? THEY WERE JUST USELESS SCRAPS OF PAPER.

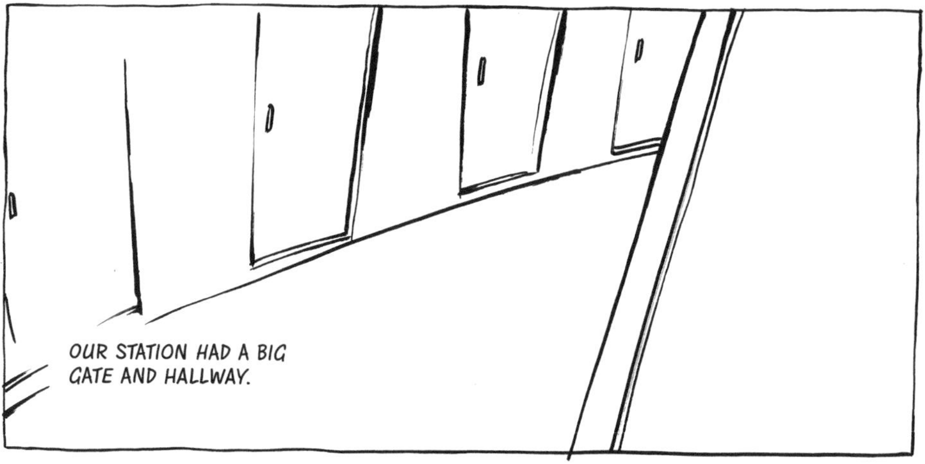
OUR STATION HAD A BIG GATE AND HALLWAY.

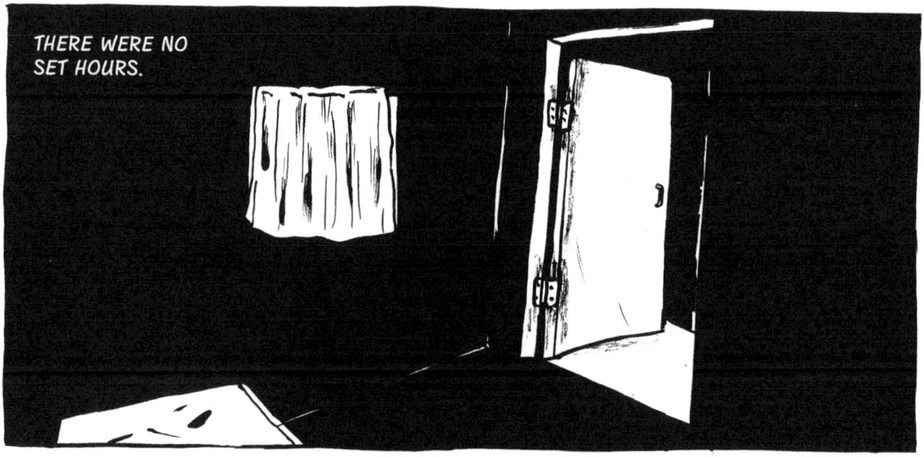
THERE WERE NO SET HOURS.

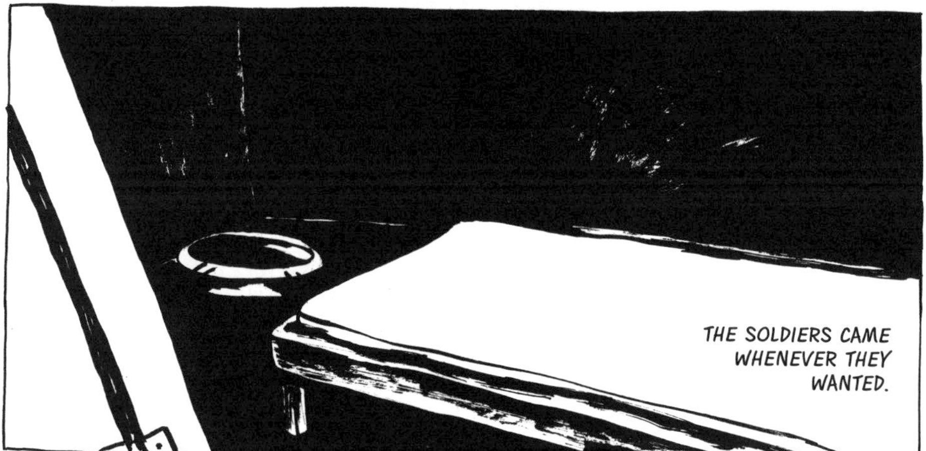
THE SOLDIERS CAME WHENEVER THEY WANTED.

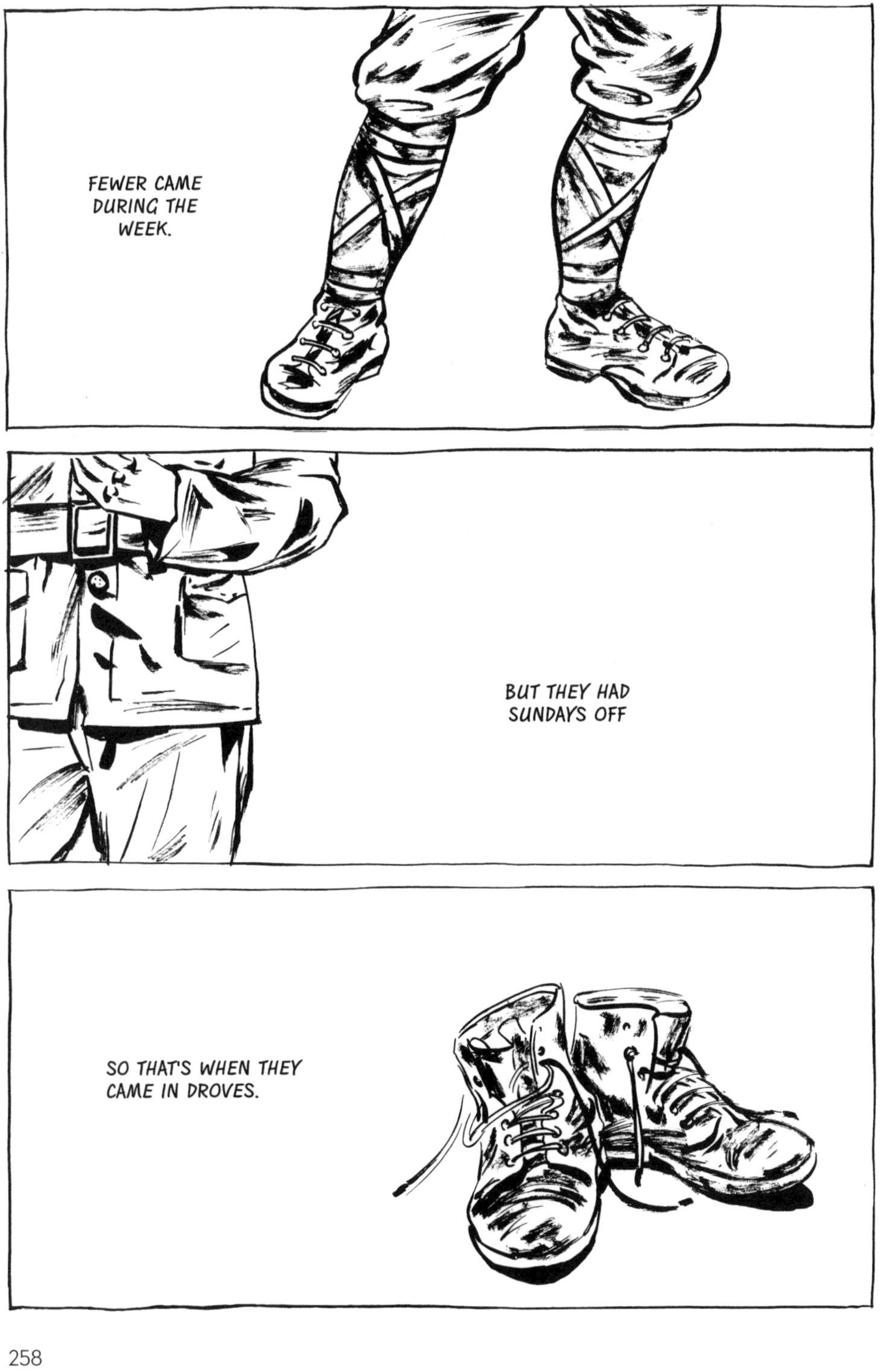
FEWER CAME DURING THE WEEK.
BUT THEY HAD SUNDAYS OFF
SO THAT'S WHEN THEY CAME IN DROVES.

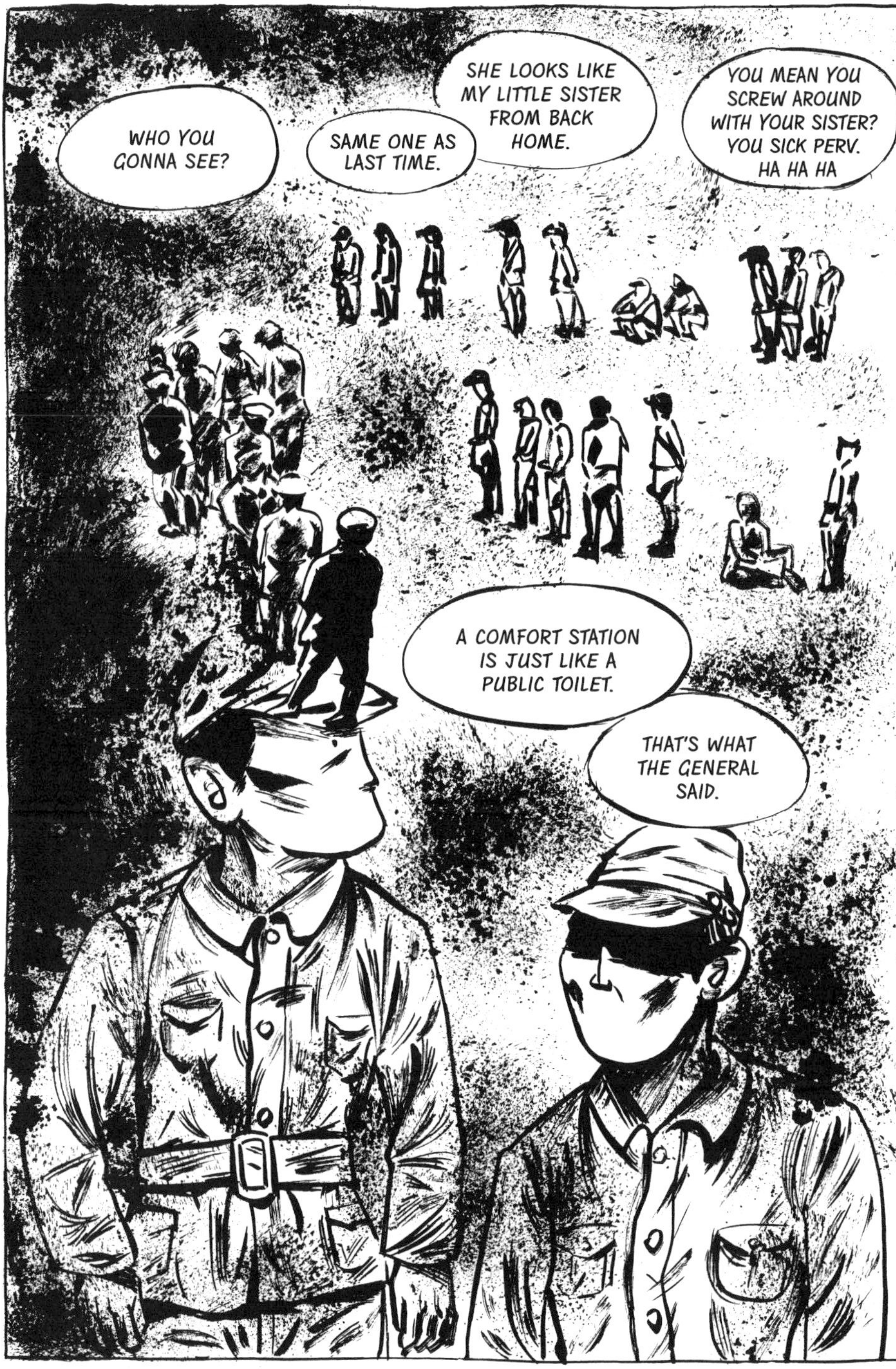
WHO YOU GONNA SEE?
SAME ONE AS LAST TIME.
SHE LOOKS LIKE MY LITTLE SISTER FROM BACK HOME.
YOU MEAN YOU SCREW AROUND WITH YOUR SISTER? YOU SICK PERV. HA HA HA
A COMFORT STATION IS JUST LIKE A PUBLIC TOILET.
THAT'S WHAT THE GENERAL SAID.

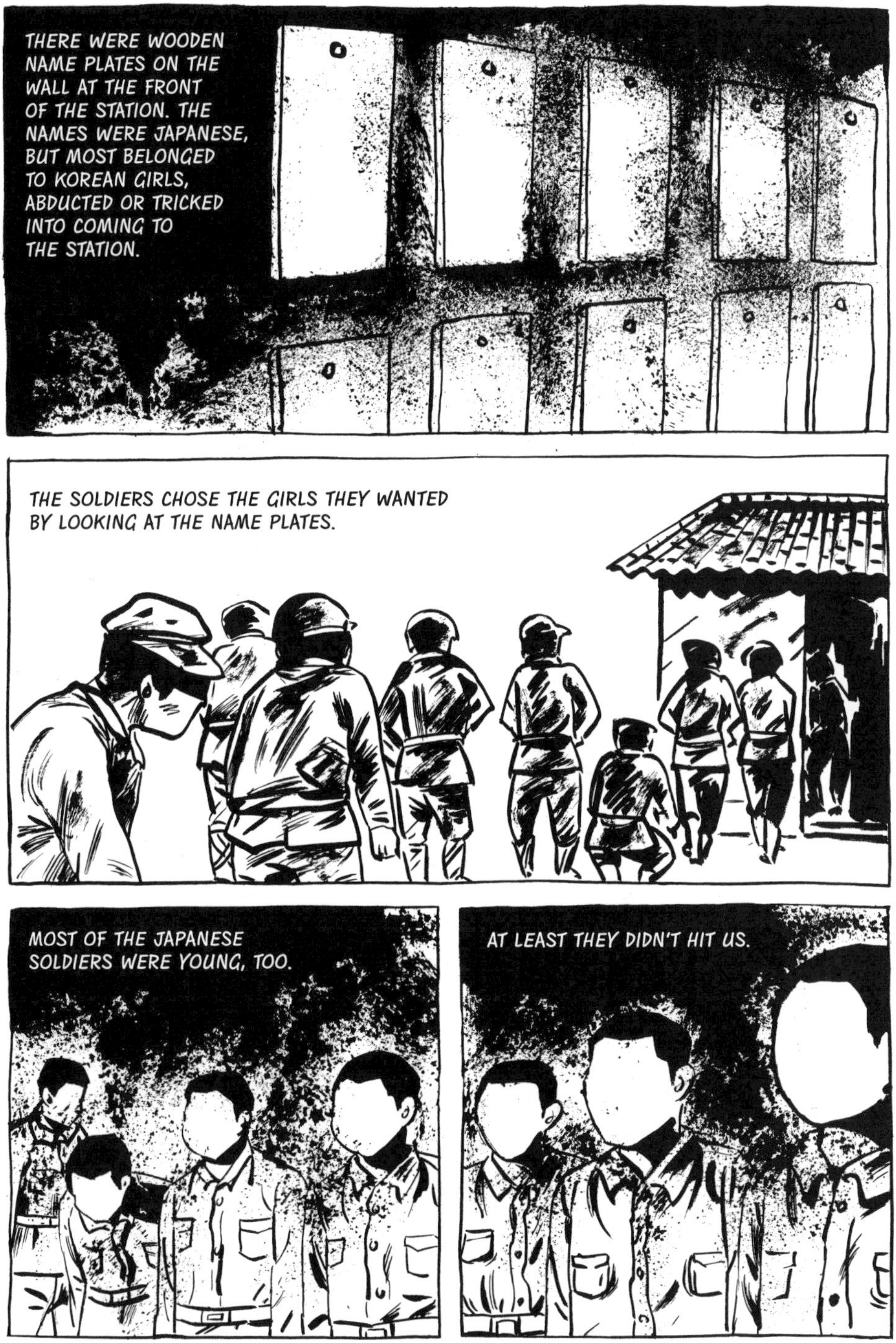
THERE WERE WOODEN NAME PLATES ON THE WALL AT THE FRONT OF THE STATION. THE NAMES WERE JAPANESE, BUT MOST BELONGED TO KOREAN GIRLS, ABDUCTED OR TRICKED INTO COMING TO THE STATION.
THE SOLDIERS CHOSE THE GIRLS THEY WANTED BY LOOKING AT THE NAME PLATES.
MOST OF THE JAPANESE SOLDIERS WERE YOUNG, TOO.
AT LEAST THEY DIDN'T HIT US.

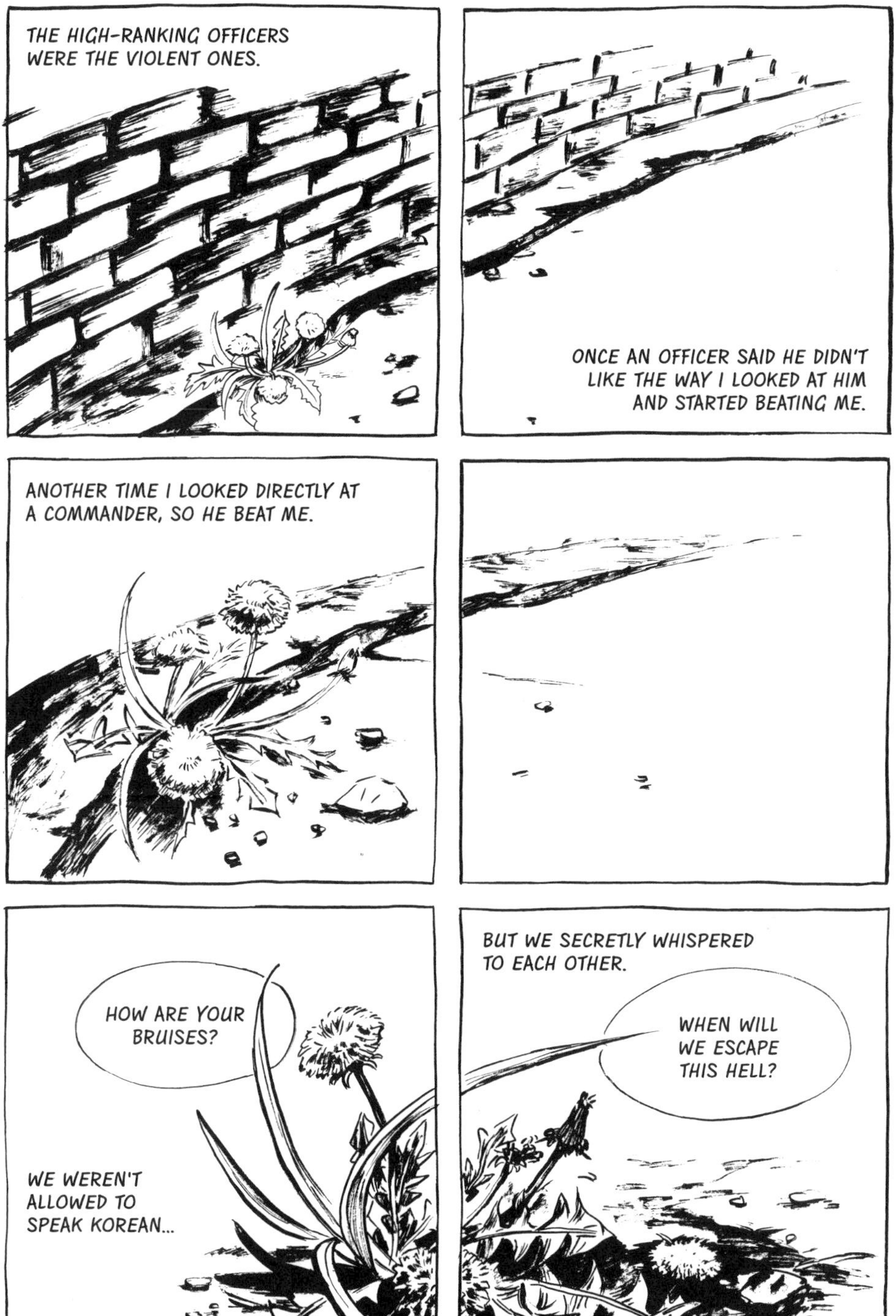
THE HIGH-RANKING OFFICERS WERE THE VIOLENT ONES.
ONCE AN OFFICER SAID HE DIDN'T LIKE THE WAY I LOOKED AT HIM AND STARTED BEATING ME.
ANOTHER TIME I LOOKED DIRECTLY AT A COMMANDER, SO HE BEAT ME.
WE WEREN'T ALLOWED TO SPEAK KOREAN...
HOW ARE YOUR BRUISES?
BUT WE SECRETLY WHISPERED TO EACH OTHER.
WHEN WILL WE ESCAPE THIS HELL?

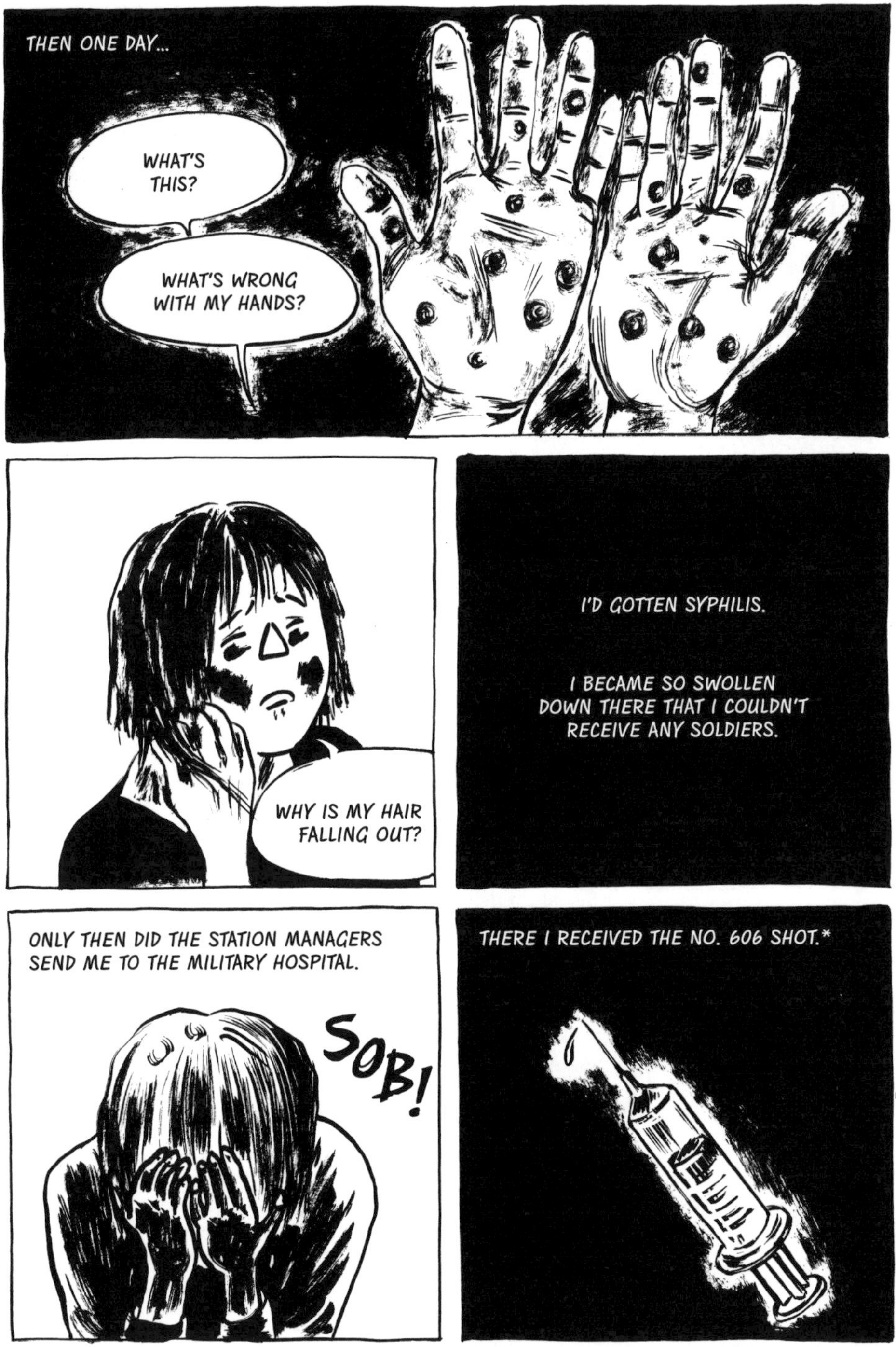
THEN ONE DAY...
WHAT'S THIS?
WHAT'S WRONG WITH MY HANDS?
WHY IS MY HAIR FALLING OUT?
I'D GOTTEN SYPHILIS.
I BECAME SO SWOLLEN DOWN THERE THAT I COULDN'T RECEIVE ANY SOLDIERS.
ONLY THEN DID THE STATION MANAGERS SEND ME TO THE MILITARY HOSPITAL.
SOB!
THERE I RECEIVED THE NO. 606 SHOT.*

*NO. 606 INJECTIONS, ALSO KNOWN AS SALVARSAN, WERE USED TO TREAT SYPHILIS AND OTHER VENEREAL DISEASES.

WHEN I DIDN'T GET BETTER FOR TWO MONTHS

THE MANAGERS GOT DESPERATE, SINCE I COULDN'T MAKE THEM ANY MONEY.

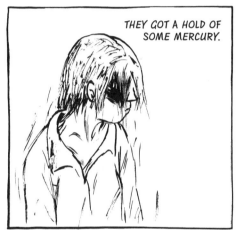

THEY GOT A HOLD OF SOME MERCURY.

THEY'D GOTTEN IT FROM THE MEDIC, WHO TOLD THEM TO BOIL THE MERCURY IN A SMALL DISH AND GET ME TO EXPOSE MY GENITALS TO THE VAPOR.

SO THE MANAGERS FORCED ME TO COVER MY FACE AND SQUAT NAKED OVER THE BOILING MERCURY.

I GOT BETTER EVENTUALLY, BUT BECAUSE OF THAT, I COULD NEVER HAVE CHILDREN.

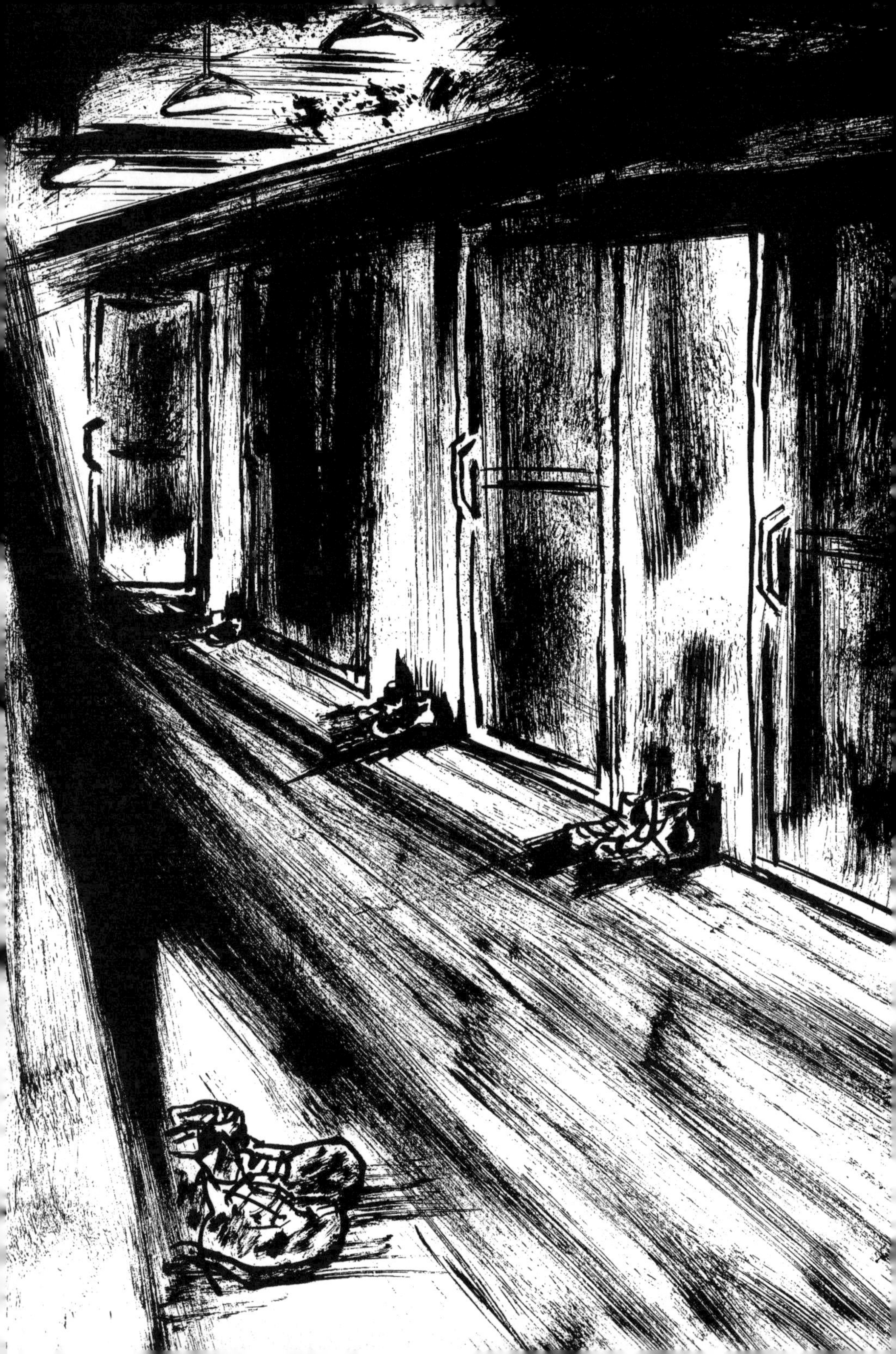

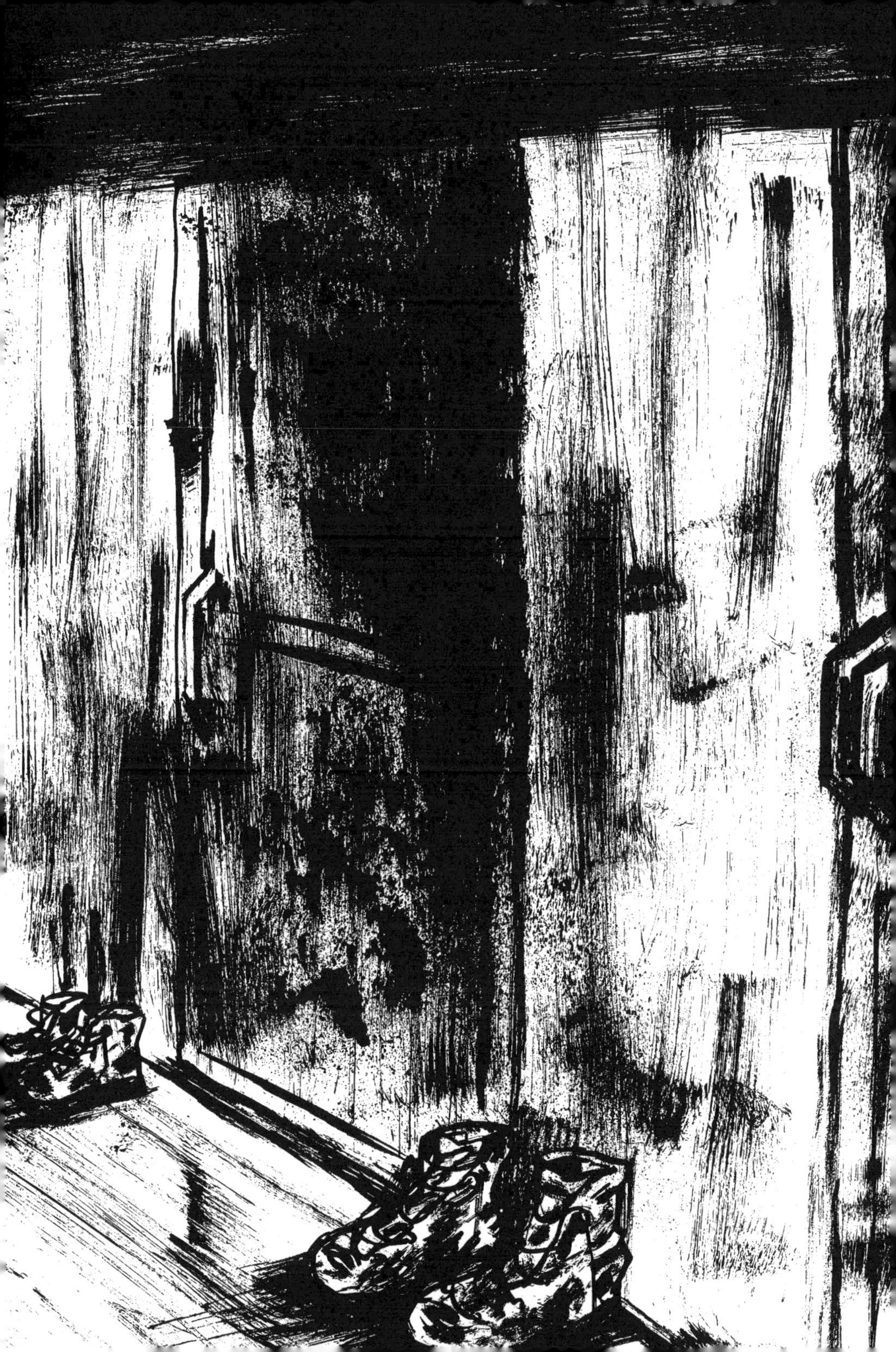

# BIG SIS MIJA

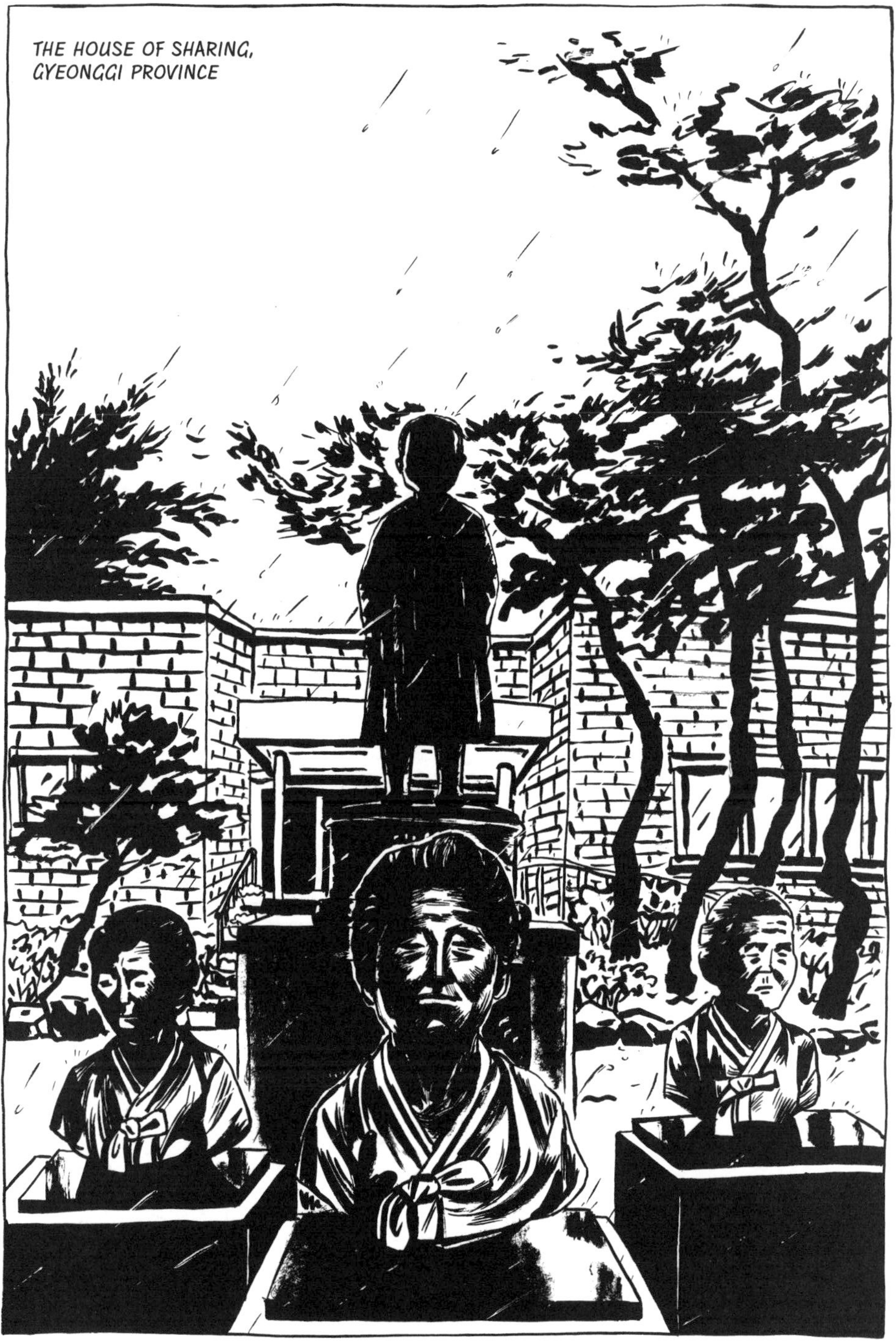
THE HOUSE OF SHARING,
GYEONGGI PROVINCE

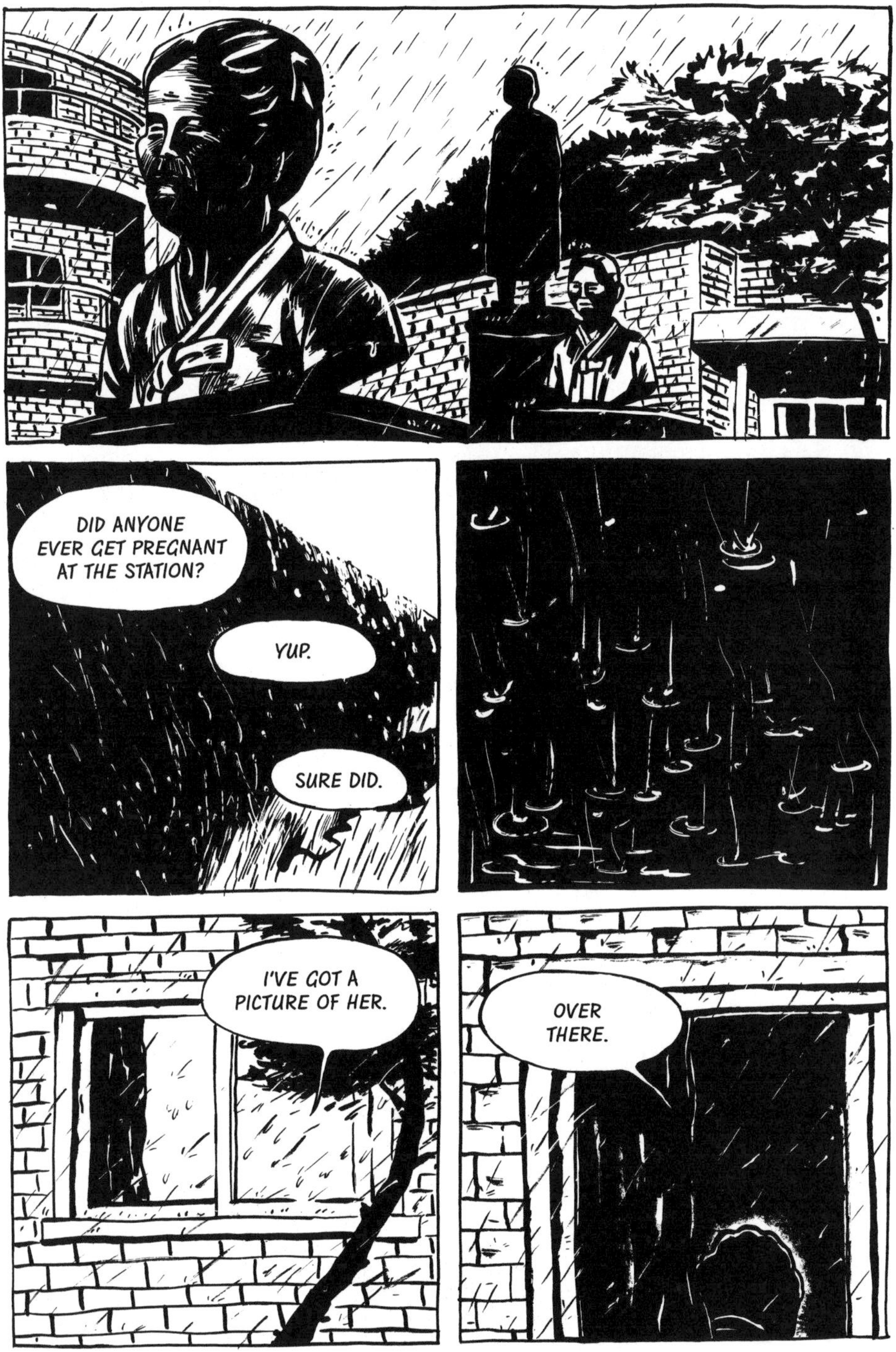
DID ANYONE EVER GET PREGNANT AT THE STATION?
YUP.
SURE DID.
I'VE GOT A PICTURE OF HER.
OVER THERE.

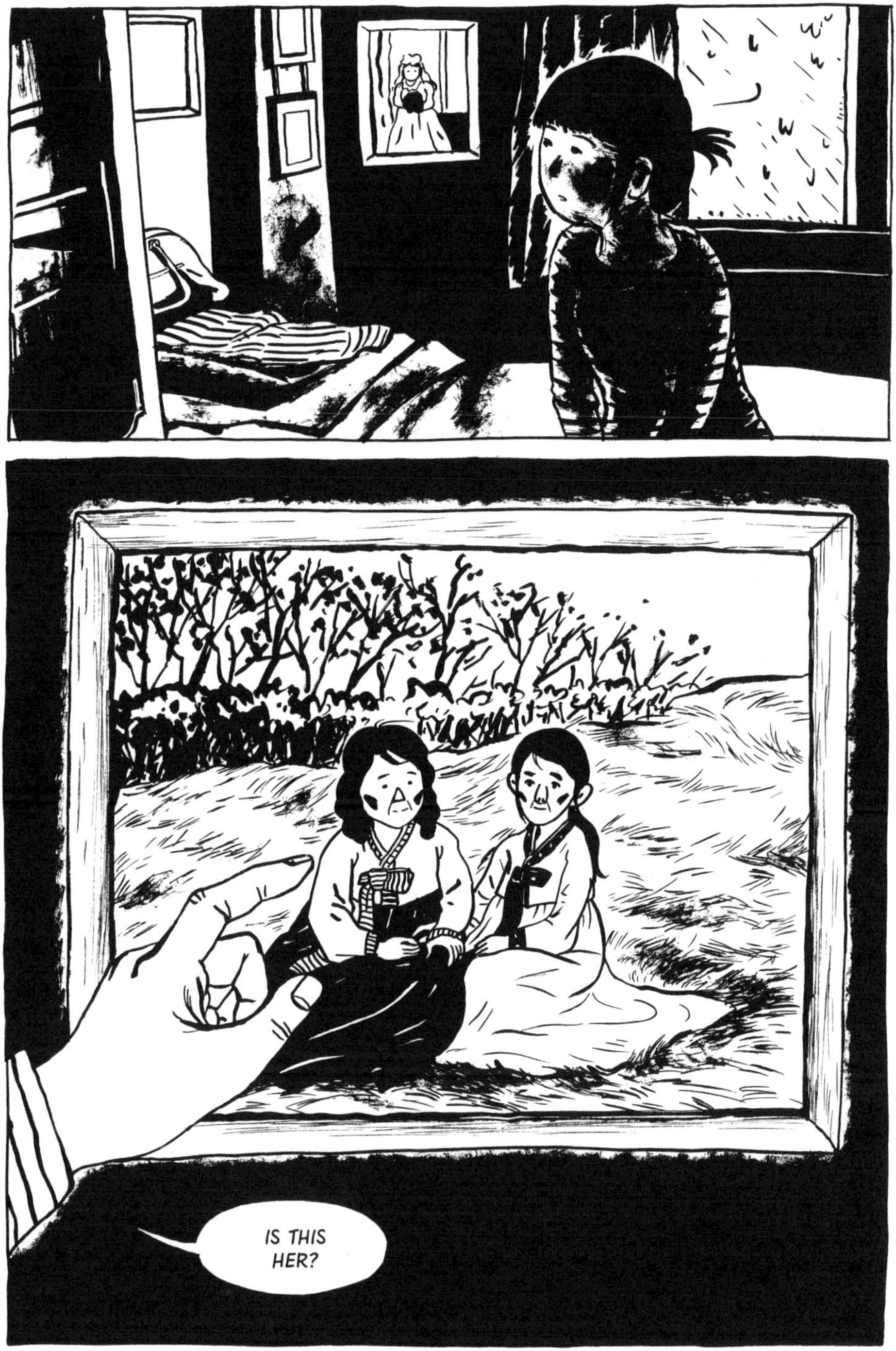
IS THIS HER?

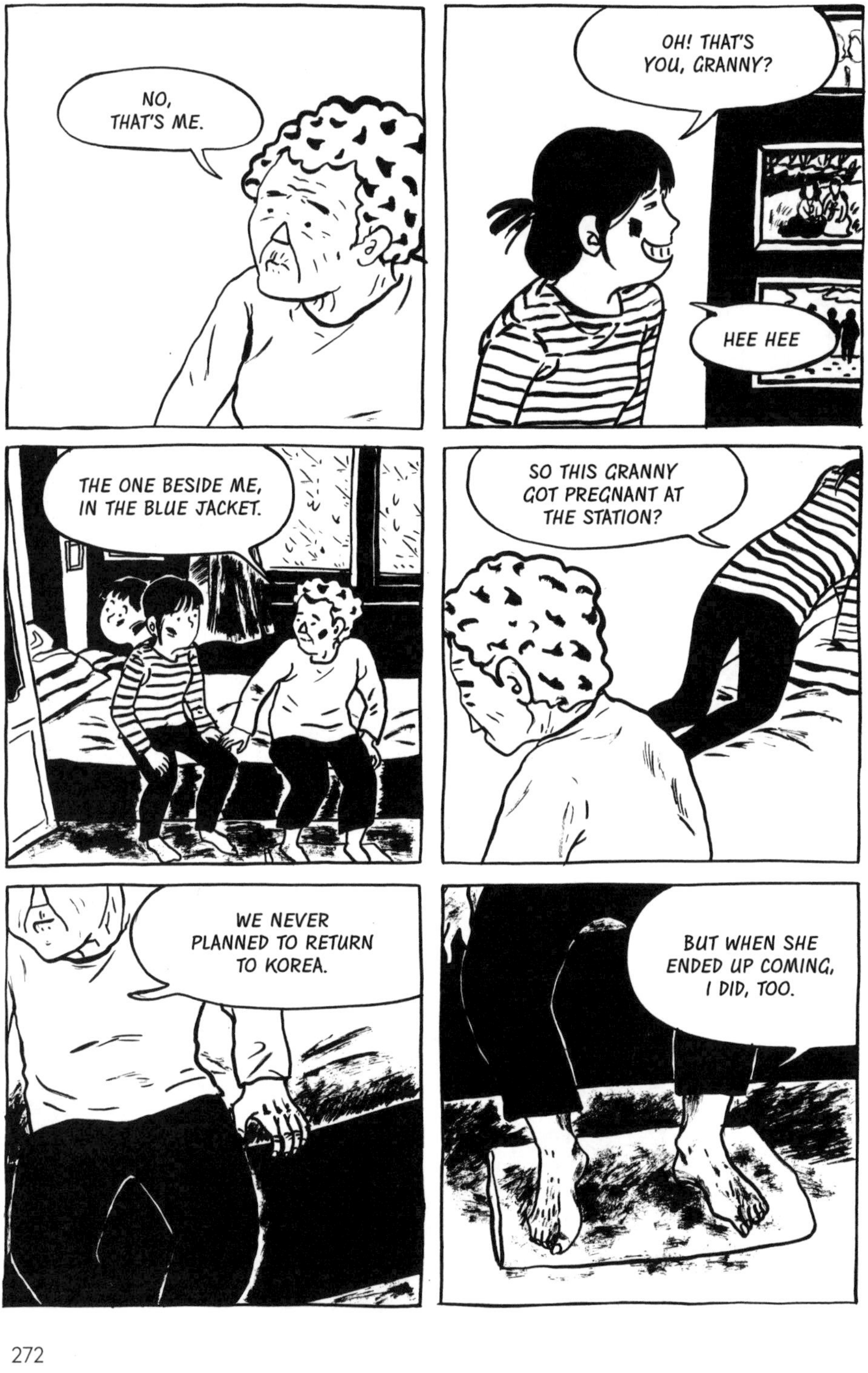
NO, THAT'S ME.
OH! THAT'S YOU, GRANNY?
HEE HEE
THE ONE BESIDE ME, IN THE BLUE JACKET.
SO THIS GRANNY GOT PREGNANT AT THE STATION?
WE NEVER PLANNED TO RETURN TO KOREA.
BUT WHEN SHE ENDED UP COMING, I DID, TOO.

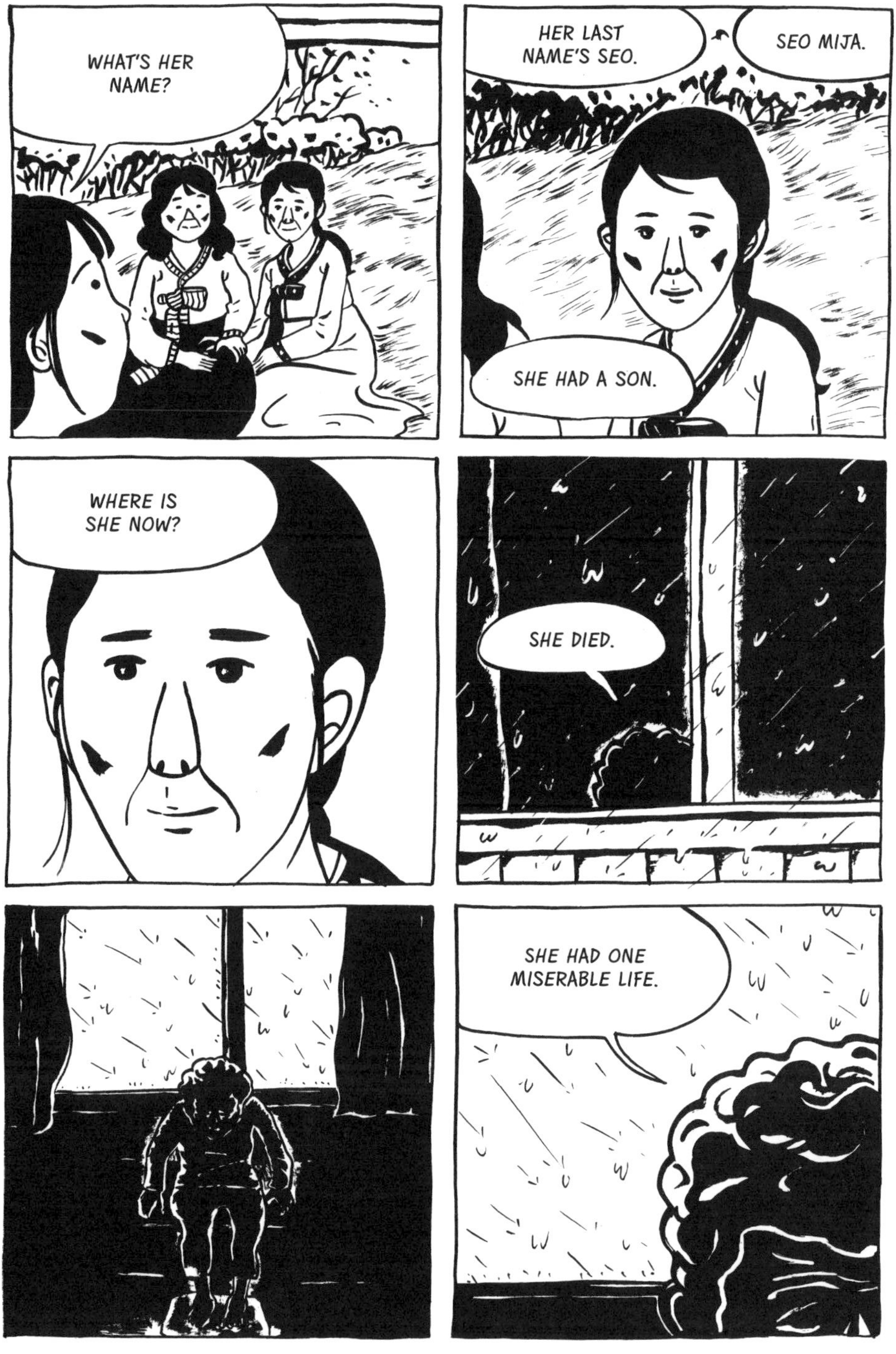
WHAT'S HER NAME?
HER LAST NAME'S SEO.
SEO MIJA.
SHE HAD A SON.
WHERE IS SHE NOW?
SHE DIED.
SHE HAD ONE MISERABLE LIFE.

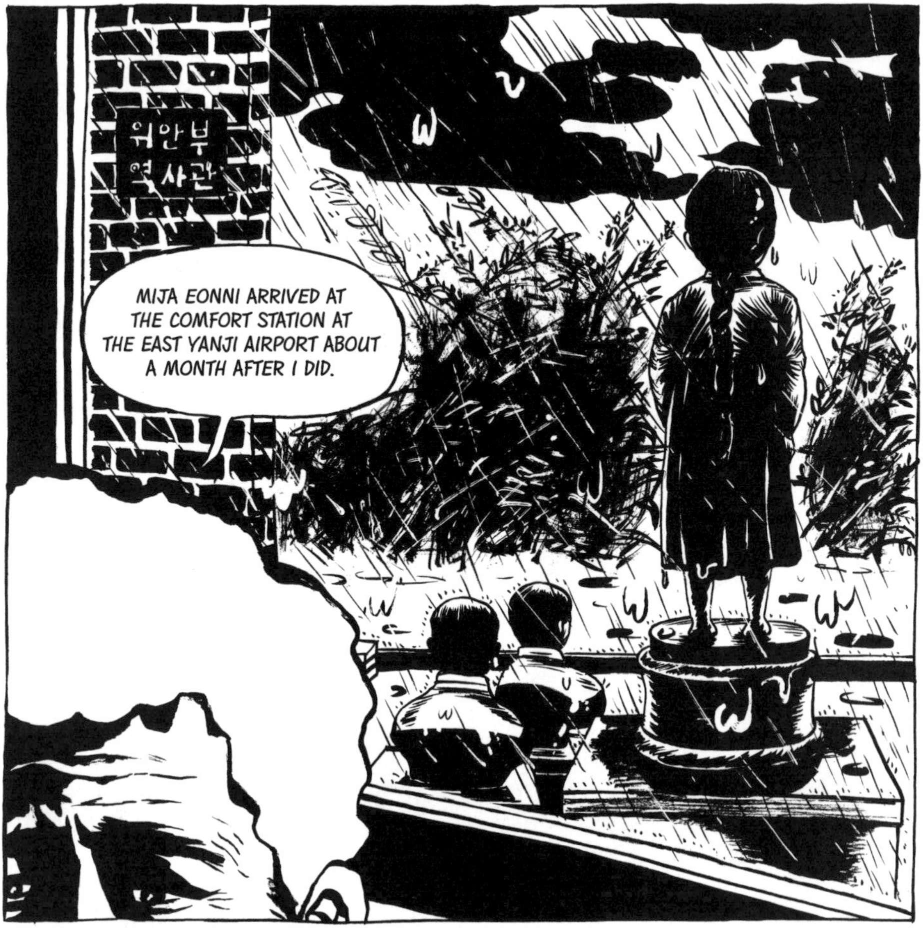
위안부
역사관
MIJA EONNI ARRIVED AT THE COMFORT STATION AT THE EAST YANJI AIRPORT ABOUT A MONTH AFTER I DID.

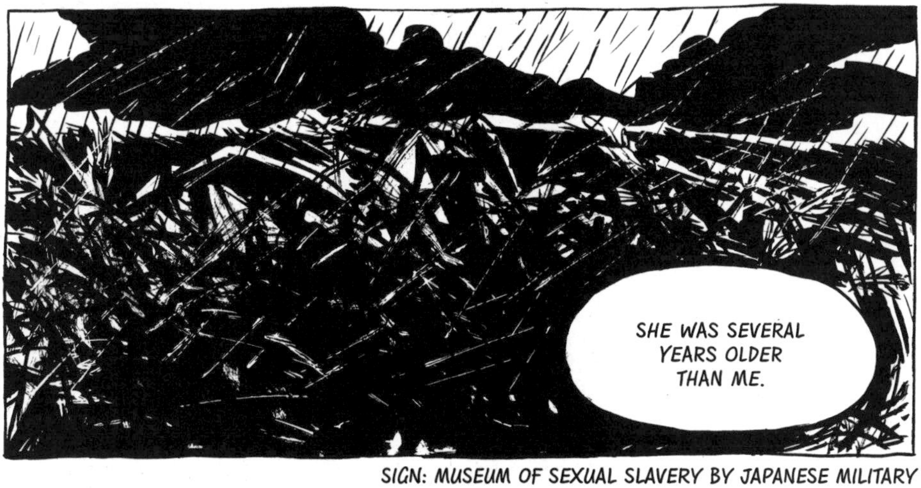
SHE WAS SEVERAL YEARS OLDER THAN ME.

SIGN: MUSEUM OF SEXUAL SLAVERY BY JAPANESE MILITARY

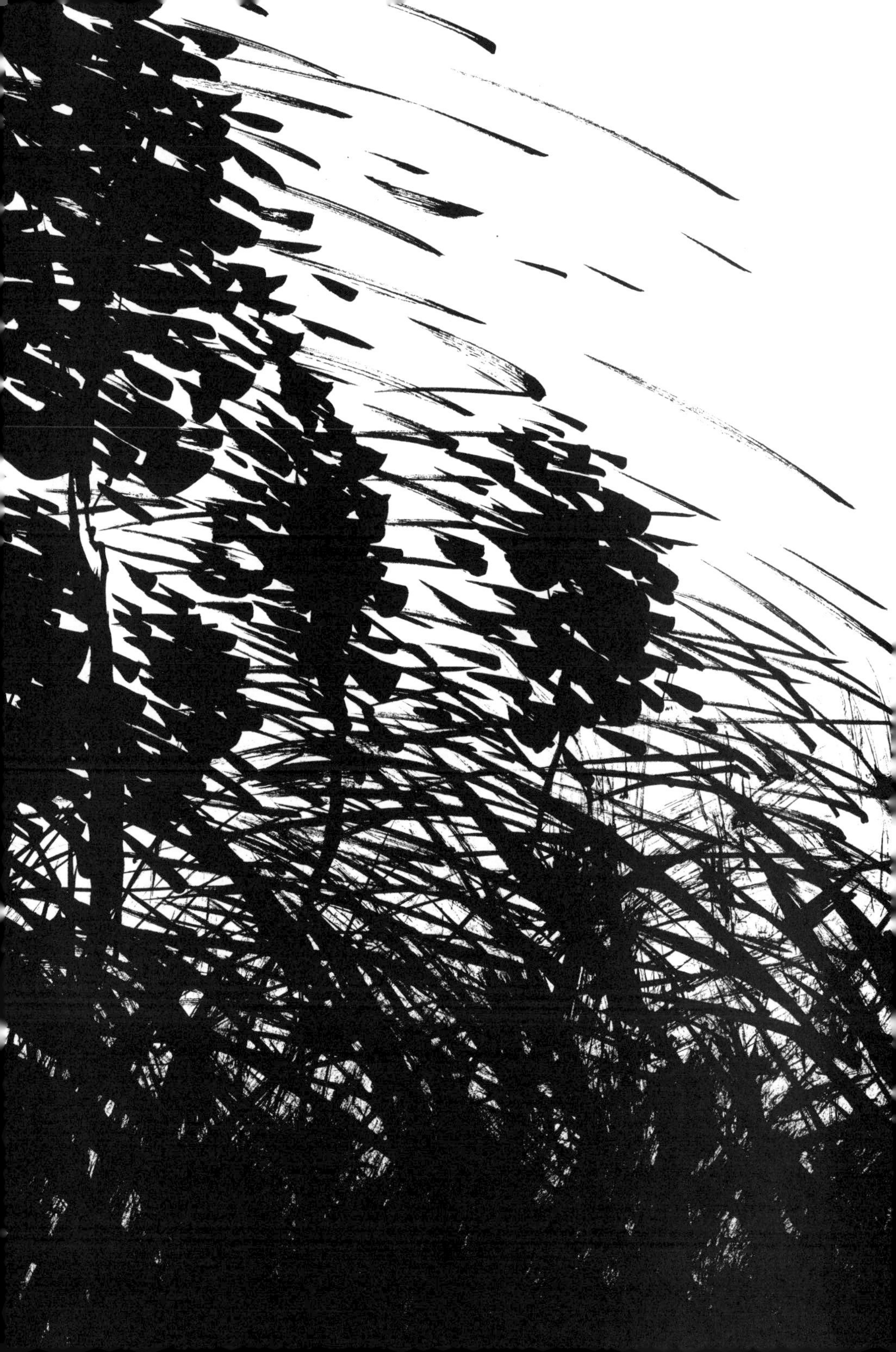

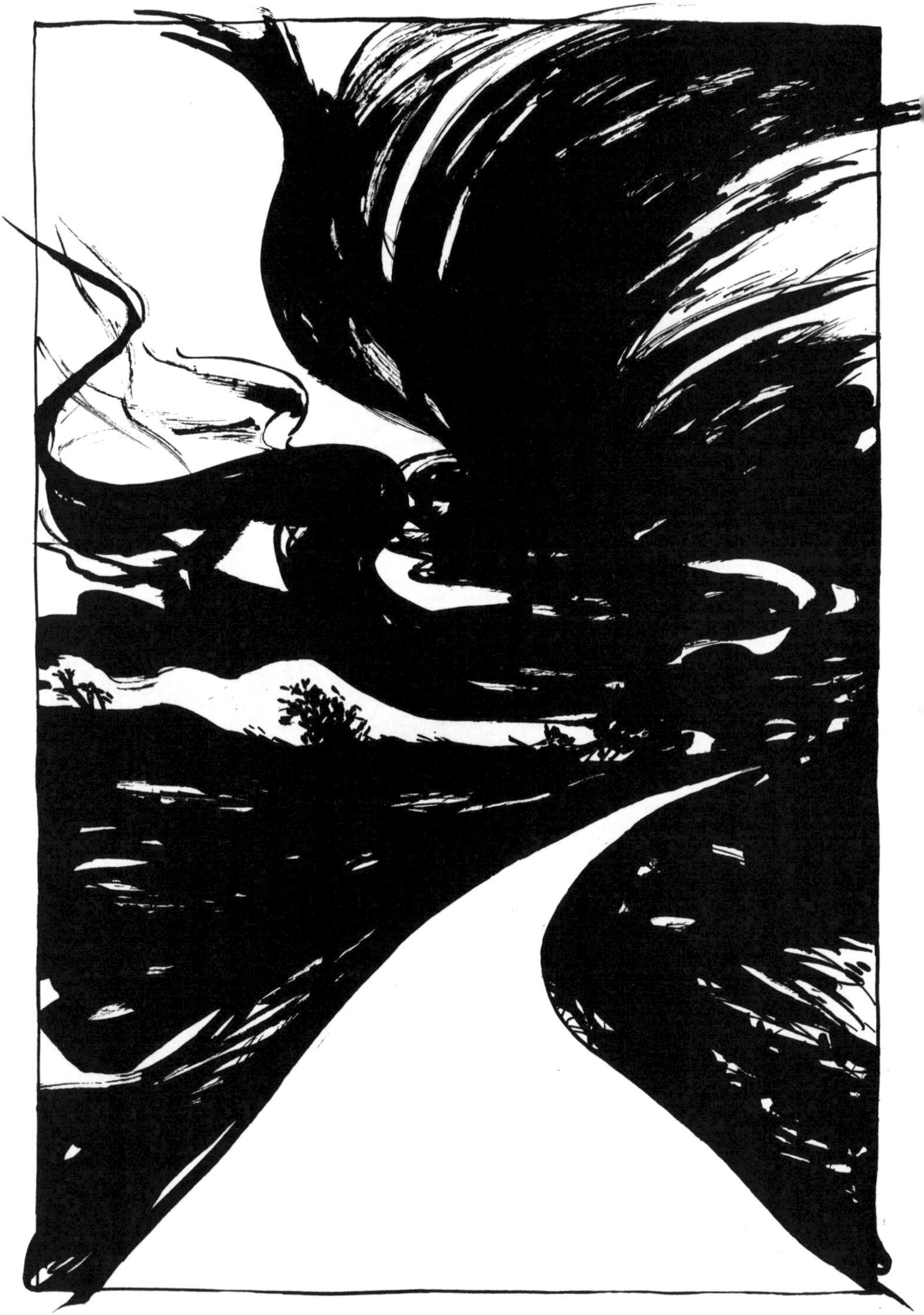

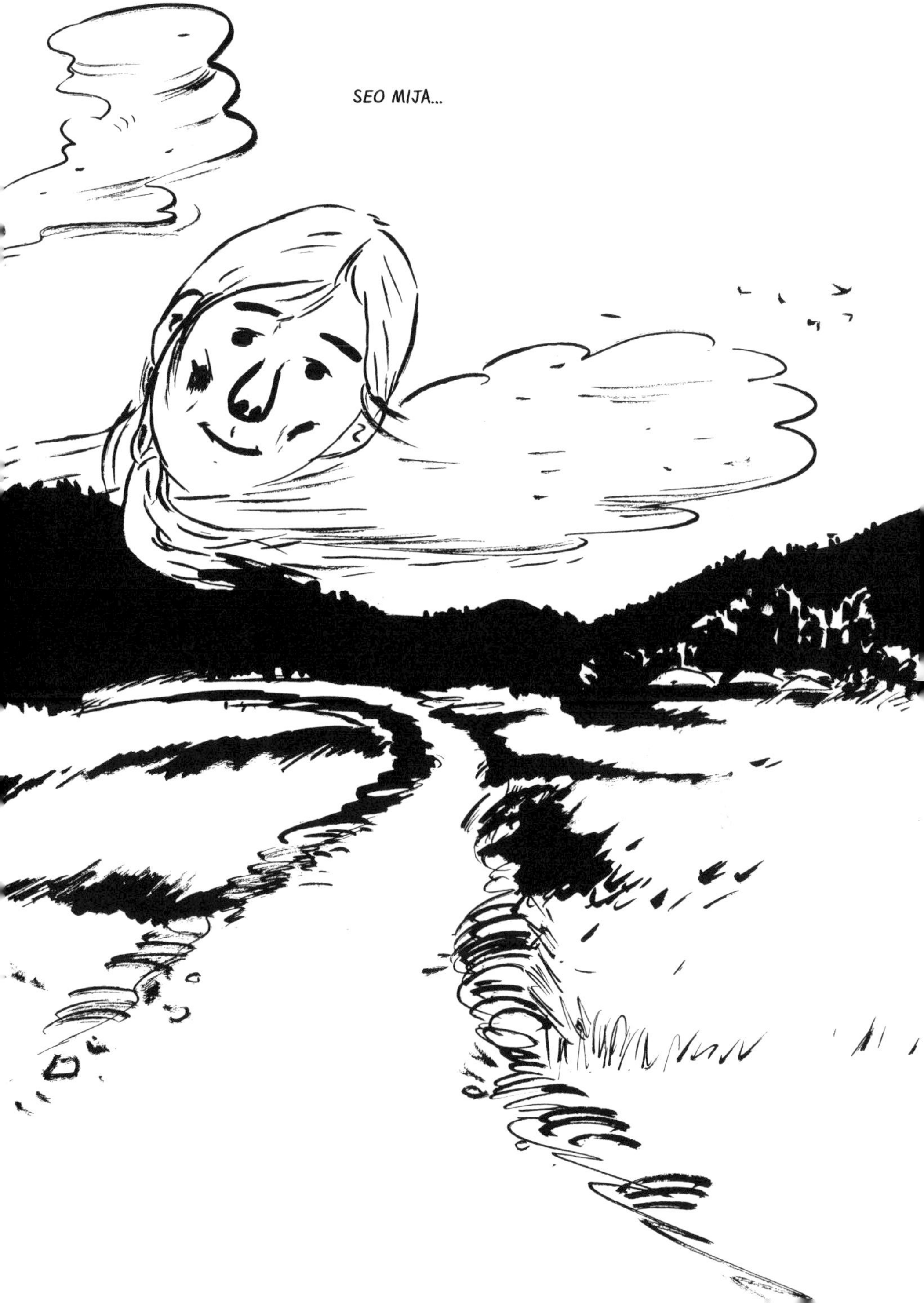
SEO MIJA...

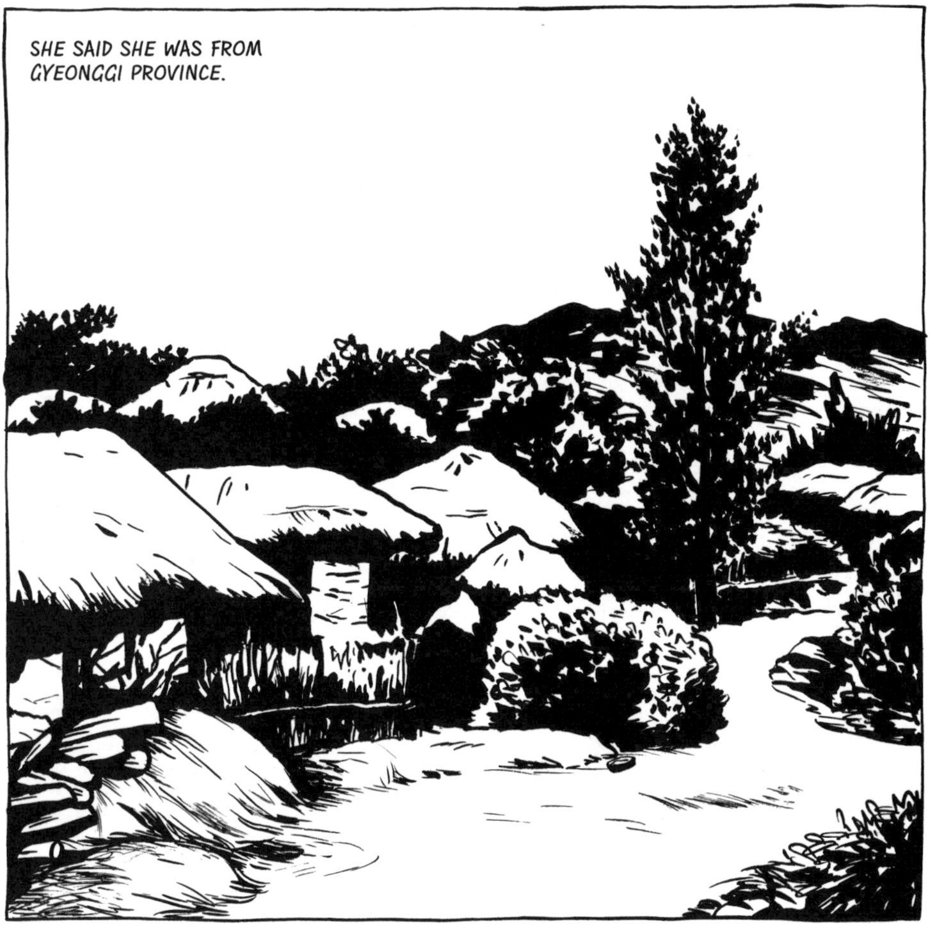
SHE SAID SHE WAS FROM GYEONGGI PROVINCE.

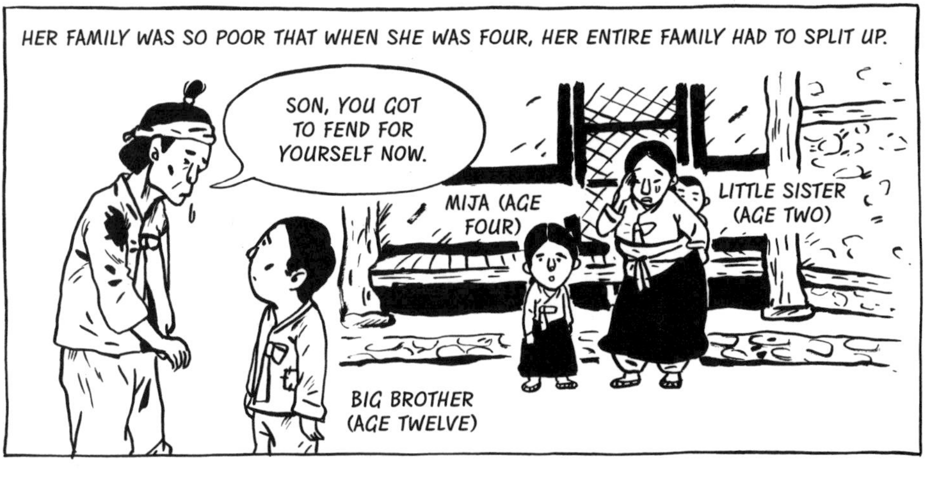
HER FAMILY WAS SO POOR THAT WHEN SHE WAS FOUR, HER ENTIRE FAMILY HAD TO SPLIT UP.
SON, YOU GOT TO FEND FOR YOURSELF NOW.
MIJA (AGE FOUR)
LITTLE SISTER (AGE TWO)
BIG BROTHER (AGE TWELVE)

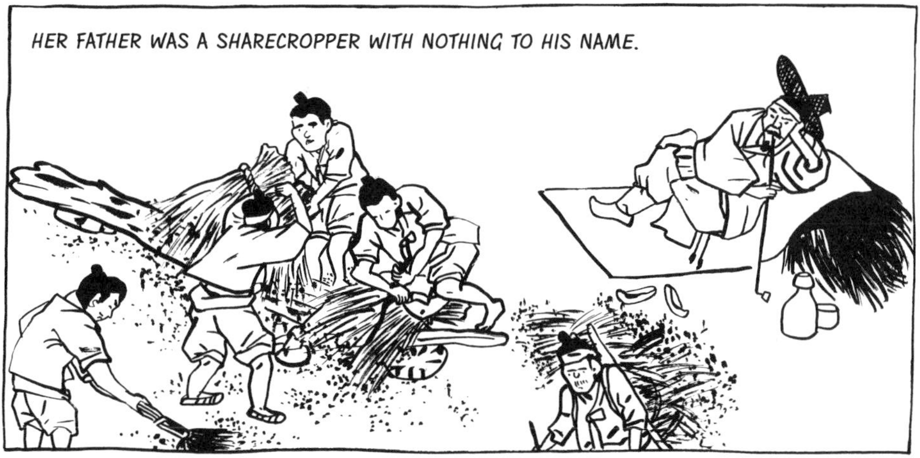
HER FATHER WAS A SHARECROPPER WITH NOTHING TO HIS NAME.

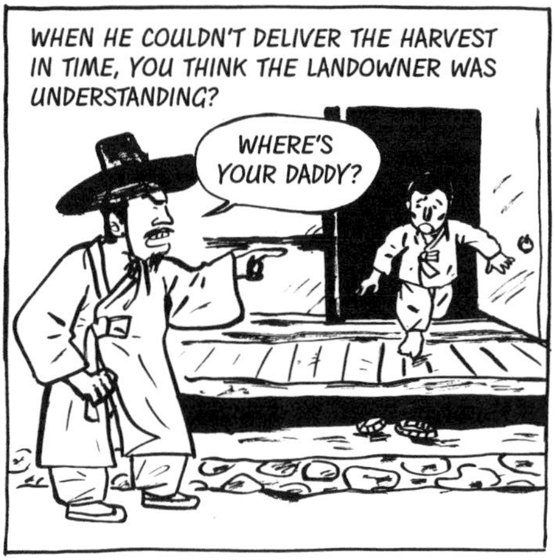
WHEN HE COULDN'T DELIVER THE HARVEST IN TIME, YOU THINK THE LANDOWNER WAS UNDERSTANDING?
WHERE'S YOUR DADDY?

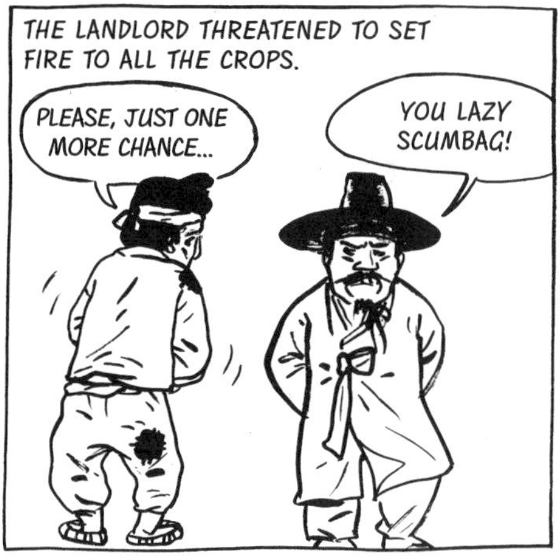
THE LANDLORD THREATENED TO SET FIRE TO ALL THE CROPS.
PLEASE, JUST ONE MORE CHANCE...
YOU LAZY SCUMBAG!

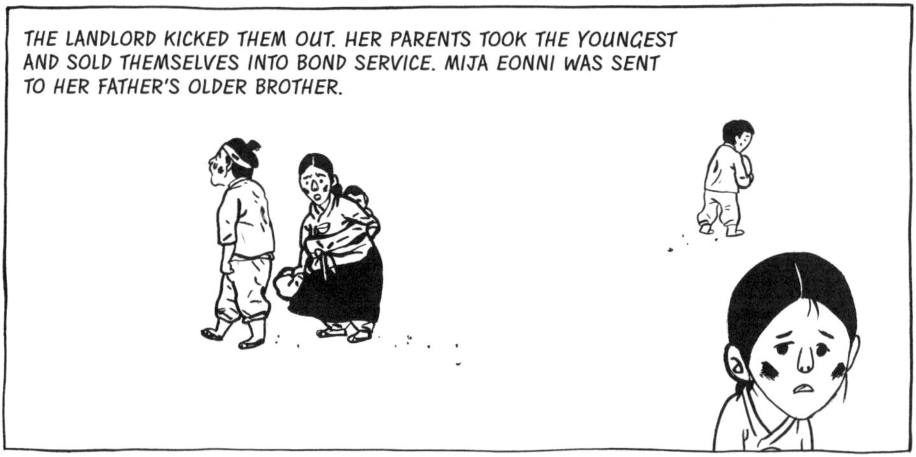
THE LANDLORD KICKED THEM OUT. HER PARENTS TOOK THE YOUNGEST AND SOLD THEMSELVES INTO BOND SERVICE. MIJA EONNI WAS SENT TO HER FATHER'S OLDER BROTHER.

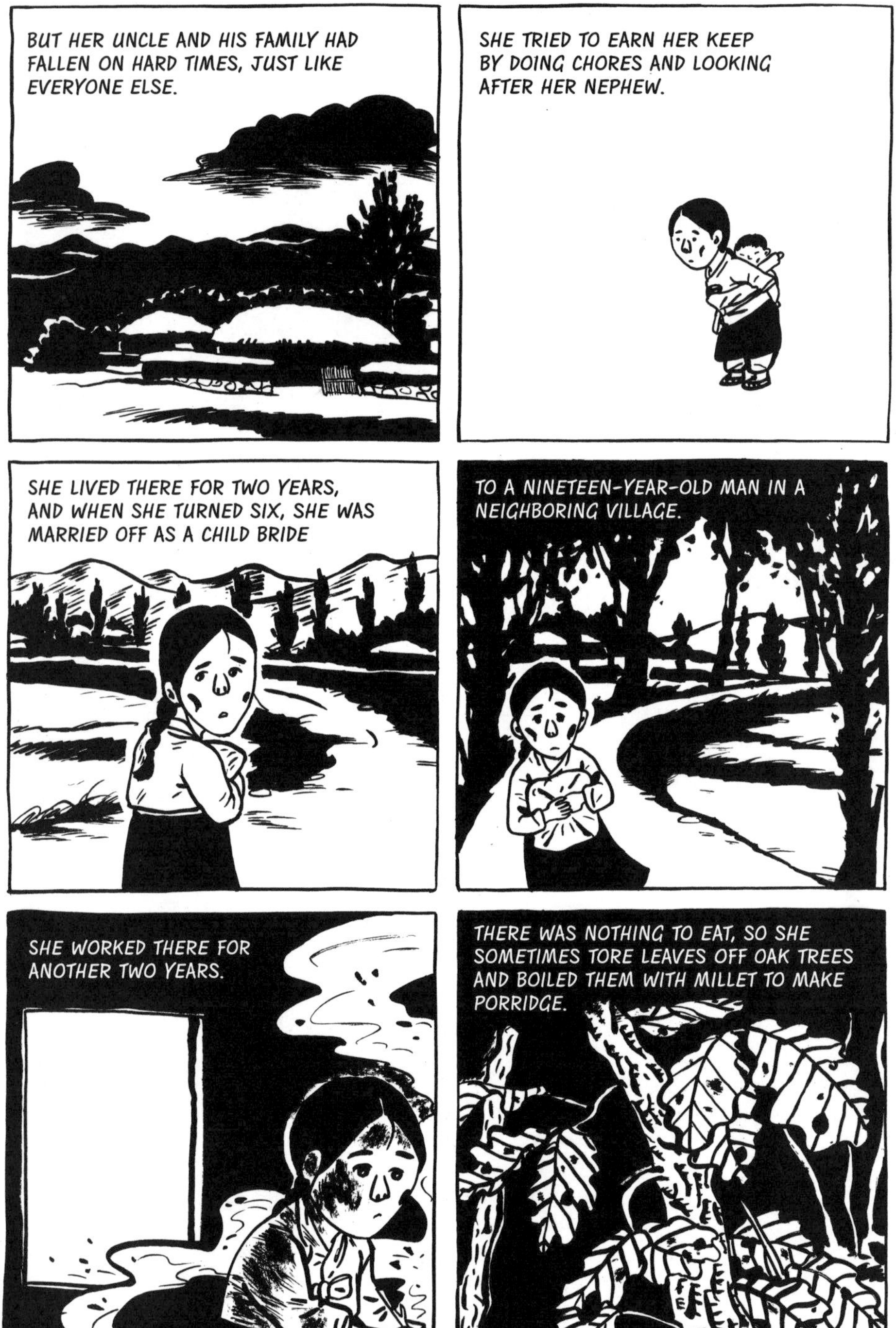
BUT HER UNCLE AND HIS FAMILY HAD FALLEN ON HARD TIMES, JUST LIKE EVERYONE ELSE.
SHE TRIED TO EARN HER KEEP BY DOING CHORES AND LOOKING AFTER HER NEPHEW.
SHE LIVED THERE FOR TWO YEARS, AND WHEN SHE TURNED SIX, SHE WAS MARRIED OFF AS A CHILD BRIDE
TO A NINETEEN-YEAR-OLD MAN IN A NEIGHBORING VILLAGE.
SHE WORKED THERE FOR ANOTHER TWO YEARS.
THERE WAS NOTHING TO EAT, SO SHE SOMETIMES TORE LEAVES OFF OAK TREES AND BOILED THEM WITH MILLET TO MAKE PORRIDGE.

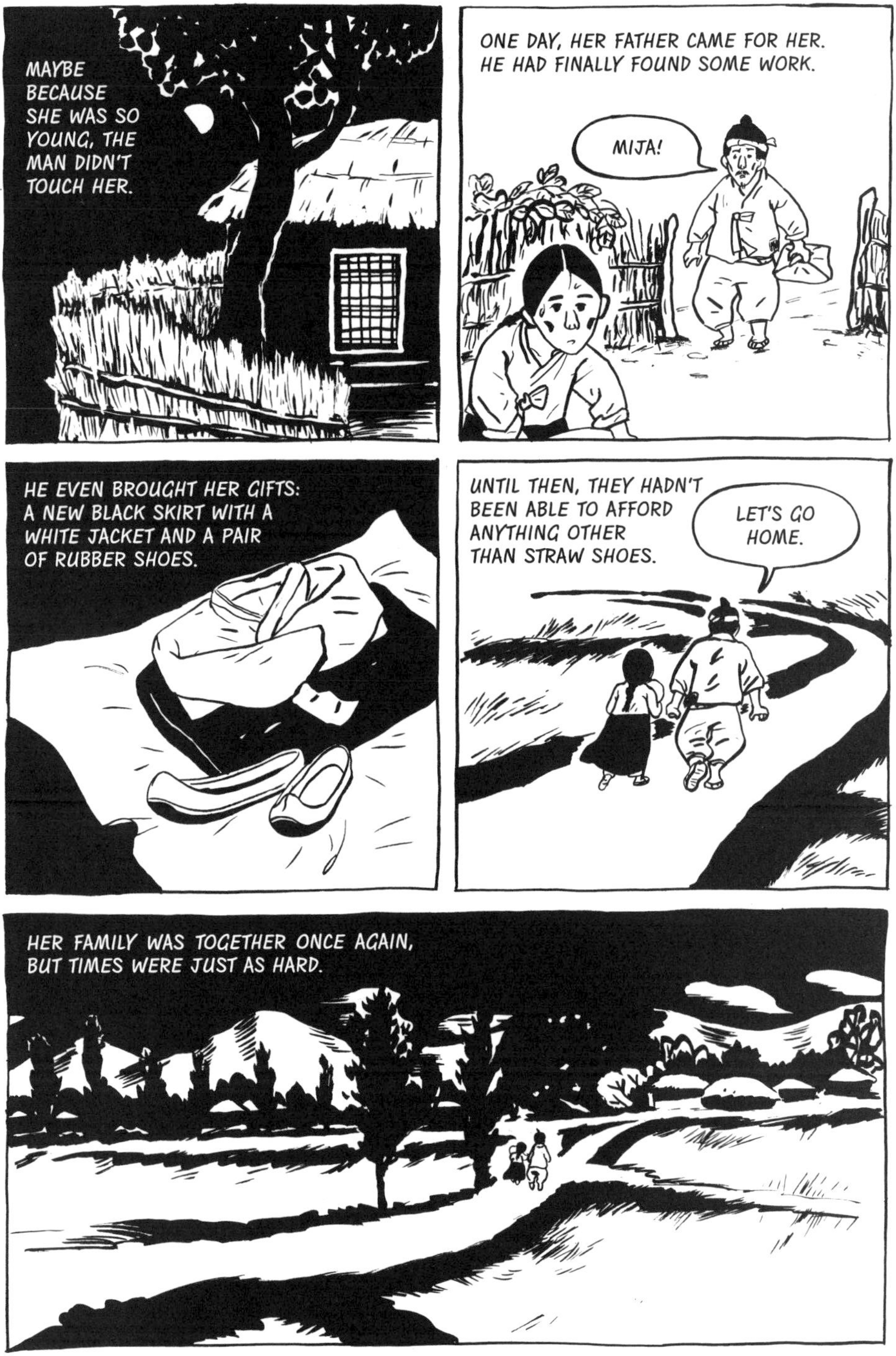

MAYBE BECAUSE SHE WAS SO YOUNG, THE MAN DIDN'T TOUCH HER.
ONE DAY, HER FATHER CAME FOR HER. HE HAD FINALLY FOUND SOME WORK.
MIJA!
HE EVEN BROUGHT HER GIFTS: A NEW BLACK SKIRT WITH A WHITE JACKET AND A PAIR OF RUBBER SHOES.
UNTIL THEN, THEY HADN'T BEEN ABLE TO AFFORD ANYTHING OTHER THAN STRAW SHOES.
LET'S GO HOME.
HER FAMILY WAS TOGETHER ONCE AGAIN, BUT TIMES WERE JUST AS HARD.

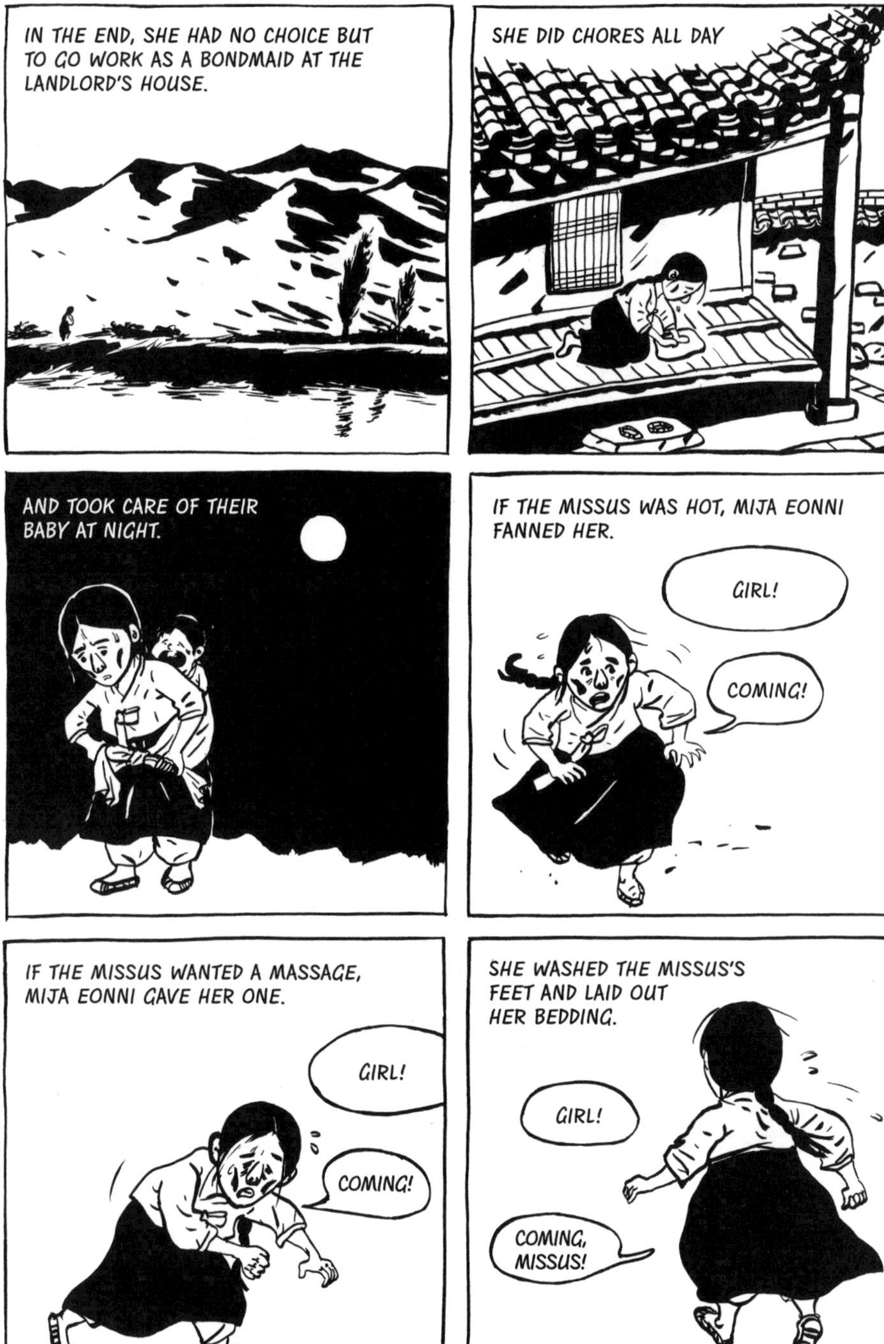
IN THE END, SHE HAD NO CHOICE BUT TO GO WORK AS A BONDMAID AT THE LANDLORD'S HOUSE.
SHE DID CHORES ALL DAY
AND TOOK CARE OF THEIR BABY AT NIGHT.
IF THE MISSUS WAS HOT, MIJA EONNI FANNED HER.
GIRL!
COMING!
IF THE MISSUS WANTED A MASSAGE, MIJA EONNI GAVE HER ONE.
GIRL!
COMING!
SHE WASHED THE MISSUS'S FEET AND LAID OUT HER BEDDING.
GIRL!
COMING, MISSUS!

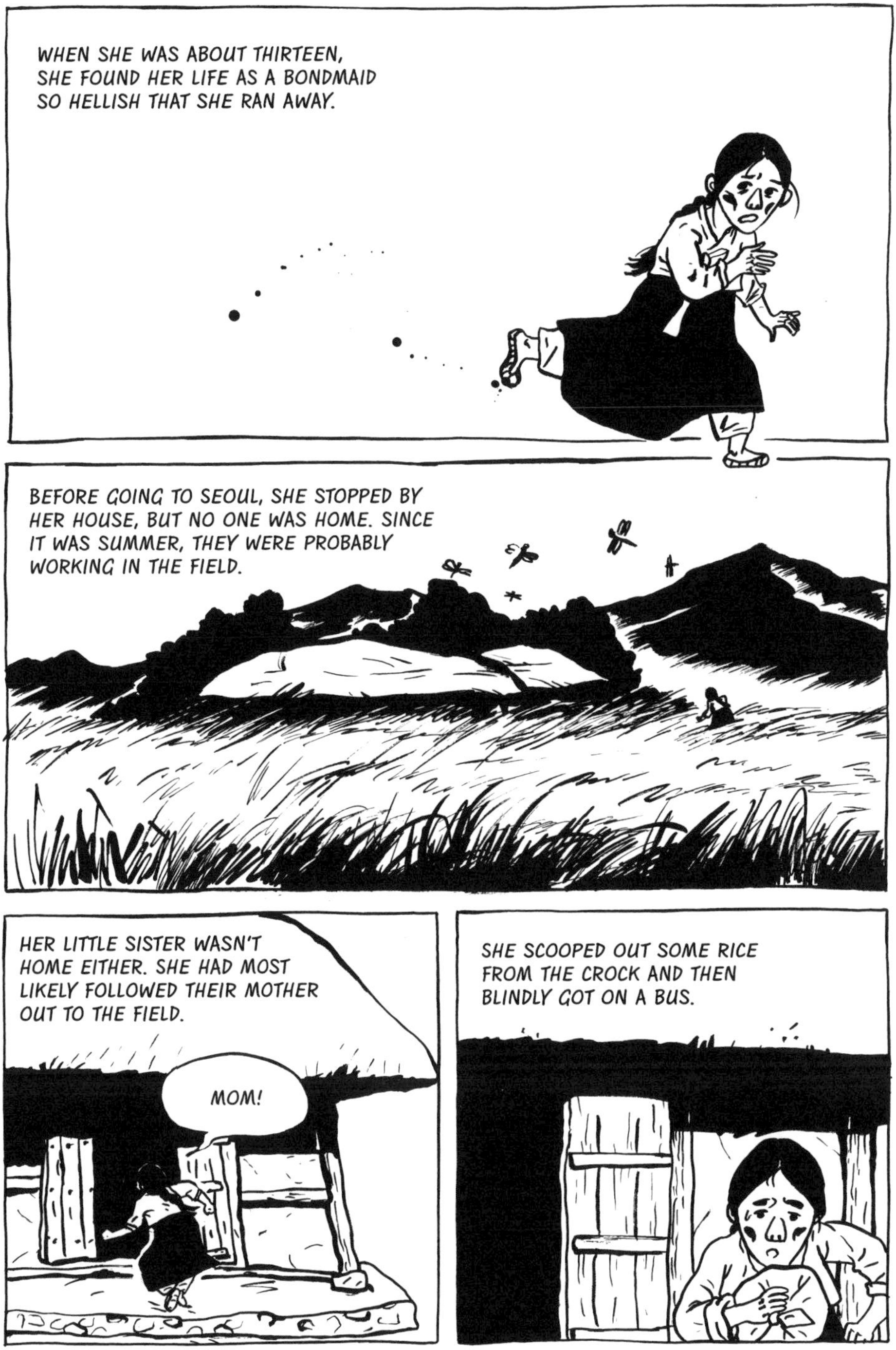
WHEN SHE WAS ABOUT THIRTEEN, SHE FOUND HER LIFE AS A BONDMAID SO HELLISH THAT SHE RAN AWAY.
BEFORE GOING TO SEOUL, SHE STOPPED BY HER HOUSE, BUT NO ONE WAS HOME. SINCE IT WAS SUMMER, THEY WERE PROBABLY WORKING IN THE FIELD.
HER LITTLE SISTER WASN'T HOME EITHER. SHE HAD MOST LIKELY FOLLOWED THEIR MOTHER OUT TO THE FIELD.
MOM!
SHE SCOOPED OUT SOME RICE FROM THE CROCK AND THEN BLINDLY GOT ON A BUS.

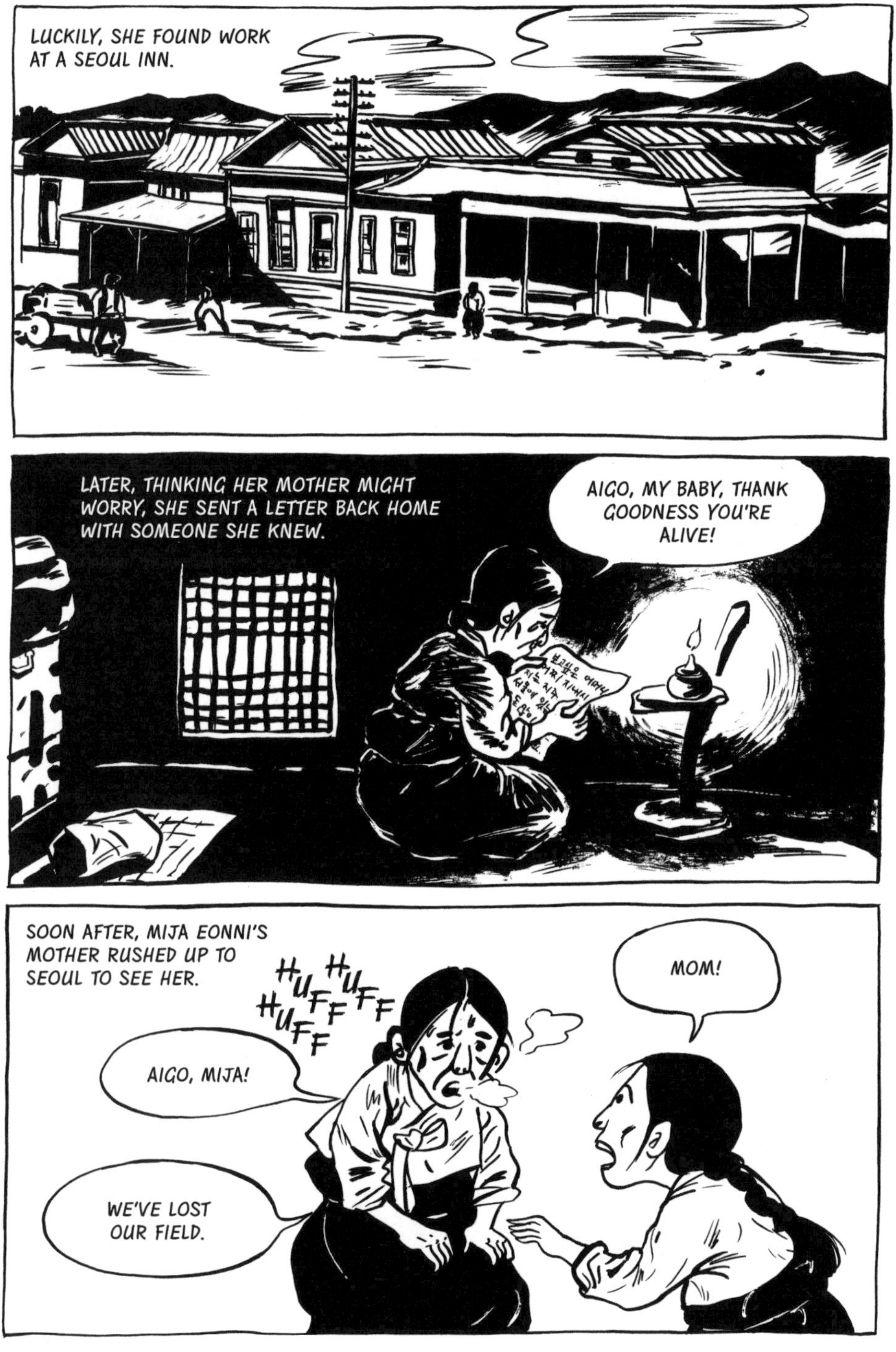
LUCKILY, SHE FOUND WORK AT A SEOUL INN.
LATER, THINKING HER MOTHER MIGHT WORRY, SHE SENT A LETTER BACK HOME WITH SOMEONE SHE KNEW.
AIGO, MY BABY, THANK GOODNESS YOU'RE ALIVE!
SOON AFTER, MIJA EONNI'S MOTHER RUSHED UP TO SEOUL TO SEE HER.
HUFF HUFF HUFF
MOM!
AIGO, MIJA!
WE'VE LOST OUR FIELD.

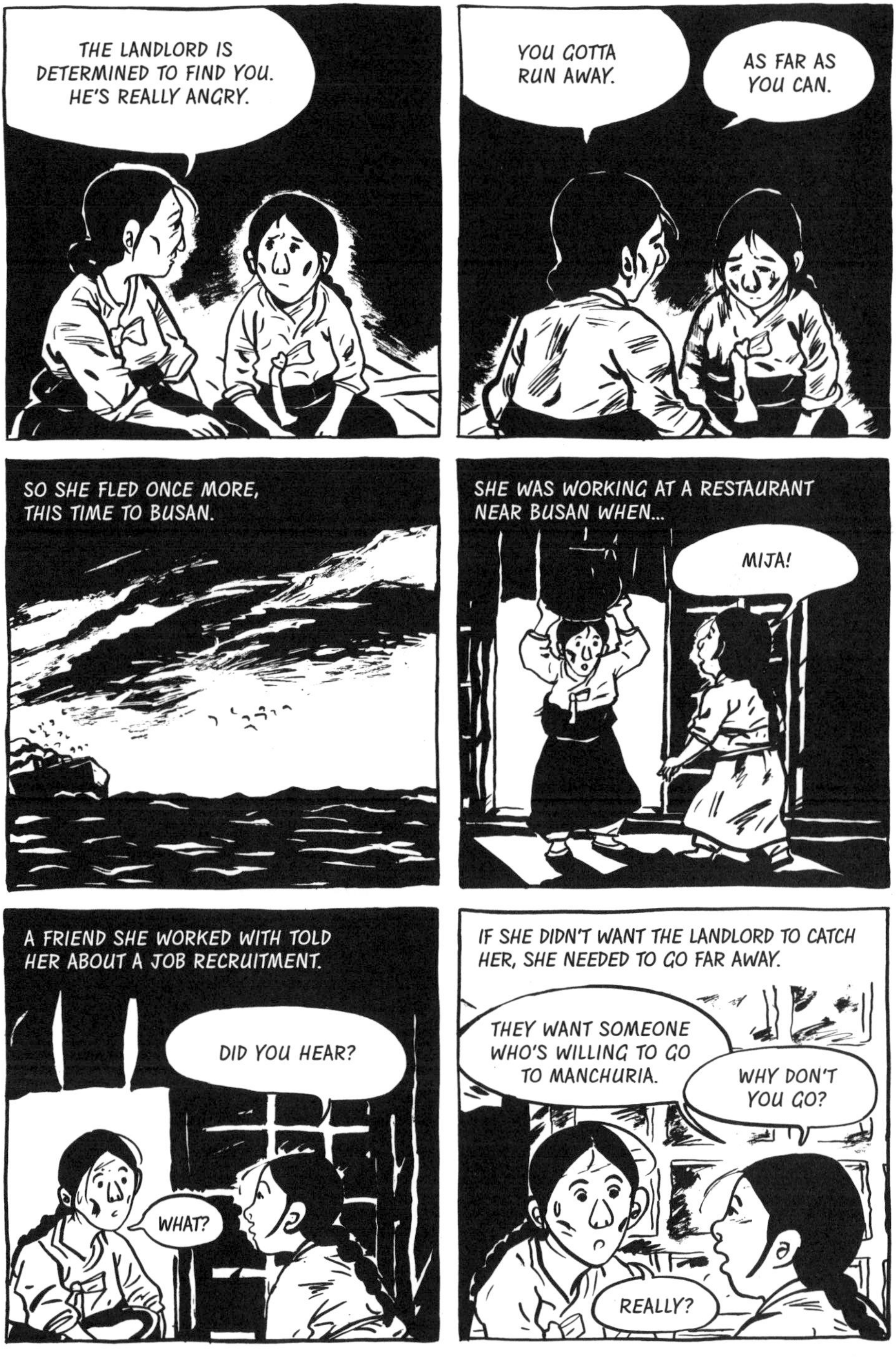
THE LANDLORD IS DETERMINED TO FIND YOU. HE'S REALLY ANGRY.
YOU GOTTA RUN AWAY.
AS FAR AS YOU CAN.
SO SHE FLED ONCE MORE, THIS TIME TO BUSAN.
SHE WAS WORKING AT A RESTAURANT NEAR BUSAN WHEN...
MIJA!
A FRIEND SHE WORKED WITH TOLD HER ABOUT A JOB RECRUITMENT.
DID YOU HEAR?
WHAT?
IF SHE DIDN'T WANT THE LANDLORD TO CATCH HER, SHE NEEDED TO GO FAR AWAY.
THEY WANT SOMEONE WHO'S WILLING TO GO TO MANCHURIA.
WHY DON'T YOU GO?
REALLY?

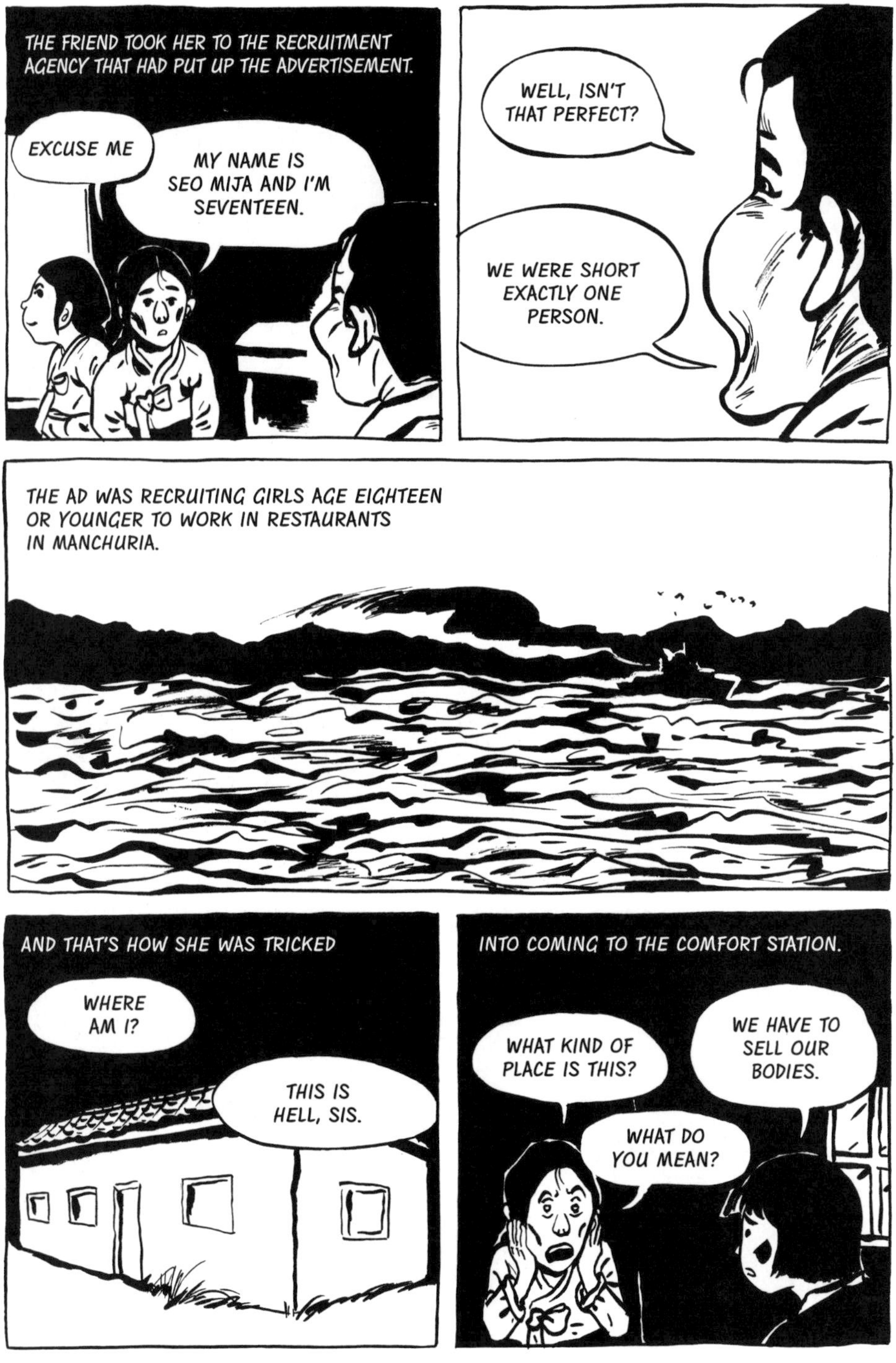
THE FRIEND TOOK HER TO THE RECRUITMENT AGENCY THAT HAD PUT UP THE ADVERTISEMENT.
EXCUSE ME
MY NAME IS SEO MIJA AND I'M SEVENTEEN.
WELL, ISN'T THAT PERFECT?
WE WERE SHORT EXACTLY ONE PERSON.
THE AD WAS RECRUITING GIRLS AGE EIGHTEEN OR YOUNGER TO WORK IN RESTAURANTS IN MANCHURIA.
AND THAT'S HOW SHE WAS TRICKED
WHERE AM I?
THIS IS HELL, SIS.
INTO COMING TO THE COMFORT STATION.
WHAT KIND OF PLACE IS THIS?
WE HAVE TO SELL OUR BODIES.
WHAT DO YOU MEAN?

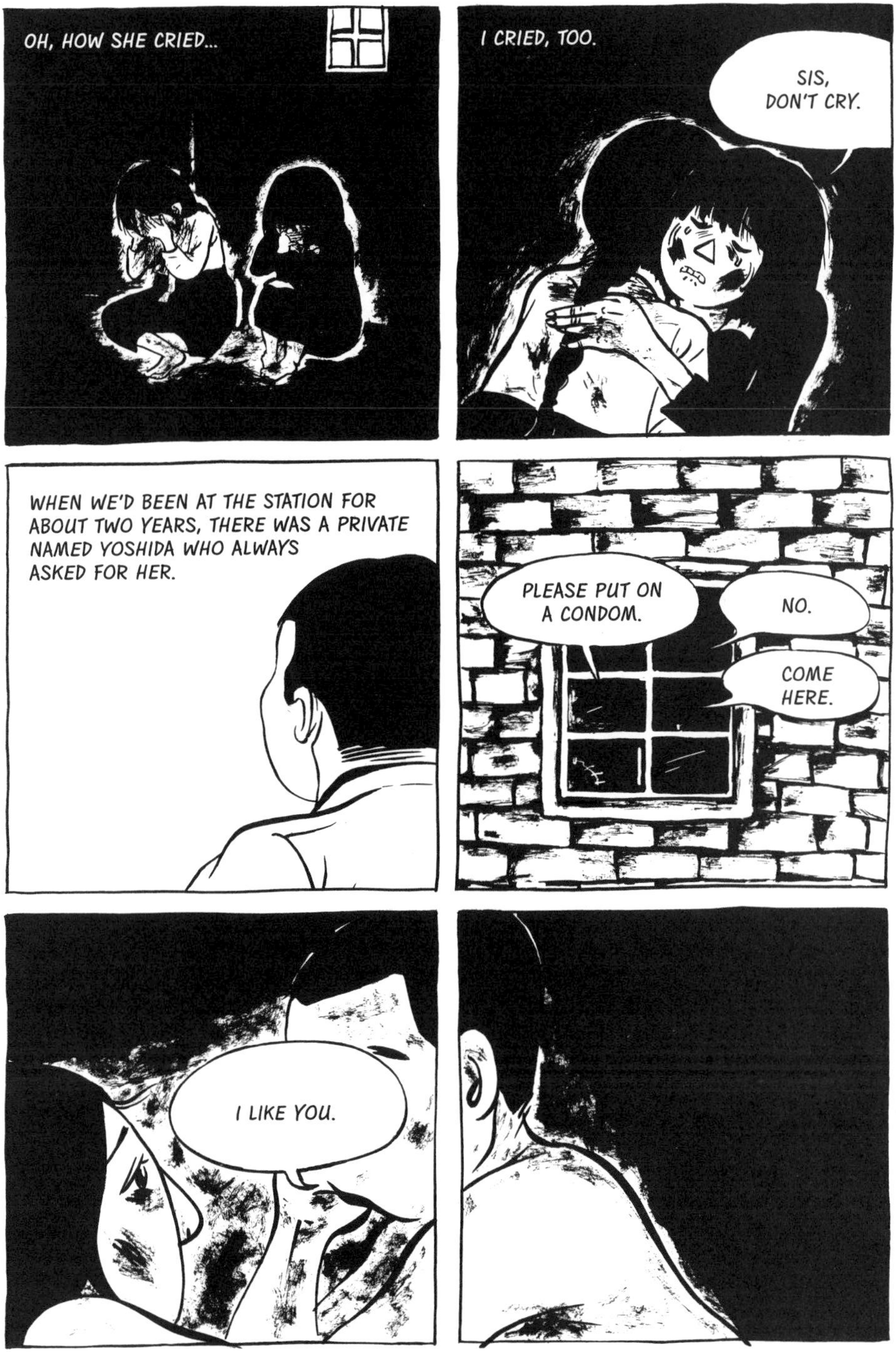
OH, HOW SHE CRIED...
I CRIED, TOO.
SIS, DON'T CRY.
WHEN WE'D BEEN AT THE STATION FOR ABOUT TWO YEARS, THERE WAS A PRIVATE NAMED YOSHIDA WHO ALWAYS ASKED FOR HER.
PLEASE PUT ON A CONDOM.
NO.
COME HERE.
I LIKE YOU.

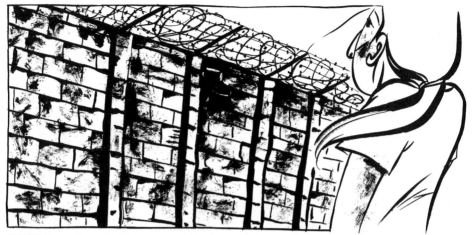

ONE DAY...

OK-SUN, I'M IN BIG TROUBLE.

HUH?

I HAVEN'T GOTTEN MY PERIOD YET.

WHAT?

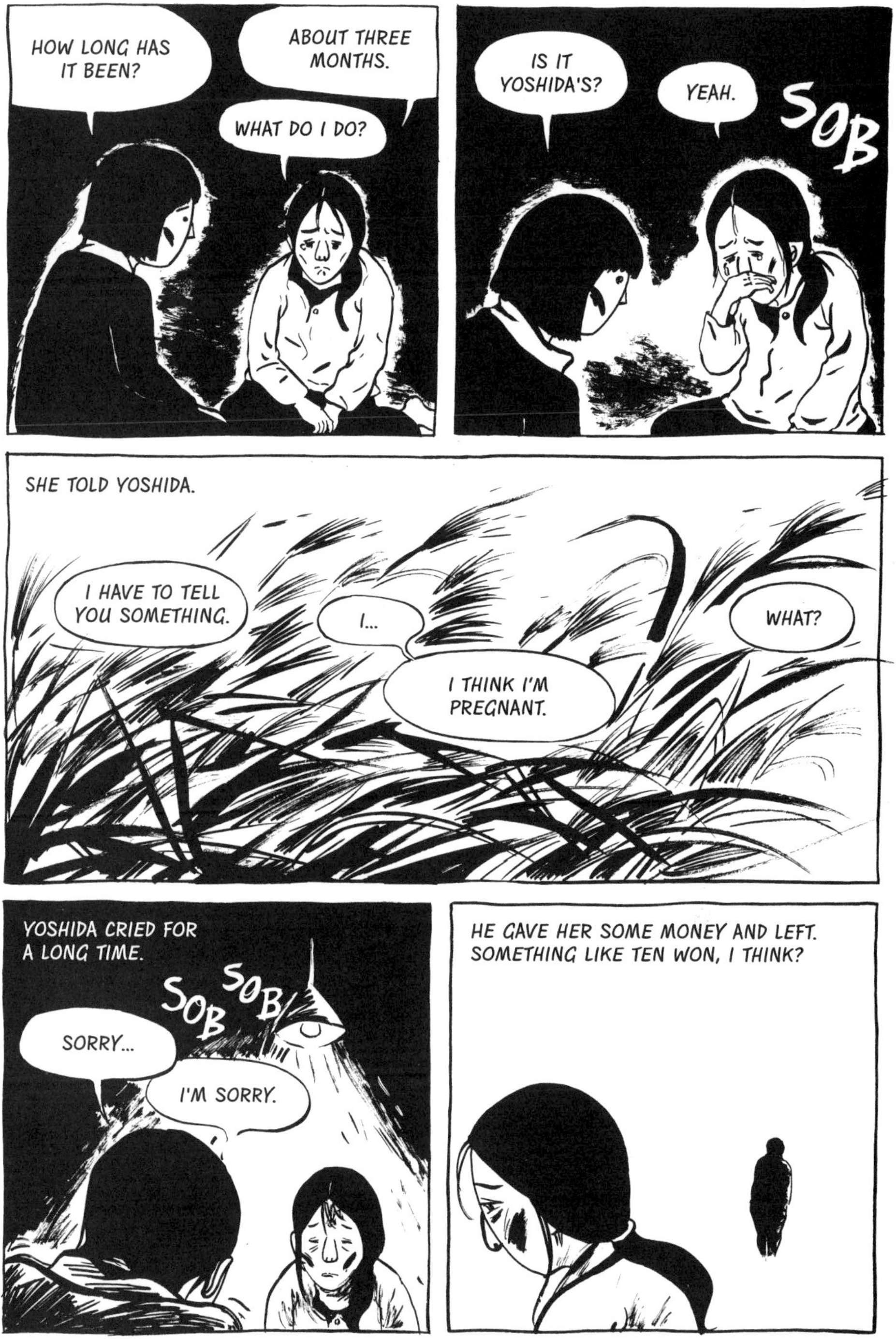
HOW LONG HAS IT BEEN?
ABOUT THREE MONTHS.
WHAT DO I DO?
IS IT YOSHIDA'S?
YEAH.
SOB
SHE TOLD YOSHIDA.
I HAVE TO TELL YOU SOMETHING.
I...
I THINK I'M PREGNANT.
WHAT?
YOSHIDA CRIED FOR A LONG TIME.
SOB
SOB
SORRY...
I'M SORRY.
HE GAVE HER SOME MONEY AND LEFT. SOMETHING LIKE TEN WON, I THINK?

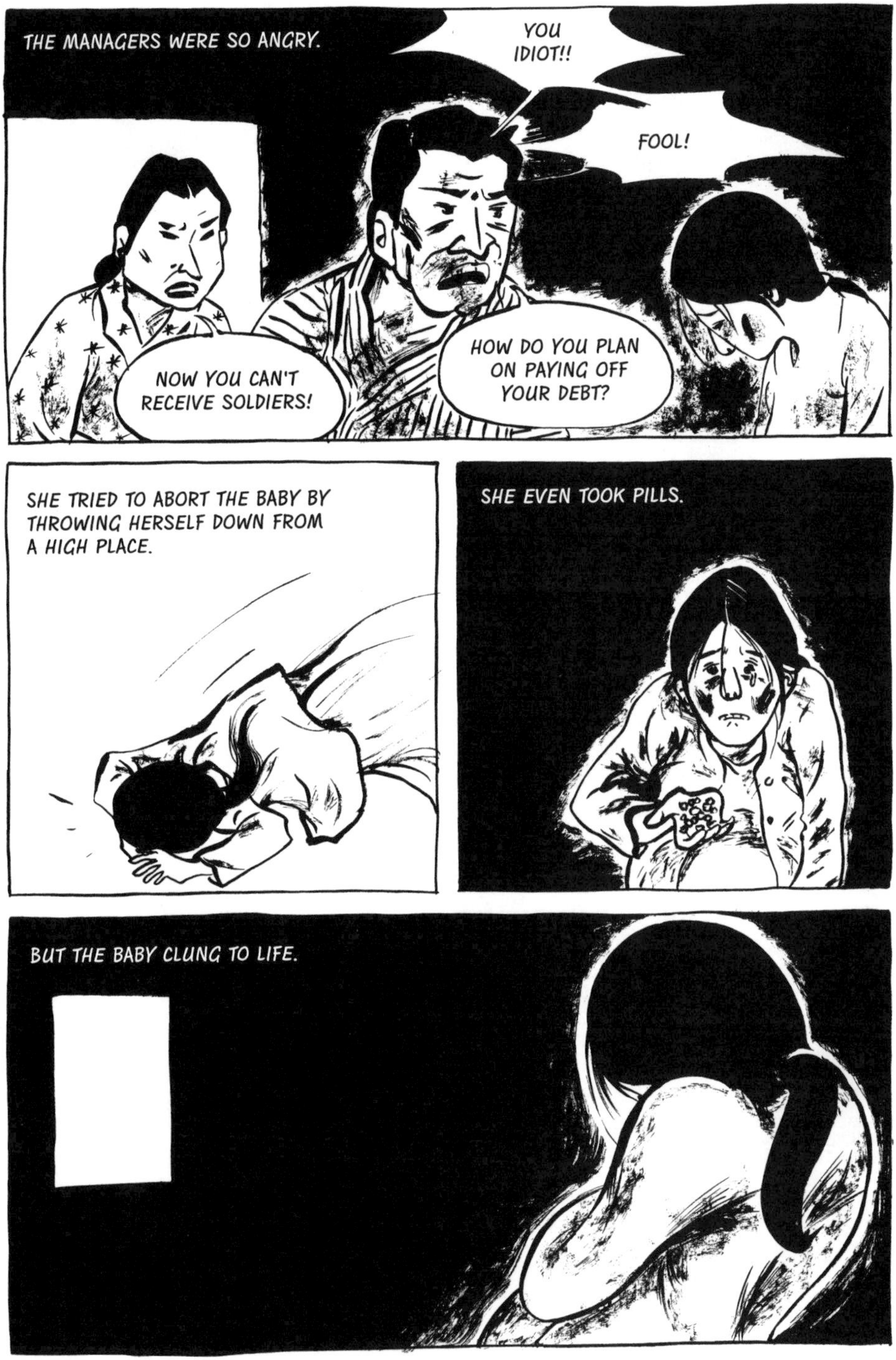
THE MANAGERS WERE SO ANGRY.
YOU IDIOT!!
FOOL!
NOW YOU CAN'T RECEIVE SOLDIERS!
HOW DO YOU PLAN ON PAYING OFF YOUR DEBT?
SHE TRIED TO ABORT THE BABY BY THROWING HERSELF DOWN FROM A HIGH PLACE.
SHE EVEN TOOK PILLS.
BUT THE BABY CLUNG TO LIFE.

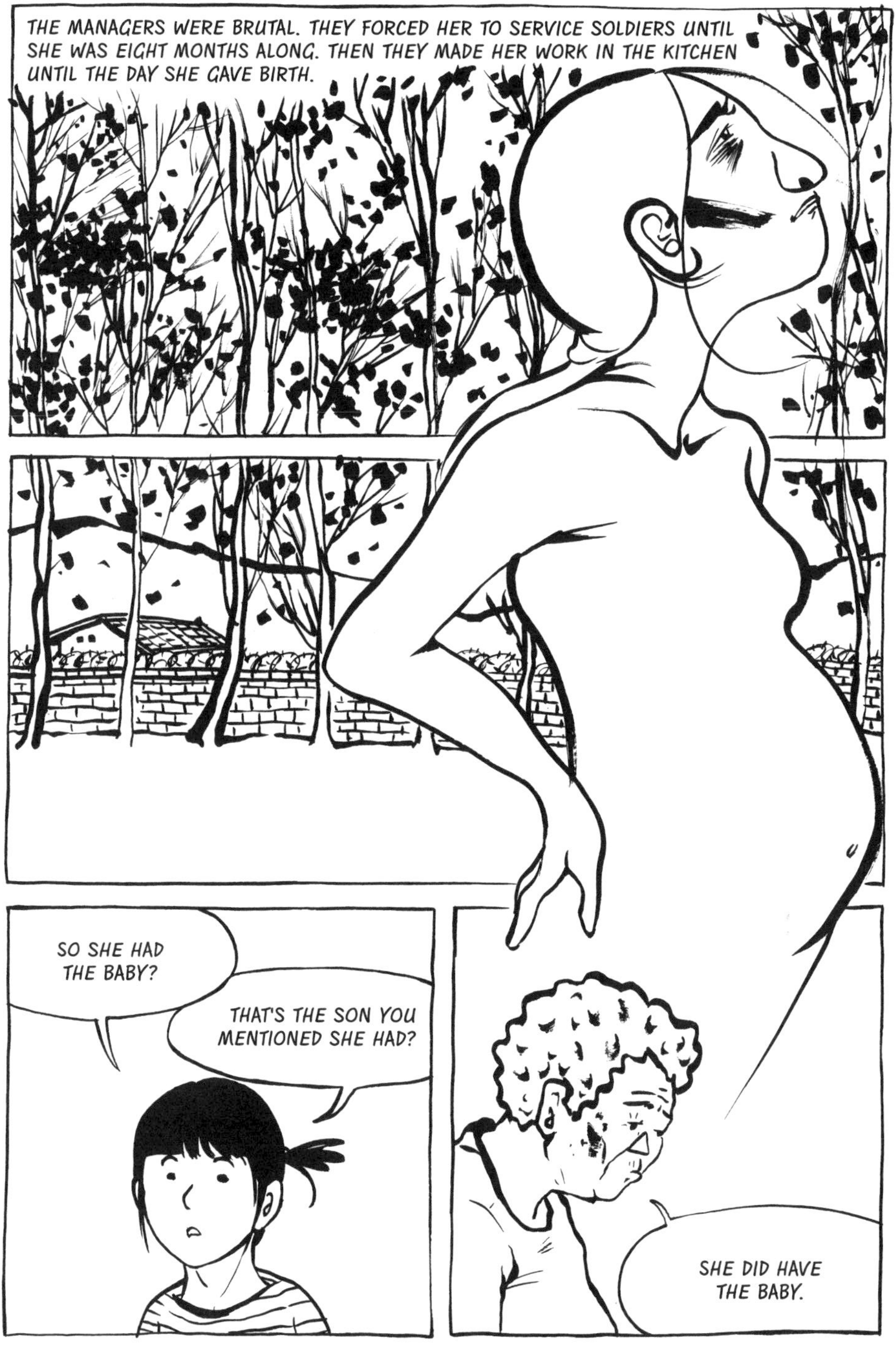
THE MANAGERS WERE BRUTAL. THEY FORCED HER TO SERVICE SOLDIERS UNTIL SHE WAS EIGHT MONTHS ALONG. THEN THEY MADE HER WORK IN THE KITCHEN UNTIL THE DAY SHE GAVE BIRTH.
SO SHE HAD THE BABY?
THAT'S THE SON YOU MENTIONED SHE HAD?
SHE DID HAVE THE BABY.

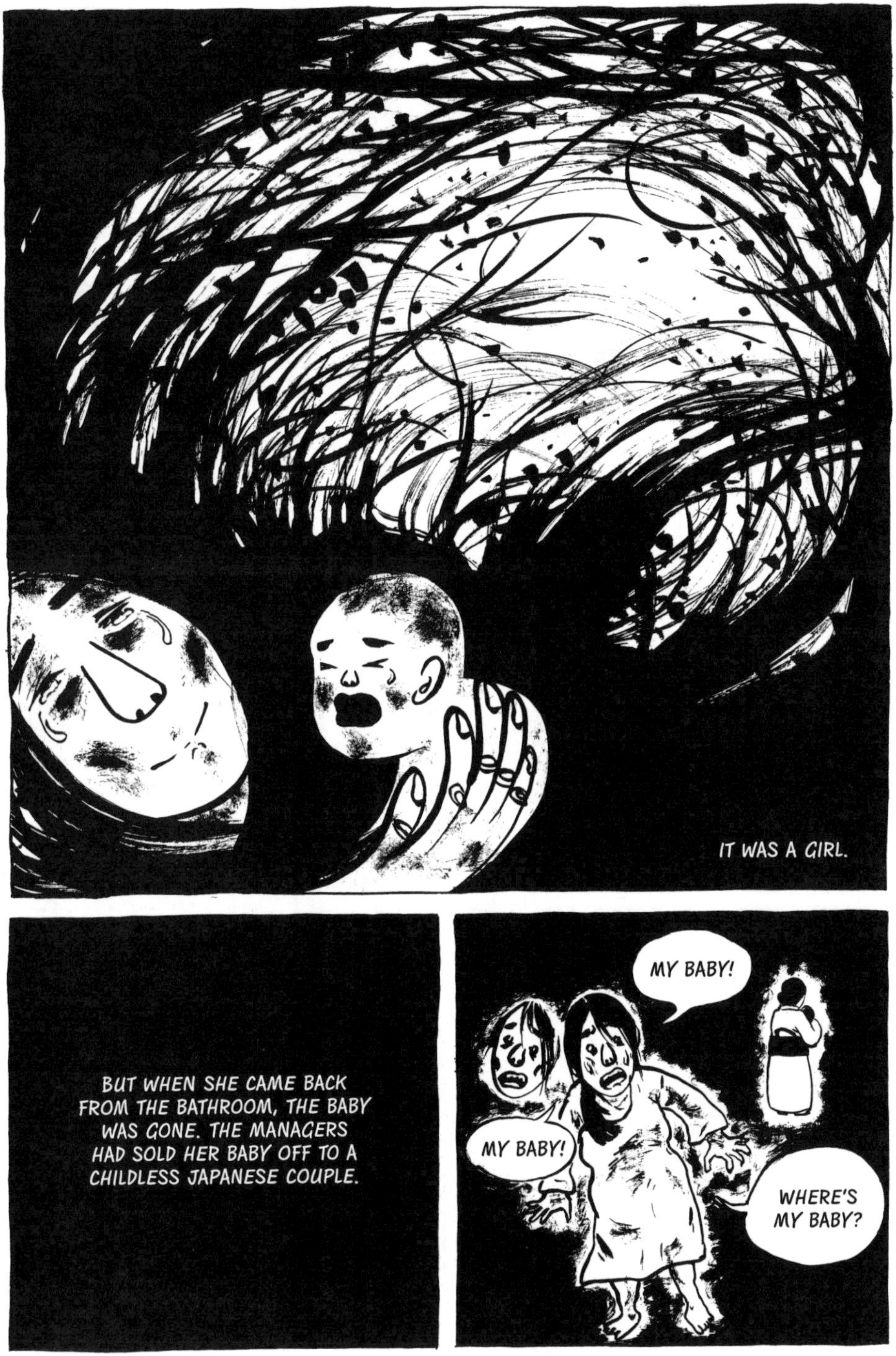
IT WAS A GIRL.
BUT WHEN SHE CAME BACK FROM THE BATHROOM, THE BABY WAS GONE. THE MANAGERS HAD SOLD HER BABY OFF TO A CHILDLESS JAPANESE COUPLE.
MY BABY!
MY BABY!
WHERE'S MY BABY?

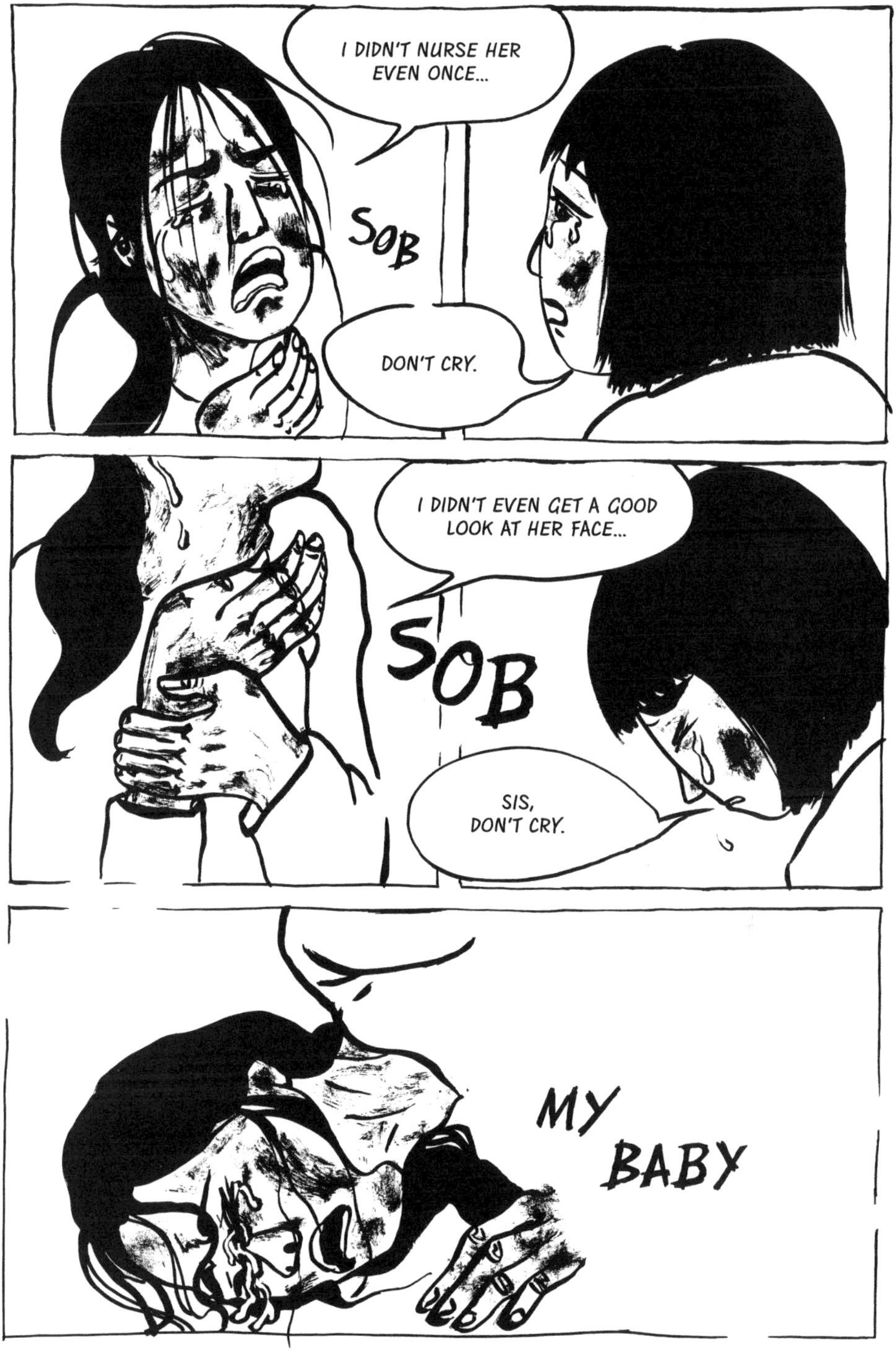
I DIDN'T NURSE HER EVEN ONCE...
SOB
DON'T CRY.
I DIDN'T EVEN GET A GOOD LOOK AT HER FACE...
SOB
SIS, DON'T CRY.
MY BABY

BEFORE SHE COULD HEAL PROPERLY, SHE WAS
FORCED TO RECEIVE SOLDIERS AGAIN.

AFTER RECEIVING THE MEN, SO MUCH BLOOD
WOULD FLOW FROM DOWN THERE THAT SHE
COULDN'T WALK AROUND.

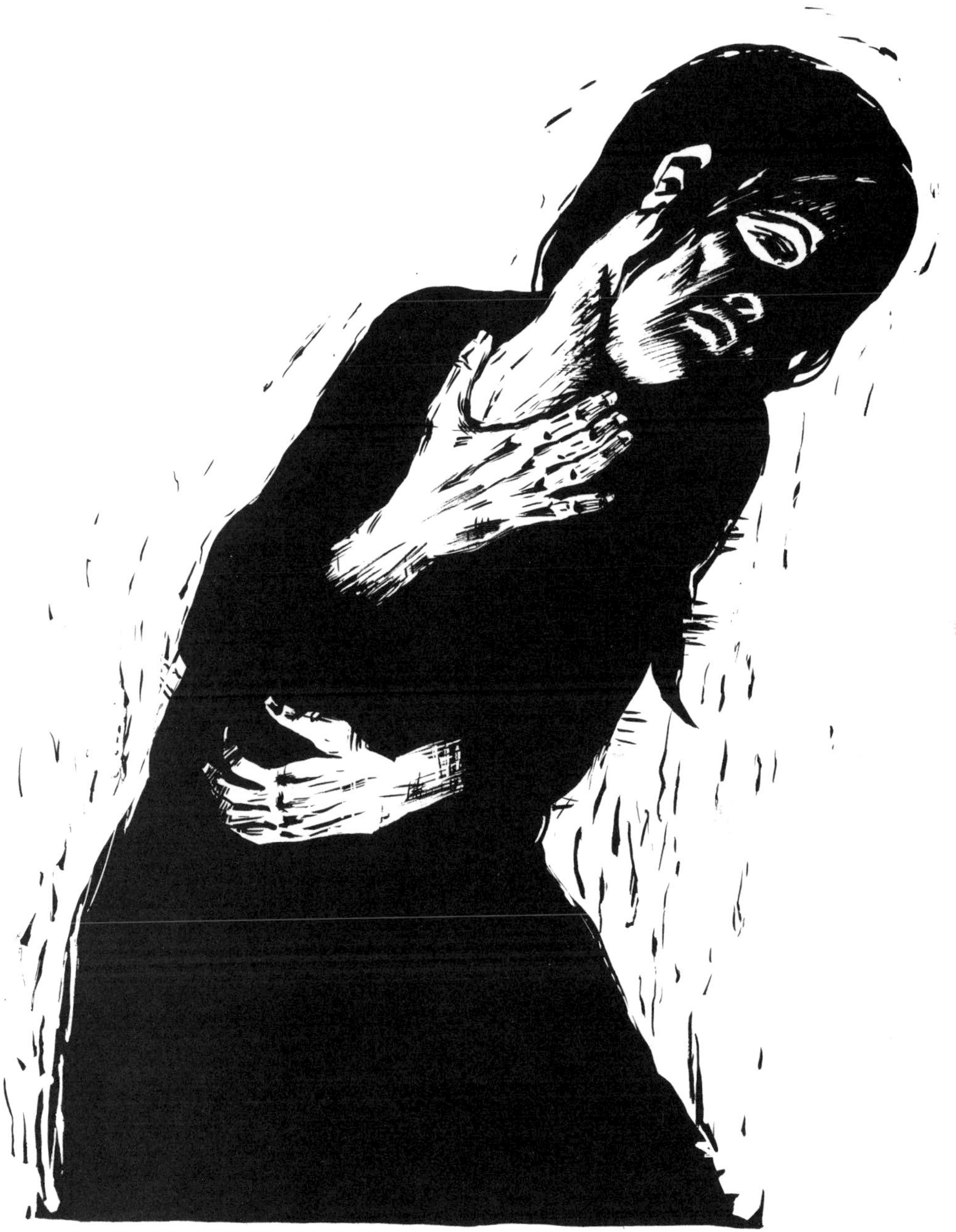

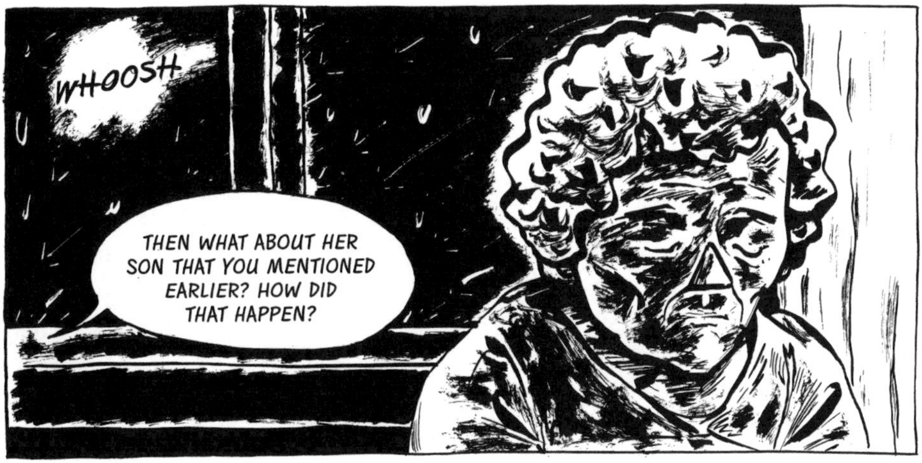
WHOOSH
THEN WHAT ABOUT HER SON THAT YOU MENTIONED EARLIER? HOW DID THAT HAPPEN?

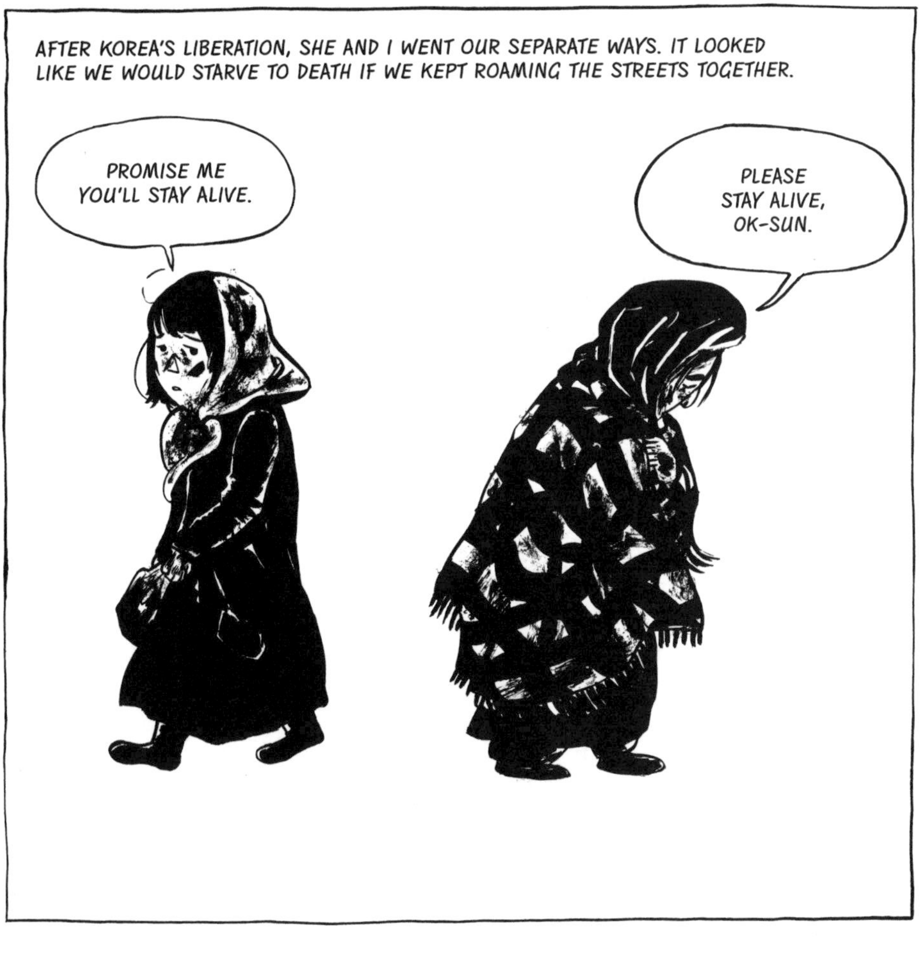
AFTER KOREA'S LIBERATION, SHE AND I WENT OUR SEPARATE WAYS. IT LOOKED LIKE WE WOULD STARVE TO DEATH IF WE KEPT ROAMING THE STREETS TOGETHER.
PROMISE ME YOU'LL STAY ALIVE.
PLEASE STAY ALIVE, OK-SUN.

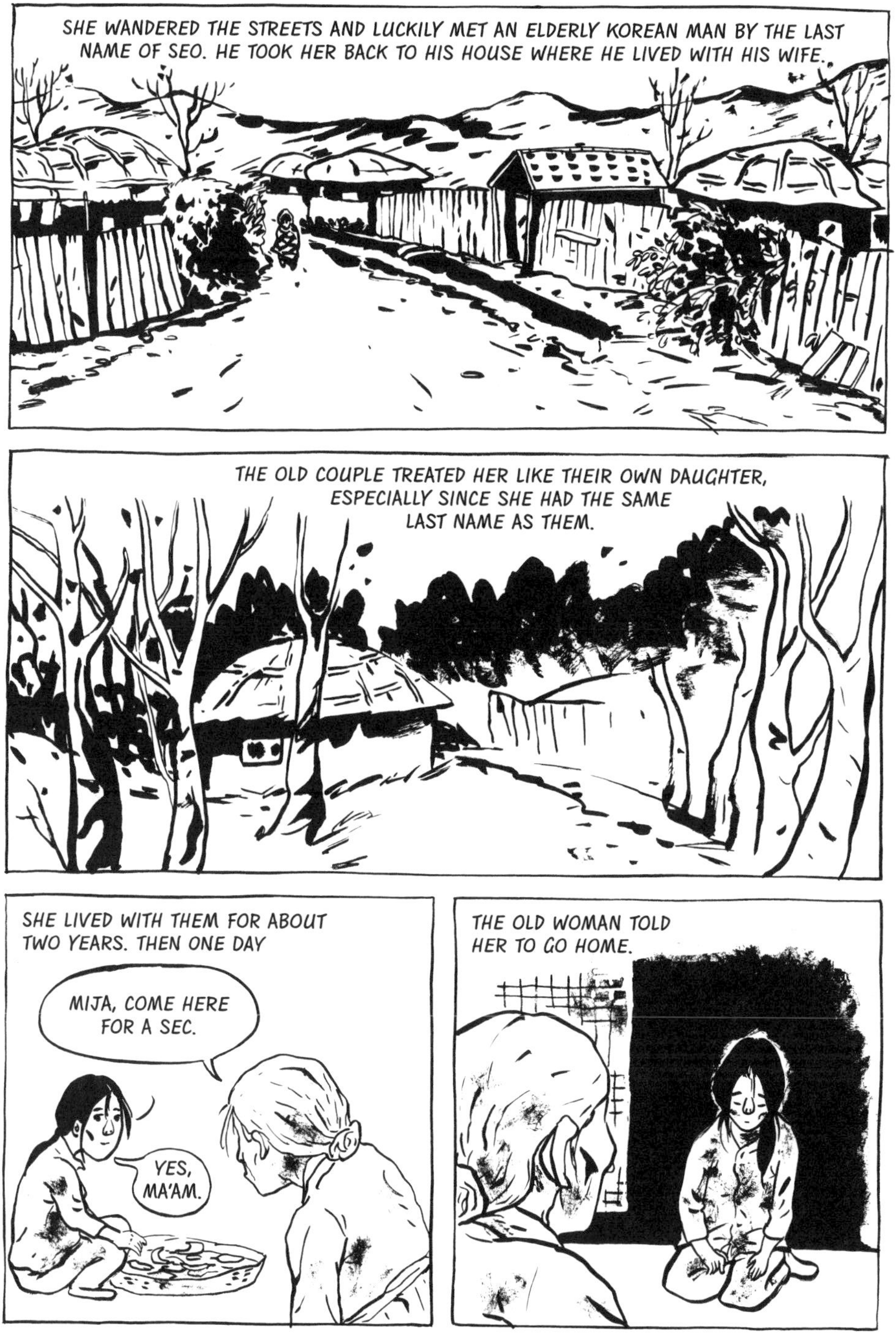
SHE WANDERED THE STREETS AND LUCKILY MET AN ELDERLY KOREAN MAN BY THE LAST NAME OF SEO. HE TOOK HER BACK TO HIS HOUSE WHERE HE LIVED WITH HIS WIFE.
THE OLD COUPLE TREATED HER LIKE THEIR OWN DAUGHTER, ESPECIALLY SINCE SHE HAD THE SAME LAST NAME AS THEM.
SHE LIVED WITH THEM FOR ABOUT TWO YEARS. THEN ONE DAY
MIJA, COME HERE FOR A SEC.
YES, MA'AM.
THE OLD WOMAN TOLD HER TO GO HOME.

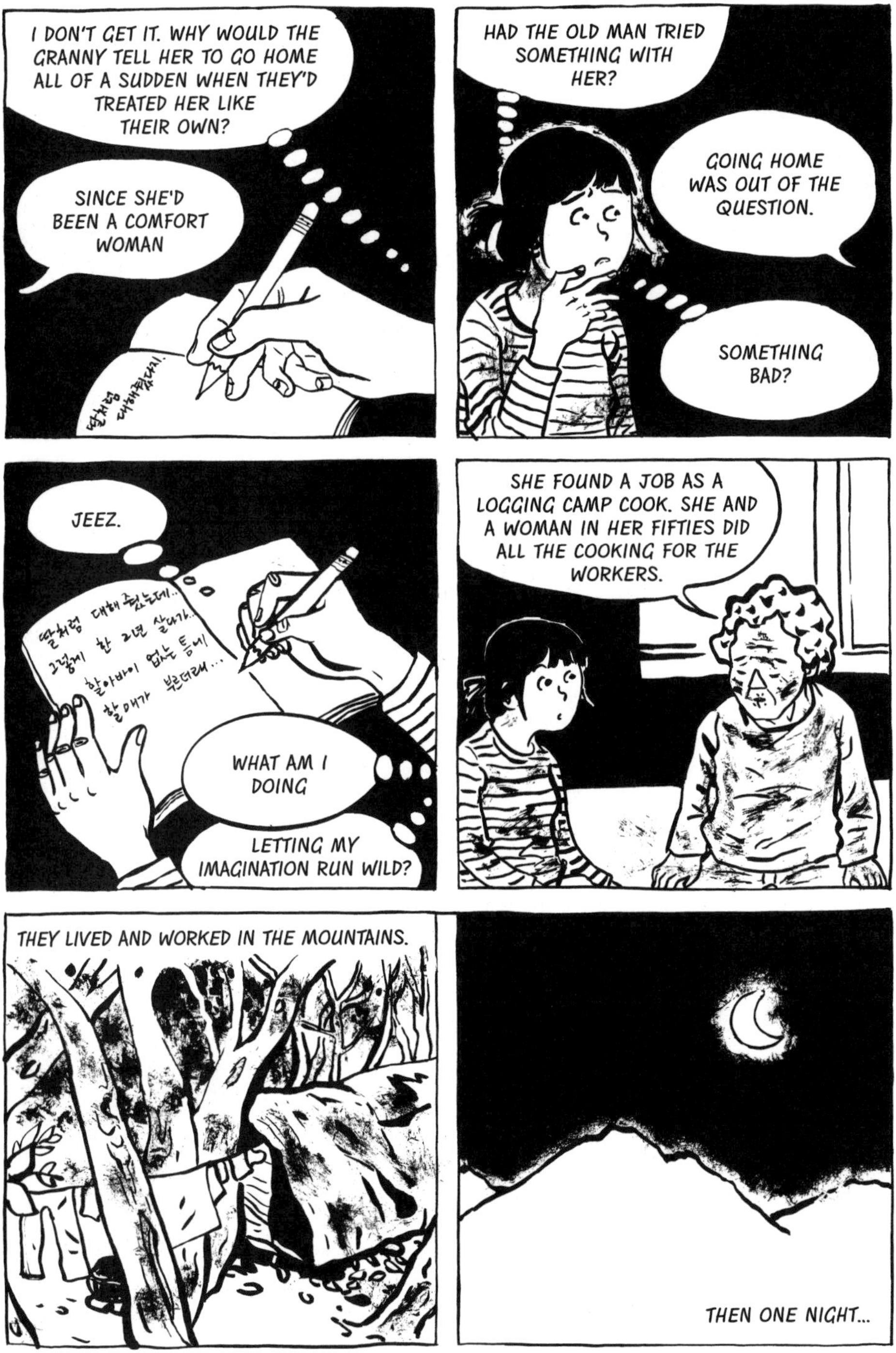
I DON'T GET IT. WHY WOULD THE GRANNY TELL HER TO GO HOME ALL OF A SUDDEN WHEN THEY'D TREATED HER LIKE THEIR OWN?
SINCE SHE'D BEEN A COMFORT WOMAN
딸처럼 대해줬다지.
HAD THE OLD MAN TRIED SOMETHING WITH HER?
GOING HOME WAS OUT OF THE QUESTION.
SOMETHING BAD?
JEEZ.
딸처럼 대해 줬는데..
그렇게 한 2년 살다가..
할아바이 없는 틈에
할매가 부르더래...
WHAT AM I DOING
LETTING MY IMAGINATION RUN WILD?
SHE FOUND A JOB AS A LOGGING CAMP COOK. SHE AND A WOMAN IN HER FIFTIES DID ALL THE COOKING FOR THE WORKERS.
THEY LIVED AND WORKED IN THE MOUNTAINS.
THEN ONE NIGHT...

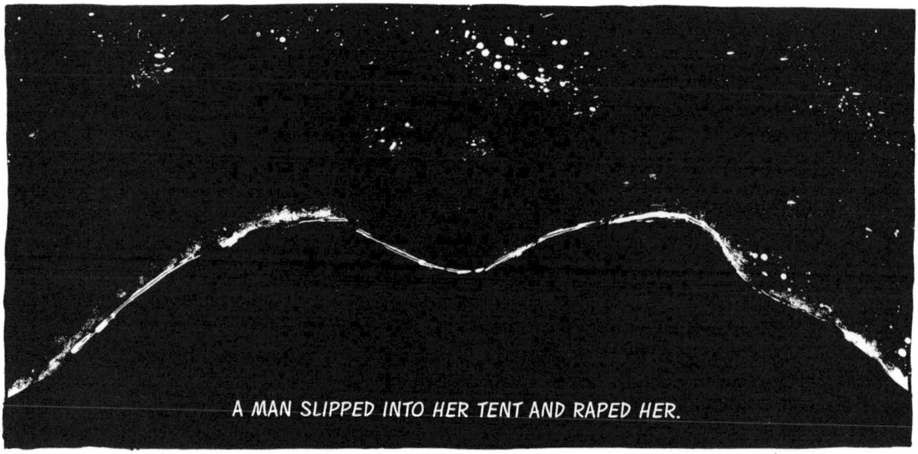
A MAN SLIPPED INTO HER TENT AND RAPED HER.

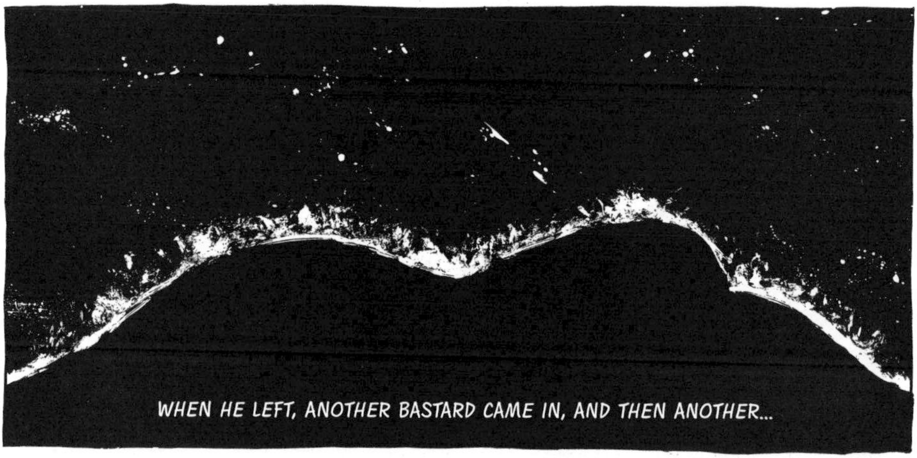
WHEN HE LEFT, ANOTHER BASTARD CAME IN, AND THEN ANOTHER...

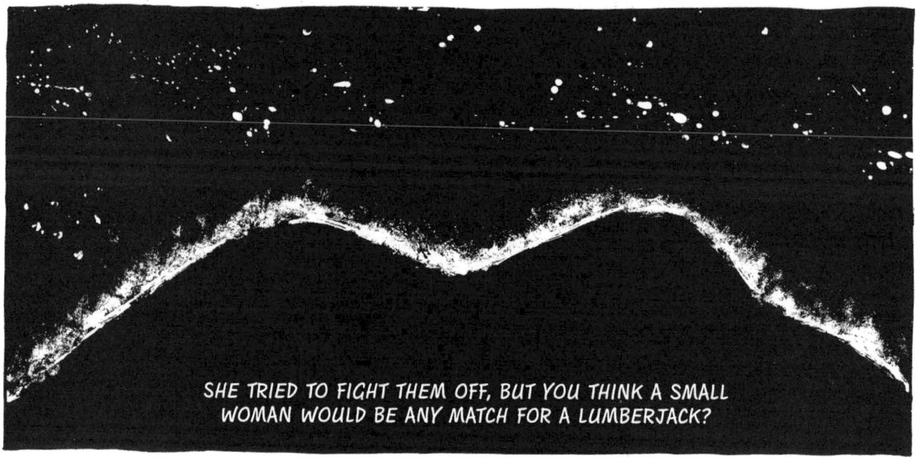
SHE TRIED TO FIGHT THEM OFF, BUT YOU THINK A SMALL
WOMAN WOULD BE ANY MATCH FOR A LUMBERJACK?

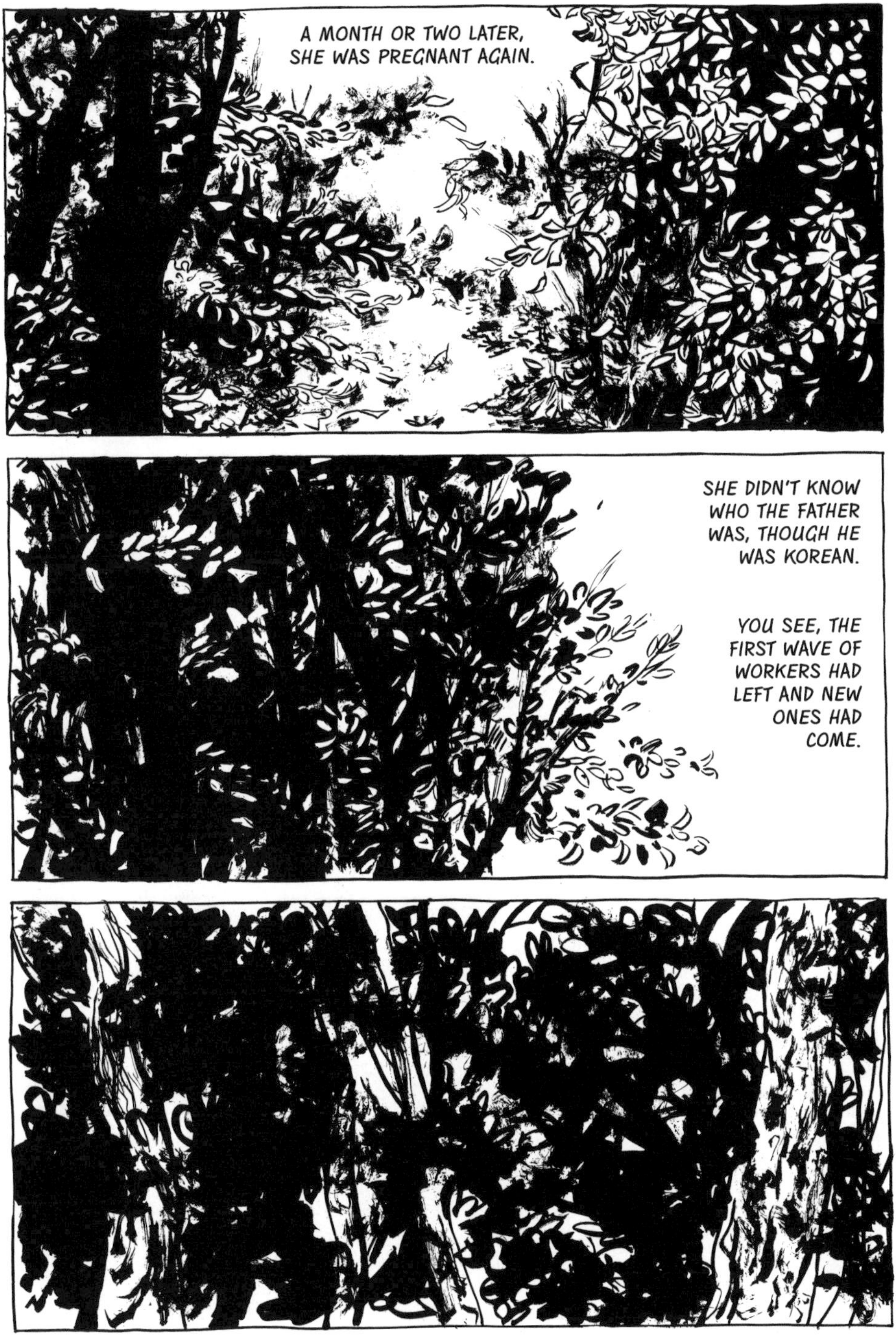
A MONTH OR TWO LATER, SHE WAS PREGNANT AGAIN.
SHE DIDN'T KNOW WHO THE FATHER WAS, THOUGH HE WAS KOREAN.
YOU SEE, THE FIRST WAVE OF WORKERS HAD LEFT AND NEW ONES HAD COME.

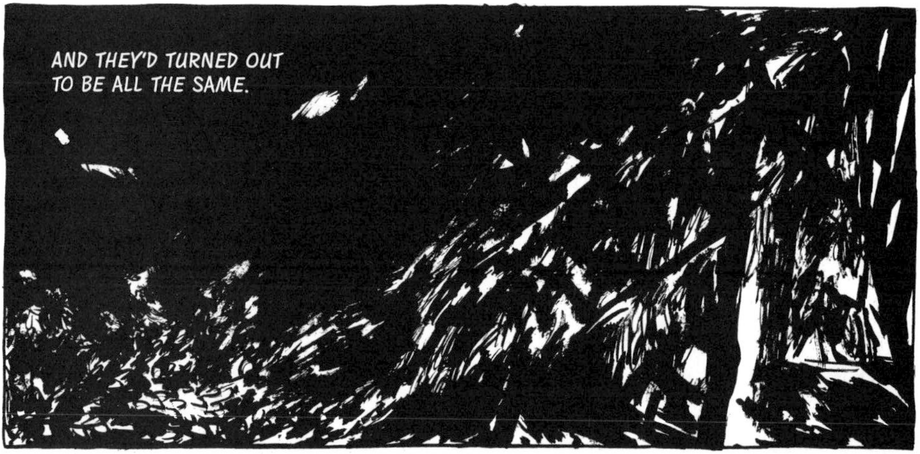
AND THEY'D TURNED OUT
TO BE ALL THE SAME.

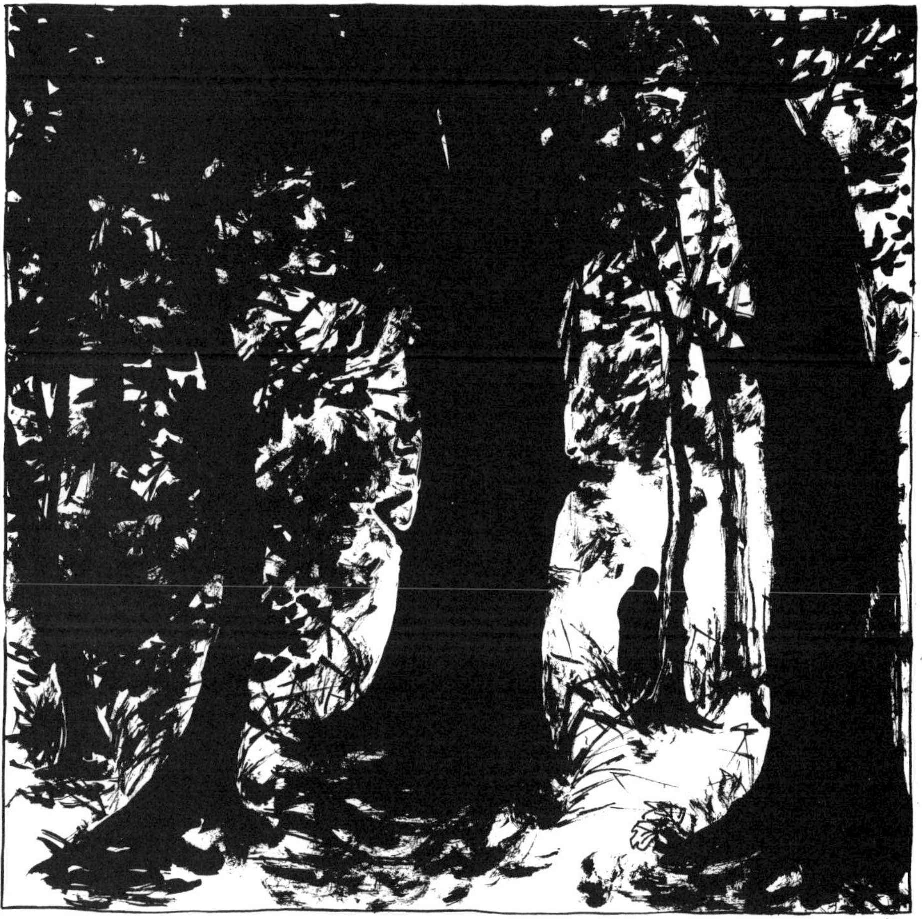

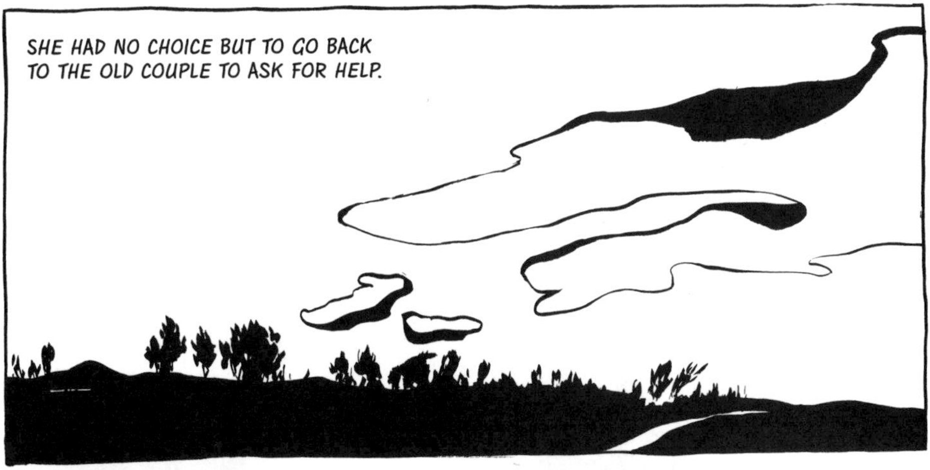
SHE HAD NO CHOICE BUT TO GO BACK
TO THE OLD COUPLE TO ASK FOR HELP.

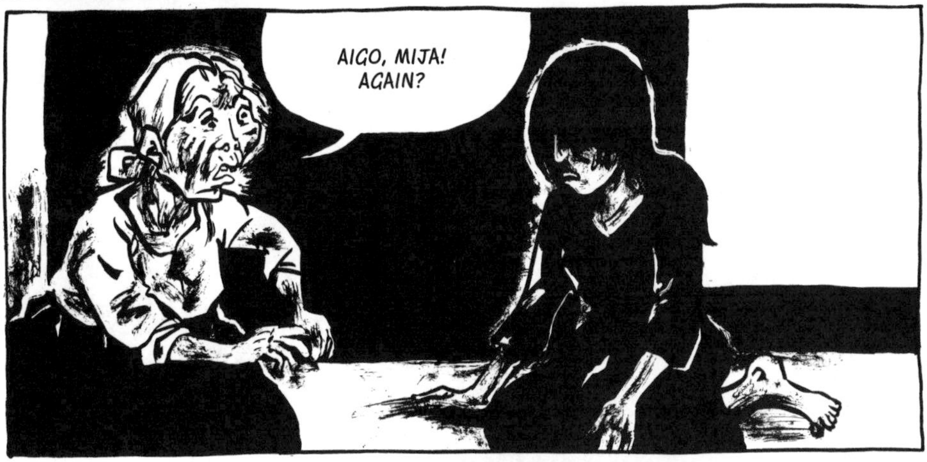
AIGO, MIJA!
AGAIN?

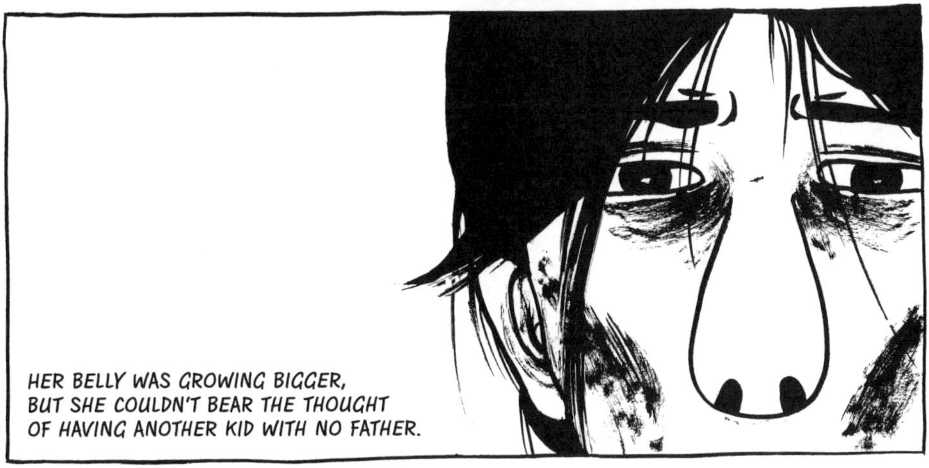
HER BELLY WAS GROWING BIGGER,
BUT SHE COULDN'T BEAR THE THOUGHT
OF HAVING ANOTHER KID WITH NO FATHER.

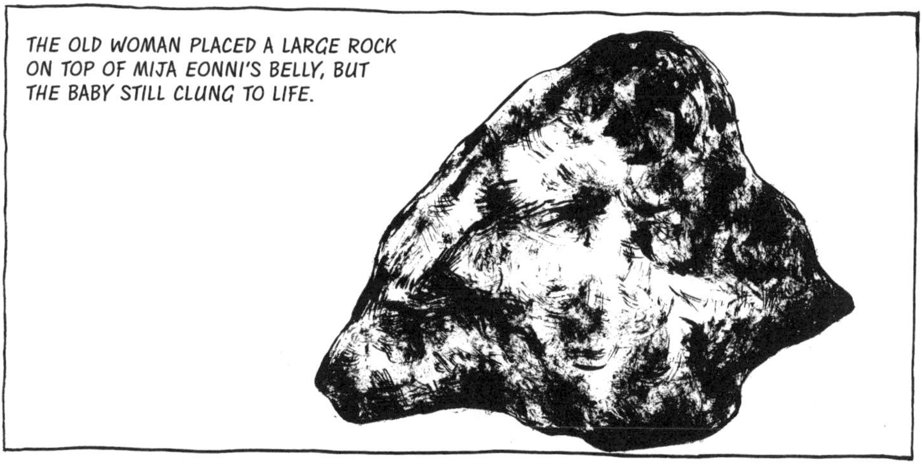
THE OLD WOMAN PLACED A LARGE ROCK ON TOP OF MIJA EONNI'S BELLY, BUT THE BABY STILL CLUNG TO LIFE.

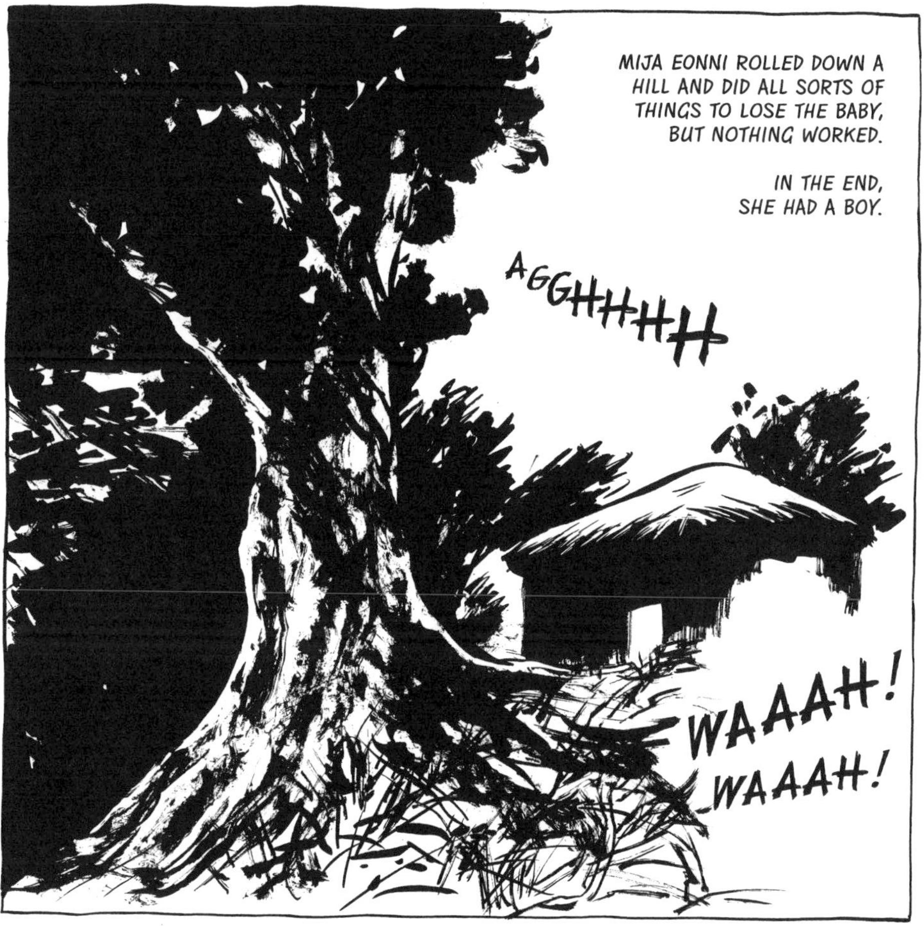
MIJA EONNI ROLLED DOWN A HILL AND DID ALL SORTS OF THINGS TO LOSE THE BABY, BUT NOTHING WORKED.
IN THE END, SHE HAD A BOY.
AGGHHHHH
WAAAH!
WAAAH!

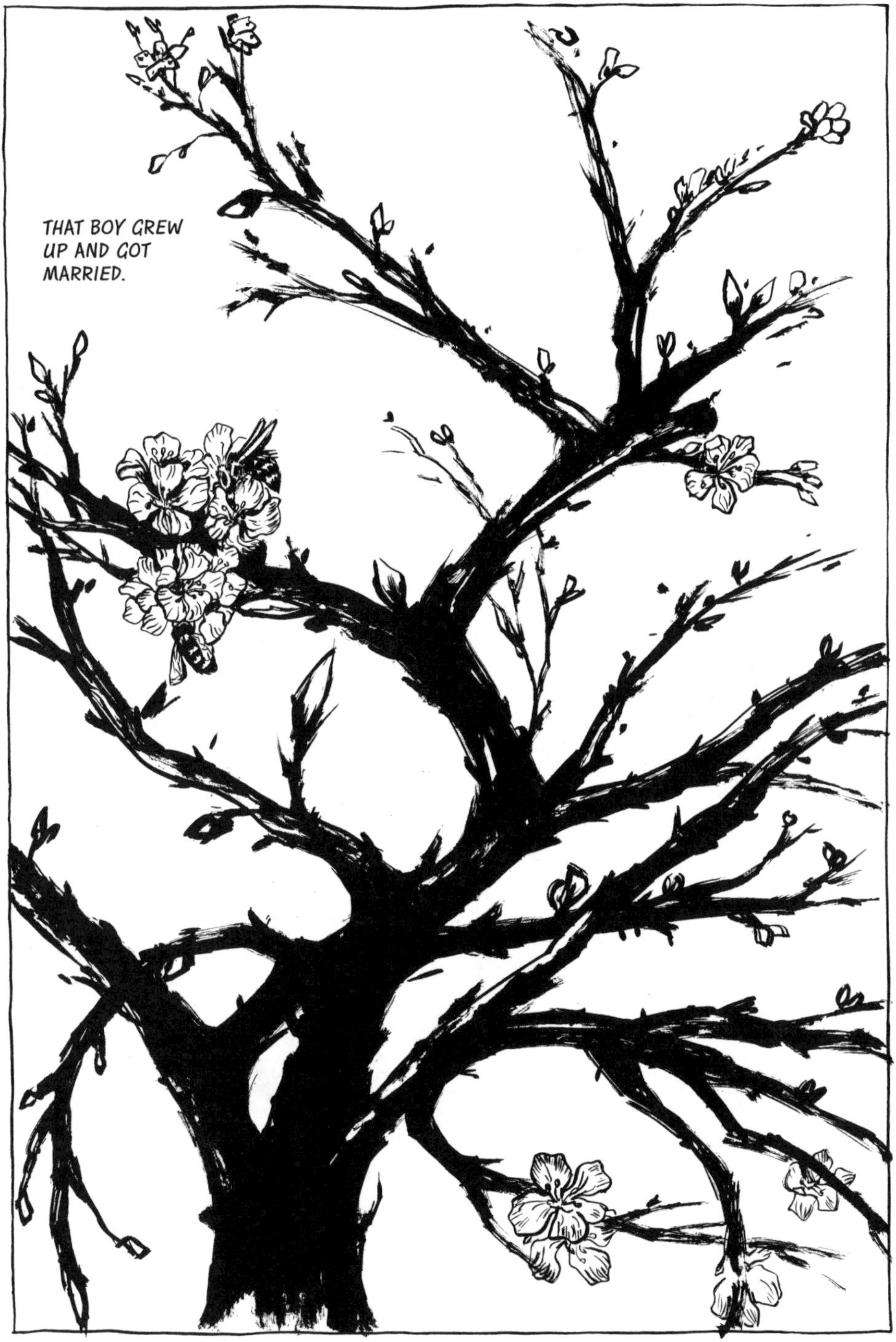
THAT BOY GREW
UP AND GOT
MARRIED.

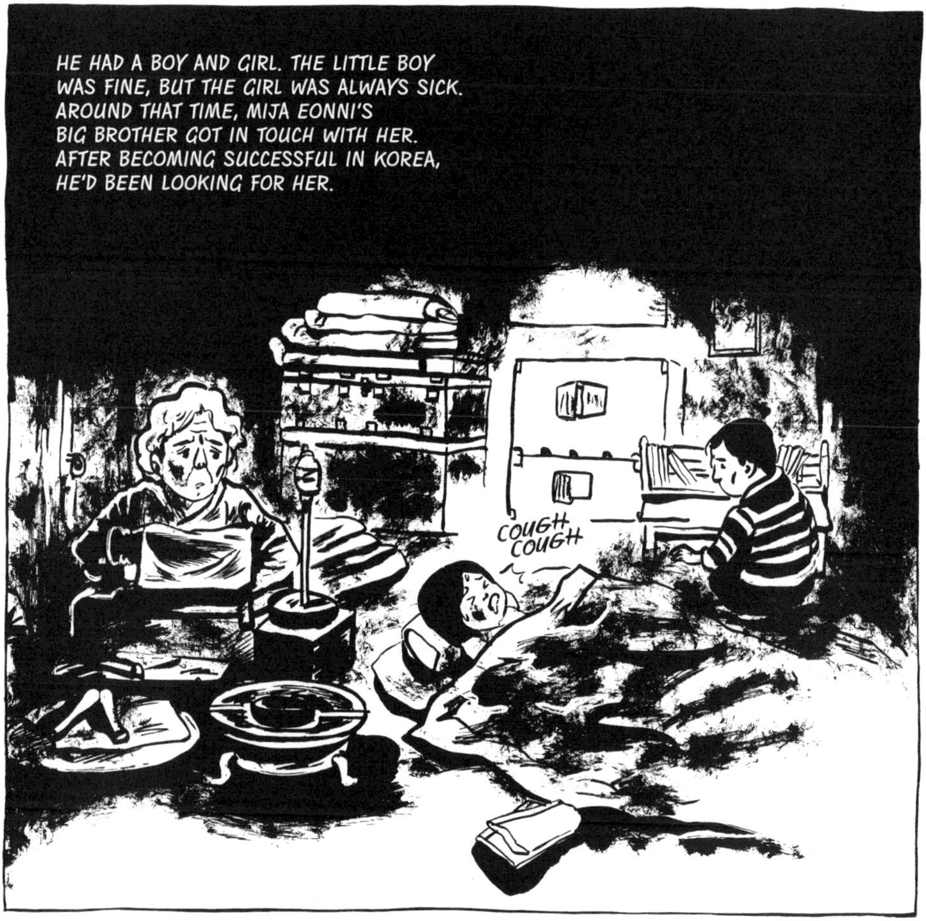
HE HAD A BOY AND GIRL. THE LITTLE BOY WAS FINE, BUT THE GIRL WAS ALWAYS SICK. AROUND THAT TIME, MIJA EONNI'S BIG BROTHER GOT IN TOUCH WITH HER. AFTER BECOMING SUCCESSFUL IN KOREA, HE'D BEEN LOOKING FOR HER.
COUGH COUGH

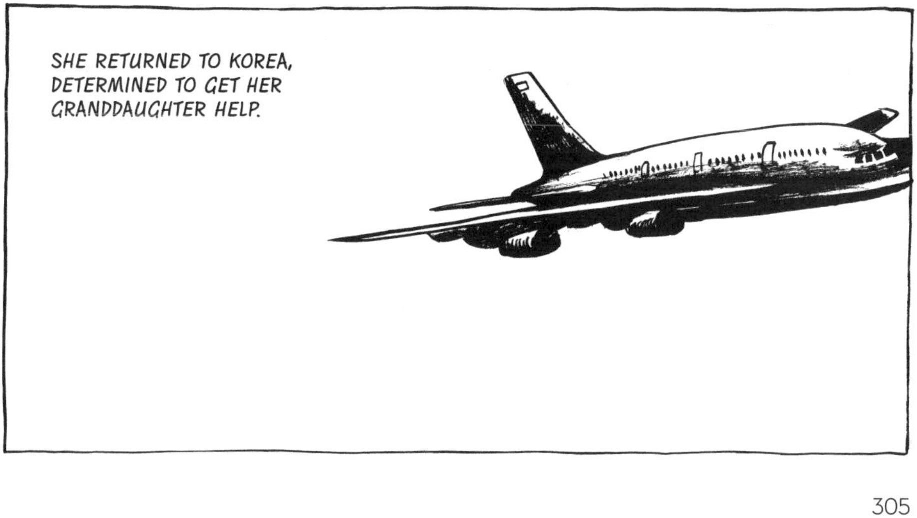
SHE RETURNED TO KOREA, DETERMINED TO GET HER GRANDDAUGHTER HELP.

MIJA *EONNI* WAS A LITTLE SMALLER THAN ME.
SHE HAD AN *OUTFIT* CUSTOM-MADE BEFORE
SHE DIED, BUT THE BLAZER WAS A BIT LOOSE,
SO I INHERITED IT. I STILL HAVE IT.

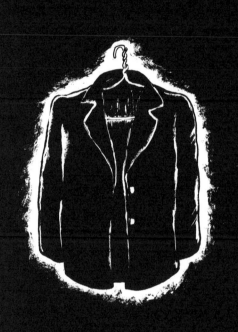

## A JAPANESE SOLDIER

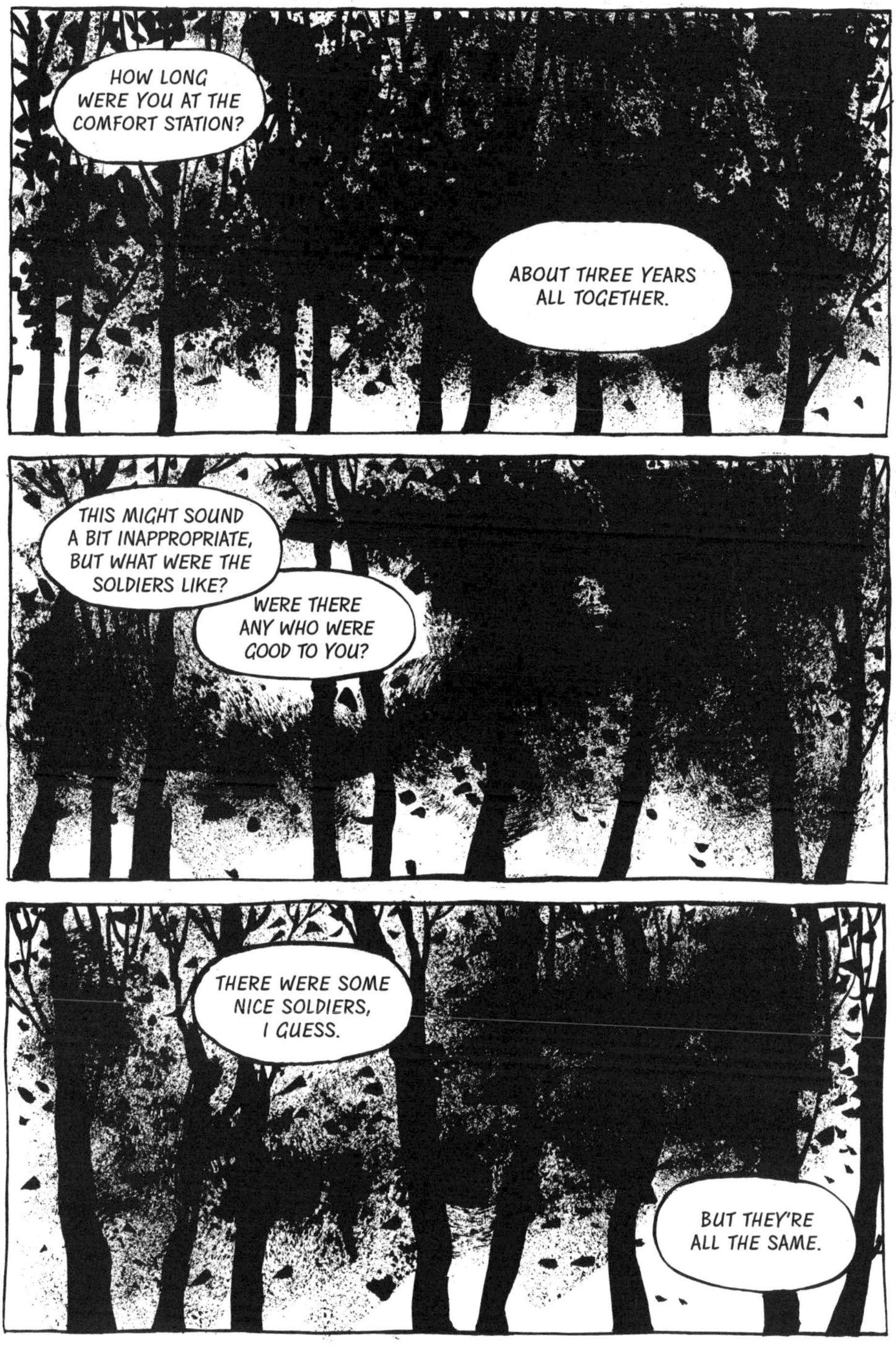
HOW LONG WERE YOU AT THE COMFORT STATION?
ABOUT THREE YEARS ALL TOGETHER.
THIS MIGHT SOUND A BIT INAPPROPRIATE, BUT WHAT WERE THE SOLDIERS LIKE?
WERE THERE ANY WHO WERE GOOD TO YOU?
THERE WERE SOME NICE SOLDIERS, I GUESS.
BUT THEY'RE ALL THE SAME.

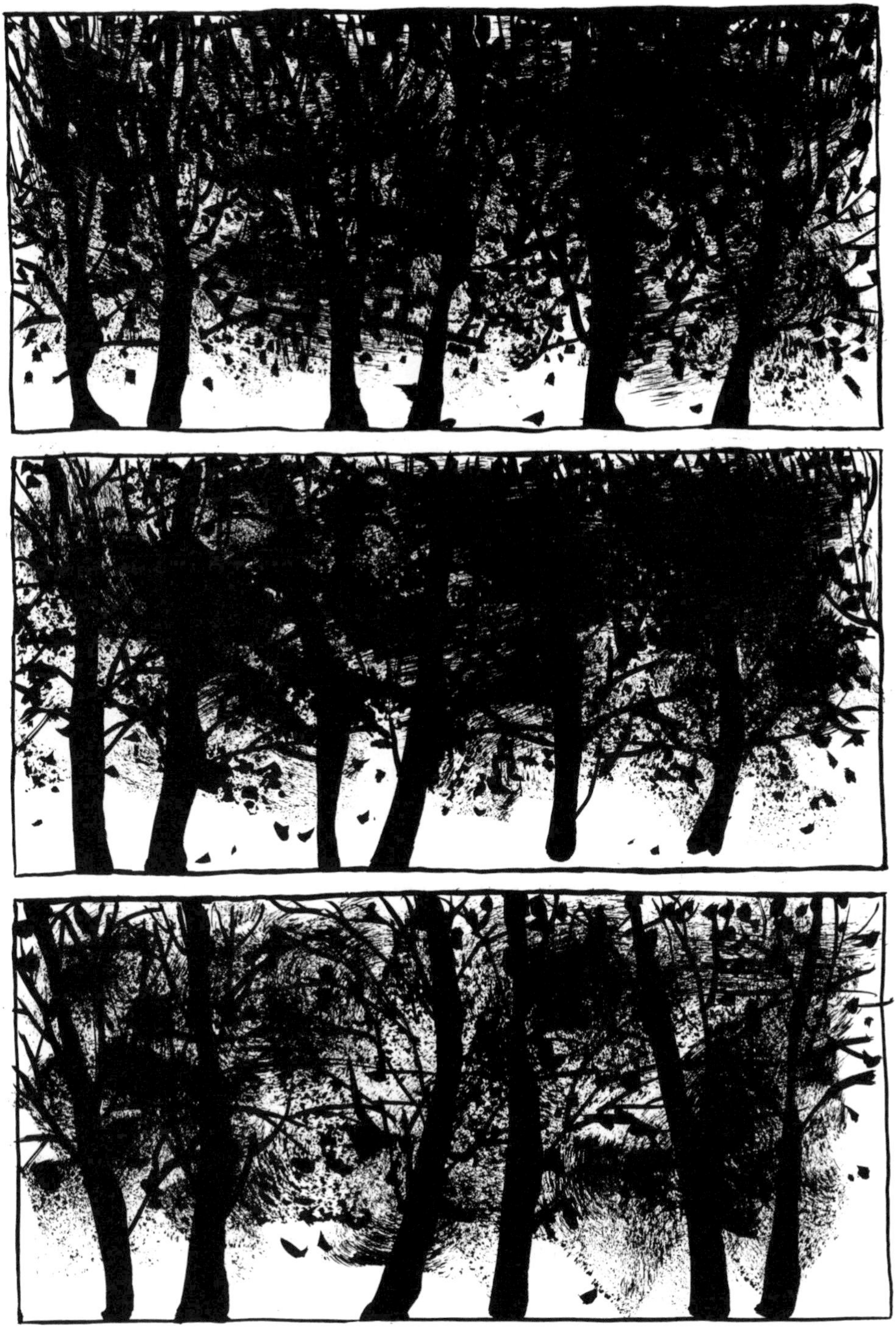

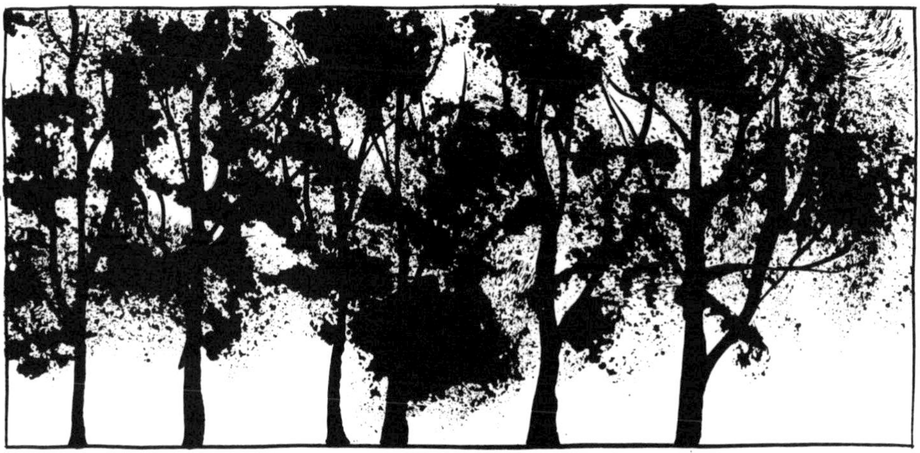
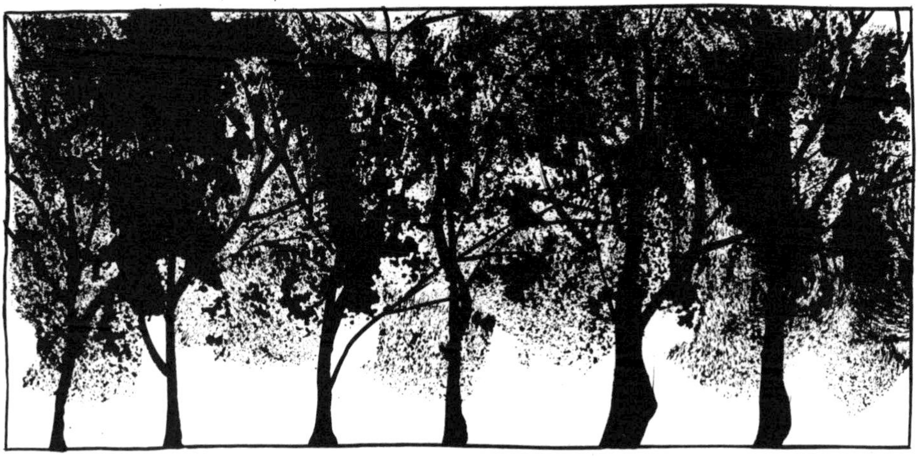
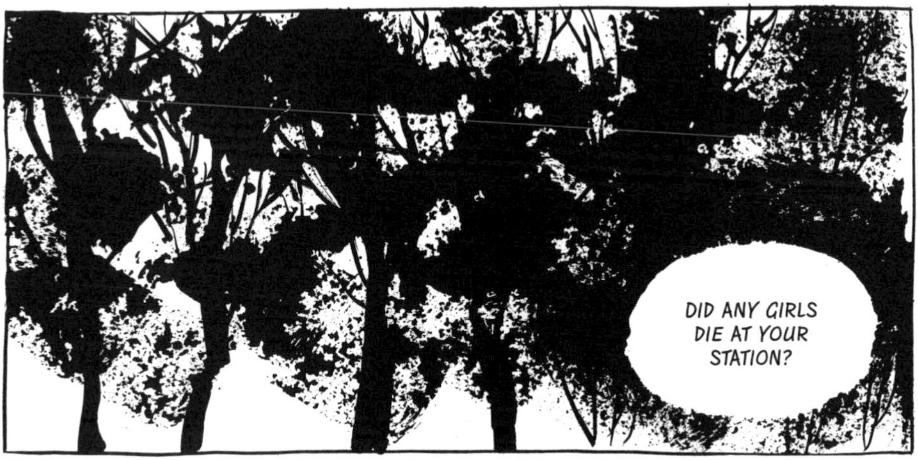
DID ANY GIRLS
DIE AT YOUR
STATION?

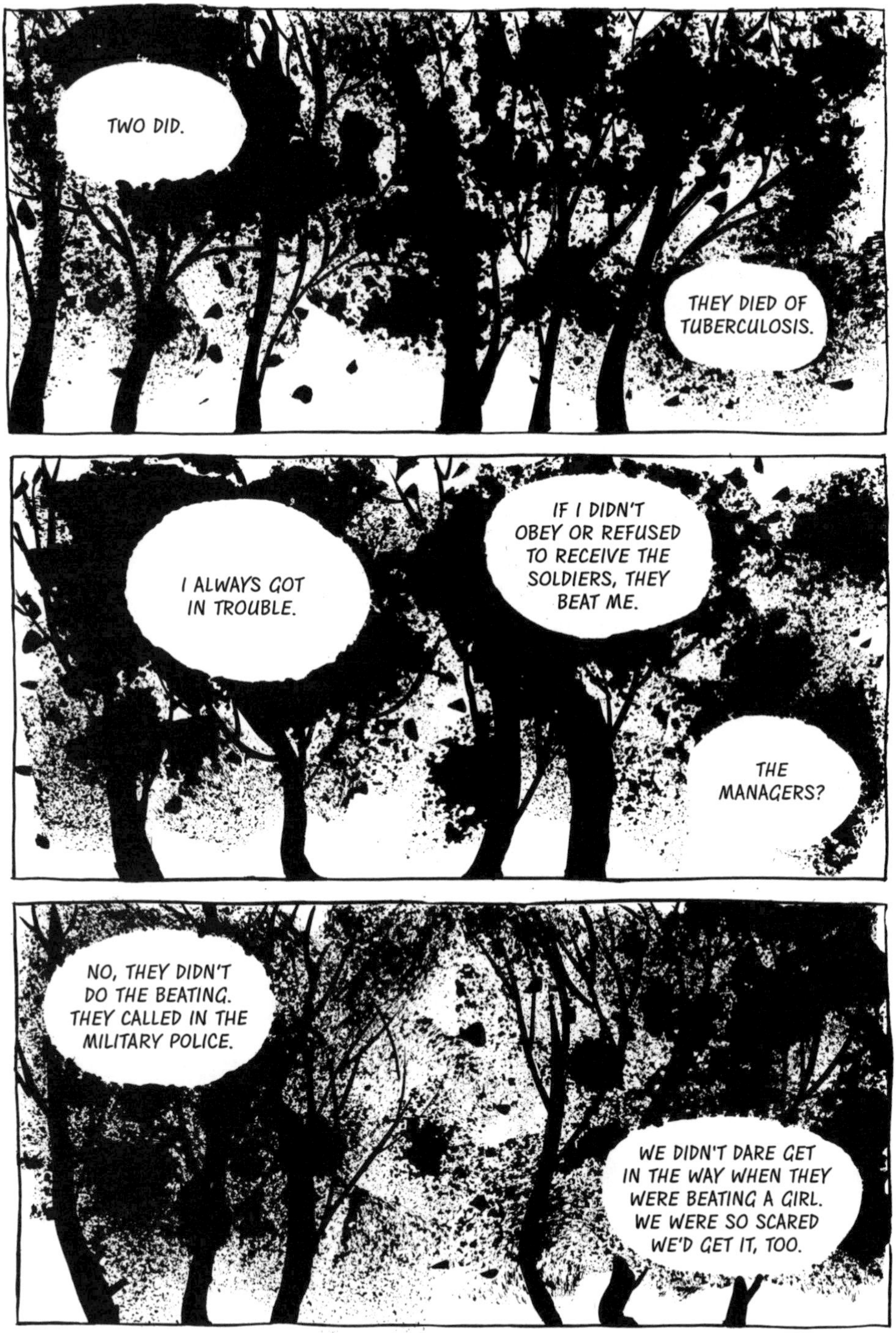
TWO DID.
THEY DIED OF TUBERCULOSIS.
I ALWAYS GOT IN TROUBLE.
IF I DIDN'T OBEY OR REFUSED TO RECEIVE THE SOLDIERS, THEY BEAT ME.
THE MANAGERS?
NO, THEY DIDN'T DO THE BEATING. THEY CALLED IN THE MILITARY POLICE.
WE DIDN'T DARE GET IN THE WAY WHEN THEY WERE BEATING A GIRL. WE WERE SO SCARED WE'D GET IT, TOO.

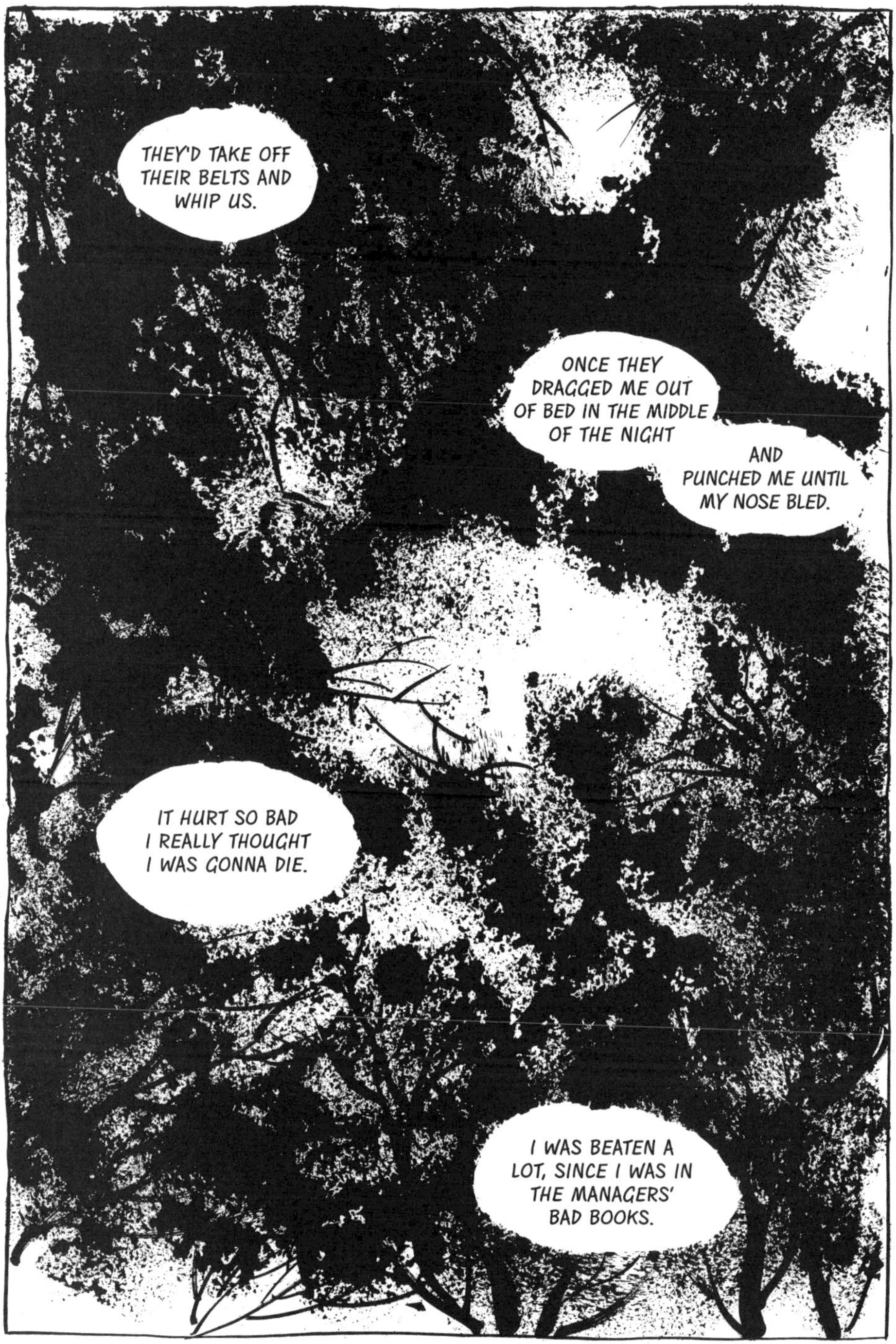
THEY'D TAKE OFF THEIR BELTS AND WHIP US.
ONCE THEY DRAGGED ME OUT OF BED IN THE MIDDLE OF THE NIGHT
AND PUNCHED ME UNTIL MY NOSE BLED.
IT HURT SO BAD I REALLY THOUGHT I WAS GONNA DIE.
I WAS BEATEN A LOT, SINCE I WAS IN THE MANAGERS' BAD BOOKS.

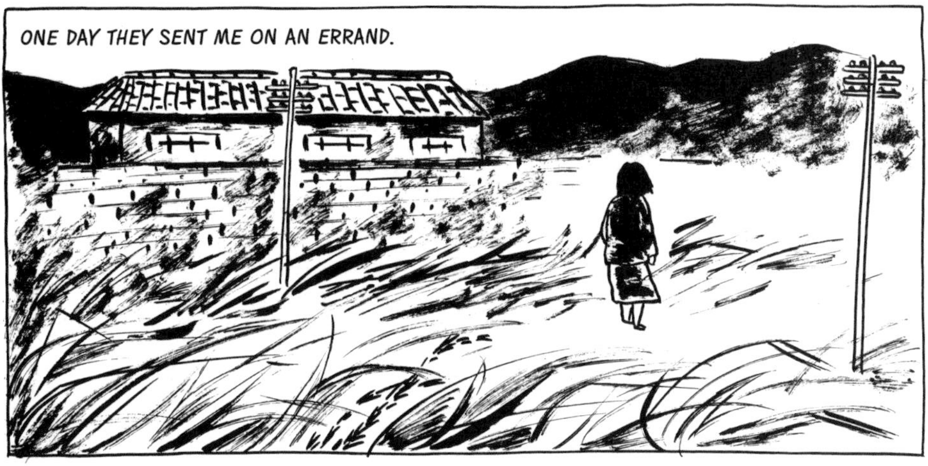
ONE DAY THEY SENT ME ON AN ERRAND.

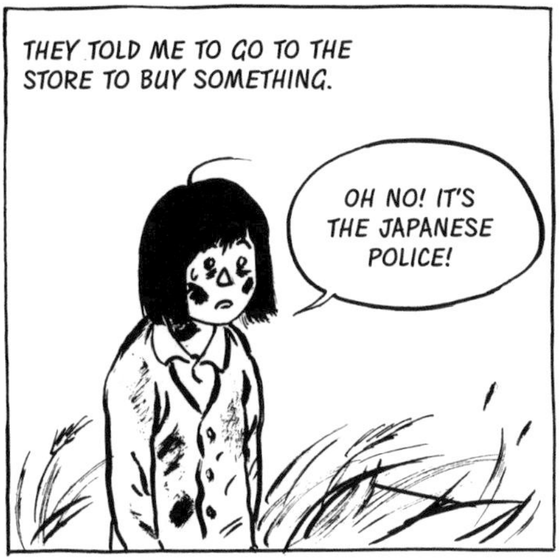
THEY TOLD ME TO GO TO THE STORE TO BUY SOMETHING.
OH NO! IT'S THE JAPANESE POLICE!

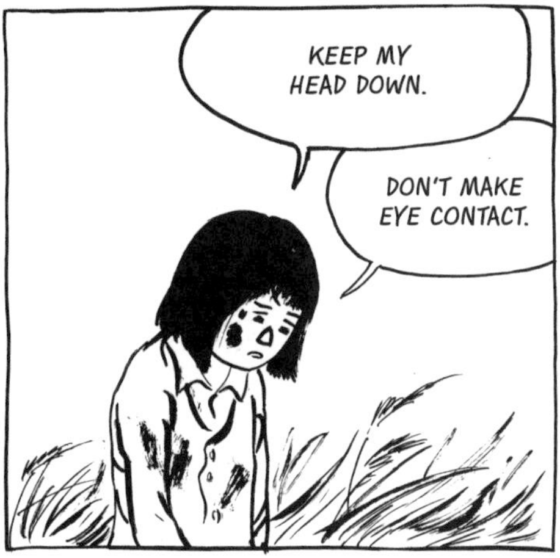
KEEP MY HEAD DOWN.
DON'T MAKE EYE CONTACT.

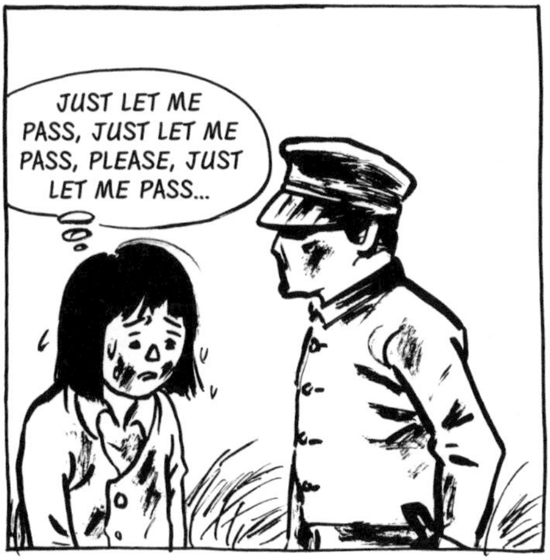
JUST LET ME PASS, JUST LET ME PASS, PLEASE, JUST LET ME PASS...

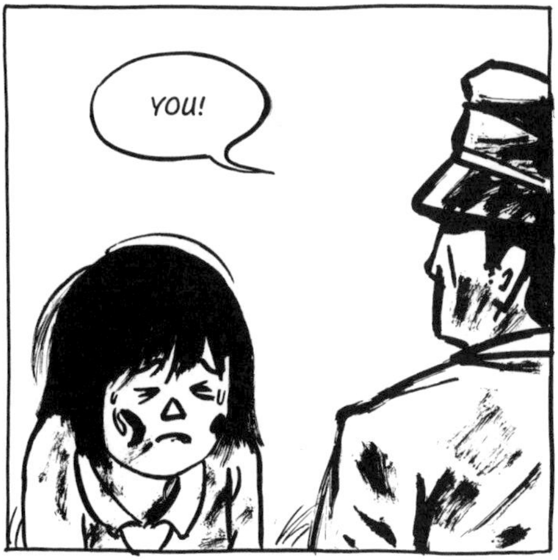
YOU!

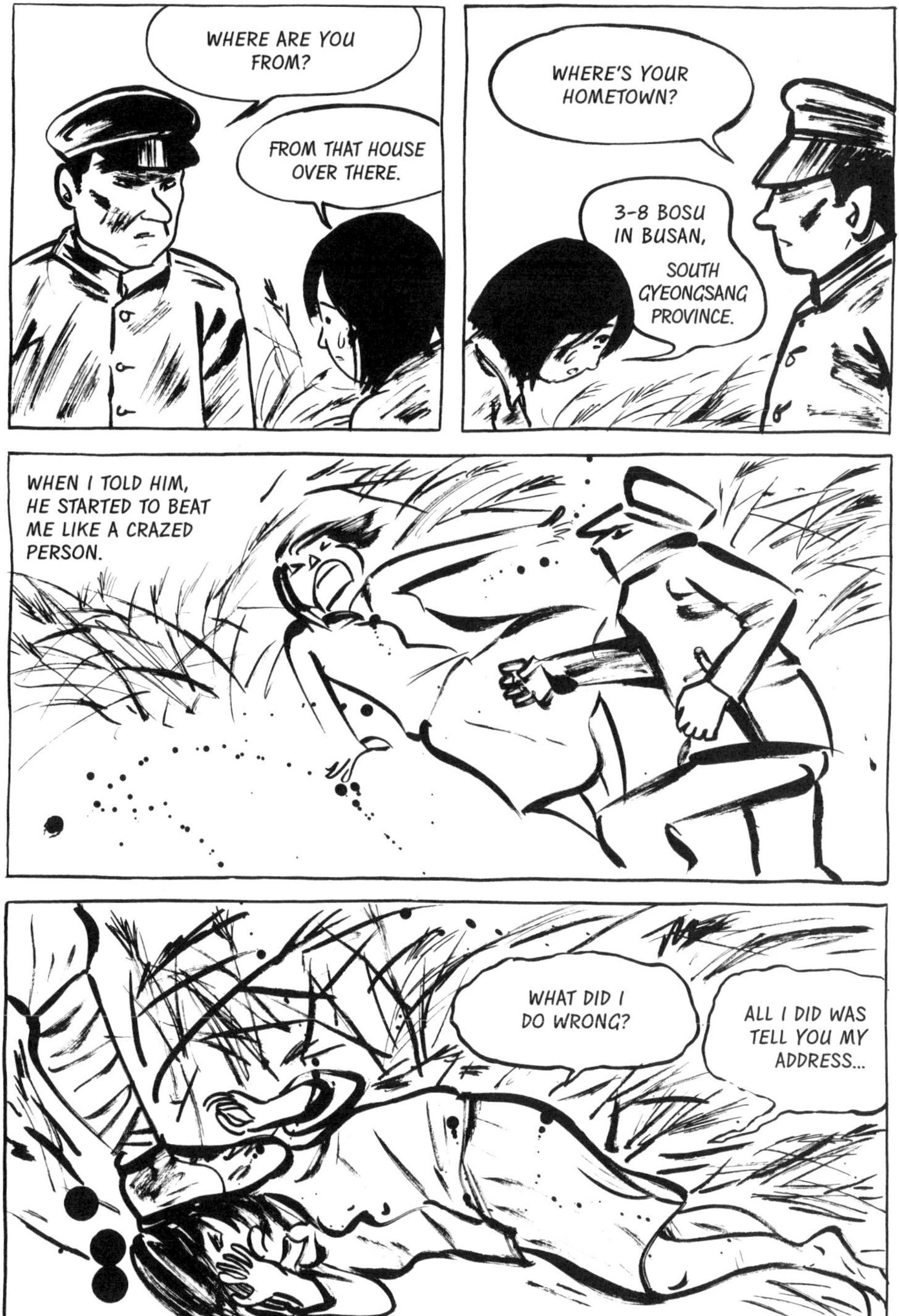
WHERE ARE YOU FROM?
FROM THAT HOUSE OVER THERE.
WHERE'S YOUR HOMETOWN?
3-8 BOSU IN BUSAN,
SOUTH GYEONGSANG PROVINCE.
WHEN I TOLD HIM, HE STARTED TO BEAT ME LIKE A CRAZED PERSON.
WHAT DID I DO WRONG?
ALL I DID WAS TELL YOU MY ADDRESS...

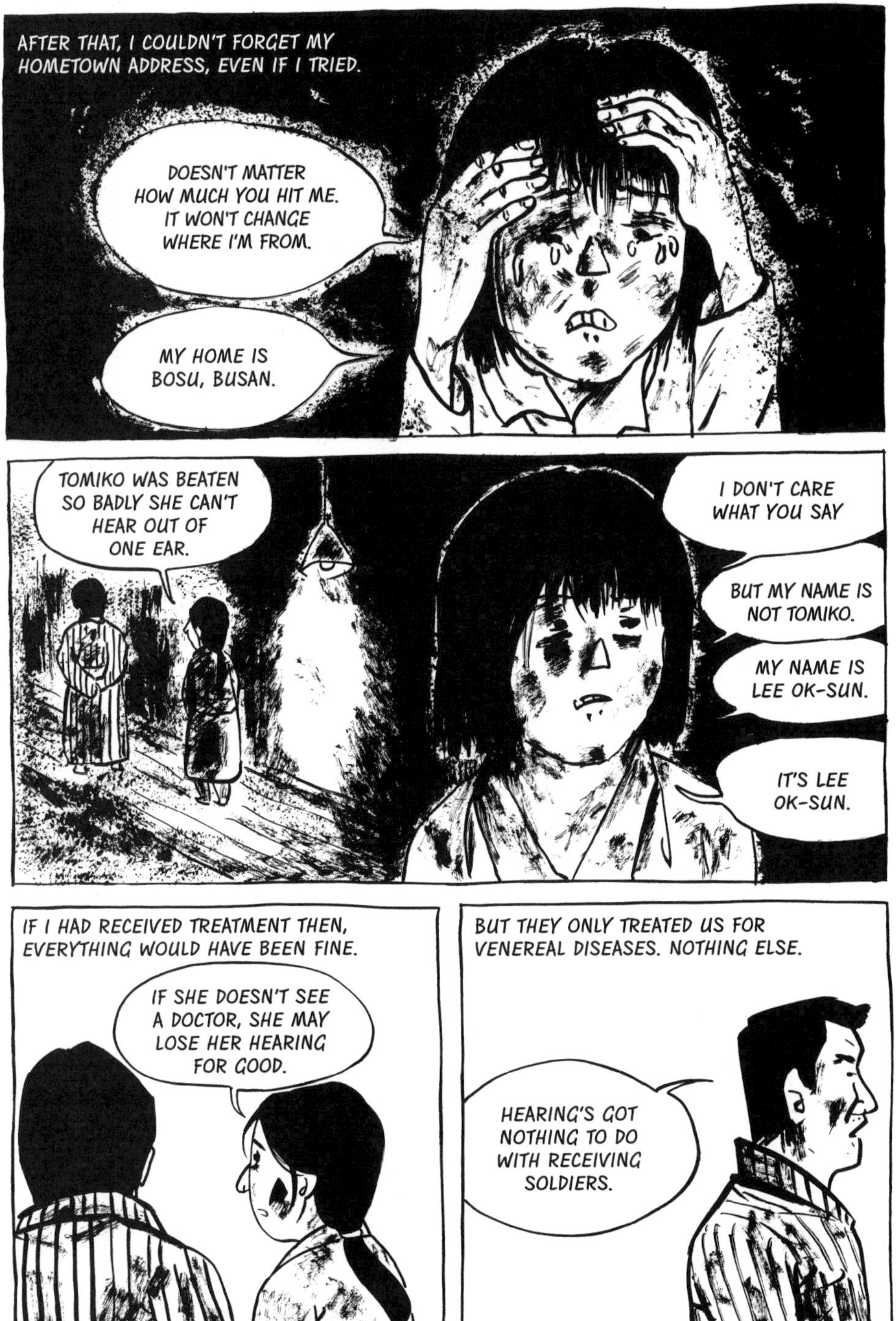
AFTER THAT, I COULDN'T FORGET MY HOMETOWN ADDRESS, EVEN IF I TRIED.
DOESN'T MATTER HOW MUCH YOU HIT ME. IT WON'T CHANGE WHERE I'M FROM.
MY HOME IS BOSU, BUSAN.
TOMIKO WAS BEATEN SO BADLY SHE CAN'T HEAR OUT OF ONE EAR.
I DON'T CARE WHAT YOU SAY
BUT MY NAME IS NOT TOMIKO.
MY NAME IS LEE OK-SUN.
IT'S LEE OK-SUN.
IF I HAD RECEIVED TREATMENT THEN, EVERYTHING WOULD HAVE BEEN FINE.
IF SHE DOESN'T SEE A DOCTOR, SHE MAY LOSE HER HEARING FOR GOOD.
BUT THEY ONLY TREATED US FOR VENEREAL DISEASES. NOTHING ELSE.
HEARING'S GOT NOTHING TO DO WITH RECEIVING SOLDIERS.

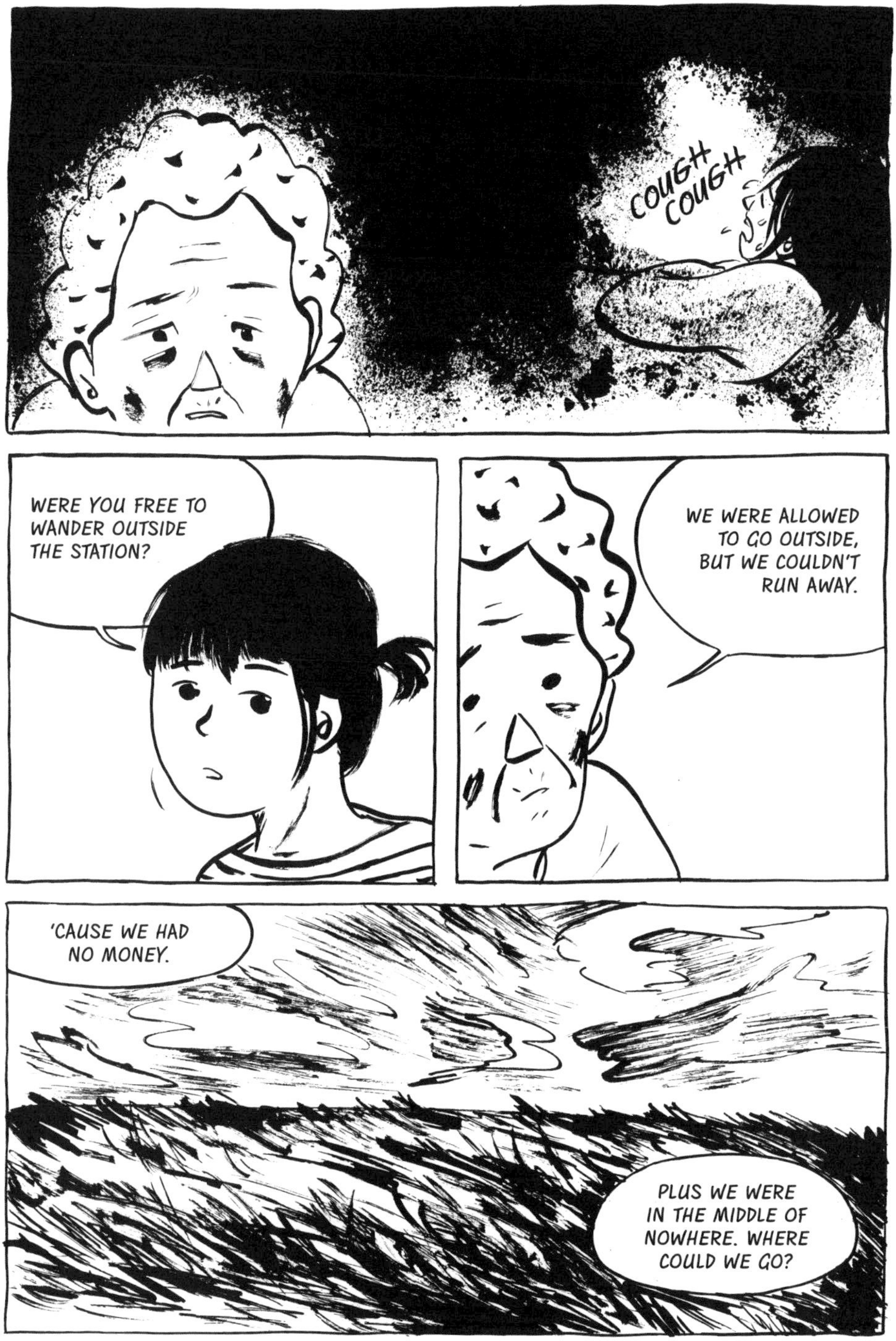
COUGH
COUGH
WERE YOU FREE TO WANDER OUTSIDE THE STATION?
WE WERE ALLOWED TO GO OUTSIDE, BUT WE COULDN'T RUN AWAY.
'CAUSE WE HAD NO MONEY.
PLUS WE WERE IN THE MIDDLE OF NOWHERE. WHERE COULD WE GO?

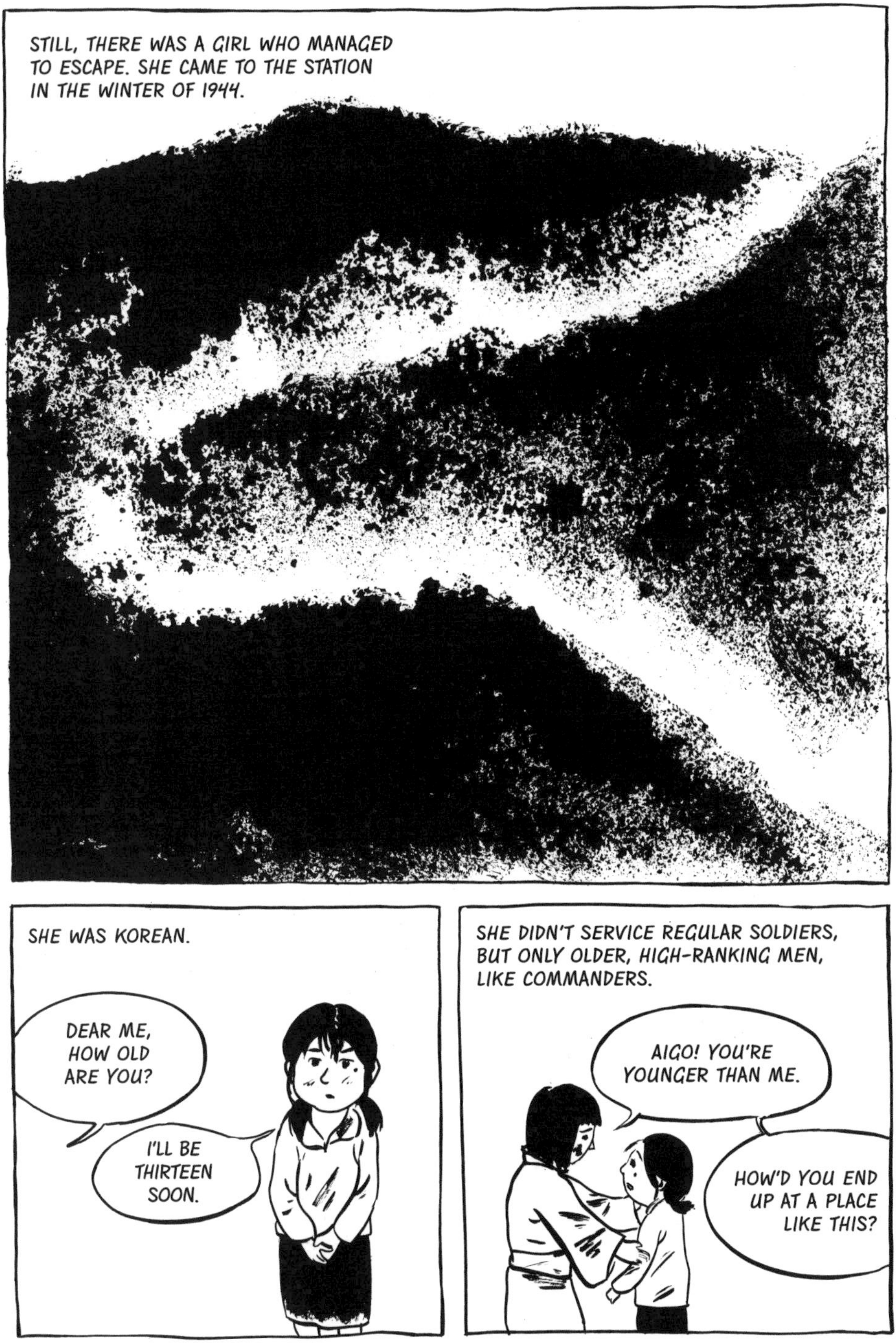
STILL, THERE WAS A GIRL WHO MANAGED TO ESCAPE. SHE CAME TO THE STATION IN THE WINTER OF 1944.
SHE WAS KOREAN.
DEAR ME, HOW OLD ARE YOU?
I'LL BE THIRTEEN SOON.
SHE DIDN'T SERVICE REGULAR SOLDIERS, BUT ONLY OLDER, HIGH-RANKING MEN, LIKE COMMANDERS.
AIGO! YOU'RE YOUNGER THAN ME.
HOW'D YOU END UP AT A PLACE LIKE THIS?

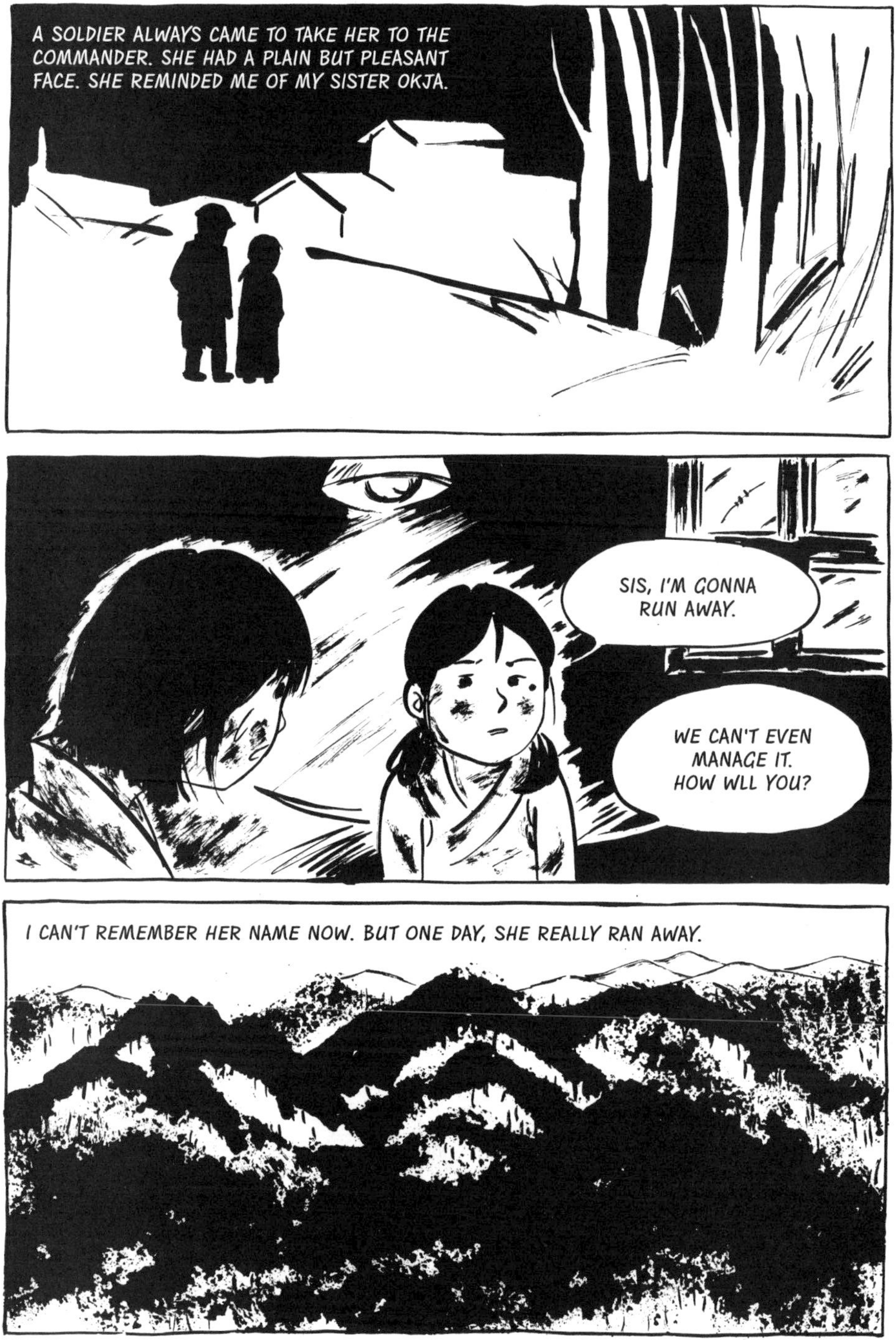
A SOLDIER ALWAYS CAME TO TAKE HER TO THE COMMANDER. SHE HAD A PLAIN BUT PLEASANT FACE. SHE REMINDED ME OF MY SISTER OKJA.
SIS, I'M GONNA RUN AWAY.
WE CAN'T EVEN MANAGE IT. HOW WLL YOU?
I CAN'T REMEMBER HER NAME NOW. BUT ONE DAY, SHE REALLY RAN AWAY.

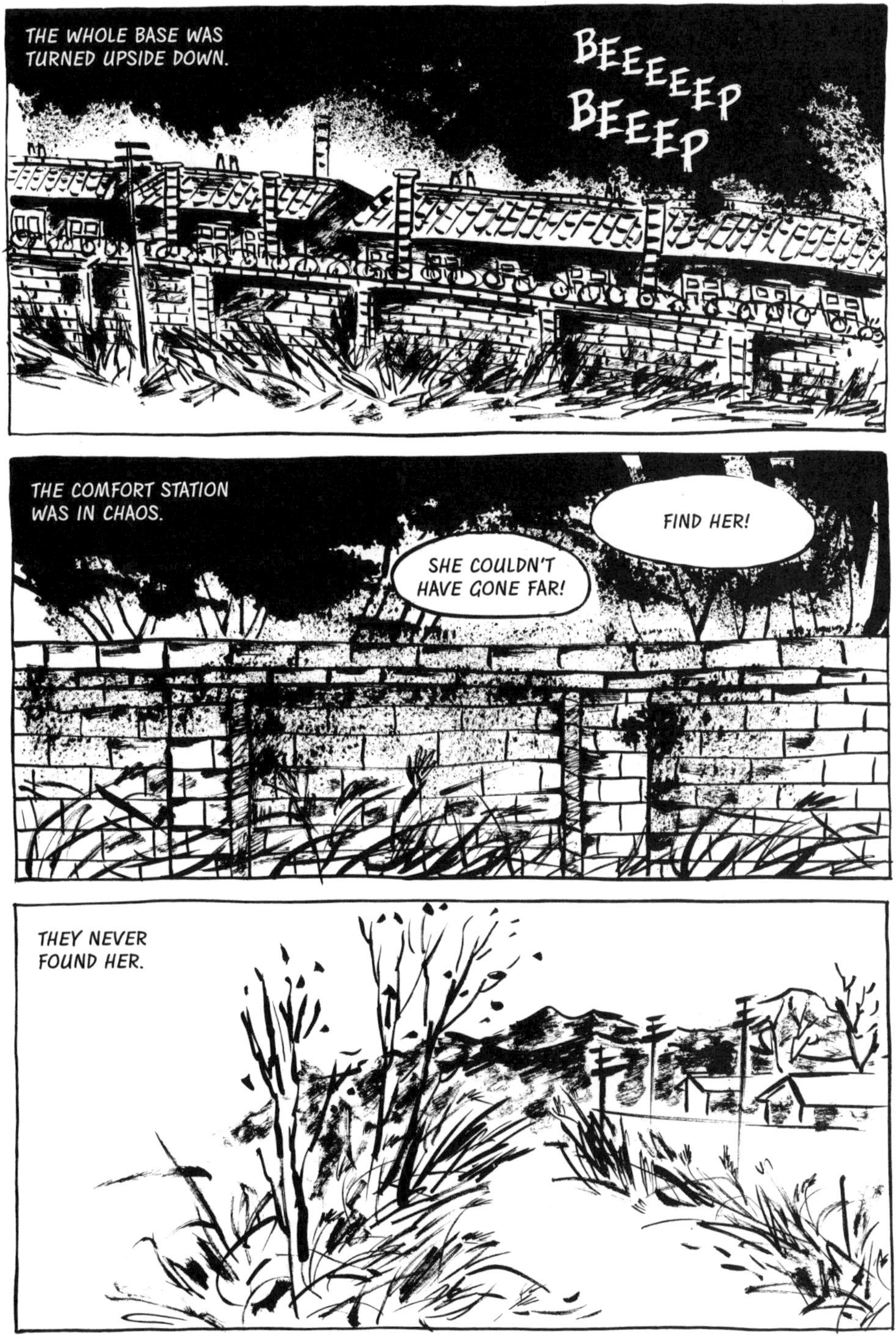
THE WHOLE BASE WAS TURNED UPSIDE DOWN.
BEEEEEP BEEEP
THE COMFORT STATION WAS IN CHAOS.
FIND HER!
SHE COULDN'T HAVE GONE FAR!
THEY NEVER FOUND HER.

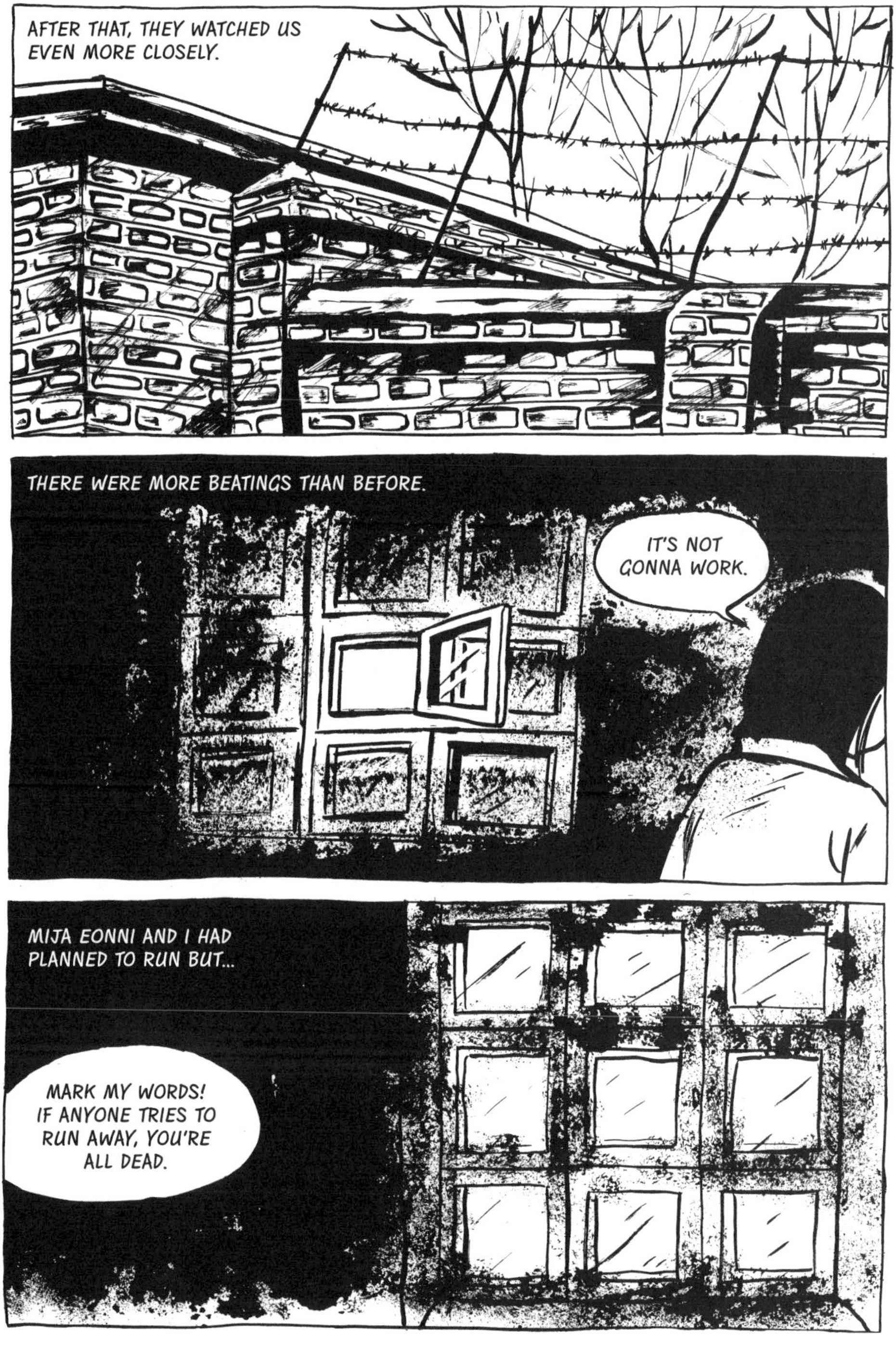
AFTER THAT, THEY WATCHED US EVEN MORE CLOSELY.
THERE WERE MORE BEATINGS THAN BEFORE.
IT'S NOT GONNA WORK.
MIJA EONNI AND I HAD PLANNED TO RUN BUT...
MARK MY WORDS! IF ANYONE TRIES TO RUN AWAY, YOU'RE ALL DEAD.

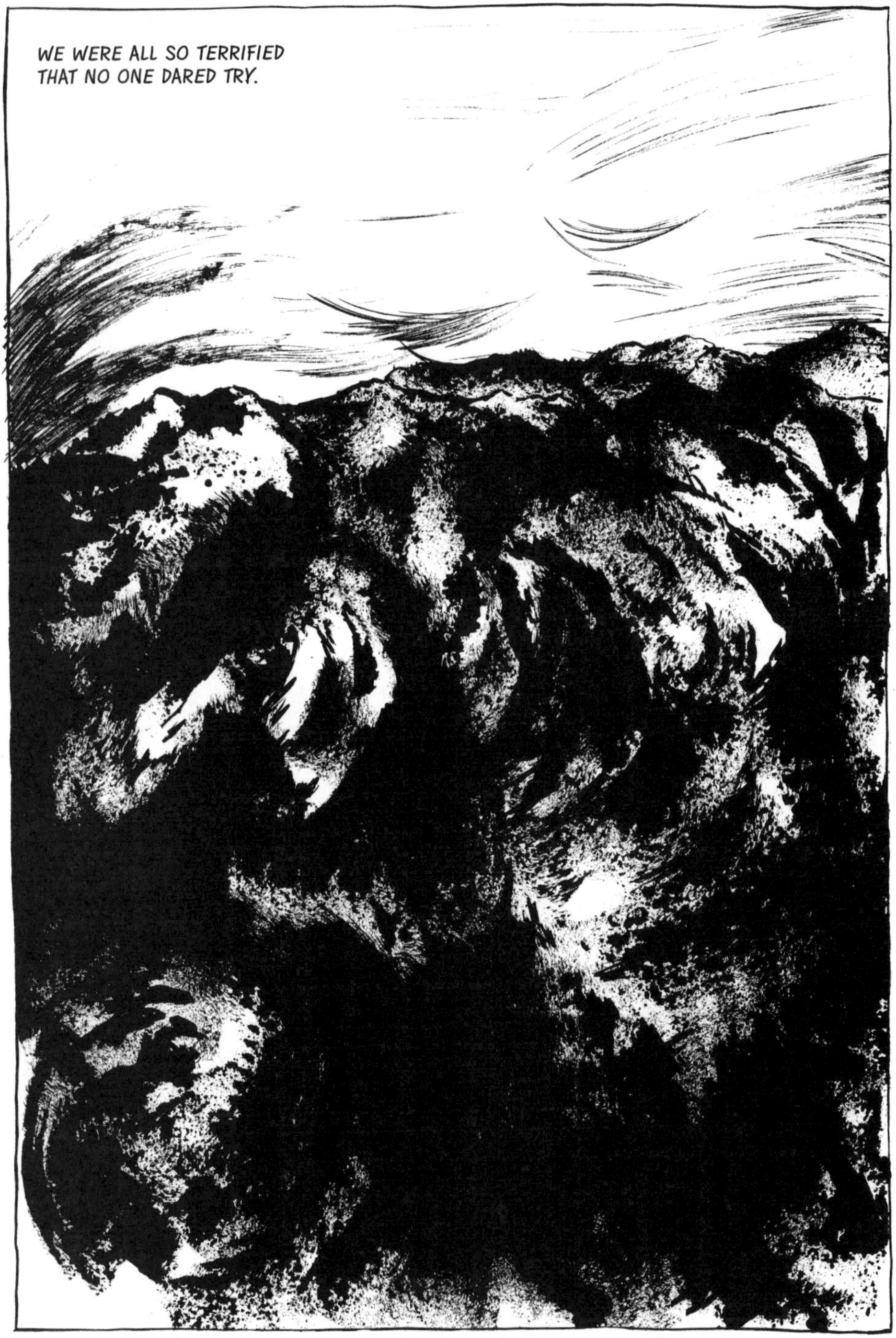
WE WERE ALL SO TERRIFIED
THAT NO ONE DARED TRY.

WHILE YOU WERE AT THE STATION, WAS THERE A SOLDIER WHO LOVED YOU? OR SOMEONE YOU HAD FEELINGS FOR?

I HAD READ AN ACCOUNT BY MOON OKJU* THAT LED ME TO BELIEVE SOMETHING LIKE THIS COULD HAPPEN.

THE TERM "LOVE" MIGHT BE INAPPROPRIATE HERE. WHEN YOU LAND IN HELL, YOU NEED THE WILL TO SURVIVE.

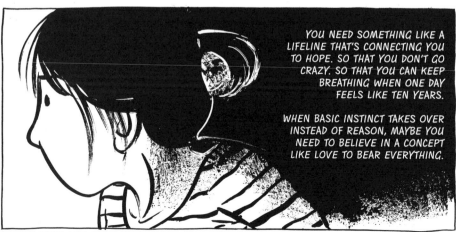

YOU NEED SOMETHING LIKE A LIFELINE THAT'S CONNECTING YOU TO HOPE. SO THAT YOU DON'T GO CRAZY. SO THAT YOU CAN KEEP BREATHING WHEN ONE DAY FEELS LIKE TEN YEARS.

WHEN BASIC INSTINCT TAKES OVER INSTEAD OF REASON, MAYBE YOU NEED TO BELIEVE IN A CONCEPT LIKE LOVE TO BEAR EVERYTHING.

*MOON OKJU WAS BORN IN DAEGU IN 1924. SHE WAS TAKEN TO HEILONGJIANG IN 1940 AND PRESENT-DAY MYANMAR IN 1942 TO SERVE AS A COMFORT WOMAN.

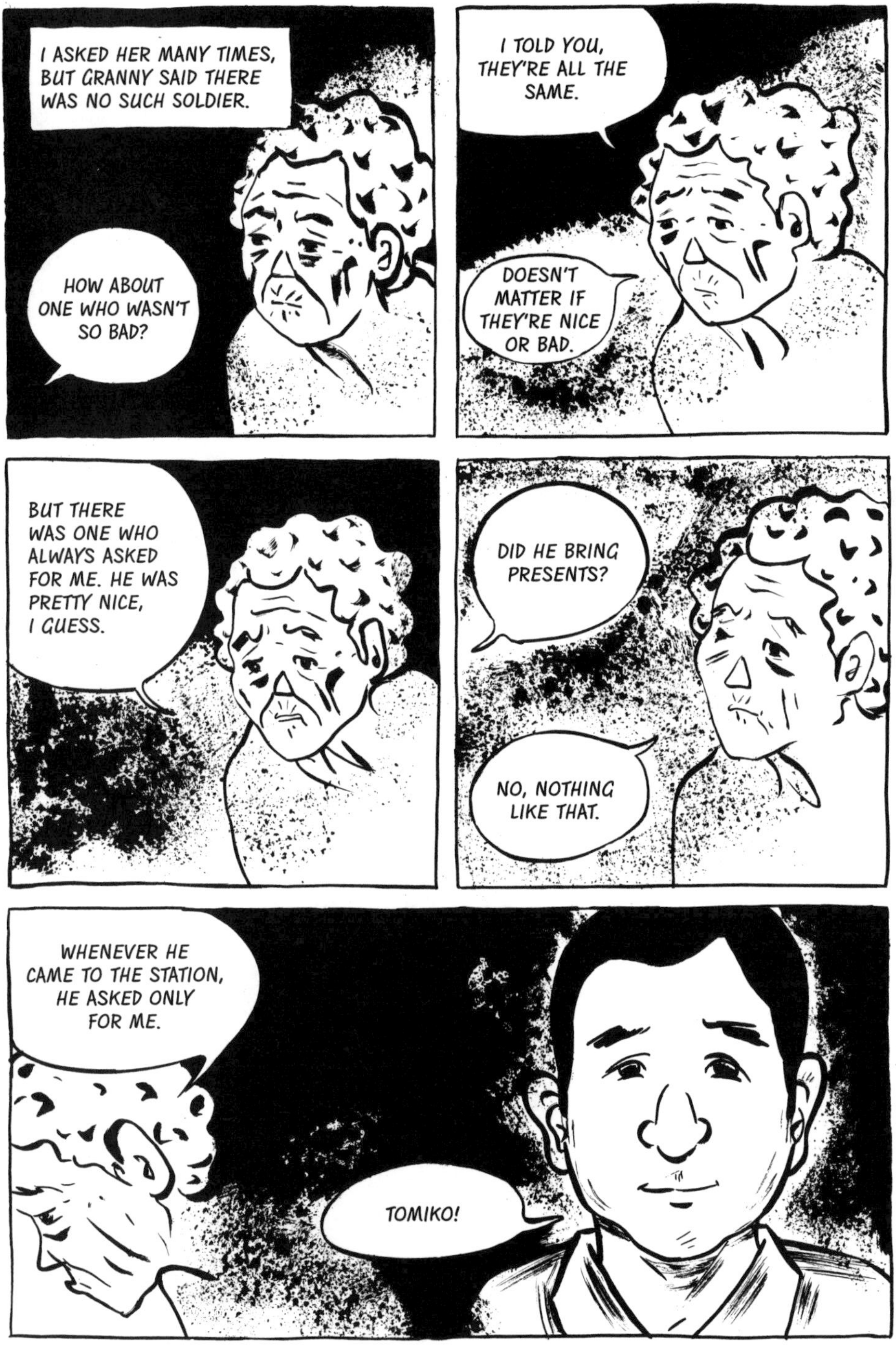
I ASKED HER MANY TIMES, BUT GRANNY SAID THERE WAS NO SUCH SOLDIER.
HOW ABOUT ONE WHO WASN'T SO BAD?
I TOLD YOU, THEY'RE ALL THE SAME.
DOESN'T MATTER IF THEY'RE NICE OR BAD.
BUT THERE WAS ONE WHO ALWAYS ASKED FOR ME. HE WAS PRETTY NICE, I GUESS.
DID HE BRING PRESENTS?
NO, NOTHING LIKE THAT.
WHENEVER HE CAME TO THE STATION, HE ASKED ONLY FOR ME.
TOMIKO!

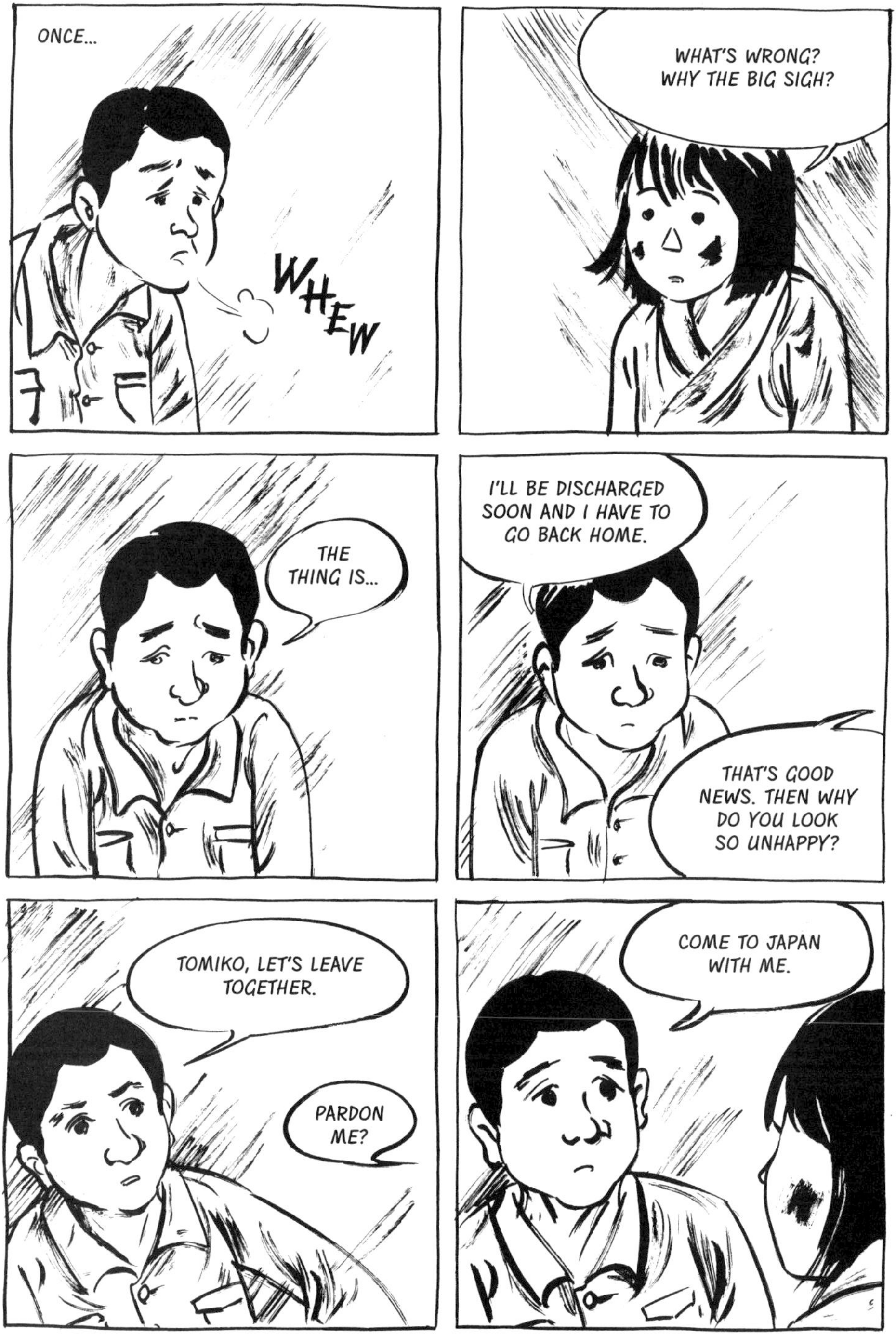
ONCE...
WHEW
WHAT'S WRONG? WHY THE BIG SIGH?
THE THING IS...
I'LL BE DISCHARGED SOON AND I HAVE TO GO BACK HOME.
THAT'S GOOD NEWS. THEN WHY DO YOU LOOK SO UNHAPPY?
TOMIKO, LET'S LEAVE TOGETHER.
PARDON ME?
COME TO JAPAN WITH ME.

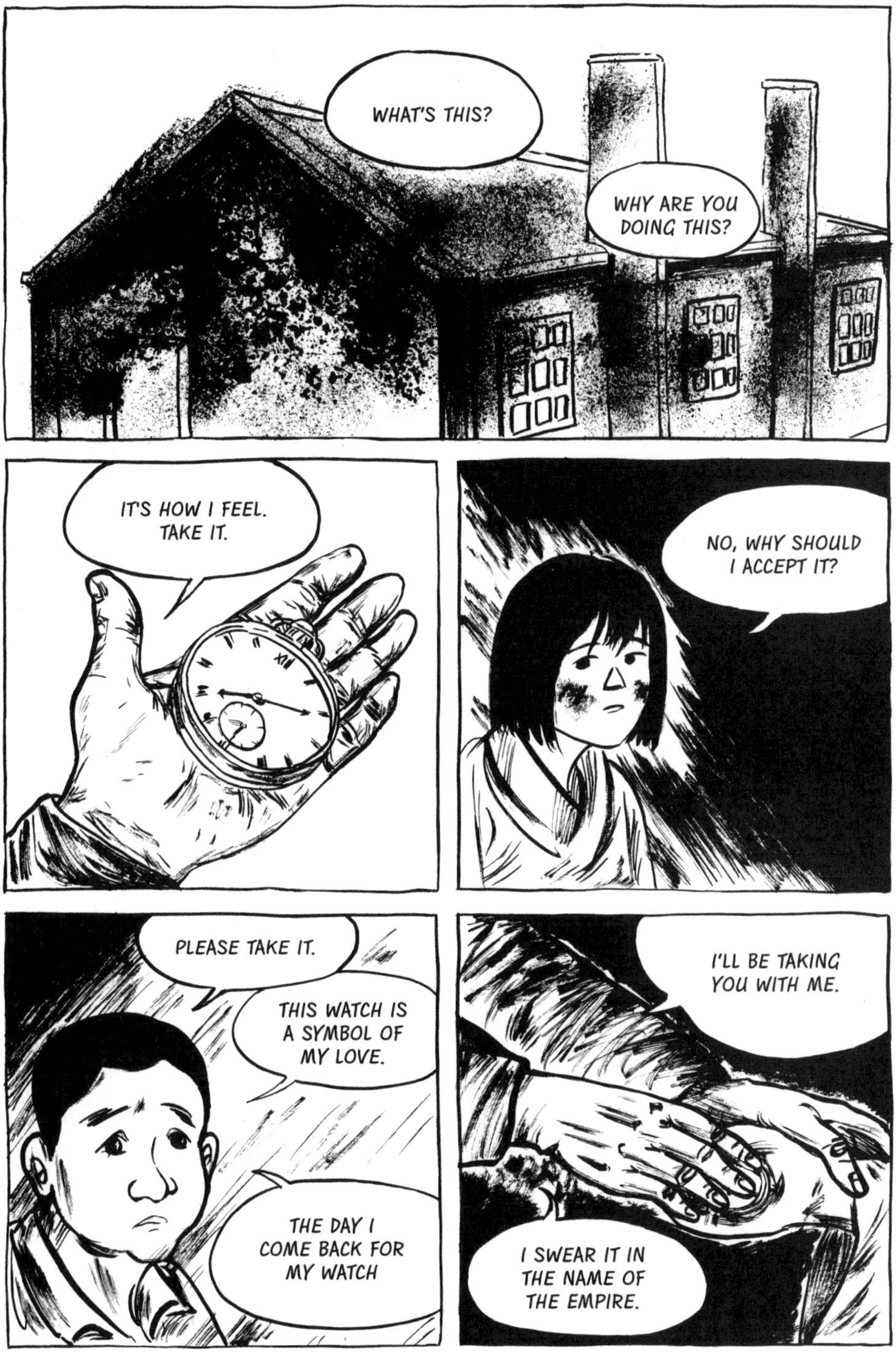
WHAT'S THIS?
WHY ARE YOU DOING THIS?
IT'S HOW I FEEL. TAKE IT.
NO, WHY SHOULD I ACCEPT IT?
PLEASE TAKE IT.
THIS WATCH IS A SYMBOL OF MY LOVE.
THE DAY I COME BACK FOR MY WATCH
I'LL BE TAKING YOU WITH ME.
I SWEAR IT IN THE NAME OF THE EMPIRE.

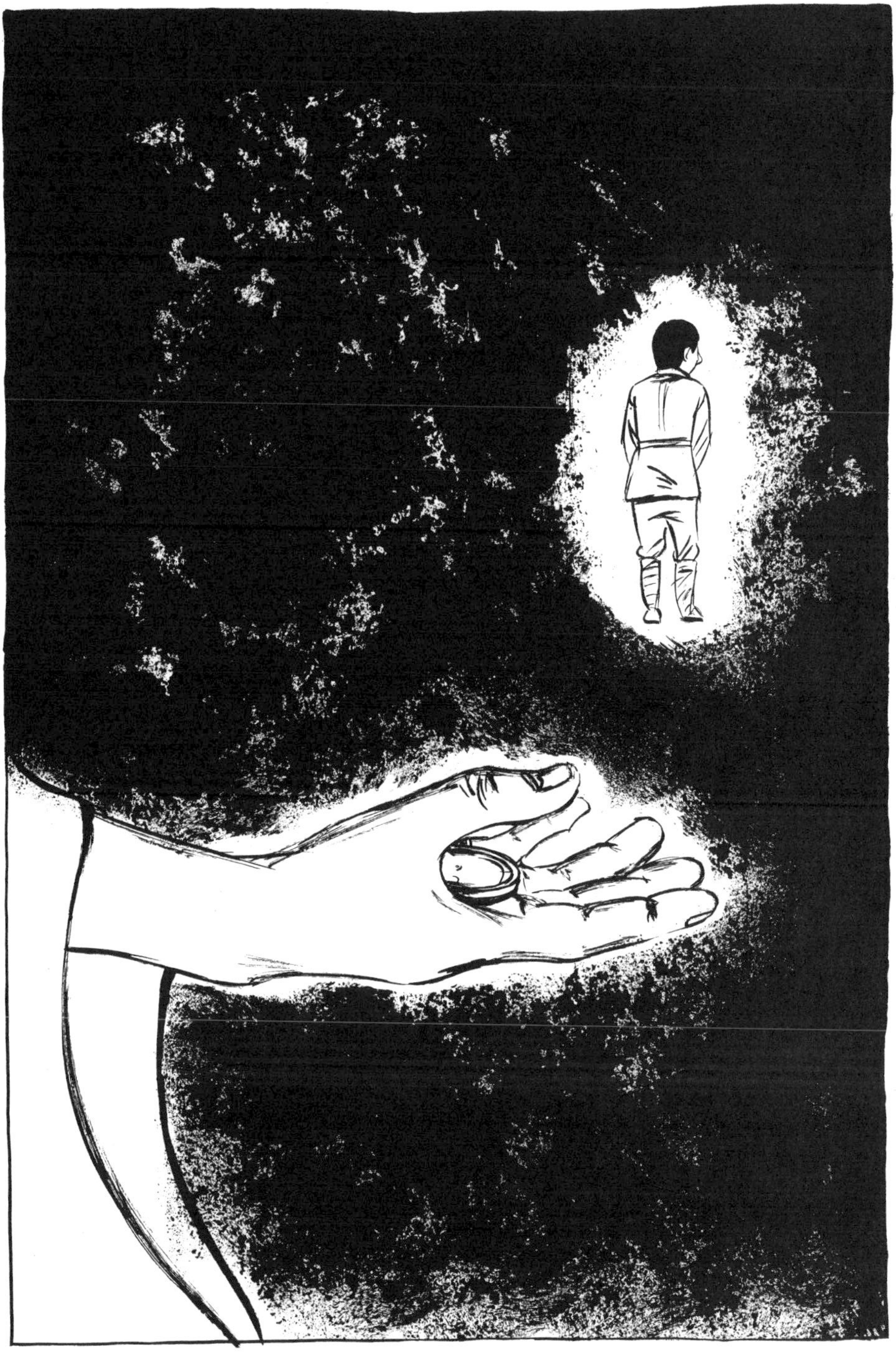

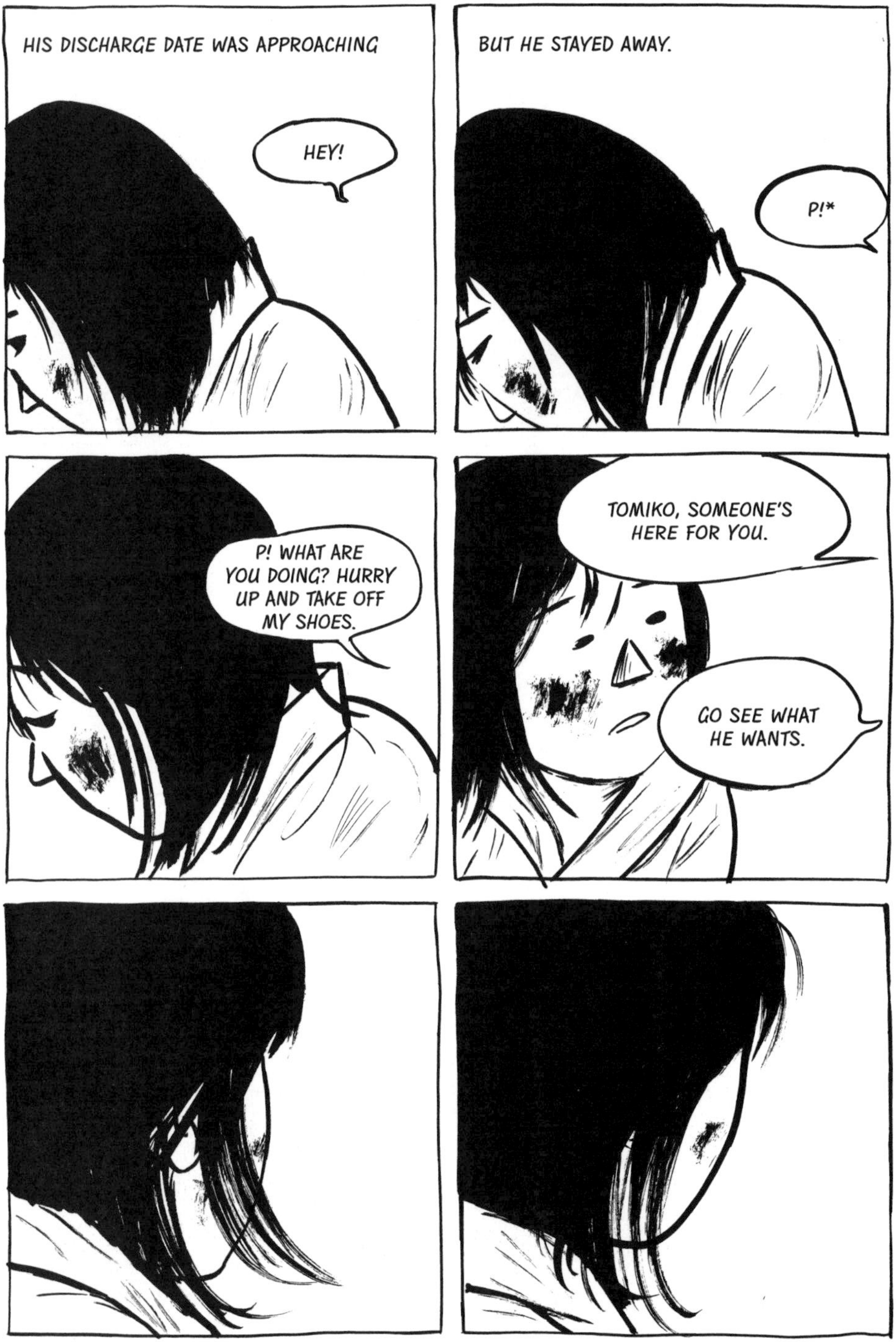
HIS DISCHARGE DATE WAS APPROACHING
HEY!
BUT HE STAYED AWAY.
P!*
P! WHAT ARE YOU DOING? HURRY UP AND TAKE OFF MY SHOES.
TOMIKO, SOMEONE'S HERE FOR YOU.
GO SEE WHAT HE WANTS.

*COMFORT WOMEN WERE SOMETIMES ADDRESSED AS P.

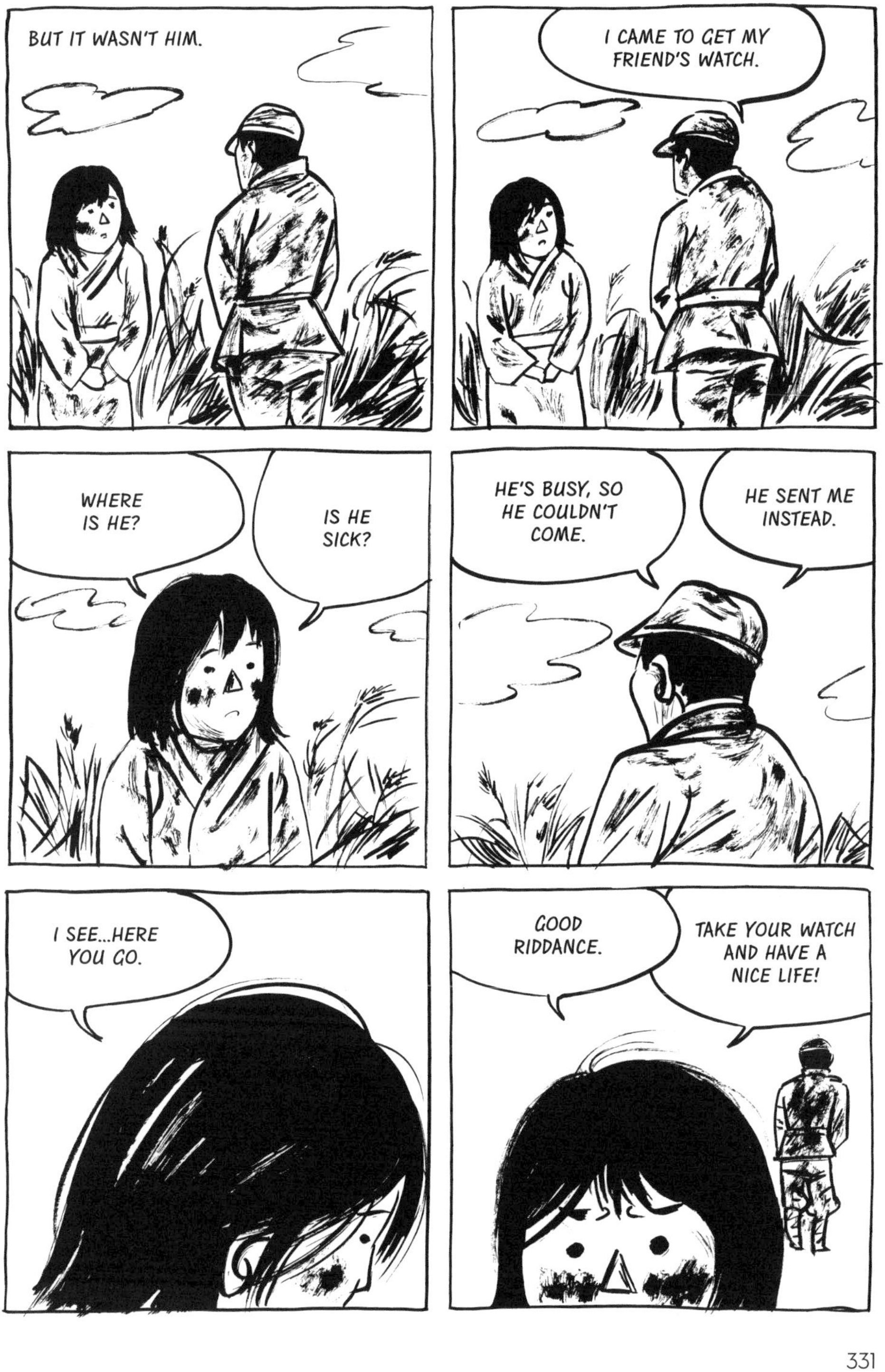
BUT IT WASN'T HIM.
I CAME TO GET MY FRIEND'S WATCH.
WHERE IS HE?
IS HE SICK?
HE'S BUSY, SO HE COULDN'T COME.
HE SENT ME INSTEAD.
I SEE...HERE YOU GO.
GOOD RIDDANCE.
TAKE YOUR WATCH AND HAVE A NICE LIFE!

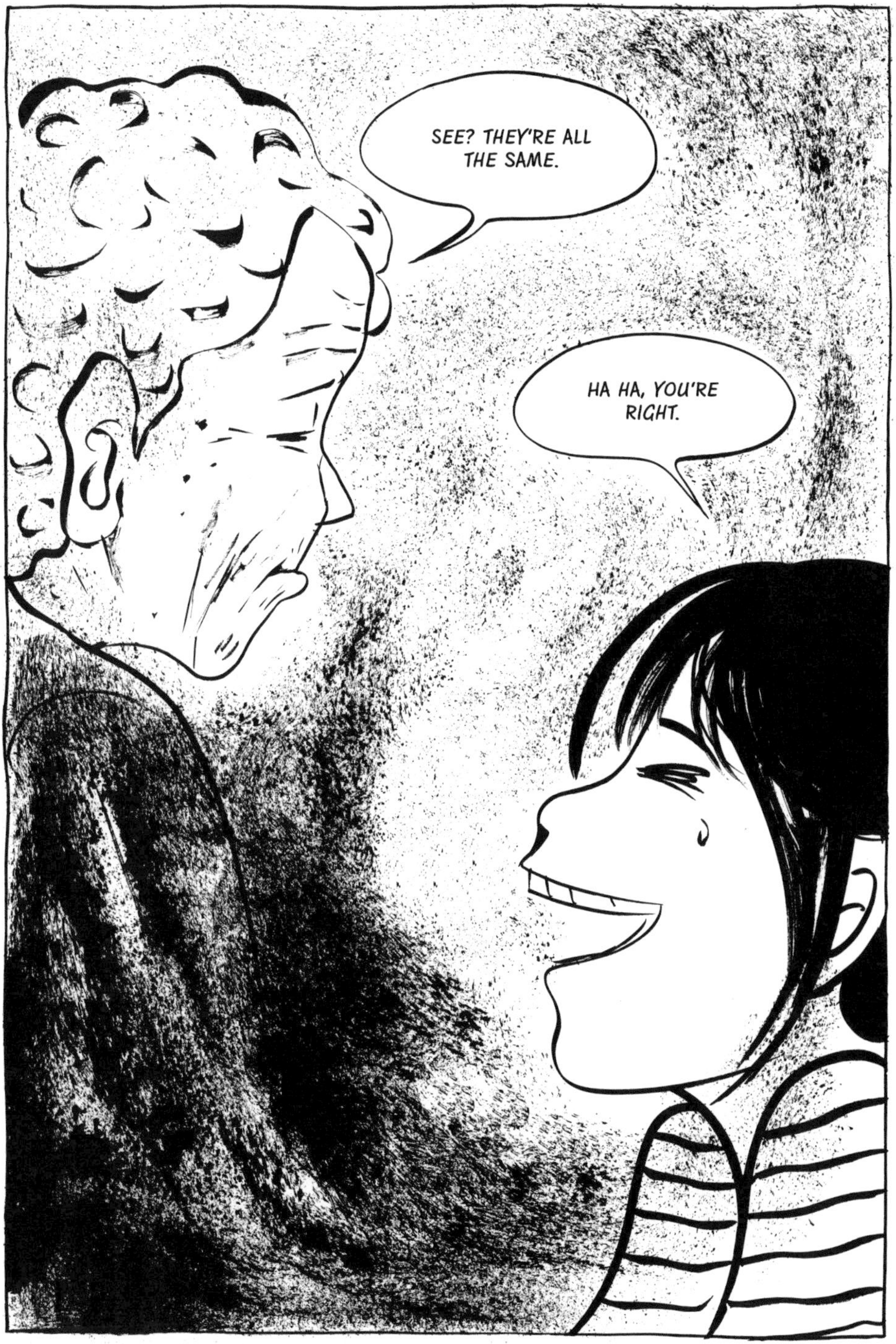
SEE? THEY'RE ALL THE SAME.
HA HA, YOU'RE RIGHT.

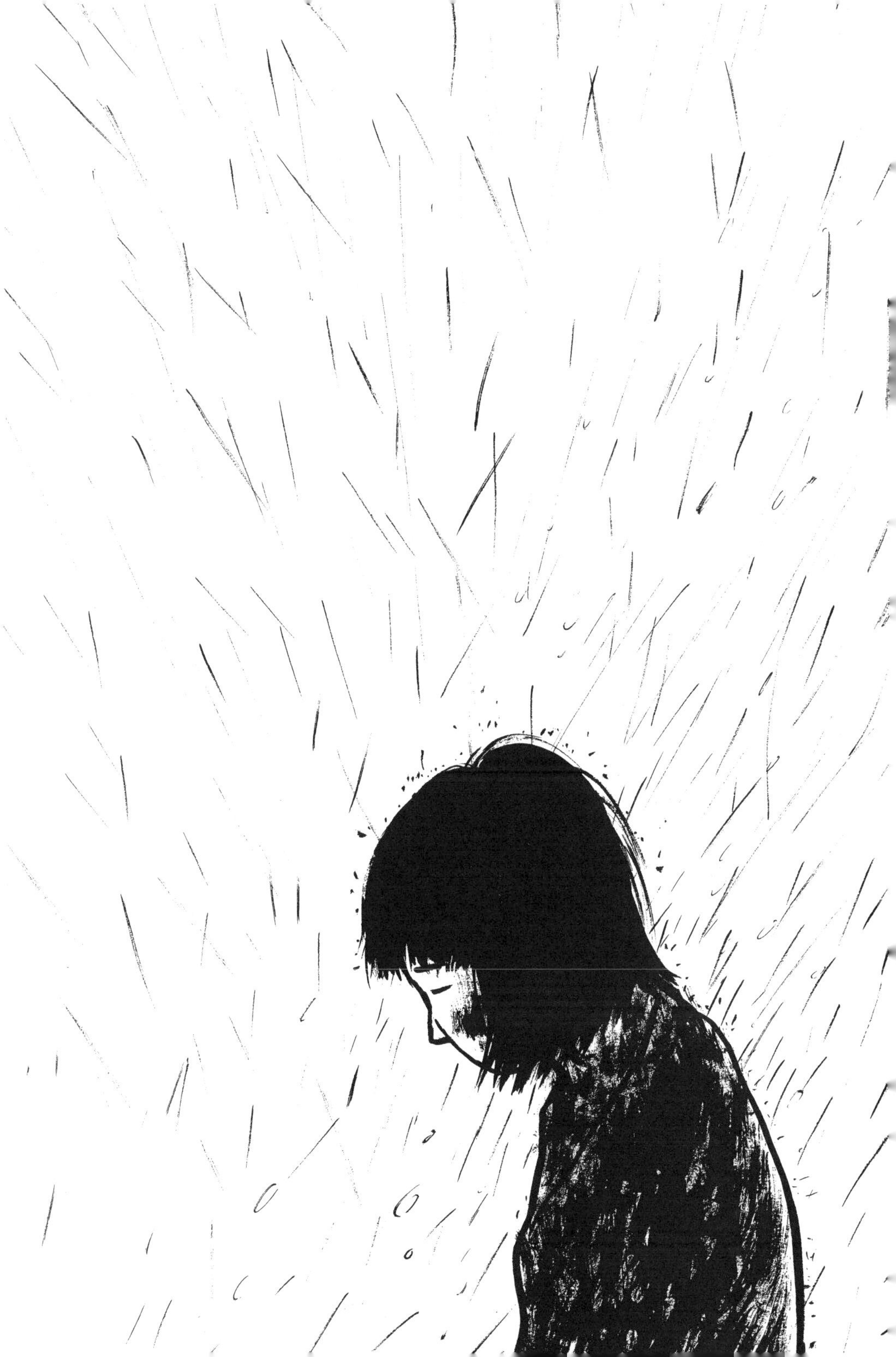

# LIBERATION AND
# THE ABANDONED GIRLS

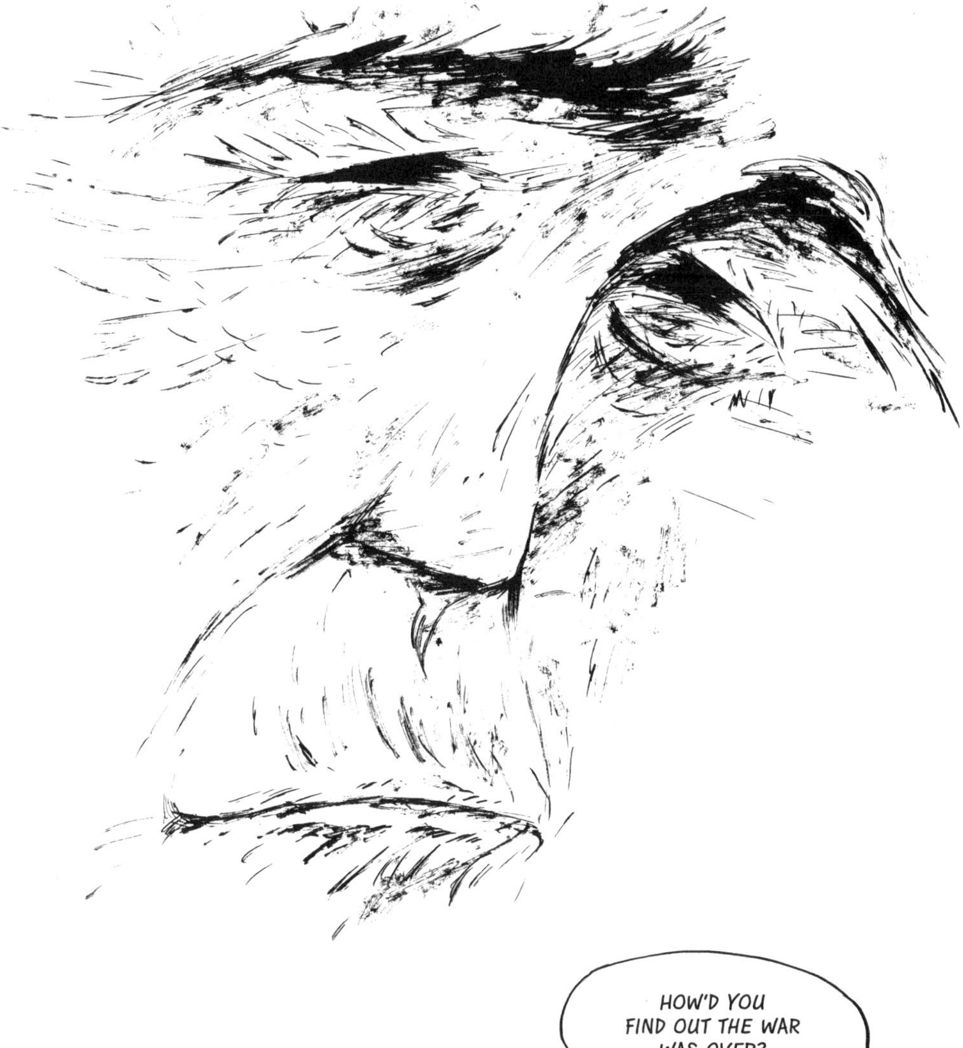
HOW'D YOU FIND OUT THE WAR WAS OVER?

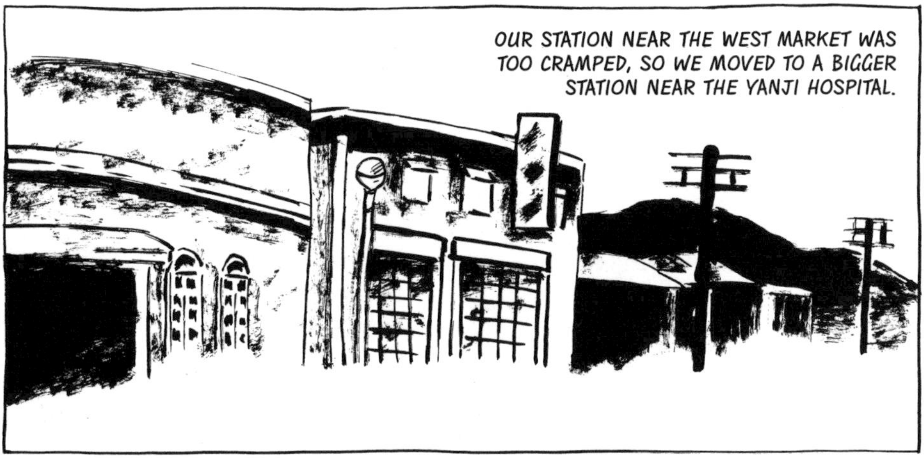
OUR STATION NEAR THE WEST MARKET WAS TOO CRAMPED, SO WE MOVED TO A BIGGER STATION NEAR THE YANJI HOSPITAL.

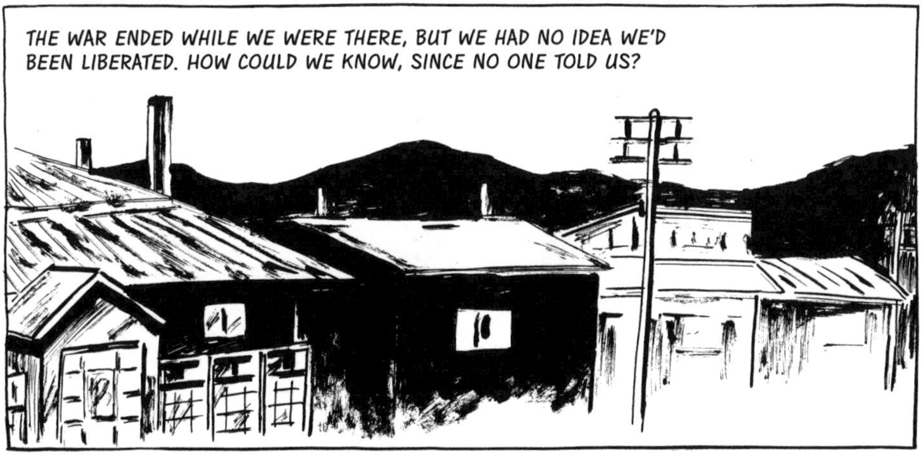
THE WAR ENDED WHILE WE WERE THERE, BUT WE HAD NO IDEA WE'D BEEN LIBERATED. HOW COULD WE KNOW, SINCE NO ONE TOLD US?

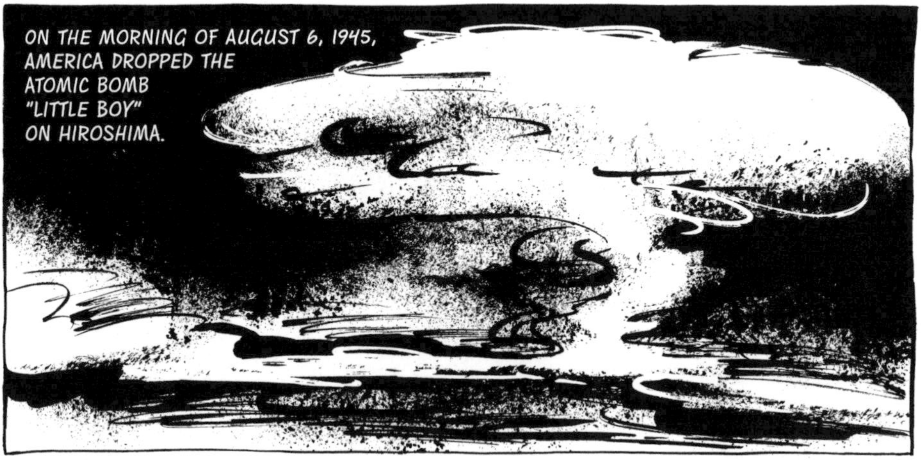
ON THE MORNING OF AUGUST 6, 1945, AMERICA DROPPED THE ATOMIC BOMB "LITTLE BOY" ON HIROSHIMA.

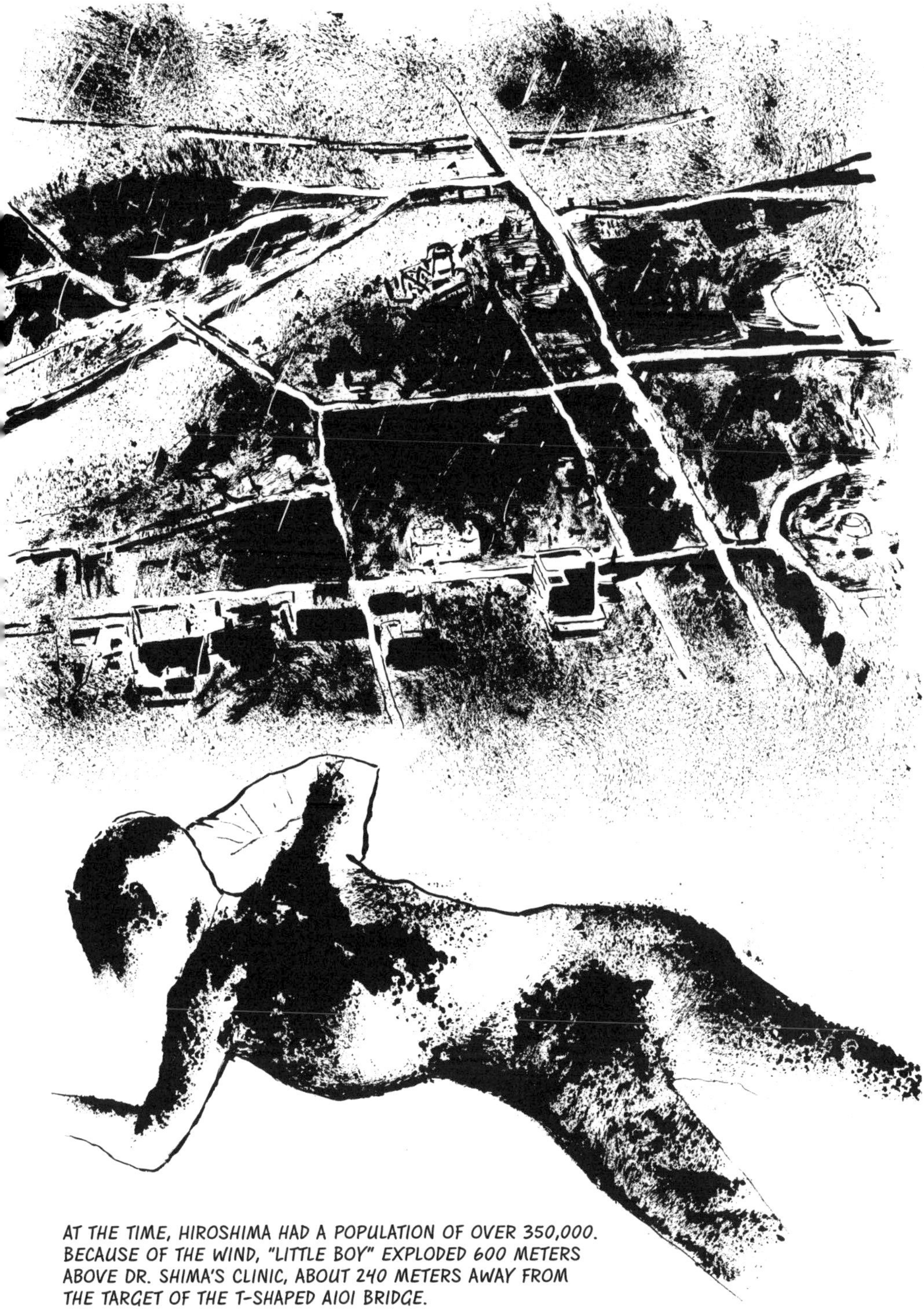

AT THE TIME, HIROSHIMA HAD A POPULATION OF OVER 350,000. BECAUSE OF THE WIND, "LITTLE BOY" EXPLODED 600 METERS ABOVE DR. SHIMA'S CLINIC, ABOUT 240 METERS AWAY FROM THE TARGET OF THE T-SHAPED AIOI BRIDGE.

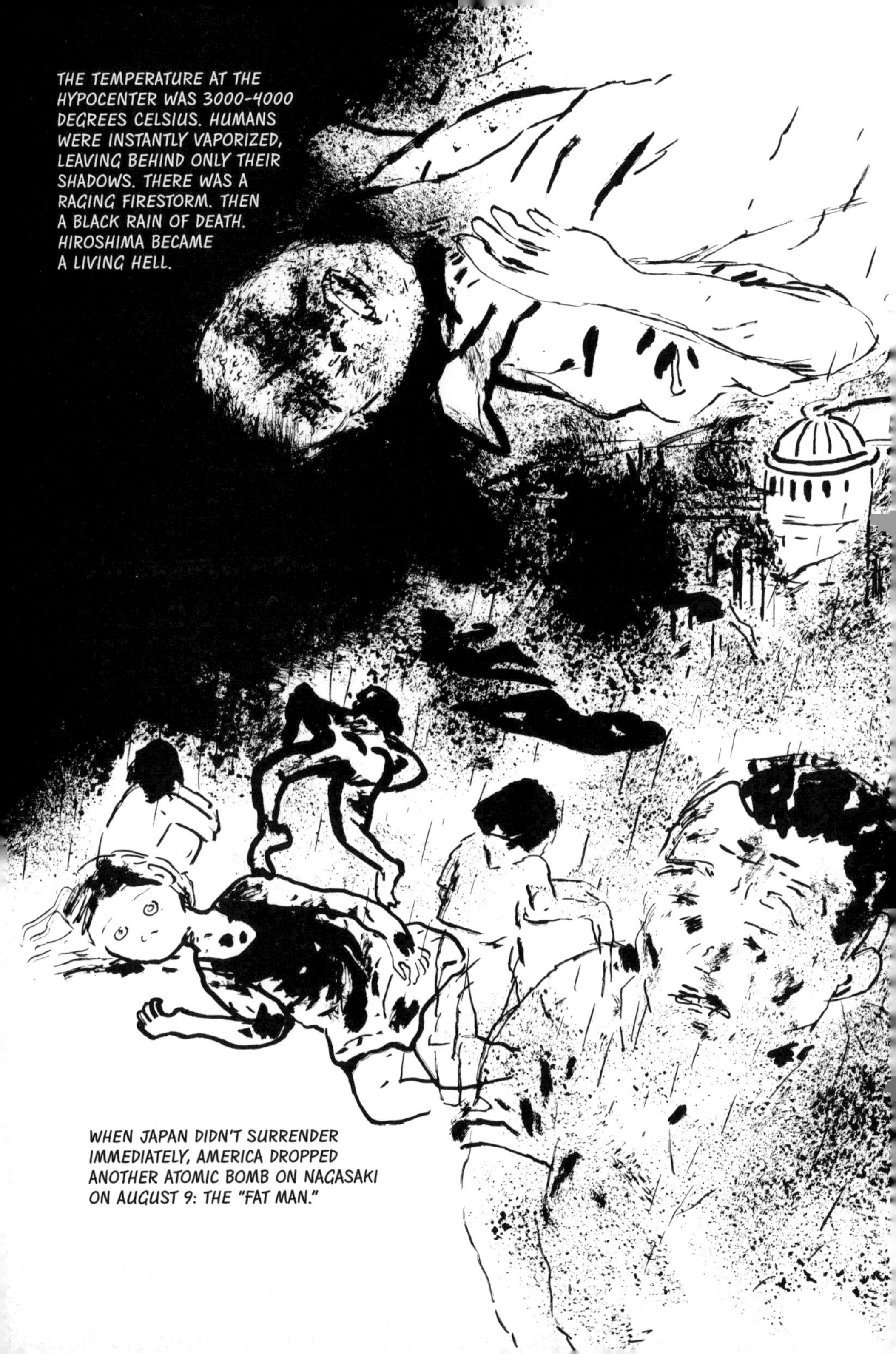
THE TEMPERATURE AT THE HYPOCENTER WAS 3000-4000 DEGREES CELSIUS. HUMANS WERE INSTANTLY VAPORIZED, LEAVING BEHIND ONLY THEIR SHADOWS. THERE WAS A RAGING FIRESTORM. THEN A BLACK RAIN OF DEATH. HIROSHIMA BECAME A LIVING HELL.
WHEN JAPAN DIDN'T SURRENDER IMMEDIATELY, AMERICA DROPPED ANOTHER ATOMIC BOMB ON NAGASAKI ON AUGUST 9: THE "FAT MAN."

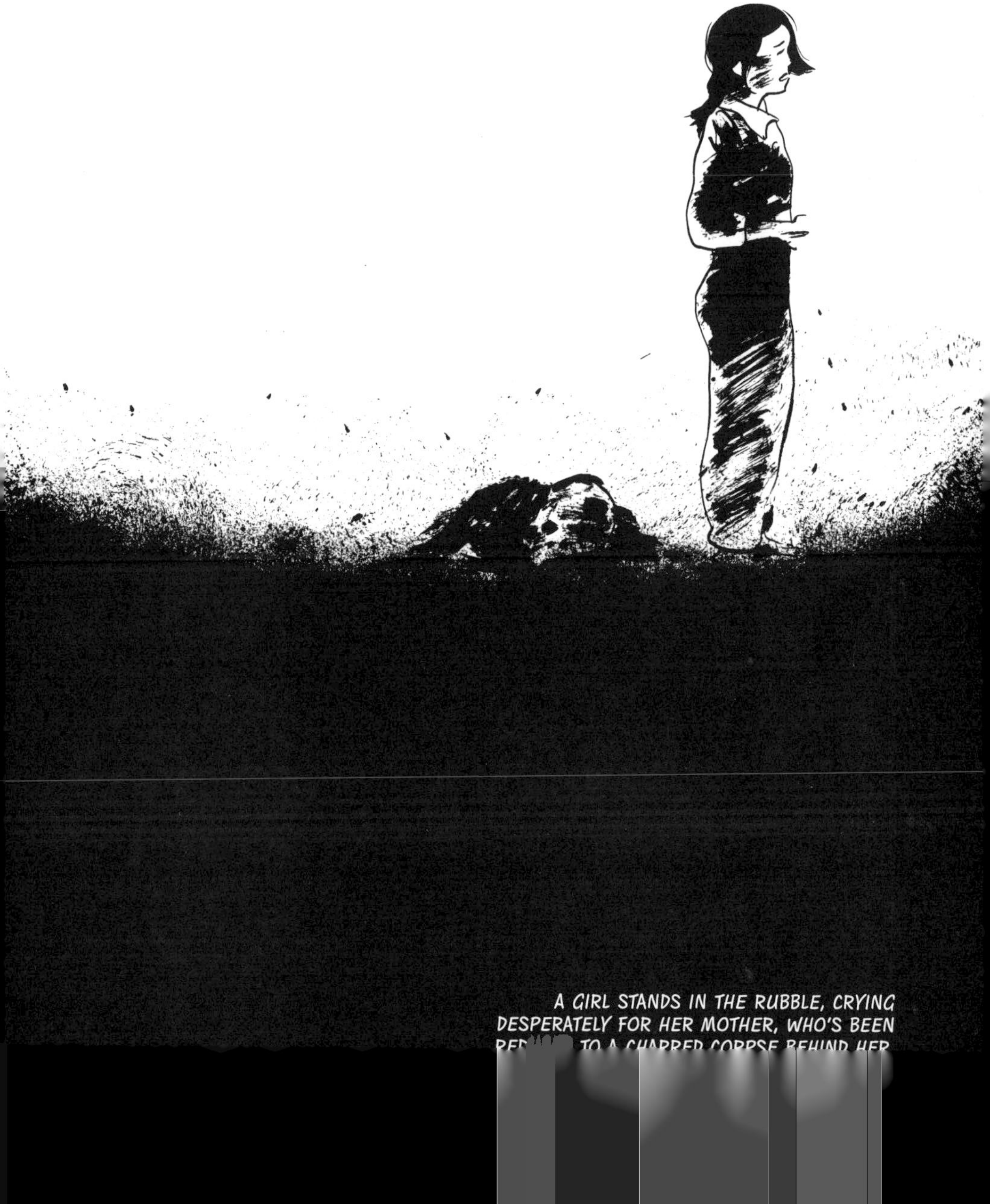
A GIRL STANDS IN THE RUBBLE, CRYING
DESPERATELY FOR HER MOTHER, WHO'S BEEN
TO A CHARRED CORPSE BEHIND HER.

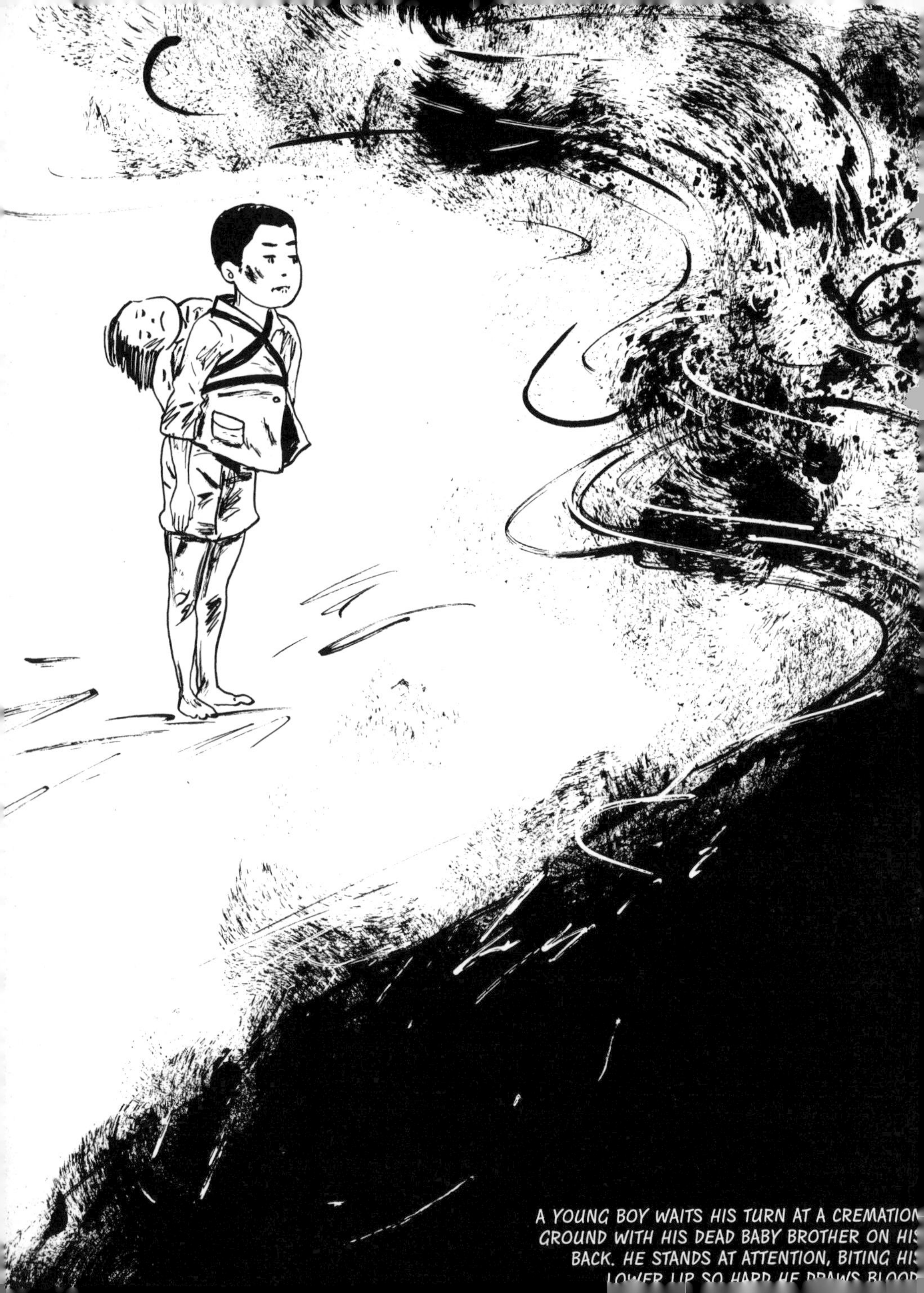
A YOUNG BOY WAITS HIS TURN AT A CREMATION
GROUND WITH HIS DEAD BABY BROTHER ON HIS
BACK. HE STANDS AT ATTENTION, BITING HIS
LOWER LIP SO HARD HE DRAWS BLOOD

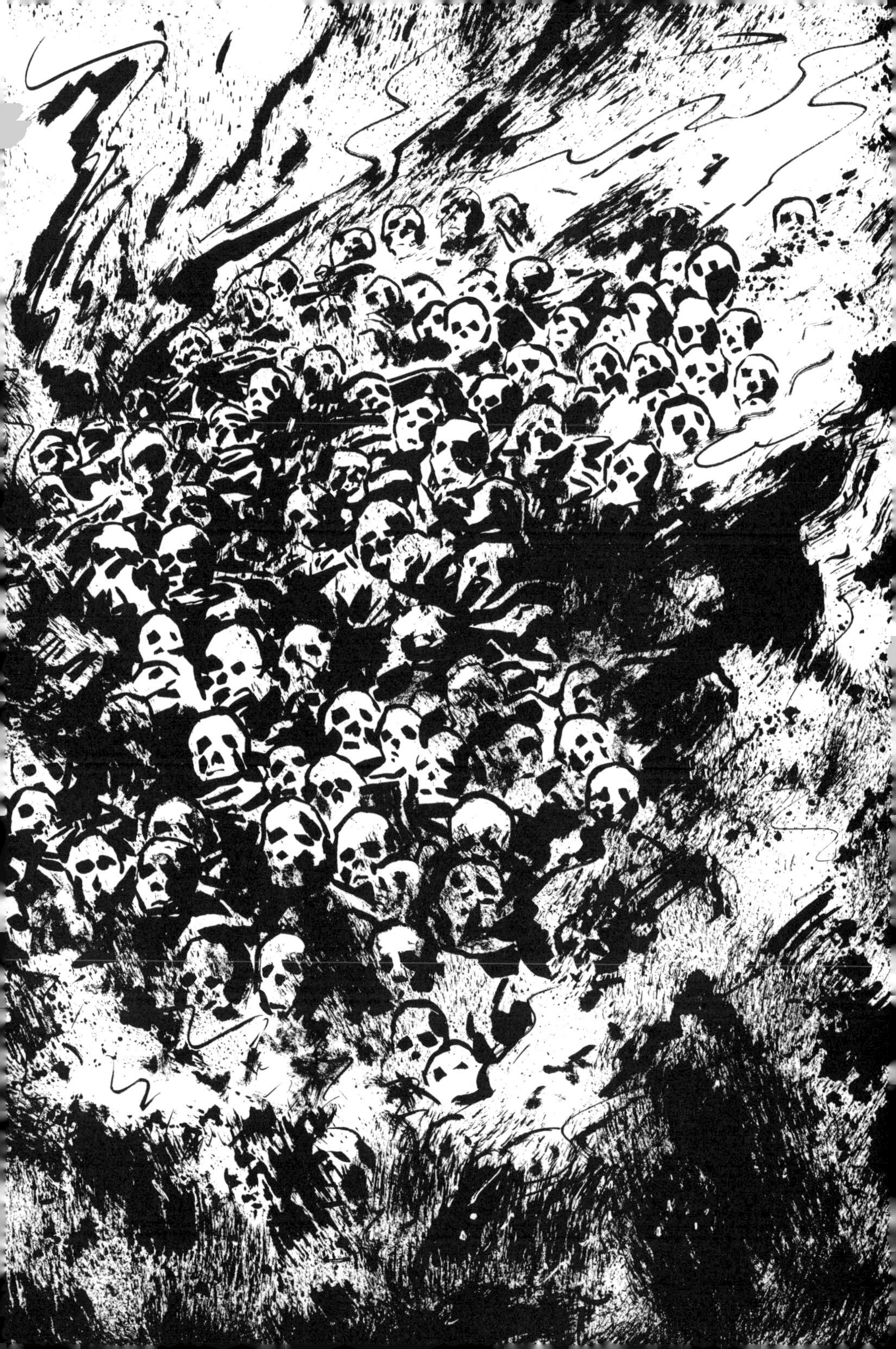

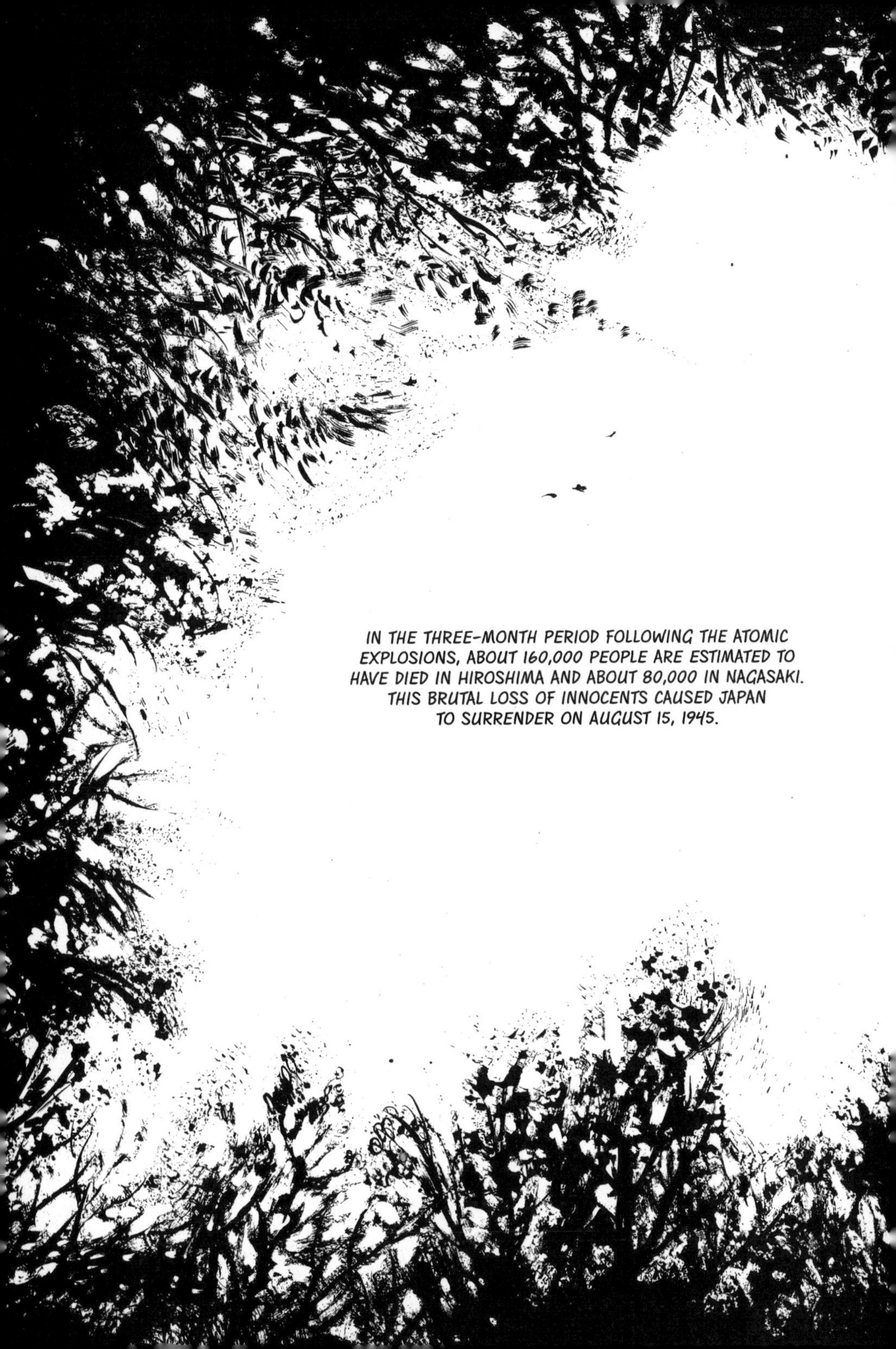
IN THE THREE-MONTH PERIOD FOLLOWING THE ATOMIC EXPLOSIONS, ABOUT 160,000 PEOPLE ARE ESTIMATED TO HAVE DIED IN HIROSHIMA AND ABOUT 80,000 IN NAGASAKI. THIS BRUTAL LOSS OF INNOCENTS CAUSED JAPAN TO SURRENDER ON AUGUST 15, 1945.

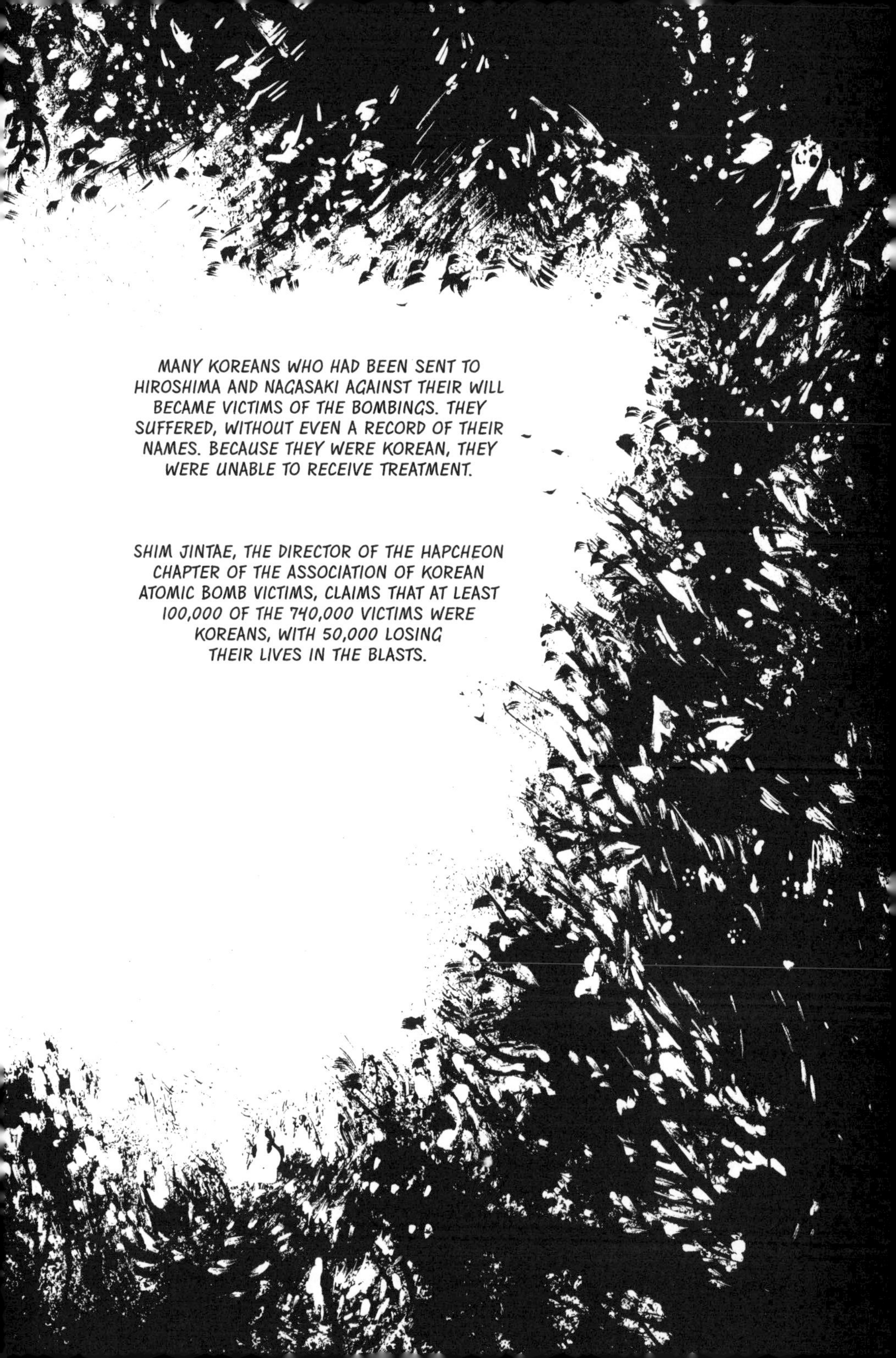
MANY KOREANS WHO HAD BEEN SENT TO HIROSHIMA AND NAGASAKI AGAINST THEIR WILL BECAME VICTIMS OF THE BOMBINGS. THEY SUFFERED, WITHOUT EVEN A RECORD OF THEIR NAMES. BECAUSE THEY WERE KOREAN, THEY WERE UNABLE TO RECEIVE TREATMENT.
SHIM JINTAE, THE DIRECTOR OF THE HAPCHEON CHAPTER OF THE ASSOCIATION OF KOREAN ATOMIC BOMB VICTIMS, CLAIMS THAT AT LEAST 100,000 OF THE 740,000 VICTIMS WERE KOREANS, WITH 50,000 LOSING THEIR LIVES IN THE BLASTS.

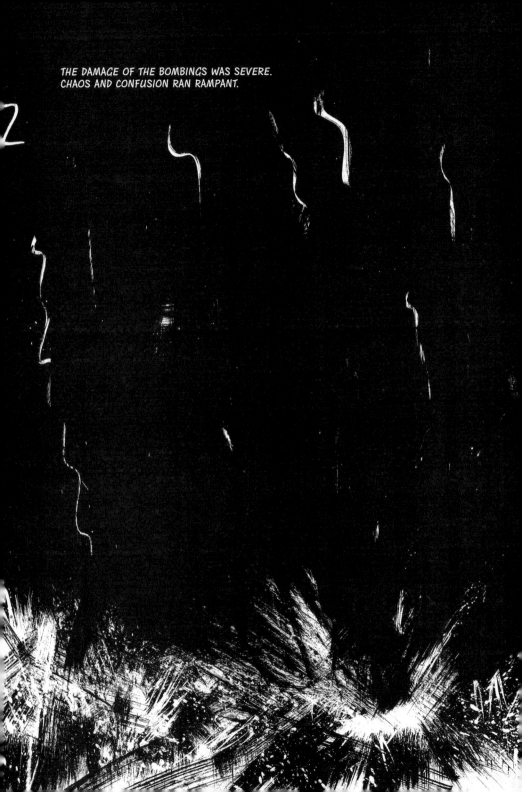

THE DAMAGE OF THE BOMBINGS WAS SEVERE.
CHAOS AND CONFUSION RAN RAMPANT.

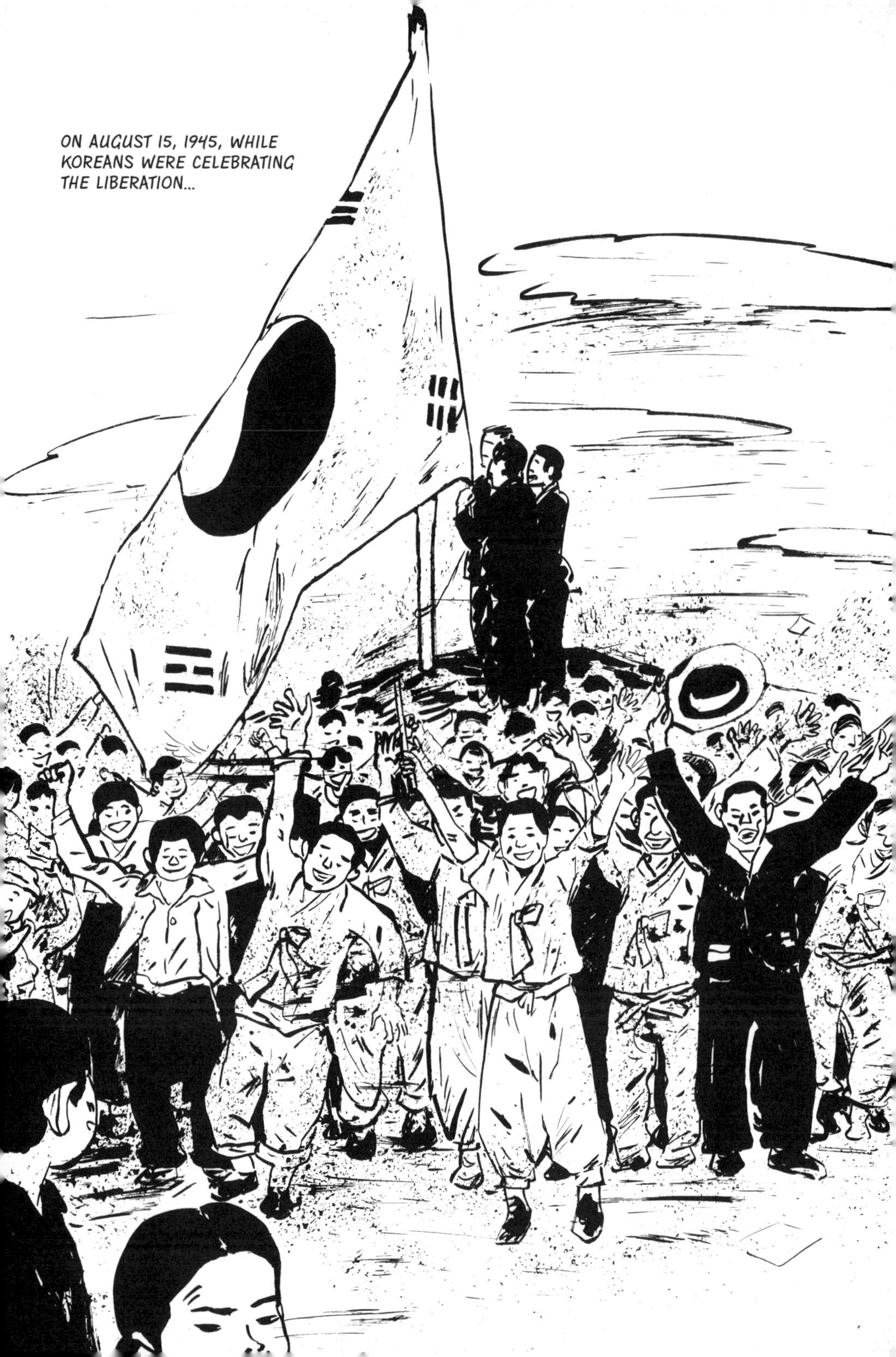
ON AUGUST 15, 1945, WHILE KOREANS WERE CELEBRATING THE LIBERATION...

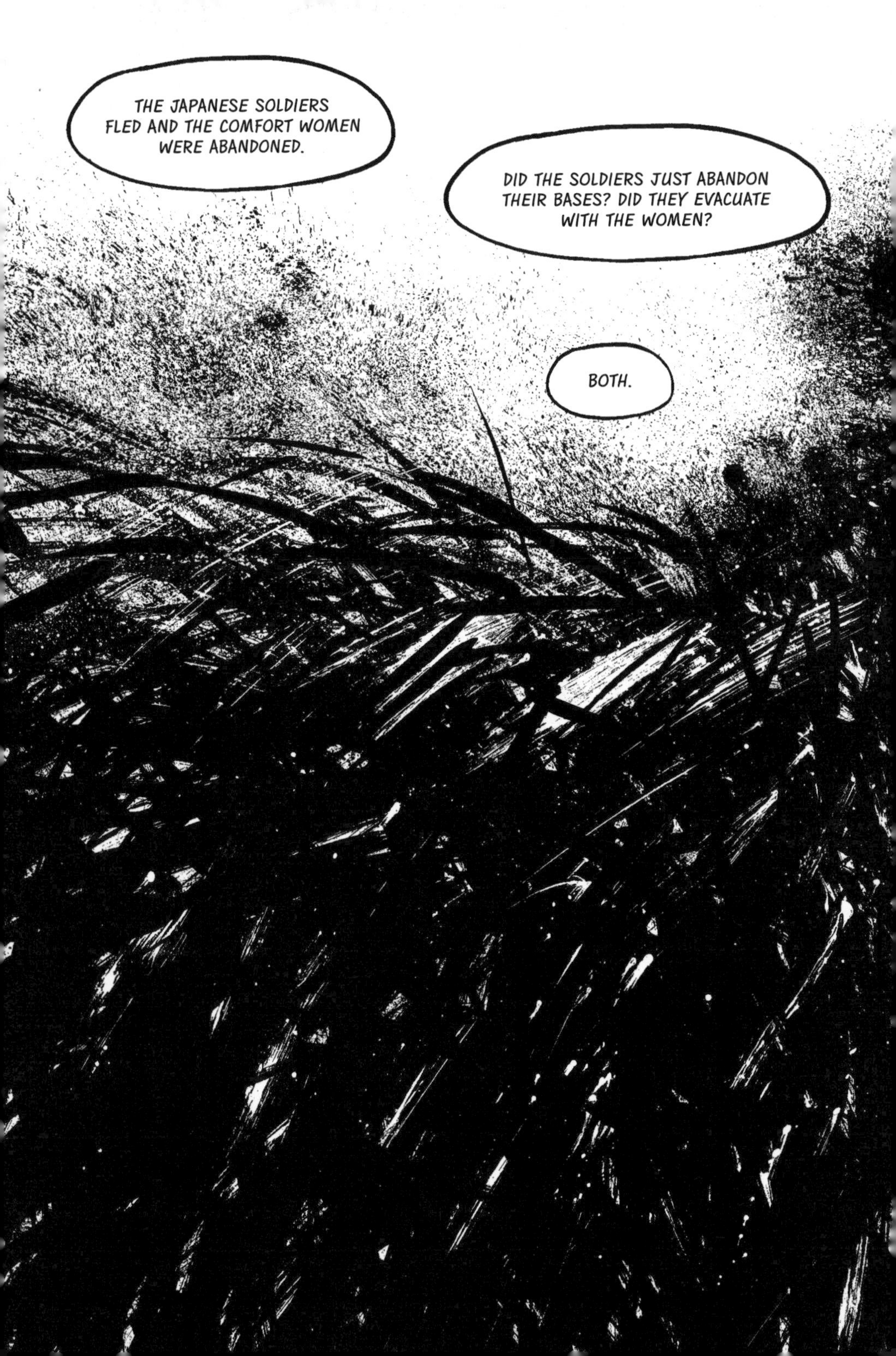
THE JAPANESE SOLDIERS FLED AND THE COMFORT WOMEN WERE ABANDONED.
DID THE SOLDIERS JUST ABANDON THEIR BASES? DID THEY EVACUATE WITH THE WOMEN?
BOTH.

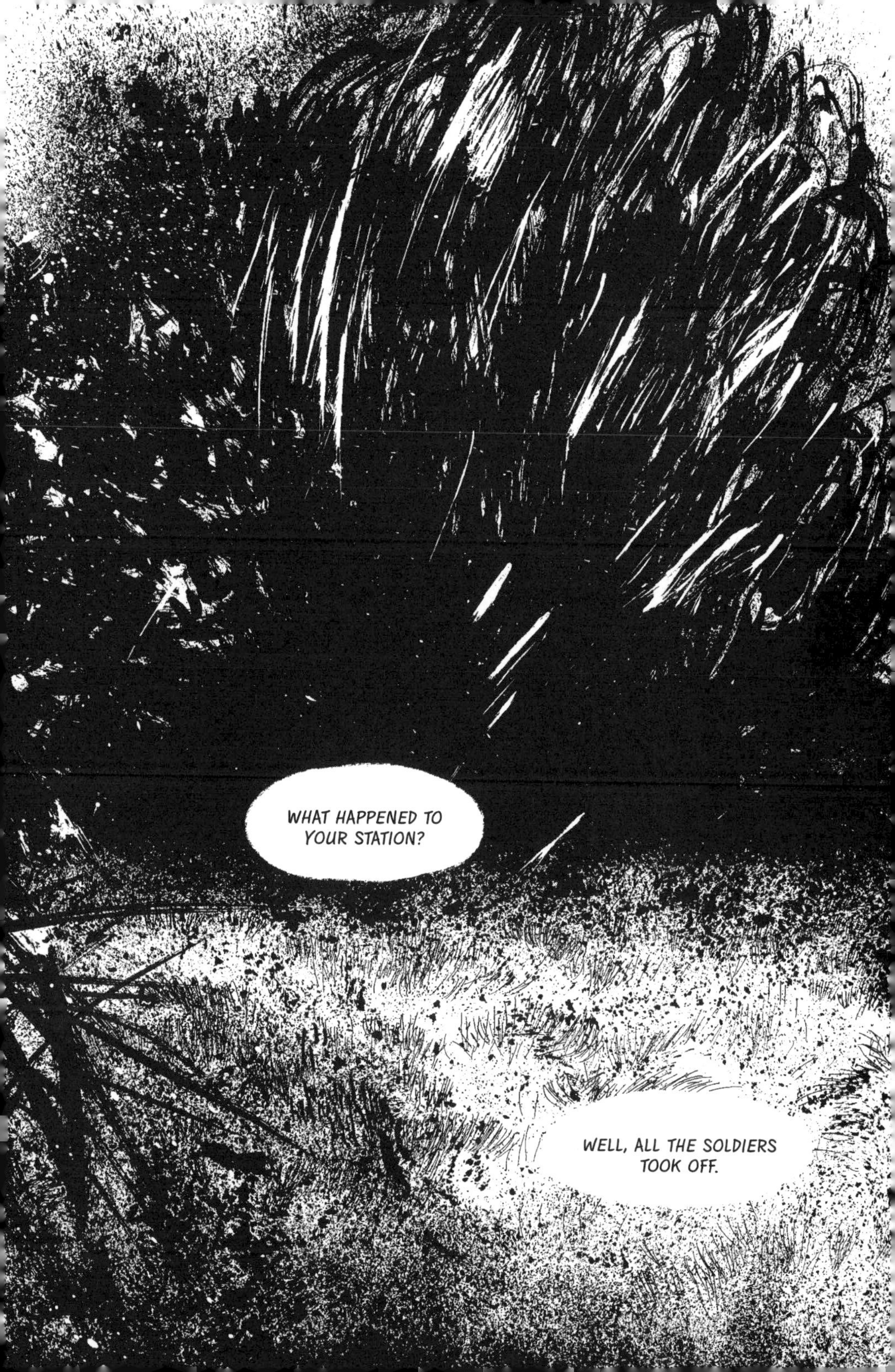
WHAT HAPPENED TO YOUR STATION?
WELL, ALL THE SOLDIERS TOOK OFF.

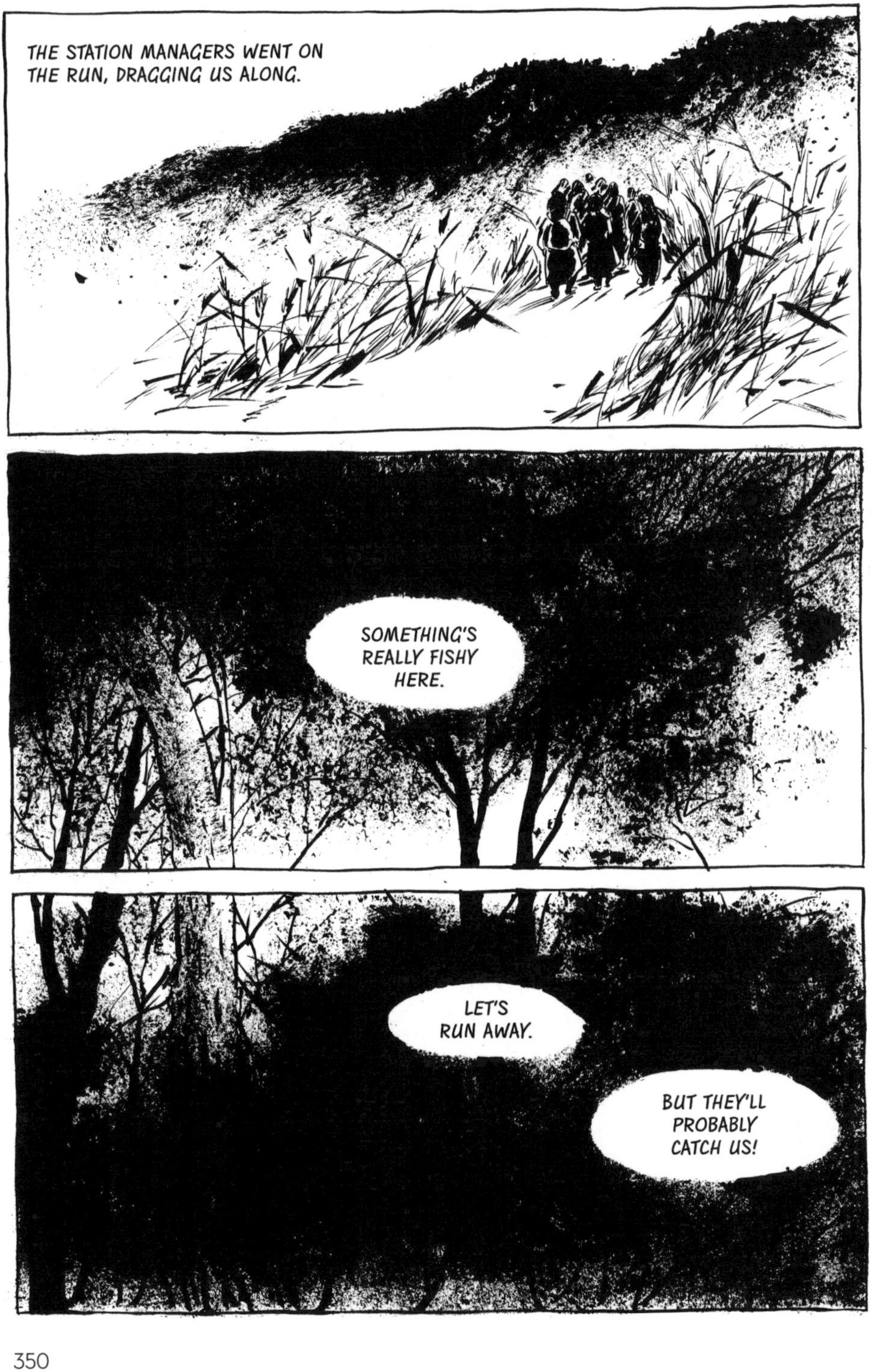
THE STATION MANAGERS WENT ON THE RUN, DRAGGING US ALONG.
SOMETHING'S REALLY FISHY HERE.
LET'S RUN AWAY.
BUT THEY'LL PROBABLY CATCH US!

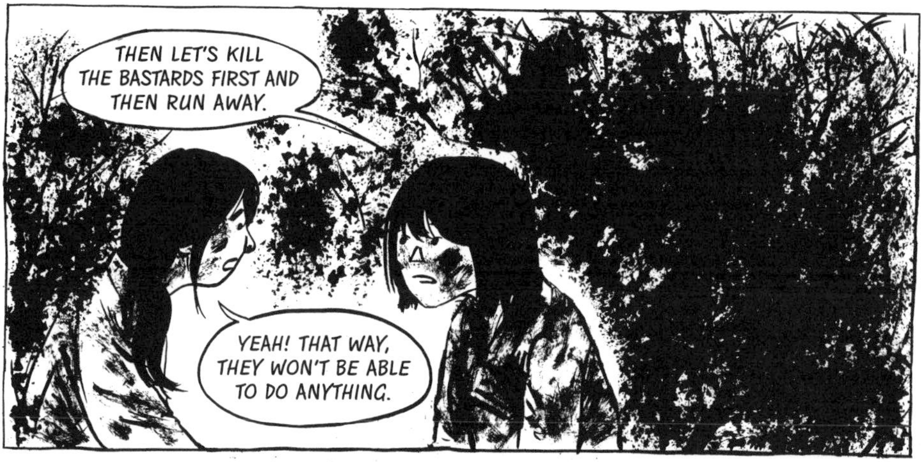
THEN LET'S KILL THE BASTARDS FIRST AND THEN RUN AWAY.
YEAH! THAT WAY, THEY WON'T BE ABLE TO DO ANYTHING.

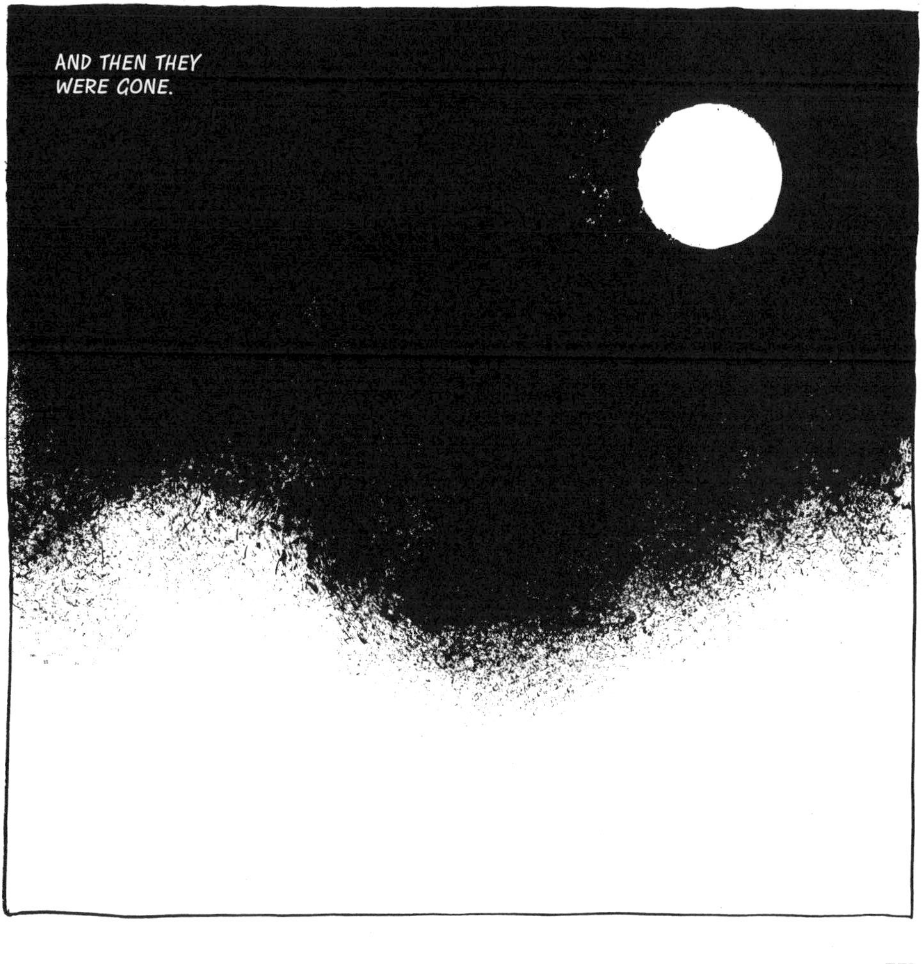
AND THEN THEY WERE GONE.

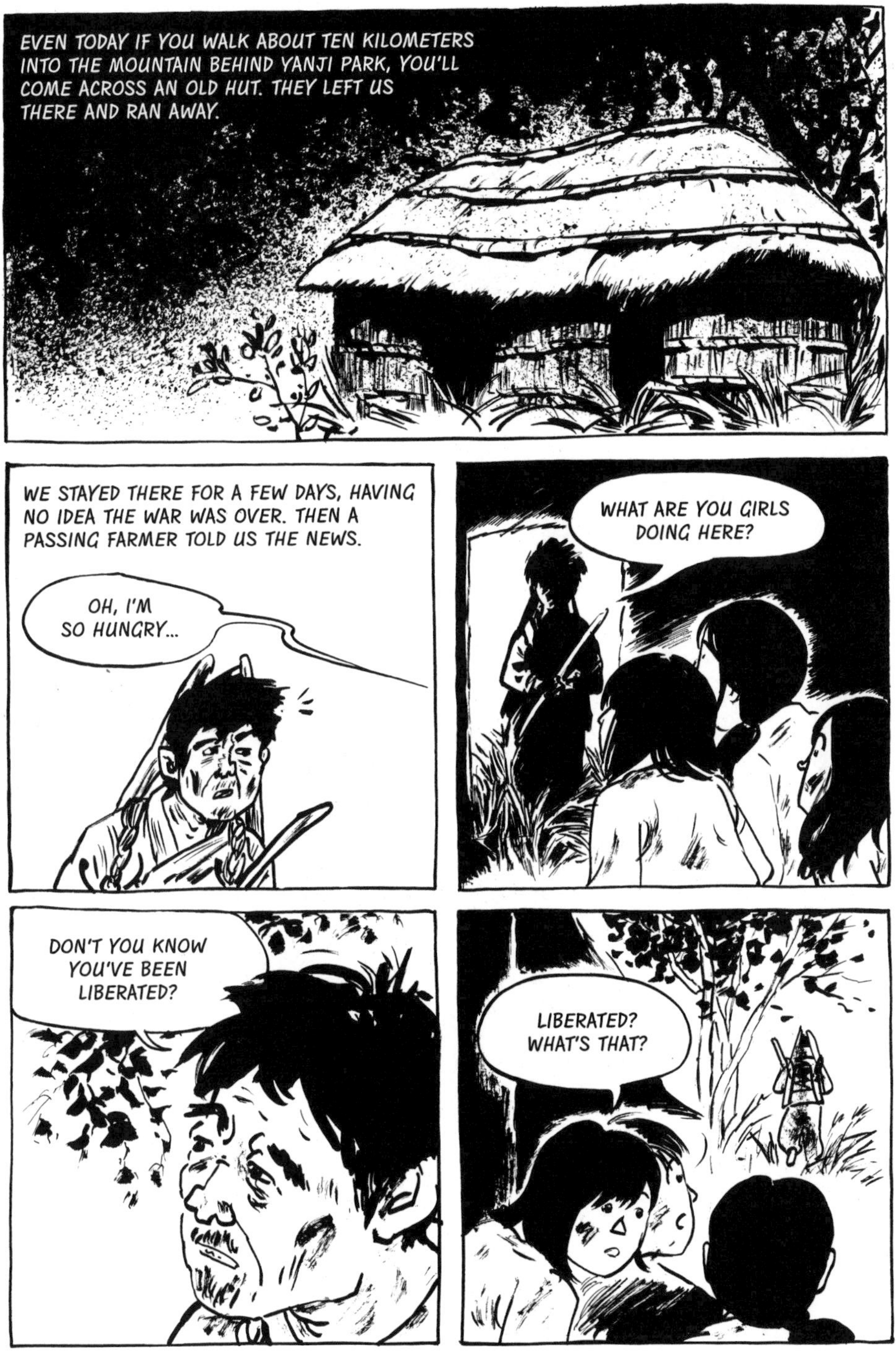
EVEN TODAY IF YOU WALK ABOUT TEN KILOMETERS INTO THE MOUNTAIN BEHIND YANJI PARK, YOU'LL COME ACROSS AN OLD HUT. THEY LEFT US THERE AND RAN AWAY.
WE STAYED THERE FOR A FEW DAYS, HAVING NO IDEA THE WAR WAS OVER. THEN A PASSING FARMER TOLD US THE NEWS.
OH, I'M SO HUNGRY...
WHAT ARE YOU GIRLS DOING HERE?
DON'T YOU KNOW YOU'VE BEEN LIBERATED?
LIBERATED? WHAT'S THAT?

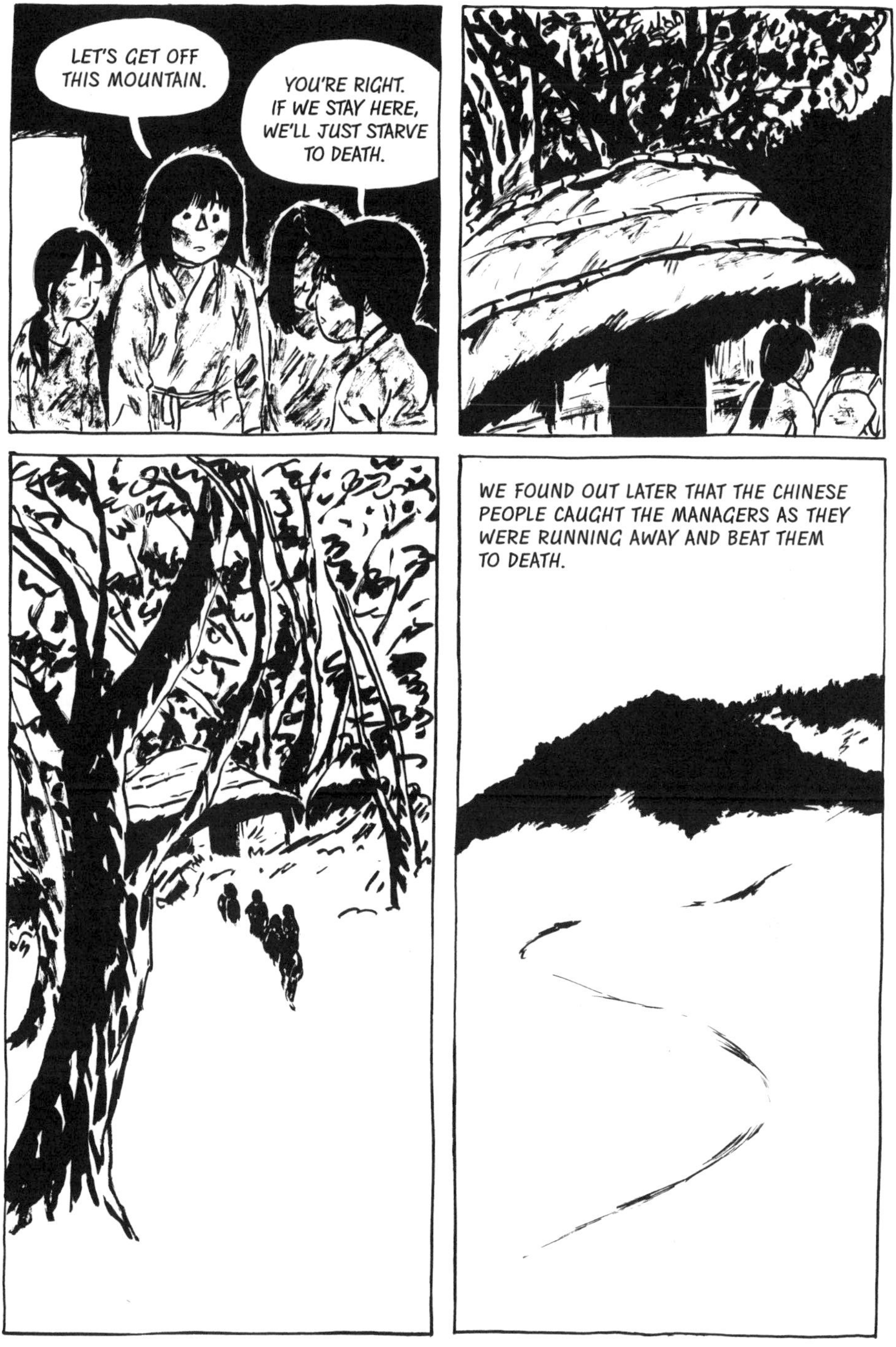
LET'S GET OFF THIS MOUNTAIN.
YOU'RE RIGHT. IF WE STAY HERE, WE'LL JUST STARVE TO DEATH.
WE FOUND OUT LATER THAT THE CHINESE PEOPLE CAUGHT THE MANAGERS AS THEY WERE RUNNING AWAY AND BEAT THEM TO DEATH.

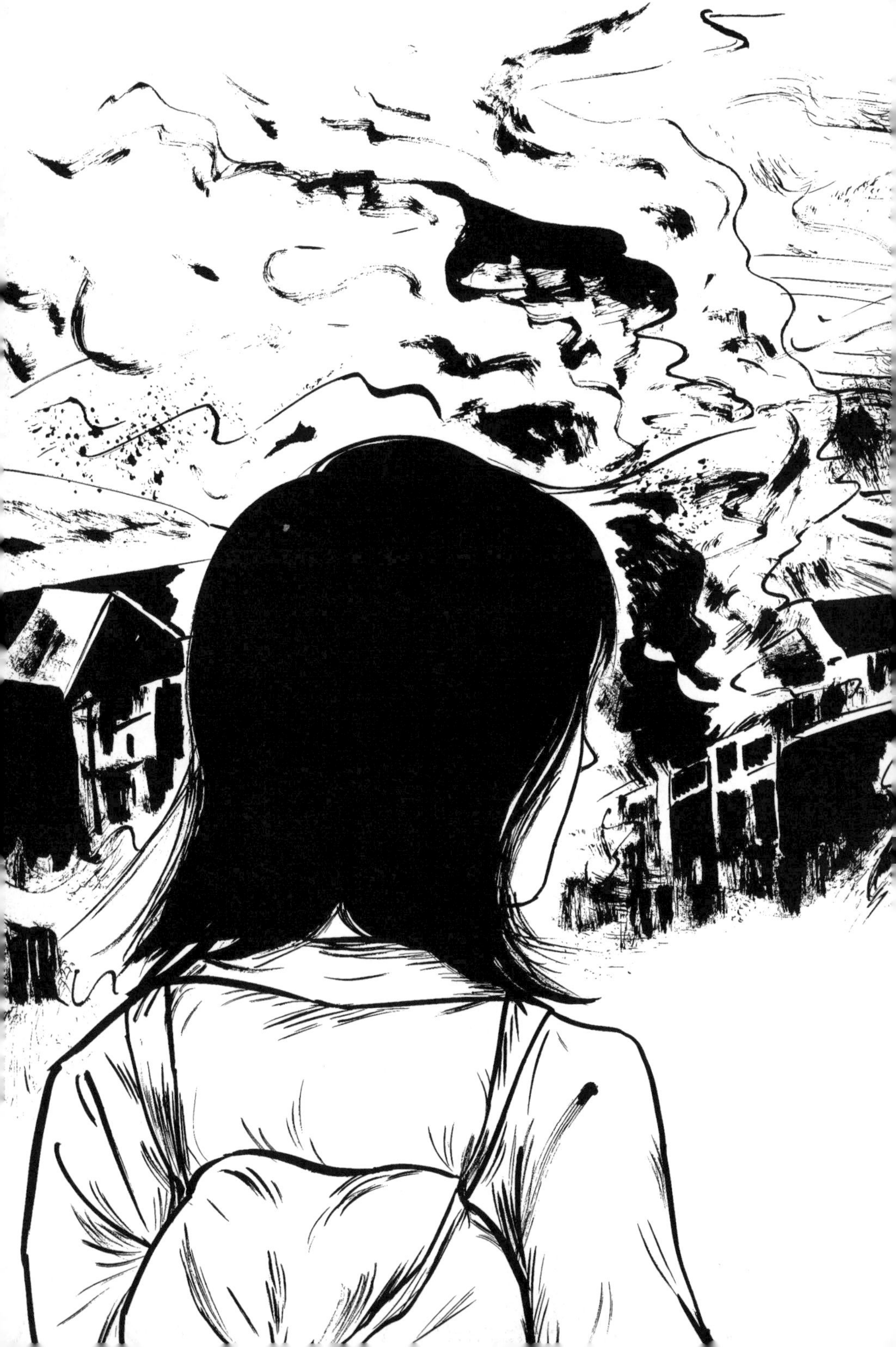

WHEN WE FINALLY GOT TO DOWNTOWN YANJI, EVERYTHING WAS ON FIRE.

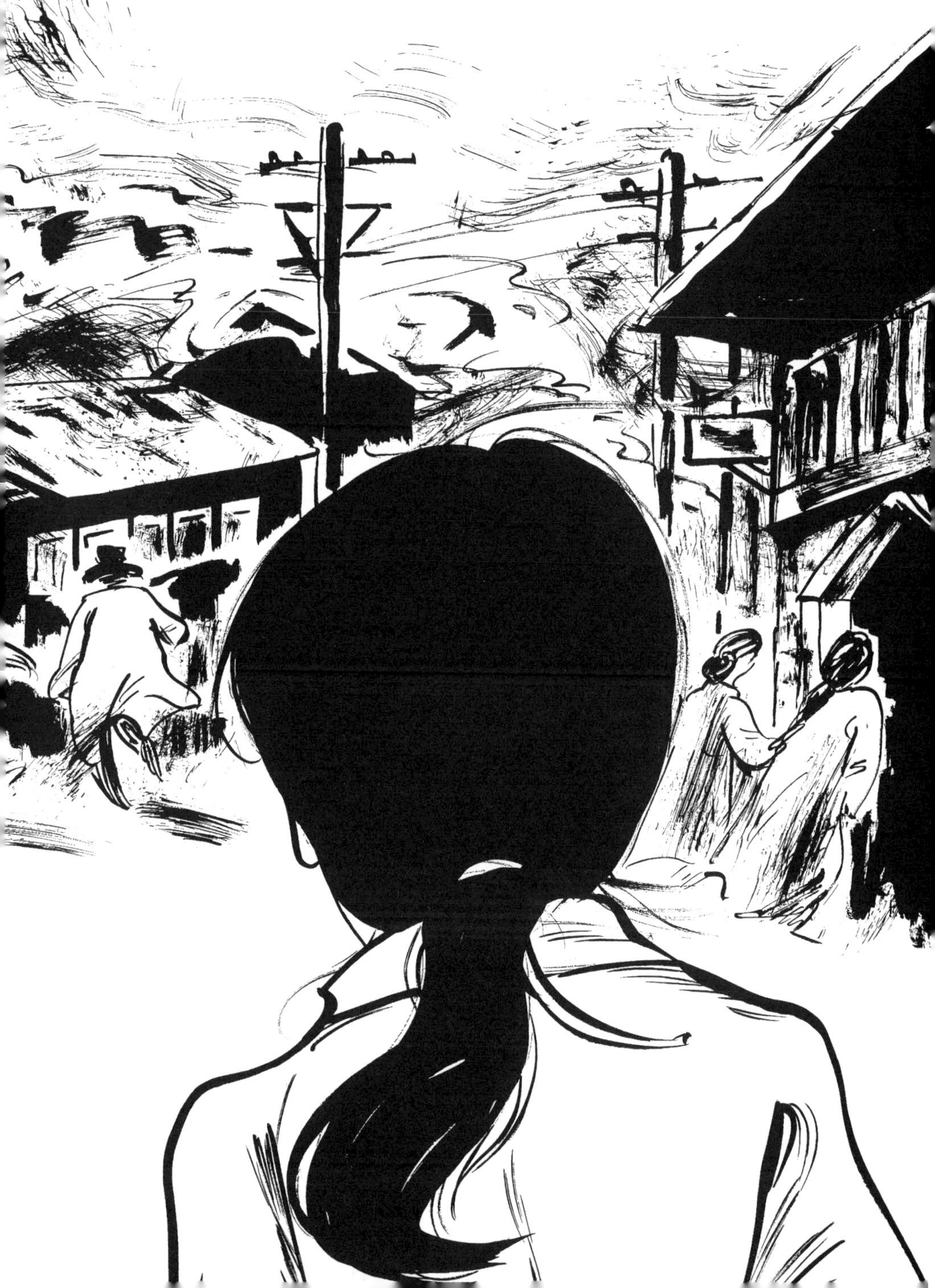

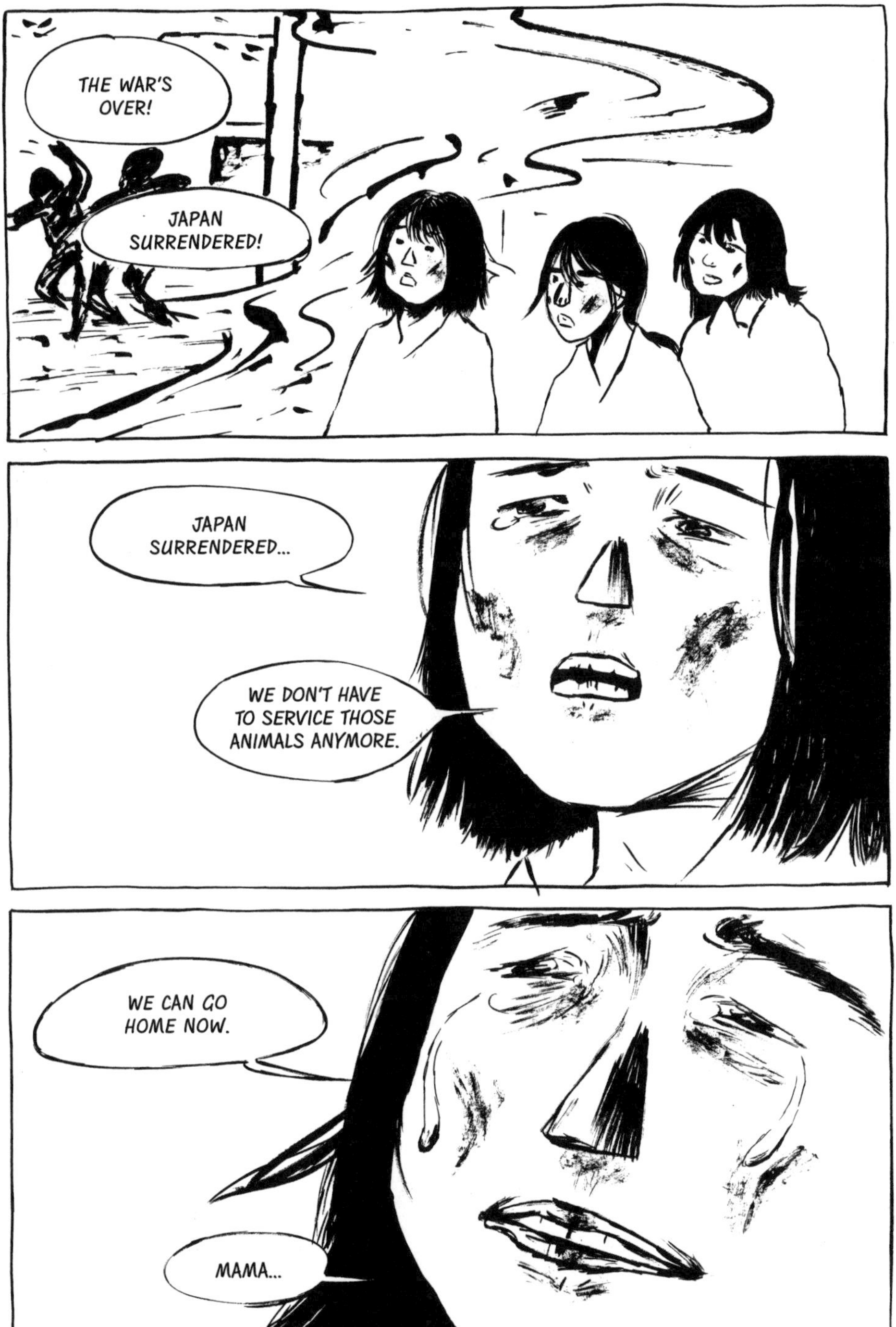
THE WAR'S OVER!
JAPAN SURRENDERED!
JAPAN SURRENDERED...
WE DON'T HAVE TO SERVICE THOSE ANIMALS ANYMORE.
WE CAN GO HOME NOW.
MAMA...

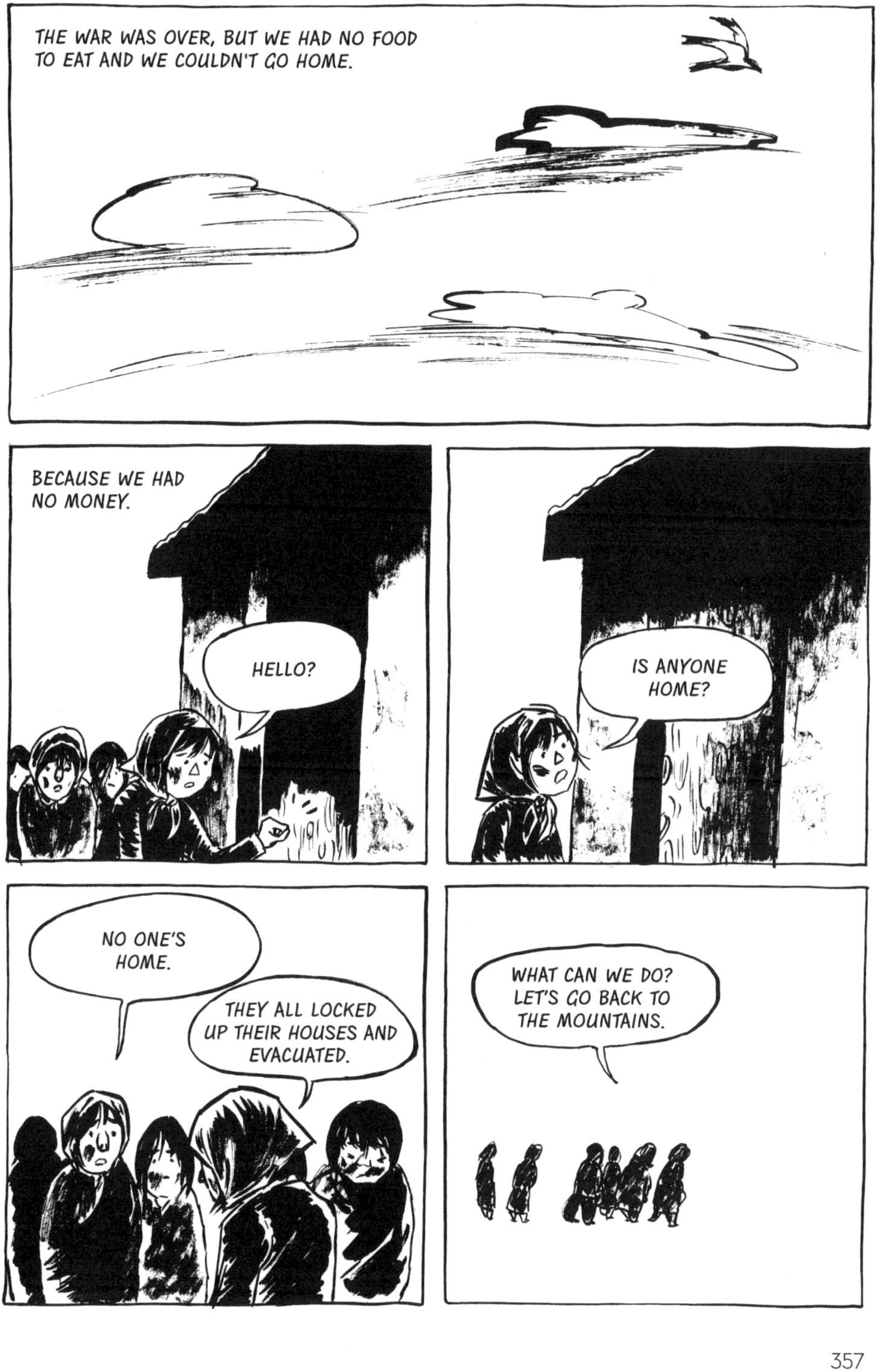
THE WAR WAS OVER, BUT WE HAD NO FOOD TO EAT AND WE COULDN'T GO HOME.
BECAUSE WE HAD NO MONEY.
HELLO?
IS ANYONE HOME?
NO ONE'S HOME.
THEY ALL LOCKED UP THEIR HOUSES AND EVACUATED.
WHAT CAN WE DO? LET'S GO BACK TO THE MOUNTAINS.

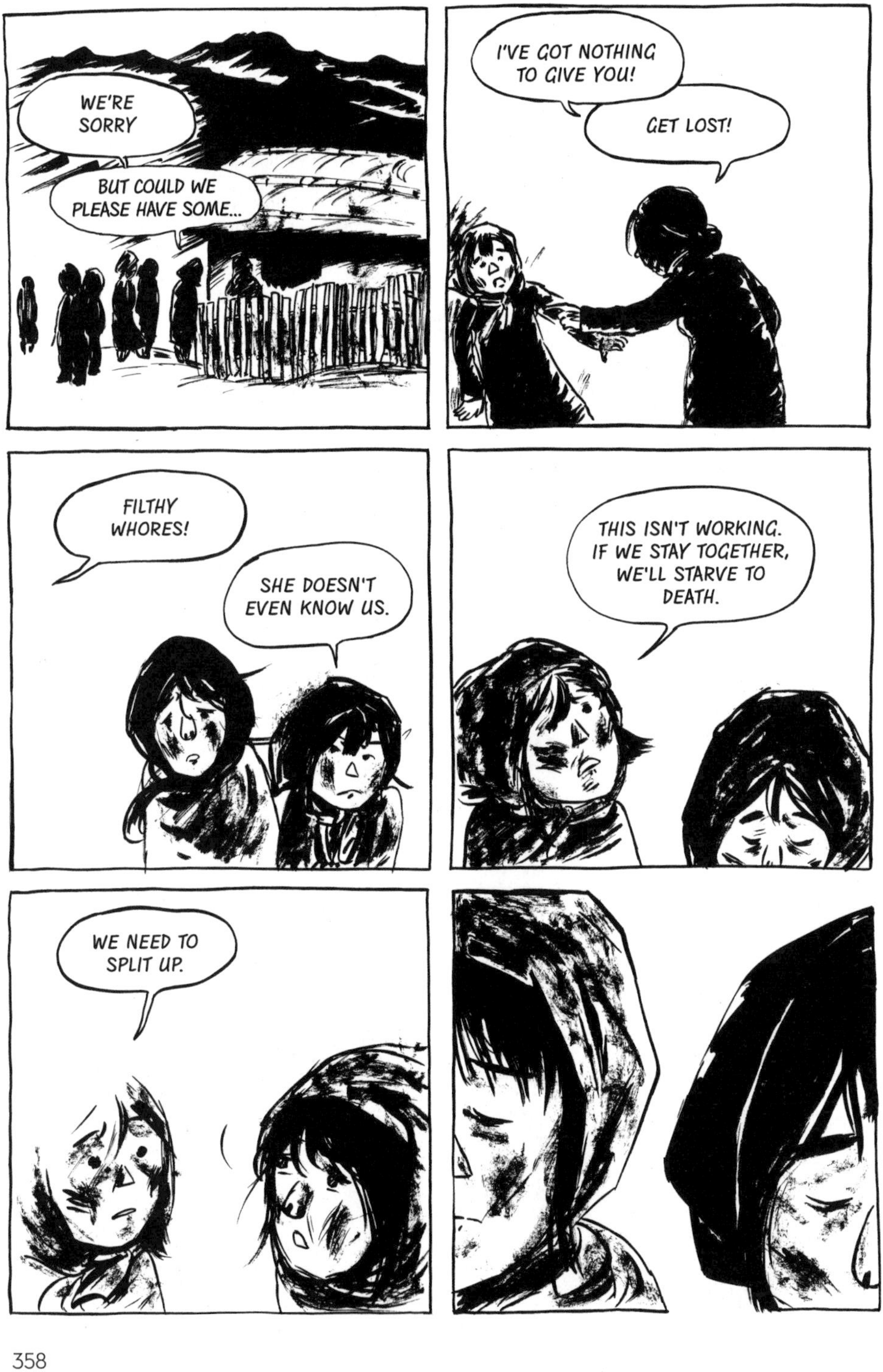
WE'RE SORRY
BUT COULD WE PLEASE HAVE SOME...
I'VE GOT NOTHING TO GIVE YOU!
GET LOST!
FILTHY WHORES!
SHE DOESN'T EVEN KNOW US.
THIS ISN'T WORKING. IF WE STAY TOGETHER, WE'LL STARVE TO DEATH.
WE NEED TO SPLIT UP.

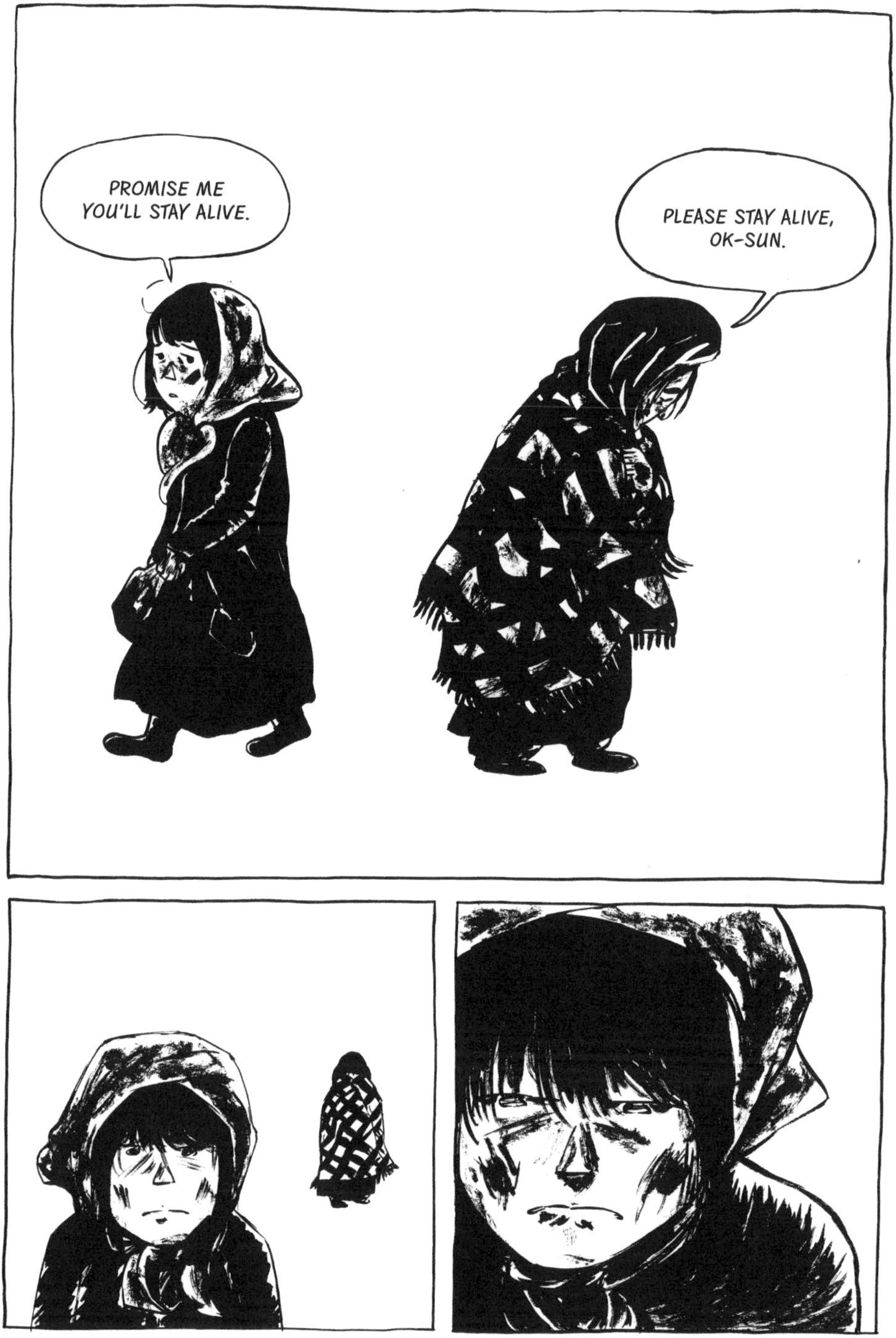
PROMISE ME YOU'LL STAY ALIVE.
PLEASE STAY ALIVE, OK-SUN.

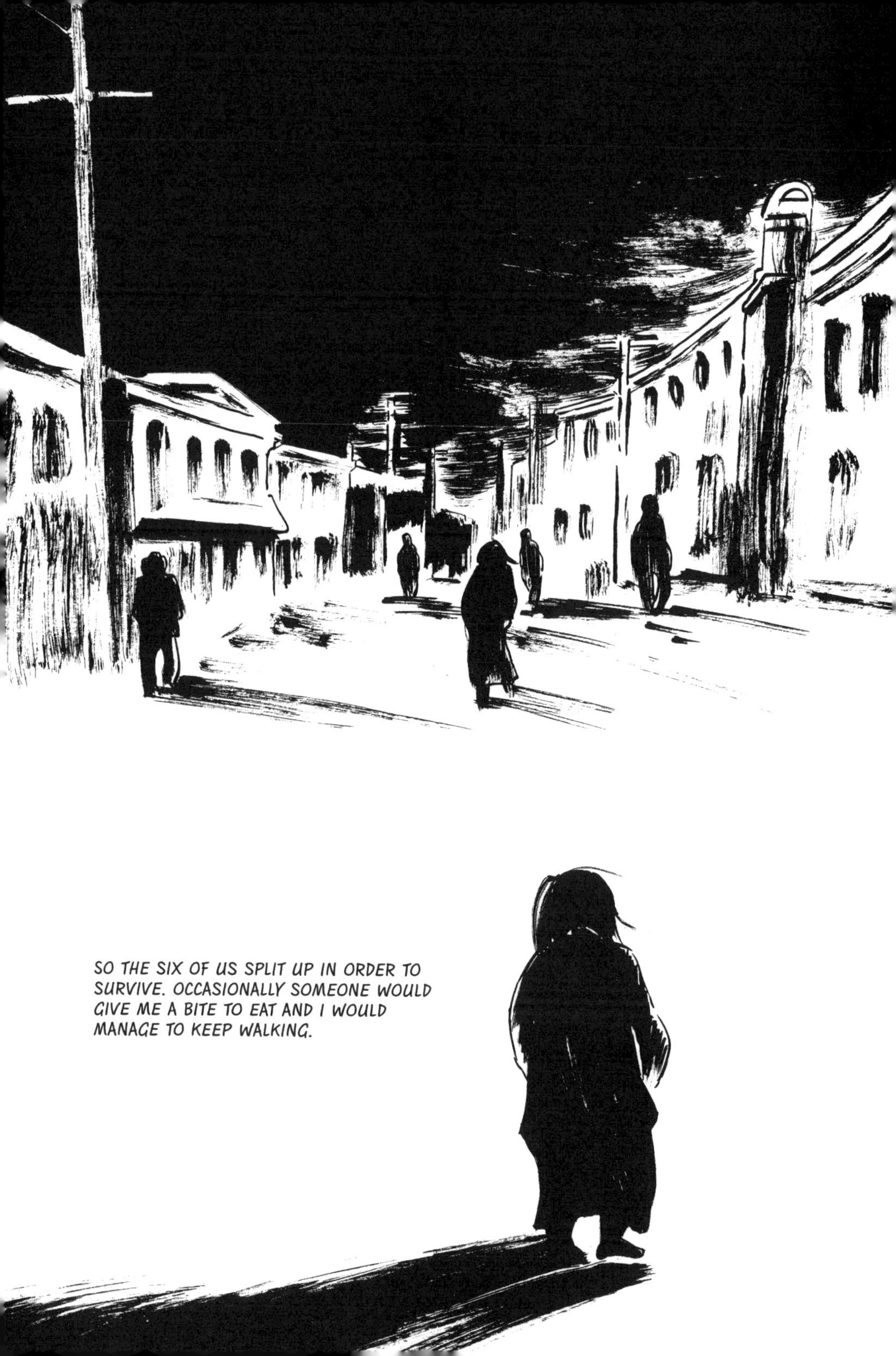
SO THE SIX OF US SPLIT UP IN ORDER TO SURVIVE. OCCASIONALLY SOMEONE WOULD GIVE ME A BITE TO EAT AND I WOULD MANAGE TO KEEP WALKING.

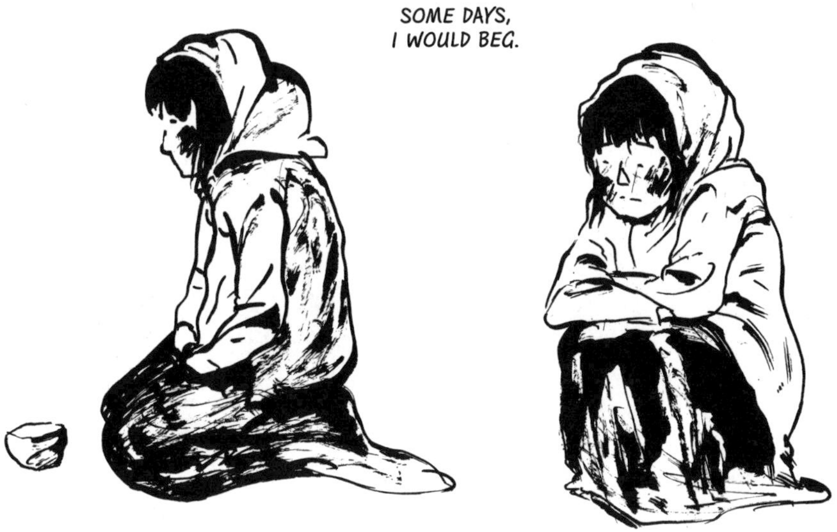
SOME DAYS, I WOULD BEG.

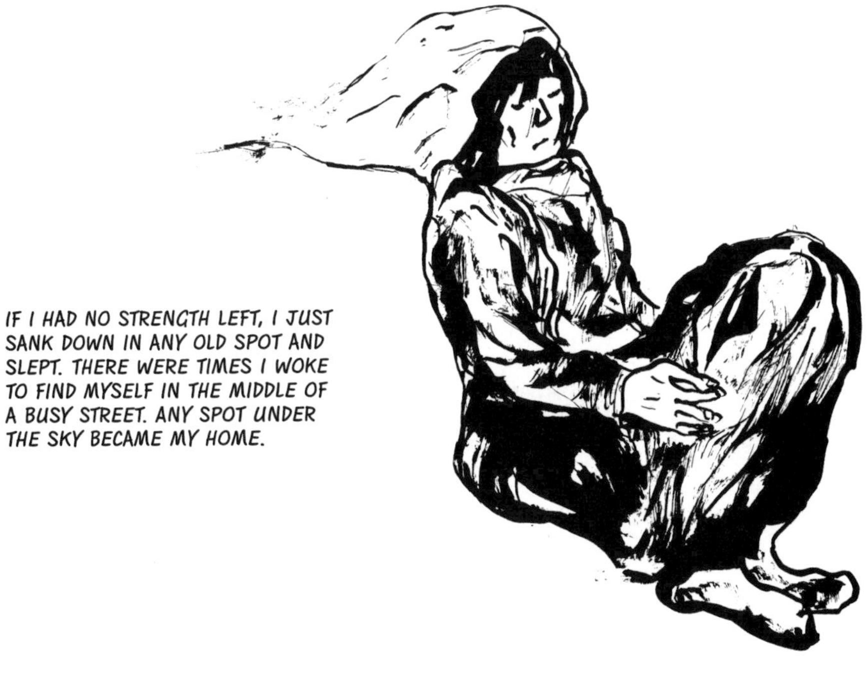
IF I HAD NO STRENGTH LEFT, I JUST SANK DOWN IN ANY OLD SPOT AND SLEPT. THERE WERE TIMES I WOKE TO FIND MYSELF IN THE MIDDLE OF A BUSY STREET. ANY SPOT UNDER THE SKY BECAME MY HOME.

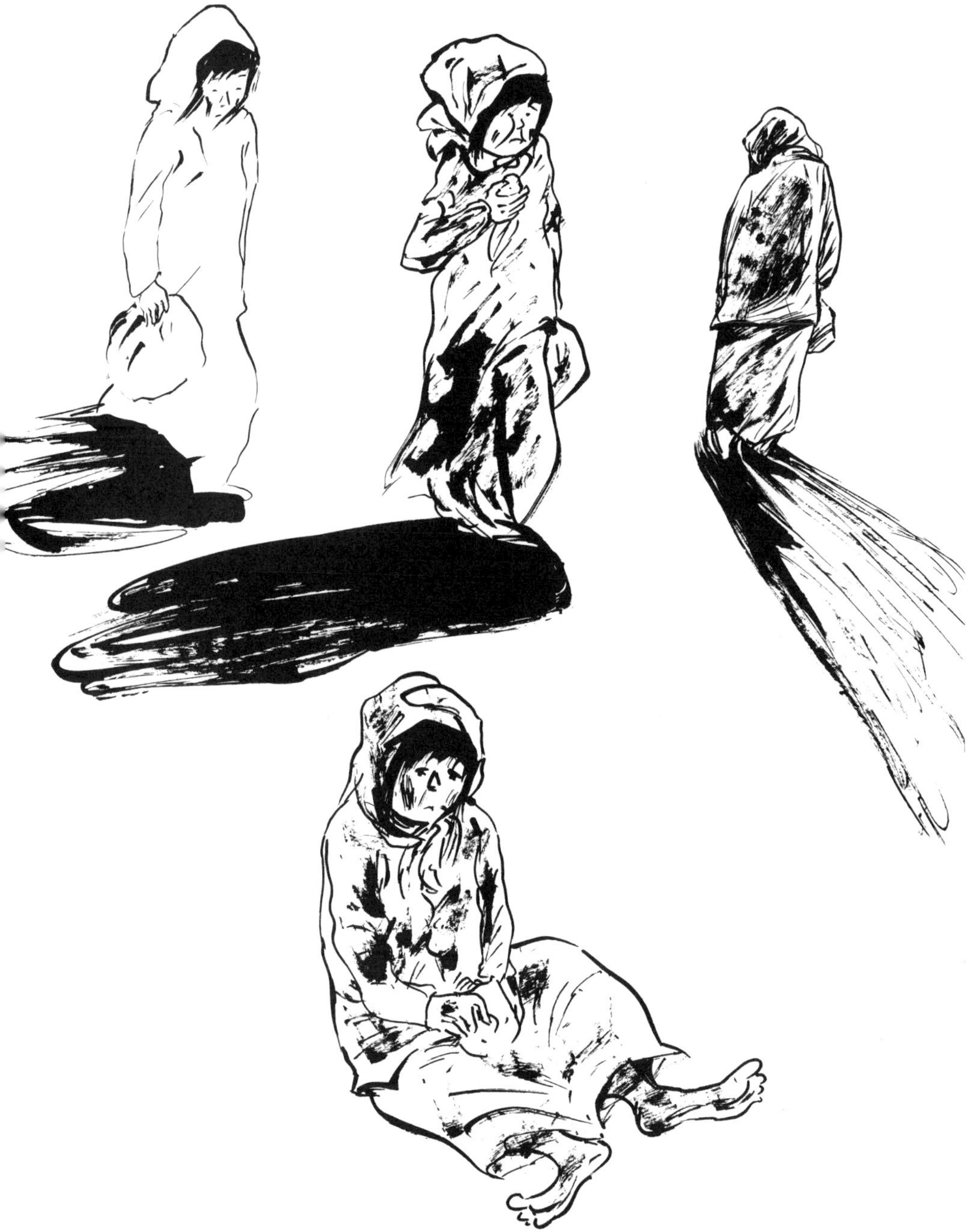

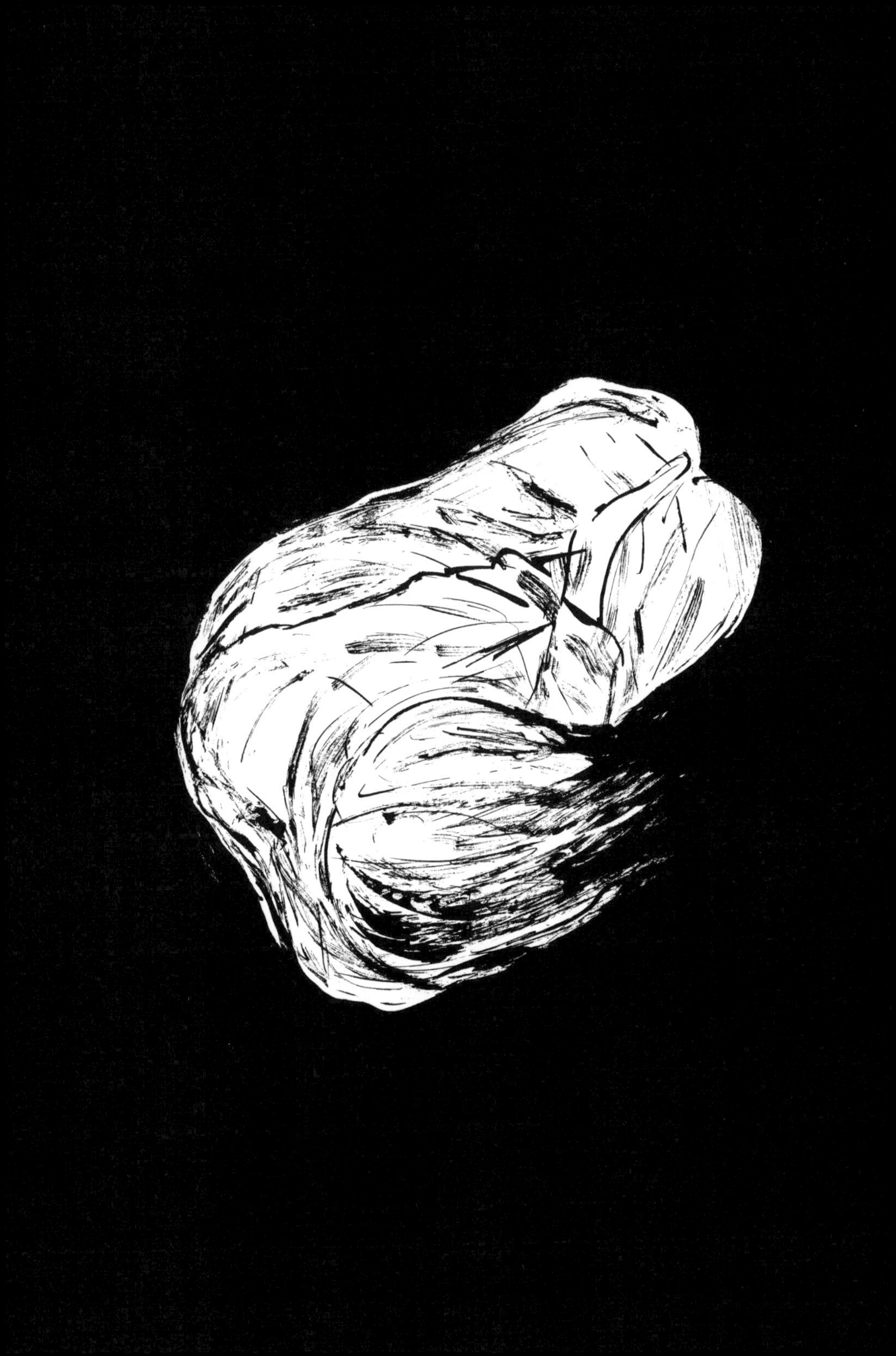

OUR SUFFERING WASN'T OVER YET. THE SOVIET
SOLDIERS CAME. THOSE BASTARDS DID BRUTAL THINGS.
THEY SNATCHED ANY GIRLS THEY SAW, RAPED THEM,
AND DID WHATEVER THEY WANTED. I SAW SO MANY
GIRLS RAPED THEN SHOT OR SET ON FIRE
BY THOSE MONSTERS.

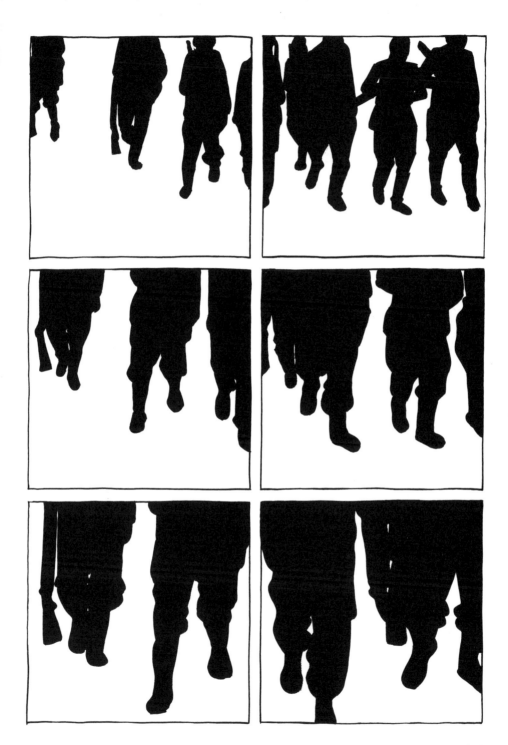

367

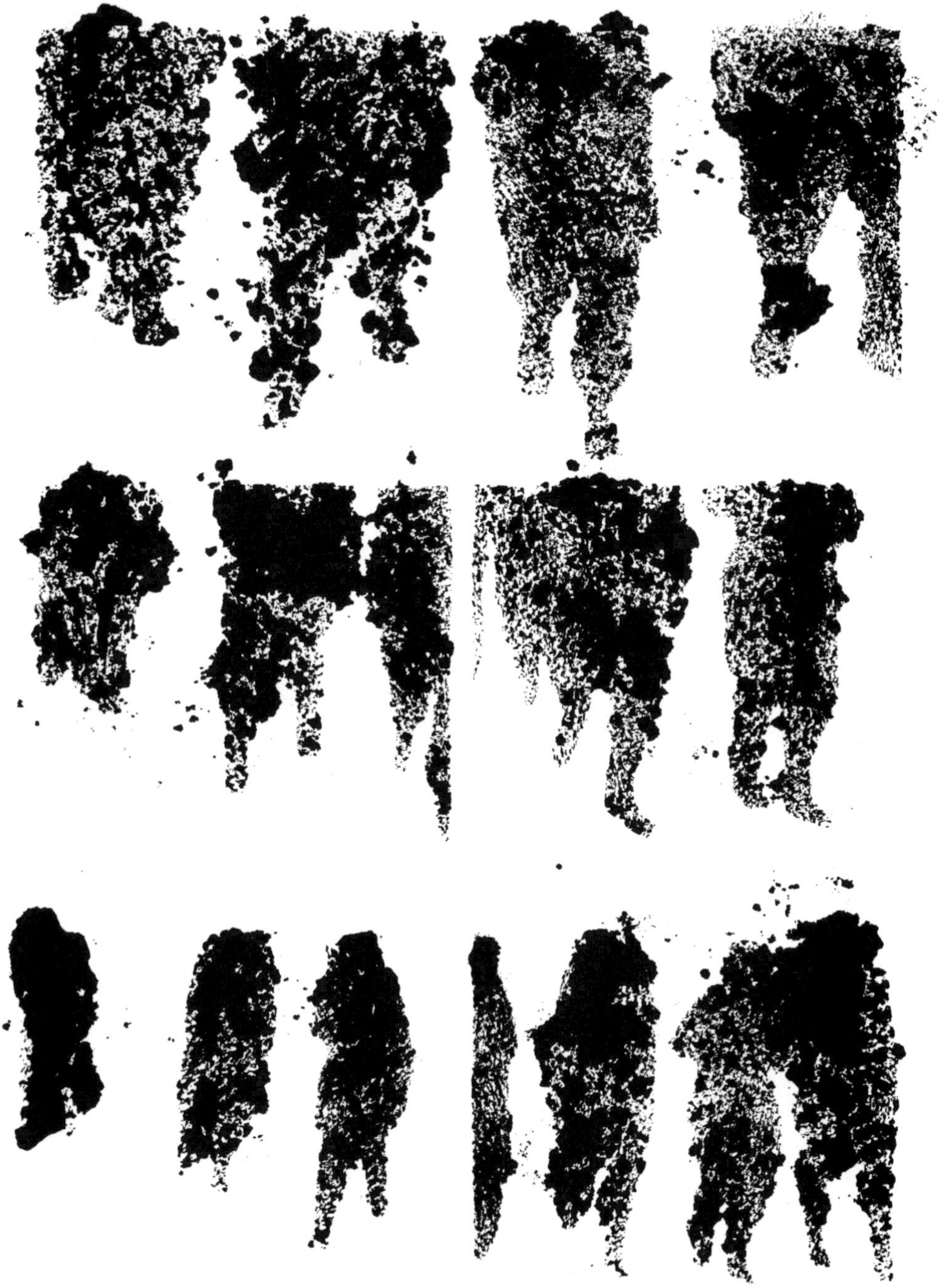

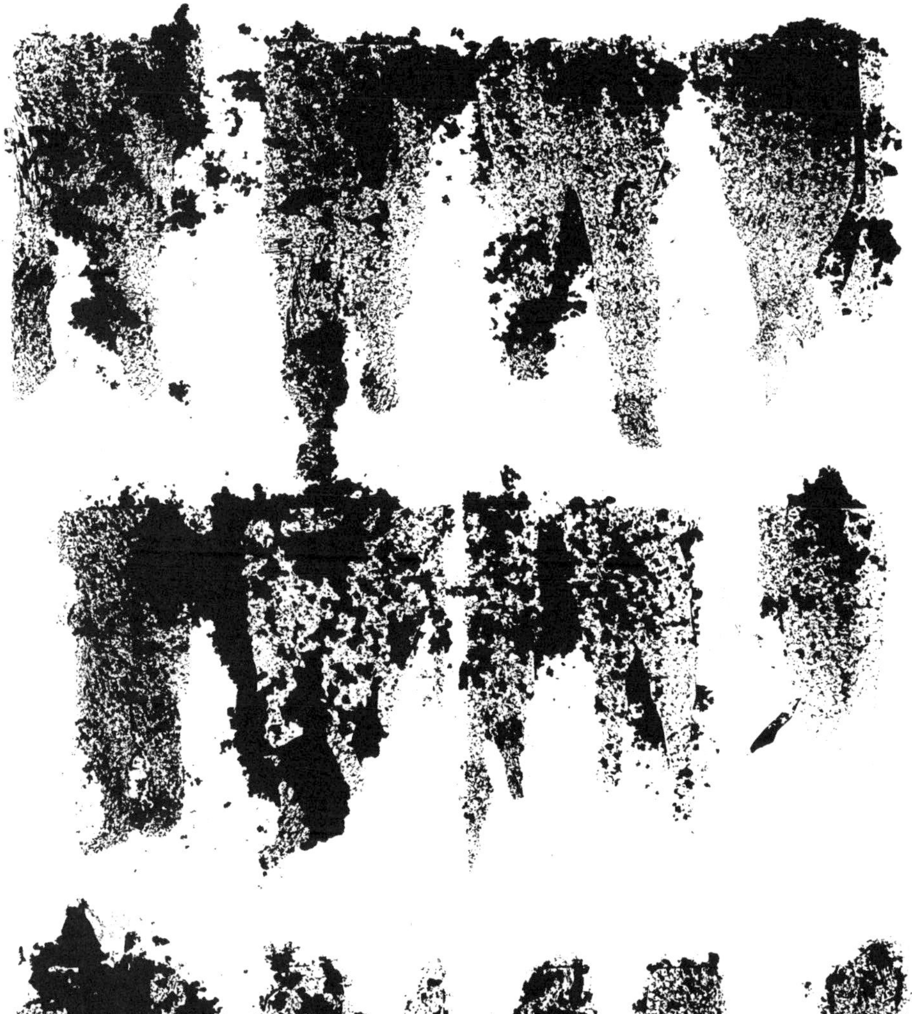

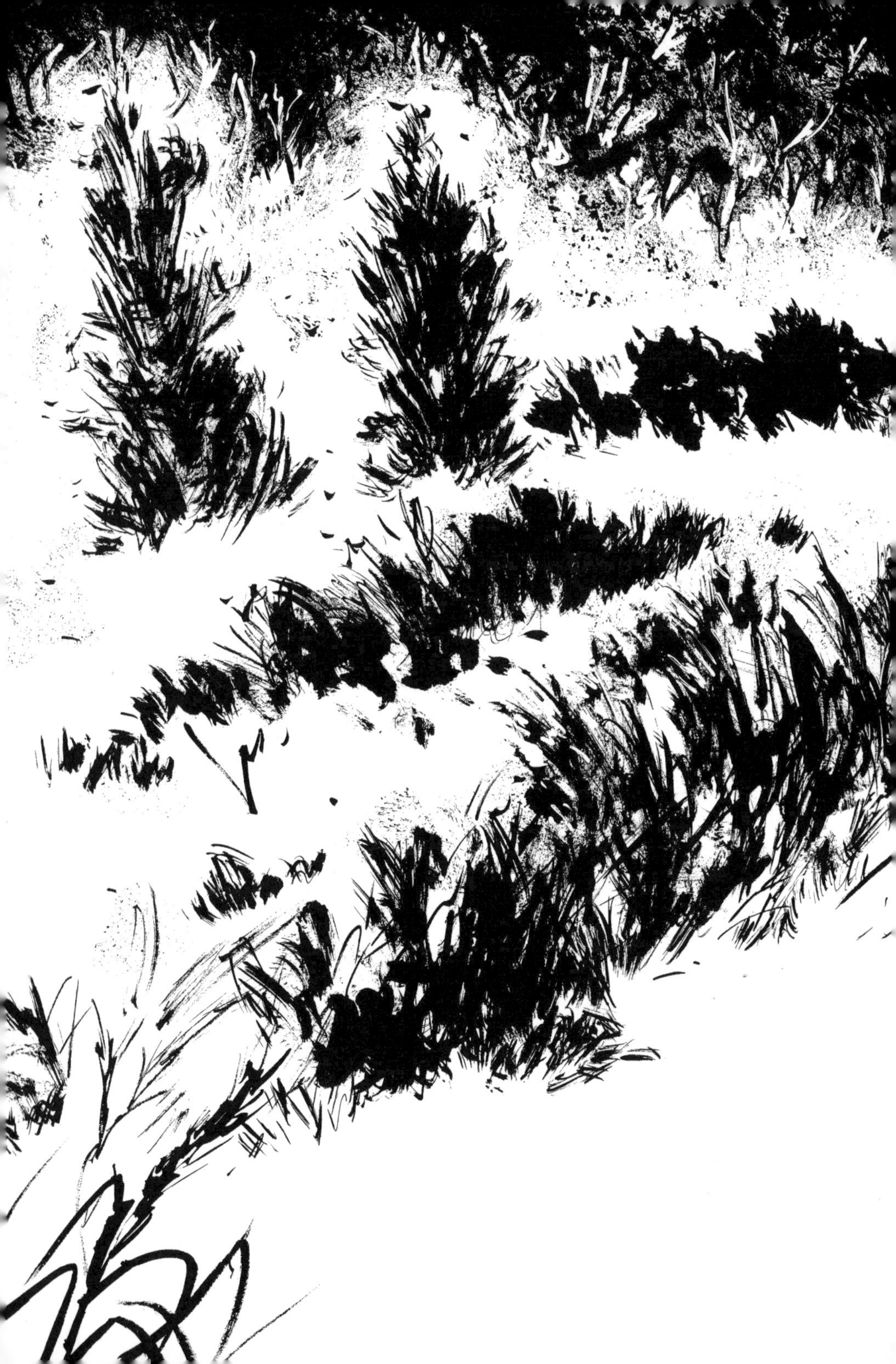

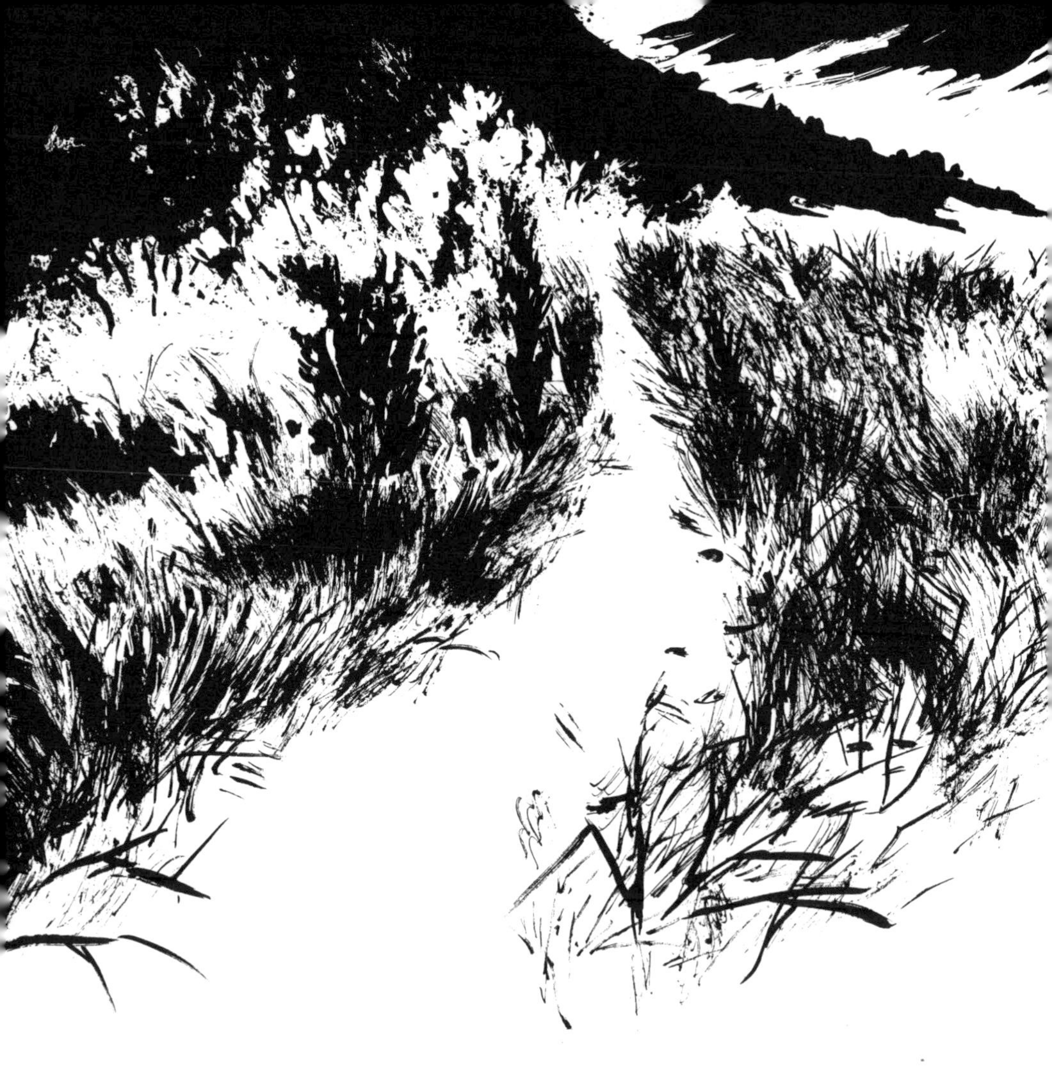

THEN ONE DAY AS I WAS WANDERING THE STREETS, I SUDDENLY THOUGHT OF HIM. SHIM YEONGSEOP, THE CAPTAIN FROM THE YANJI AIRFIELD. HE'D TOLD ME HIS HOME WAS IN LONGJING.

I DECIDED TO GO
LOOK FOR HIM.

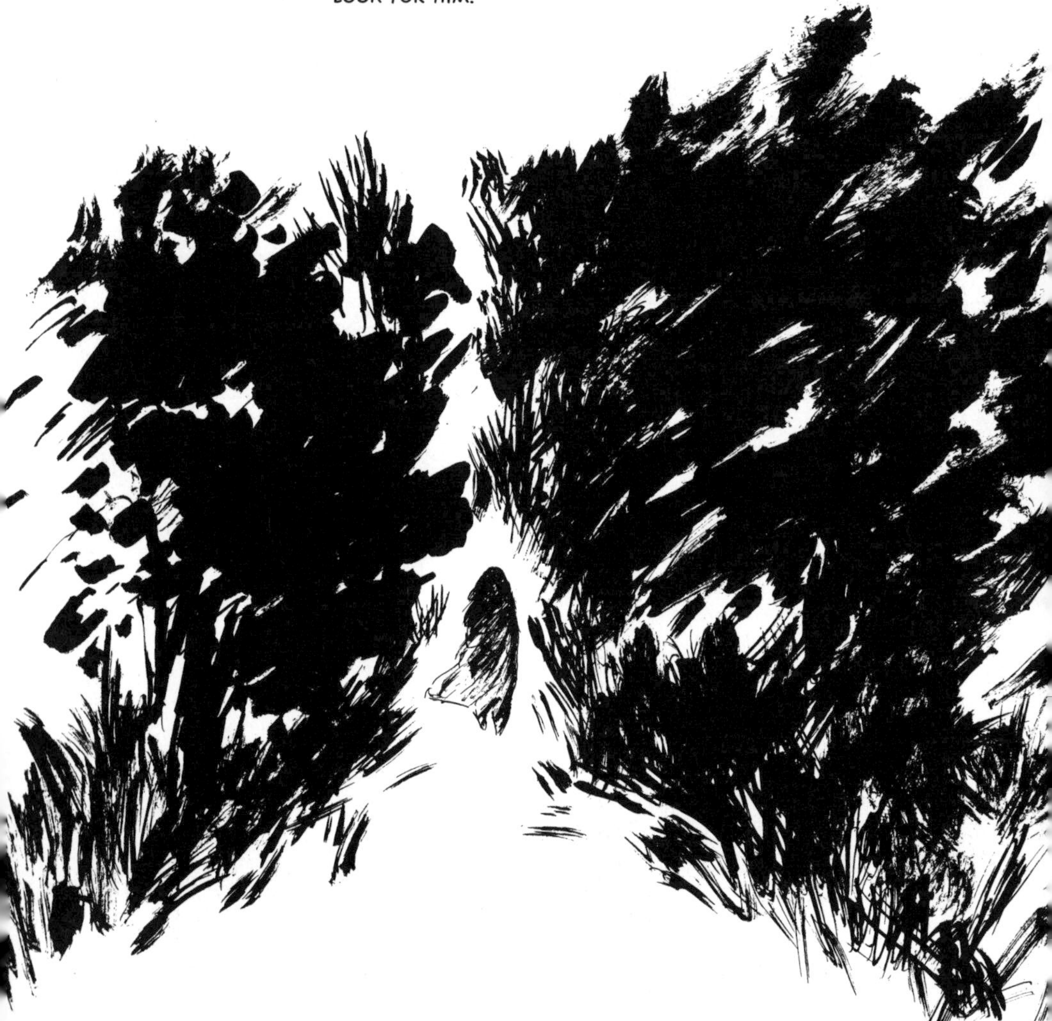

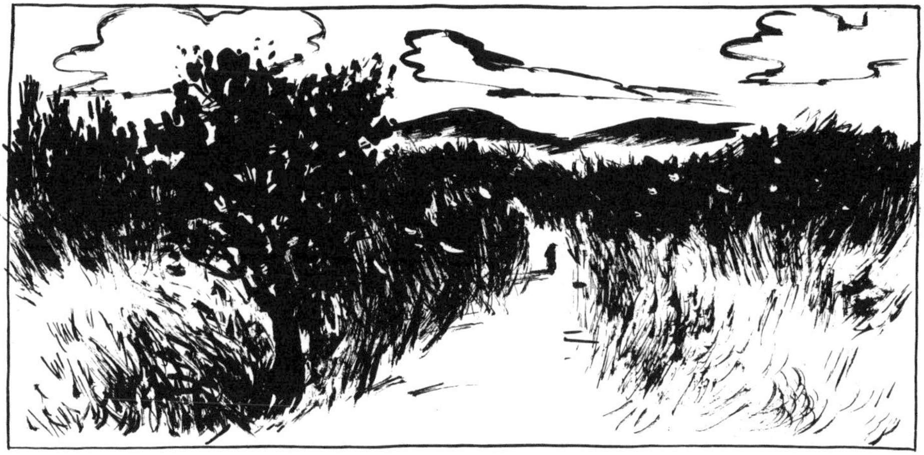

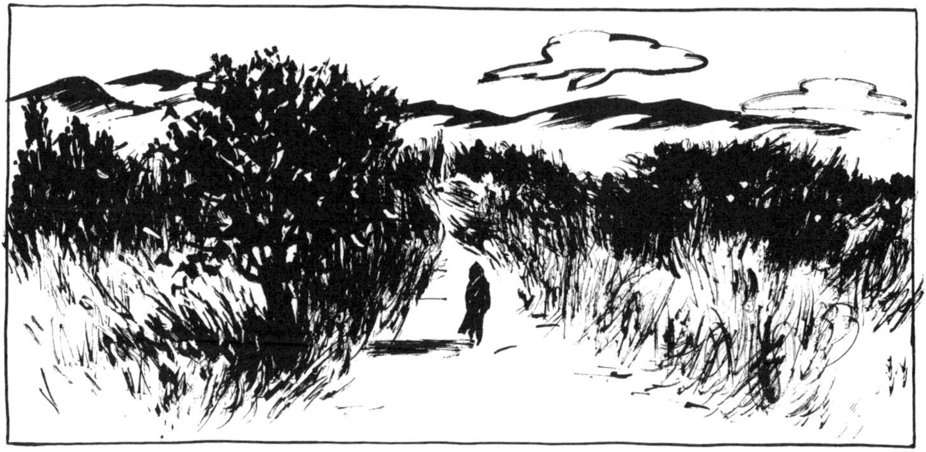

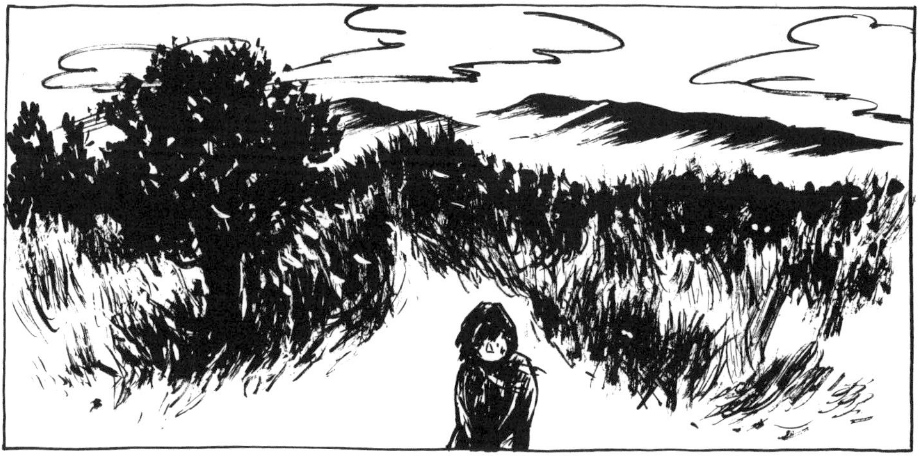

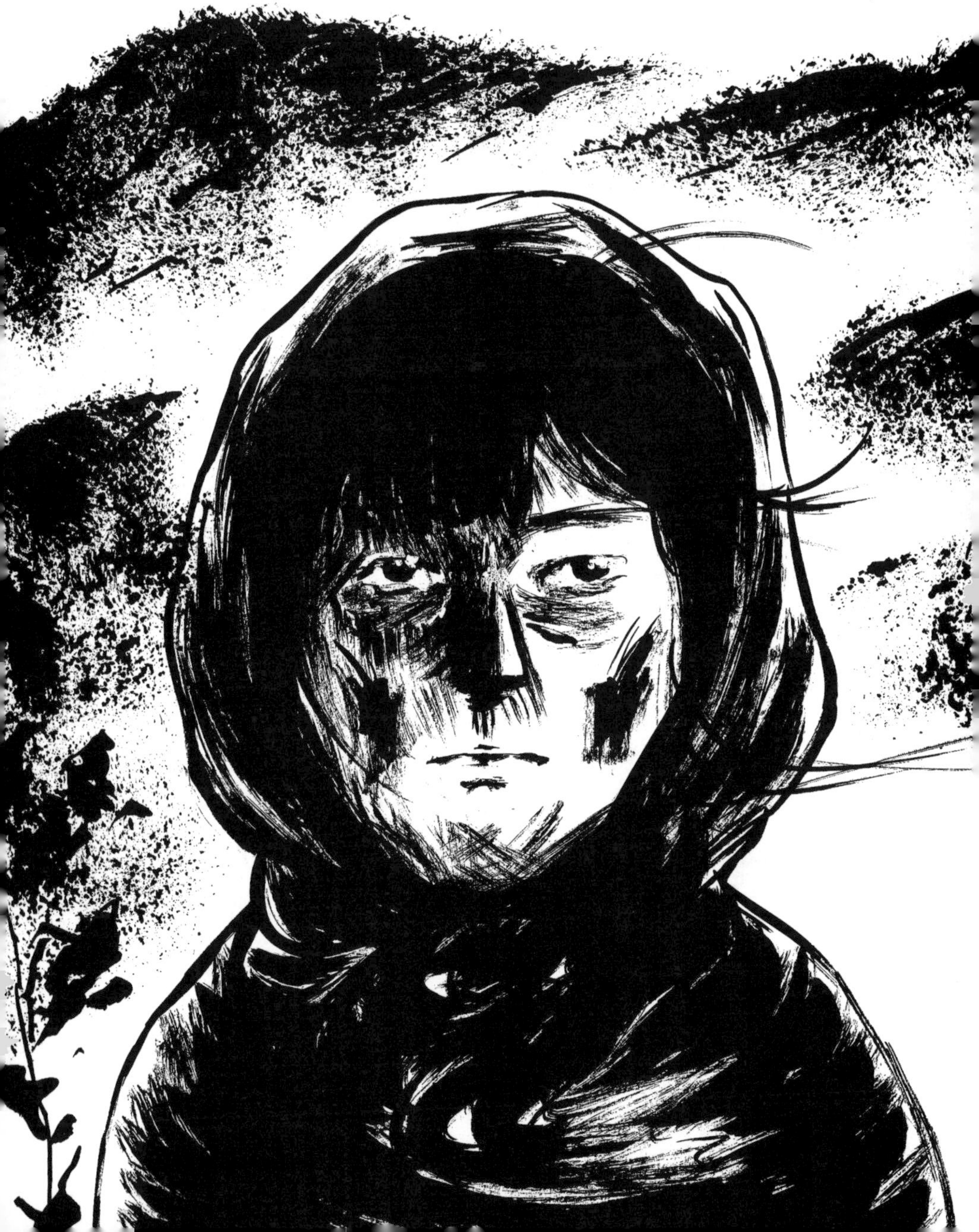

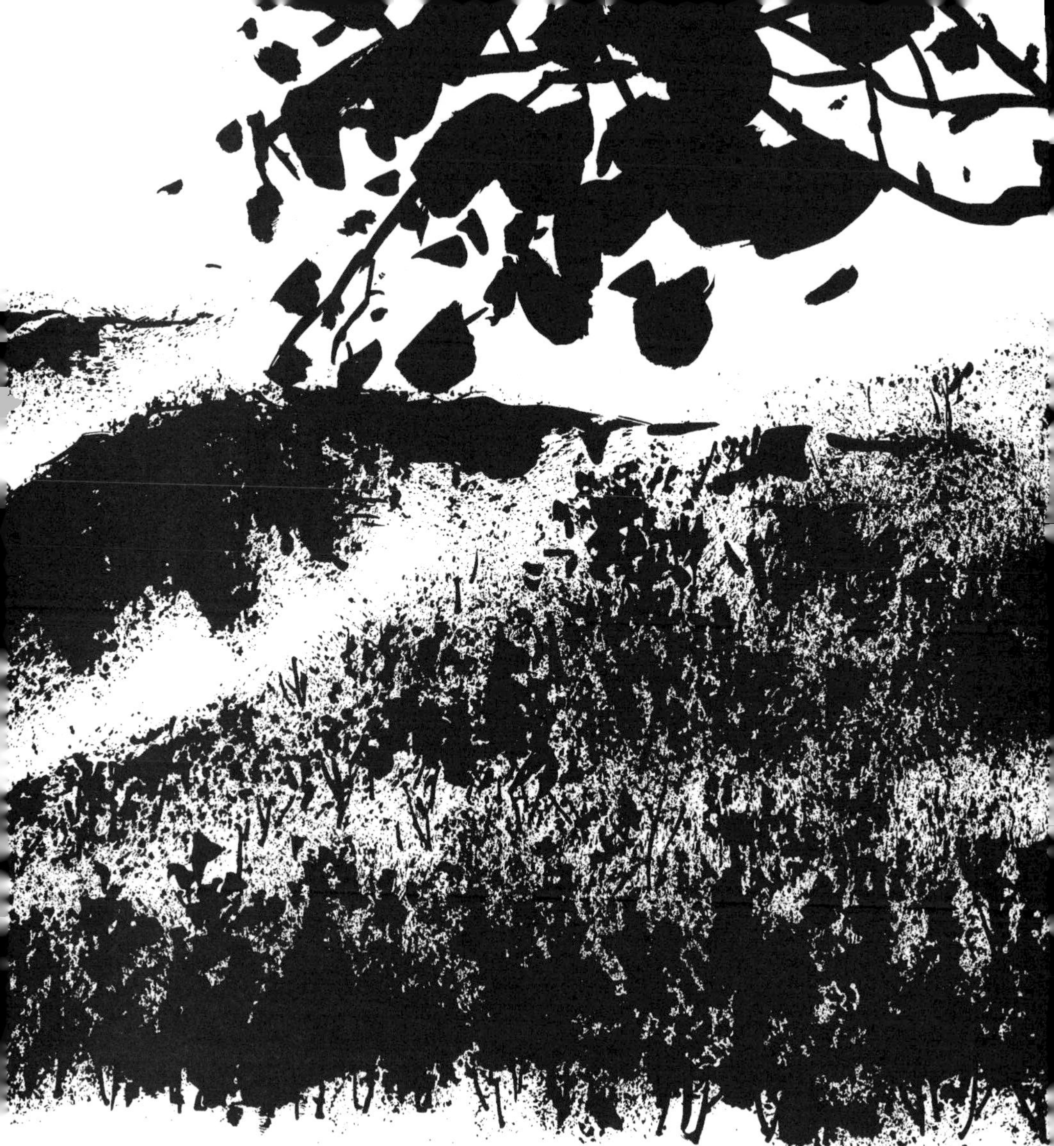

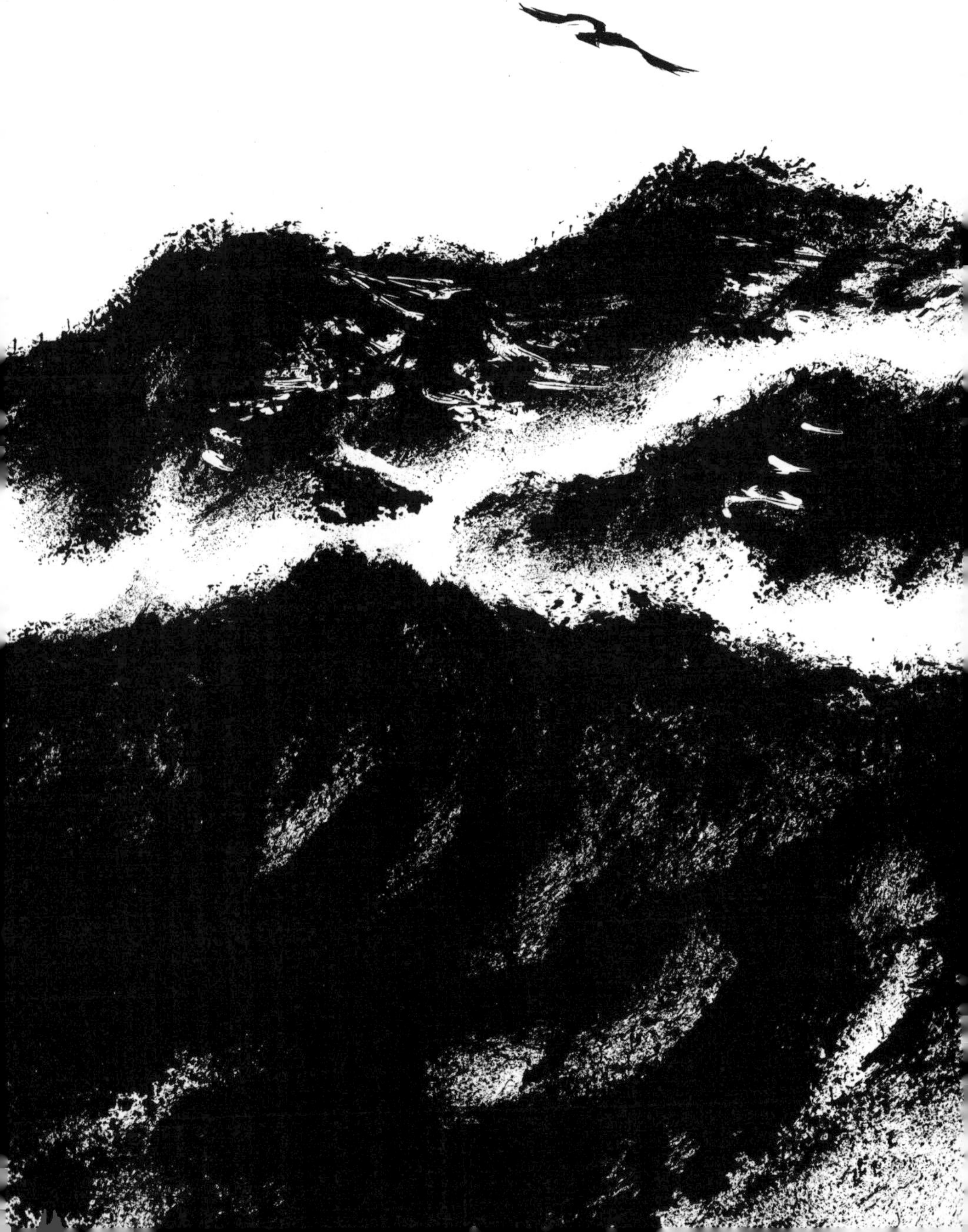

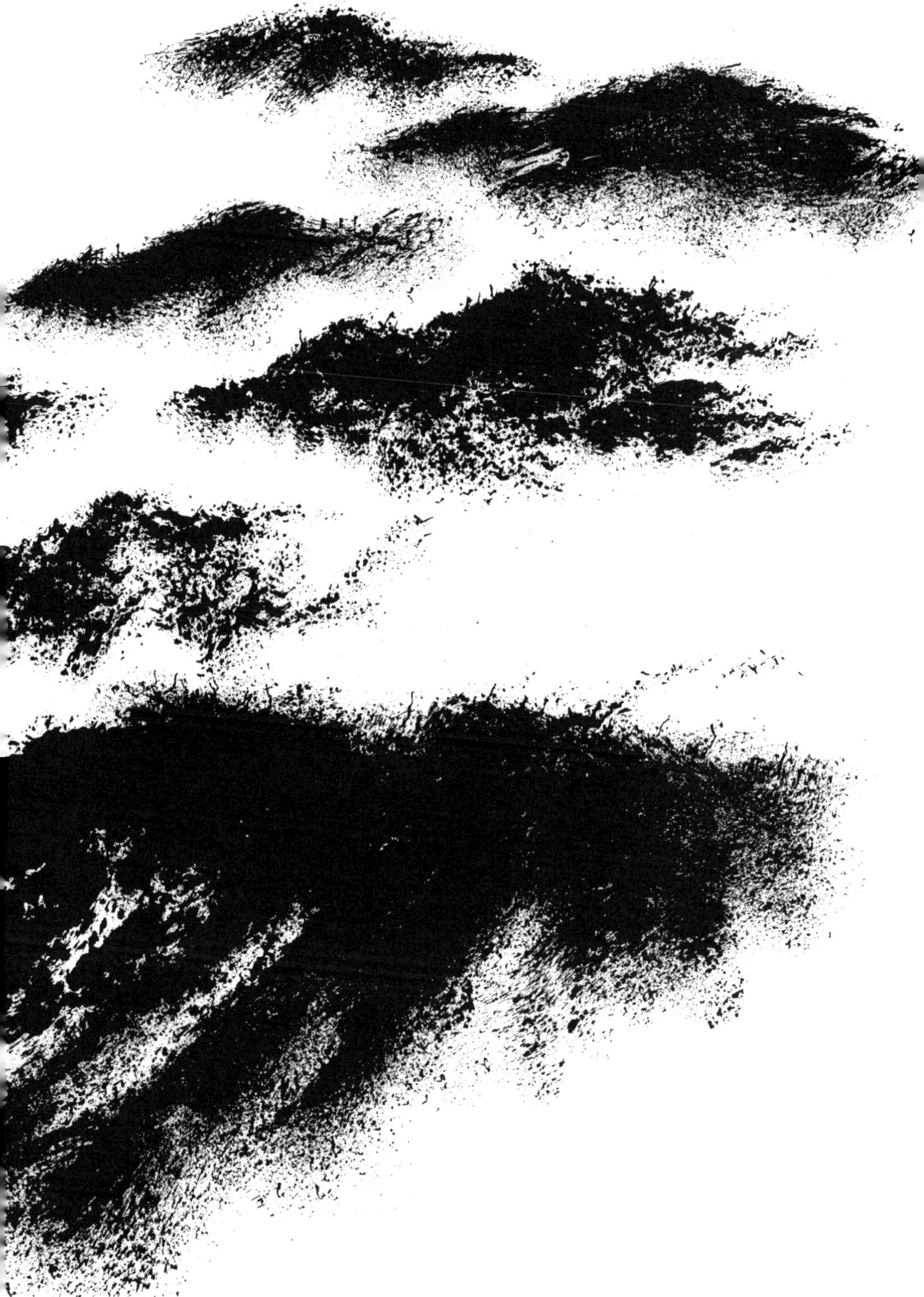

# FIRST MARRIAGE

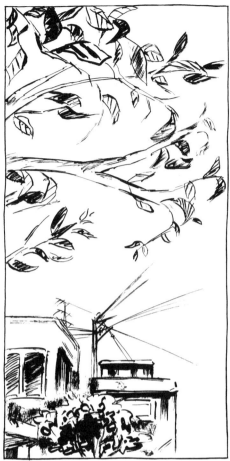

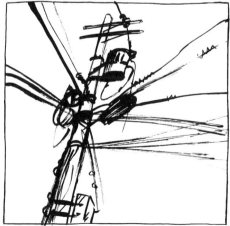

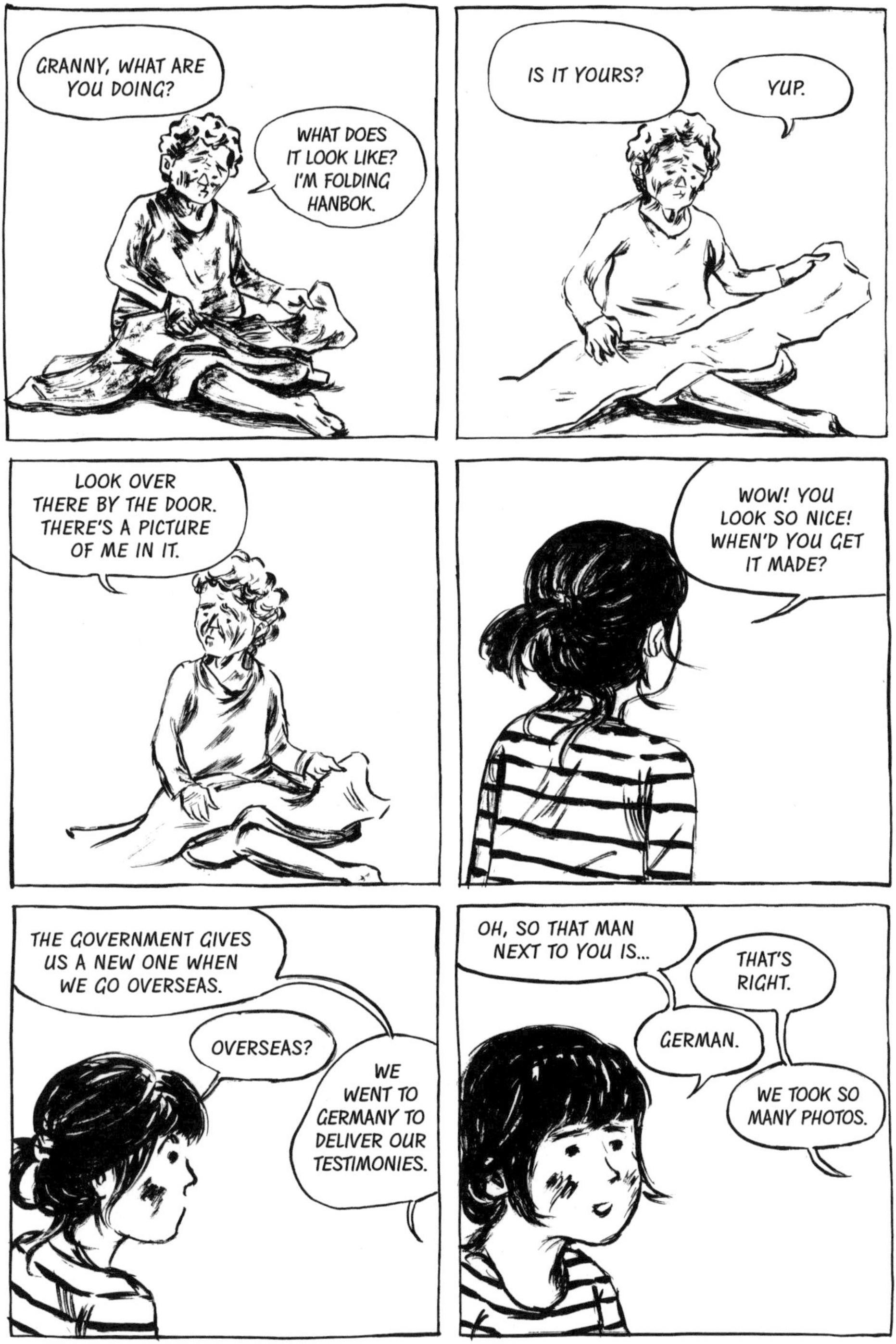
GRANNY, WHAT ARE YOU DOING?
WHAT DOES IT LOOK LIKE? I'M FOLDING HANBOK.
IS IT YOURS?
YUP.
LOOK OVER THERE BY THE DOOR. THERE'S A PICTURE OF ME IN IT.
WOW! YOU LOOK SO NICE! WHEN'D YOU GET IT MADE?
THE GOVERNMENT GIVES US A NEW ONE WHEN WE GO OVERSEAS.
OVERSEAS?
WE WENT TO GERMANY TO DELIVER OUR TESTIMONIES.
OH, SO THAT MAN NEXT TO YOU IS...
GERMAN.
THAT'S RIGHT.
WE TOOK SO MANY PHOTOS.

I GUESS THE HANBOK KEEPS YOU COOL DURING THE SUMMER?
NO WAY, IT'S UNCOMFORTABLE.
OH! WHAT'S THIS?
I TOLD YOU, I TOOK IT IN GERMANY.
NO.
NOT THE ONE WITH THE HANBOK.
THE PICTURE OF THE YOUNG WOMAN.
OH, THAT?
THAT'S ME.
WOW, YOU WERE QUITE A LOOKER!
WHEN WAS IT TAKEN?
AFTER THE WAR.
I WANTED TO HAVE AT LEAST ONE PICTURE OF WHEN I LOOKED GOOD, BUT...
YOU WERE BEAUTIFUL, GRANNY.
TRULY.

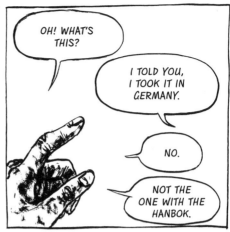

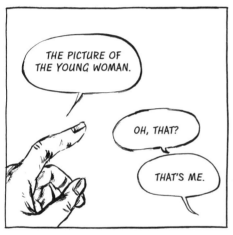

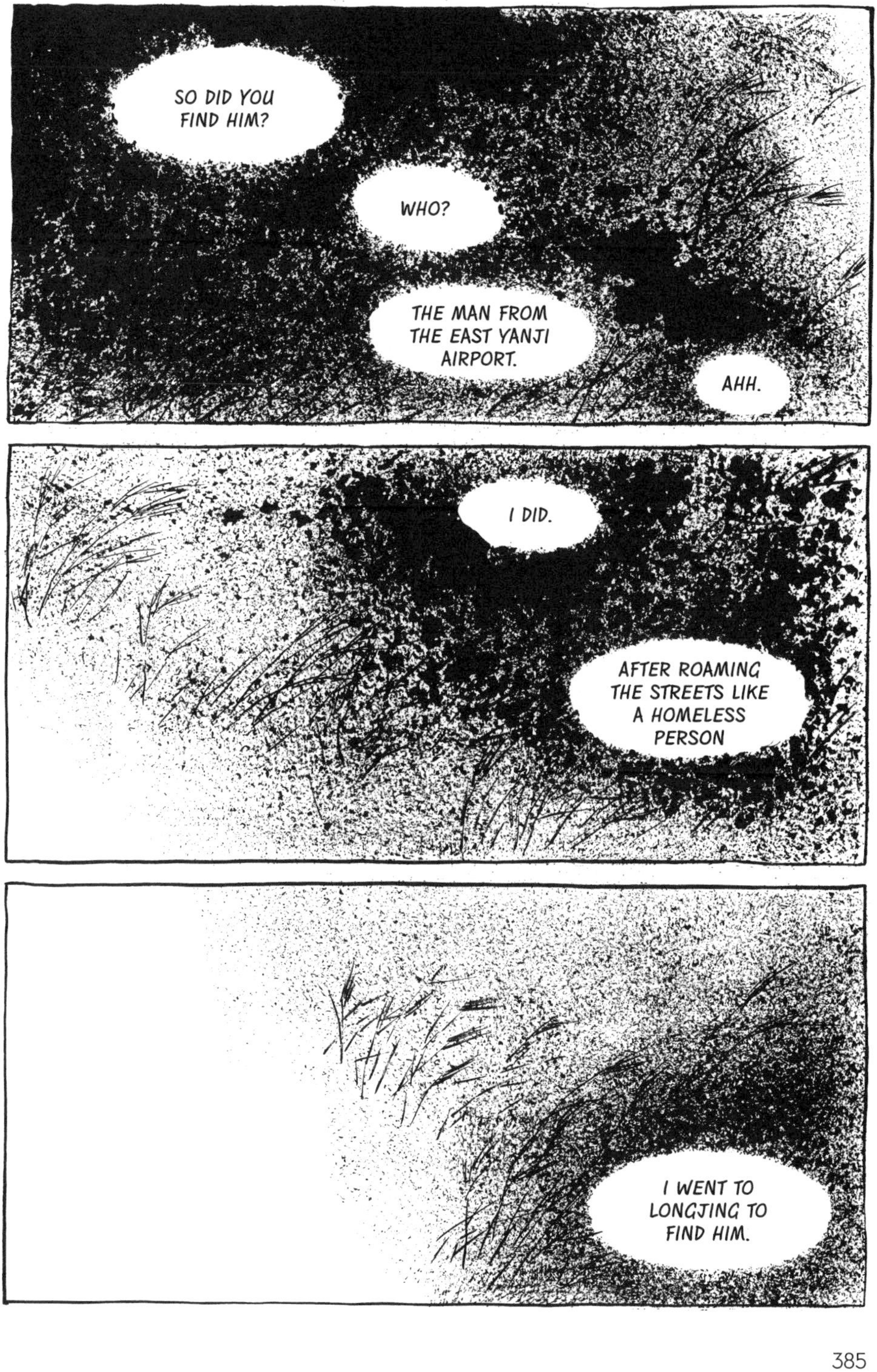
SO DID YOU FIND HIM?
WHO?
THE MAN FROM THE EAST YANJI AIRPORT.
AHH.
I DID.
AFTER ROAMING THE STREETS LIKE A HOMELESS PERSON
I WENT TO LONGJING TO FIND HIM.

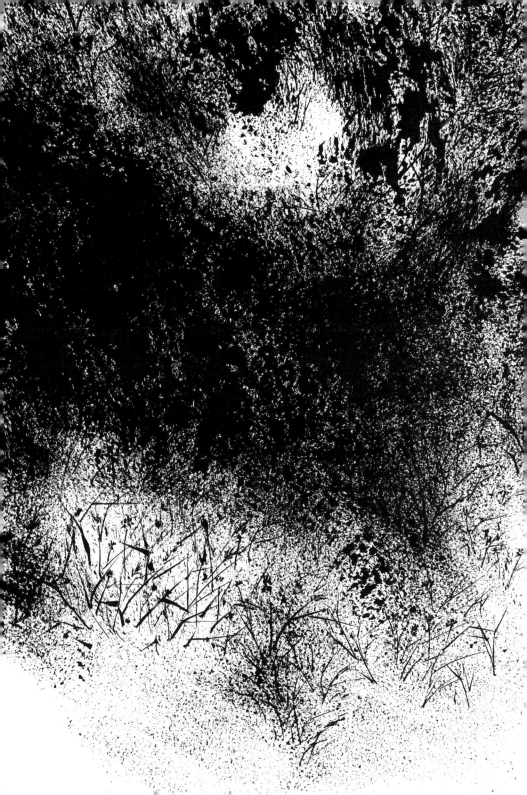

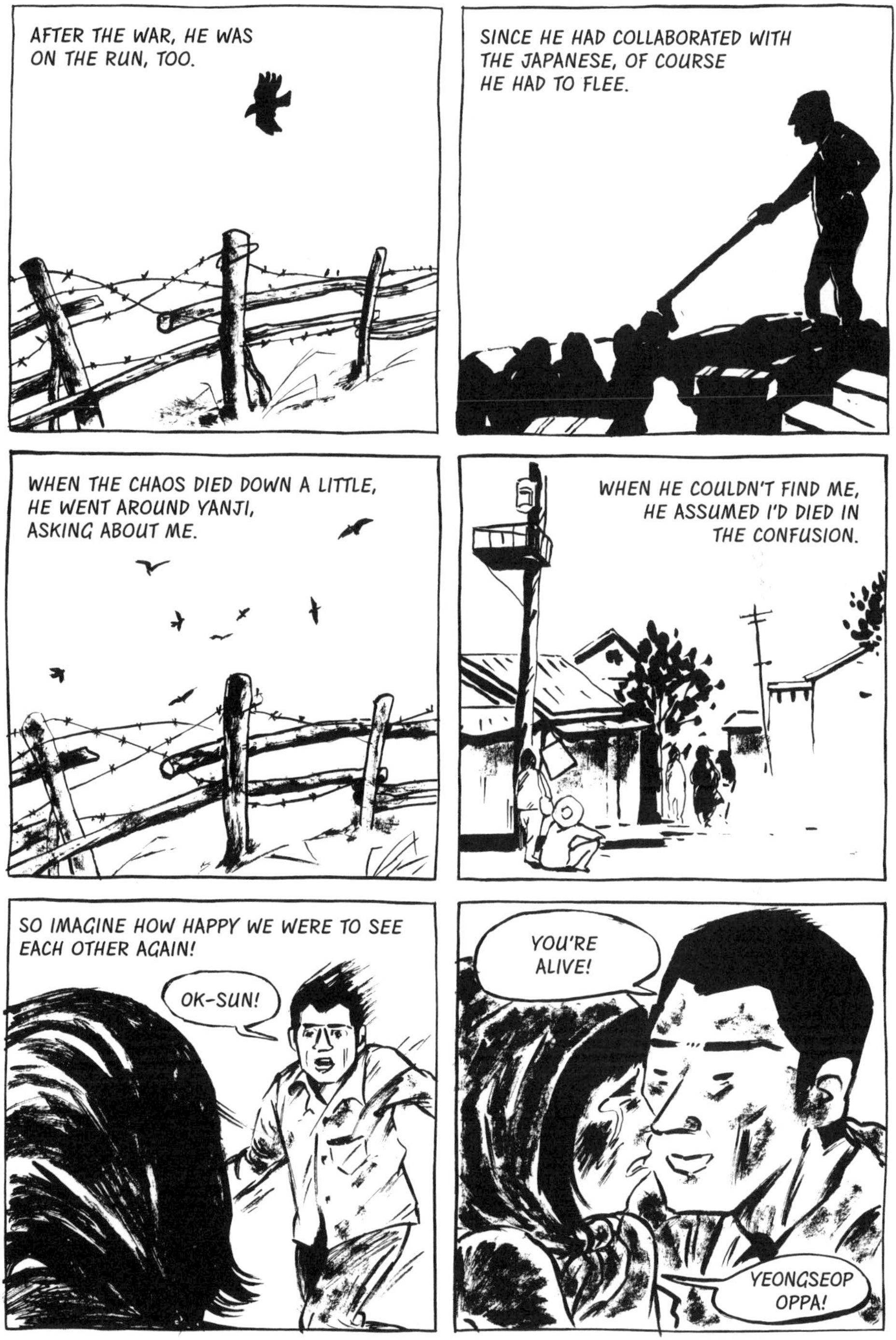
AFTER THE WAR, HE WAS ON THE RUN, TOO.
SINCE HE HAD COLLABORATED WITH THE JAPANESE, OF COURSE HE HAD TO FLEE.
WHEN THE CHAOS DIED DOWN A LITTLE, HE WENT AROUND YANJI, ASKING ABOUT ME.
WHEN HE COULDN'T FIND ME, HE ASSUMED I'D DIED IN THE CONFUSION.
SO IMAGINE HOW HAPPY WE WERE TO SEE EACH OTHER AGAIN!
OK-SUN!
YOU'RE ALIVE!
YEONGSEOP OPPA!

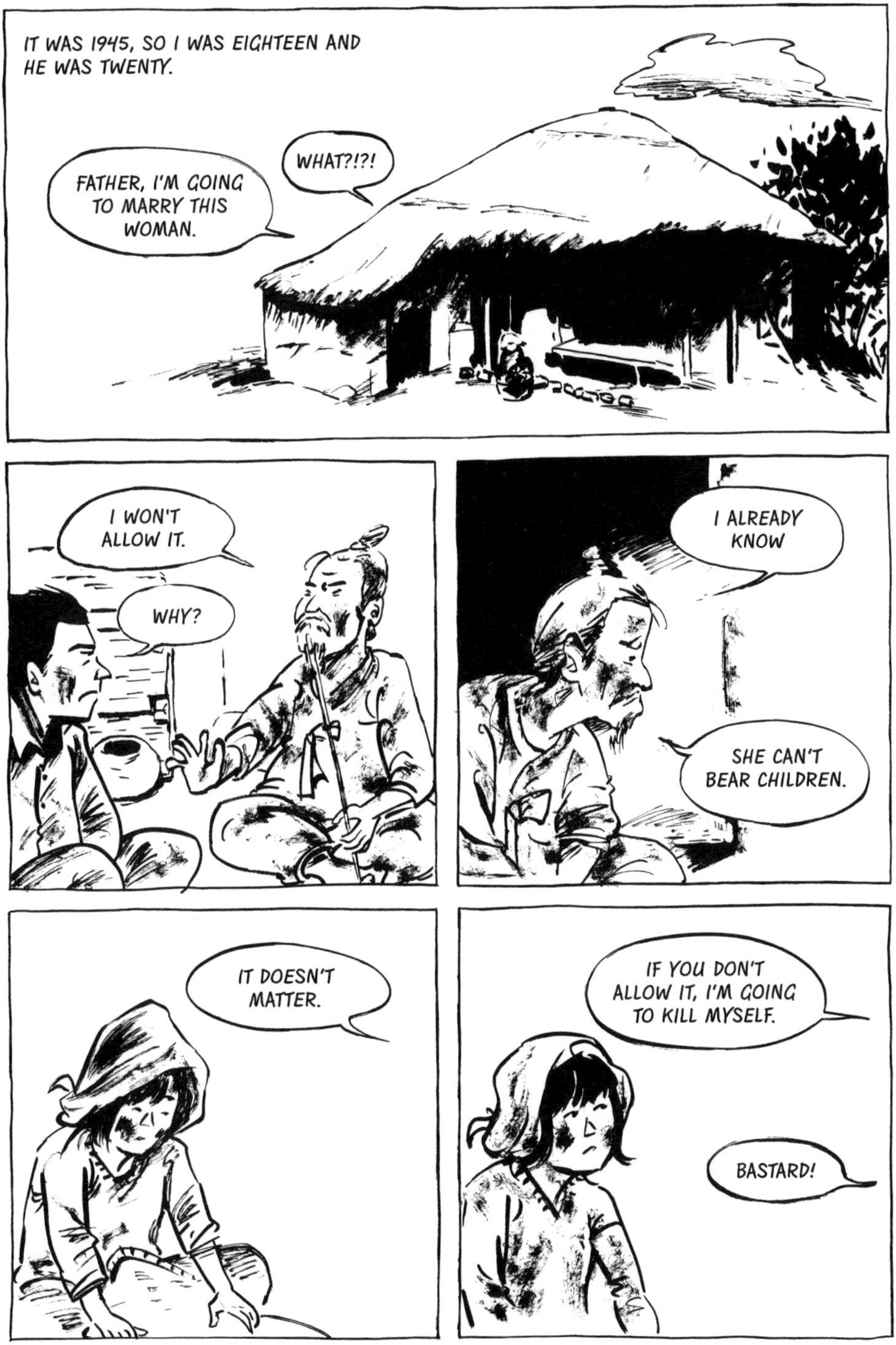
IT WAS 1945, SO I WAS EIGHTEEN AND HE WAS TWENTY.
FATHER, I'M GOING TO MARRY THIS WOMAN.
WHAT?!?!
I WON'T ALLOW IT.
WHY?
I ALREADY KNOW
SHE CAN'T BEAR CHILDREN.
IT DOESN'T MATTER.
IF YOU DON'T ALLOW IT, I'M GOING TO KILL MYSELF.
BASTARD!

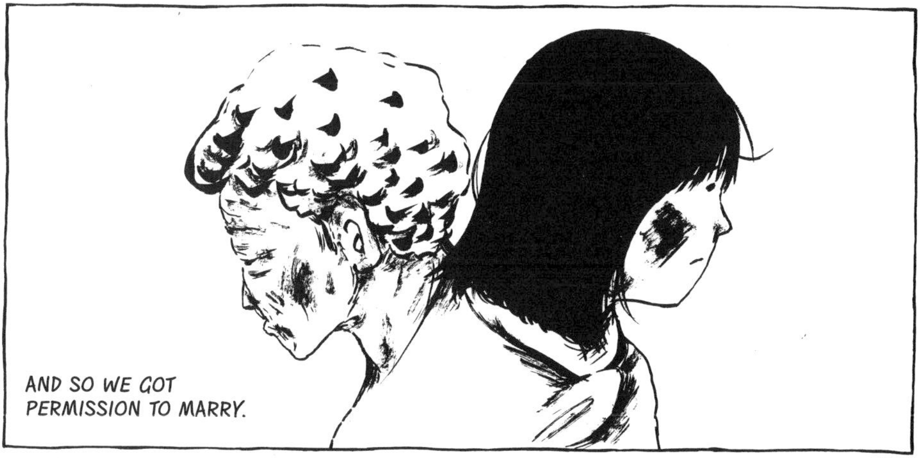
AND SO WE GOT PERMISSION TO MARRY.

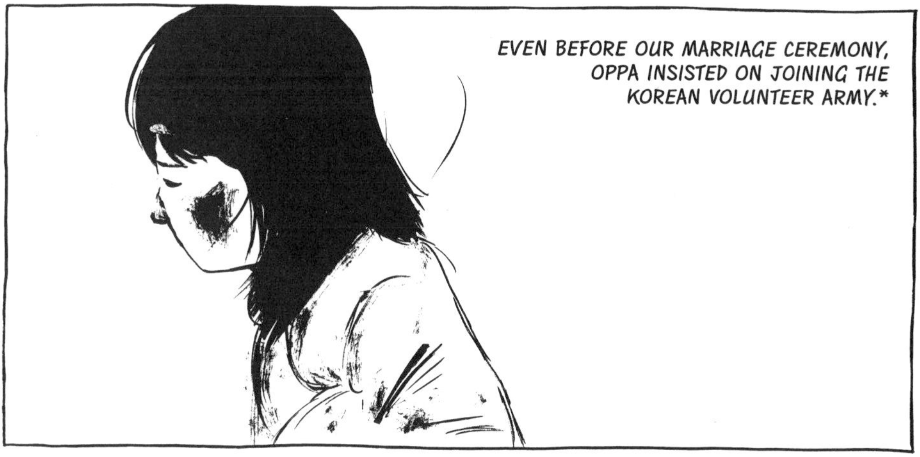
EVEN BEFORE OUR MARRIAGE CEREMONY, OPPA INSISTED ON JOINING THE KOREAN VOLUNTEER ARMY.*

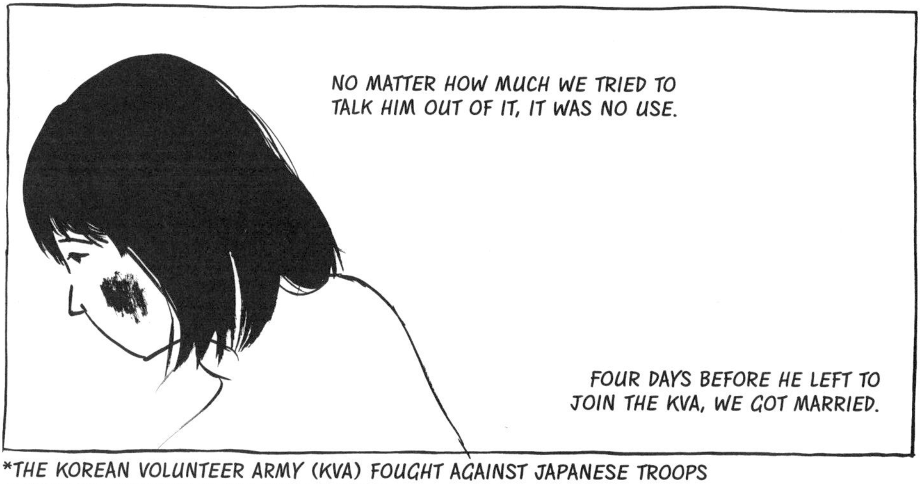
NO MATTER HOW MUCH WE TRIED TO TALK HIM OUT OF IT, IT WAS NO USE.
FOUR DAYS BEFORE HE LEFT TO JOIN THE KVA, WE GOT MARRIED.

*THE KOREAN VOLUNTEER ARMY (KVA) FOUGHT AGAINST JAPANESE TROOPS ALONGSIDE CHINESE COMMUNIST FORCES.

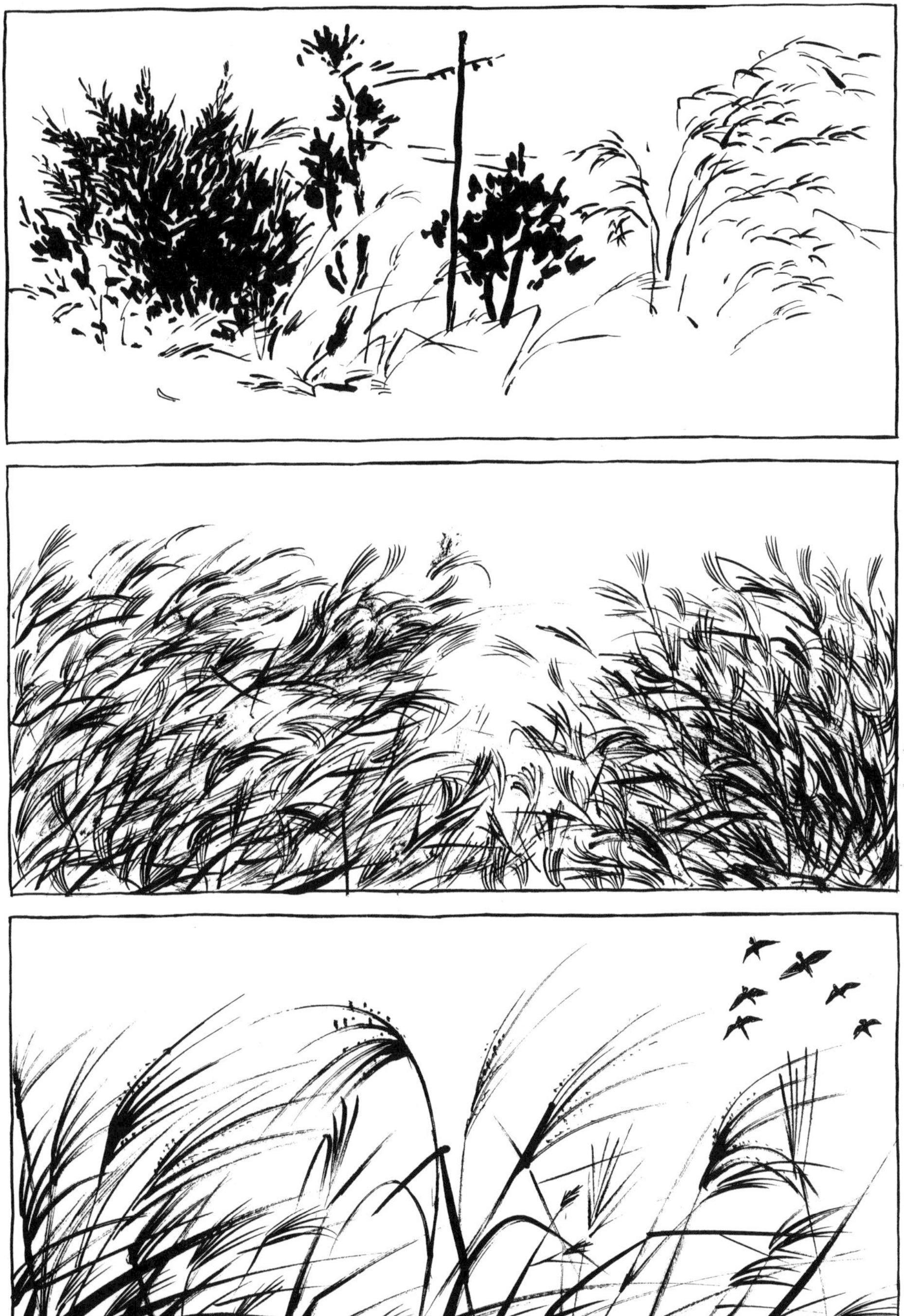

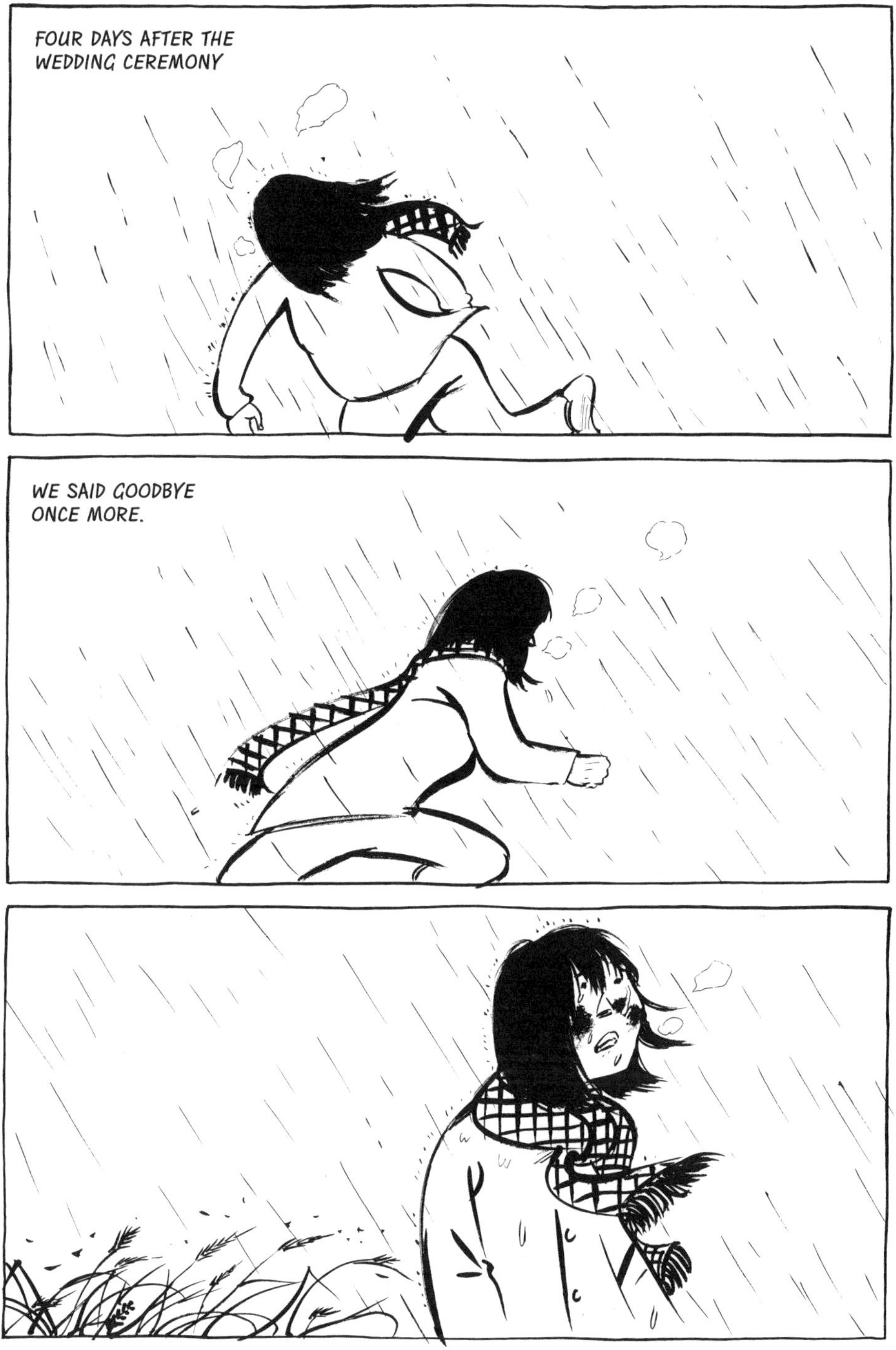
FOUR DAYS AFTER THE WEDDING CEREMONY
WE SAID GOODBYE ONCE MORE.

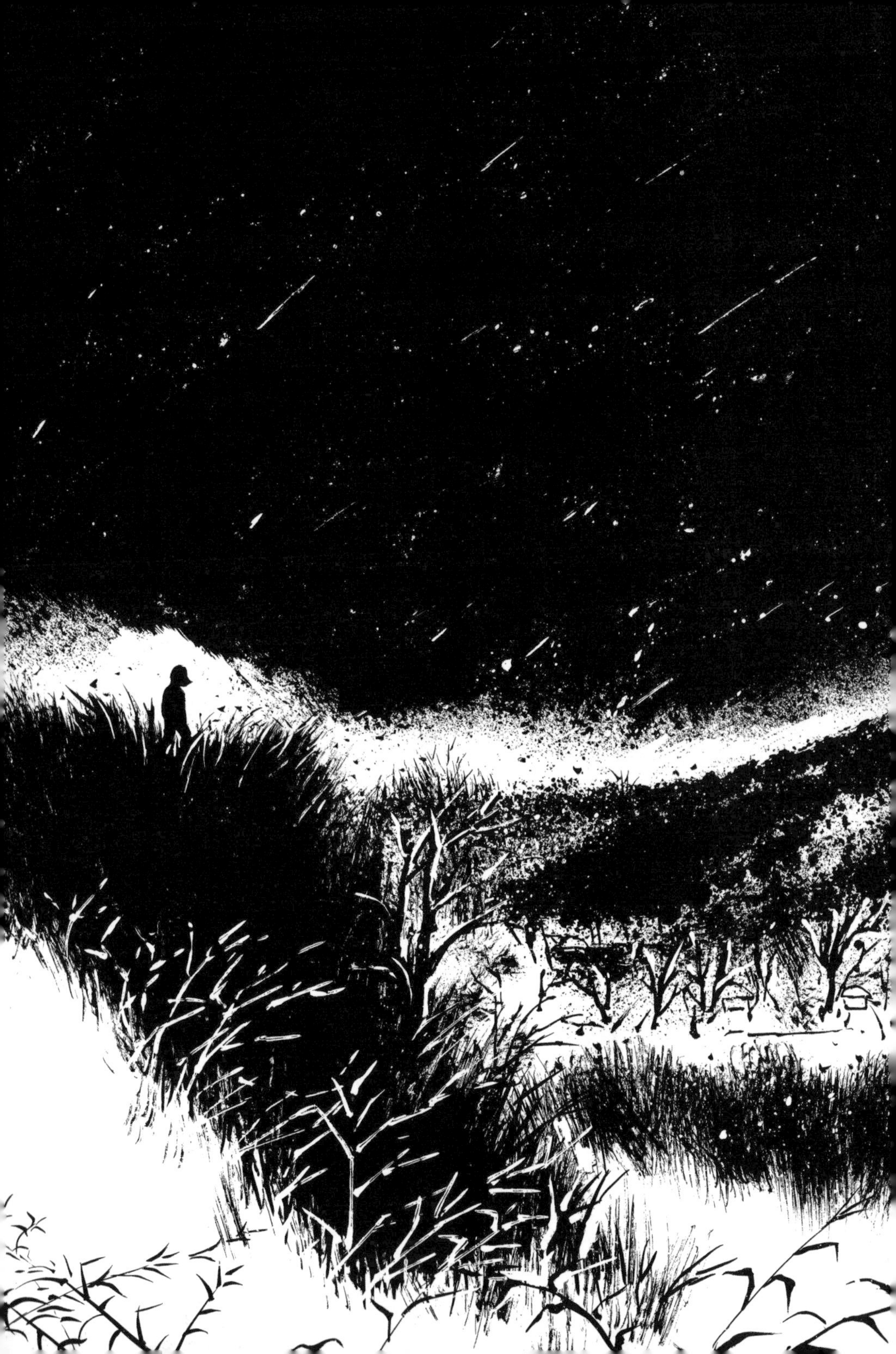

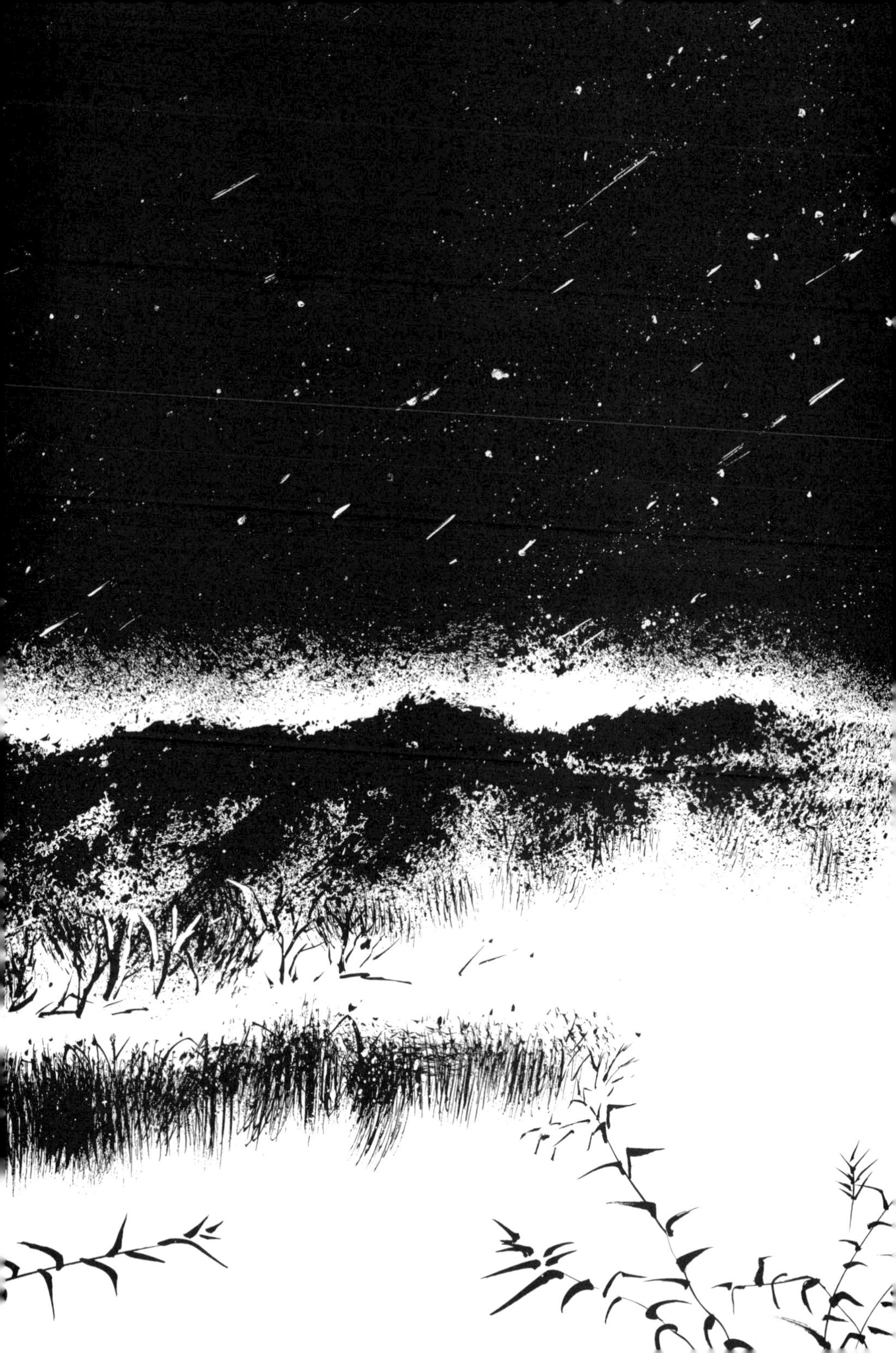

I HEARD LATER THAT THE KVA HAD
SENT HIM TO NORTH KOREA.

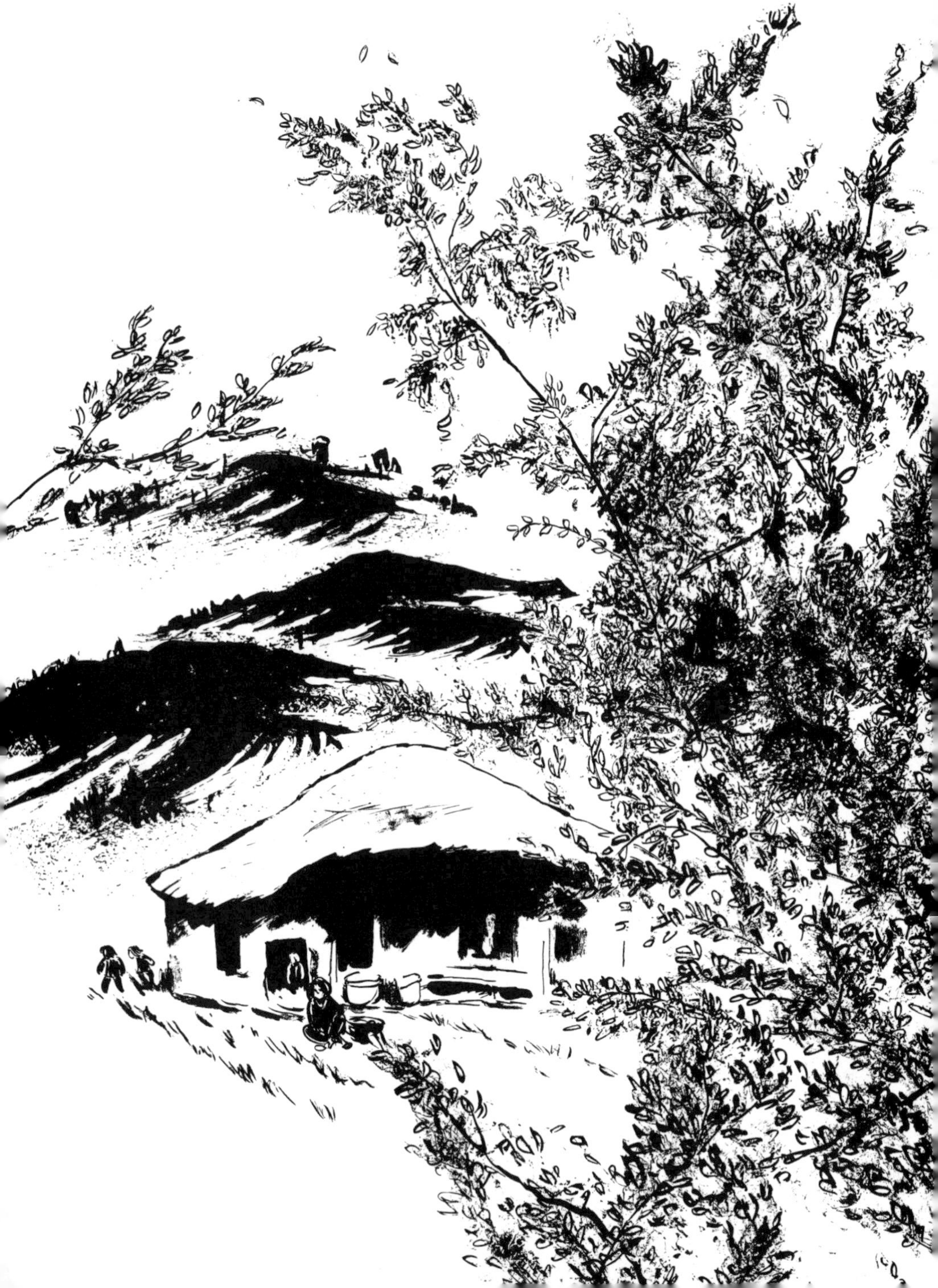

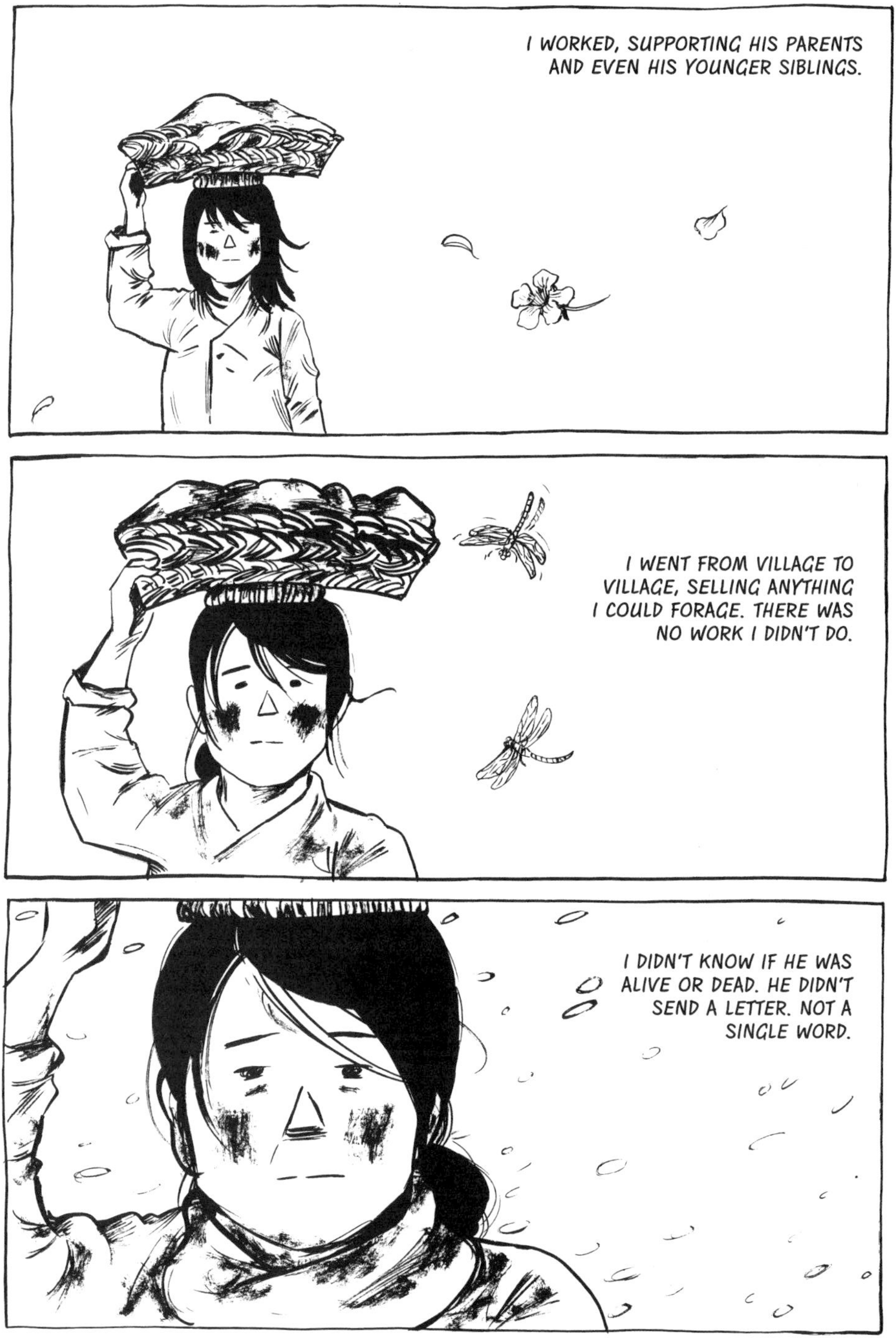
I WORKED, SUPPORTING HIS PARENTS AND EVEN HIS YOUNGER SIBLINGS.
I WENT FROM VILLAGE TO VILLAGE, SELLING ANYTHING I COULD FORAGE. THERE WAS NO WORK I DIDN'T DO.
I DIDN'T KNOW IF HE WAS ALIVE OR DEAD. HE DIDN'T SEND A LETTER. NOT A SINGLE WORD.

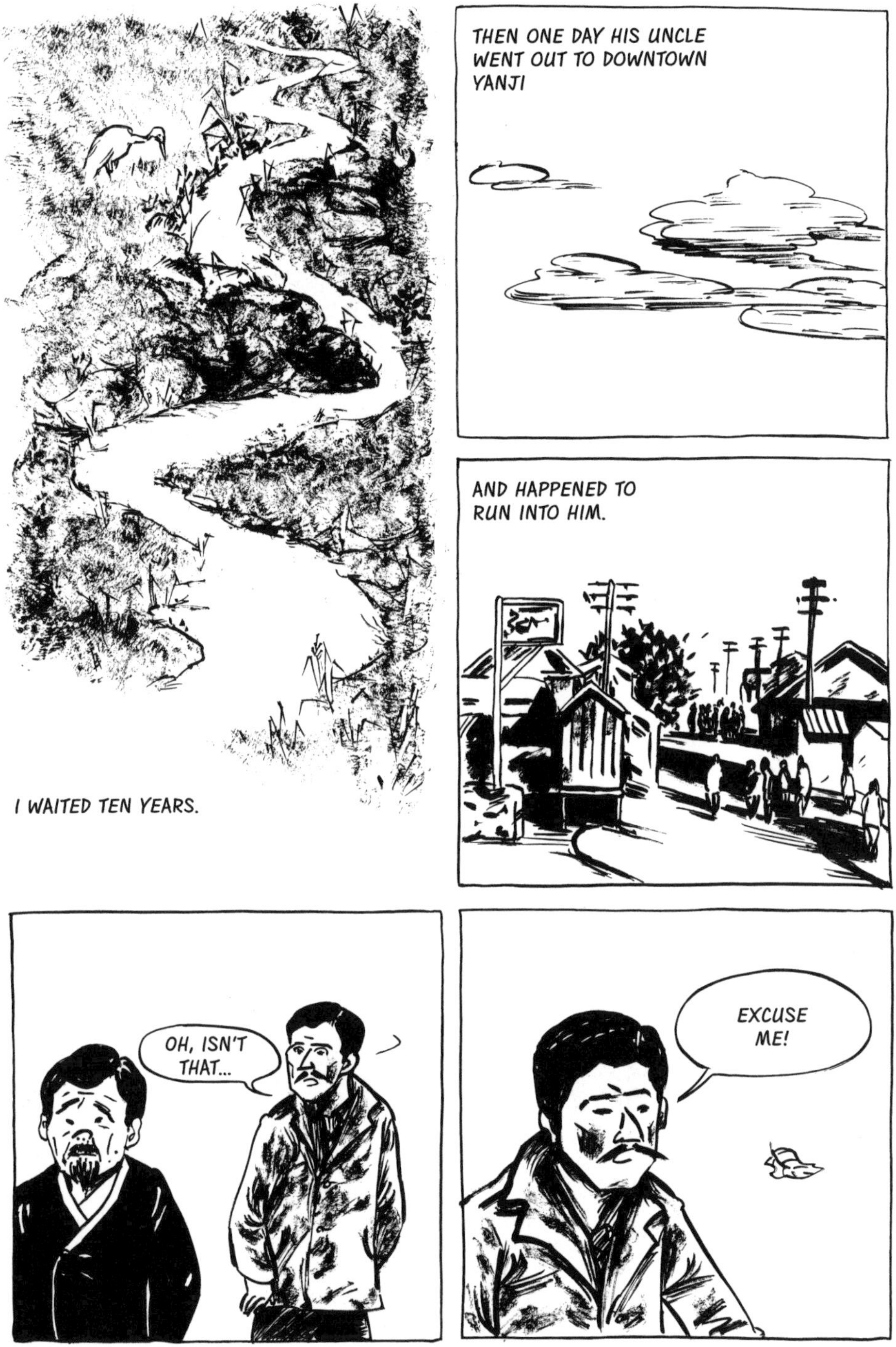
I WAITED TEN YEARS.
THEN ONE DAY HIS UNCLE WENT OUT TO DOWNTOWN YANJI
AND HAPPENED TO RUN INTO HIM.
OH, ISN'T THAT...
EXCUSE ME!

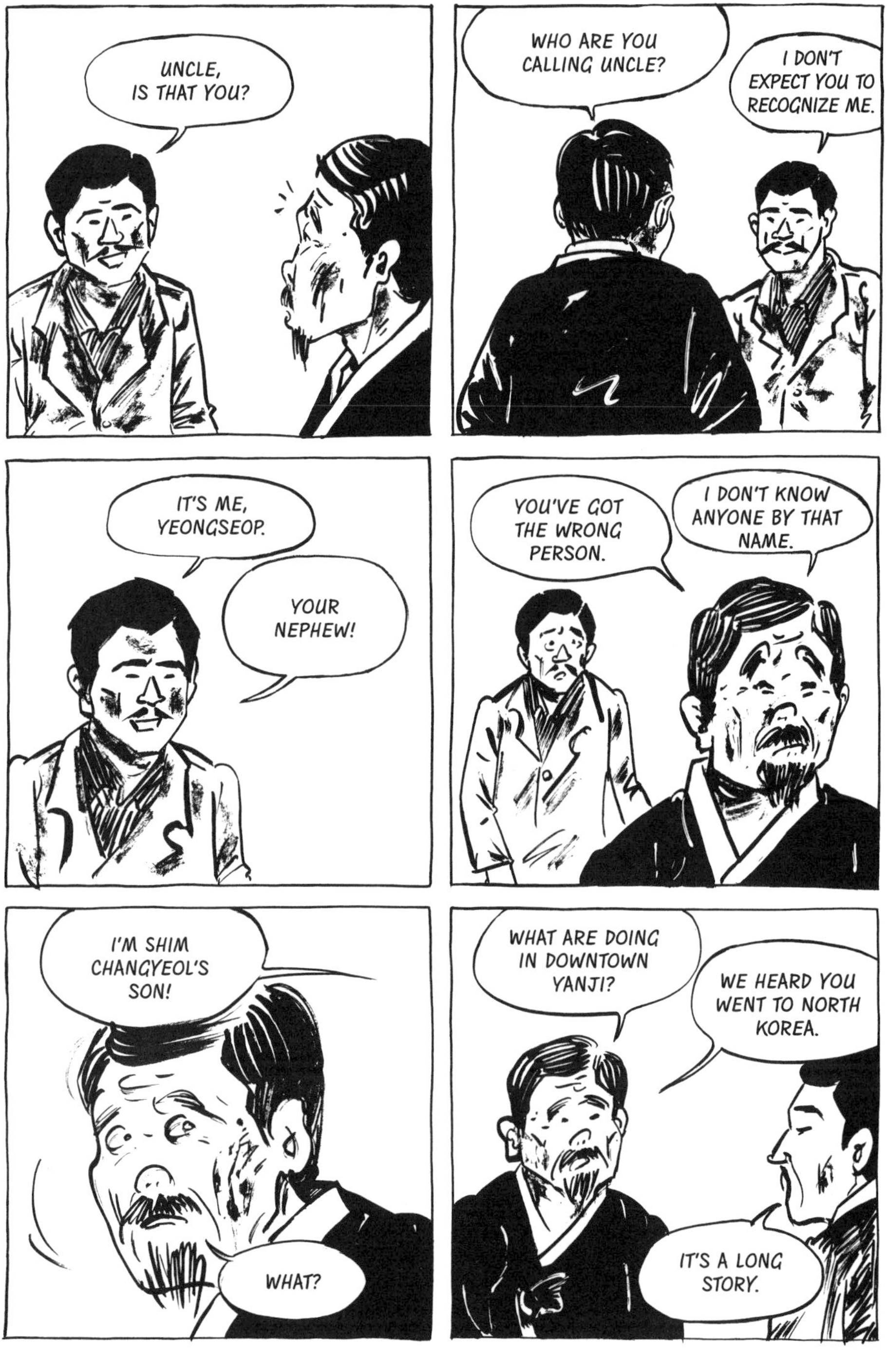
UNCLE, IS THAT YOU?
WHO ARE YOU CALLING UNCLE?
I DON'T EXPECT YOU TO RECOGNIZE ME.
IT'S ME, YEONGSEOP.
YOUR NEPHEW!
YOU'VE GOT THE WRONG PERSON.
I DON'T KNOW ANYONE BY THAT NAME.
I'M SHIM CHANGYEOL'S SON!
WHAT?
WHAT ARE DOING IN DOWNTOWN YANJI?
WE HEARD YOU WENT TO NORTH KOREA.
IT'S A LONG STORY.

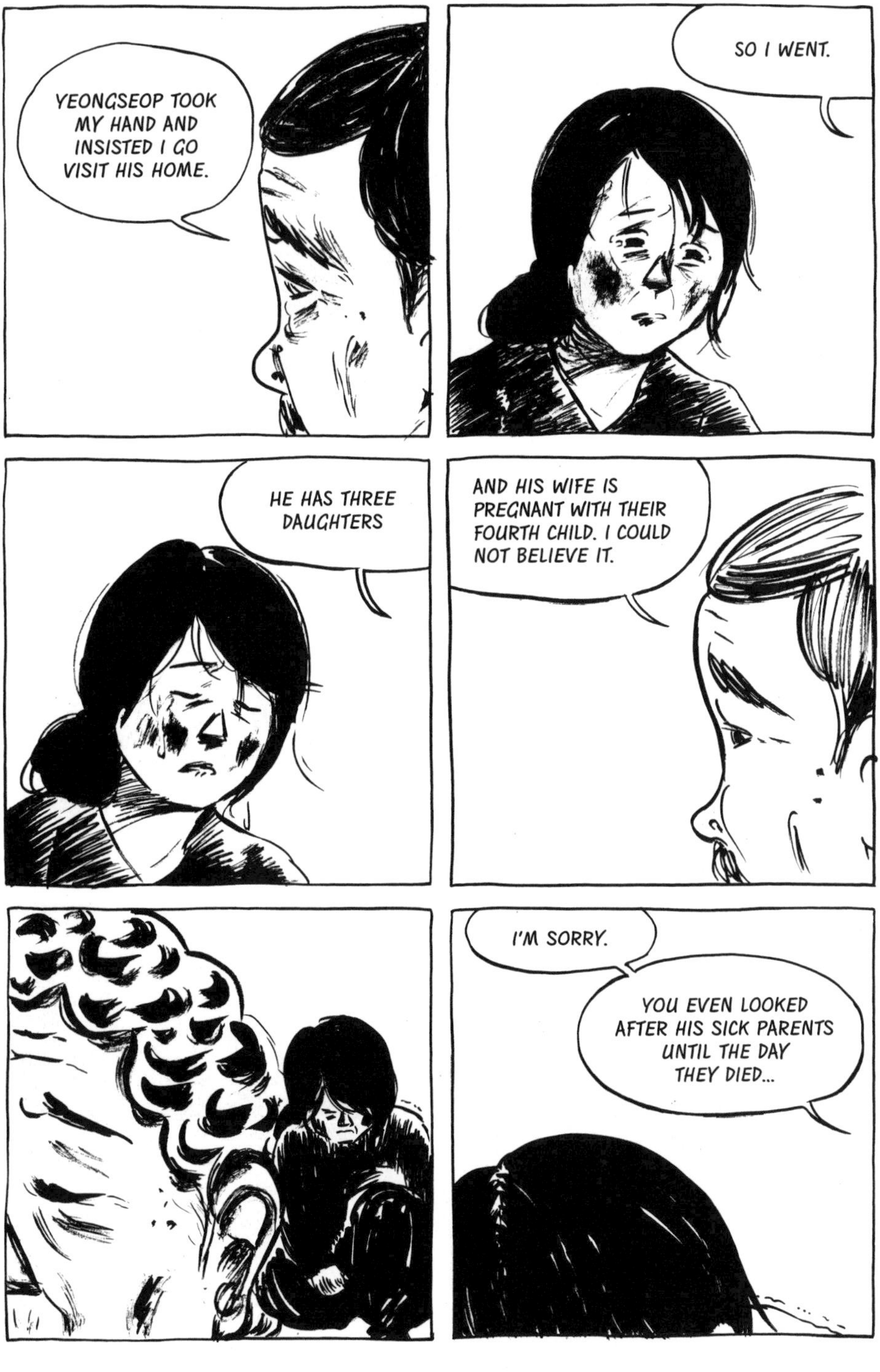
YEONGSEOP TOOK MY HAND AND INSISTED I GO VISIT HIS HOME.
SO I WENT.
HE HAS THREE DAUGHTERS
AND HIS WIFE IS PREGNANT WITH THEIR FOURTH CHILD. I COULD NOT BELIEVE IT.
I'M SORRY.
YOU EVEN LOOKED AFTER HIS SICK PARENTS UNTIL THE DAY THEY DIED...

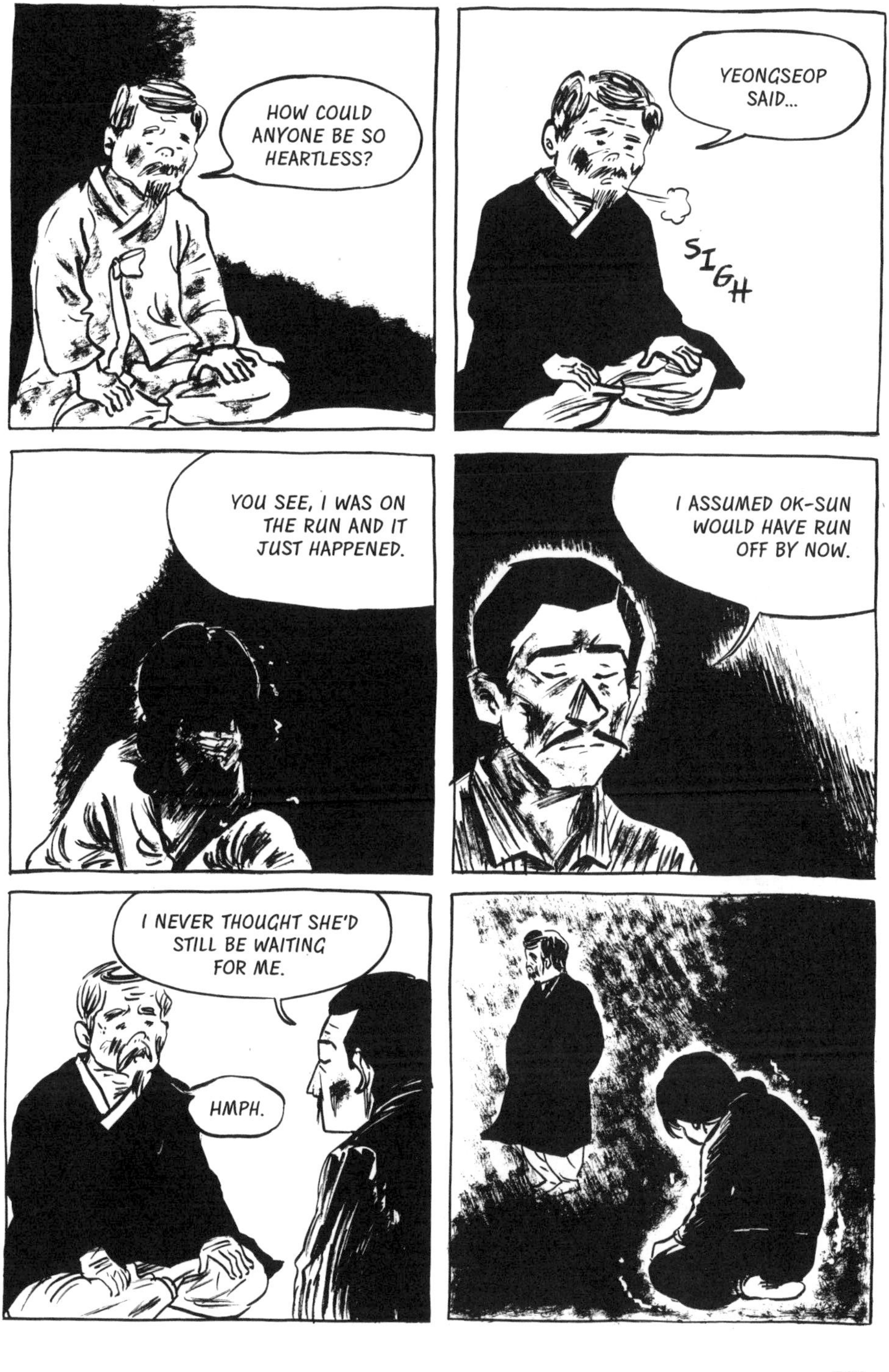
HOW COULD ANYONE BE SO HEARTLESS?
YEONGSEOP SAID...
SIGH
YOU SEE, I WAS ON THE RUN AND IT JUST HAPPENED.
I ASSUMED OK-SUN WOULD HAVE RUN OFF BY NOW.
I NEVER THOUGHT SHE'D STILL BE WAITING FOR ME.
HMPH.

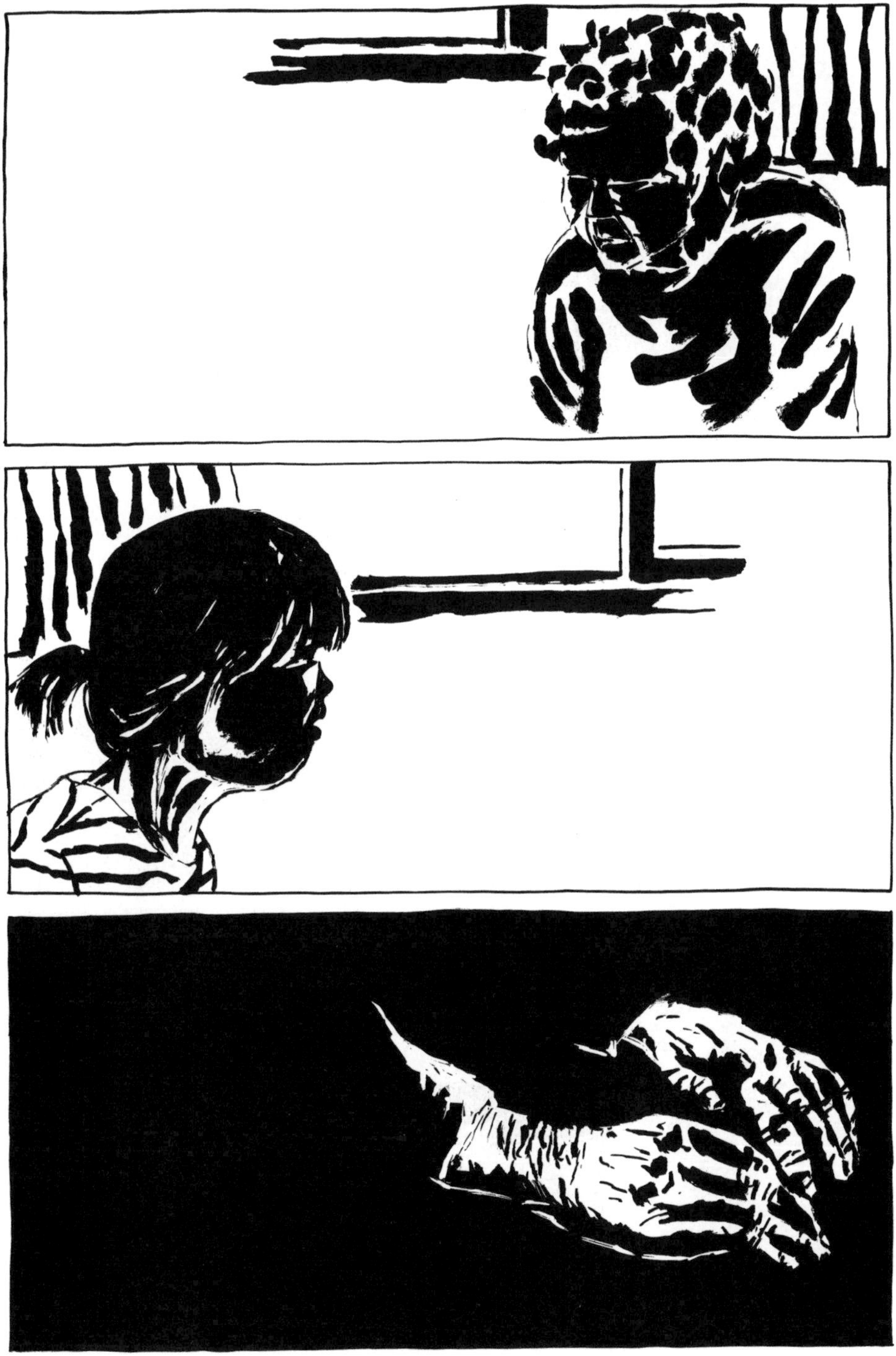

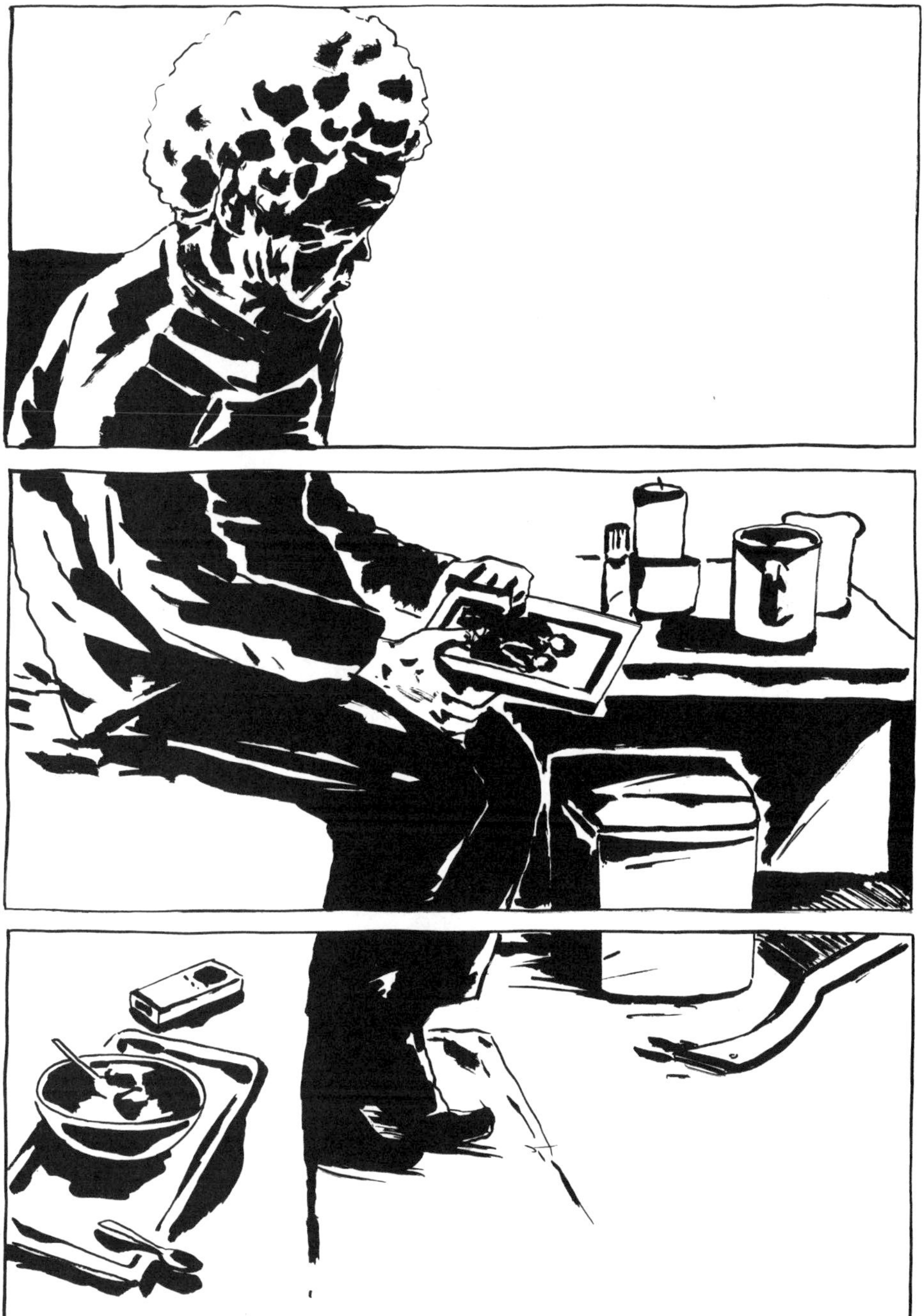

# MY SON

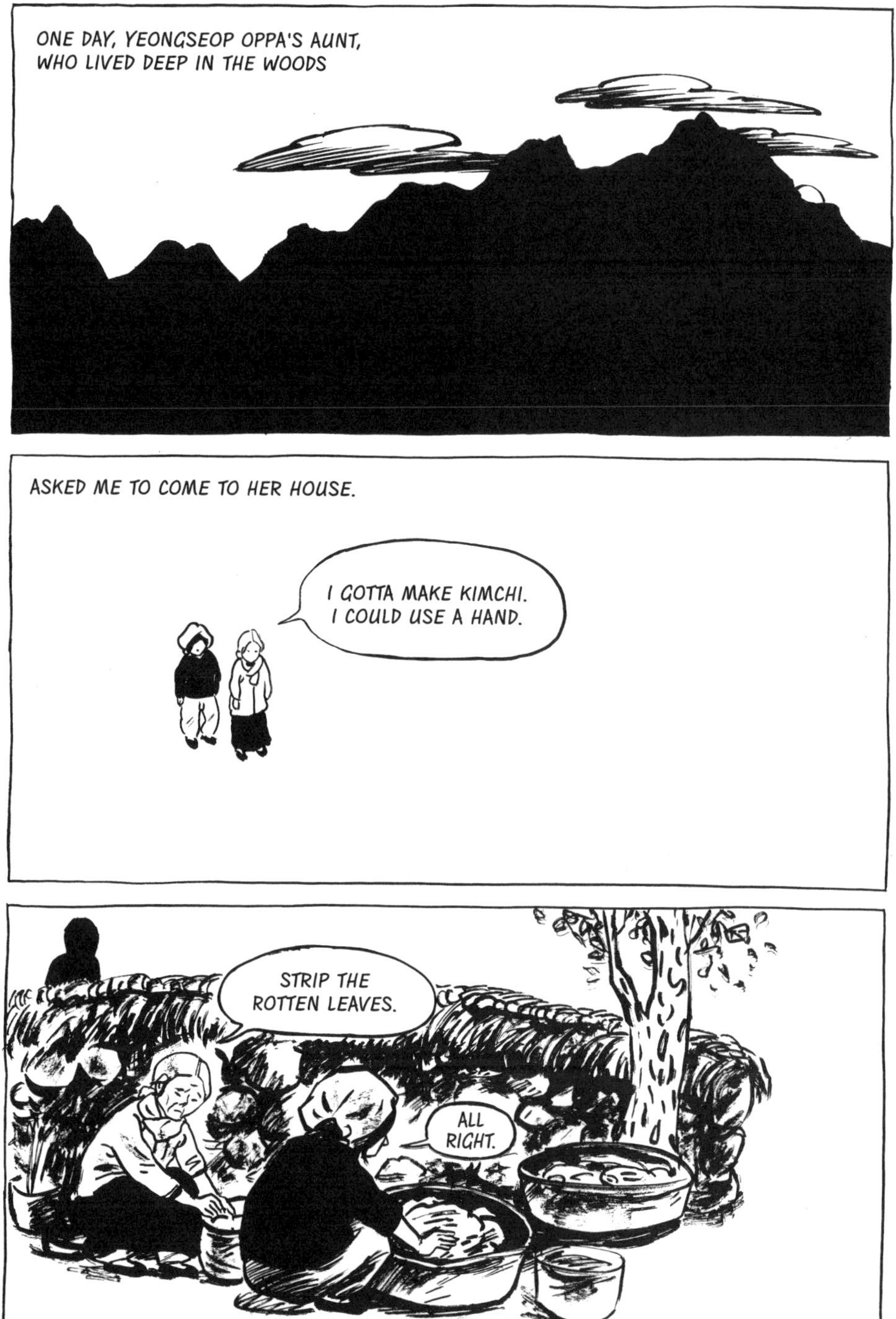
ONE DAY, YEONGSEOP OPPA'S AUNT, WHO LIVED DEEP IN THE WOODS
ASKED ME TO COME TO HER HOUSE.
I GOTTA MAKE KIMCHI. I COULD USE A HAND.
STRIP THE ROTTEN LEAVES.
ALL RIGHT.

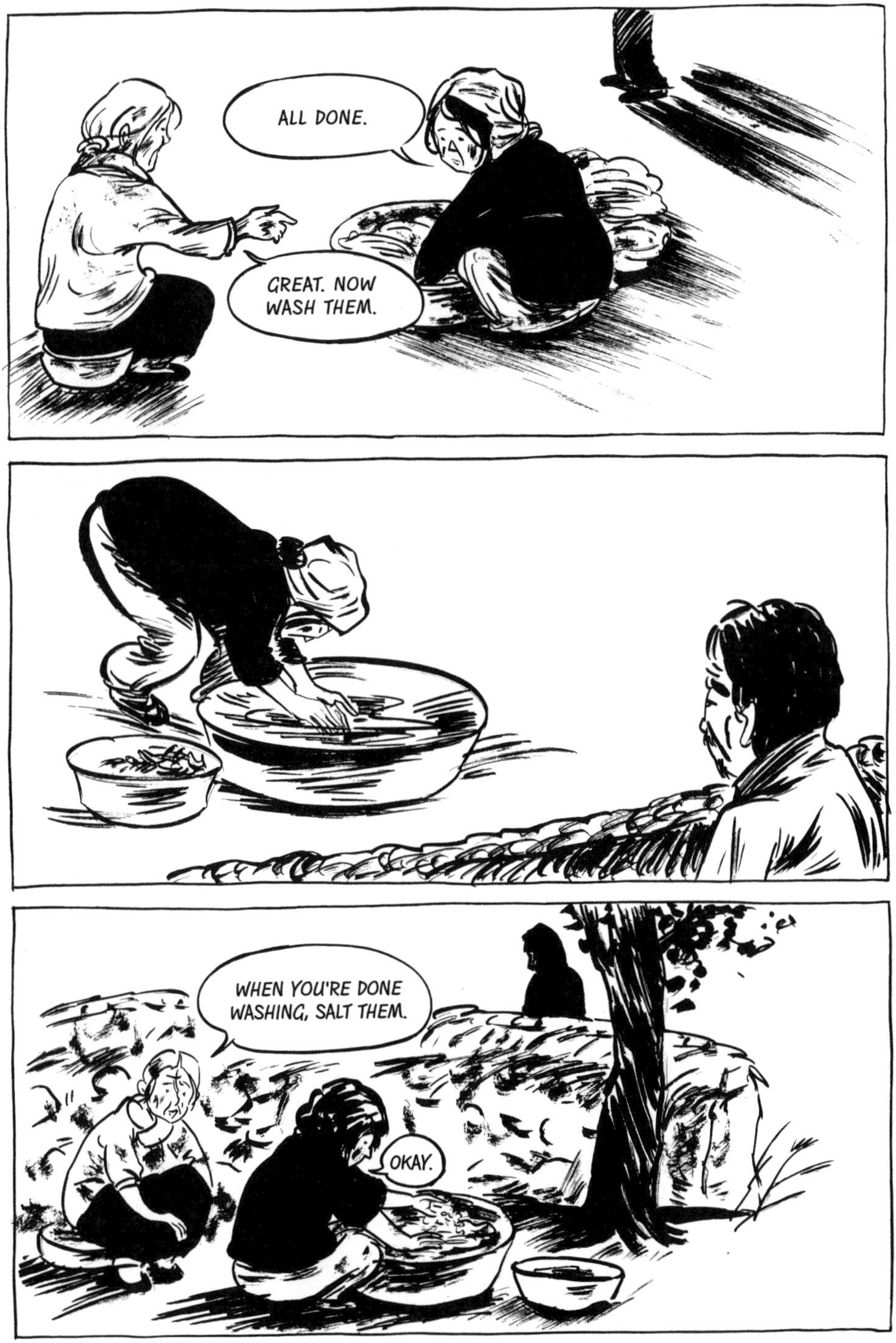
ALL DONE.
GREAT. NOW WASH THEM.
WHEN YOU'RE DONE WASHING, SALT THEM.
OKAY.

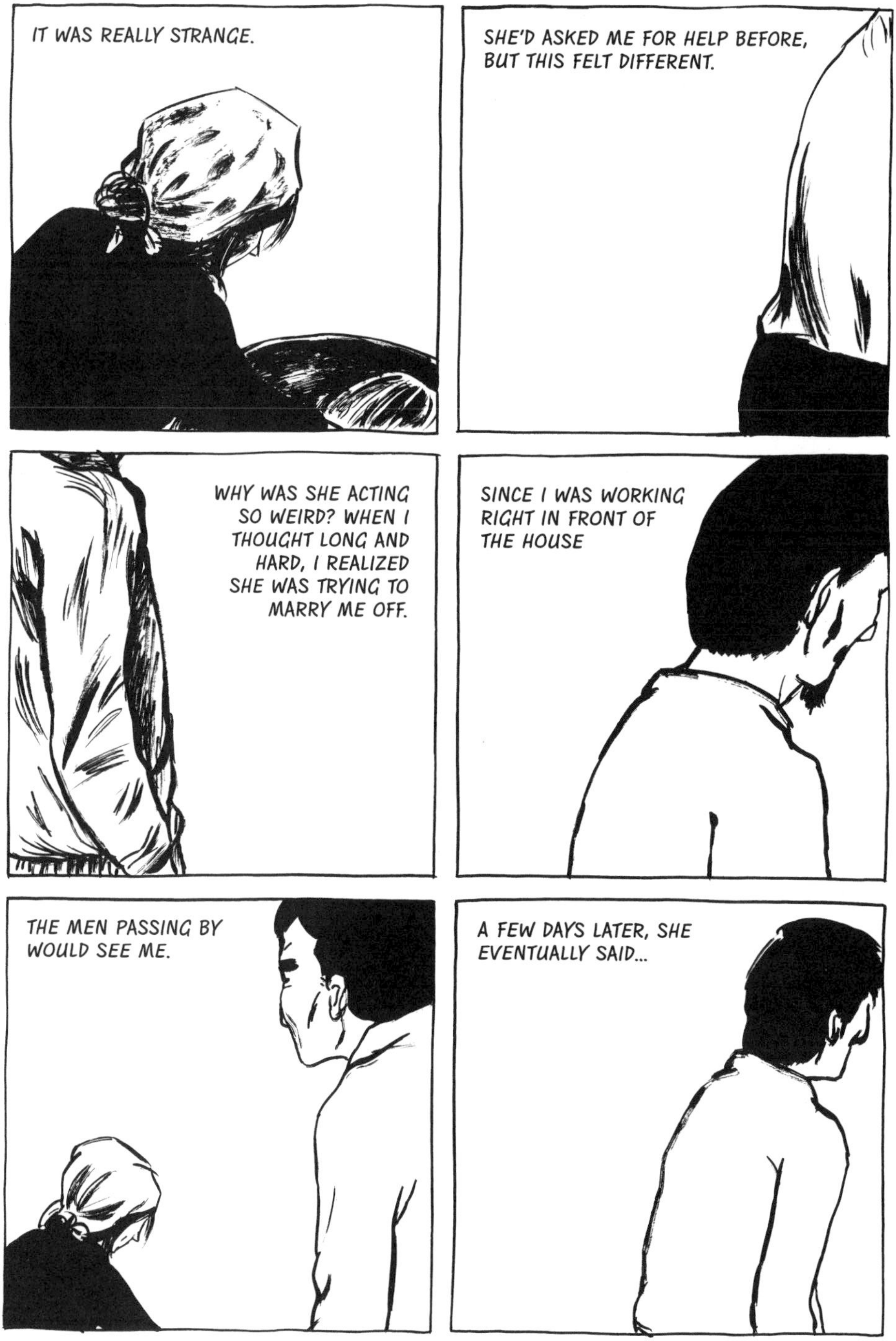
IT WAS REALLY STRANGE.
SHE'D ASKED ME FOR HELP BEFORE, BUT THIS FELT DIFFERENT.
WHY WAS SHE ACTING SO WEIRD? WHEN I THOUGHT LONG AND HARD, I REALIZED SHE WAS TRYING TO MARRY ME OFF.
SINCE I WAS WORKING RIGHT IN FRONT OF THE HOUSE
THE MEN PASSING BY WOULD SEE ME.
A FEW DAYS LATER, SHE EVENTUALLY SAID...

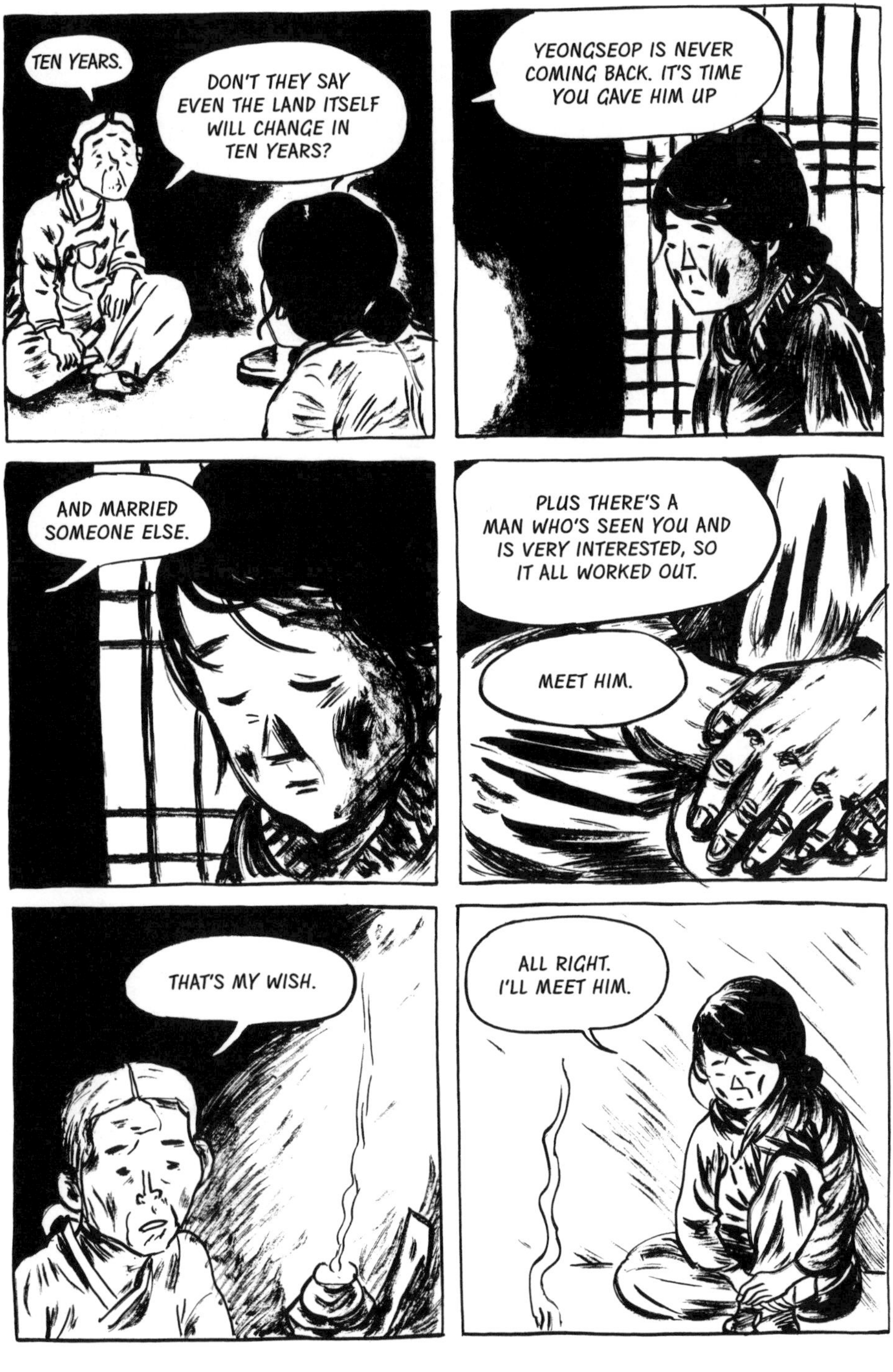
TEN YEARS.
DON'T THEY SAY EVEN THE LAND ITSELF WILL CHANGE IN TEN YEARS?
YEONGSEOP IS NEVER COMING BACK. IT'S TIME YOU GAVE HIM UP
AND MARRIED SOMEONE ELSE.
PLUS THERE'S A MAN WHO'S SEEN YOU AND IS VERY INTERESTED, SO IT ALL WORKED OUT.
MEET HIM.
THAT'S MY WISH.
ALL RIGHT. I'LL MEET HIM.

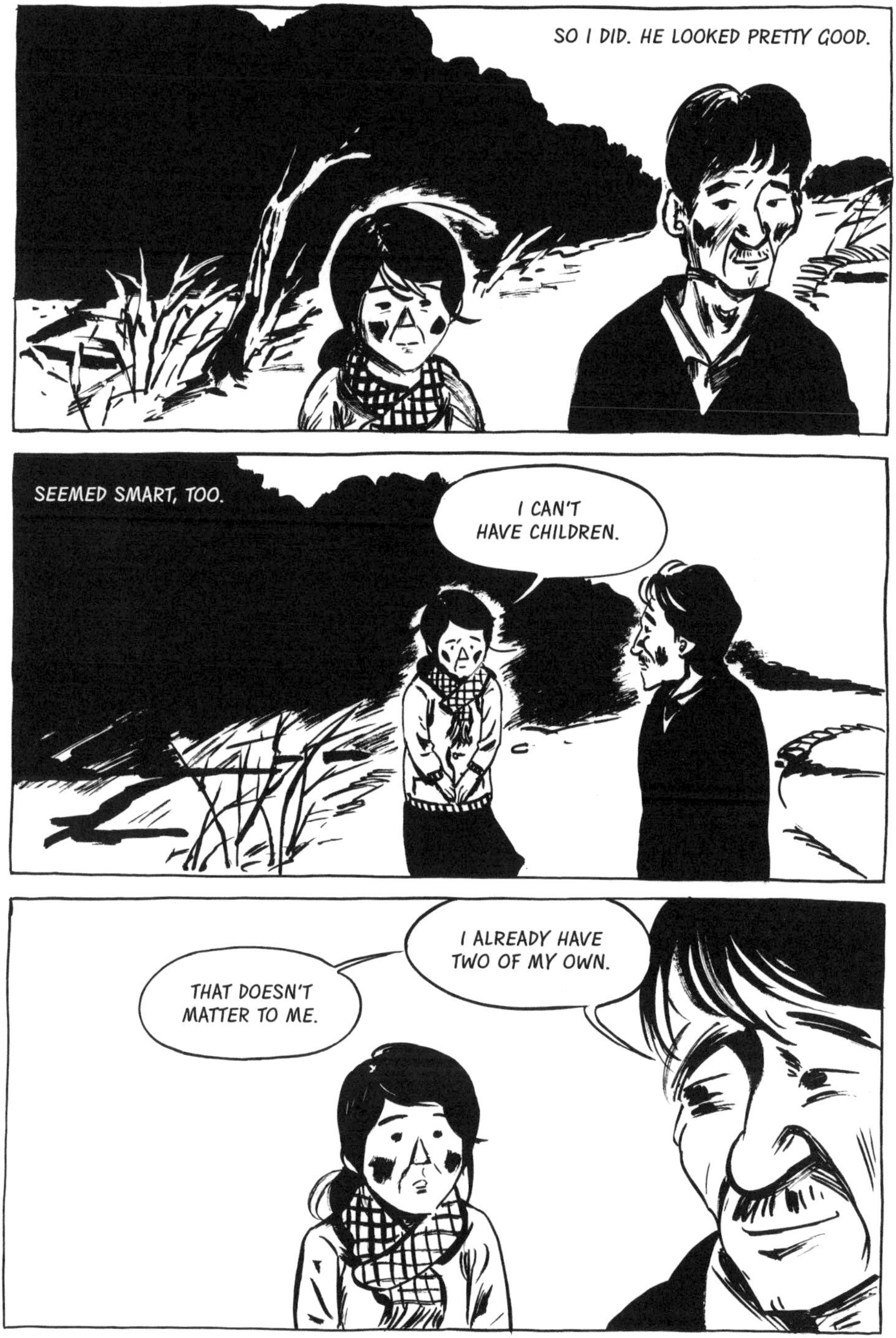
SO I DID. HE LOOKED PRETTY GOOD.
SEEMED SMART, TOO.
I CAN'T HAVE CHILDREN.
I ALREADY HAVE TWO OF MY OWN.
THAT DOESN'T MATTER TO ME.

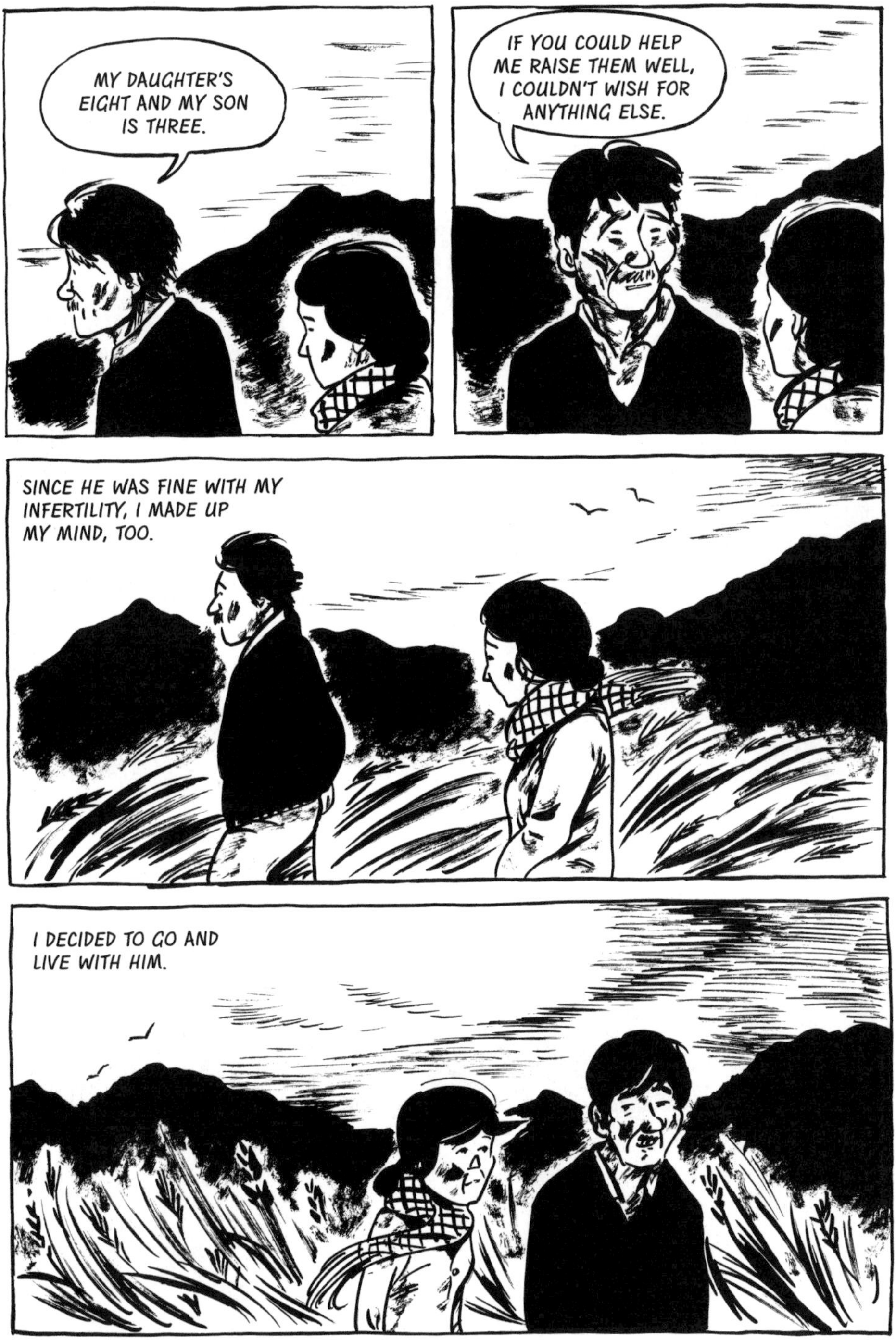

MY DAUGHTER'S EIGHT AND MY SON IS THREE.
IF YOU COULD HELP ME RAISE THEM WELL, I COULDN'T WISH FOR ANYTHING ELSE.
SINCE HE WAS FINE WITH MY INFERTILITY, I MADE UP MY MIND, TOO.
I DECIDED TO GO AND LIVE WITH HIM.

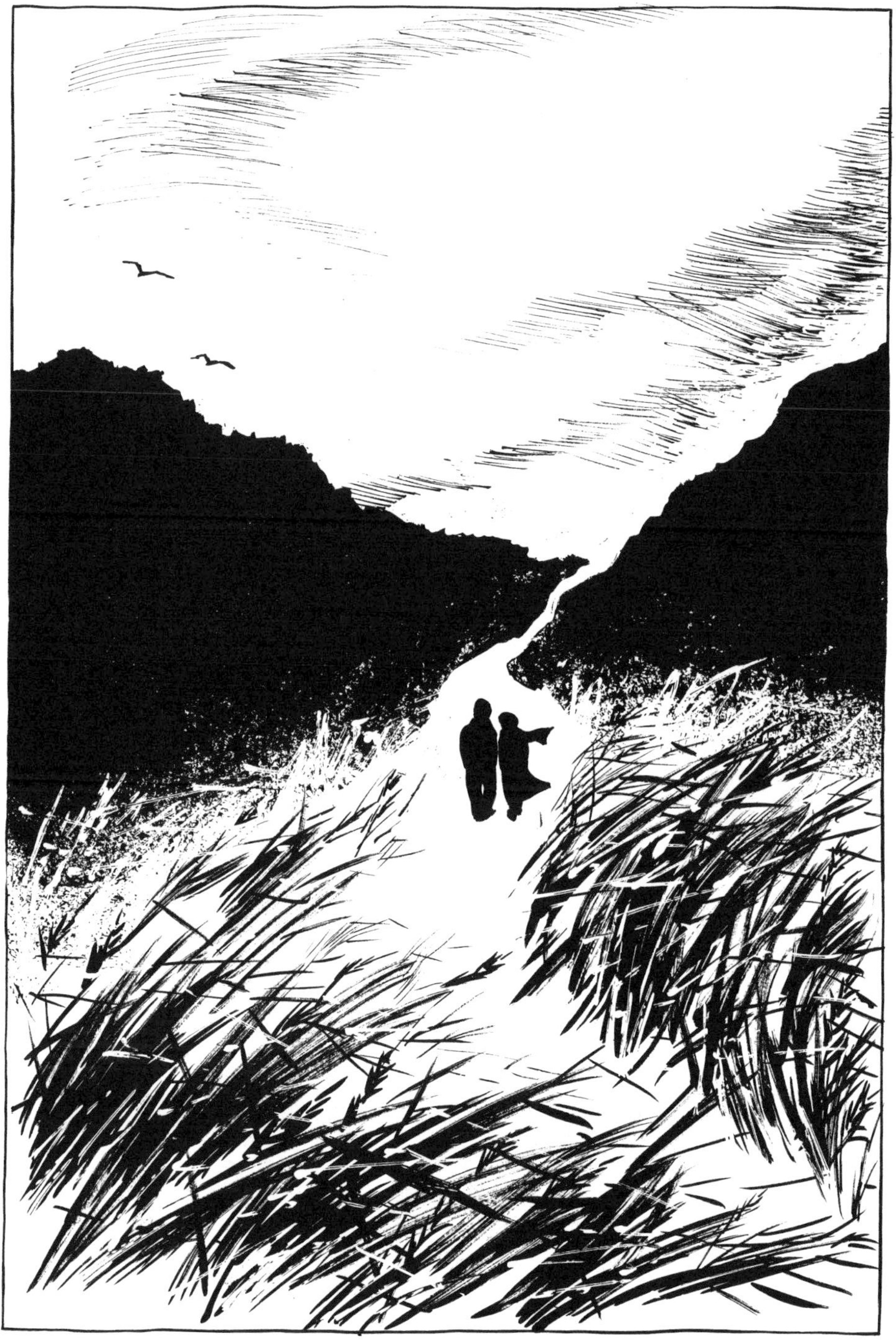

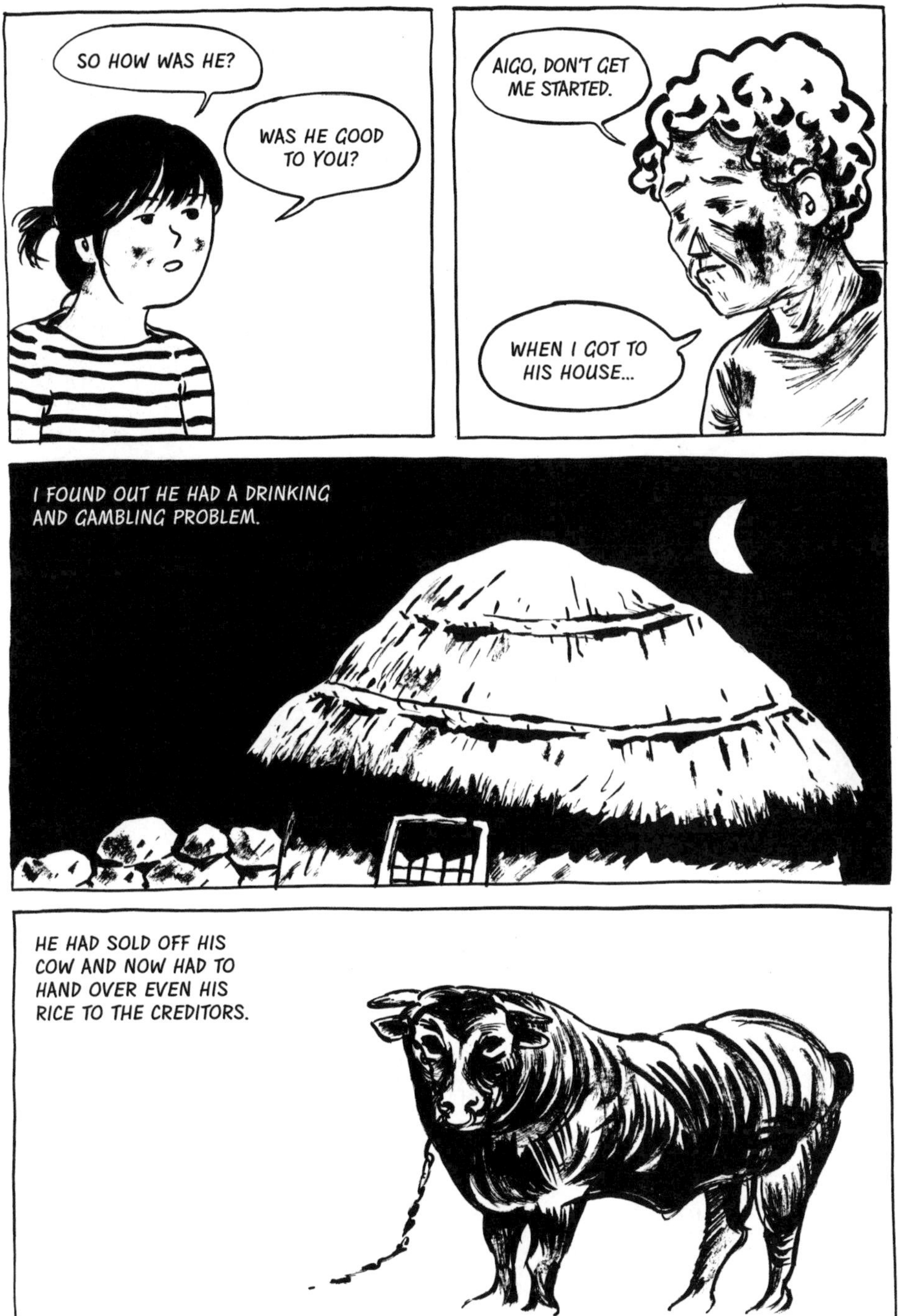
SO HOW WAS HE?
WAS HE GOOD TO YOU?
AIGO, DON'T GET ME STARTED.
WHEN I GOT TO HIS HOUSE...
I FOUND OUT HE HAD A DRINKING AND GAMBLING PROBLEM.
HE HAD SOLD OFF HIS COW AND NOW HAD TO HAND OVER EVEN HIS RICE TO THE CREDITORS.

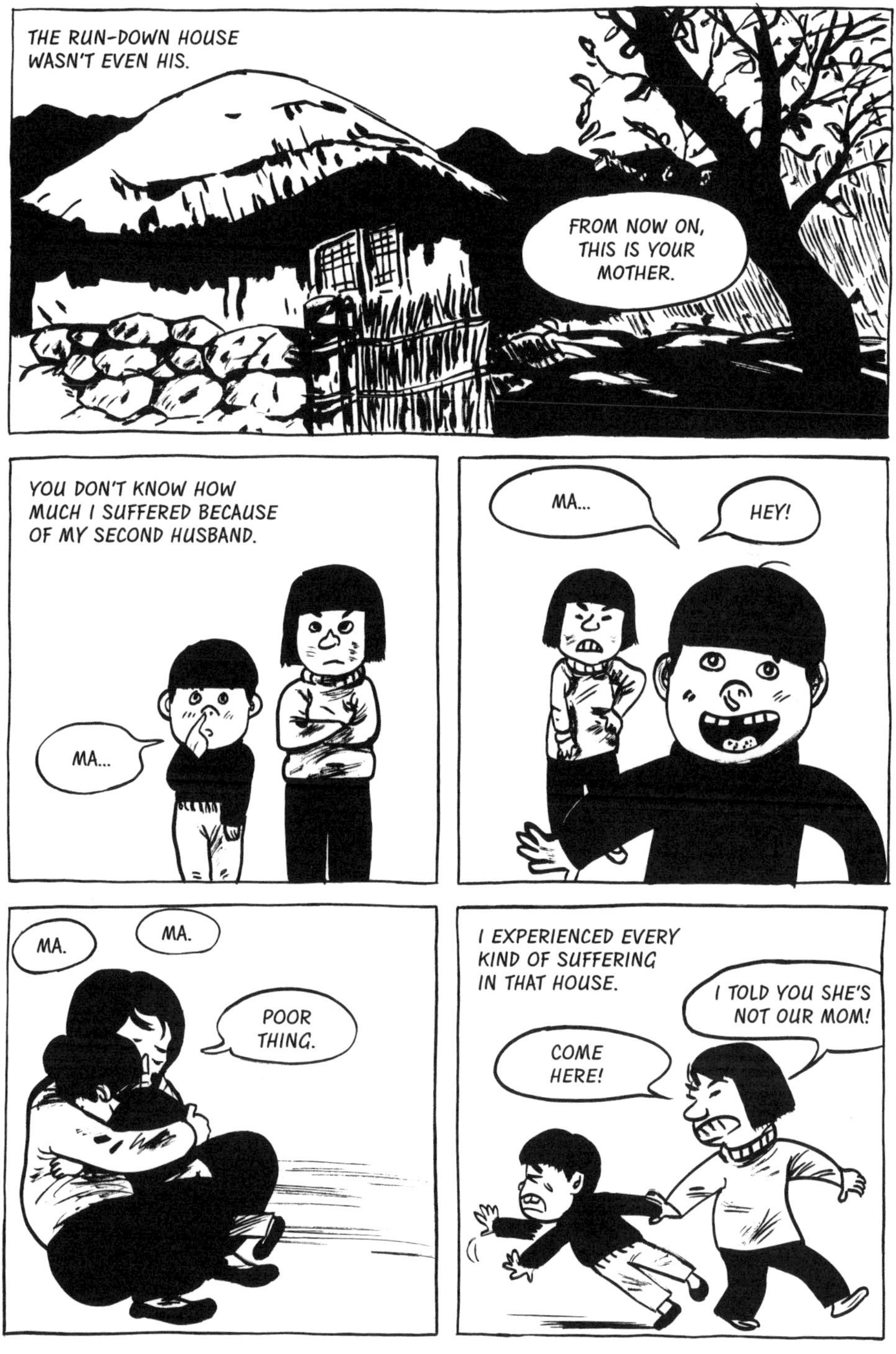
THE RUN-DOWN HOUSE WASN'T EVEN HIS.
FROM NOW ON, THIS IS YOUR MOTHER.
YOU DON'T KNOW HOW MUCH I SUFFERED BECAUSE OF MY SECOND HUSBAND.
MA...
MA...
HEY!
MA.
MA.
POOR THING.
I EXPERIENCED EVERY KIND OF SUFFERING IN THAT HOUSE.
I TOLD YOU SHE'S NOT OUR MOM!
COME HERE!

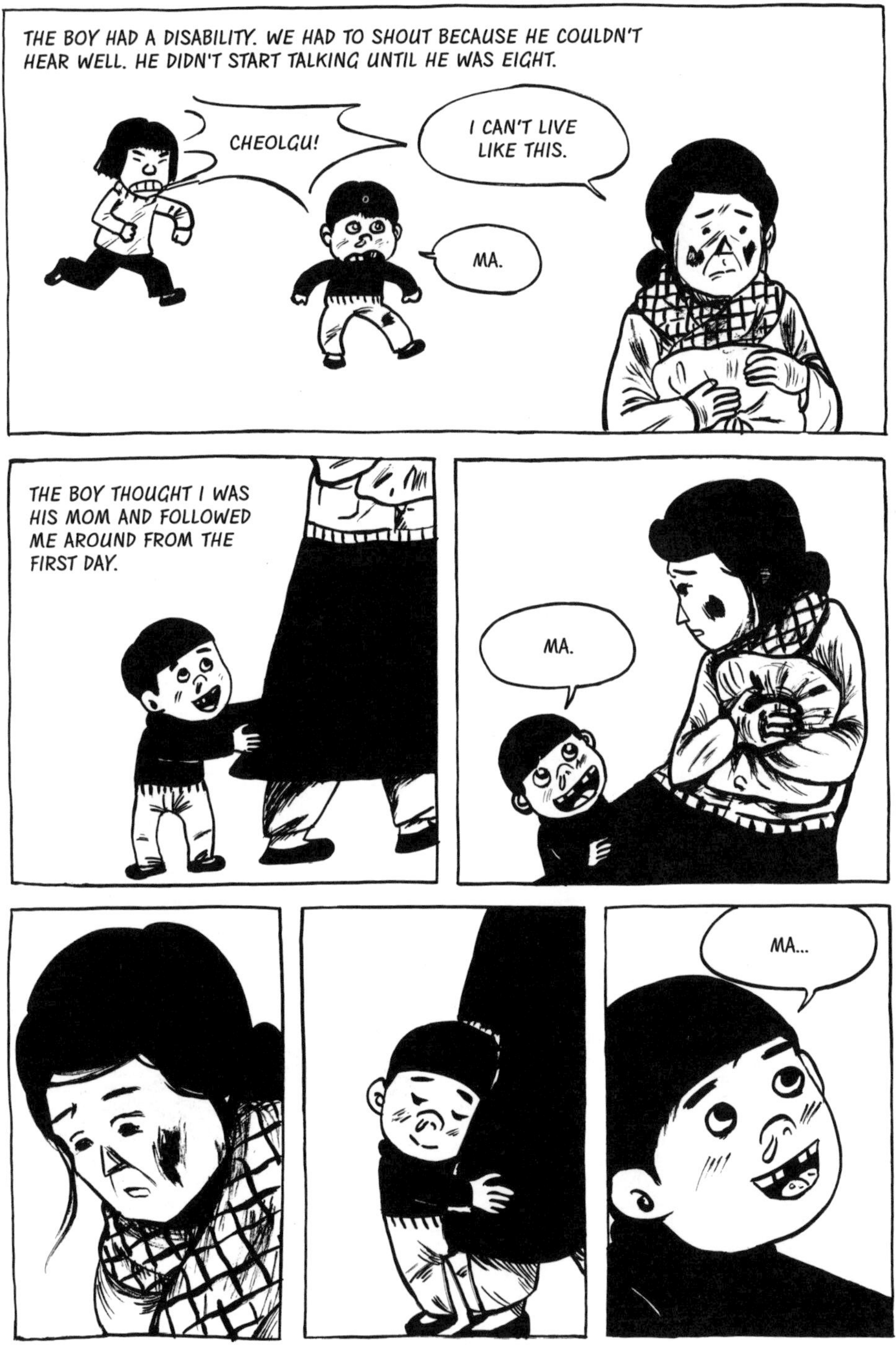
THE BOY HAD A DISABILITY. WE HAD TO SHOUT BECAUSE HE COULDN'T HEAR WELL. HE DIDN'T START TALKING UNTIL HE WAS EIGHT.
CHEOLGU!
I CAN'T LIVE LIKE THIS.
MA.
THE BOY THOUGHT I WAS HIS MOM AND FOLLOWED ME AROUND FROM THE FIRST DAY.
MA.
MA...

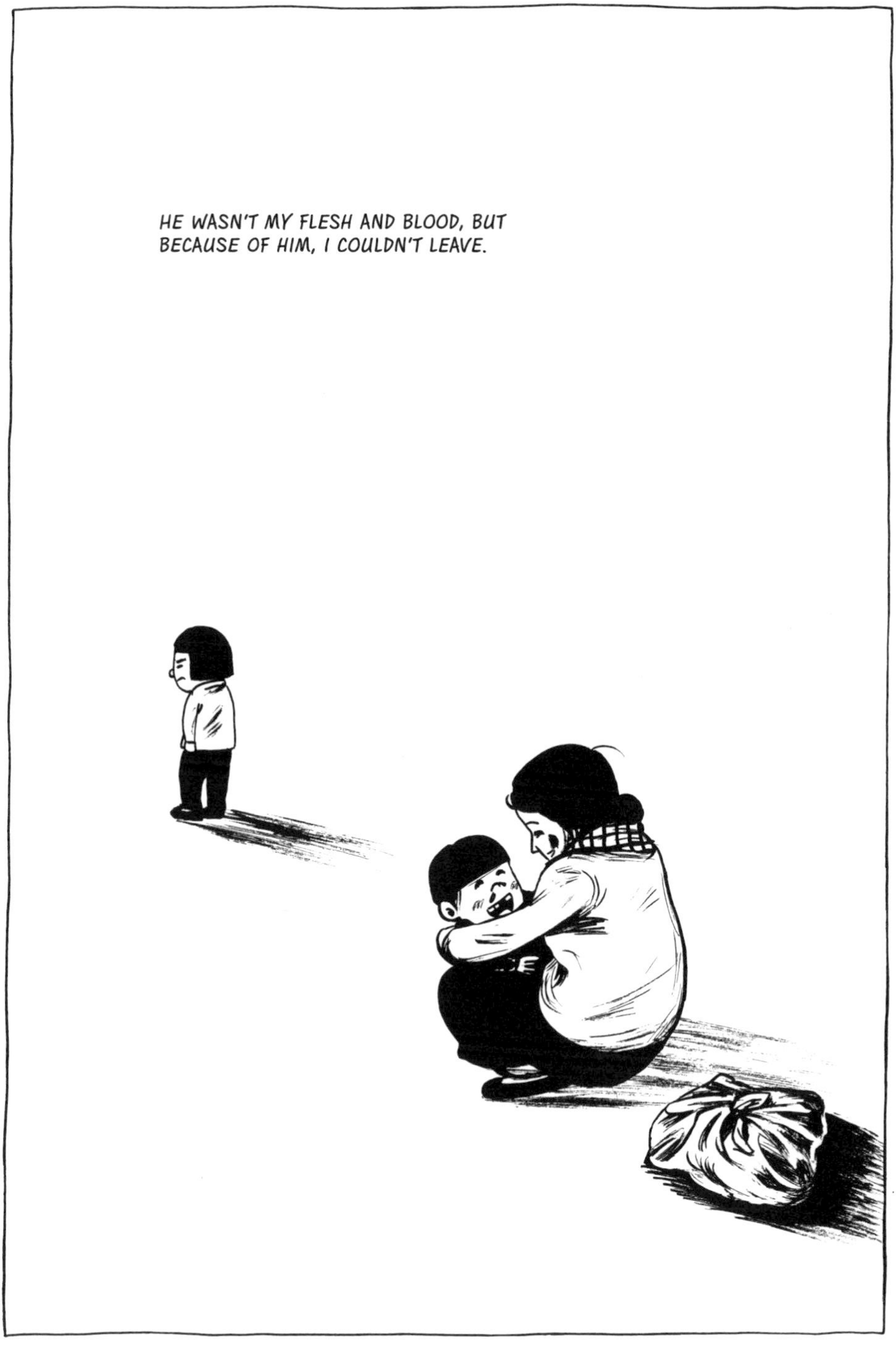
HE WASN'T MY FLESH AND BLOOD, BUT
BECAUSE OF HIM, I COULDN'T LEAVE.

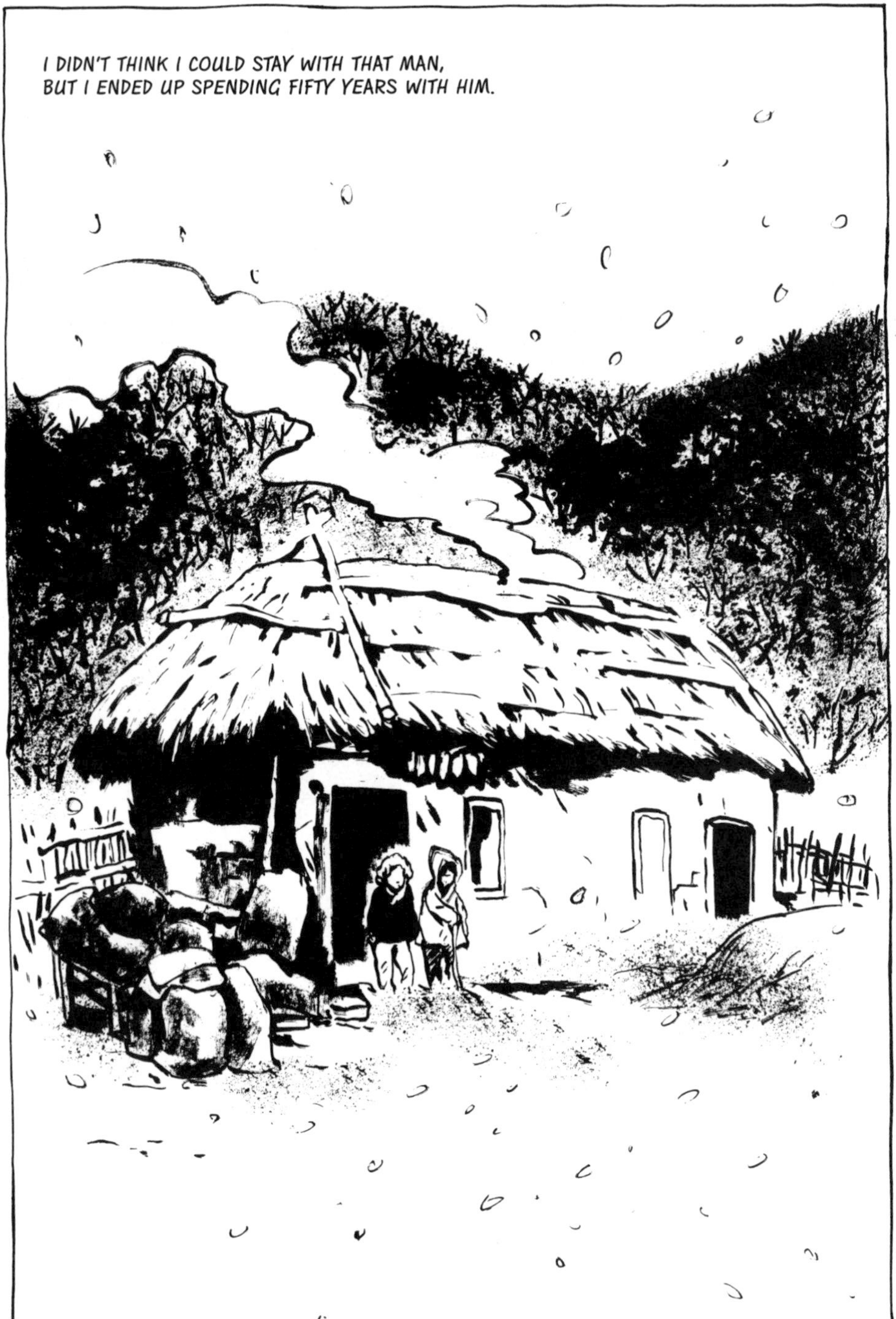
I DIDN'T THINK I COULD STAY WITH THAT MAN,
BUT I ENDED UP SPENDING FIFTY YEARS WITH HIM.

# THE RETURN

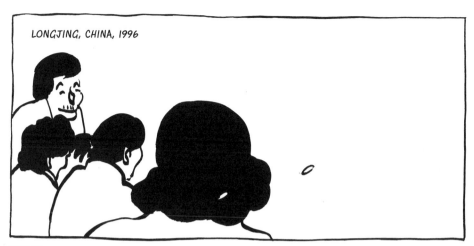

LONGJING, CHINA, 1996

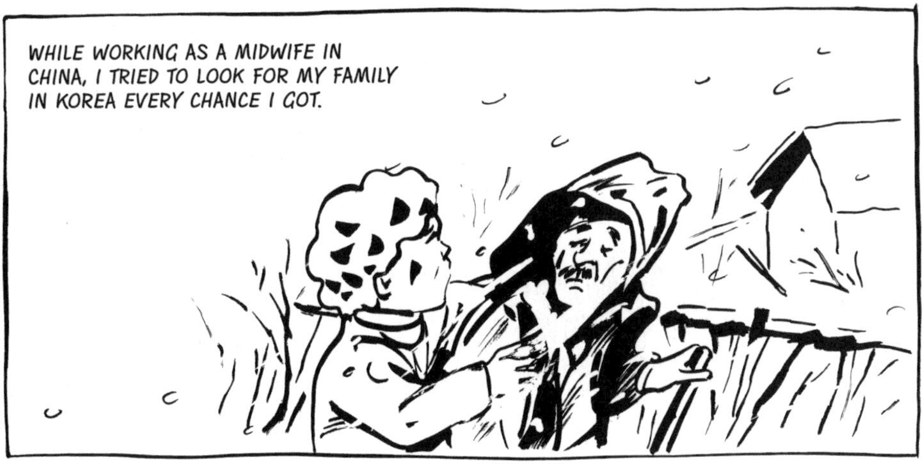
WHILE WORKING AS A MIDWIFE IN CHINA, I TRIED TO LOOK FOR MY FAMILY IN KOREA EVERY CHANCE I GOT.

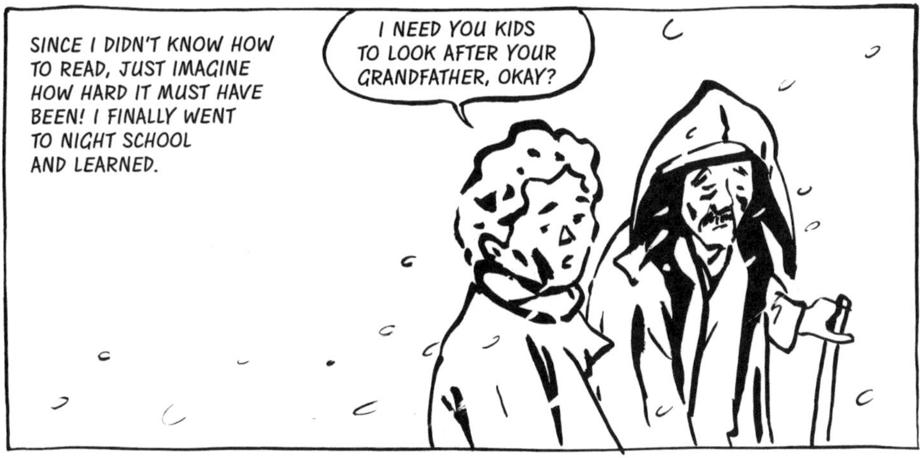
SINCE I DIDN'T KNOW HOW TO READ, JUST IMAGINE HOW HARD IT MUST HAVE BEEN! I FINALLY WENT TO NIGHT SCHOOL AND LEARNED.
I NEED YOU KIDS TO LOOK AFTER YOUR GRANDFATHER, OKAY?

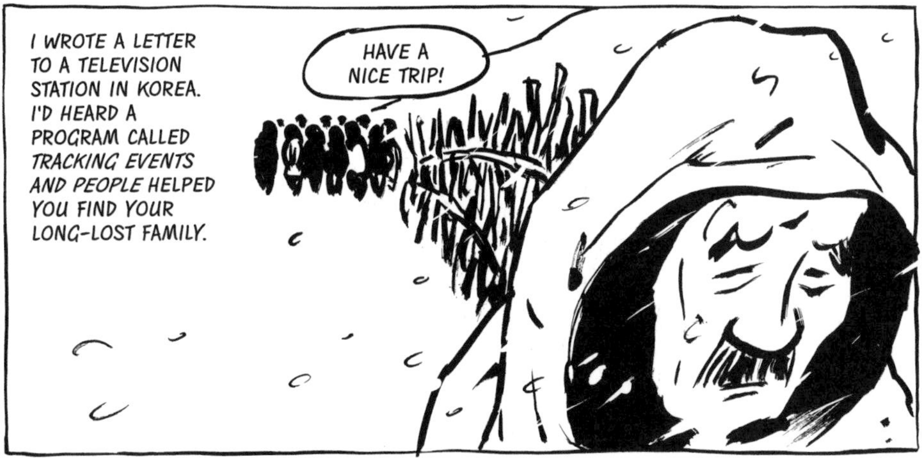
I WROTE A LETTER TO A TELEVISION STATION IN KOREA. I'D HEARD A PROGRAM CALLED *TRACKING EVENTS AND PEOPLE* HELPED YOU FIND YOUR LONG-LOST FAMILY.
HAVE A NICE TRIP!

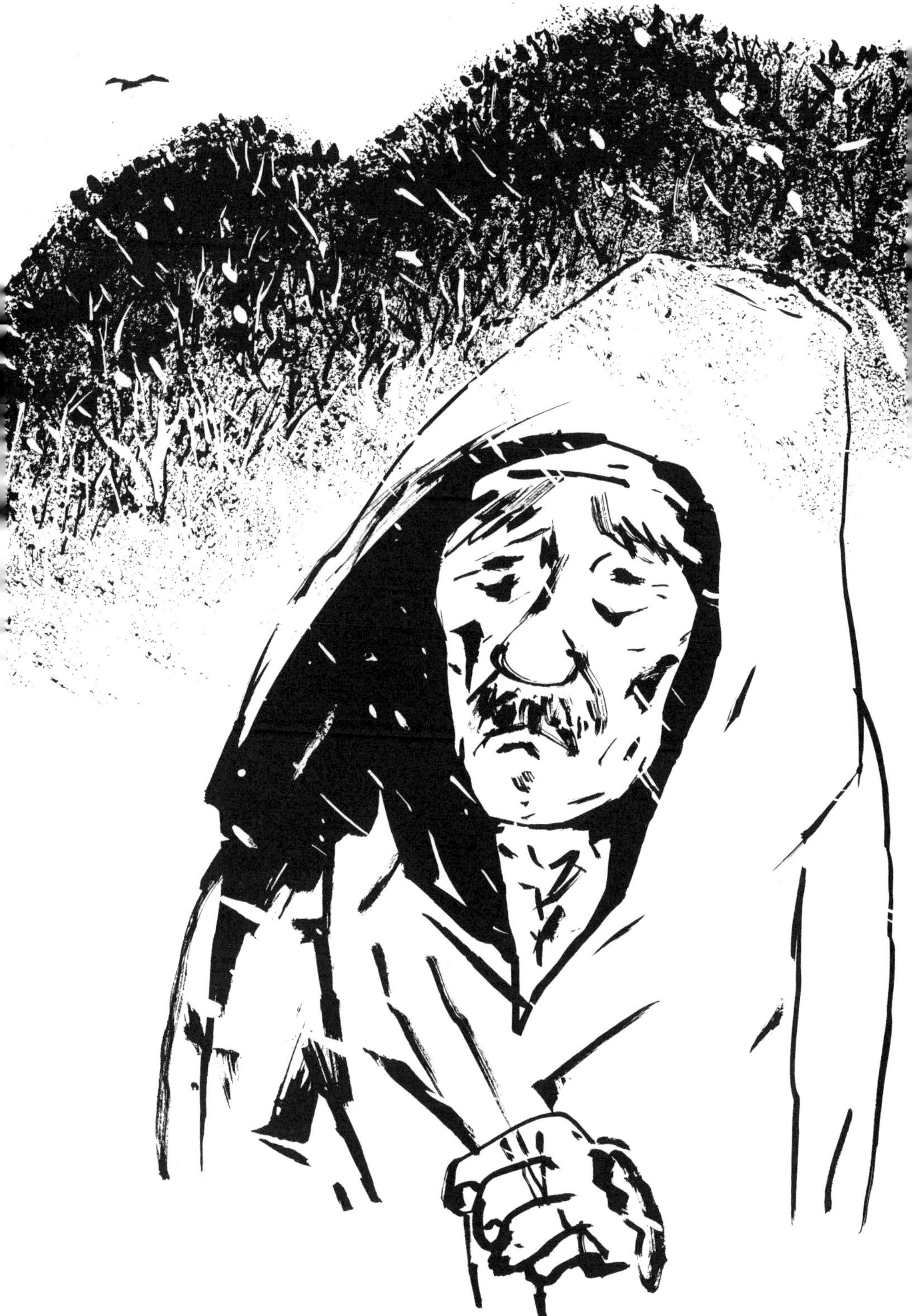

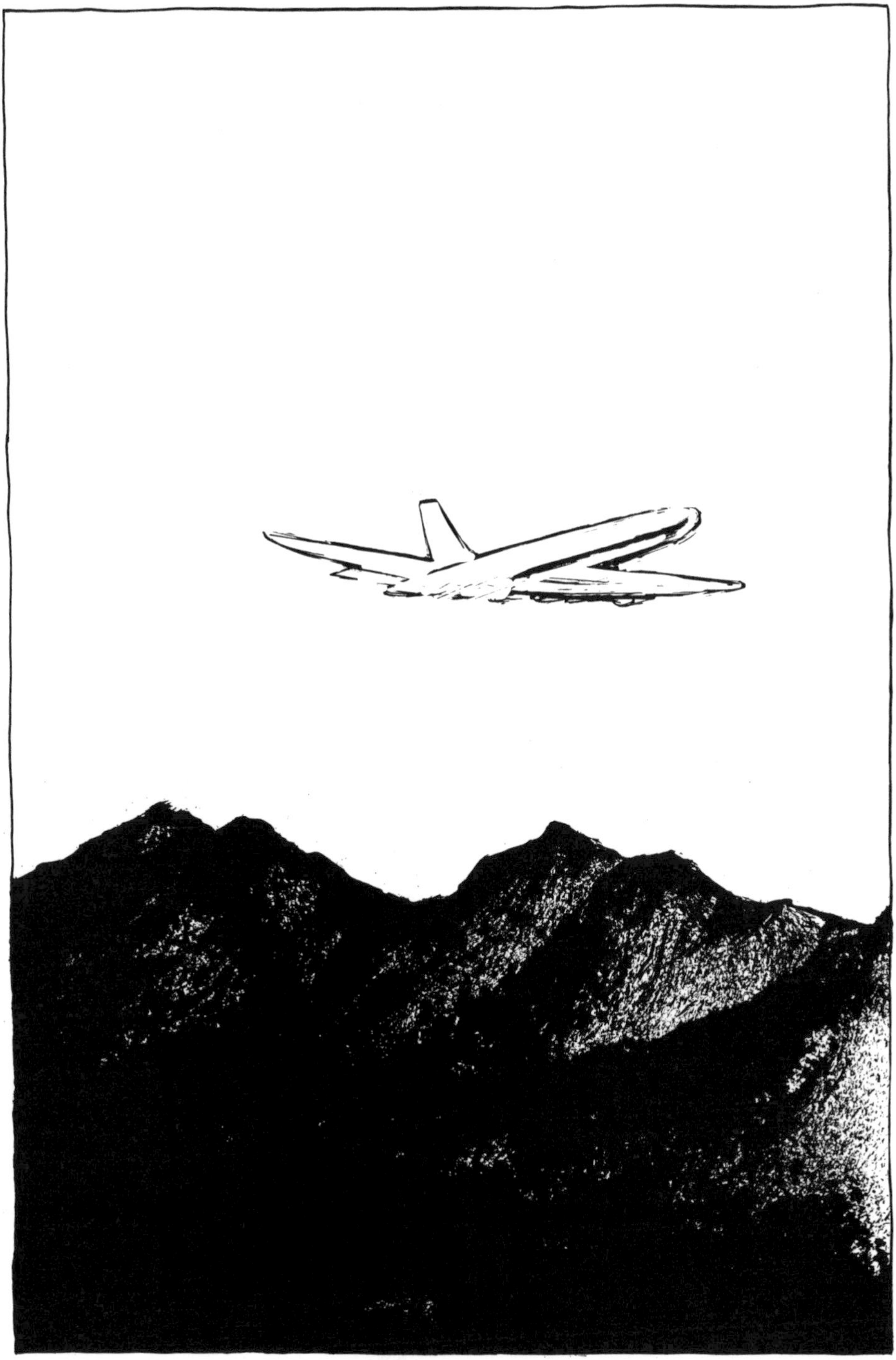

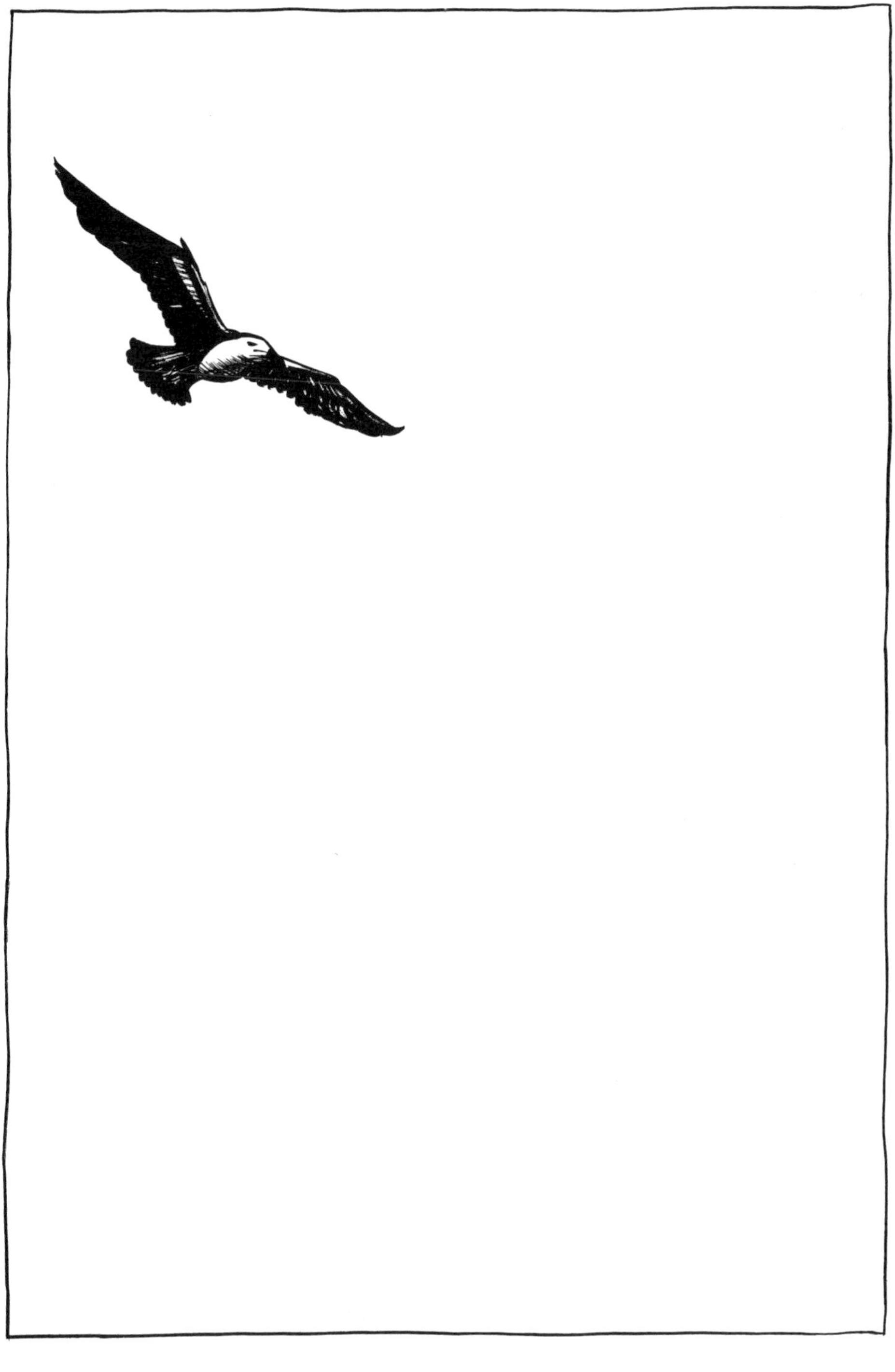

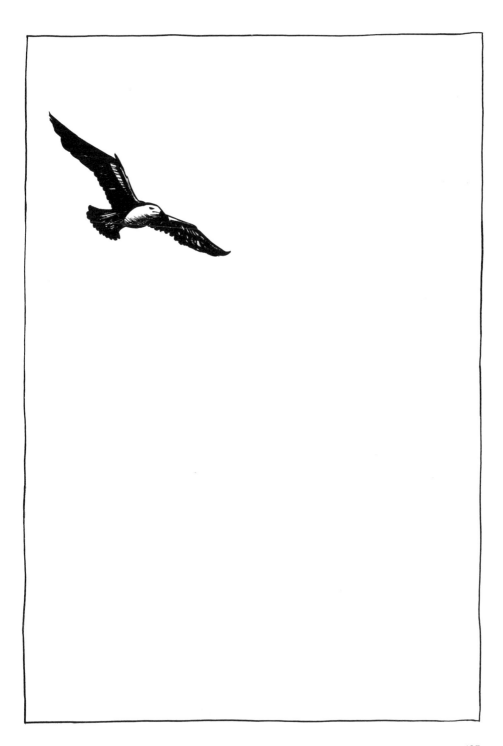

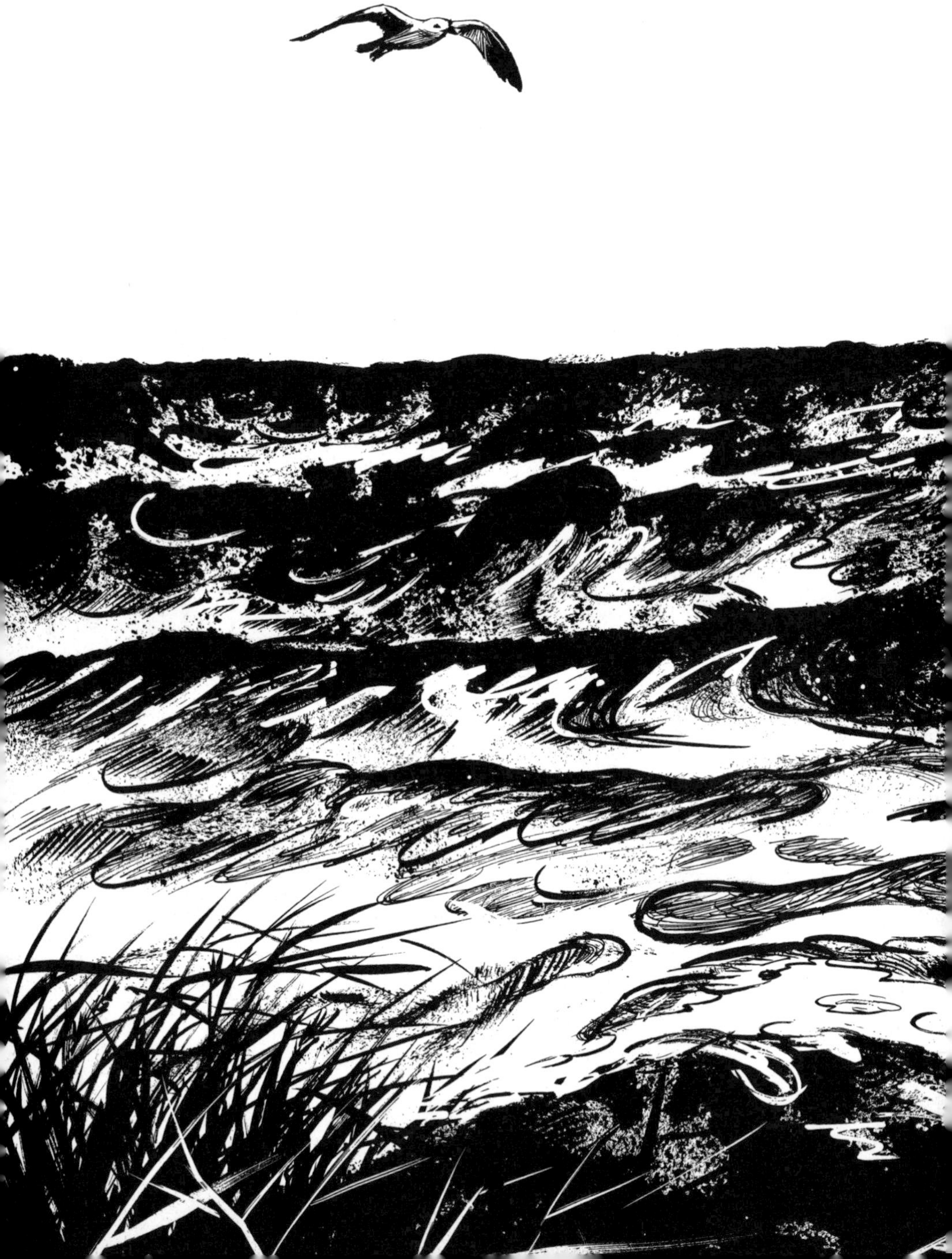

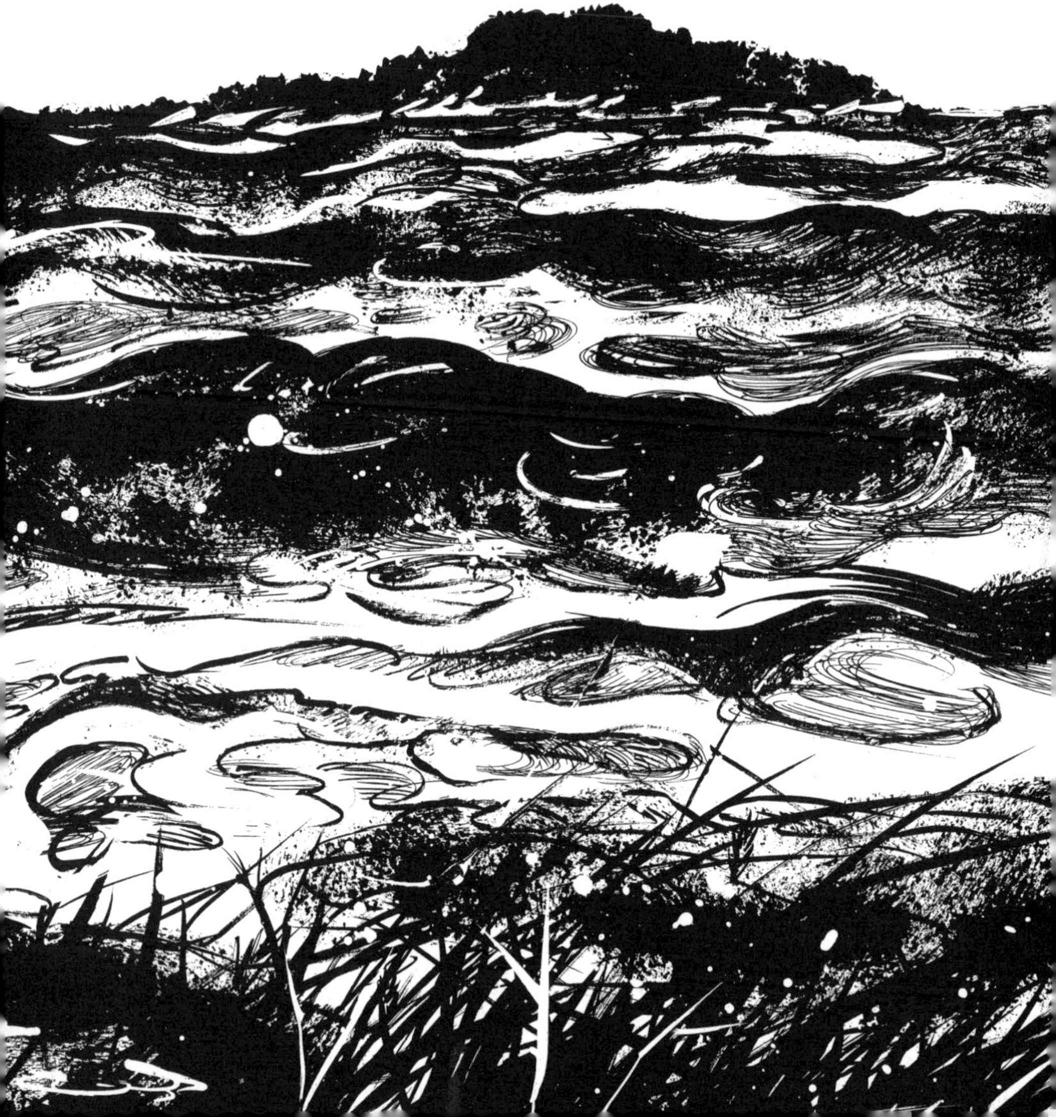

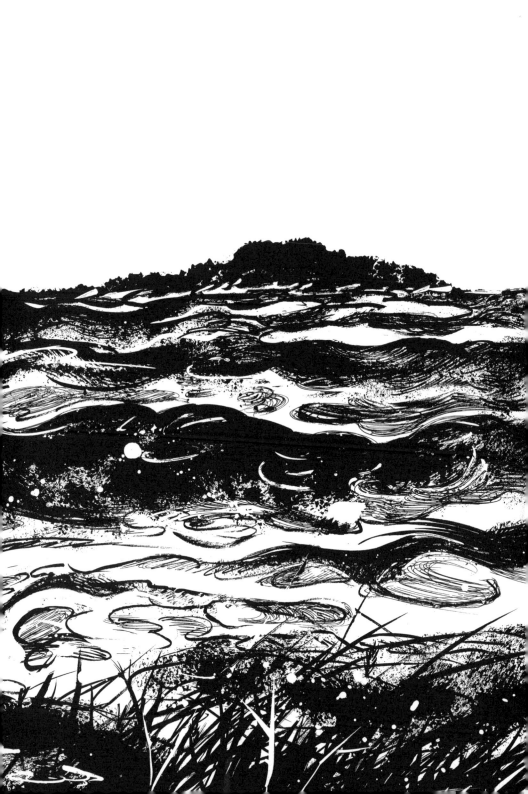

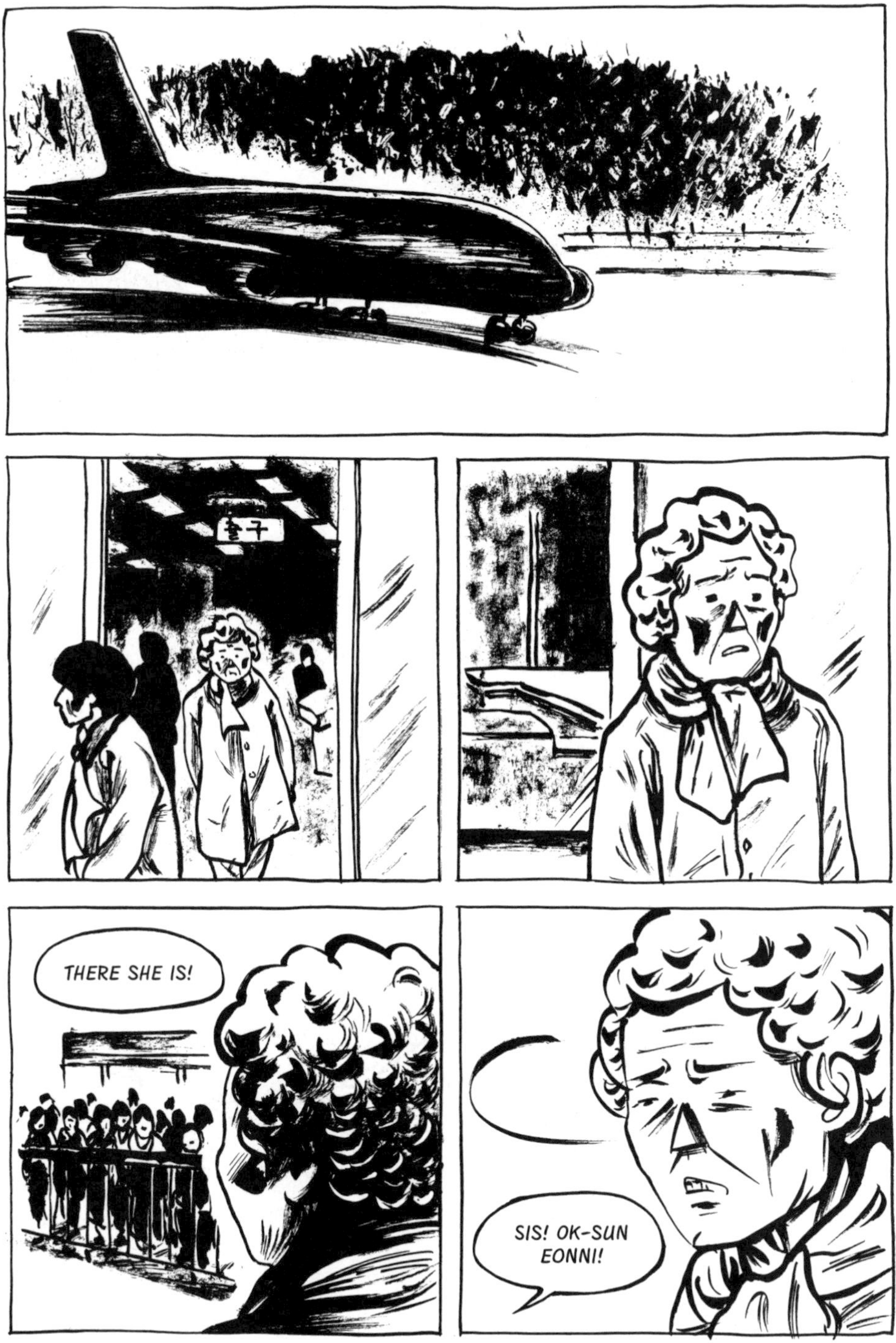
출구
THERE SHE IS!
SIS! OK-SUN EONNI!

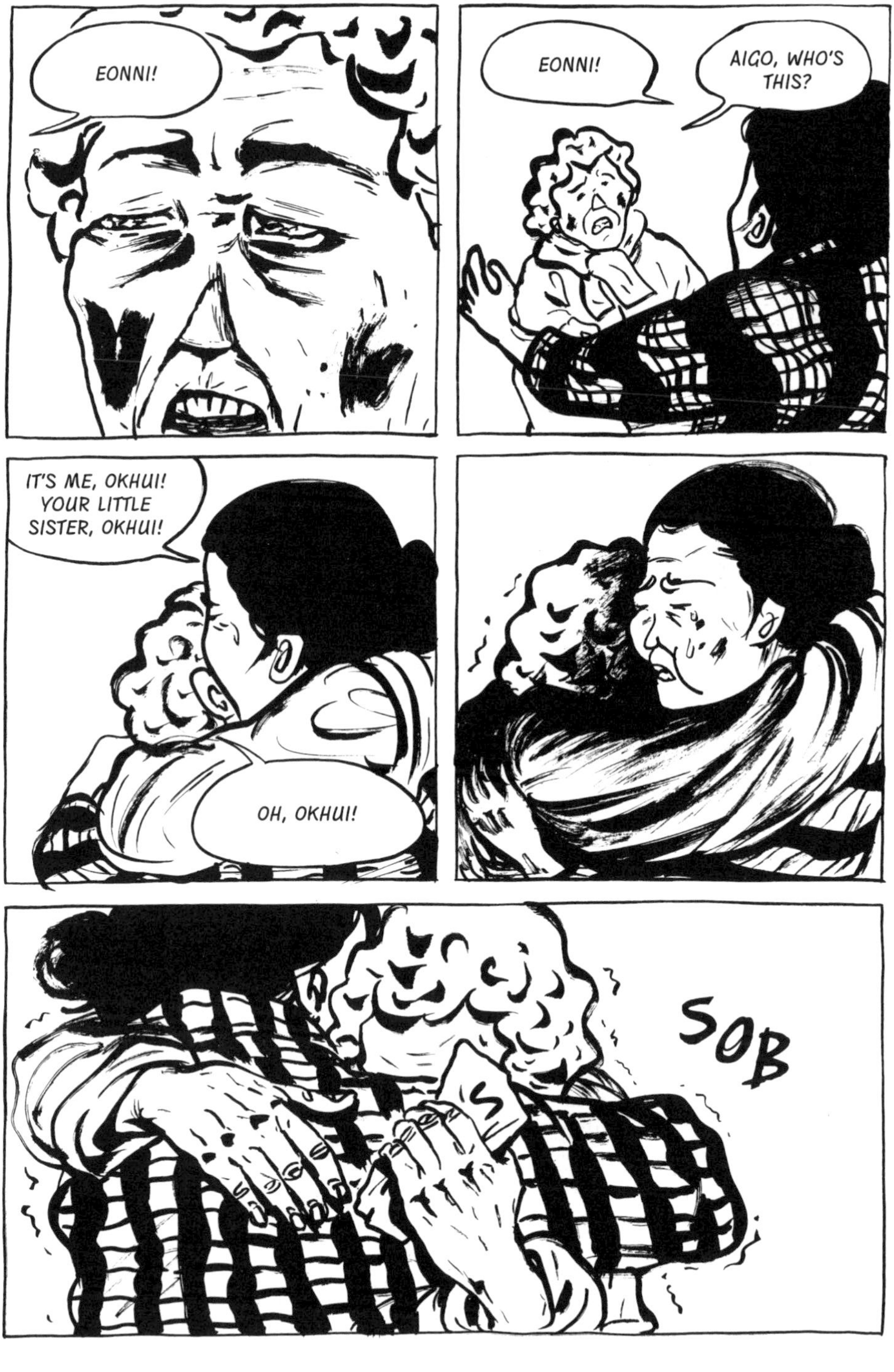
EONNI!
EONNI!
AIGO, WHO'S THIS?
IT'S ME, OKHUI! YOUR LITTLE SISTER, OKHUI!
OH, OKHUI!
SOB

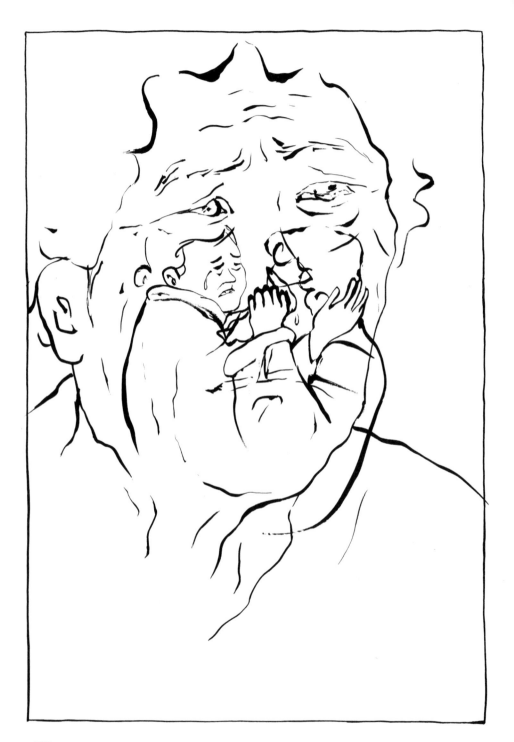

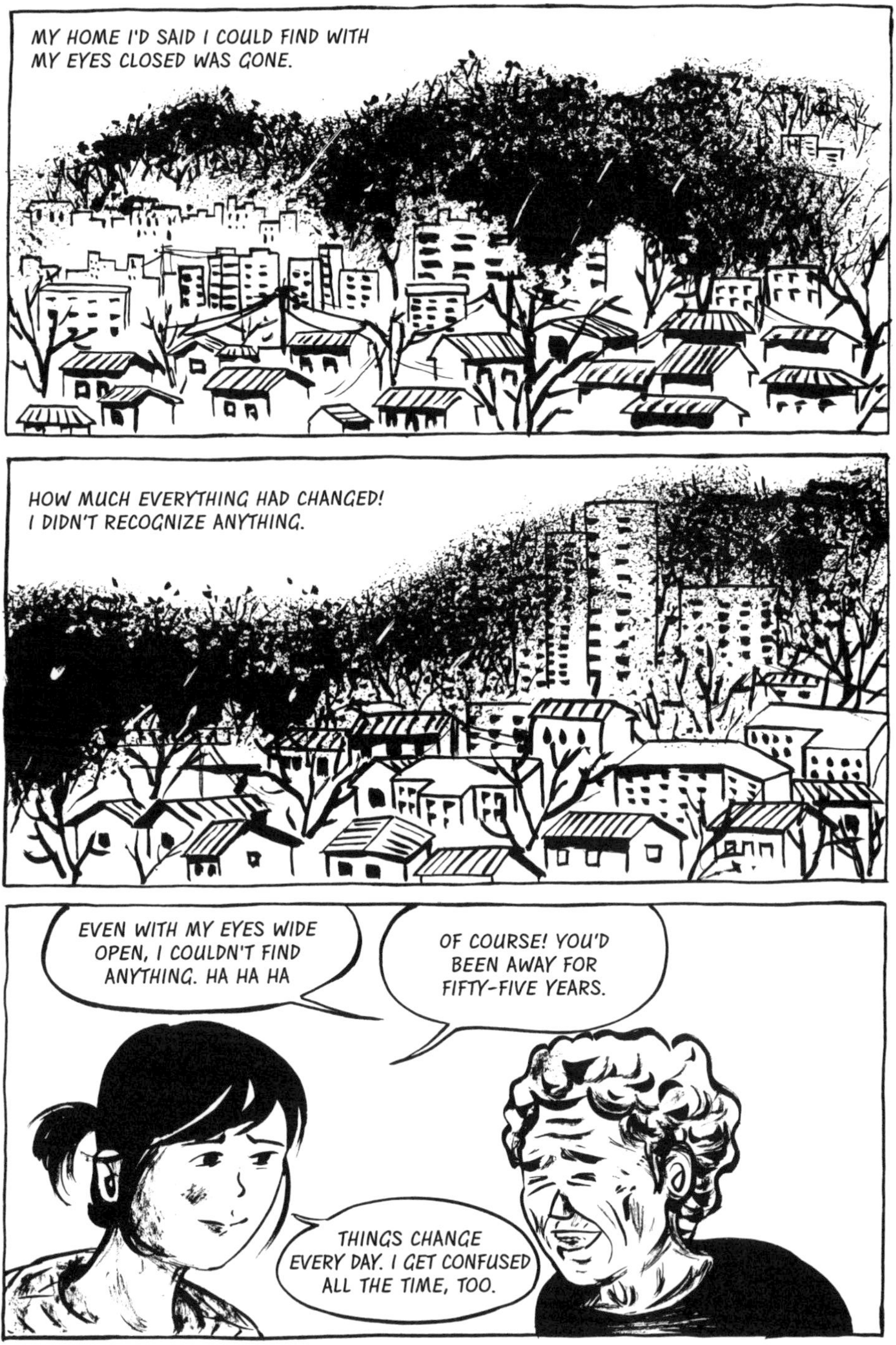
MY HOME I'D SAID I COULD FIND WITH MY EYES CLOSED WAS GONE.
HOW MUCH EVERYTHING HAD CHANGED! I DIDN'T RECOGNIZE ANYTHING.
EVEN WITH MY EYES WIDE OPEN, I COULDN'T FIND ANYTHING. HA HA HA
OF COURSE! YOU'D BEEN AWAY FOR FIFTY-FIVE YEARS.
THINGS CHANGE EVERY DAY. I GET CONFUSED ALL THE TIME, TOO.

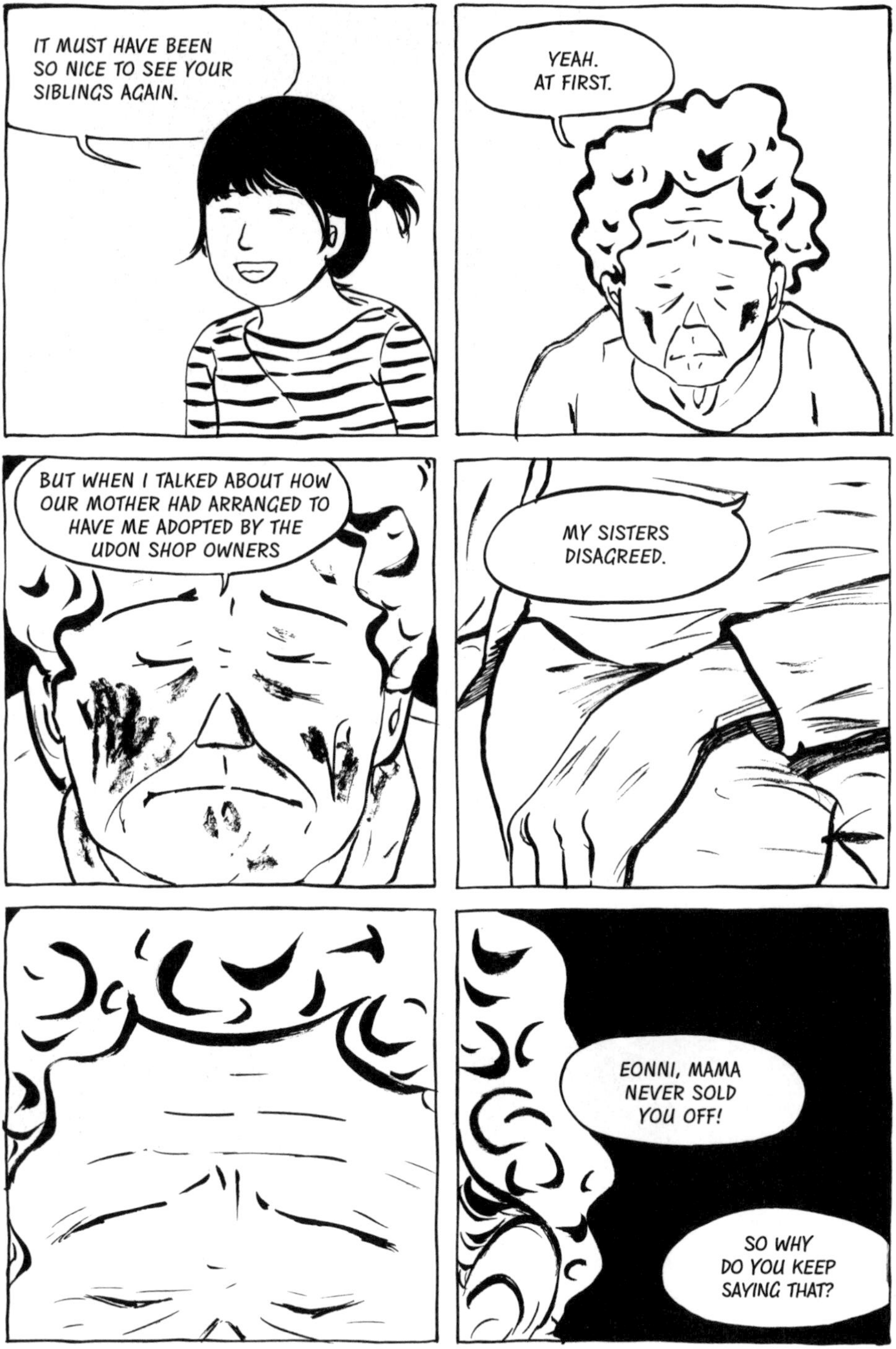
IT MUST HAVE BEEN SO NICE TO SEE YOUR SIBLINGS AGAIN.
YEAH. AT FIRST.
BUT WHEN I TALKED ABOUT HOW OUR MOTHER HAD ARRANGED TO HAVE ME ADOPTED BY THE UDON SHOP OWNERS
MY SISTERS DISAGREED.
EONNI, MAMA NEVER SOLD YOU OFF!
SO WHY DO YOU KEEP SAYING THAT?

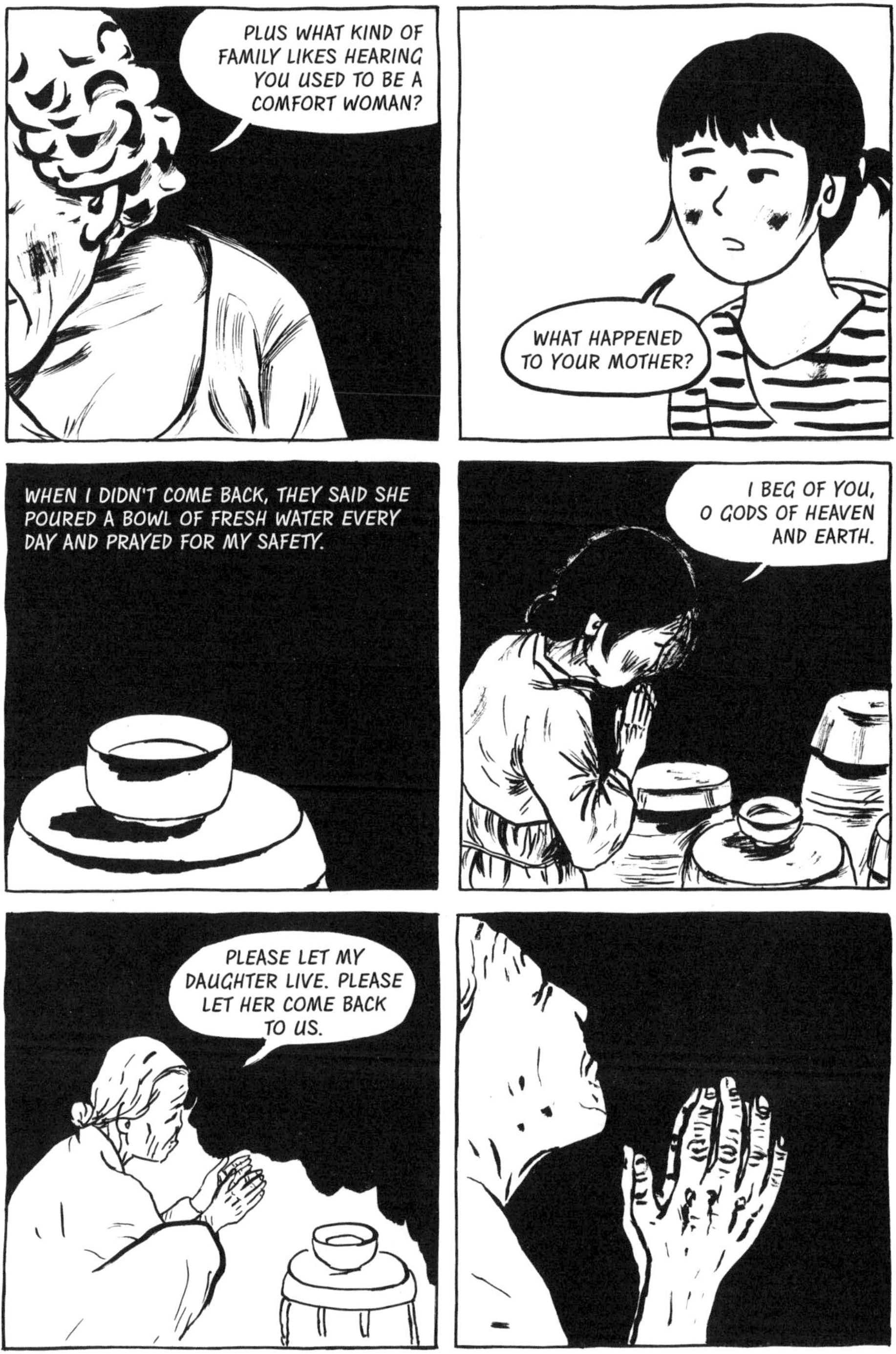
PLUS WHAT KIND OF FAMILY LIKES HEARING YOU USED TO BE A COMFORT WOMAN?
WHAT HAPPENED TO YOUR MOTHER?
WHEN I DIDN'T COME BACK, THEY SAID SHE POURED A BOWL OF FRESH WATER EVERY DAY AND PRAYED FOR MY SAFETY.
I BEG OF YOU, O GODS OF HEAVEN AND EARTH.
PLEASE LET MY DAUGHTER LIVE. PLEASE LET HER COME BACK TO US.

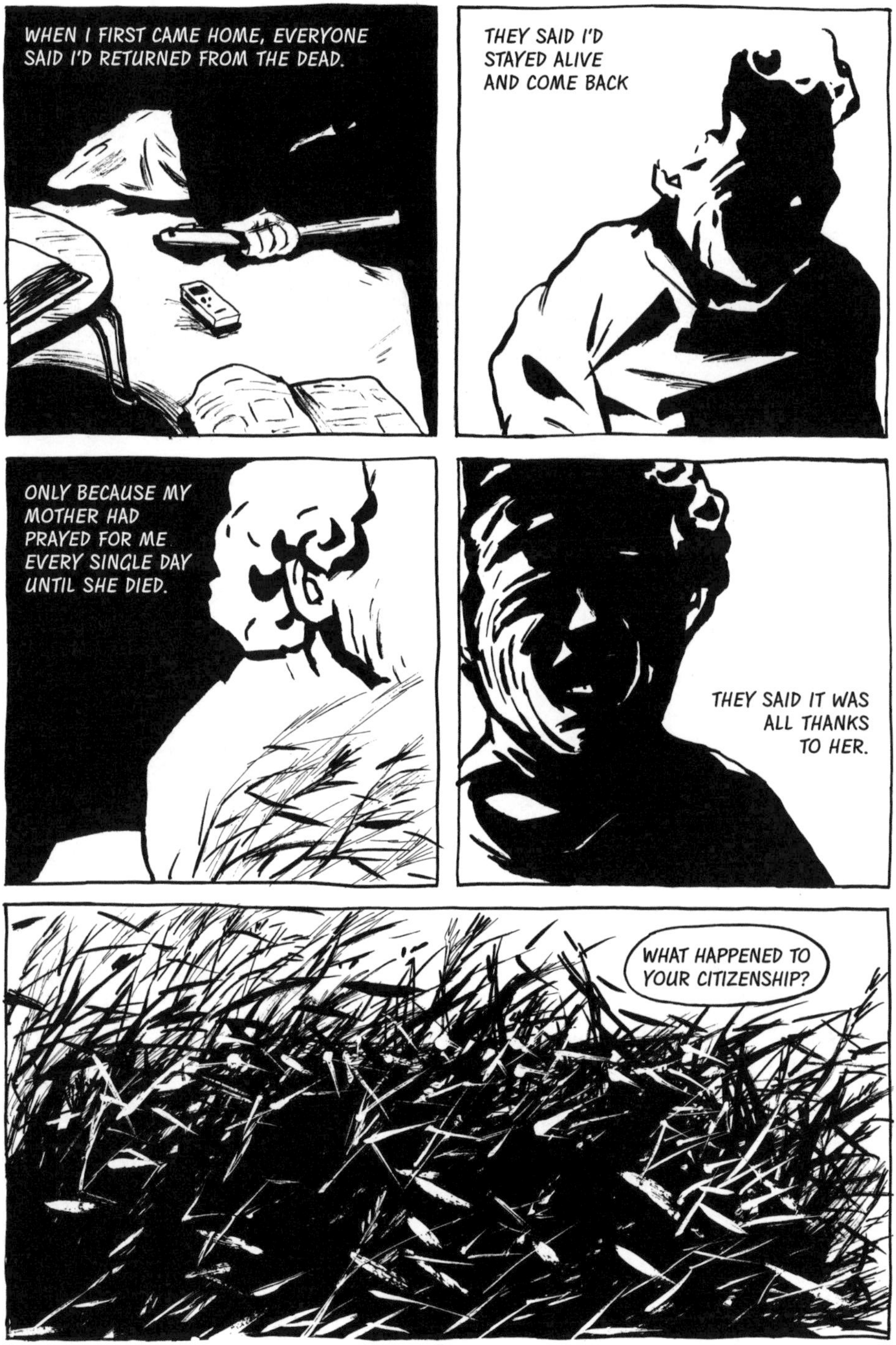
WHEN I FIRST CAME HOME, EVERYONE SAID I'D RETURNED FROM THE DEAD.
THEY SAID I'D STAYED ALIVE AND COME BACK
ONLY BECAUSE MY MOTHER HAD PRAYED FOR ME EVERY SINGLE DAY UNTIL SHE DIED.
THEY SAID IT WAS ALL THANKS TO HER.
WHAT HAPPENED TO YOUR CITIZENSHIP?

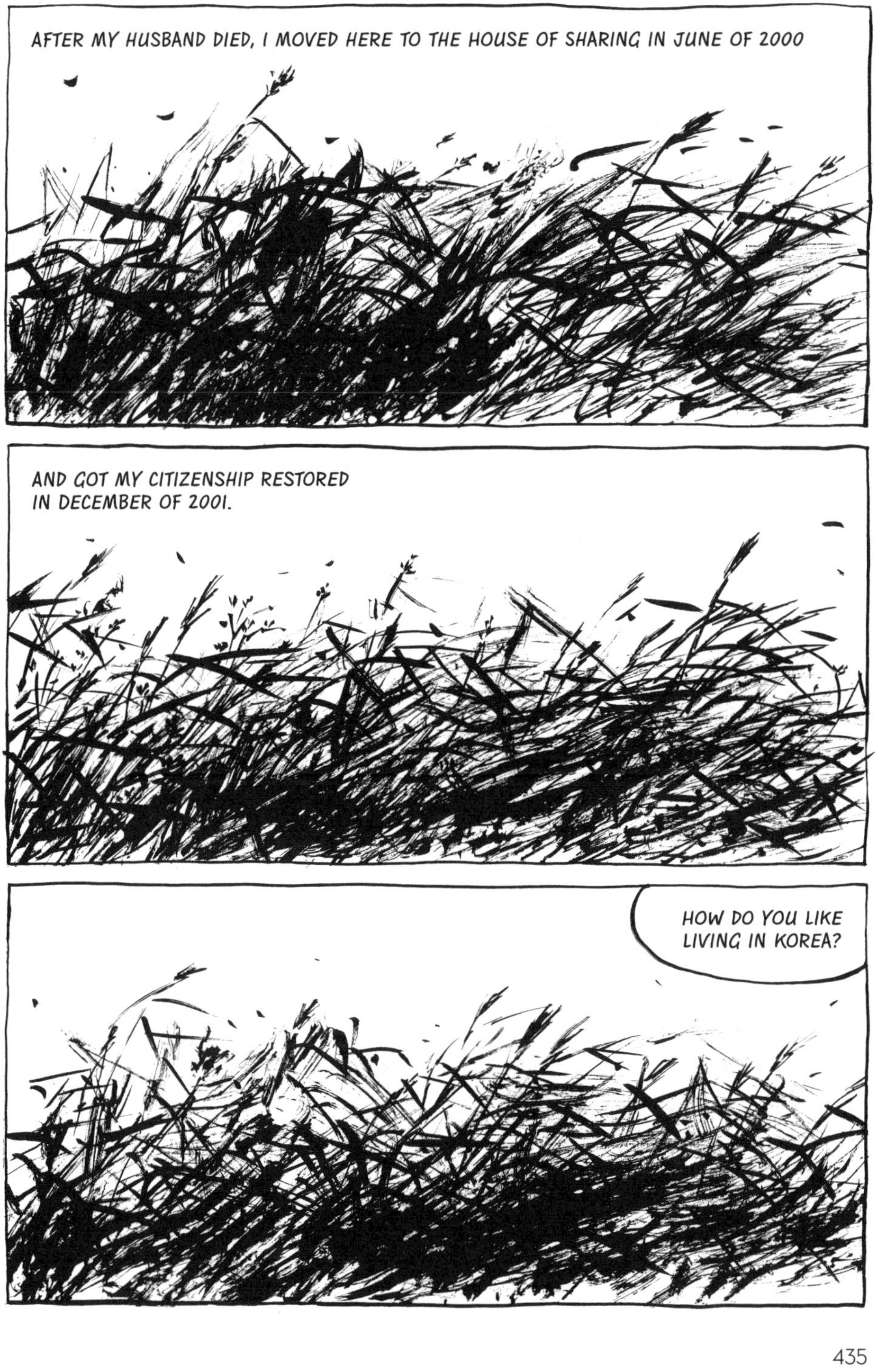
AFTER MY HUSBAND DIED, I MOVED HERE TO THE HOUSE OF SHARING IN JUNE OF 2000
AND GOT MY CITIZENSHIP RESTORED IN DECEMBER OF 2001.
HOW DO YOU LIKE LIVING IN KOREA?

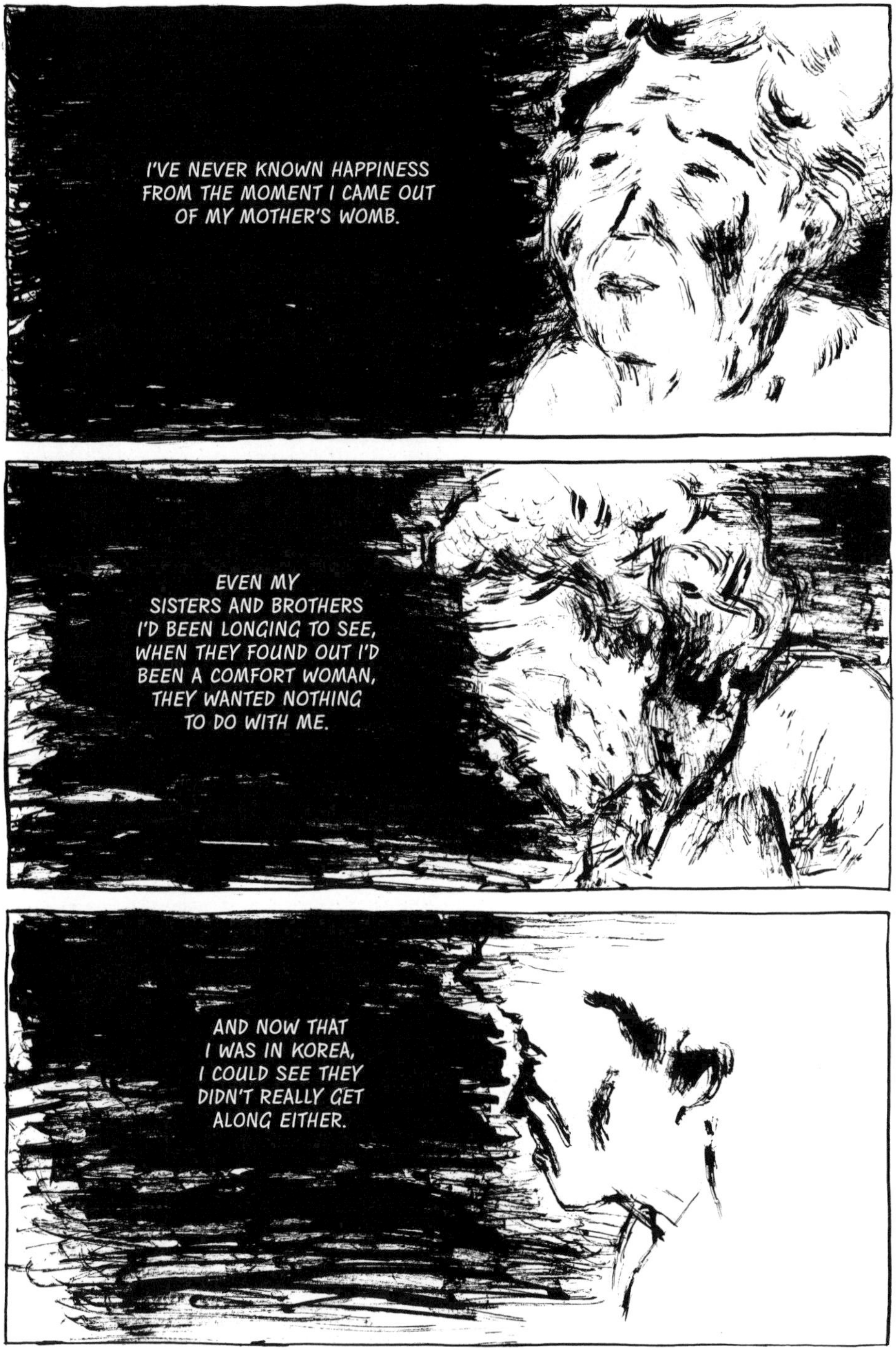
I'VE NEVER KNOWN HAPPINESS FROM THE MOMENT I CAME OUT OF MY MOTHER'S WOMB.
EVEN MY SISTERS AND BROTHERS I'D BEEN LONGING TO SEE, WHEN THEY FOUND OUT I'D BEEN A COMFORT WOMAN, THEY WANTED NOTHING TO DO WITH ME.
AND NOW THAT I WAS IN KOREA, I COULD SEE THEY DIDN'T REALLY GET ALONG EITHER.

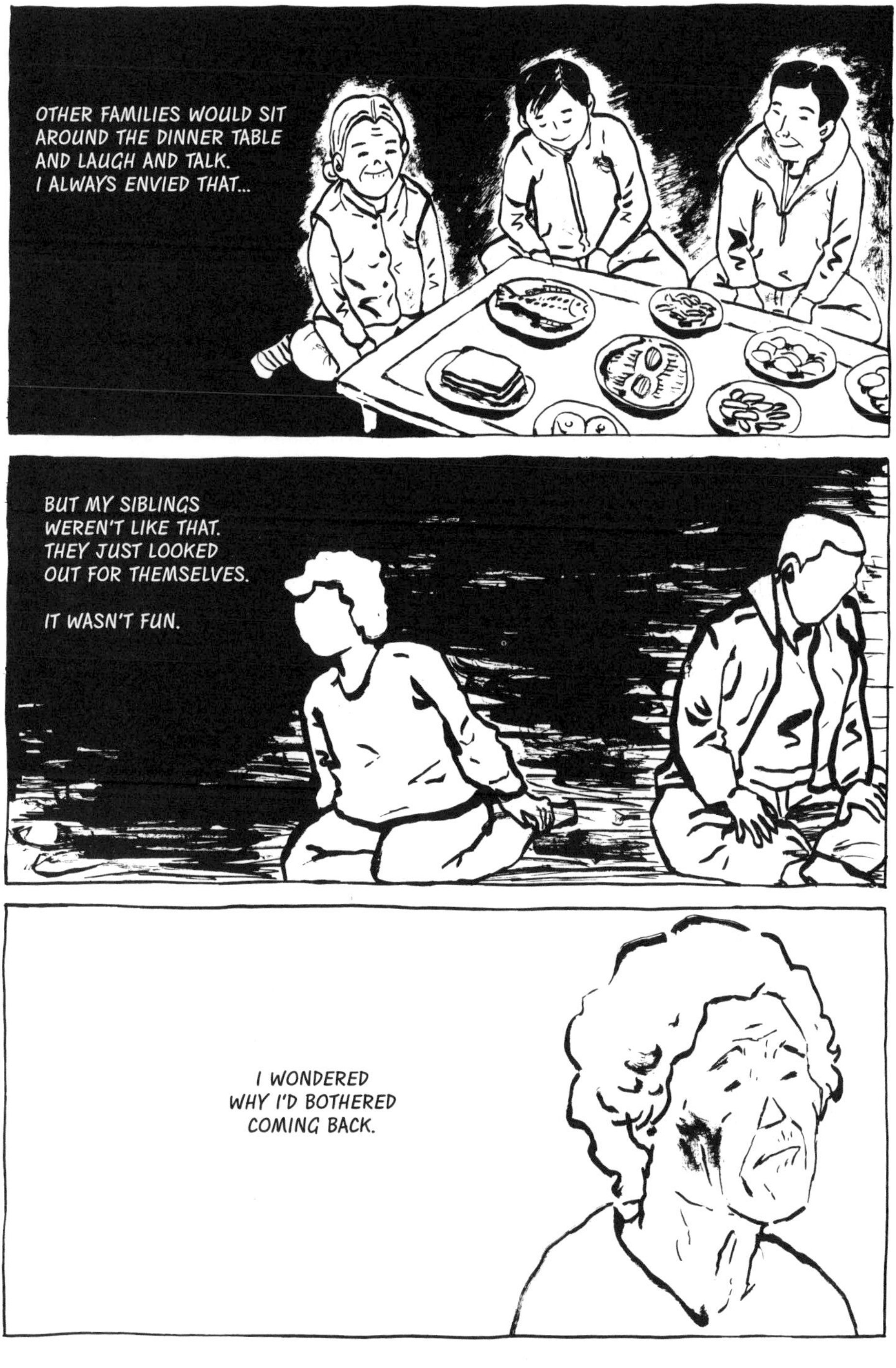
OTHER FAMILIES WOULD SIT AROUND THE DINNER TABLE AND LAUGH AND TALK. I ALWAYS ENVIED THAT...
BUT MY SIBLINGS WEREN'T LIKE THAT. THEY JUST LOOKED OUT FOR THEMSELVES.
IT WASN'T FUN.
I WONDERED WHY I'D BOTHERED COMING BACK.

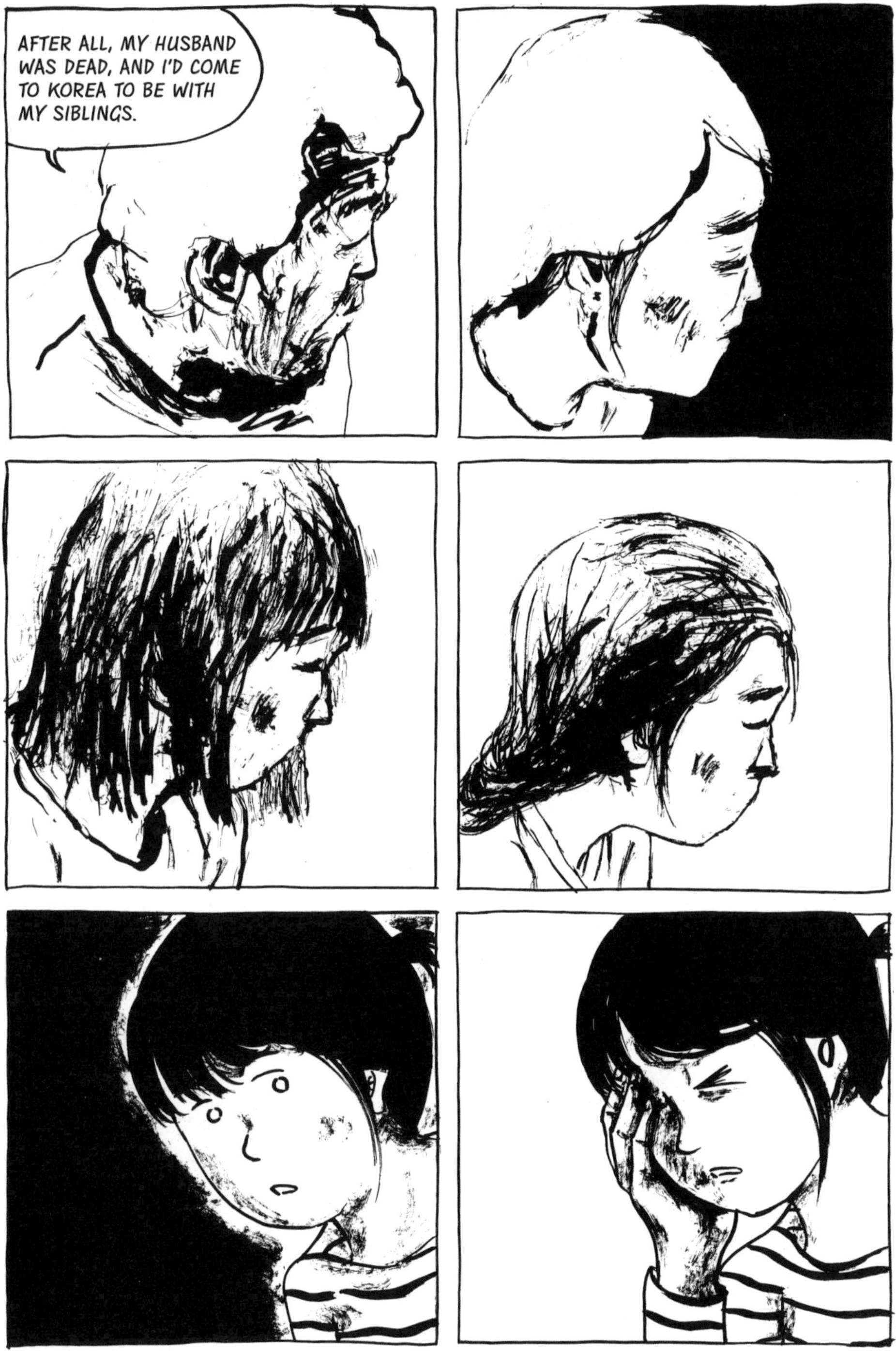
AFTER ALL, MY HUSBAND WAS DEAD, AND I'D COME TO KOREA TO BE WITH MY SIBLINGS.

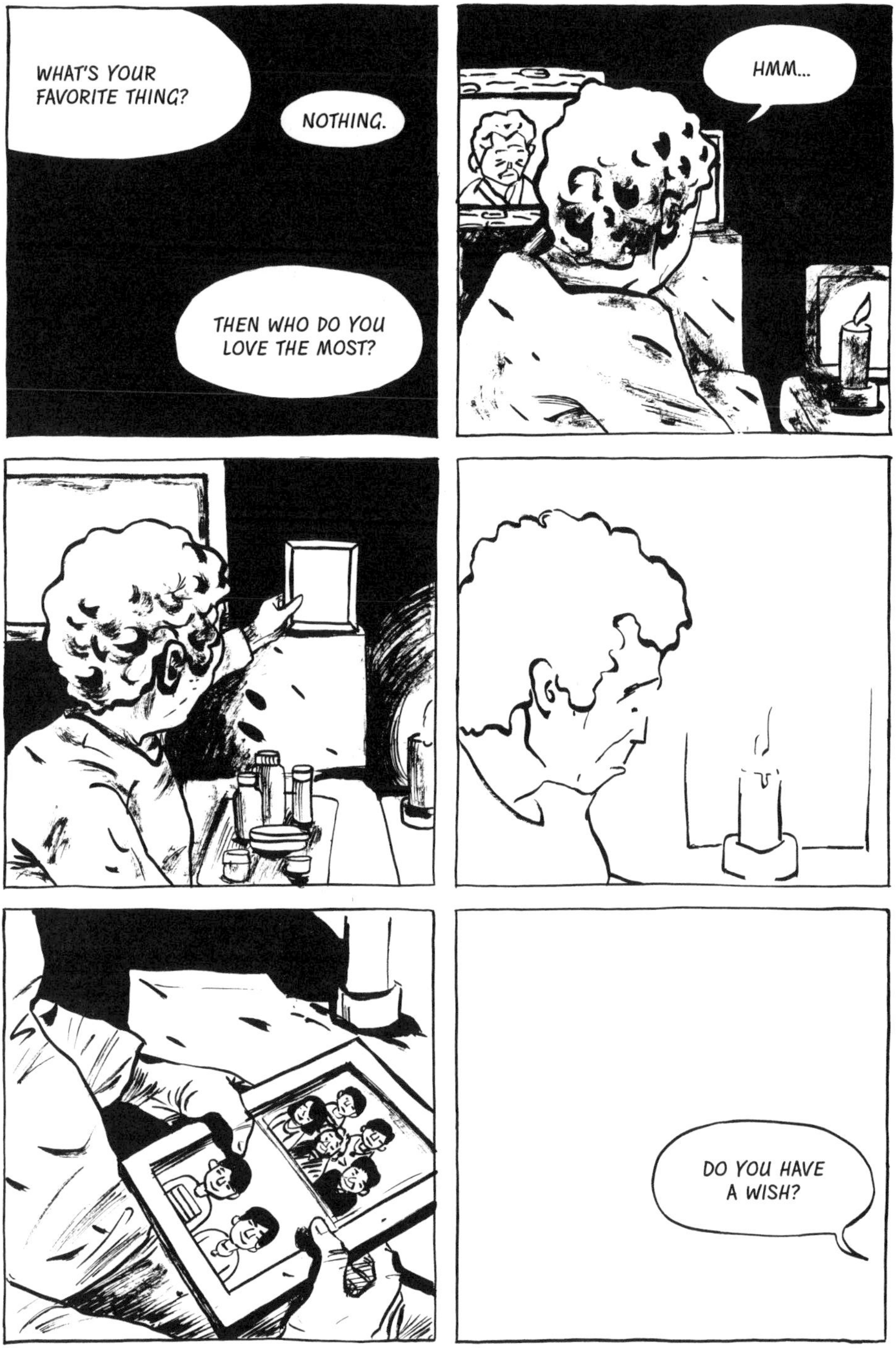
WHAT'S YOUR FAVORITE THING?
NOTHING.
THEN WHO DO YOU LOVE THE MOST?
HMM...
DO YOU HAVE A WISH?

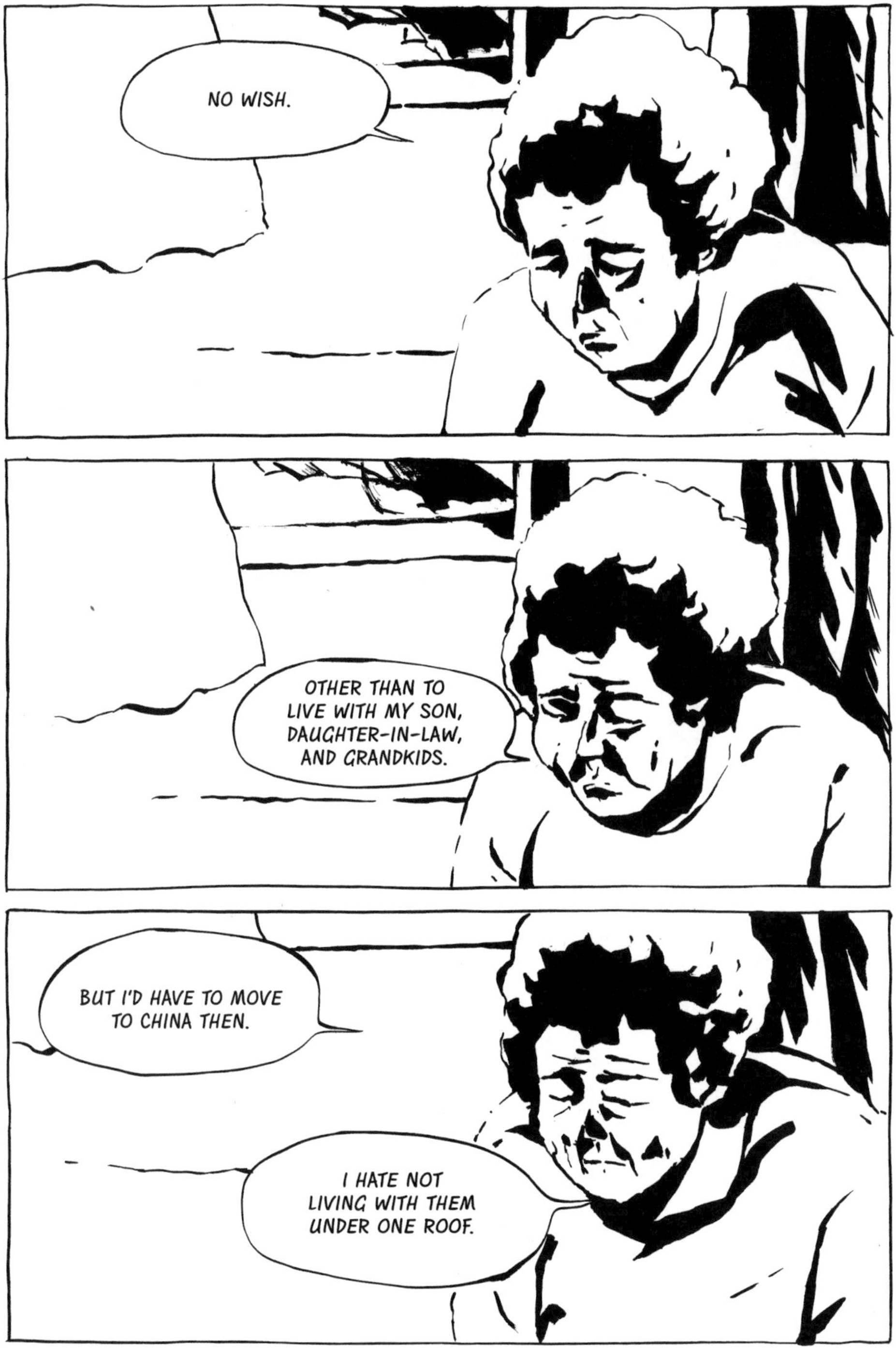
NO WISH.
OTHER THAN TO LIVE WITH MY SON, DAUGHTER-IN-LAW, AND GRANDKIDS.
BUT I'D HAVE TO MOVE TO CHINA THEN.
I HATE NOT LIVING WITH THEM UNDER ONE ROOF.

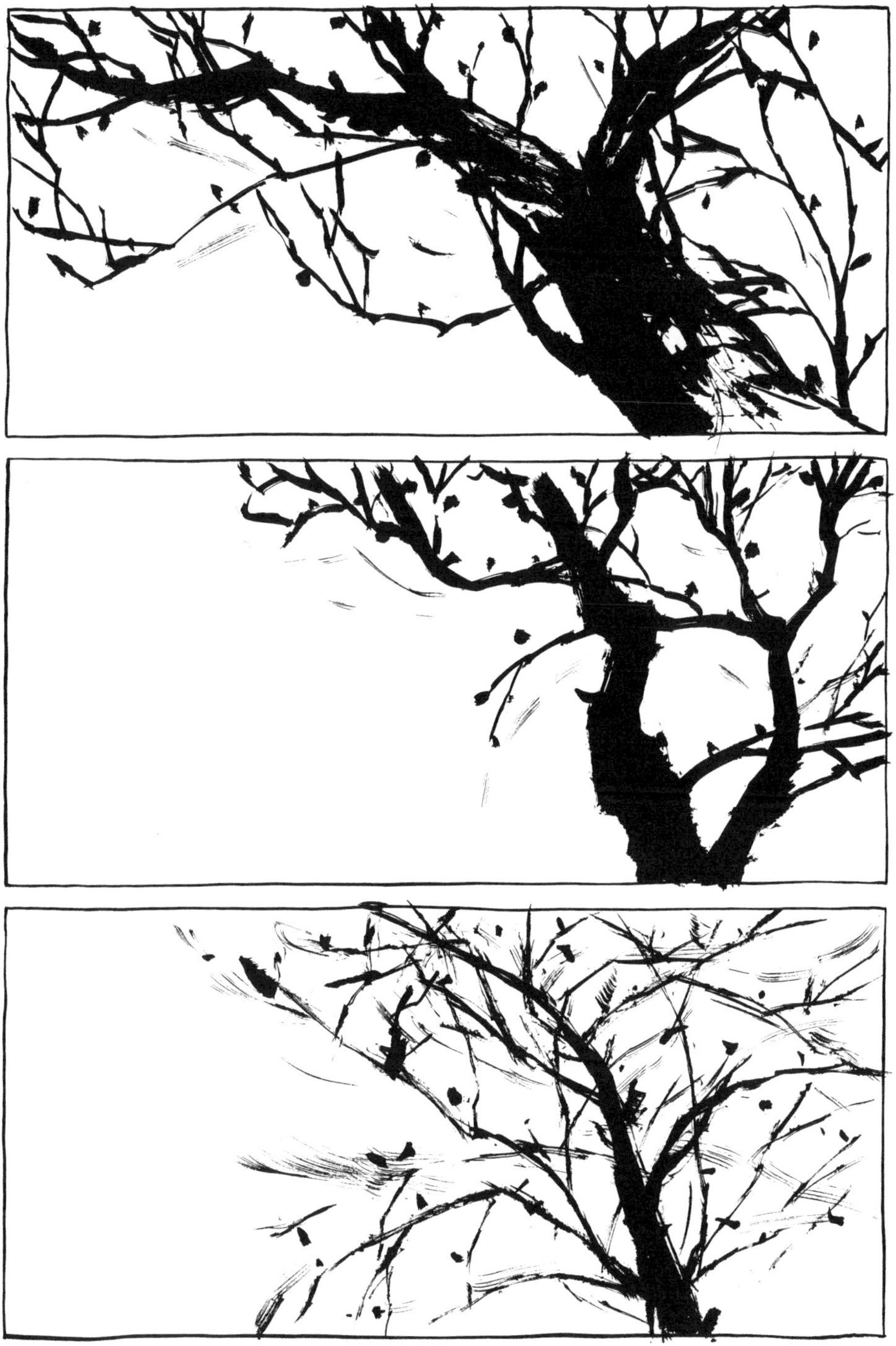

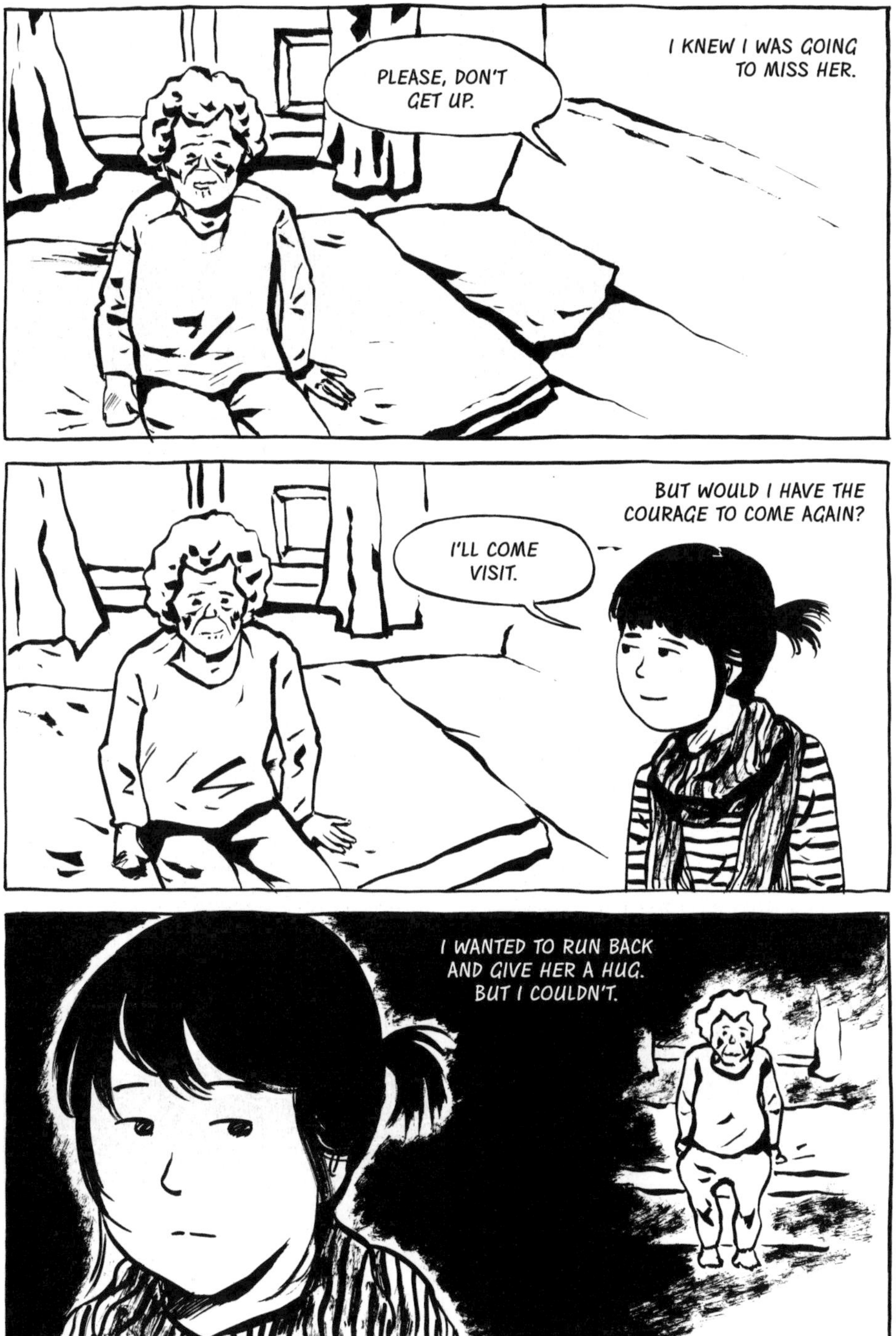
PLEASE, DON'T GET UP.
I KNEW I WAS GOING TO MISS HER.
I'LL COME VISIT.
BUT WOULD I HAVE THE COURAGE TO COME AGAIN?
I WANTED TO RUN BACK AND GIVE HER A HUG. BUT I COULDN'T.

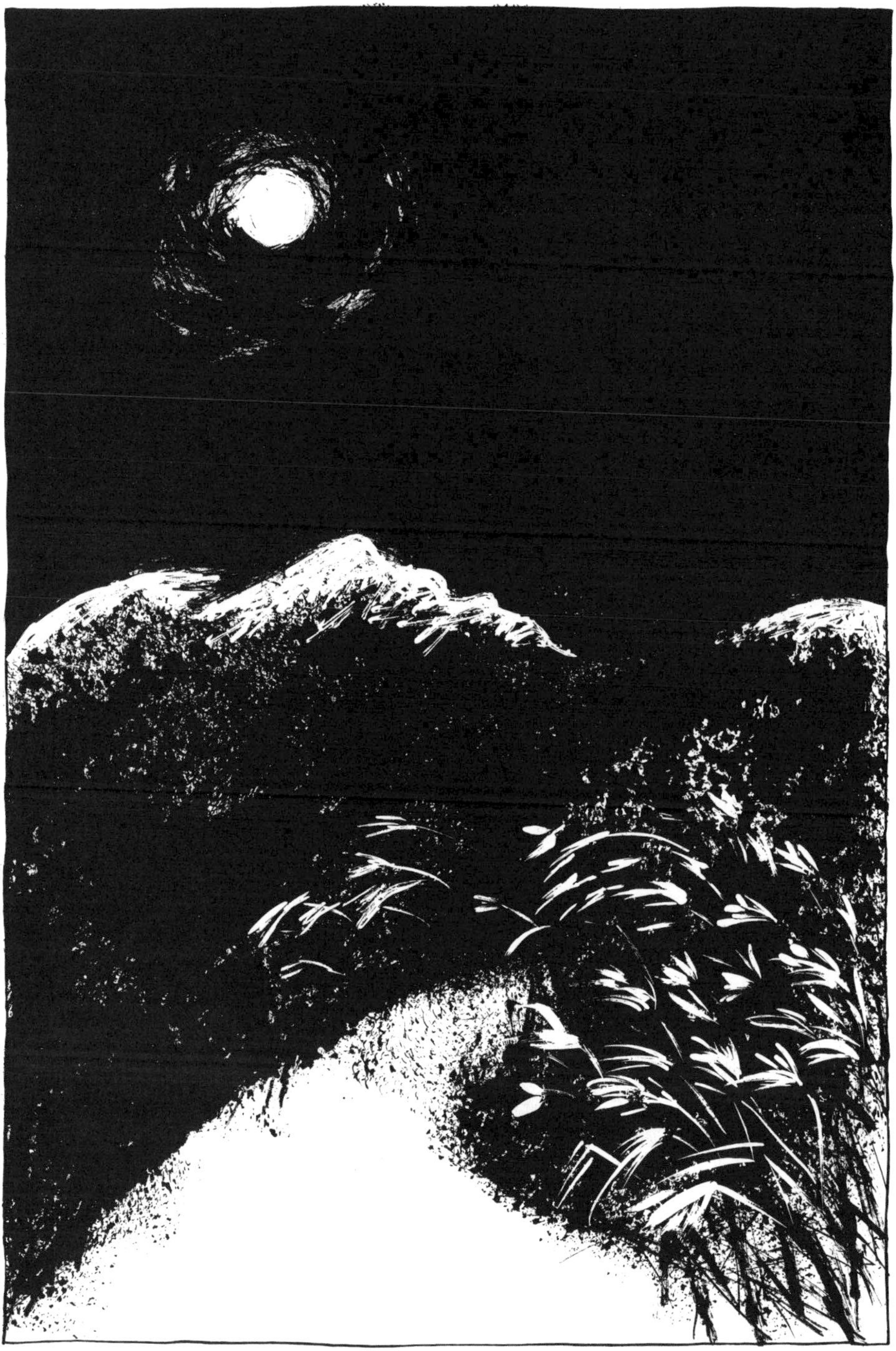

# TRACING THE STEPS
# OF GRANNY LEE

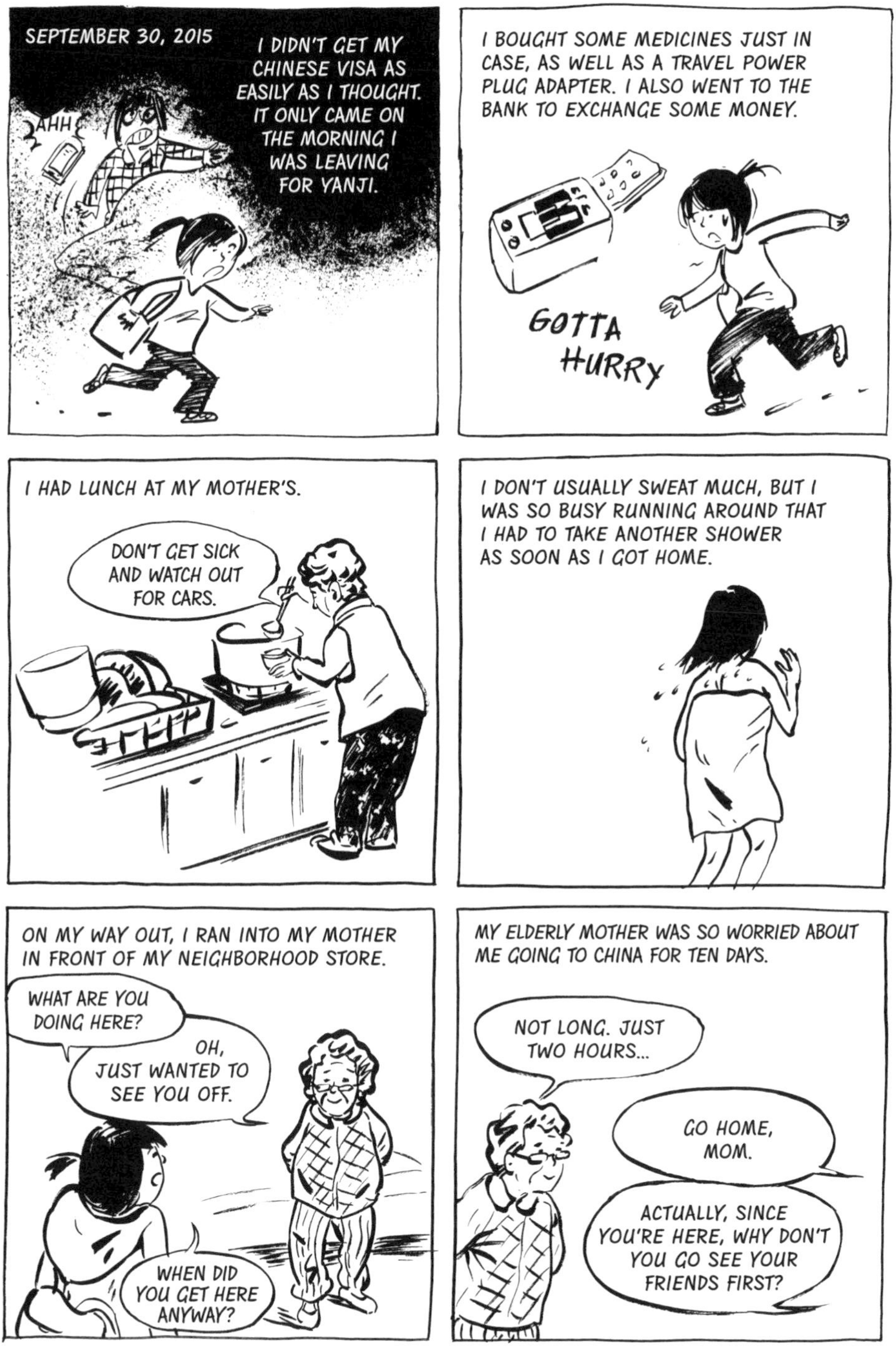
SEPTEMBER 30, 2015
I DIDN'T GET MY CHINESE VISA AS EASILY AS I THOUGHT. IT ONLY CAME ON THE MORNING I WAS LEAVING FOR YANJI.
AHH
I BOUGHT SOME MEDICINES JUST IN CASE, AS WELL AS A TRAVEL POWER PLUG ADAPTER. I ALSO WENT TO THE BANK TO EXCHANGE SOME MONEY.
GOTTA HURRY
I HAD LUNCH AT MY MOTHER'S.
DON'T GET SICK AND WATCH OUT FOR CARS.
I DON'T USUALLY SWEAT MUCH, BUT I WAS SO BUSY RUNNING AROUND THAT I HAD TO TAKE ANOTHER SHOWER AS SOON AS I GOT HOME.
ON MY WAY OUT, I RAN INTO MY MOTHER IN FRONT OF MY NEIGHBORHOOD STORE.
WHAT ARE YOU DOING HERE?
OH, JUST WANTED TO SEE YOU OFF.
WHEN DID YOU GET HERE ANYWAY?
MY ELDERLY MOTHER WAS SO WORRIED ABOUT ME GOING TO CHINA FOR TEN DAYS.
NOT LONG. JUST TWO HOURS...
GO HOME, MOM.
ACTUALLY, SINCE YOU'RE HERE, WHY DON'T YOU GO SEE YOUR FRIENDS FIRST?

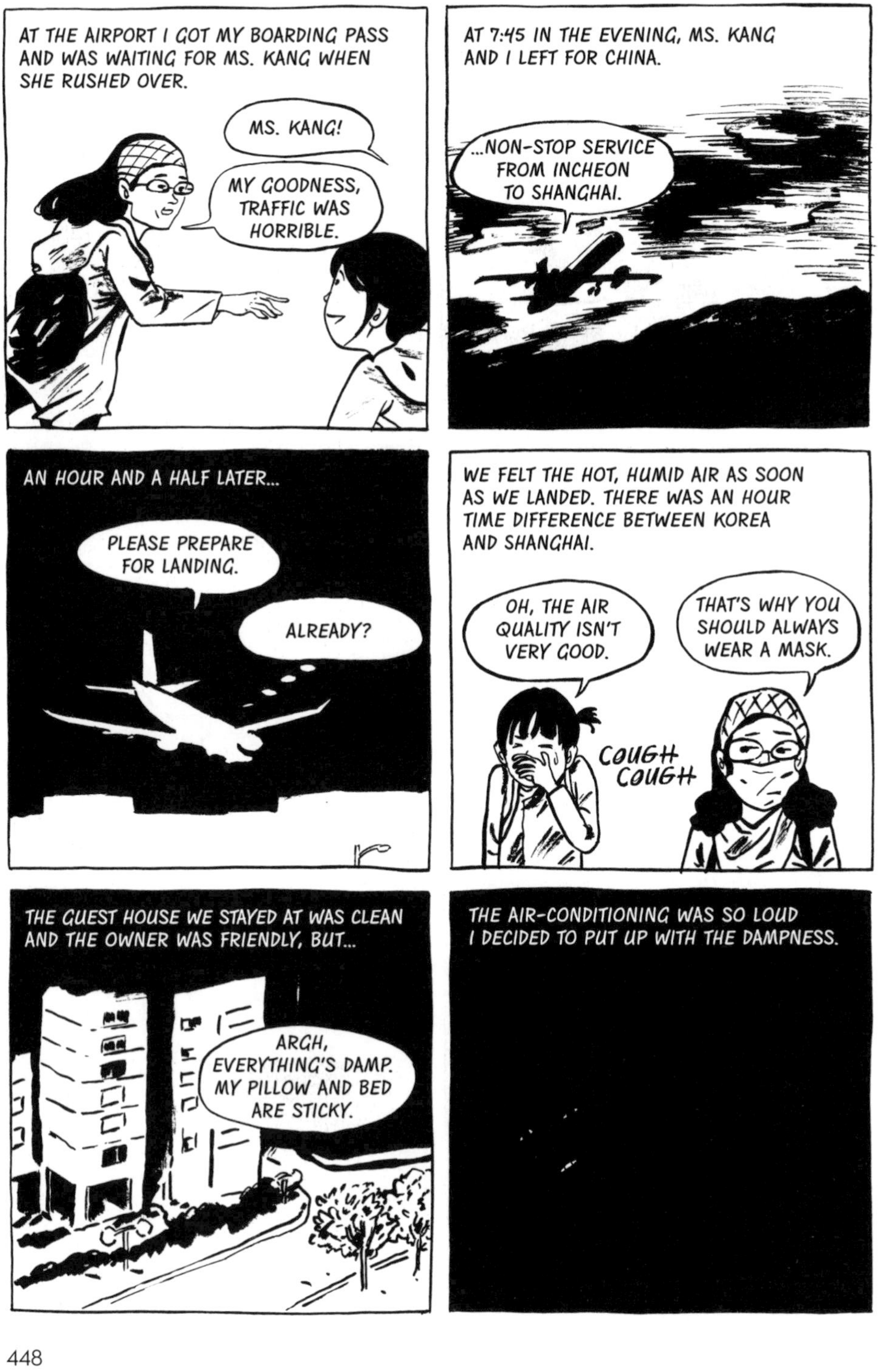
AT THE AIRPORT I GOT MY BOARDING PASS AND WAS WAITING FOR MS. KANG WHEN SHE RUSHED OVER.
MS. KANG!
MY GOODNESS, TRAFFIC WAS HORRIBLE.
AT 7:45 IN THE EVENING, MS. KANG AND I LEFT FOR CHINA.
...NON-STOP SERVICE FROM INCHEON TO SHANGHAI.
AN HOUR AND A HALF LATER...
PLEASE PREPARE FOR LANDING.
ALREADY?
WE FELT THE HOT, HUMID AIR AS SOON AS WE LANDED. THERE WAS AN HOUR TIME DIFFERENCE BETWEEN KOREA AND SHANGHAI.
OH, THE AIR QUALITY ISN'T VERY GOOD.
COUGH COUGH
THAT'S WHY YOU SHOULD ALWAYS WEAR A MASK.
THE GUEST HOUSE WE STAYED AT WAS CLEAN AND THE OWNER WAS FRIENDLY, BUT...
ARGH, EVERYTHING'S DAMP. MY PILLOW AND BED ARE STICKY.
THE AIR-CONDITIONING WAS SO LOUD I DECIDED TO PUT UP WITH THE DAMPNESS.

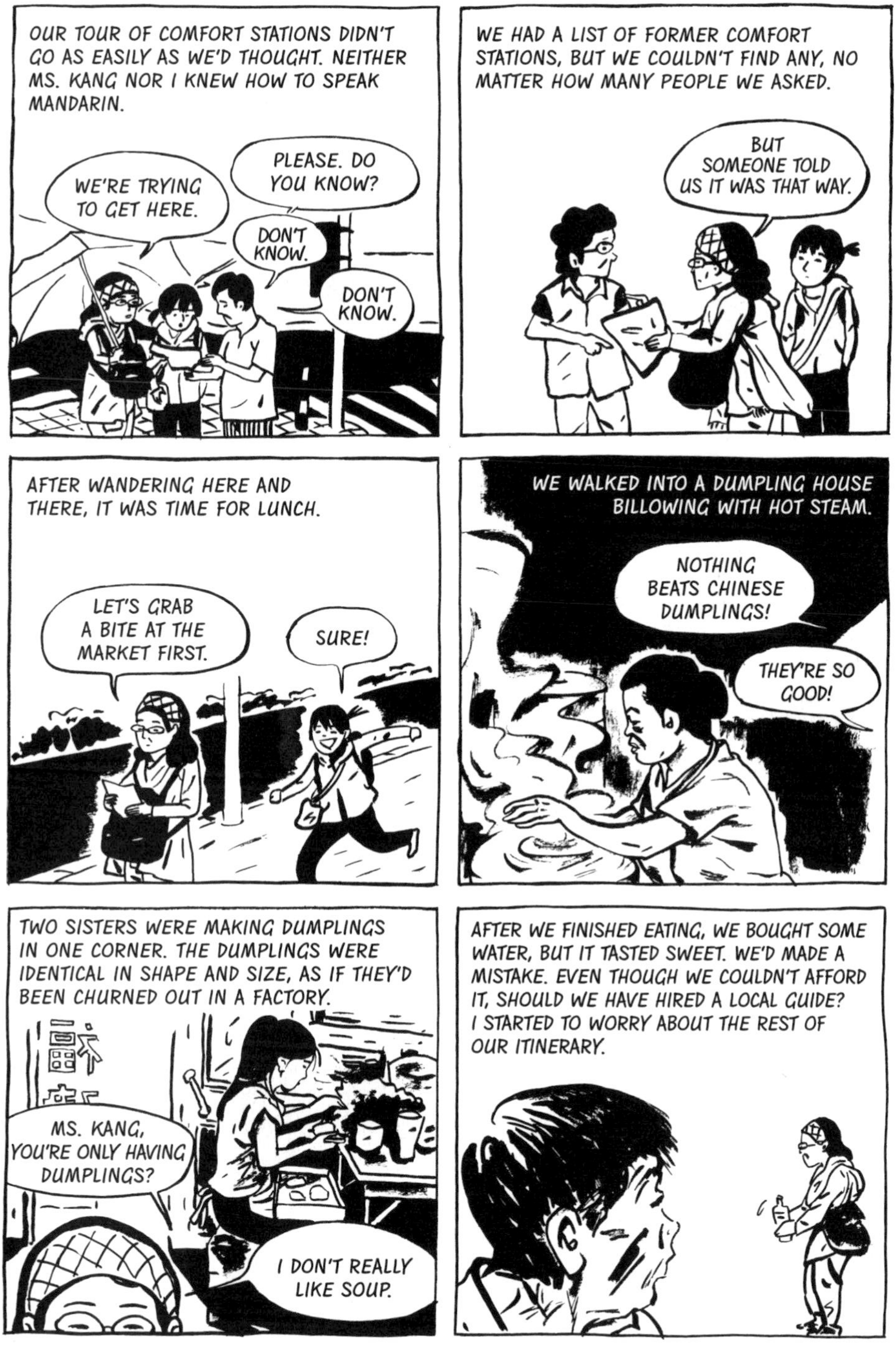
OUR TOUR OF COMFORT STATIONS DIDN'T GO AS EASILY AS WE'D THOUGHT. NEITHER MS. KANG NOR I KNEW HOW TO SPEAK MANDARIN.
WE'RE TRYING TO GET HERE.
PLEASE. DO YOU KNOW?
DON'T KNOW.
DON'T KNOW.
WE HAD A LIST OF FORMER COMFORT STATIONS, BUT WE COULDN'T FIND ANY, NO MATTER HOW MANY PEOPLE WE ASKED.
BUT SOMEONE TOLD US IT WAS THAT WAY.
AFTER WANDERING HERE AND THERE, IT WAS TIME FOR LUNCH.
LET'S GRAB A BITE AT THE MARKET FIRST.
SURE!
WE WALKED INTO A DUMPLING HOUSE BILLOWING WITH HOT STEAM.
NOTHING BEATS CHINESE DUMPLINGS!
THEY'RE SO GOOD!
TWO SISTERS WERE MAKING DUMPLINGS IN ONE CORNER. THE DUMPLINGS WERE IDENTICAL IN SHAPE AND SIZE, AS IF THEY'D BEEN CHURNED OUT IN A FACTORY.
MS. KANG, YOU'RE ONLY HAVING DUMPLINGS?
I DON'T REALLY LIKE SOUP.
AFTER WE FINISHED EATING, WE BOUGHT SOME WATER, BUT IT TASTED SWEET. WE'D MADE A MISTAKE. EVEN THOUGH WE COULDN'T AFFORD IT, SHOULD WE HAVE HIRED A LOCAL GUIDE? I STARTED TO WORRY ABOUT THE REST OF OUR ITINERARY.

AFTER ASKING AROUND, WE FINALLY MANAGED TO
FIND A RUN-DOWN BUILDING THAT HAD BEEN
USED AS A COMFORT STATION. LUCKILY, IT WAS
CLOSE TO THE MARKET. NEAR THE ALLEY
ENTRANCE SAT A STREET COBBLER.

MS. KANG SAID SHE SMELLED SOMETHING
DELICIOUS, BUT I ALSO CAUGHT A WHIFF
OF URINE.

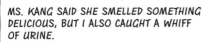

450

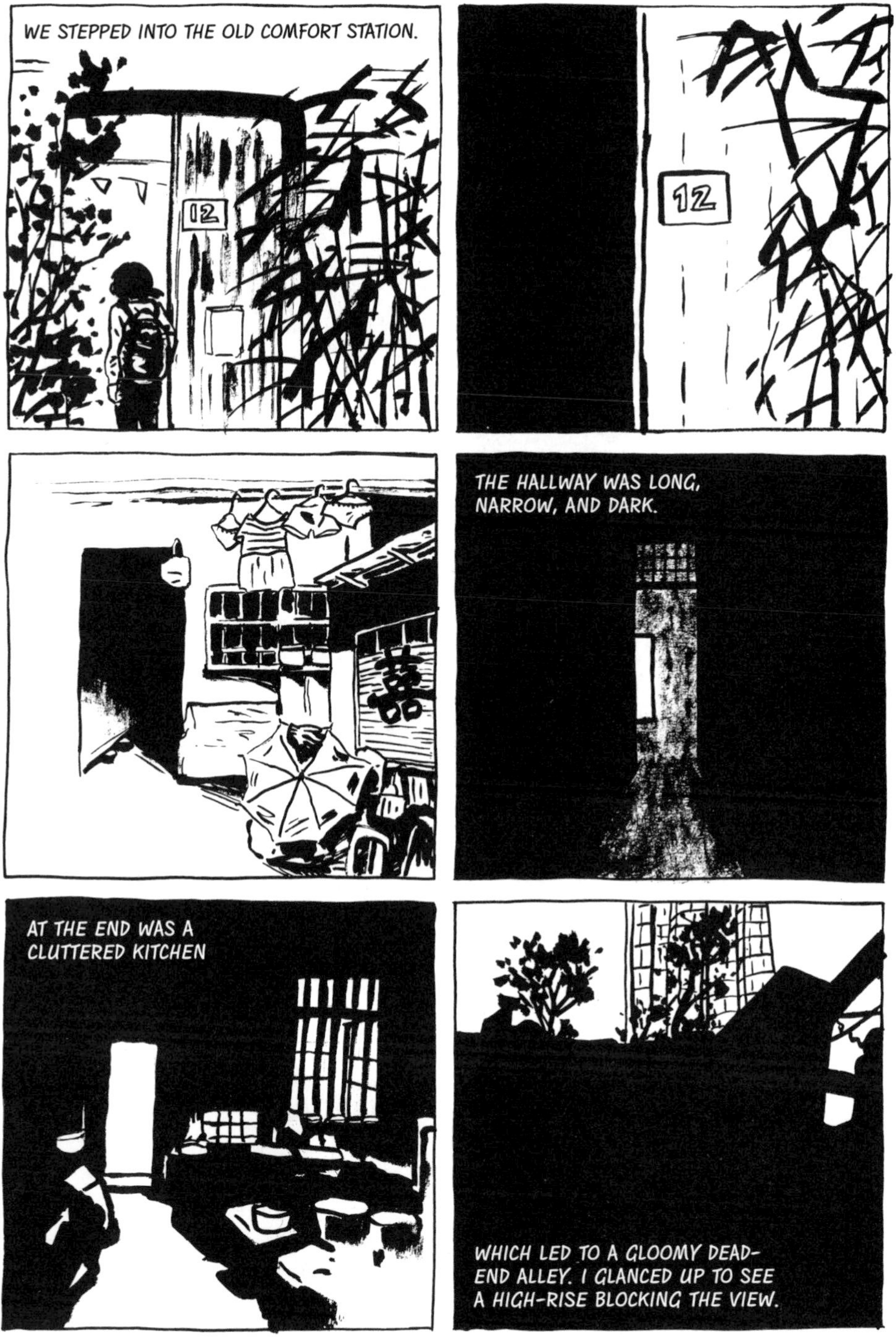
WE STEPPED INTO THE OLD COMFORT STATION.
12
12
THE HALLWAY WAS LONG, NARROW, AND DARK.
囍
AT THE END WAS A CLUTTERED KITCHEN
WHICH LED TO A GLOOMY DEAD-END ALLEY. I GLANCED UP TO SEE A HIGH-RISE BLOCKING THE VIEW.

AS I WAS MAKING MY WAY BACK, MY HEART DROPPED. THE LIGHT CREEPING INTO THE BUILDING HIT THE SHADOWY STEPS AND I THOUGHT I SAW A WILD ANIMAL CROUCHING THERE.

THE JAPANESE SOLDIERS MUST HAVE GONE UP THOSE STAIRS...

MY IMAGINATION TOOK OFF. I TREMBLED, FEELING A CHILL RUN THROUGH MY BODY.

WHEN I STEPPED OUT INTO THE COURTYARD, I FELT AS IF FACES OF GIRLS WERE PEERING OUT AT ME FROM BETWEEN ALL THE LAUNDRY. RIGHT THEN—

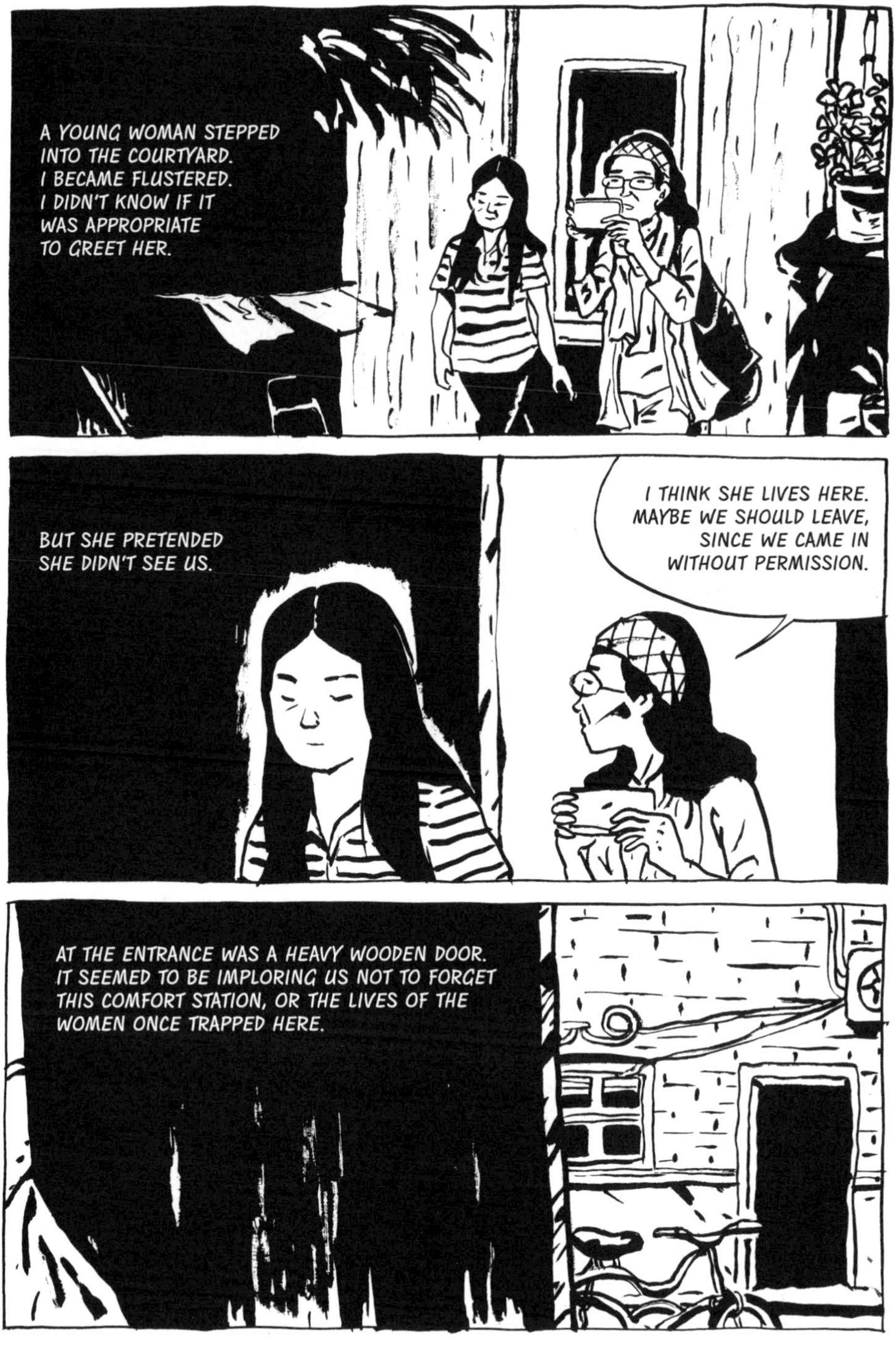
A YOUNG WOMAN STEPPED INTO THE COURTYARD. I BECAME FLUSTERED. I DIDN'T KNOW IF IT WAS APPROPRIATE TO GREET HER.
BUT SHE PRETENDED SHE DIDN'T SEE US.
I THINK SHE LIVES HERE. MAYBE WE SHOULD LEAVE, SINCE WE CAME IN WITHOUT PERMISSION.
AT THE ENTRANCE WAS A HEAVY WOODEN DOOR. IT SEEMED TO BE IMPLORING US NOT TO FORGET THIS COMFORT STATION, OR THE LIVES OF THE WOMEN ONCE TRAPPED HERE.

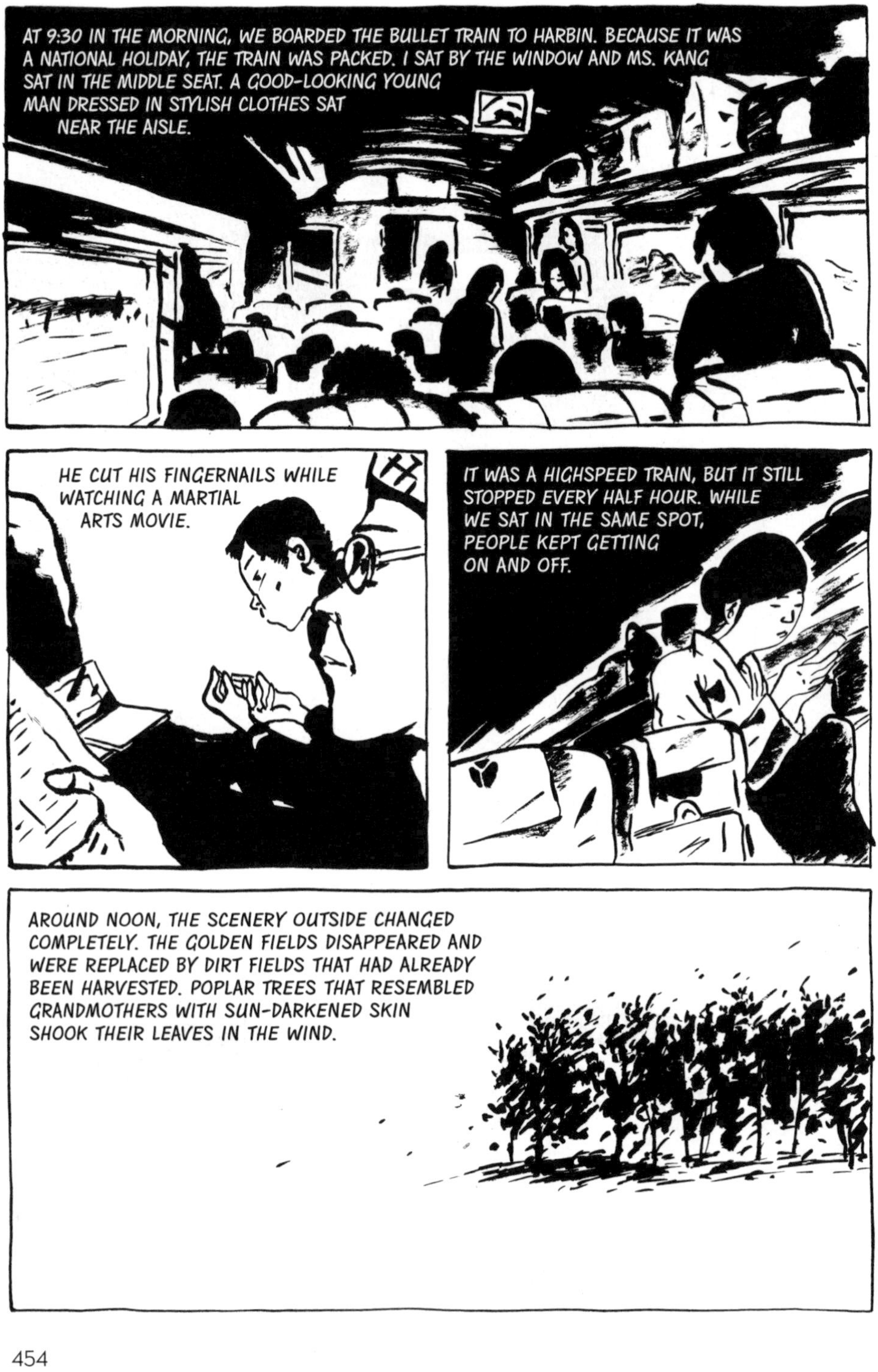
AT 9:30 IN THE MORNING, WE BOARDED THE BULLET TRAIN TO HARBIN. BECAUSE IT WAS A NATIONAL HOLIDAY, THE TRAIN WAS PACKED. I SAT BY THE WINDOW AND MS. KANG SAT IN THE MIDDLE SEAT. A GOOD-LOOKING YOUNG MAN DRESSED IN STYLISH CLOTHES SAT NEAR THE AISLE.
HE CUT HIS FINGERNAILS WHILE WATCHING A MARTIAL ARTS MOVIE.
IT WAS A HIGHSPEED TRAIN, BUT IT STILL STOPPED EVERY HALF HOUR. WHILE WE SAT IN THE SAME SPOT, PEOPLE KEPT GETTING ON AND OFF.
AROUND NOON, THE SCENERY OUTSIDE CHANGED COMPLETELY. THE GOLDEN FIELDS DISAPPEARED AND WERE REPLACED BY DIRT FIELDS THAT HAD ALREADY BEEN HARVESTED. POPLAR TREES THAT RESEMBLED GRANDMOTHERS WITH SUN-DARKENED SKIN SHOOK THEIR LEAVES IN THE WIND.

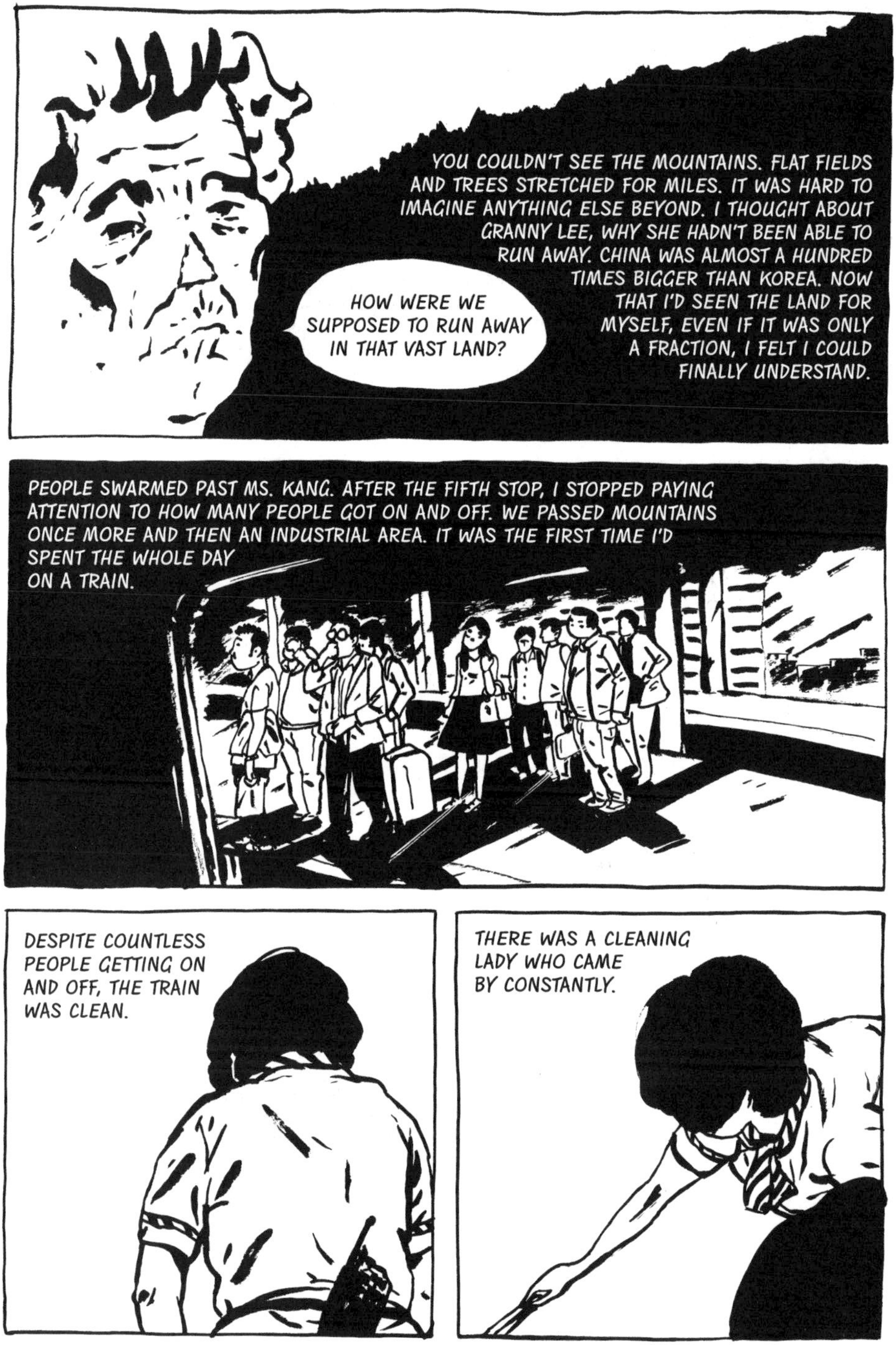
YOU COULDN'T SEE THE MOUNTAINS. FLAT FIELDS AND TREES STRETCHED FOR MILES. IT WAS HARD TO IMAGINE ANYTHING ELSE BEYOND. I THOUGHT ABOUT GRANNY LEE, WHY SHE HADN'T BEEN ABLE TO RUN AWAY. CHINA WAS ALMOST A HUNDRED TIMES BIGGER THAN KOREA. NOW THAT I'D SEEN THE LAND FOR MYSELF, EVEN IF IT WAS ONLY A FRACTION, I FELT I COULD FINALLY UNDERSTAND.
HOW WERE WE SUPPOSED TO RUN AWAY IN THAT VAST LAND?
PEOPLE SWARMED PAST MS. KANG. AFTER THE FIFTH STOP, I STOPPED PAYING ATTENTION TO HOW MANY PEOPLE GOT ON AND OFF. WE PASSED MOUNTAINS ONCE MORE AND THEN AN INDUSTRIAL AREA. IT WAS THE FIRST TIME I'D SPENT THE WHOLE DAY ON A TRAIN.
DESPITE COUNTLESS PEOPLE GETTING ON AND OFF, THE TRAIN WAS CLEAN.
THERE WAS A CLEANING LADY WHO CAME BY CONSTANTLY.

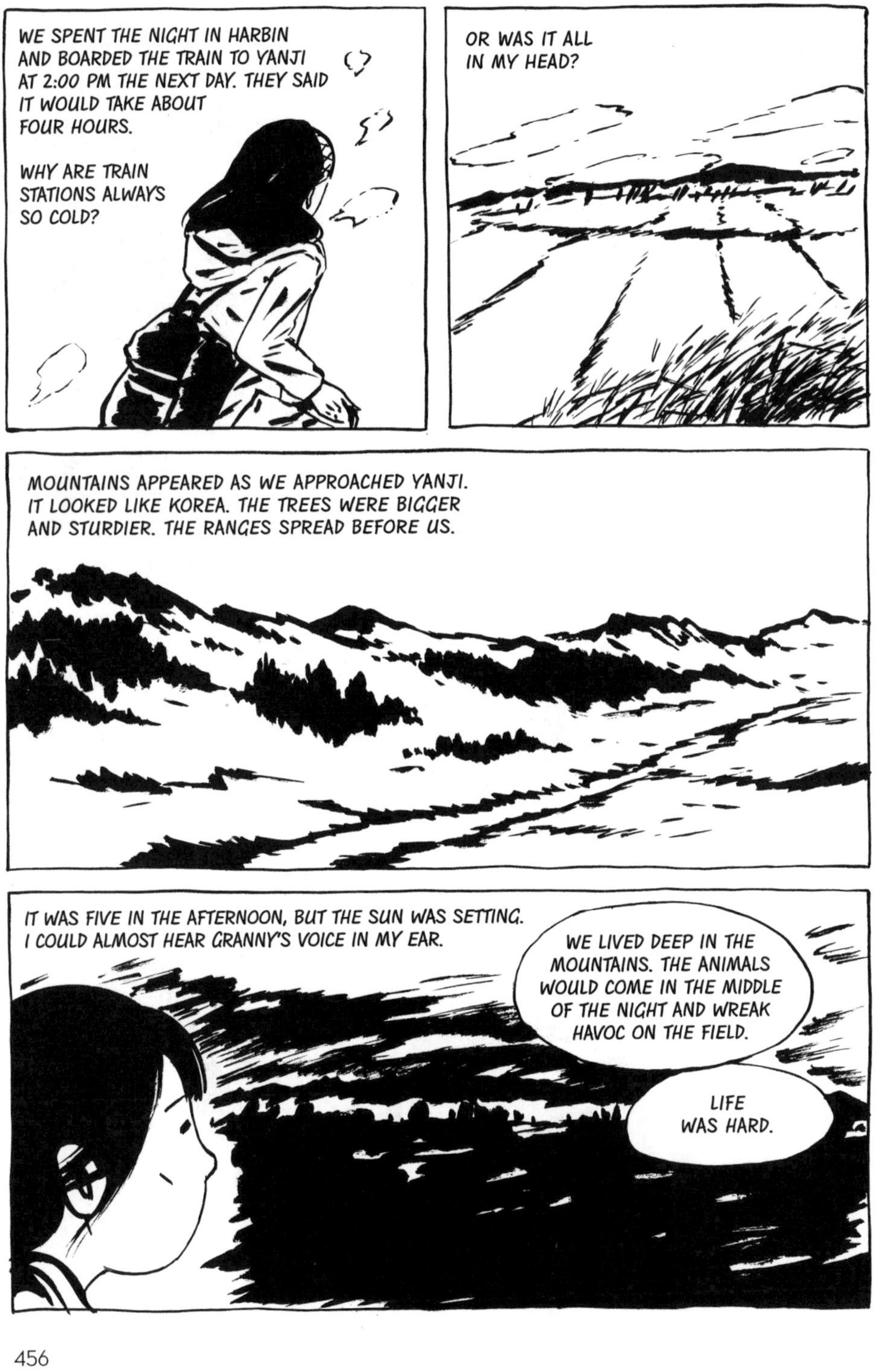
WE SPENT THE NIGHT IN HARBIN AND BOARDED THE TRAIN TO YANJI AT 2:00 PM THE NEXT DAY. THEY SAID IT WOULD TAKE ABOUT FOUR HOURS.
WHY ARE TRAIN STATIONS ALWAYS SO COLD?
OR WAS IT ALL IN MY HEAD?
MOUNTAINS APPEARED AS WE APPROACHED YANJI. IT LOOKED LIKE KOREA. THE TREES WERE BIGGER AND STURDIER. THE RANGES SPREAD BEFORE US.
IT WAS FIVE IN THE AFTERNOON, BUT THE SUN WAS SETTING. I COULD ALMOST HEAR GRANNY'S VOICE IN MY EAR.
WE LIVED DEEP IN THE MOUNTAINS. THE ANIMALS WOULD COME IN THE MIDDLE OF THE NIGHT AND WREAK HAVOC ON THE FIELD.
LIFE WAS HARD.

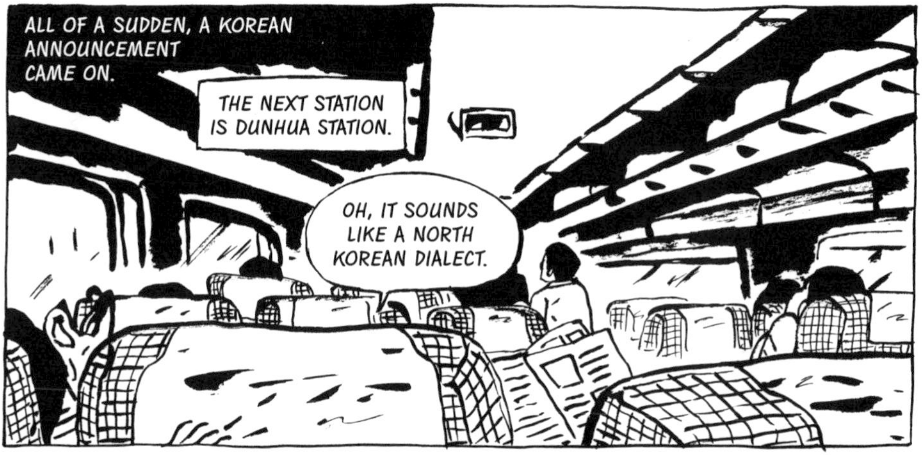
ALL OF A SUDDEN, A KOREAN ANNOUNCEMENT CAME ON.
THE NEXT STATION IS DUNHUA STATION.
OH, IT SOUNDS LIKE A NORTH KOREAN DIALECT.

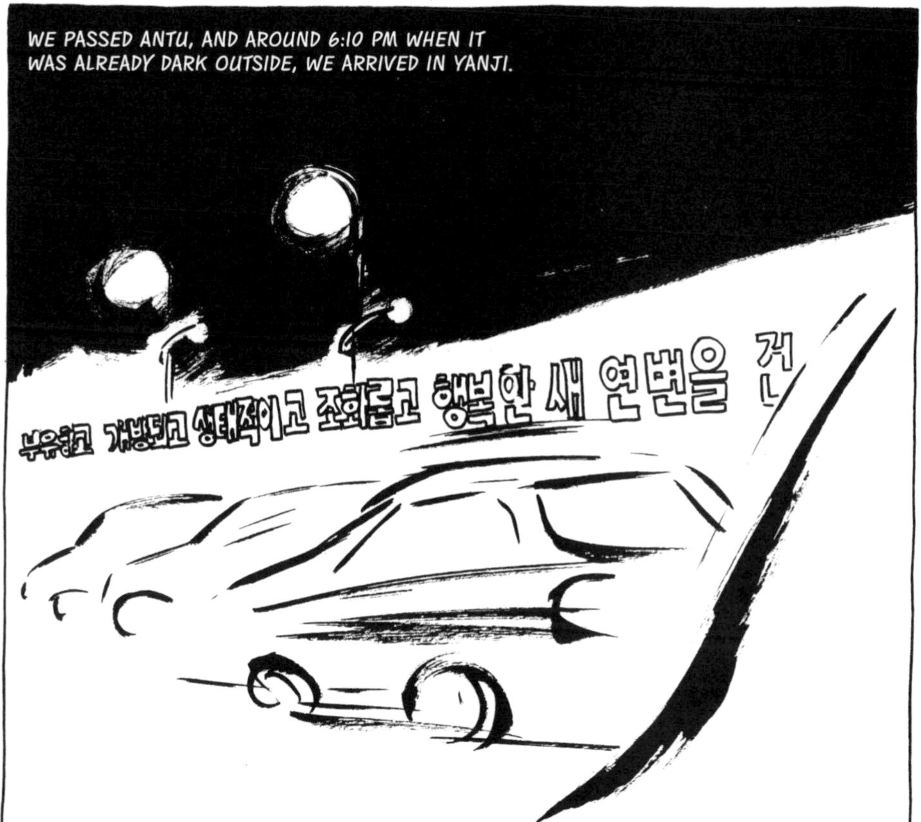
WE PASSED ANTU, AND AROUND 6:10 PM WHEN IT WAS ALREADY DARK OUTSIDE, WE ARRIVED IN YANJI.
부유하고 개방되고 생태적이고 조화롭고 행복한 새 연변을 건

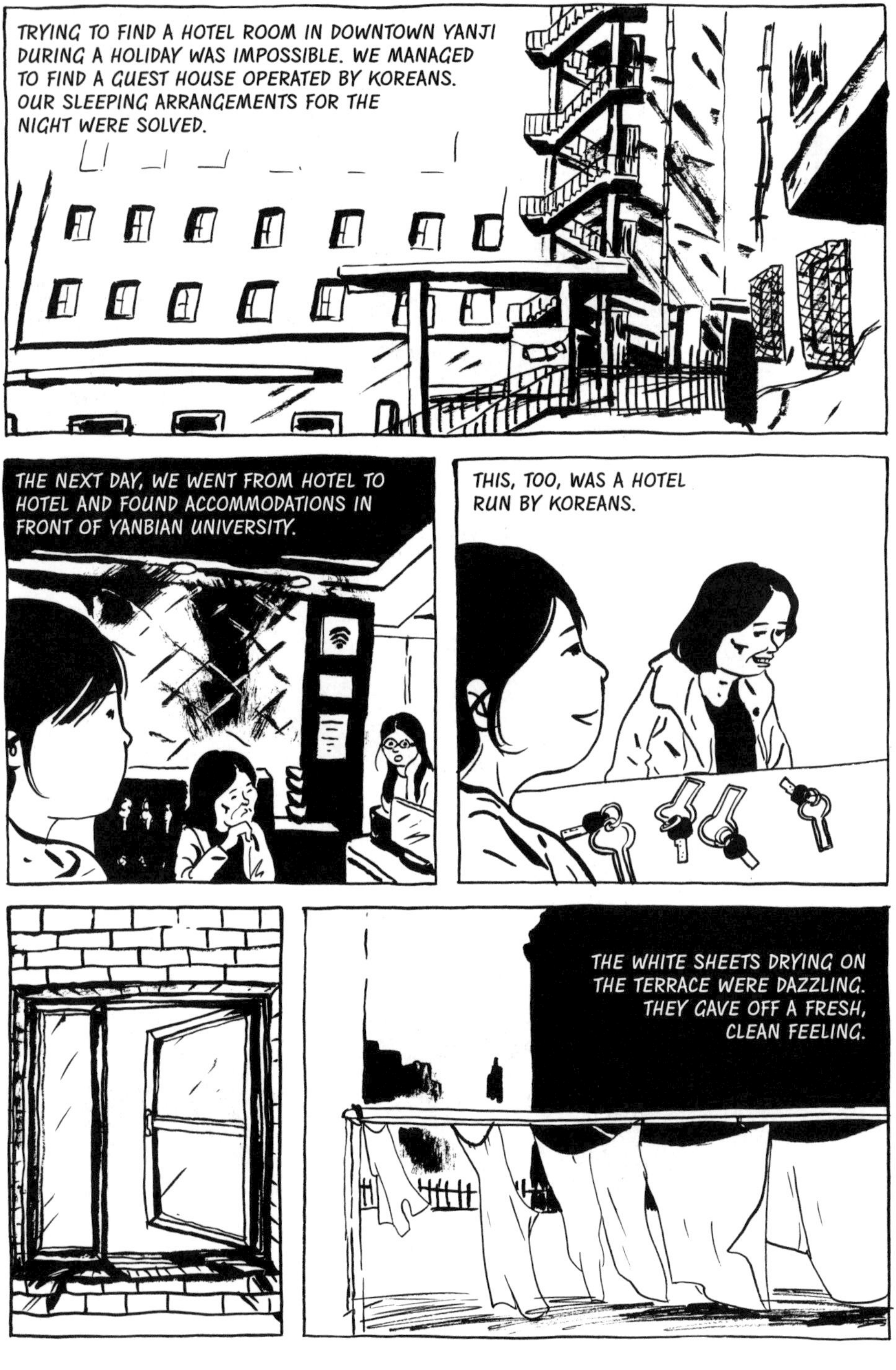
TRYING TO FIND A HOTEL ROOM IN DOWNTOWN YANJI DURING A HOLIDAY WAS IMPOSSIBLE. WE MANAGED TO FIND A GUEST HOUSE OPERATED BY KOREANS. OUR SLEEPING ARRANGEMENTS FOR THE NIGHT WERE SOLVED.
THE NEXT DAY, WE WENT FROM HOTEL TO HOTEL AND FOUND ACCOMMODATIONS IN FRONT OF YANBIAN UNIVERSITY.
THIS, TOO, WAS A HOTEL RUN BY KOREANS.
THE WHITE SHEETS DRYING ON THE TERRACE WERE DAZZLING. THEY GAVE OFF A FRESH, CLEAN FEELING.

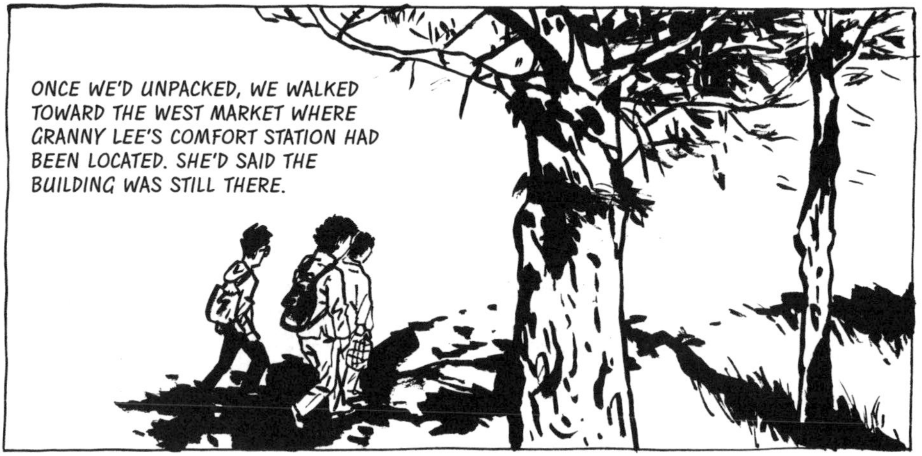
ONCE WE'D UNPACKED, WE WALKED TOWARD THE WEST MARKET WHERE GRANNY LEE'S COMFORT STATION HAD BEEN LOCATED. SHE'D SAID THE BUILDING WAS STILL THERE.

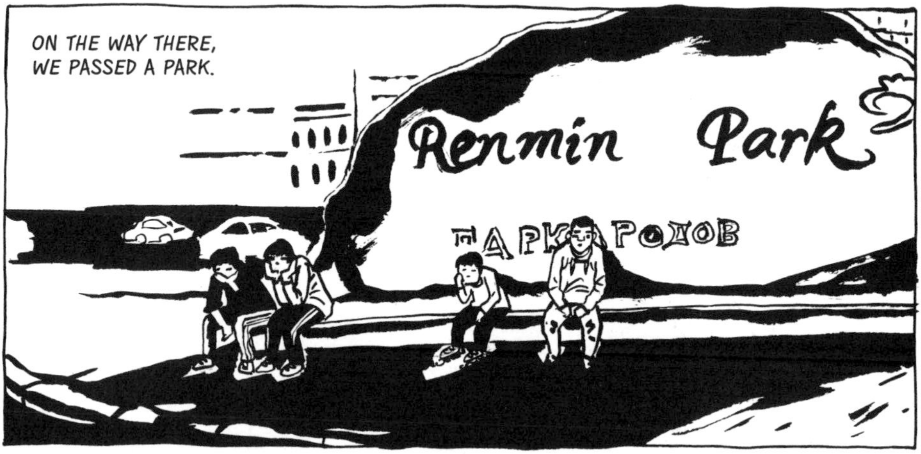
ON THE WAY THERE, WE PASSED A PARK.
Renmin Park

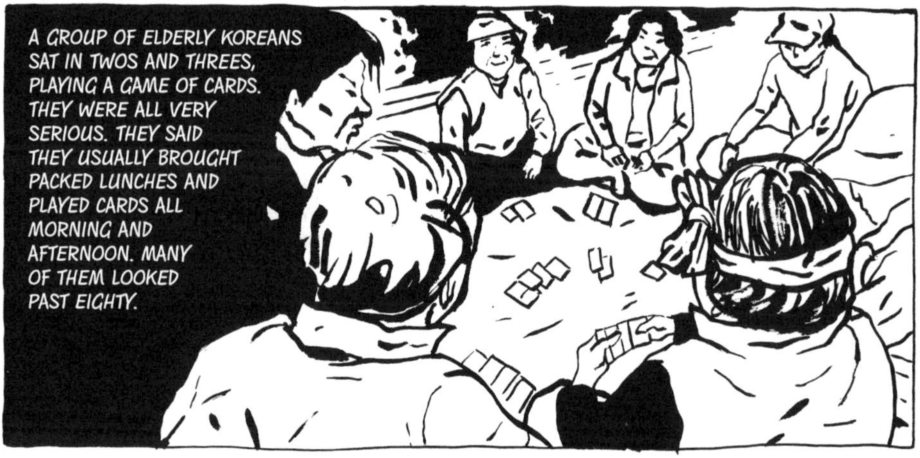
A GROUP OF ELDERLY KOREANS SAT IN TWOS AND THREES, PLAYING A GAME OF CARDS. THEY WERE ALL VERY SERIOUS. THEY SAID THEY USUALLY BROUGHT PACKED LUNCHES AND PLAYED CARDS ALL MORNING AND AFTERNOON. MANY OF THEM LOOKED PAST EIGHTY.

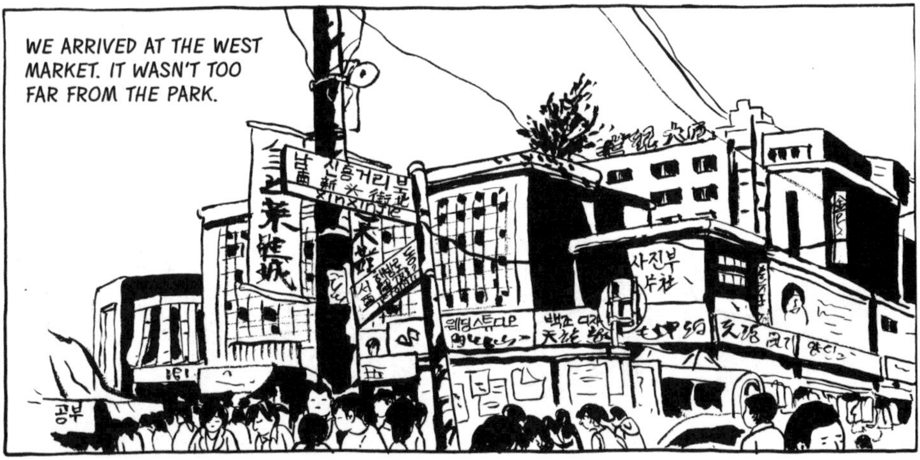
WE ARRIVED AT THE WEST MARKET. IT WASN'T TOO FAR FROM THE PARK.
사진부
공부

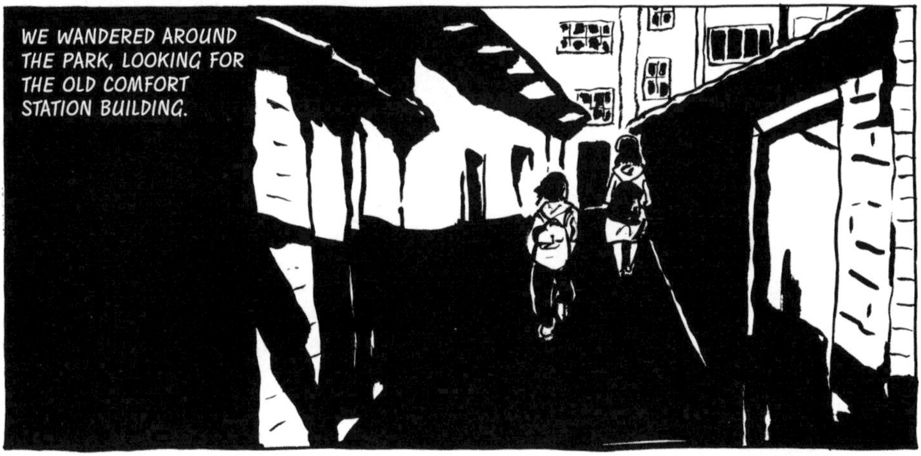
WE WANDERED AROUND THE PARK, LOOKING FOR THE OLD COMFORT STATION BUILDING.

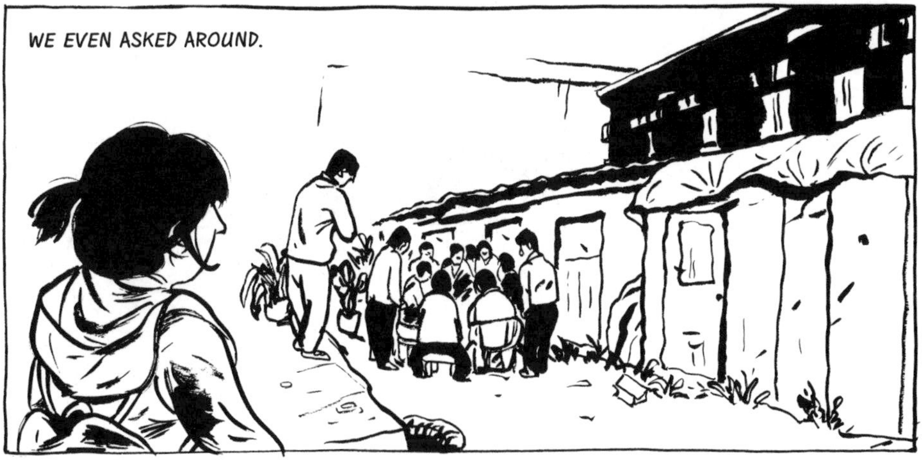
WE EVEN ASKED AROUND.

BUT NO ONE KNEW.

I SHOULD HAVE ASKED GRANNY FOR MORE DETAILS.

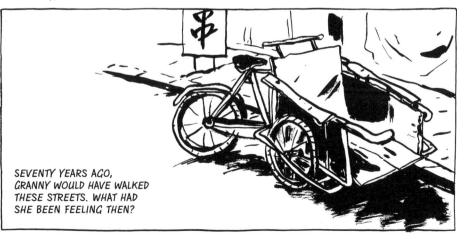

SEVENTY YEARS AGO, GRANNY WOULD HAVE WALKED THESE STREETS. WHAT HAD SHE BEEN FEELING THEN?

THE SUN WAS SETTING.
WE COULDN'T FIND THE BUILDING.

IT WOULD HAVE BEEN NICE TO COME
WITH GRANNY...NO. STOP. I WASN'T GOING
TO STIR UP PAIN FOR HER ANYMORE.

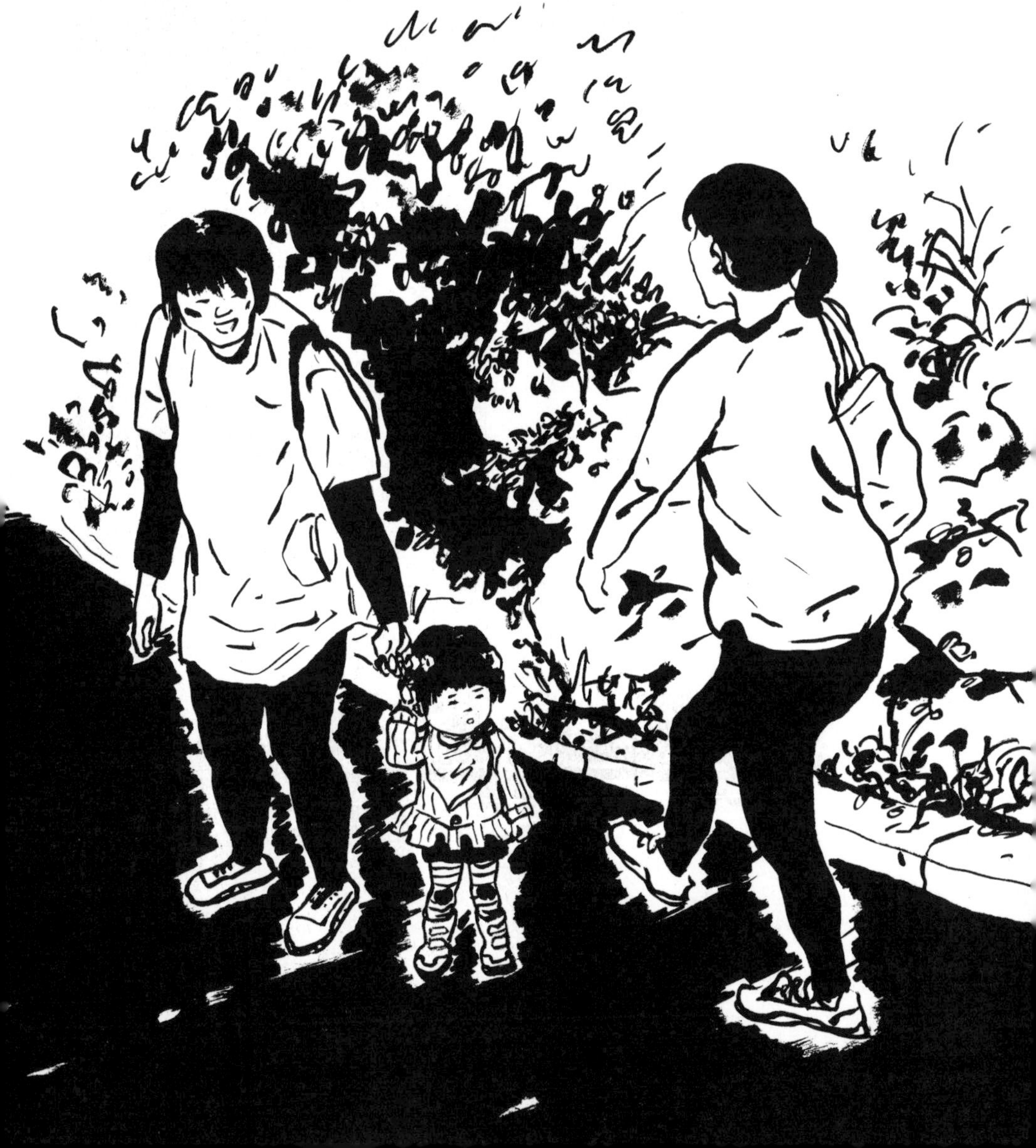

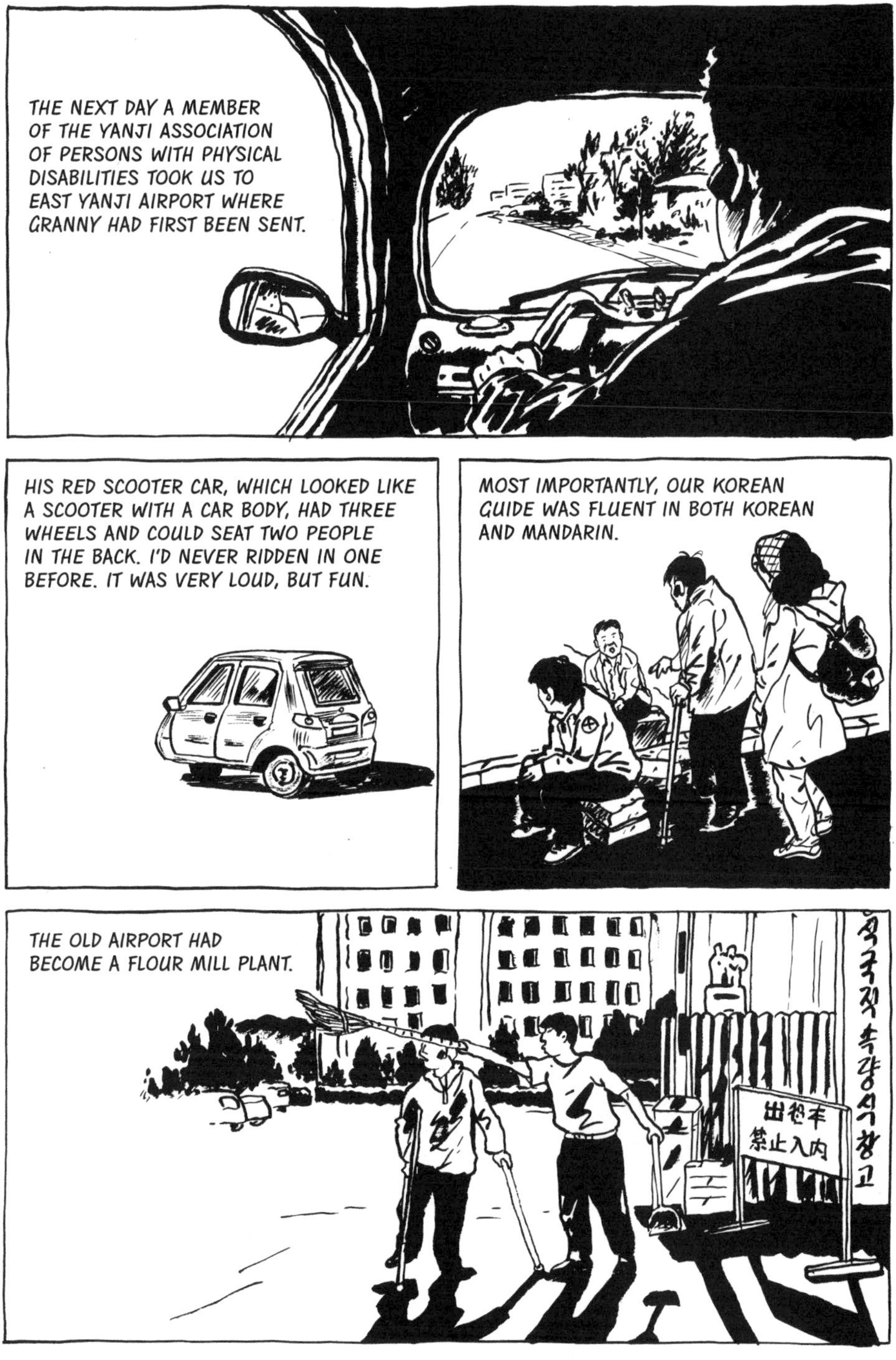
THE NEXT DAY A MEMBER OF THE YANJI ASSOCIATION OF PERSONS WITH PHYSICAL DISABILITIES TOOK US TO EAST YANJI AIRPORT WHERE GRANNY HAD FIRST BEEN SENT.
HIS RED SCOOTER CAR, WHICH LOOKED LIKE A SCOOTER WITH A CAR BODY, HAD THREE WHEELS AND COULD SEAT TWO PEOPLE IN THE BACK. I'D NEVER RIDDEN IN ONE BEFORE. IT WAS VERY LOUD, BUT FUN.
MOST IMPORTANTLY, OUR KOREAN GUIDE WAS FLUENT IN BOTH KOREAN AND MANDARIN.
THE OLD AIRPORT HAD BECOME A FLOUR MILL PLANT.
국직속량식창고
出租车
禁止入内

BUT IN ONE CORNER OF THE SITE STOOD A BUILDING FROM THE TIME OF THE JAPANESE OCCUPATION.

IT HAD BEEN THE JAPANESE MILITARY OFFICE.

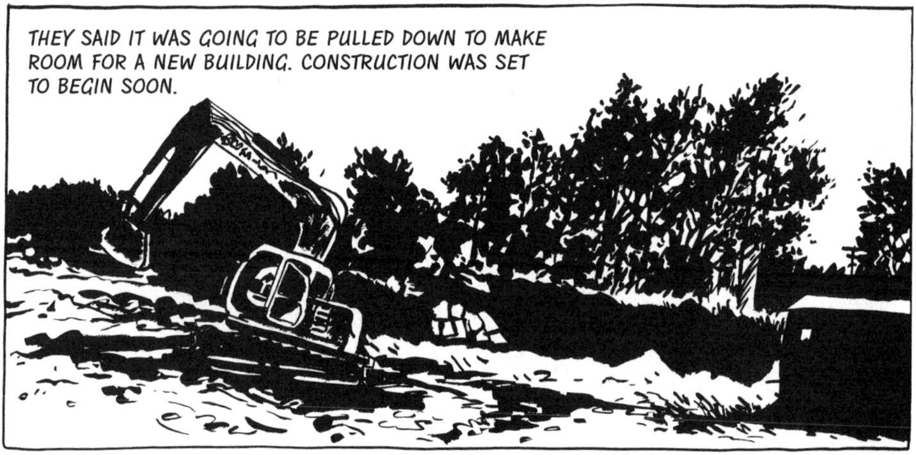
THEY SAID IT WAS GOING TO BE PULLED DOWN TO MAKE ROOM FOR A NEW BUILDING. CONSTRUCTION WAS SET TO BEGIN SOON.

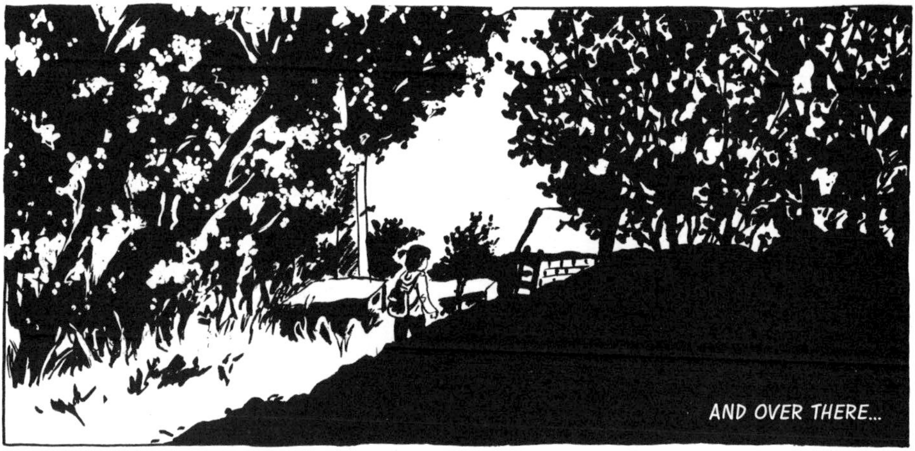
AND OVER THERE...

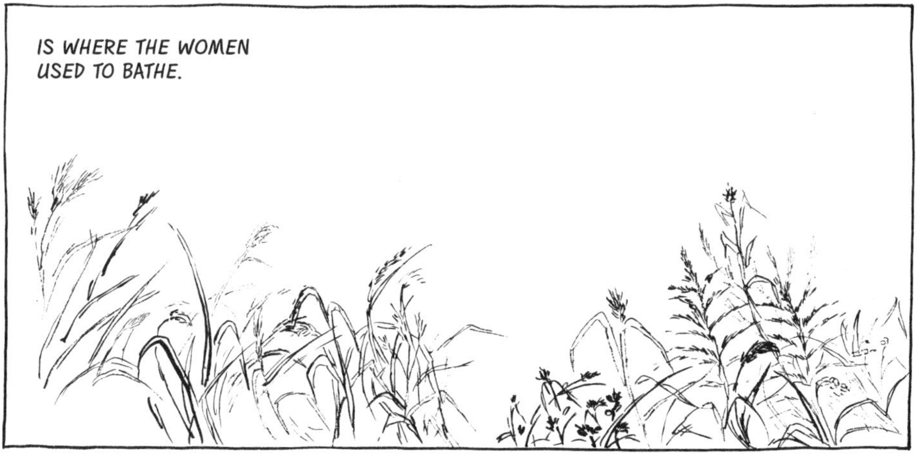
IS WHERE THE WOMEN USED TO BATHE.

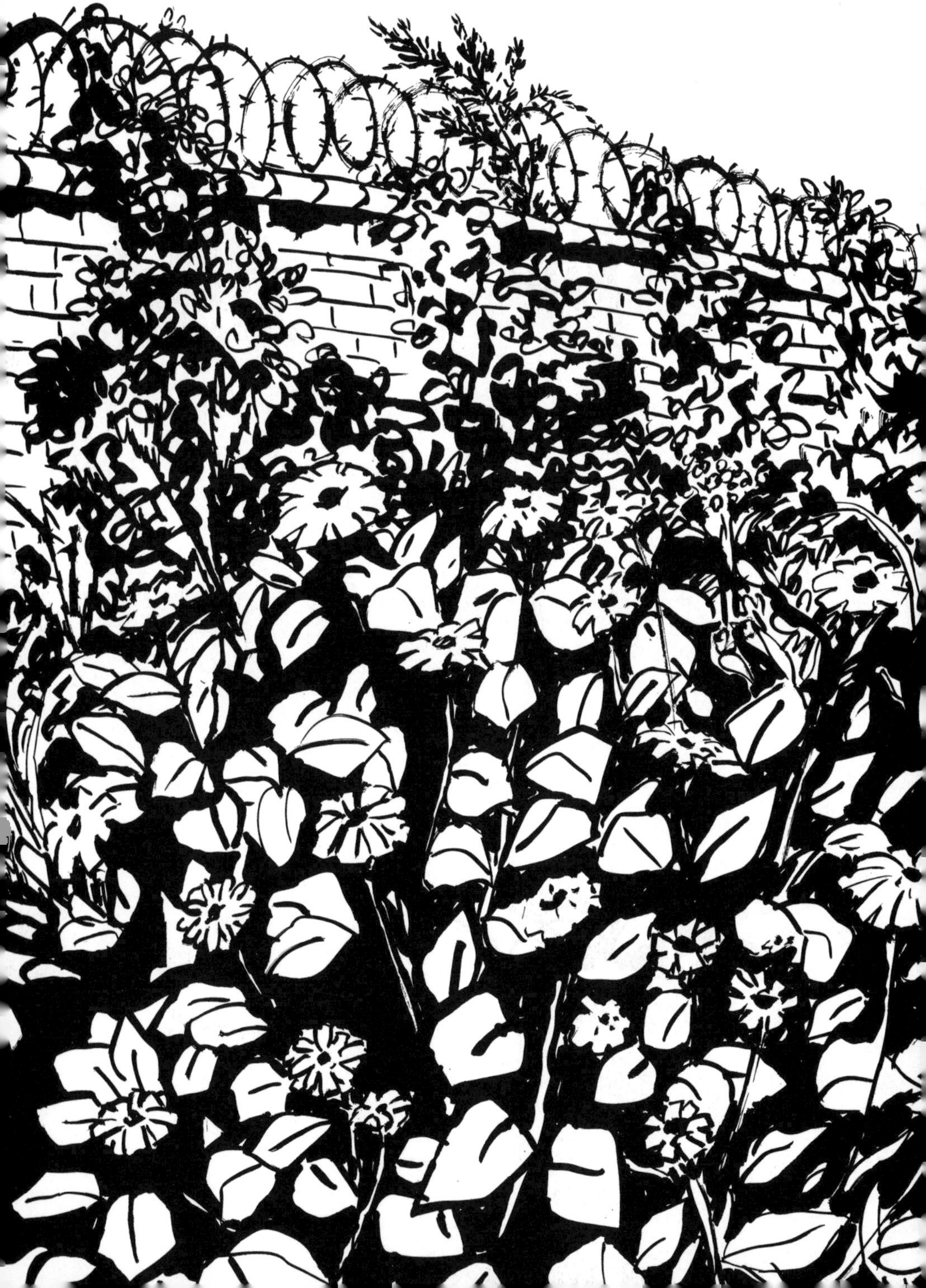

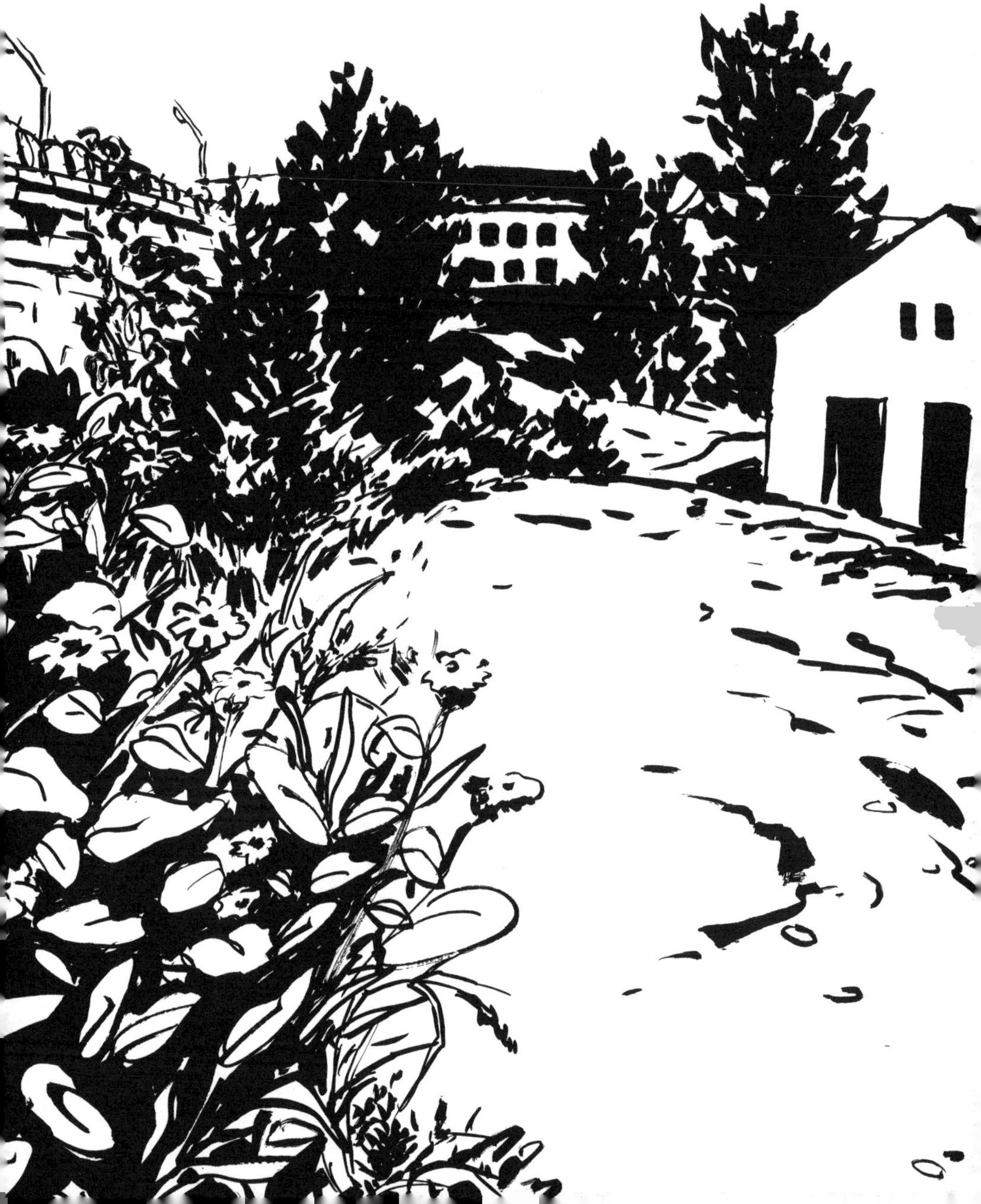

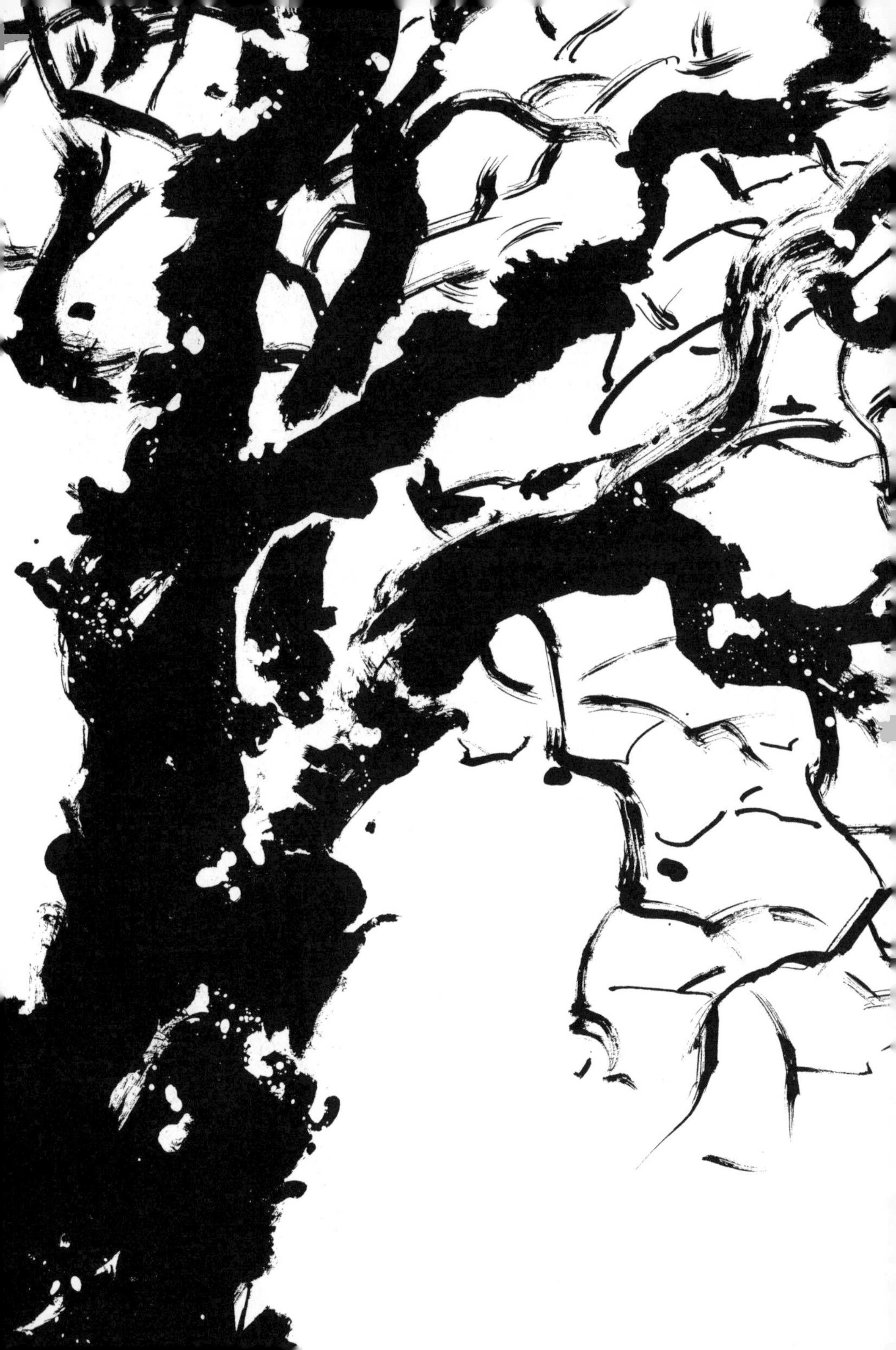

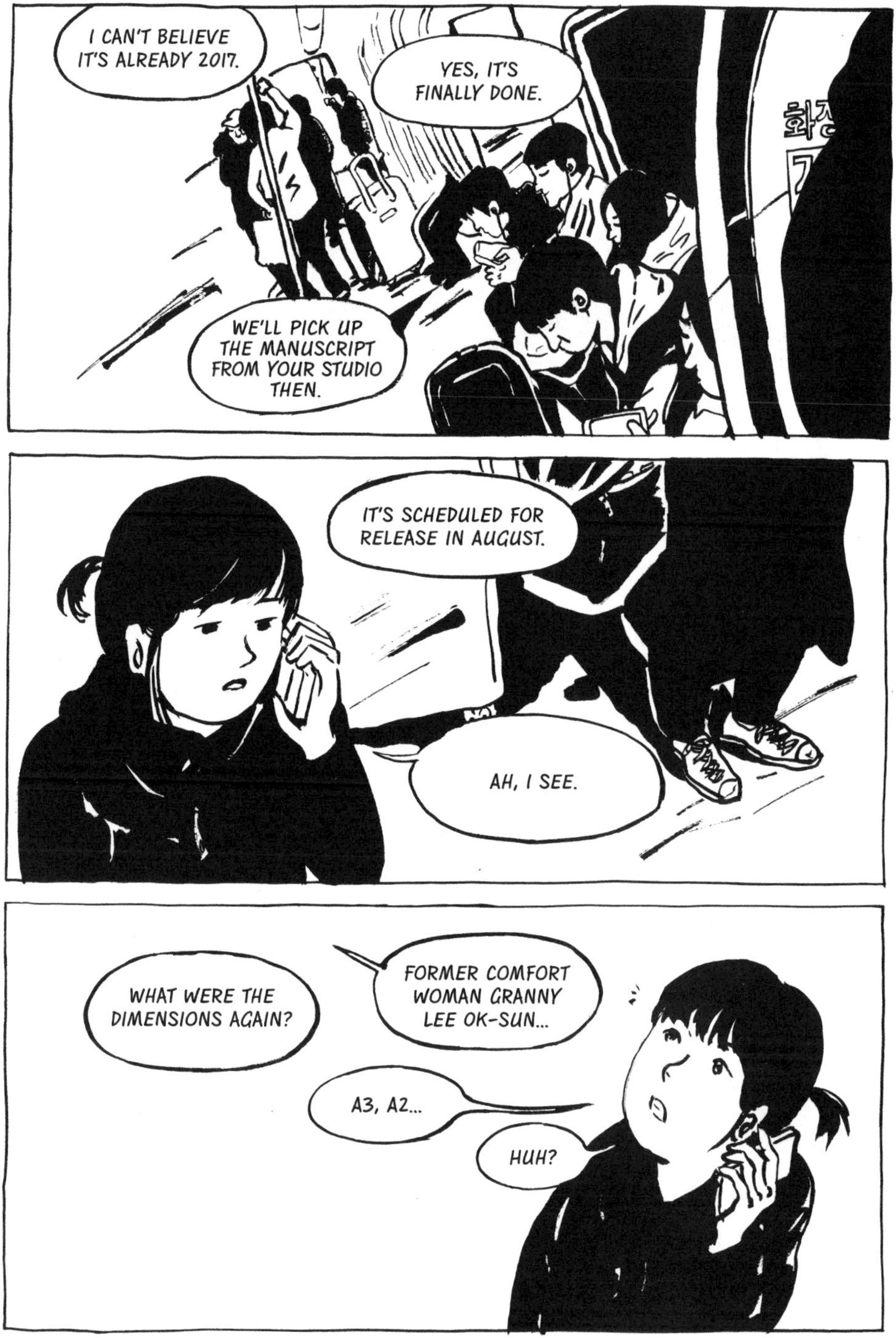

I CAN'T BELIEVE IT'S ALREADY 2017.
YES, IT'S FINALLY DONE.
WE'LL PICK UP THE MANUSCRIPT FROM YOUR STUDIO THEN.
IT'S SCHEDULED FOR RELEASE IN AUGUST.
AH, I SEE.
FORMER COMFORT WOMAN GRANNY LEE OK-SUN...
WHAT WERE THE DIMENSIONS AGAIN?
A3, A2...
HUH?

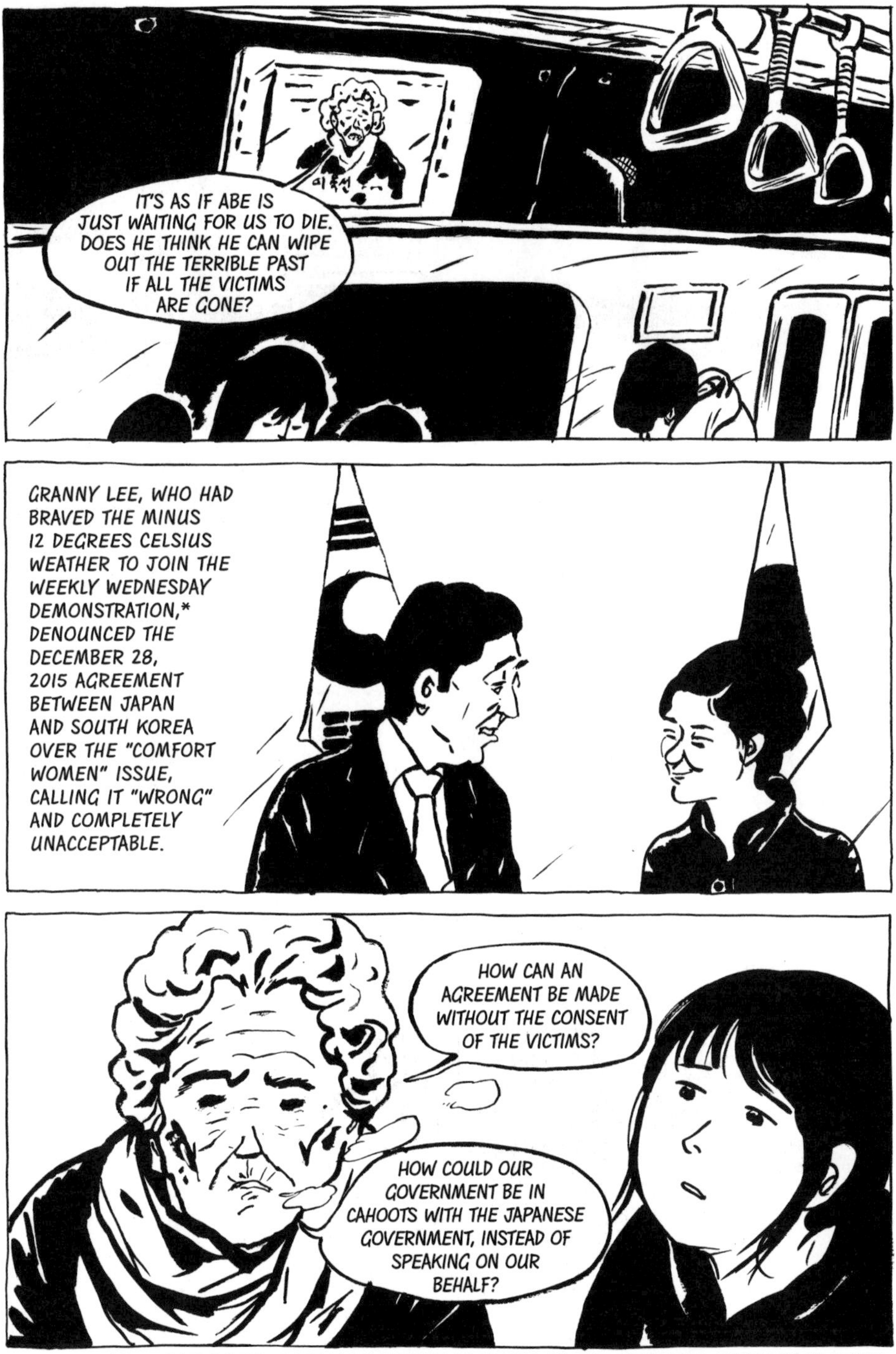
IT'S AS IF ABE IS JUST WAITING FOR US TO DIE. DOES HE THINK HE CAN WIPE OUT THE TERRIBLE PAST IF ALL THE VICTIMS ARE GONE?
GRANNY LEE, WHO HAD BRAVED THE MINUS 12 DEGREES CELSIUS WEATHER TO JOIN THE WEEKLY WEDNESDAY DEMONSTRATION,* DENOUNCED THE DECEMBER 28, 2015 AGREEMENT BETWEEN JAPAN AND SOUTH KOREA OVER THE "COMFORT WOMEN" ISSUE, CALLING IT "WRONG" AND COMPLETELY UNACCEPTABLE.
HOW CAN AN AGREEMENT BE MADE WITHOUT THE CONSENT OF THE VICTIMS?
HOW COULD OUR GOVERNMENT BE IN CAHOOTS WITH THE JAPANESE GOVERNMENT, INSTEAD OF SPEAKING ON OUR BEHALF?

*A PROTEST HELD EVERY WEDNESDAY IN FRONT OF THE JAPANESE EMBASSY IN SEOUL, DEMANDING JUSTICE FROM JAPAN FOR ITS PAST TREATMENT OF COMFORT WOMEN.

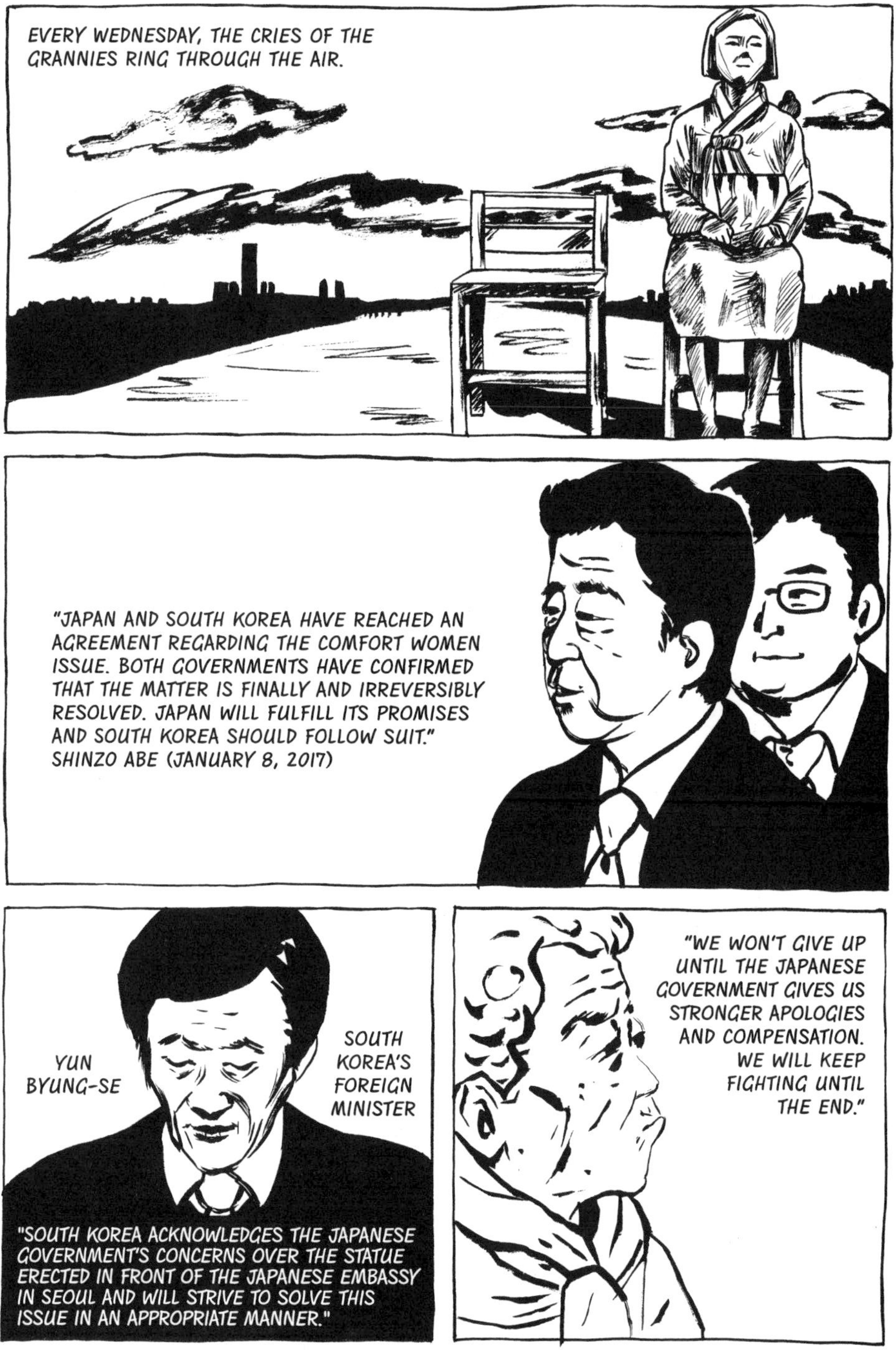
EVERY WEDNESDAY, THE CRIES OF THE GRANNIES RING THROUGH THE AIR.
"JAPAN AND SOUTH KOREA HAVE REACHED AN AGREEMENT REGARDING THE COMFORT WOMEN ISSUE. BOTH GOVERNMENTS HAVE CONFIRMED THAT THE MATTER IS FINALLY AND IRREVERSIBLY RESOLVED. JAPAN WILL FULFILL ITS PROMISES AND SOUTH KOREA SHOULD FOLLOW SUIT."
SHINZO ABE (JANUARY 8, 2017)
YUN BYUNG-SE
SOUTH KOREA'S FOREIGN MINISTER
"SOUTH KOREA ACKNOWLEDGES THE JAPANESE GOVERNMENT'S CONCERNS OVER THE STATUE ERECTED IN FRONT OF THE JAPANESE EMBASSY IN SEOUL AND WILL STRIVE TO SOLVE THIS ISSUE IN AN APPROPRIATE MANNER."
"WE WON'T GIVE UP UNTIL THE JAPANESE GOVERNMENT GIVES US STRONGER APOLOGIES AND COMPENSATION. WE WILL KEEP FIGHTING UNTIL THE END."

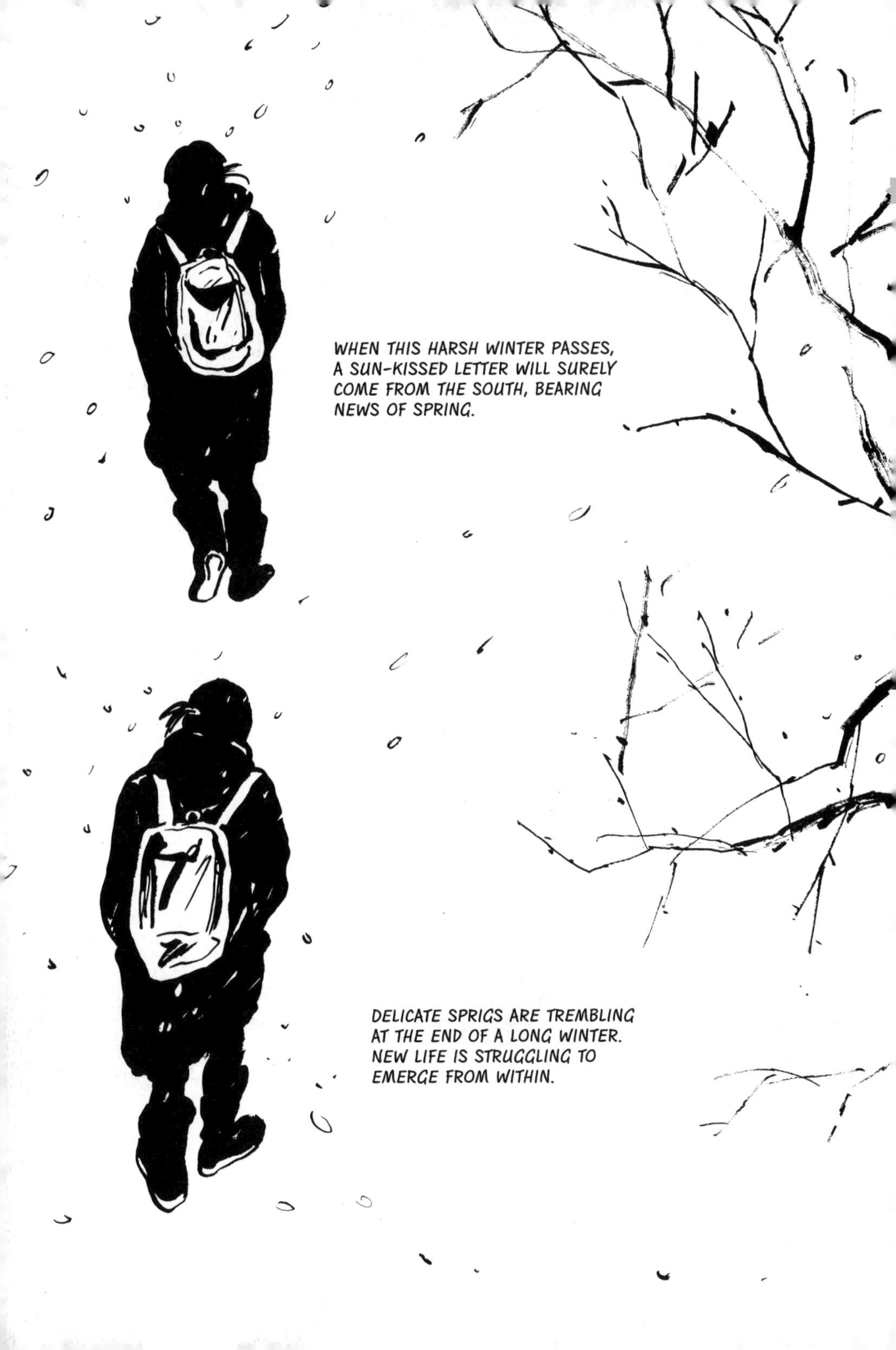
WHEN THIS HARSH WINTER PASSES, A SUN-KISSED LETTER WILL SURELY COME FROM THE SOUTH, BEARING NEWS OF SPRING.
DELICATE SPRIGS ARE TREMBLING AT THE END OF A LONG WINTER. NEW LIFE IS STRUGGLING TO EMERGE FROM WITHIN.

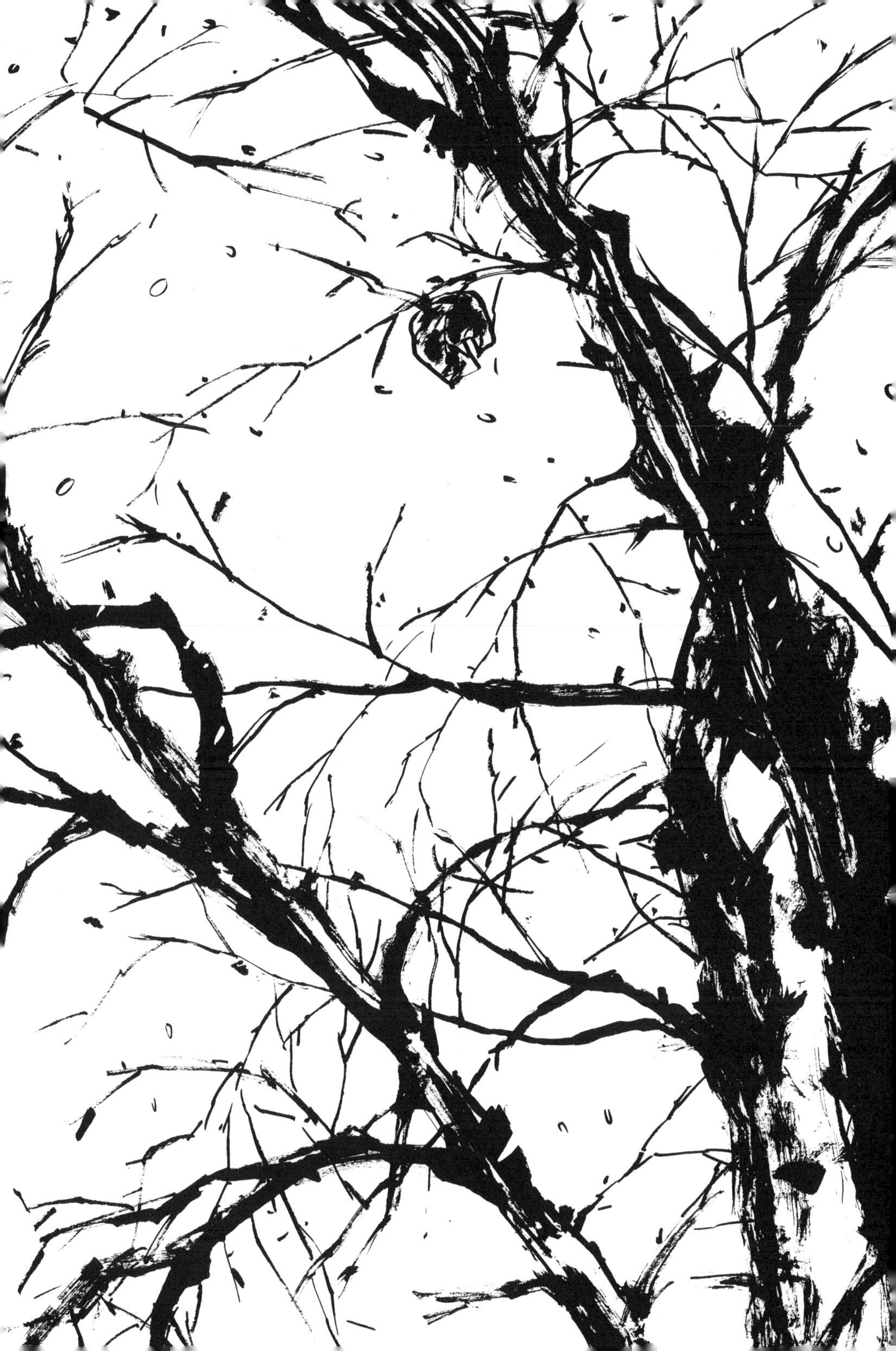

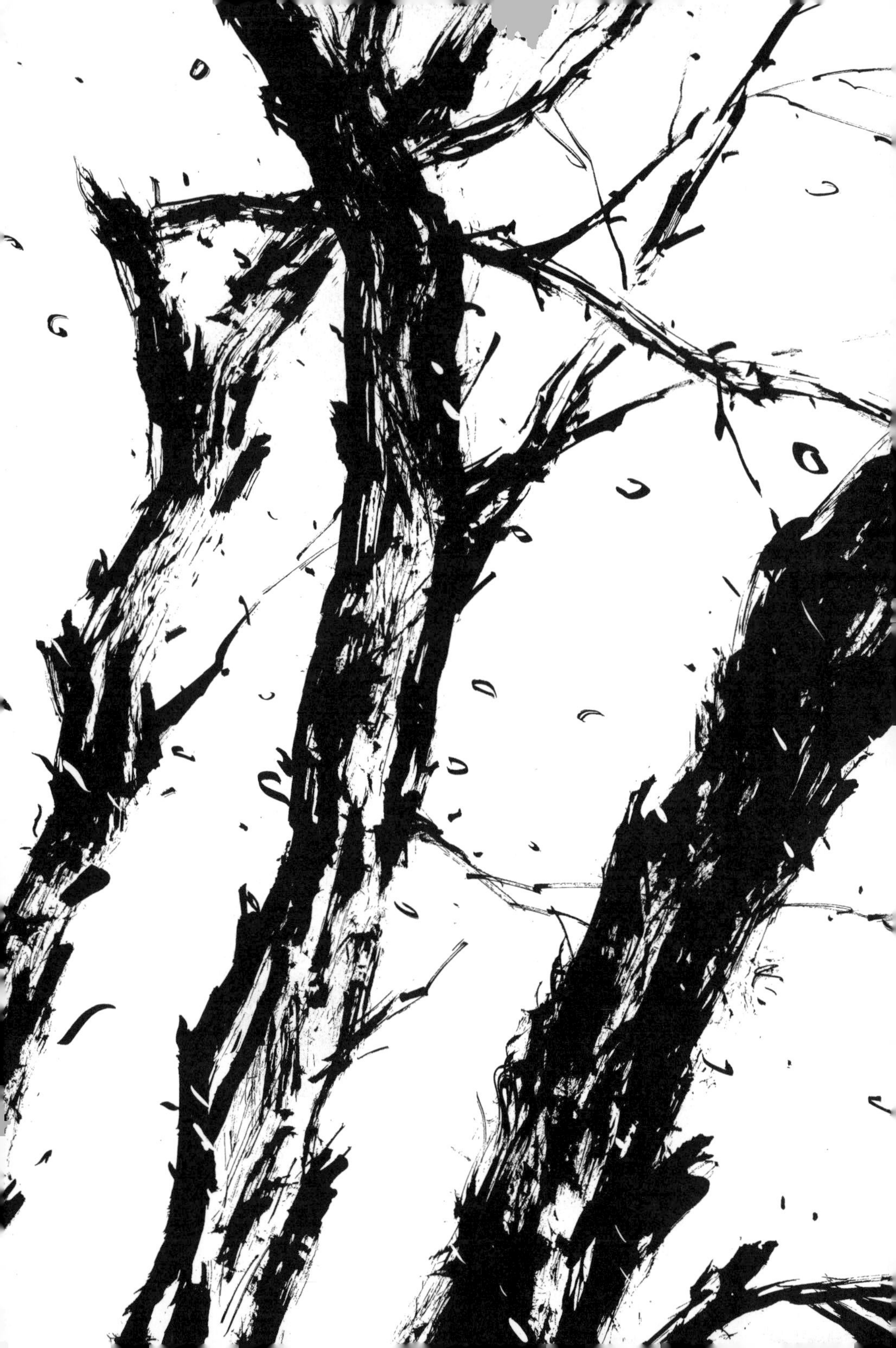

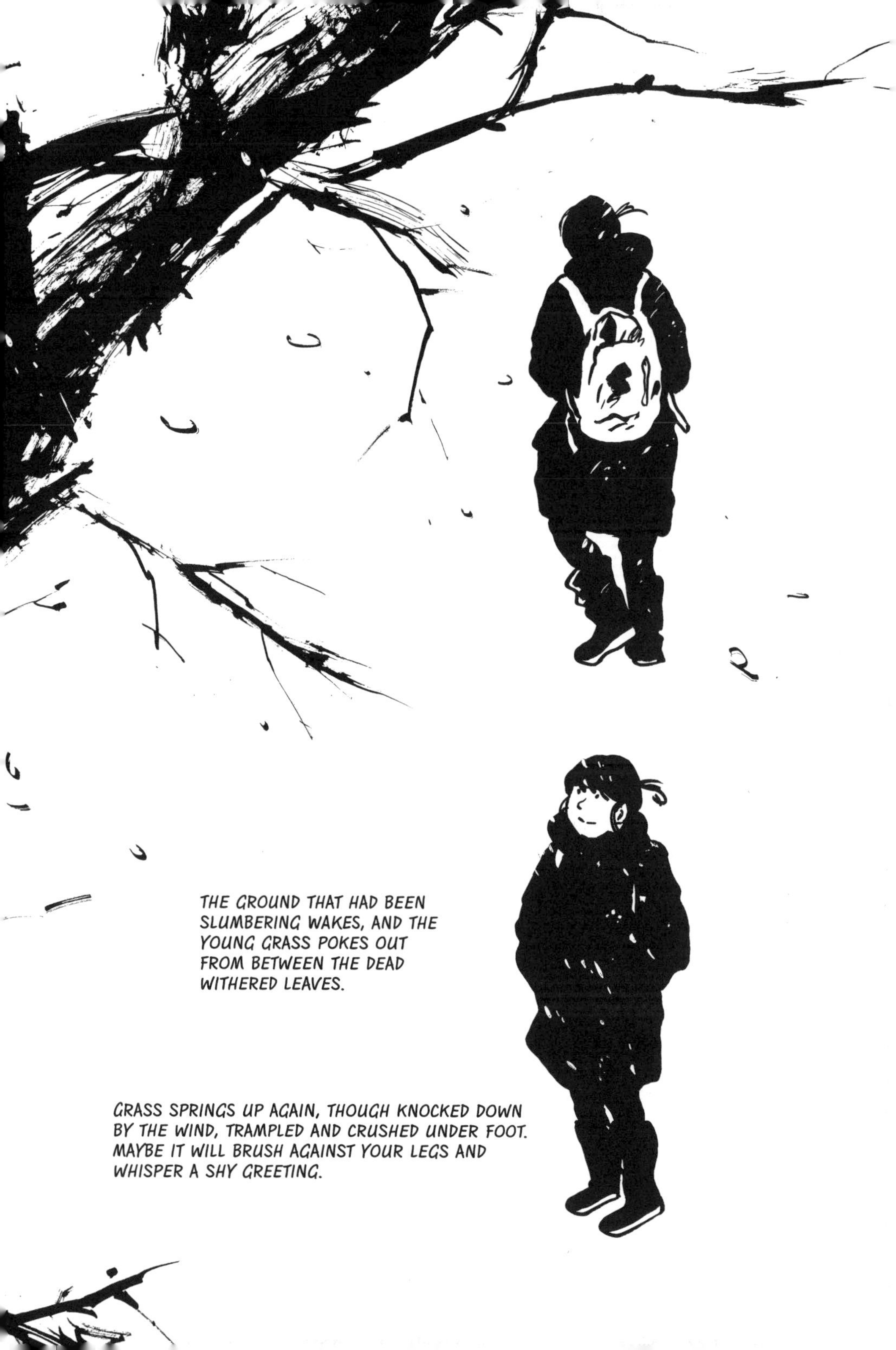
THE GROUND THAT HAD BEEN SLUMBERING WAKES, AND THE YOUNG GRASS POKES OUT FROM BETWEEN THE DEAD WITHERED LEAVES.
GRASS SPRINGS UP AGAIN, THOUGH KNOCKED DOWN BY THE WIND, TRAMPLED AND CRUSHED UNDER FOOT. MAYBE IT WILL BRUSH AGAINST YOUR LEGS AND WHISPER A SHY GREETING.

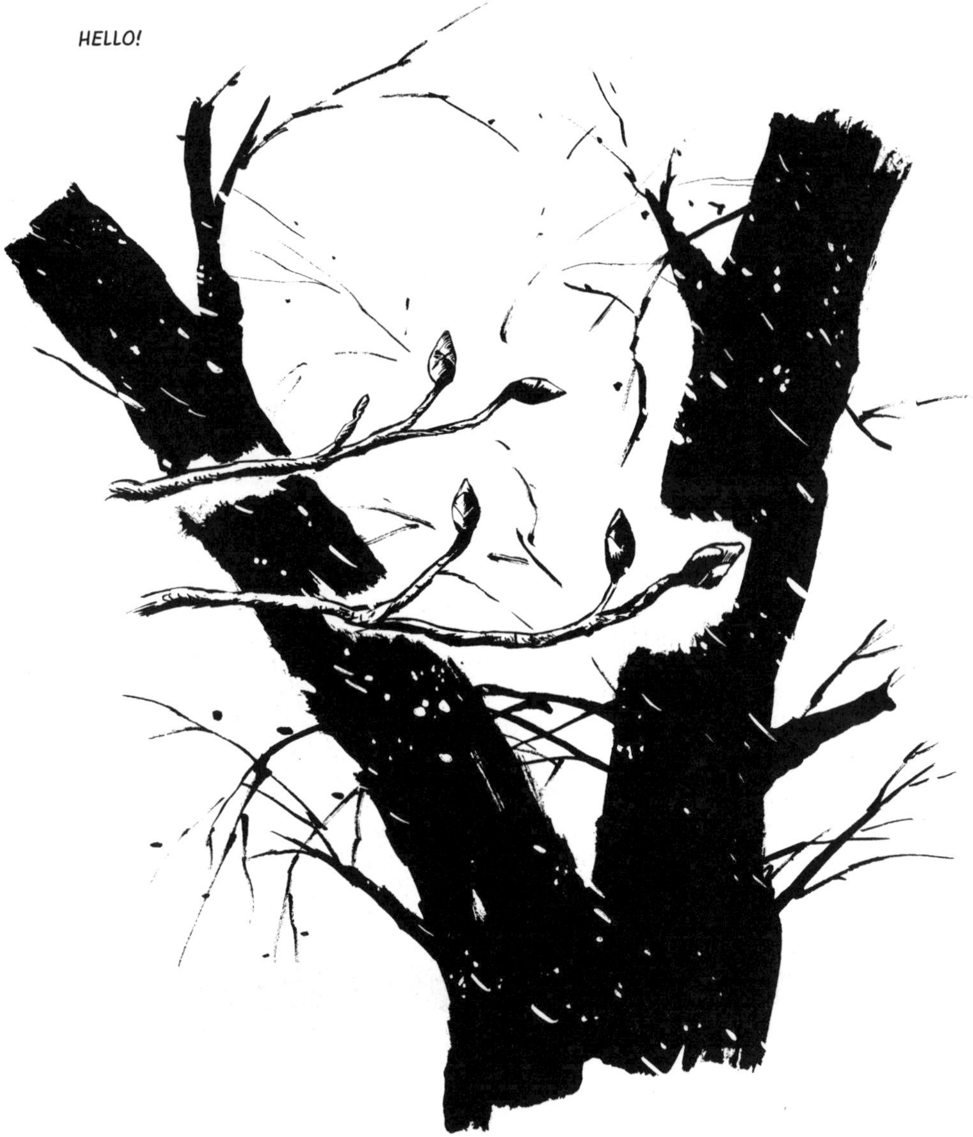
HELLO!
THE WINTER IS OVER, AND THE COLD THAT SEEMED TO LAST FOREVER IS THAWING. SPRING HAS FINALLY COME.

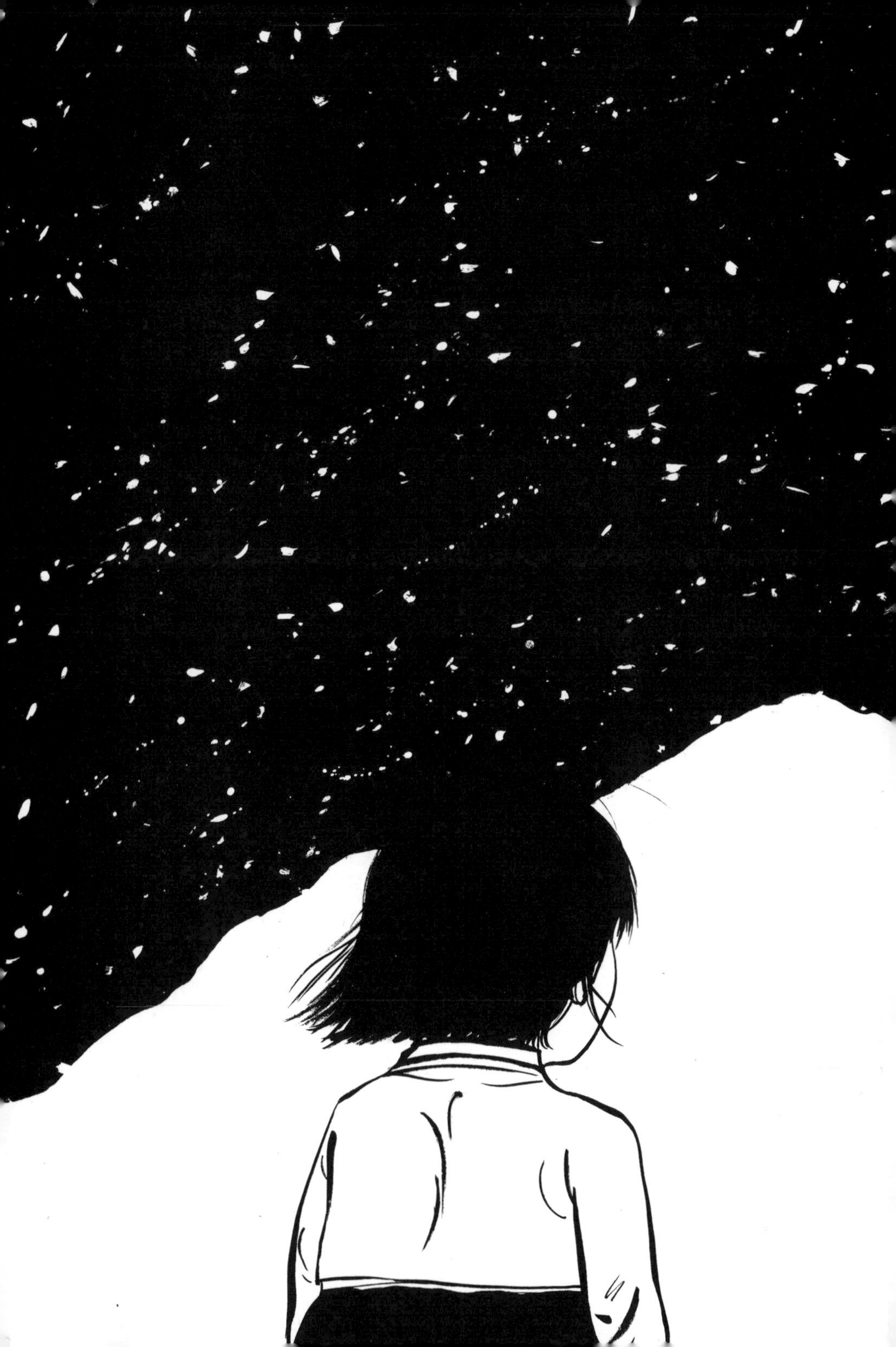